W9-BXF-216

INTERNATIONAL TRADE AND THIRD WORLD DEVELOPMENT

International Development Resource Books
Pradip K. Ghosh, editor

INTERNATIONAL TRADE AND THIRD WORLD DEVELOPMENT

Pradip K. ₍Ghosh, *Editor*

Dilip Ghosh, *Associate Editor*

Foreword by Gamani Corea, Secretary-General of UNCTAD

Prepared under the auspices of the Center for International Development,
University of Maryland, College Park, and the World Academy of Development
and Cooperation, Washington, D.C.

International Development Resource Books, Number 16

Greenwood Press
Westport, Connecticut • London, England

231123

Library of Congress Cataloging in Publication Data

Main entry under title:

International trade and Third World development.

(International development resource books,
ISSN 0738-1425 ; no. 16)
    Includes bibliographical references and index.
    1. Developing countries—Commercial policy—
Addresses, essays, lectures.   2. Commercial policy—
Addresses, essays, lectures.   3. Developing countries—
Commerce—Bibliography.   4. Developing countries—
Economic policy—Information services.   I. Ghosh,
Pradip K., 1947—   . II. Series.
HF1413.I675   1984   382'.091724   83-27457
ISBN 0-313-24152-X (lib. bdg.)

Library of Congress Catalog Card Number: 83-27457
ISBN: 0-313-24152-X
ISSN: 0738-1425

First published in 1984

Greenwood Press
A division of Congressional Information Service, Inc.
88 Post Road West, Westport, Connecticut 06881

Printed in the United States of America

10   9   8   7   6   5   4   3   2   1

TO

THE RESEARCHERS
AT THE UNITED NATIONS CONFERENCE ON TRADE AND DEVELOPMENT

IN GRATEFUL RECOGNITION OF THEIR LEADERSHIP ROLE
IN THIRD WORLD DEVELOPMENT RESEARCH

"THE ULTIMATE OBJECTIVE OF DEVELOPMENT MUST BE TO BRING ABOUT A SUSTAINED IMPROVEMENT IN THE WELL-BEING OF THE INDIVIDUAL AND BESTOW BENEFITS ON ALL. IF UNDUE PRIVILEGES, EXTREMES OF WEALTH AND SOCIAL INJUSTICES PERSIST, THEN DEVELOPMENT FAILS IN THE ESSENTIAL PURPOSE"

– UNITED NATIONS GENERAL ASSEMBLY RESOLUTION 2626 (XXV), 24 OCTOBER 1970.

Contents

EXPORTS IN THE NEW WORLD ENVIRONMENT: THE CASE OF LATIN
AMERICA

ANNEX

The Third World

Afghanistan
  Republic of Afghanistan
Algeria
  Democratic and Popular
  Republic of Algeria
Angola
  People's Republic of Angola
Argentina
  Argentine Republic
Bahamas
  Commonwealth of the Bahamas
Bahrain
  State of Bahrain
Bangladesh
  People's Republic of
  Bangladesh
Barbados
  People's Republic of
  Barbados
Benin
  People's Republic of Benin
Bhutan
  People's Republic of Bhutan
Bolivia
  Republic of Bolivia
Botswana
  Republic of Botswana
Brazil
  Federative Republic of Brazil
Burma
  Socialist Republic of the
  Union of Burma
Burundi
  Republic of Burundi

Cambodia
  Democratic Kampuchea

Cameroon
  United Republic of Cameroon
Cape Verde
  Republic of Cape Verde
Central African Empire
Chad
  Republic of Chad
Chile
  Republic of Chile
Colombia
  Republic of Colombia
Comoro Islands
  Republic of the Comoros
Congo
  People's Republic of the
  Congo
Costa Rica
  Republic of Costa Rica
Cuba
  Republic of Cuba
Dominican Republic
Ecuador
  Republic of Ecuador
Egypt
  Arab Republic of Egypt
El Salvador
  Republic of El Salvador
Equatorial Guinea
  Republic of Equatorial
  Guinea
Ethiopia
Fiji
  Dominion of Fiji
Gabon
  Gabonese Republic
Gambia
  Republic of the Gambia

Ghana
Republic of Ghana
Grenada
State of Grenada
Guatemala
Republic of Guatemala
Guinea
Republic of Guinea
Guinea-Bissau
Republic of Guinea-Bissau
Guyana
Cooperative Republic of
Guyana
Haiti
Republic of Haiti
Honduras
Republic of Honduras
India
Republic of India
Indonesia
Republic of Indonesia
Iran
Imperial Government of Iran
Iraq
Republic of Iraq
Ivory Coast
Republic of Ivory Coast
Jamaica
Jordan
Hashemite Kingdom of Jordan
Kenya
Republic of Kenya
Kuwait
State of Kuwait
Laos
Lao People's
Democratic Republic
Lebanon
Republic of Lebanon
Lesotho
Kingdom of Lesotho
Liberia
Republic of Liberia
Libya
People's Socialist
Libyan Arab Republic

Madagascar
Democratic Republic
of Madagascar
Malawi
Republic of Malawi
Malaysia
Maldives
Republic of Maldives
Mali
Republic of Mali
Mauritania
Islamic Republic
of Mauritania
Mauritius
Mexico
United Mexican States
Mongolia
Mongolian People's Republic
Morocco
Kingdom of Morocco
Mozambique
People's Republic
of Mozambique
Nepal
Kingdom of Nepal
Nicaragua
Republic of Nicaragua
Niger
Republic of Niger
Nigeria
Federal Republic of Nigeria
Oman
Sultanate of Oman
Pakistan
Islamic Republic of Pakistan
Panama
Republic of Panama
Papua New Guinea
Paraguay
Republic of Paraguay
Peru
Republic of Peru
Philippines
Republic of the Philippines
Qatar
State of Qatar

Adopted from THE THIRD WORLD: PREMISES OF U.S. POLICY by W. Scott
Thompson, Institute for Contemporary Studies, San Francisco, 1978.

Rhodesia
Ruanda
Republic of Ruanda
Samoa
Sao Tome and Principe
Democratic Republic of
Sao Tome and Principe
Saudi Arabia
Kingdom of Saudi Arabia
Senegal
Republic of Senegal
Seychelles
Sierra Leone
Republic of Sierra Leone
Singapore
Republic of Singapore
Somalia
Somali Democratic Republic
Sri Lanka
Republic of Sri Lanka
Sudan
Democratic Republic of
the Sudan
Surinam
Swaziland
Kingdom of Swaziland
Syria
Syrian Arab Republic
Tanzania
United Republic of Tanzania

Thailand
Kingdom of Thailand
Togo
Republic of Togo
Trinidad and Tobago
Tunisia
Republic of Tunisia
Uganda
Republic of Uganda
United Arab Emirates
Upper Volta
Republic of Upper Volta
Uruguay
Oriental Republic of Uruguay
Venezuela
Republic of Venezuela
Vietnam
Socialist Republic of Vietnam
Western Sahara
Yemen
People's Democratic Republic
of Yemen
Yemen
Yemen Arab Republic
Zaire
Republic of Zaire
Zambia
Republic of Zambia

Countries which have social and economic characteristics in
common with the Third World but, because of political
affiliations or regimes, are not associated with Third
World organizations:

China
People's Republic of China
Cyprus
Republic of Cyprus
Israel
State of Israel
Kazakhstan
Kirghizia
Korea
Democratic People's Republic
of Korea
Romania
Socialist Republic of Romania

South Africa
Republic of South Africa
South West Africa
Namibia
Tadzhikistan
Turkmenistan
Uzbekistan
Yugoslavia
Socialist Federal Republic
of Yugoslavia

Abbreviations

ADC	Andean Development Corporation
AsDB	Asian Development Bank
ASEAN	Association of South-East Asian Nations
CARIFTA	Caribbean Free Trade Association
DAC	Development Assistance Committee (of OECD)
ECA	Economic Commission for Africa
ECE	Economic Commission for Europe
ECLA	Economic Commission for Latin America
ECOWAS	Economic Commission of West African States
EDF	European Development Fund
EEC	European Economic Community
EFTA	European Free Trade Association
ESCAP	Economic and Social Commission for Asia and the Pacific
FAO	Food and Agriculture Organization of the United Nations
GATT	General Agreement on Tariffs and Trade
GDP	gross domestic product
GNP	gross national product
IBRD	International Bank for Reconstruction and Development (World Bank)
IDA	International Development Association
IDB	Inter-American Development Bank
IFC	International Finance Corporation
IIEP	International Institute for Educational Planning
ILO	International Labour Office
IMF	International Monetary Fund
LAFTA	Latin American Free Trade Association
ODA	official development assistance
OECD	Organisation for Economic Co-operation and Development
OPEC	Organization of Petroleum Exporting Countries
UNDP	United Nations Development Programme
UNEP	United Nations Environment Programme
UNESCO	United Nations Educational, Scientific and Cultural Organization
UNHCR	Office of the United Nations High Commissioner for Refugees
UNITAR	United Nations Institute for Training and Research
UNICEF	United Nations Children's Fund
UNIDO	United Nations Industrial Development Organization
WFP	World Food Programme
WHO	World Health Organization

Foreword

I am pleased to know of the International Development Resources Book project. The 20 resource books which are published under this project, covering the whole spectrum of issues in the fields of development economics and international co-operation for development, and containing not only current reading materials but also up-to-date statistical data and bibliographical notes, will, I am sure, prove to be extremely useful to a wide public.

I would like to commend the author for having undertaken this very ambitious and serious project and, by so doing, rendered a most valuable service. I am confident that it will have a great success.

Gamani Corea

Secretary-General
United Nations Conference on Trade and Development

Preface

Stimulus for the publication of an international resource book series was developed in 1980, while teaching and researching various topics related to third world development. Since that time, I have built up a long list of related resource materials on different subjects, usually considered to be very important for researchers, educators, and public policy decision makers involved with developing country problems. This series of resource books makes an attempt for the first time to give the reader a comprehensive look at the current issues, methods, strategies and policies, statistical information and comprehensive resource bibliographies, and a directory of various information sources on the topic.

This topic is very important because within the framework of the current international economic order, developing an effective international trade and third world development policy is envisaged as a dynamic instrument of growth essential to the rapid economic and social development of the developing countries, in particular of the least developed countries of Asia, Africa and Latin America.

Much of this work was completed during my residency as a visiting scholar in the Center for Advanced Study of International Development at Michigan State University. Suzanne Wilson, Mary Ann Kozak, Kathy White and Susan Costello, students at the University, provided much needed assistance with the project. I am thankful to the M.S.U. Sociology department for providing necessary support services and Dr. James T. Sabin, Vice President, editorial of Greenwood Press who encouraged me in pursuing the work and finally agreeing to publish in book form.

I would also like to gratefully acknowledge the encouragement given to me by Dr. Denton Morrison to pursue this project and Dr. Mark Van de Vall who has been an inspiration to me since my graduate school days.

Finally, preparation of this book would not have been completed without the contributions from Richard Jolly, Jack P. Barnouin, Jukio A. Lacarte, Jagdish N. Bhagwati, Samuel Laird,

Gerald K. Helleiner, Daniel Chudnovsky, F. Fiallo, L. Perez, I. M. D. Little, Ezriel M. Brook, Enzo R. Grilli, Barend A. de Vries and many respects from the U.N. Department of Economic and Social Affairs, UNCTAD and the OECD. I am gratefully indebted to Journal of Economic Literature, U.N. Documents and World Bank Publications for the much needed annotations, and a very special thanks to Tom and Jackie Minkel for their assistance in the preparation of this book in camera ready form.

PART I
CURRENT ISSUES, TRENDS, ANALYTICAL METHODS, STRATEGIES AND POLICIES, COUNTRY STUDIES

Introduction

This resource book has two multifaceted purposes. Firstly, to document and analyze the current trends in the development of an effective world trade policy for accelerated progress of the third world countries--and to evaluate the progress made by them during the past decade in attaining long term objectives of a sustained economic growth and improvement in the quality of living future populations.

We are all very much familiar with the problems of Third World countries, usually described by Latin America (excluding Cuba) the whole of Africa, Asia (excluding its socialist countries, Japan and Israel) and Oceania (excluding Australia and New Zealand). They are plagued by poverty, very high rates of population growth, low growth rates of gross domestic product, low rates of industrialization, extremely high dependence on agriculture, rate of unemployment, and uneven income distribution. Although the expression "Third World countries" no longer has a clear meaning, majority of the international development experts would consider the poor developing countries to belong in the third world irrespective [1] of their affiliation as aligned or non-aligned characteristic.

Secondly, major purpose of this volume is to provide the researchers with the much needed knowledge about the different sources of information and available data related to objectives and goals of international trade programs for the development of the third world countries. International trade policies in the developing countries have raised many complex issues. While these issues are largely dependent on national policies and priorities, their solution is of international concern.

The pace and pattern of international trade have varied widely among the developing countries partly because of differences in the availability of natural, human and capital resources and in factors such as size and location, and partly because of differences in objectives, strategies and policies regarding international trade that countries have pursued. The issues affecting strategies and policies differ considerably at the present time from those that were important decade ago and policy design is thus now more complex and difficult than before.

Foreign trade is a key factor in the development strategy of these countries and must be channelled towards the creation of employment and the attainment of economic growth, external assistance is a necessary complement to it. Whatever good effects the measures taken in the sphere of trade may have, it will still be necessary to finance their balance-of-payments deficits to allow for co-operation in development projects, to provide financial and technical support for the trade measures adopted, and in general to supplement internal saving. In the current Development Decade, therefore, external assistance must continue to be an important means of promoting employment and development.

Exports from the developing countries account for high percentages of their national product. Consequently, the multiplier effect of any increase in such exports must be felt on broad sectors of their economies, and particularly on employment. The diversification and stepping up of their exports will thus provide the developing countries with the stimulus they need to increase employment.

The development of world trade has not, however, led to an improvement in the relative position of the developing countries. On the contrary, their share in trade declined steadily during the First United Nations Development Decade and has in general continued to consist mainly of a small number of primary products. Despite the efforts to promote and liberalize world trade, the developing countries are still encountering serious quota and tariff barriers on world markets. These barriers, which are often a violation of the principles advocated and accepted in international forums, have the greatest effect on precisely those products in which the developing countries are most competitive and which would permit more intensive use of their abundant manpower.

Moreover, not only do the developing countries find it difficult to enter markets because of the obstacles referred to above, they also meet competition from products from the developed countries, which in many cases are subsidized to enable them to enter foreign markets. Thus, not only are conditions deteriorating on the international market but misuse of the world's resources is also being encouraged.

The developing countries themselves have sometimes failed to take the measures related to their production and exports without which they cannot hope to achieve the desired improvement in their position.[2]

This volume examines the experience of a substantial number of the third world countries in implementing development plans during approximately the 1970's and draws some general conclusions for policy action during the years ahead.

Attention has been focused on some of the major problems faced by hard core developing countries and policy issues posed by those problems. However, the development needs of hard-core developing countries are very large and call for much greater interest and attention from world community than has been the case for. A systematic attack on the acute problems of countries facing extreme poverty and underdevelopment should therefore now be at the center of the policies designed to usher in a new international economic order.

It is hoped that this resource book will be of use not only to those directly involved in the formulation and implementation of development policies but also will help to acquaint a wide reading audience with the thrusts planned by developing countries for accelerated progress. In addition, the intercountry comparative analysis may be of use to planners and policy makers in developing countries, especially from the viewpoint of harmonizing national plans in order to strengthen economic co-operation with respect to international trade among interested countries.

The plan of the reading materials in Part I of the book and the selection of the twenty one pieces represents a specific orientation, or bias. They present current international issues and trends affecting trade policies in third world development, analytical methods, strategies and policies for development and selected third world country studies.

Part II includes statistical information and a descriptive bibliography of information sources related to international trade and development in the third world countries.

Part III is a select bibliography of books, documents and periodical articles published since 1970, relevant to foreign trade development of the developing countries. Annotations for the different titles have been compiled from The Journal of Economic Literature, International Social Sciences Index, U.N. Documents Index, World Bank Publications, Finance and Development, Book Publisher's promotion brochures and the IMF-IBRD Joint Library Publications.

Part IV consists of a directory of information sources. This section is in four parts, directory of United Nations information sources, listing of bibliographic sources, titles of selected periodicals published around the world and a directory of institutions involved in research relevant to development problems in the third world countries.

---

[1]Rodwin Lloyd, "Regional Planning Perspectives in Third World Countries," in TRAINING FOR REGIONAL DEVELOPMENT PLANNING: PERSPECTIVES FOR THE THIRD DEVELOPMENT DECADE, ed. by, Om Prakash Mathur, UNCRD, 1981.
Thompson, W. Scott, THE THIRD WORLD: PREMISES OF U.S. POLICY Institute for Contemporary Studies, San Francisco, 1978.

[2]Lacarte, Julio A., "Aspects of International Trade and Assistance Relative to the Expansion of Employment in the Developing Countries", JOURNAL OF DEVELOPMENT PLANNING, Vol 5, 1972, pp. 115-143.

Trade and Structural Change

THE WORLD BANK

Proving their ability to compete in international markets, the developing countries boosted their sales of manufactures to the industrial countries and to other developing countries during the 1970s at an average of 13 percent a year in real terms (see Table 1). Countries that participated in this trade boom came from all levels of development and enjoyed more rapid growth than those that did not participate.

Though some of the successful countries tried to develop domestic production to replace imports at early stages of industrialization, they quickly moved away from an import-substitution policy toward what is often called an outward orientation. The policies of the successful countries have been generally supportive of industrialization and commerce but have avoided directing that support toward any particular sector. Decisions about the activities and processes that could be built up profitably have been left to individual firms, which succeed or fail as their decisions prove to be correct or incorrect.

I. WHAT ARE THE ADVANTAGES

Outward-looking strategies have been shown to raise income. Major studies undertaken by the Organisation for Economic Co-operation and Development (OECD) and the National Bureau of Economic Research in the early 1970s analyzed the foreign-trade regimes of twenty countries in the post-World War II period and revealed the superior performance of those that encouraged exports

From **TRADE AND EMPLOYMENT POLICIES FOR INDUSTRIAL DEVELOPMENT**, **WORLD BANK**, 1982 (8-29), reprinted by permission of the publisher.

Table 1. Exports of Manufactures from
Developing Countries

	All developing countries	Low-income developing countries	Middle-income developing countries
Value of exports, 1980 (1978 US$ billion)	97.4	6.0	91.4
Annual growth of exports, 1970-80 (%)	12.9	6.9	13.4
Destination, 1977 (%)	n.a.	100.0	100.0
Industrial countries	n.a.	51.0	58.0
Developing countries	n.a.	27.0	30.0
Centrally planned economies	n.a.	12.0	6.0
Capital-surplus oil exporters	n.a.	10.0	6.0

Note: n.a. = not available
Source: *World Development Report 1981* (New York: Oxford University Press, 1981).

compared with those that were biased toward import-substitution.[1] A subsequent World Bank study contrasted the experience of ten developing countries. It estimated that the 1966-73 increase in per capita incomes in Chile, India, and Mexico, for example -- which all favored inward-looking policies -- would have been 21 percent, 22 percent, and 17 percent higher, respectively, if those countries had reached the average export growth of the sample. In contrast, per capita income in Korea -- which took an outward orientation -- would have been 43 percent lower than it actually was if Korea's exports had only matched the average for the same sample.[2] Later research has found similar relationships between exports and growth of gross domestic product (GDP) in a larger group of countries.[3] The most recent study examined the performance of fifty-five developing countries between 1960 and 1977. It found a significant positive relationship between the growth of manufactured exports and economic growth.[4]

Manufacturing for export as well as for domestic consumption encourages efficient allocation of resources, permits the exploitation of economies of scale, generates technological improvements in response to competition abroad, and, in labor-surplus countries, contributes to increased employment. Furthermore, the strong growth and balance-of-payments positions that countries can attain by promoting exports enable them to borrow abroad to supplement domestic savings. By contrast, once the "easy" stage of import substitution is completed (for products in which local producers have advantages over foreign producers in the domestic market), substituting domestic production for imports entails rising costs because of the loss of economies of scale in small national markets. In short, trade has proved a more effective instrument for promoting efficient structural change than has economic autarky.

It is now being argued that there are limits to the extent to which new exporters can benefit from outward-oriented strategies. There are three sets of issues, which will be examined here. The first is whether good export performance is attributable to special characteristics of the most successful countries or whether their success can be readily replicated in other countries. The second is whether the penetration of the markets of industrial countries has reached or will soon reach a limit. The third is whether trade in manufactures among the developing countries can continue to expand.

II. REPLICABILITY OF SUCCESSFUL PERFORMANCE

Initially, a large percentage of manufactured exports from developing countries came from a handful of countries. The principal East Asian exporters still account for nearly 50 percent of all exports of manufactures.[5] This creates the impression that the characteristics of these countries -- relatively resource-poor economies with energetic entrepreneurs and a disciplined, hard-working labor force and with special ties to the main importing countries -- are the main factors behind their export performance. But the suppliers of the balance of manufactured exports include a wide range of countries. The number of developing countries that realized more than $500 million in exports of manufactures (in constant 1975 U.S. dollars) rose from seven in 1965 to fifteen in 1975. Those with exports exceeding $50 million went up from twenty-seven in 1975 to fifty-eight in 1978.[6]

These countries differ in size, resource endowment, geographical location, extent of industrialization, and other factors. After examining the characteristics of twenty-eight countries that achieved an average annual growth of manufactured exports of between 8 percent and 36 percent from 1965 to 1975, a World Bank study grouped the countries into four broad categories:[7]

1. Countries that specialized relatively early in export of manufactures and have followed generally outward-looking policies. This group includes Hong Kong, Singapore, Korea, Israel, Portugal, and Greece. They are all characterized by limited natural resources, relatively educated labor, and the need to export manufactures (or services) in order to develop. With local variations, their exports initially were built around labor-intensive, technologically stable products, such as textiles, clothing, footwear, assembled electronic components, and toys. In recent years they have begun to diversify their exports into more sophisticated, skill-intensive products, such as ships.

2. Large semi-industrial countries that have achieved considerable success in industrialization based mainly upon the home market, and in recent years have also tried to promote exports of manufactures. Among those on this list are Brazil, Mexico, and Turkey. Most of these countries began to expand manufactured exports as a remedy for shortages of foreign exchange. These countries have managed to develop export markets for their capital goods, chemicals, and other intermediate goods for which their domestic markets, augmented by exports, provided sufficient economies of scale.

3. Countries now shifting away from specialization in primary exports to diversify their exports and accelerate development. Such countries include Malaysia, Colombia, Ivory Coast, Morocco, Tunisia, the Philippines, and Thailand. The optimal timing of such a shift into manufactured exports depends in part on the prospects of (and effects on) primary exports. It has proved difficult for resource-rich countries, whose current exchange rates are based on specialization, to accomplish this shift through the market. Conversely, countries in this group that still have relatively low wage levels (for example, Thailand) find this shift easier.

4. Large poor countries that have achieved a significant volume of manufactured exports. All countries in this group had income levels below $300 per capita in 1975; examples include Egypt and Pakistan. This is a heterogeneous group with a diverse industrial background and structure.

It is clear from the export success of this wide variety of countries that entrepreneurship, organization, and hard work are not unique to East Asia. The key to good performance is to avoid adopting inappropriate policies that suppress these characteristics and to make full use of whatever comparative advantages a country possesses. But which policies work best?

The diversity of national endowments and situations means that a single policy prescription would not be useful. Each country is unique, and policies should be adapted to the particular circumstances of each. Nevertheless, it would be equally wrong to imply that no general lessons can be drawn from past experiences. There are some common elements in the strategies of developing countries that have been most successful in promoting industrial exports.[8]

Realistic Foreign Exchange Rates

Exchange-rate policy plays a crucial role. The extent to which exports of all kinds are promoted depends above all on the relationship between the exchange rate effectively applied to exports and domestic prices and costs. If, in real terms, people are well rewarded for producing exports, they will be encouraged to produce more; if not, they will turn their attention in other directions. The exchange rate also determines the rewards for saving foreign exchange by producing goods or services that will compete with imports. Import substitution is rewarded when the real rate of exchange is shifted so that imports are made more expensive. Local production is discouraged when imports are made cheap.

It is not easy to determine the optimal exchange rate. A resource-rich economy may build up a strong balance-of-payments position by exporting a simple primary (nonrenewable) commodity. This may make importing too easy, in effect, and block the development of a wide range of activities, notably in manufacturing, that compete with imports and have the potential to promote exports. Here the key seems to be to tax the main exports, while sustaining a unified exchange rate that is favorable to export production and import substitution in other sectors.

It is also recognized that an equilibrium exchange rate cannot be defined without roughly specifying how fast the economy is to grow. More inputs, including foreign exchange, are required to make an economy grow faster. Crucial growth-related activities, such as capital investment and technology transfer, use foreign exchange intensively, and much learning-by-doing in industry depends on imported inputs. Furthermore, foreign exchange plays a special role in overcoming shortages, not only in energy, food, or construction, but also in skilled manpower and technical know-how. In order to earn enough foreign exchange for these purposes, a rapidly growing economy needs to maintain its exchange rate at a level that makes its products and services competitive in foreign markets.

There are limits, of course, to the extent to which economic growth can be stimulated by adjustments to the exchange rate. Devaluation or other exchange policies will have the desired effects when there are underutilized factors of production -- underemployed labor, idle capital equipment, and so forth -- that can be brought into the production of tradable goods. Otherwise devaluation may lead to inflation, which will negate its initially favorable effect on the balance of payments. Inflation is especially likely if wages rise to compensate for the higher domestic prices of tradables. Experience has shown that exchange-rate policies cannot be used in isolation. They must be combined with other tools of economic management.

Easy, Duty-Free Access to Imported Inputs

Exporters will not be able to survive in a competitive world market if they are forced to depend for their inputs on suppliers that are isolated from such competition. In what are called the footloose export industries, such as clothing or electronics, nearly all exports from developing countries come from those countries where imported inputs are given what amounts to a free-trade regime.

Because these exports generally involve modest capital requirements, low labor costs, and low profit margins, the bulk of the cost of the final product (60 percent to 70 percent at world prices) goes for raw materials and intermediate inputs. Any significant tax on these inputs, or even unusually high transport and handling costs, can knock a country out of the running in export markets. Quality defects in raw materials or parts are equally fatal.

In several countries, export processing zones have proved to be a useful means of avoiding the bureaucratic entanglements and taxation often associated with inward-looking industrialization efforts. But sometimes such zones create "enclave" industries apart from the rest of the economy. One solution has been to allow producers to import inputs to the extent they choose and to pay the local tariff and other indirect taxes on the portion sold domestically, while waiving these expenses on the portion exported. While this helps the exporter, it does nothing positive for the local producer of goods that complete with imported inputs.

This problem has been met by providing subsidies of one kind or another to producers of import-competing inputs and, to the extent feasible, giving them the same treatment as is given to direct exporters, including preferential credit facilities. Such schemes are used in Korea, but they may not be practical in countries with less sophisticated administrative systems and higher collection and disbursement costs.[9] Furthermore, export subsidies may provoke countervailing duties from importing countries, even if the subsidies are provided indirectly. The chances of retaliation are minimized by the use of export taxes on those primary products facing less than infinitely elastic foreign demand, rather than by explicit export subsidies on manufactured goods. This permits a balance-of-payments equilibrium to be reached at a higher exchange rate (that is, a higher price of foreign exchange), thus increasing the amount of domestic currency that exporters of other primary products and manufactured goods receive per dollar earned.[10]

Competitive Labor/Wage Policies

Usually, the initial industrial exports from developing countries are marketable because their labor costs are relatively low for the quality and productivity of the labor when it is properly trained and managed.[11] But rising real wages and improved working conditions have been shown to be compatible with competitive unit labor costs in countries that enjoy high rates of capital accumulation and rapid technological progress. In Korea, real wages in manufacturing rose by over 7 percent a year between 1966 and 1976.[12] In Singapore, the government has recently intervened in the labor market to force up wage rates in order to accelerate a structural shift toward more capital- and skill-intensive industries better adapted to its current factor endowment.

Collective bargaining and labor legislation can play positive roles in democratic societies. They are means of ensuring wider participation and equity in economic development, and if exercised with discretion they need not inhibit economic growth. In some countries, however, these instruments have become barriers to economic and social progress. The lesson seems to be that governments should not attempt to impose minimum wages significantly above the market rate or to hold down wages artificially when market forces are pushing them up.

Policies to Foster Foreign Investment and Other Cooperative Arrangements

In some industries, at least, countries that fail to encourage foreign investment may pay a substantial price in manufactured exports forgone.[13] Foreign-owned companies contribute substantially to exports of processed foods, for example. Subsidiaries of transnational corporations play a dominant role in the thriving market for electronics, machinery, transport equipment, fabricated metal products, instruments, and the like. In these industries, exports of the developing countries may be built around labor-intensive parts of the production and marketing processes controlled by transnational corporations. Foreign firms provide technical and managerial know-how and easy access to patented technology, as well as additional capital. This does not mean that developing countries should give foreign investors special treatment not accorded to local entrepreneurs. Moderate levels of taxation provide greater incentive to companies in the long run than do tax holidays. Developing countries, however, should offer guarantees for the security of the investment and the repatriation of profits and capital. They should also provide a supportive working environment: Ports and telephones have to work; paperwork must not be an untoward burden.

Foreign cooperation may also be obtained through other forms of association. These include licensing, international subcontracting, and consultancy contracts. In the developing countries that are major exporters of manufactures, most labor-intensive consumer goods, such as clothing, shoes, and textiles, tend to be made in firms owned locally. But trade in these products is largely organized by major foreign buyers and trading companies, whose role in exporting the goods is often crucial.

Trade Policy and Efficient Import Substitution

Trade policy covers not only measures promoting exports but also those affecting the import of goods that compete with local industry in the domestic market. The need for some protection of infant industry (to allow a learning process) is generally accepted, but should it be a uniform or a made-to-measure system? A uniform system, advocates argue, minimizes distortions and simplifies administration and policy making. Others prefer made-to-measure protection on the grounds that industries should get only as much protection as they "need"; to give them more is considered wasteful. The issue here is how to determine need. Such a determination requires that tariff authorities estimate costs of production -- a complicated task, involving judgement and discretion on the part of the authorities.

The choice is not simple. If a tariff is set too low, the domestic firm may not survive. If it is too high, the primary aim of stimulating efficiency is not achieved. If selective, case-by-case protection is implemented through quantitative controls (quotas, licenses, and the like), as well as tariffs, additional uncertainty is introduced into business planning. Bureaucratic delays and corruption may be encouraged. On the whole, the most effective trade policies seem to be those that emphasize uniformity rather than discretion and that provide low overall levels of protection.[14]

Concern has been expressed that the benefits of outward-looking strategies might accrue largely to the importing countries (through lower prices), or to the entrepreneurs engaged in export production and marketing, and might even be at the expense of domestic industry and local consumers. Also, excessive export promotion through export subsidies can be costly. But the experience of the most successful exporters demonstrates that these risks can be avoided. Export growth has been associated in these countries with rapid increase in industrial output for the domestic market and significant diversification and deepening of the industrial structure. Industrial employment and real wages have risen substantially, as have domestic savings and investment rates. Indigenous skills have been developed, and managerial and technical know-how have been broadly diffused. Consumers have been offered a wider choice of product, and rapidly rising incomes have allowed them to take advantage of this choice.

Several factors and mechanisms have contributed to these results. Perhaps most relevant is the roughly equal incentive an outward-looking strategy provides to exports and import substitution. Thus an efficient use of resources is encouraged for both domestic and export production. Exports supply the foreign exchange to pay for those imported inputs essential for industrial expansion (a major constraint on output in many countries). Rapid growth allows high rates of capital accumulation and provides the revenues to expand educational and training programs. This investment, in turn, generates further growth and brings about a progressive shift in comparative advantage toward more skill- and capital-intensive industries. Clearly, exports need not be in conflict with efficient import substitution. They can be mutually reinforcing, if supported by moderate and balanced incentives.

Construction Government Intervention

The role of government in the industrialization process varies widely in the market or mixed economies represented in the list of top exporters. In no case has government assumed a laissez faire posture. All have shown a commitment to industrial growth and export expansion. Strong leadership has been exhibited in the formulation and execution of industrial policies. But the extent and forms of direct government intervention have differed considerably among countries, with varying degrees of success.

In some countries, the state has acquired ownership of the "commanding heights" of the economy. In Korea, public enterprises are responsible for about 15 percent of nonagricultural output, roughly on a par with the proportions in the United Kingdom and Italy.[15] Their share is also significant in Brazil.[16] The Korean public enterprise sector has been financially profitable overall, although less cost-efficient than the private sector.[17] In several countries, however, public enterprises have been a substantial burden on the central government budget. These financial losses have been attributed to (1) inadequate planning and poor feasibility studies, resulting in ill-conceived investments, (2) lack of skilled managers and administrators, (3) over-centralized decision making, (4) state intervention in the day-to-day operations of the firm, (5) unclear or conflicting objectives, and (6) political patronage.[18] Public enterprises have performed best in countries where they are granted a large measure of autonomy and where they are subject to competition from other domestic firms and from the foreign-trade sector.

Industrial licensing and price controls are other forms of state intervention often used to overrule market forces. The aims are multiple: to control investments and to allocate resources to conform with predetermined priorities and targets, to prevent market structures from becoming monopolized, to promote regionally balanced industrial development, to protect consumers from excessive price mark-ups, to ensure an adequate supply of raw materials and intermediate inputs at reasonable prices to "priority" sectors, and to prevent or mitigate inflation. These objectives are laudable, but experience in many developing countries indicates that these administrative controls have given rise to a variety of economic costs and to few of the expected benefits.

Various studies have shown that the state has not been more knowledgeable than the market in selecting the most beneficial industrial investments. Licenses have been frequently allocated ad hoc, without regard to sound economic criteria. Delays in the planning and the execution of projects have resulted. Additional costs thus imposed on the society include diversion of skilled manpower to handle the administration of the system, bribery and corruption to lubricate the process, and a negative impact on indigenous research and development. Price controls tend to constrict investment (in part because they hamper the internal generation of investment funds) and often lead to chronic shortages of output.[19] Indirect measures (such as fiscal incentives or tariff policies) have proved to be superior to direct controls as means of furthering broad industrial development objectives.

Korea and Japan are often cited as examples of where constructive intervention by governments has occurred. Korea's rapid economic growth since the early 1960s has been described as "a government directed development in which the principal engine has been private enterprise."[20] The effectiveness of the government's direction of economic activity can be ascribed to the leadership's single-minded commitment to economic growth and, at a deeper level, to its identification of rapid growth with export-led development. But Korea's successful export performance derived primarily from initiatives taken by firms acting within a de-centralized system and in response to general incentives as well as strong government prodding. The government has relied on market incentives to ensure that firms earn adequate profits on their exports. These incentives are applied across the board and generally operate through taxes and measures that affect market prices; they apply to all firms automatically.[21]

In Japan, strong leadership coincided with a broad consensus that economic or industrial growth was the road to independence and national revival after occupation.[22] However, a recent World Bank study concludes that the explosive growth of the Japanese economy did not come about because Japan developed (either by government alone or in cooperation with business) a precise plan and then stuck to it. There were many instances in which firms and industries that were not government-picked "winners" did well. The growth came from the interaction of a high savings rate, an abundance of private entrepreneurship, and a supportive business atmosphere. The government, through its multifaceted contact with business and its influence over the flow of capital, has stressed economies of scale, quality control and exports.[23]

Infrastructure and Human Resource Development

There is little doubt that industrial expansion is fostered more readily in countries that have already reached relatively high levels of human resource development and that have large domestic markets and a substantial physical infrastructure. Basic minimum levels in these areas are probably preconditions for effective industrial development. Furthermore, adequate transport facilities, communications systems, technical and organizational skills would seem to be required for the export of primary commodities as well as for manufactures.[24] However, it is difficult to assess what would constitute such minimum levels of infrastructure or to identify countries in which the absence of the preconditions has prevented the economy from responding to the policies and incentives discussed here. Several countries with small populations and limited domestic markets have been successful in penetrating world markets.

While manufactures accounted for only 11 percent of total merchandise exports from low-income countries (excluding China and India) in 1978, their total exports of goods and nonfactor services represented a higher share (20 percent) of their GDP than is the case for the middle-income oil importers (18 percent) or the industrial market economies (19 percent). The share of total exports in GDP for sub-Saharan Africa, which is the most backward region in terms of infrastructure and human resource development, was 23 percent. Nonetheless, this proportion has not changed markedly since 1960, when it was 22 percent. Subsequent development in the majority of low-income countries was marked by the failure to ensure an adequate rate of manufacturing growth by diversifying output and exports.

This failure seems to stem largely from inappropriate policies rather than from constraints on infrastructure or human resources. In the few low-income countries that did diversify successfully, there does not appear to be a close correlation between educational levels and manufacturing growth. The annual growth of manufacturing output averaged 6.7 percent in Malawi, 7.1 percent in Haiti, and 11.4 percent in Kenya from 1970 to 1979. Their adult literacy rates in 1976 were only 25 percent, 23 percent, and 45 percent, respectively. Some low-income countries with much higher literacy levels, such as Sri Lanka (85 percent) and Tanzania (66 percent), achieved little growth in manufacturing output (1.7 percent and 3.6 percent, respectively) over the same period. Nor is there a close correlation between the disappointing industrial growth of the low-income countries overall and their expenditure on education, roads, and domestic energy production. Education accounted for 14.0 percent and roads for 5.0 percent of central government expenditure in low-income countries in 1978. In middle-income countries, their share was 11.5 percent and 5.6 percent, respectively. In low-income Africa (sub-Sahara), expenditures were as high as 15.2 percent on education and 5.3 percent on roads. Commercial energy production rose by 8.4 percent a year in low-income countries (21.2 percent in low-income Africa) between 1974 and 1979, compared with a decline of 0.5 percent in middle-income countries.[25]

Although the importance of these complementary factors should not be underestimated, differences in growth performance appear to be more directly related to differences in policy. Perceptive government leadership and sensible economic policies can go a long way to overcome initial constraints. Gaps in skills and know-how can be filled through cooperation with foreign firms and expatriates, who in turn help to develop local manpower by means of in-plant training. Appropriate incentives and price structures not only stimulate industrial entrepreneurship, but also encourage private initiatives in transport and road maintenance services. Changes in pricing policies for transport, power, and telephone services to reflect their real costs to society as a whole has led to a modification of design standards (reducing capital costs) and to greater operational efficiency. The more successful countries have shown that, in regard to infrastructure, it is possible to do more with less.[26] Much can also be done to encourage local initiatives and mobilize resources, such as labor, building materials, finance, and teaching talent.[27]

Malawi is a good example of how a small African country with little apparent industrial potential can enjoy a high rate of manufacturing growth while following an agriculture-oriented development strategy. It is one of the poorest countries in the world. It is land-locked, has no significant mineral resources, and has a very small domestic market. Seventy-five percent of its adult population is illiterate. Its main natural resource is land, but even land has become scarce under the pressure of its dense and rapidly growing population of 5.8 million. Its approach to industry has been far from laissez faire -- the government has provided protection for infant industries and has actively promoted industry through parastatal investment, within strict limits. There is a moderate protective tariff, which ranges from 7.5 to 40 percent. Parastatal enterprises, which account for more than half of industrial output, have been profitable and have generally remained free from government interference. Most important, quantitative restrictions have not been used to protect industry, and the exchange rate has been kept at a level that not only encourages export growth but also maintains external balance.

These policies help explain Malawi's economic performance, which compares favorably with most other countries with similar resources and income levels. During 1968-77, total industrial value added in real terms grew at an annual average rate of 6.5 percent, while agriculture grew at 4.5 percent. Manufacturing employment grew 6.5 percent annually over the same period, because of the labor-intensive nature of the industry that has developed (food processing, textiles and footwear, tobacco and tea processing, and metal manufactures), and because of a wage policy that has held down urban wages. Given the obstacles to industrial growth in Malawi, it is doubtful whether industrial output would have grown any faster with higher protection, while agricultural output, manufacturing employment, and total GDP would almost certainly have grown more slowly.[28]

III. PENETRATION OF MARKETS IN INDUSTRIAL COUNTRIES

Are the developing countries that adopt outward-oriented strategies likely to face increasing barriers to their exports in industrial countries? Several studies have allayed such misgivings by showing that the adverse impact of manufactured exports from developing countries on industrial countries has been greatly exaggerated. Although their market penetration grew by about 8 percent a year in the 1970s, at the end of the decade products from developing countries still accounted for less than 3.5 percent of consumption (production plus imports minus exports) in the industrial countries. Even in the clothing, textiles, and leather industries, where penetration of the markets in industrial countries was highest, it had not reached 10 percent of total consumption.

If market penetration by developing countries were to continue to rise in the 1980s at the rate it did in the 1970s, the developing countries' share in the consumption of manufactured goods in the industrial countries would only rise to about 5 percent. In the most successful industries, such as clothing and textiles, that share might rise to 15 percent. Even so, the production of these goods in the industrial countries would still increase at an average annual rate of 2 percent.[29]

The fears of undue dependence on imports by important domestic industries in industrial countries are being stressed and may have merit in some cases in terms of national defense.[30] However, with market penetration by developing countries well below 5 percent overall, such dependence is some time away in most sectors. Greater diversification of exports by developing countries should also reduce such fears.

Similarly, the effect of imports from developing countries on job displacement in the industrial countries is generally exaggerated. The essence of outward-oriented policy is greater involvement in world trade -- on the import as well as on the export side. In fact, the volume of manufactured exports from industrial to developing countries has increased by much more than the counterflow (Table 2).

When the direct and indirect impact of an expansion of trade between industrial and developing countries is taken into account, several studies show positive net effects on employment for the industrial countries.[31]

In times of recession and high unemployment, there is, of course, considerable political pressure in the industrial countries to shore up weak industries by giving them tariffs, subsidies, or other protection. Many of these defensive measures have been ill

Table 2. Increase in the Volume of Trade in Manufactures between Developing and Industrial Countries, 1960-78

(1970 US$ billion)

Period and direction of trade	Increase of trade
1960-70	
Industrial to developing countries	15.22
Developing to industrial countries	5.78
1970-78	
Industrial to developing countries	31.83
Developing to industrial countries	11.48

Source: J. M. Finger, "Industrial Country Policy and Adjustment to Imports from Developing Countries," World Bank Staff Working Paper No. 470 (Washington, D.C.: World Bank, July 1981).

advised, encouraging wasteful investment in industries that should have been abandoned or left free to adjust to changing comparative advantages.

Despite these defensive measures, the process of global trade liberalization continued throughout the decade.[32] Traditional exports of manufactures from the developing countries grew quite rapidly in the 1970s, and, in recent years, have become more diversified. The developing countries have begun to compete in a wide range of new nondurable and durable consumer goods, as well as in intermediate and capital products. In particular, there has been a rapid growth of exports of machinery (see Table 3).

The very character of North-South trade is thus changing. Instead of consisting predominantly of trade between different industries, it is moving toward intraindustry trade, that is, trade in components within an industry, which is characteristic of the trade among industrial countries. In the more advanced developing countries, the emphasis in promoting exports is therefore shifting from industries, such as clothing, with a comparative advantage in low labor costs to firms with a comparative entrepreneurial advantage. Firms in countries such as Brazil, Argentina, and Korea are thus taking part in world trade in such sophisticated capital goods as hydroelectric generating equipment and earth-moving machinery. The scope for more rapid and more widespread diversification of exports by developing countries during the 1980s will be influenced, of course, by the economic climate in the industrial countries. The ability of the industrial countries to get inflation under control and to lower interest rates appears to be a prerequisite for sustained growth in their markets.[33]

IV. EXPANSION OF TRADE TO MARKETS IN DEVELOPING COUNTRIES

About a third of the exports of the developing countries go to other developing countries. As these countries continue to industrialize, their mutual trade in manufactures can be expected to increase rapidly. The petroleum-exporting countries, in particular, are important markets.

Overall in the mid and late 1970s, the developing countries' exports of manufactures to other developing countries grew more rapidly than their exports to industrial countries. The developing countries participating in this trade were primarily those that followed outward-oriented policies. In other developing countries, high tariffs and other forms of protection limited exports and retarded the expansion of export capacity.

Mainly from this latter group, there have been calls urging "collective self-reliance" in the form of closer economic integration and cooperation among developing countries. Various attempts at economic integration have been made -- notably, the East African Community and the Central American Common Market (CACM) -- but it is generally agreed that these integration schemes have not lived up to their expectations.[34] Various factors

Table 3. Structure of Merchandise Exports

(percent)

	Low-income developing countries	Middle-income developing countries
Agricultural commodities		
1960	69	60
1978	38	29
Fuels, minerals, and metals		
1960	13	27
1978	32	35
Textiles and clothing		
1960	13	3
1978	12	9
Machinery and transport equipment		
1960	(.)	2
1978	3	12
Other manufactures		
1960	5	8
1978	15	17

Note: (.) indicates a value substantially less than 1.
Source: *World Development Report 1981.*

account for the limited progress so far. First, item-by-item negotiations on tariff reductions have encountered serious opposition from special interests. Second, differences in the level of industrial development have made agreements on trade liberalization difficult. Third, in view of the distortions in relative prices because of protection, it has been difficult to determine the benefits of integration, and there has been a tendency to consider changes in the trade balance as signs of gain or loss. Finally, the governments of the individual countries have been reluctant to proceed with integration because they were anxious to safeguard their freedom of action. In particular, this has hampered agreement on the allocation of industries among member countries. While it is still argued that the problems associated with integration schemes can be overcome, the evidence suggests that they are inherent.[35]

The experience of Costa Rica illustrates the limitations of regional integration schemes. In 1963, Costa Rica joined the Central American Common Market and adopted the instruments of integration, which, in essence, promoted a strategy of regional import substitution. An open economy was created for imports of raw materials, intermediate products, and capital goods, but high levels of protection (nominal tariff rates averaging about 100 percent, and effective rates averaging 230 percent) were established for industries making consumer goods, but did not apply to trade among the members of CACM. These policies paid early dividends. Manufacturing output grew by 9 percent a year between 1963 and 1977. Exports of manufactured goods, which constituted only 4 percent of exports in 1963, grew to 28 percent in 1977, but 80 percent of these manufactured exports went to other members of the CACM. Industrial expansion began to slow in the late 1970s after the first "easy" stage of regional import substitution. Economies of scale and scarcities of domestic raw materials now severely limit the possibility for additional import substitution, and the economy is stagnating. The highly skewed structure of protection, combined with an overvalued exchange rate, has resulted in a pronounced bias against exports to non-CACM countries and a heavy reliance on imported inputs in manufacturing. Excluding the food products sector, raw material and intermediate imports for manufacturing exceed manufactured exports by about 70 percent. In 1980, the balance-of-payments deficit on current account amounted to 14 percent of GDP. Diminished availability of foreign exchange is exercising a severe constraint on overall development. Overcoming this constraint requires changing the orientation of Costa Rica's development policies away from import substitution, toward the promotion of nontraditional exports to markets outside the CACM.

The experience of Costa Rica and similar experiences in other regions point to the need for trade-creating rather than trade-diverting policies and relationships. These would stimulate innovation of products and processes more suitable to the consumption levels, tastes, and factor endowments of countries at similar levels of development. The policy instruments to bring about these goals have already been discussed -- realistic exchange rates, reduced tariff protection, and simplification or abolition

of quantitative controls and licensing procedures. Supporting
measures would include improvement in port services, simplified
customs procedures, and standardized products. [36]

In short, although there is ample scope for greater economic
cooperation among developing countries, outward-looking strategies
that stimulate entrepreneurs to take advantage of market
opportunities in all directions -- north and south, east and
west -- hold out greater prospects for continued growth and balance
development than does reliance on membership in restricted
economic communities. It should be stressed that outward-looking
strategies do not imply completely open economies. Moderate and
balanced protection for domestic industry, agriculture, and
services is justified while these sectors are in the process of
learning by doing. But protection in the domestic market must be
balanced by adequate incentives, supporting services, and access to
resources for exporters. As the Central American experience
demonstrates, the opening up of an economy to trade with its
neighbors in a regional grouping is not a substitute for a truly
outward-looking strategy.

NOTES

[1] See Jagdish N. Bhagwati and T. N. Srinivasan. "Trade Policy and
Development" in Rudigar Dornbusch and Jacob A. Frenkel, eds.,
International Economic Policy: Theory and Evidence (Baltimore
and London: The Johns Hopkins University Press, 1978).

[2] See Bela Balassa, "Exports and Economic Growth: Further
Evidence," Journal of Development Economics, vol. 5 (1978), pp.
181-89.

[3] See Michael Michaely, "Exports and Growth: An Empirical
Investigation," Journal of Development Economics, vol. 4 (1977),
pp. 49-54; Anne O. Krueger, Foreign Trade Regimes and Economic
Development (Cambridge, Mass." Ballinger, 1978); and William G.
Tyler, "Growth and Export Expansion in Developing Countries:
Some Empirical Evidence," Journal of Development Economics, vol.
9 (August 1981), pp. 121-30.

[4] Pearson and Spearman rank correlation coefficients of 0.55 and
0.50, respectively, were reported for the non-OPEC developing
countries covered. See Tyler, "Growth and Export Expansion."

[5] See Donald B. Keesing, "World Trade and Output of Manufactures:
Structural Trends and Developing Countries' Exports," World Bank
Staff Working Paper No. 316 (Washington, D.C.: World Bank,
January 1080). It has been pointed out that this figure

overstates the export share of these countries as it includes considerable reexports.

[6]See Hollis B. Chenery and Donald B. Keesing, "The Changing Composition of Developing Country Exports," World Bank Staff Working Paper No. 314 (Washington, D.C.: World Bank, January 1979); and World Development Report 1981 (New York: Oxford University Press, 1981), table 12. This list includes twelve countries in the low-income group and eleven from Africa. It should also be noted that although the most successful exporters are mainly middle-income countries, some began their export drive at low income levels and with few natural resources. Per capita income in Korea, for example, was well below the average for Africa in 1950 and was only 41 percent of the level in Ghana in that year. See David Morawetz, Twenty-five Years of Economic Development, 1950 to 1975 (Baltimore and London: The Johns Hopkins University Press, 1977).

[7]See Chenery and Keesing, "Changing Composition of Exports."

[8]The following section draws upon John Cody, Helen Hughes, and David Wall, eds., Policies for Industrial Progress in Developing Countries (New York: Oxford University Press, 1980); and Donald Keesing, "Trade Policy for Developing Countries," World Bank Staff Working Paper No. 353 (Washington, D.c.: World Bank, August 1979).

[9]It should also be noted that by providing free-trade treatment to exports as well as to the production of inputs for exports, Korea has little need for export subsidies. Subsidies have been extensively used in Latin American countries to offset the adverse effects of high input costs.

[10]For a fuller discussion of these issues and the practical remedies open to developing countries, see Bela Balassa and Michael Sharpston, "Export Subsidies by Developing Countries: Issues of Policy," Commercial Policy Issues (November 1977), pp. 13-50.

[11]Apart from exports by capital-intensive industries that enjoy other comparative advantages because of location, climate, energy supplies, or natural resources. In labor-intensive industries, competitive unit wage costs are critical. An International Labour Office (ILO) survey in 1979 showed that the median wage for textile workers in ten African countries was 50 percent higher than in Pakistan and more than twice as high as in Bangladesh. African labor productivity also tends to compare unfavorably with many other parts of the world. See ILO, Bulletin of Labour Statistics (Geneva, 1980).

[12]See Wontack Hong, Trade, Distortions and Employment Growth in Korea (Seoul: Korea Development Institute, 1979).

[13]Direct foreign investment in East Asia and the Pacific, the region that achieved the highest growth of manufactured exports, grew elevenfold in current prices between 1965 and 1977, reaching $1.5 billion in the latter year. In Africa south of the Sahara (excluding South Africa and Nigeria), which had a disappointing export performance on the whole, foreign investment rose by only 85 percent in current prices during this period, amounting to $184 million in 1977. See World Tables 1980 (Baltimore and London: The John Hopkins Univeristy Press, 1980), table 7.

[14]The optimal level of protection will vary according to the level of development and industrial experience of each country. Higher tariffs and greater assistance in export promotion (including incentives to foreign investors) may be justified in low-income countries on grounds of protecting infant industries.

[15]See Armeane M. Choksi, "State Intervention in the Industrialization of Developing Countries: Selected Issues," World Bank Staff Working Paper No. 314 (Washington, D.C.: World Bank, January 1979).

[16]See   William G. Tyler,   The   Brazilian   Industrial   Economy

[17]See L. P. Jones, Public Enterprise and Economic Development: The Korean Case (Seoul: Korea Development Institute, 1975).

[18]See Choksi, "State Intervention."

[19]See Stephen E. Guisinger, "Direct Controls in the Private Sector," in Cody, Hughes, and Wall, eds., Policies for Industrial Progress; and Choksi, "State Intervention."

[20]Edward S. Mason Et al., The Economic and Social Modernization of the Republic of Korea (Cambridge, Mass.: Council on East Asian Studies, distributed by Harvard University Press, 1980). (Lexington, Mass.: Lexington Books, 1981).

[21]See Larry E. Westphal, "the Private Sector as 'Principal Engine' of Development: Korea," in Economic Development and the Private Sector (Washington, D.C.: World Bank, September 1981).

[22]Philip H. Trezise and Yukio Suzuki, "Politics, Government and Economic Growth in Japan," in Hugh Patrick and Henry Rosovsky, eds., Asia's New Giant (Washington, D.C.: Brookings Institution, 1976).

[23]See J. M. Finger, "Industrial Country Policy and Adjustment to Imports from Developing Countries," World Bank Staff Working Paper No. 470 (Washington, D.C.: World Bank, July 1981).

[24]Large-scale plantations, mining, and timber operations have required extensive transport networks but have drawn upon the organizational skills and expertise of multinational companies. However, it has been pointed out by Peter Bauer, in a lecture

delivered at the World Bank in February 1982, that a developed
infrastructure was not a precondition for the emergence of the
major cash crops of Southeast Asia and West Africa.
Infrastructural facilities were developed in the course of the
expansion of the economy.

[25]See Accelerated Development in Sub-Saharan Africa: An Agenda for
Action (Washington, D.C.: World Bank, 1981).

[26]See Christopher R. Willoughby, "Infrastructure: Doing More with
Less," in Economic Development and the Private Sector.

[27]See Education Sector Policy Paper (Washington, D.C.: World Bank,
1980).

[28]See Accelerated Development in Sub-Saharan Africa.

[29]See Bela Balassa, "The Process of Industrial Development and
Alternative Development Strategies," Graham Memorial Lecture,
Princeton University, April 17, 1980.

[30]The defense issue is raised mostly by imported inputs originating
from the mining sectors of developing countries. For example,
developing countries were responsible for 49 percent of world
trade in iron ore and 60 percent of exports of nonferrous ore in
1978. But their share has also become significant in some
manufactured products, such as transistors, valves, and other
electronic components; they were responsible for over a third of
world trade in these items in 1978.

[31]See Robert E. Baldwin, "Trade and Employment Effects in the
United States Multilateral Tariff Reductions," American Economic
Review, Papers and Proceedings (May 1976); H. F. Lydall, Trade
and Employment (Geneva, ILO, 1975); and Errol Grinols and Erik
Thorbecke, "The Effects of Trade between the US and Developing
Countries on US Employment," Working Paper No. 171 (Ithaca,
N.Y.: Cornell University, Department of Economics, 1978).

[32]See General Agreement on Tariffs and Trade (GATT), International
Trade 1980/81 (Geneva, 1981).

[33]See statements by the U.S. secretary of the treasury and the
spokesman for the European Economic Community to the 1981 annual
meeting of the World Bank and International Monetary Fund (IMF).
World Development Report 1981, chapter 3, discusses more
comprehensively the risks of limits of access to industrial
country markets.

[34]See Bela Balassa and E. J. Stoutjesdijk, "Economic
Integration among Developing Countries" (Washington, D.C.: World
Bank 1974), processed, and Bela Balassa, "Types of Economic
Integration," in Fritz Machlup, ed., Economic Integration:
Worldwide, Regional, Sectoral (New York: Wiley, 1976).

[35]See Constantine V. Vaitsos, "Crisis in Regional Economic Cooperation (Integration) among Developing Countries: A Survey," World Development (June 1978).

[36]See Helen Hughes, "Inter-Developing Country Trade and Employment," a paper presented at the International Economic Association (IEA) Sixth World Congress on Human Resources, Employment and Development, Mexico City, August 4-9, 1980.

Restructuring Out of Recession

RICHARD JOLLY

Given unemployment and excess capacity in the industrialised countries, it seems only obvious to ask how some measures to stimulate investment and restructuring in the South might be combined with measures which would also stimulate higher levels of economic activity in the North. To the extent that the process brought into use resources which would otherwise be idle, the real costs of the programme would be by that much reduced. To the extent that a higher level of economic activity was stimulated in the industrialised countries, unemployment would be reduced and thus also one of the main factors which leads to popular and political opposition to imports and restructuring.

The link between unemployment and opposition to restructuring and adjustment is worth stressing. More adjustment took place in the 1960s in most industrial countries than has occurred in the last 5 years. Yet there was relatively little opposition, a comforting contrast with the present, usually attributed in part to the lower unemployment and greater economic dynamism of the 1960s.

There is little doubt that a "massive transfer of additional resources" from the North to the South -- or even just a sizeable transfer -- could make a significant impact on levels of economic activity in both developing and developed countries.

Holsen and Waelbroeck estimated that balance of payments borrowing by developing countries in 1975 and 1976, to a value of $8 and $11 billion respectively, avoided the need for a fall in the GNP of the LDCs by 5.0 and 6.9% in these two years and thereby contributed 0.4% and 0.6% in the aggregate demand sustaining the GNPs of the developed countries. They added:

> It is not unusual in analysing business-cycle developments to think of developing countries as capable

From **INTERNATIONAL DEVELOPMENT REVIEW**, 1980, Vol 2-3, (80-83), reprinted by permission of the publisher.

TABLE 1

Transfer of $20.0 billion per year to non-OPEC developing regions, maintained for three years
(Per Cent Increase)

Effect on:	Year of Transfer:		
	First	Second	Third
World Exports ($)	2.6	2.6	2.0
World Exports (Volume)	3.0	2.8	1.8
OECD Exports ($)	3.1	3.1	2.3
OECD Imports ($)	1.3	1.6	1.5
LDC Exports ($)	1.4	1.7	1.4
LDC Imports ($)	8.4.	7.1	4.6
OECD GNP (real)	0.5	0.6	0.4
LDC GNP (real)	1.7	1.8	1.5

Source: US Bureau of Intelligence and Research, Department of State: INR Report No. 1081, 1978, p. 3. The final 2 lines are calculated from data given in later tables of the report.

of affecting aggregate demand. This is because they are
thought of as adjusting their purchases passively to the
level permitted by their foreign exchange earnings. This
assumption is not correct any more. Less-developed
countries' import policies influence demand today in the
same way as the US deficit of the late 1960s and early
1970s, and the OPEC balance of payments surplus.[1]

Calculations made for UNCTAD by the University of Pennsylvania
using the link econometric model for the world economy suggested
that "an increase of the growth rate by 3 percentage points in the
non-oil-producing developing countries would result in an increase
of the growth rate by 1 per cent point in the OECD countries."
Since then more disaggregated analyses on alternative hypotheses
have been undertaken by various groups. The results of the
simulations undertaken by the US Bureau of Intelligence and
Research[2] summarised in Table 1 make clear some of the issues.

These simulations consider a transfer of an additional $20
billion a year to non-OPEC developing countries sustained for three
years. Three ways of financing the transfers were simulated: (a)
a "costless" transfer, analogous to transferring profits from the
sale of International Monetary Fund reserves of gold or allocating
newly created SDRs to the developing countries. In essence, this
corresponds to a Keynesian stimulus to demand which calls into use
resources which would otherwise be idle. The results shown in
Table 1 correspond to these simulations. Exports and imports in
both developed and developing countries would rise considerably.
So also would GNP: by roughly one half a per cent per year for 3
years in the industrial countries; by one and a half per cent or
slightly more per year for those years in non-OPEC developing
countries. The employment impact of such increases was not
calculated but, following Okun's rule of thumb, the increase in GNP
might be the equivalent to a direct increase in employment of
perhaps 0.2% or roughly 500,000 jobs throughout the industrial
countries.

The other two simulations are based on alternative ways of
raising the finance: (b) assumes that the $20 billion is obtained
by diverting government expenditure from domestic goods and
services to the transfer programme in each of the 13 industrial
countries. The sum involved is roughly 1% of GDP in these
countries, so the net effect is also roughly just over twice that
of increasing official development assistance (ODA) from the
present average level of 0.31% of GNP in the DAC donor countries to
the target level of 0.7 per cent of GNP. Simulation (c) assumes
that the $20 billion is raised from additional direct taxation.

In both these simulations, the net impact on both developed
and developing countries is substantially smaller than that of the
first simulation, essentially because the positive impacts of the
transfer on economic activity in both developed and developing
countries s offset by the negative impact of the withdrawals of
effective purchasing power in the industrial countries. In the
case of the transfer financed by a diversion of government
expenditures the combined effect on the GNP of the developed
countries is negative: total GNP with the programme would be

something under one tenth of one per cent less than without the transfer -- though, of course, GNP in developing countries would be one and a half per cent higher.

In the case of the transfer financed by increasing direct taxation, however, the impact on both developed and developing countries would be positive; on developed countries by some 0.2 per cent of GNP, on developing countries by about the same amount as in other simulations.

These simulations only offer a rough guide to the possible effects of transfers of resources but they can help to illuminate some of the issues, particularly the differential impact on the various parties involved.

I. STRUCTURAL CHANGE - THE SECOND OBJECTIVE

Development, however, means much more than a Keynesian expansion of demand. If a programme of additional transfers is to stimulate more balanced and sustainable growth, the transfers much be directed towards restructuring, to deal with structural problems and global imbalance in key sectors such as agriculture, energy, certain sectors of industry and certain, but not all, commodities. Without this, there is a real risk that several of the existing structural imbalances in the world economy could rapidly become more serious if higher levels of economic activity were to be resumed in industrial countries. This in turn could stimulate inflationary pressures on a scale which could slow or even stop recovery.

Taken together, under-utilisation of capacity and the need for restructuring provide the possibility of and suggest the need for a new international initiative, under which a major increase of transfers from developed to developed countries would be combined with measures to stimulate investment in developing countries in projects or sectors which would ease structural bottlenecks in the medium and longer run. If undertaken on a reasonable scale, the transfers and investment could provide an important stimulus towards higher levels of economic activity in the industrial economies of the West -- though their probable scale and timing suggest that any initiative should primarily be judged for its medium-term impact rather than for its short-term countercyclical efforts.[3]

Various policy inducements would be available to implement such a programme of transfers: major increases in ODA (Official Development Assistance), especially but not only from Germany and Japan, which currently combine relatively low ODA performance with very large balance-of-payments surpluses; additional flows of private finance, possibly stimulated through new institutional mechanisms or a major increase in co-financing; an increase in SDRs, made possible by more ambitious reforms of the international monetary system; or a combination of such instruments and measures, old and new, but operated on a much larger scale than at present and adding up to a co-ordinated, identifiable international initiative.

In my view the critical points for such an initiative to be politically acceptable and economically effectives are four:

1. That the programme combine both additional flows of private finance with at least some reasonable proportion of additional ODA. Without this, the poorer countries of the Third World are likely to receive very little benefit and there will be little capacity to stimulate additional investment in activities which are important for development and structural change but initially only marginally viable in commercial terms, such as small-scale agriculture, small-scale transportation or even energy exploration.

2. That the programme clearly be directed towards stimulating investment of a sort which promotes structural change internationally. The particular sectors to be covered could be for later discussion -- though investment (and other related supporting expenditure) to increase Third World production in agriculture, energy, and some sectors of industry and raw-material production and processing should certainly qualify. So also would major regional or global projects and programmes, of the sort which have been proposed for the Third Development Decade, and international stockpiling schemes which might form part of commodity agreements.

3. That responsibility for initiating the programme and control of its key operations clearly involve both developed and developing countries on an equitable basis. This is more important than the question of where administrative responsibility for the initiative would rest. As regards administration, it would obviously be desirable to work through existing institutions, if possible relying considerably upon the regional development banks, as a way of incorporating greater developing-country involvement and of strengthening the regional focus.

4. In size, I believe the total situation well justifies a sizable not a minor initiative. A programme building up within two to four years to total additional flows of some $10-20 billion a year would not seem to me excessive.

The number of voices, official and non-official, calling for such a programme has been growing: Chancellor Kreisky in 1976, Claude Cheysson in 1977, the Swedish proposal for a massive programme of transfers in 1978. Over the last 18 months there have been proposals from Nakajima for a Global Infrastructure Investment Fund, for an OPEC/OECD global stimulation plan, for a 20-year Marshall Plan for the Third World. The 1979 ICFTU Review of the World Economic Situation states: "There has been growing recognition over the past year of the need for a massive, planned international effort to assist the developing countries -- for a new, world-wide 'Marshall Plan', as advocated by the ICFTU for some years."[4]

Most recently, the Arusha Declaration of the Group of 77, in preparation for UNCTAD V, observed that "the extent and persistence of considerable under-utilisation of resources leading to unemployment in the developed world should no longer be seen as an exceptionally prolonged trough to the business cycle with a more or less automatic recovery to follow. This situation inhibits an effective international adjustment process. What would be required to restore full employment is a new impulse on a historic scale comparable for example with the transfer of resources to Europe for post-war reconstruction; this time, meeting the needs of the Third World would have a decisive role to play in a situation where purely domestic reflation in developed economies would be no substitute against the existing background of production capacities geared to export markets that have been developed over three decades of export-led growth."[5]

Mr. Roy Jenkins, giving the first Jean Monnet Lecture in October 1978, said: "We also need to view the present economic recession in a longer-term perspective. The extent and persistence of unemployment can no longer be seen as an exceptionally low and long bottom to the business cycles. To restore full employment requires a new impulse on a historic scale. We require a new driving force comparable with the major rejuvenations of the past 2000 years; the industrial revolution itself, the onset of the railway age, the impact of Keynes, the need for post-war reconstruction, the spread of what were previously regarded as middle-class standards to the mass of the populations in the industrial countries. I believe that the needs of the Third World have a major part to play here. The sources of new growth have in the past sometimes come together, the one world-wide and the other regional."[6]

One must frankly recognise that, in spite of these attempts to stimulate serious action on these broad lines, most governments of industrial countries have to date been cautious and hesitant. Among the industrial countries, caution has, I believe, been mainly the result of three concerns: the fear of inflation; the uncertainty of the impact on the balance of payments of different countries; the reluctance to consider any initiative which might involve increasing public expenditure.

As indicated in Arusha, Third World governments have been more open to such proposals -- but not without conditions. Third World responses have been particularly sensitive to a strong emphasis on transferring resources in ways which would support international structural change, the inclusion of a component of ODA in order that poorer as well as better-off developing countries may benefit from the initiative, and a broad base of control which will provide for strong participation by developing countries in the management of any such scheme.

The risk of inflation is in my view the most legitimate of such objections. There is no strong evidence to suggest that a stimulus to greater economic activity within the industrial countries would be less inflationary if effected by means of a transfer to developing countries than by a direct expansion of domestic demand. This has led some critics to argue that a major transfer to developing countries must be rejected for the simple reason that industrial countries have "obviously been unwilling to undertake major domestic programmes of Keynesian expansion".

In my view, the general argument that almost any expansion of demand, output and production would be inflationary needs to be challenged. The evidence for such a rigid view of a Phillips-curve relationship does not exist -- and this implication for policy is both oversimplified and misleading. In contrast one can argue that continuing high unemployment stimulates uncertainty and generates increasing reactions within the organised section of the labour force in ways which may result in greater wage-push, cost-push and inflationary effects rather than less. Moreover, these reactions often lead to institutional changes which create further imperfections and rigidities within both labour and other markets.

Moreover, clear evidence exists of the favourable effects of trade links with developing countries on inflation. The recent World Development Report shows that textile prices over the past 5 years have risen by 26% compared with a general rise in the wholesale price index of 66%. A recent Brookings study shows that imports from less-developed countries into the United States retail at prices 16% lower than comparable domestically-produced goods. The OECD itself has recognised that trade with the NICs has been a moderating influence on inflationary pressures within the industrial countries both in the short run and, by encouraging increases in productivity and efficiency, over the longer run.

Except for inflation, the other effects of the programme are matters of policy, not inevitability. The impact on the balance of payments of different industrial countries, for example, will primarily reflect how the size of each country's "contribution" to the programme compares with the amount of additional exports it gets from the programme, which in turn will primarily reflect the sectors and countries supported and the institutional arrangements governing the use of the transfer funds. All these are matters of policy, which can be adjusted to match the goals and constraints affecting the countries participating in the programme. So also is the form in which the funds are raised and administered.

The need now is for one of the major governments of the industrial powers to give a strong political lead: to recognise the need for a significant international initiative along the lines proposed and to provide the impetus and leadership for it to be converted rapidly into a programme for implementation. The idea in general terms has already been much debated, but with the years not really engaged, because strong political leadership has been lacking. For a proposal now to be seriously developed,

-- a time limit should be set for preparing a specific programme;

-- a clear mandate should be given for an international group or groups to work out the elements of a feasible programme within clear and broad basic guidelines, which recognise the different interest of the various parties involved;

-- for both North and South to be involved in whatever formal meetings are required to reach agreement on the proposal.

It is not argued that an initiative on these lines would solve all the major economic problems of the North or the South. In particular, special attention would be needed if the mass of the rural population in the poorer developing countries were to gain much benefit. But a major initiative for restructuring out of recession could provide a more dynamic context in which other long-standing problems could be tackled.

REFERENCES

[1] J.A. Holsen & H.L. Waelbroeck, "The LDCs & the International Monetary Mechanism", AER Papers and Proceedings, May 1976, pp. 171-76.

[2] US Bureau of Intelligence and Research, Department of State, Financial Transfers from Industrial to Developing Nations: A Reexamination, INR Report No. 1081, 1978 (mimeo).

[3] Unless used for general balance-of-payments support, it would probably take several years to build up the programme of investment to a sizable scale. Moreover, estimates suggest that no more than 70% of the OECD multiplier effects would take place in the first year.

[4] Op. cit. ICFTU Brussels, Belguim, December 1978, p. 23.

[5] Arusha Declaration, advance (consolidated) text, 22 Feb. 1979, pp. 61-3.

[6] The Right Honourable Roy Jenkins: Europe's present challenge and future opportunity, Florence, 27 October 1977, p. 17.

Trade and Economic Cooperation Among Developing Countries

JACK P. BARNOUIN

The need for strengthening economic cooperation among developing countries (which has come to be known as ECDC) has been increasingly recognized by the international community in recent years (see box). Although global cooperation among developing countries has only recently been the focus of international discussion, the concept in itself is not a novel one. As the box shows, regional attempts to implement it may be traced back to the early 1960s. But while these were based on the concept of cooperation, the early efforts were considerably more limited in scope and content than the new approach favored now by the Group of 77 (developing countries). First, they embraced regional and subregional groupings of countries while the new approach involves all developing countries. Second, the regional agreements were concerned with trade, and the new approach is geared toward forging links not only in trade but also in a large number of other areas. Finally, while regional integration efforts had relied only to a limited extent on the support of the United Nations system, mainly through the United Nations regional commissions, the sponsors of the new approach have called for broader involvement of existing international institutions.

I. RATIONALE

This article will attempt to identify the principal efforts at regional and multilateral economic cooperation among developing countries, as an adjunct to their economic ties to the developed

From **FINANCE AND DEVELOPMENT**, June 1982, (24-26), reprinted by permission of the publisher.

countries. The aim is to provide a concise outline of the discussions to date and the prospects for implementing certain policies, especially in the area of trade. Data on trade flows accompany this article.

Two major factors may explain the recent shift among the Group of 77 toward efforts at global cooperation. First, with a marked slowdown in the expansion of South-North trade as a result of the reduced rate of economic growth in the industrial countries, the developing countries began to consider the fostering of the largely untouched intra-South trade as a major tool to maintain a relatively satisfactory rate of growth of their economies. Since they felt that, by their very nature, regional integration efforts were somewhat limited in scope, they came to the conclusion that an attempt should be made to reduce barriers against trade among themselves at the world level. A second factor has been the disappointment of the developing countries with the results of the North-South dialogue. This led them to the view that their negotiating position should be strengthened through the establishment of worldwide economic links among themselves.

These two factors are emphasized by the Brandt Commission, which defines the purpose of economic cooperation among developing countries as being to forge "links among the countries of the Third World for more fully exploiting their potential for economic and social development and for strengthening their collective bargaining capability in international economic relations."

II. PROGRAM SCOPE, CONTENT

The final report endorsed by the Caracas Conference in 1981 (see chronology) identifies seven sectors in which cooperation among Third World countries should be strengthened in the near future. While no specific priority is assigned to any of these sectors, the parts of the program dealing with finance, the transfer of technology, and trade are considerably more detailed and specific than those dealing with other sectors, such as food and agriculture, energy, raw materials, and industrialization.

In the area of finance, the basic aim of the program is to bring about a substantial increase in the direct flow of funds from the developing countries with structural balance of payments (BOP) surpluses (the oil exporting countries) toward the rest. The program therefore recommends, inter alia, the strengthening of existing subregional and regional payment arrangements, incorporating an important element of reciprocal credits to support mutual trade flows; the examination of the feasibility for a financing facility to meet the BOP needs of developing countries with contributions from the developing countries themselves; the establishment of new regional and interregional trade development banks as well as an expansion of the activities of existing ones; and further study of the feasibility of establishing a development bank for developing countries.

The program also contemplates a number of other self-help measures. These include the increase in the deposits of governmental and semigovernmental institutions of developing countries in the banks of other developing countries; a larger participation of developing countries in the purchase of financial instruments issued by other developing countries in the international capital market; and the conclusion of bilateral and multilateral arrangements to enhance the soundness and attractiveness of direct investment by developing countries in other developing countries. Finally, the program recommends that "developing countries should intensify collective efforts in international forums to ensure that developed countries join the developing countries in establishing a mechanism to alleviate the financial burden imposed on the developing countries on account of oil price adjustment and the continued inflation of the prices of their imports of goods and services from developed countries."

Regarding technology, the program has two aims: to upgrade the collective technical capabilities of the developing countries through an exchange of experience and to improve the terms under which technology is being transferred from the industrial countries to the Third World. It recommends better dissemination of information on the technological capabilities of the developing countries, the conclusion of scientific and technical cooperation agreements among them, the pooling of information on the terms and conditions for the transfer of technology from the developed countries, and, when appropriate, joint negotiations for the purchase of specific technologies from the industrial countries.

The Caracas program makes a number of other suggestions for possible cooperation among developing countries. The most interesting of them would strengthen existing associations of raw material producers in the developing countries and establish new associations; foster cooperation among developing countries in specific industrial sectors, establishing, among others, multinational production enterprises; undertake joint efforts to explore and exploit additional sources of energy in the energy-importing developing countries; establish multinational enterprises for the production of energy-related capital goods such as drilling, pipelines, and storage equipment; set up a scheme for acquiring and maintaining food reserves, including infrastructure arrangements; and adopt cooperative measures for the production and marketing of agricultural inputs such as fertilizers, pesticides, and agricultural machinery and implements, as well as improved seed and livestock breeds.

Main elements of the international recognition of
economic cooperation among developing countries;
Regional phase

1959   West African Customs Union begun (replaced in 1974 by the
            West African Economic Community)
         Equatorial African Customs Union begun (replaced in 1966
            by the Central African Customs and Economic Union)

1960   Latin American Free Trade Association created
        Central American Common Market created
        Andean Group established
        Caribbean Free Trade Association established

1964   Arab Common Market established

1967   Association of South-East Asian Nations established
        East African Community created (dissolved in 1977)

1975   Economic Community of West African States established

International phase

1974   United Nations Sixth Special Session adopts Program of Action
        for establishing a New International Economic Order
        (NIEO), emphasizing ECDC

1976   Group of 77 includes ECDC program in Manila Declaration and
        Program of Action
        UNCTAD IV in Nairobi approves resolution to support ECDC
        Nonaligned heads of state adopt action program on ECDC in
        Colombo
        Group of 77 Mexico City conference on ECDC

1979   Group of 77 adopts Arusha Program for Collective
        Self-Reliance, which is partly endorsed by UNCTAD V
        in Manila

1981   Group of 77 in Caracas issues blueprint for ECDC

III. TRADE COOPERATION

     While the scope of the Caracas program is very broad, it is in
the area of trade that considerable attention has been focused.
The section on trade is based on the premise that while trade among
developing countries has expanded rapidly in recent years, there
remains considerable room for growth, particularly if these
countries are, by the year 2000, to account for at least 25 per
cent of the world's industrial production as set forth at the
United Nations Industrial Development Organization Conference held
in Lima, Peru, in 1975. By 1978 only 26 per cent of the exports
(excluding mineral fuels) of developing countries went to other
developing countries, while only 14 per cent of their imports (also
excluding mineral fuels) came from them.
     To strengthen existing weak areas of marketing, distribution,
and all levels of infrastructure needed for trade to expand, the
program envisages cooperation arrangements among the state-trading
organizations of the developing countries; the promotion of

multinational marketing enterprises among them; the establishment of national enterprises in the fields of transportation, communications, shipping and insurance, and the conclusion of cooperation arrangements between these enterprises at the subregional, regional, and interregional levels and the fostering of technical cooperation among the developing countries through the establishment of multinational research and training institutions.

In addition to these institutional changes designed to promote intra-South trade, the Caracas program contains a specific agreement on the need to establish a system of trade preferences among developing countries. This is based on the premise that although trade among developing countries is likely to grow spontaneously (see the article on South-South trade by Havrylyshyn and Wolf in the March 1982 issue of Finance & Development), a major reorientation in its geographical distribution cannot be expected without specific encouragement. Preferences would be a direct way of providing this encouragement.

Notwithstanding the substantial consensus among the developing countries on the desirability of trade preferences among developing countries, the implementation of a comprehensive program of preferences, it is now recognized, is a task fraught with difficulties. Some of these difficulties have already emerged during the preliminary discussions in 1980 and 1981 held by a United Nations Conference on Trade and Development-sponsored group of experts from developing countries on the establishment of the preference system.

A major issue of whether the liberalization of trade should be limited to a reduction of tariff and nontariff barriers or whether it should also encompass direct measures of trade promotion, such as long-term supply and purchase contracts that would provide importers with assured supplies and exporters with stable markets. The more advanced developing countries favor the first approach. By contrast, other developing countries, which rely significantly on state trade, insist on a long-term supply approach, arguing that because of their weak export structure and competitiveness they are unlikely to be able to take substantial advantage of the export opportunities arising from a mere reduction in tariff and nontariff barriers.

A second important and debated issue is whether tariffs should be reduced product by product or across the board. Most of its proponents favor an identical across-the-board tariff reduction for all customs items and all countries. Their argument is that, because of the emphasis of the Third World's industrialization policies on the development of consumer goods industries, protection is high for those goods which are the most susceptible to be traded among developing countries, and low or nonexistent for intermediate and capital goods for which the supply capability of these countries is very limited. An across-the-board reduction of tariffs among developing countries would not modify substantially the current situation for capital and intermediate goods but it could greatly foster intra-Third World trade in consumer goods for which it would provide a significant preference margin. This reasoning presupposes that a reduction would, in fact, increase trade. However, in some developing countries, tariff rates on consumer goods are so high that even after an across-the-board reduction they would remain prohibitive. Obviously some selection would have to be introduced, either through the stipulation of maximum post-cut tariff level or through the adoption of a progressive formula that would call for greater cuts in the higher rates. Reaching agreement on any of these proposals, however, promises to be difficult.

Another delicate problem is how to maintain tariff preferences that developing countries have extended to each other in the framework of existing regional groupings. It is clear that if individual members of such groupings grant preferences to nonmember developing countries, the effect could erode the group system. To avoid such an erosion, the grouping would need to increase group preferences. This might well be difficult in view of the numerous obstacles that anyway exist to the strengthening of existing regional and subregional trade arrangements.

Althoughthe experts of the Group of 77 have not yet been able to reach conclusions of these difficult issues, they did reach agreement at their meeting in November 1980 in Geneva on some broad guidelines for the initiation of negotiations on the global system. These guidelines stipulate, inter alia, that the system should be negotiated and established step by step; that the negotiations be reserved for the exclusive participation of the developing country members of the Group of 77; that the existing subregional, regional, and interregional groupings of such countries should participate fully in the negotiations; that the least developed countries should not be required to make concessions on a reciprocal basis; that the products covered by the system should include manufactures as well as commodities and agricultural products; and that, at the start of the negotiations, the participants should submit information concerning the areas in which they consider appropriate to offer concessions. Beyond these guidelines, it was agreed that a meeting of senior officials would be convened to consider the procedural and institutional arrangements needed for an effective launching of the negotiations.

Whatever those procedural decisions might be, it is clear that the establishment of the Global System of Trade Preferences will be a time-consuming exercise. In this connection, it may be recalled that the countries participating in the Tokyo Round of negotiations on the mutual reduction of tariff and nontariff trade barriers took some six years to reach agreement. Since commercial policies diverge more widely among developing than developed countries, it is likely that the negotiations on the global system will be complex and could require even more time than the Tokyo Round.

RELATED READINGS

The Brandt Commission Papers: Selected Papers prepared for the Independent Commission on International Development Issues, 1978-79 (Geneva-The Hague, Independent Bureau for International Development Issues, 1981).

Group of 77, Manila Declaration and Program of Action (UNCTAD IV, document TD/195, 1976).

, Arusha Program for Collective Self-Reliance and Framework for Negotiations (UNCTAD V, document TD/236, 1979).

, Final Report of the High-Level Conference on Economic Cooperation among Developing Countries, Caracas, May 1981 (Caracas/G.77/F.R.).

New Directions and New Structures for Trade and Development: Report by the Secretary-General of the United Nations Conference on Trade and Development to UNCTAD IV (UNCTAD TD/183/Rev.1, 1977).

Gamani Seneviratne: "Economic Cooperation Among Developing Countries, New Dimensions in the Thrust for Collective Self-Reliance" (New York, United Nations, 1980).

Promoting Trade Among Developing Countries: An Assessment

OLI HAVRYLYSHYN and
MARTIN WOLF

For two centuries economists have been developing different theories of the underlying causes of patterns of trade, combining natural and policy determinants in an effort to illuminate and predict the nature of trade between countries. But the direction of trade has rarely been explicitly treated as a separate issue in the literature; the fundamental notion that trade will mirror the pattern of comparative advantage has always been understood to apply to the trade of a country with the rest of the world, its direction being until recently ignored. Now, however, arguments are being raised which suggest that the direction of the trade of developing countries, in particular, is important. The contention seems to be based on two premises: first, that developing countries benefit more from trading with each other than with the industrial world; and, second, that obstacles exist resulting in less South-South trade than may be desirable.

This article attempts to evaluate the economic and empirical validity of these arguments on the basis of trade movements among developing countries between 1963 and 1977.

The findings generally do not lend support to the view that South-South trade should be actively encouraged under the prevailing conditions. There are several grounds for this conclusion. For example, no bias against trade among developing countries could be identified; in fact, exports among developing countries were greater than relative market size would seem to indicate. Nor did exports to other developing countries appear to be a vital first stage for export of capital goods. The analysis also supplied support for new hypotheses. While the share of manufactured goods traded among developing countries fell, that of primary nonfuel products increased unexpectedly, indicating a new direction for expansion. Far from there being a need for policy

From **FINANCE AND DEVELOPMENT**, March, 1982, (17-21), reprinted by permission of the publisher.

intervention to promote South-South trade, however, the best policy is probably to reduce existing overall commercial barriers and allow trade to expand in directions dictated by market.

I. PATTERNS IN THEORY

There are three theoretical perspectives that are widely used in the analysis of trade. The first, the Hecksher-Ohlin approach, postulates that a country will export those goods embodying its most abundant factor, usually labor or capital, and import those using intensively the scarcer factor. Krueger (1977) and Baldwin (1979) have extended this idea to predict that of a country's exports, the more labor-intensive goods will go to countries more generously endowed with capital than itself and the more capital-intensive ones will go to countries less well-endowed with capital.

Product-cycle theory, the second perspective, is based on the notion that technical knowledge is unevenly distributed throughout the world, so at any given moment trade is occurring in manufactured goods embodying different degrees of sophistication. The idea is that each country will import goods produced by a technology it does not yet have, while it exports its own products to countries below it on the scale of technology.

There is a third model developed by Linder that the greater the similarity in the domestic demand of two countries, the higher trade will be between them. This hypothesis would, therefore, seem to have explicit relevance to trade among developing countries.

Actual trade flows will not only be determined by the underlying factors isolated by these models but also by natural and policy barriers--the cost of transport and communications, marketing channels, commercial policies, and so on. Marketing and policy barriers are believed to be particularly important. Developing countries lack key institutions, such as large retailers, specialized importers, and wholesalers; moreover, their levels of protection have not fallen over the past 35 years, as have those of developed countries. Differences in market size and growth are also bound to play a decisive role in determining trade patterns: developed countries account for as much as 65 per cent of world product and 67 per cent of global imports.

Analysis of the underlying theoretical determinants of trade, barriers, and market size leads to a number of hypotheses about the trade pattern to be expected of the developing countries. In the first place, only a small part of the trade of any developing country is likely to be with countries at similar income levels. Comparative advantage, the relatively greater protectionism of developing than of industrial countries, and the overwhelming relative size of the latter's markets will all lead developing nations to trade more with developed countries. There is, of course, potential for intraindustry specialization among those developing countries sufficiently advanced to produce

Table 1
Trade among developing countries as share of their total exports of selected commodities, 1963–77
(In per cent)

	1963	1968	1971	1973	1975	1977
Food and beverages	16	19	18	19	21	23
Nonfood agriculture	18	24	26	25	27	29
Metals and minerals	11	9	10	11	11	12
All nonfuels primary	16	19	18	20	20	23
Manufactures	40	30	27	25	28	25
Capital goods	66	53	44	38	45	38
All nonfuels	22	23	22	22	24	24
Fuels	35	31	31	26	28	31
Developing countries' share of world income	15.6	14.7	14.6	14.8	16.7	17.3

Source: Computations based on United Nations trade data tapes, prepared by World Bank staff. Havrylyshyn and Wolf, Trade among Developing Countries: Theory, Policy Issues, and Principal Trends, World Bank Staff Working Paper No. 479.

Table 2
Commodity composition of developing country exports to different markets in 1977
(In per cent)

	World	Industrial countries	Capital-surplus countries[1]	Developing countries	Oil exporters[2]	Newly industrialized countries[3]
Food and beverages	34.3	35.1	25.7	32.3	31.1	38.4
Nonfood agriculture	8.3	7.8	2.7	9.9	4.3	18.9
Metals and minerals	5.2	6.3	2.0	2.7	1.5	3.9
Manufactures	51.3	49.9	69.4	54.4	62.4	38.8
Of which, capital goods	(12.6)	(9.4)	(16.5)	(20.4)	(23.8)	(11.7)
Total nonfuels[4]	100.0	100.0	100.0	100.0	100.0	100.0
			As per cent of total exports			
Fuels	15.1	16.0	1.7	18.2	4.5	10.6

Source: Computations based on United Nations trade data tapes, prepared by World Bank staff. Havrylyshyn and Wolf, *Trade among Developing Countries: Theory, Policy Issues, and Principal Trends*, World Bank Staff Working Paper No. 479.
[1]Capital-surplus countries include Iran, Iraq, Kuwait, the Libyan Arab Jamahiriya, Qatar, Saudi Arabia, and the United Arab Emirates.
[2]Oil exporters include Algeria, Angola, Bahrain, Bolivia, Brunei, Congo, Ecuador, Egypt, Gabon, Indonesia, Malaysia, Mexico, Nigeria, Oman, Peru, Syrian Arab Republic, Trinidad and Tobago, Tunisia, and Venezuela.
[3]Newly industrialized countries include Argentina, Brazil, Greece, Hong Kong, Israel, Mexico, Portugal, Singapore, South Korea, Spain, and Yugoslavia.
[4]Components may not add to total due to rounding.

Table 3
The role of newly industrialized country (NIC) markets in developing country (LDC) trade, 1963 and 1977
(In per cent)

	1963		1977	
	Exports to NICs from LDCs[1]	NICs share of LDC markets[2]	Exports to NICs from LDCs[1]	NICs share of LDC markets[2]
Food and beverages	5.9	36.6	10.2	44.3
Nonfood agriculture	11.8	68.0	20.7	71.4
Metals and minerals	4.4	40.4	7.0	55.8
All primary nonfuels	7.4	46.1	11.7	51.0
Manufactures	7.0	17.4	6.9	27.6
All nonfuels	7.4	33.8	9.2	38.2

Source: Computations based on United Nations trade data tapes, prepared by World Bank staff. Havrylyshyn and Wolf, *Trade among Developing Countries: Theory, Policy Issues, and Principal Trends*, World Bank Staff Working Paper No. 479.
[1]Developing country exports to newly industrialized countries as a percentage of developing country exports to the world.
[2]Developing country exports to newly industrialized countries as a percentage of developing country exports to all developing countries.

48

FIGURE 1. Percentage Share of Developing Country Exports Going to the Developing Countries

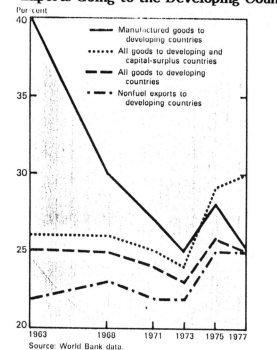

Per cent

Manufactured goods to developing countries

All goods to developing and capital-surplus countries

All goods to developing countries

Nonfuel exports to developing countries

Source: World Bank data.

differentiated goods, namely, the newly industrialized countries. But restrictive commercial policy has so far precluded this development, with few exceptions--such as Hong Kong and Singapore--and is likely to do so in the future. Second, one, would expect some of the larger and more inward-looking developing countries to tend to trade relatively more with developing countries, because their available exports are largely determined by domestic demand and a policy-induced shift toward products that require capital-intensive methods of production.

Third, there will have been a strong long-term pull toward trade with developed countries, because of the liberalization of their trade barriers and the commercial policies of some developing countries that promote their comparative advantage in labor-intensive goods. Fourth, because of wide differences among developing countries in natural resource endowments and because of the demand for raw materials and food of rapidly industrializing developing countries, exports of primary commodities to developing countries are likely to grow faster than those of manufactures.

Finally, a particularly dynamic component of trade among developing countries should be between the rapidly growing, resource-poor newly industrializing countries and other countries, which should, in turn, provide markets for their most capital-intensive and skill-intensive manufactures.

II. POTENTIAL BENEFITS

As long as the prices at which goods are traded fully equal their social costs and as long as there are no policy-induced distortions, trade is likely to be as beneficial in one direction as in any other. To establish that trade between developing countries is to be preferred to trade elsewhere and should be promoted means, therefore, establishing that divergences or distortions exist and that they can only be corrected by actively encouraging trade among developing countries.

Some market distortions, for example in the relative cost of labor, may actually argue against South-South trade. Thus trade with developed countries in manufactures tends to be more labor intensive than with developing countries. Since developing countries generally suffer from unemployment, the social returns on exporting to developing countries are higher than on exporting to developed countries (Krueger); this indicates that trade with developed countries should, in fact, be larger than it is now. One argument of the proponents of more South-South trade is that there are external benefits from competitive trade among developing countries--it stimulates managerial and organizational efficiency, innovation, and the exploitation of economies of scale (Hughes argues this case for trade in manufactures). A related proposition is that more sophisticated and capital-intensive goods can initially be produced only for the home market. If the latter is small, subsidization or protection may be required. Trade with other developing countries, it is suggested, permits the country to produce these goods on a larger scale, which lowers the costs of infant industry promotion.

Another argument for emphasizing trade among developing countries is that more diversification in the direction of trade means more diversification in the products traded, which in turn provides insurance against adverse developments in major products, ensures a wider range of domestic skills and knowledge, and reduces the potential for coercion by any one trading partner.

III. REMOVING BIASES

There are two main arguments that suggest present trade patterns are detrimental to developing countries. Those working in the "dependency" tradition (Stewart, 1976, for example) argue that colonial and neocolonial coercion has forced developing countries, through a straitjacket of transport, financial, and marketing constraints, to trade more with developed countries and less with one another than they should. The consequences are excessive specialization and consequent vulnerability to price changes on the one hand; and, on the other, the loss of the dynamic benefits of trade with one another that come from opportunities of learning by doing, the shared technological requirements of the South, and the advantages of the appropriate technology supposedly embodied in capital exports of developing countries.

Another argument is that of the export pessimists—a view popular in the 1950s and now returning (see Lewis, 1980). The proposition is that for almost all developing countries a certain rate of growth of trade is virtually essential for any target growth rate of national income. If developed countries grow slowly, the required overall growth of trade can then be achieved only by accelerated trade among developing countries. This view does not regard trade among developing countries as superior except in a global environment when industrial country markets may be sluggish.

In general, economists seem to make policy recommendations on the basis of their views about the benefit of foreign trade. Those who believe that trade among developing countries is particularly valuable tend to recommend discriminatory trade liberalization via customs unions or free trade areas (United Nations Conference on Trade and Development, 1979). Those who think that trade among developing countries is discriminated against by institutional and technical constraints focus upon policy reform in particular areas. Even those who are wary of the economic costs of discriminatory trading arrangements and are well aware that they have been collapsing like ninepins (Hughes, 1980; Vaitsos, 1978) sometimes still argue that discriminatory policies are the best available vehicles for wider liberalization by developing countries but that care must be taken to avoid costly trade-diverting plans and to look instead for opportunities for trade creation. Many others would argue, however, that a general reduction in trade barriers is needed (Frank).

IV. THE EVIDENCE

To test the validity of some of the arguments, a study was made in the World Bank of the destination of the exports of 33 developing countries between 1963 and 1977. The sample includes countries from Southern Europe, Asia, Africa, and Latin America and also represents a range of different stages of development and resource endowments by including newly industrializing countries and oil producers. A sample cannot be fully representative (this one may underrepresent small, low-income countries and overrepresent exporters of manufactures) but the patterns traced by the analysis serve sufficiently well as a general proxy for measuring trade among developing countries.

According to the analysis, and contrary to a widespread impression, there has been no large shift toward trade among developing countries since 1963, at least when the focus is upon nonfuel trade and where the capital-surplus oil exporting countries are excluded. Aggregate nonfuel exports to developing countries were quite stable at about 23 per cent of their total exports between 1963 and 1973, whereupon they rose to 24 per cent in 1975 and 1977. Only the share of exports to oil exporting (nonsurplus) countries and to capital-surplus countries increased sharply, from 5.1 per cent in 1973 to 6.9 per cent in 1977 for the first group, and from 2.4 per cent to 7.1 per cent for the second.

These movements are the most important direct consequence of oil price increases on the direction of exports. However, at a more disaggregated level, exports of manufactures and nonfuel primary commodities have not been so stable. Manufactured exports were the developing countries' most dynamic export sector in the 1960s and 1970s and the share of developing countries as markets fell from 40 per cent in 1963 to 27 per cent in 1971 and 25 per cent in 1977. In the 1960s and early 1970s, the industrial countries received most of the increase in the manufactured exports of the developing countries; in the late 1970s the capital-surplus, oil exporting countries' share increased--from 2 per cent in 1973 to 7 per cent in 1977. Within manufactures, capital goods exports have tended to go more to other developing countries at any moment, but the decline in the importance of these markets has been noteworthy, from 66 per cent in 1963 to 38 per cent of total capital goods exports in 1977.

The changes in the direction of developing countries' manufactured exports fit with the factor endowment theory. In the 1960s and early 1970s exports to industrial countries soared as a number of countries exploited their opportunities for exporting labor-intensive manufactures to rapidly growing industrial country markets, encouraged by declining trade barriers there. The developing countries, meanwhile, remained strongly protectionist.

In the 1970s, with a large shift in global income toward oil exporters--and to some extent toward the newly industrialized countries--and slower growth in industrial countries, the direction of developing countries' exports of manufactures shifted toward the former two groups.

Also in conformity with the theory, it was found that developing countries' manufactured exports to other developing countries were twice as capital intensive as those to the industrial world.

Primary commodity exports from the sample of developing countries, especially nonfood agriculture and food and beverages, shifted toward developing country markets, offsetting the decline in the importance of developing countries' markets for manufactures. The existence of wide differences in relevant factor endowments, the failure of some developing countries to achieve rapid growth in food production, and--most important--the rapid industrialization of some resource-poor developing countries seem to explain these trends in primary commodities. It should be stressed, however, that even though exports of nonfuel primary commodities grew more rapidly to developing countries' markets than to the rest of the world, the importance of manufactures rose in all markets.

V. THE DEBATE ASSESSED

On the basis of the evidence, it is difficult to argue that there is an effective bias against trade among developing countries. Taking into account such factors as their weight in the world economy, their comparative advantage, and the fact that industrial countries have not only been liberalizing their trade policies (at least in manufactures, and certainly until the mid-1970s) but have also substantially more open trade regimes in general, one might expect trade between developing countries and industrial countries actually to exceed that indicated by the latter's weight in the world economy. In fact, exports to developing countries of all nonfuel commodities, manufactures, and nonfuel primary commodities have been greater than might be expected on this basis.

Nor did the analysis support the arguments that existing trade patterns are undesirable because of divergences between private and social costs. On the contrary, there is evidence that casts doubt on the infant industry argument that markets in developing countries are needed by those developing countries beginning to produce sophisticated capital goods. In fact, exports of capital goods from developing countries have been going increasingly to developed countries; for the sample, the share of developing country markets declined from 66 to 38 per cent between 1963 and 1977. And although it is probably true that trade with developing countries leads to export diversification, the benefits of this are uncertain. In the case of manufactured exports, at least, it

appears that the countries that specialized increasingly in trade
with developed countries on the lines of comparative advantage (the
East Asian economies, the Mediterranean ones, plus a few in Latin
America) have shown themselves to be more flexible than the others
in meeting changing opportunities.

Nor do we find evidence to support the export pessimism
argument. For many primary commodities, there is no discernible
link between the growth of developed countries and exports by
developing countries, especially since the industrial countries are
dominant exporters of many primary products other than fuel and
tropical tree crops. Further, the evidence suggests that the link
is still weaker for manufactured exports. Thus, although more
trade opportunities can hardly hurt, it is far from clear from past
evidence of actual trade flows that trade among developing
countries is essential for the growth of developing countries.
While we have not considered here the related argument that the
terms of trade movements favor the North, it should be pointed out
that several recent studies cast considerable doubt on this.

However, there does seem to be a good case for the export of
primary commodities to developing countries. Discussions of trade
among developing countries are almost always exclusively
concerned with manufactured goods. Nonetheless, both theory and
experience suggest that trade in primary goods among developing
countries has been particularly valuable (see Table 3). This
points to the potential importance of complementarities between
more and less industrialized developing countries in exporting and
processing primary products or exchanging food and raw materials
for manufactured goods, particularly given the rapid growth of the
more industrialized developing countries.

VI. POLICY OPTIONS FOR TRADE

The arguments and the evidence do not seem to find inherent
reasons to favor trade in any particular direction but rather
emphasize that a country should seek to maximize its gains from all
exports regardless of destination. In the current world
environment (which is not a given but an outcome of prior policy
decisions) there may, in fact, be reason for interest in the
prospects of South-South trade, but probably no reason for direct
intervention to promote it for its own sake; indeed if anything,
not more but less intervention seems to be needed. Three elements
are relevant: slower growth in the industrial countries, high
protection levels in developing countries, and the continued
existence of domestic market distortions in developing countries.

Slower growth of industrial countries, while by no means
precluding increased penetration by efficient exporters from the
South, simply means that markets in the South become relatively
more important. The natural consequence of this would be increased
flows to these markets--as has indeed occurred most recently--to
the extent allowed by the other two elements. But the higher the

protection in the South and the greater the internal market distortions, the less successfully will exporters of the South adapt to slower growth in the North and the less will South-South trade grow--which perhaps explains why its increase has not been greater.

The policy implications of this are then clear: new policies to promote expressly South-South trade are not needed; rather the desirable policies are the reduction of protective barriers to the South-South trade and the reduction of internal policy-induced market distortions in developing countries.

Where constraints are not caused by trade policies, the best approach is to deal with the problem directly; a labor market distortion, for instance, should ideally be corrected by equating market wages to shadow wages, a second best solution is to subsidize labor-intensive output, and a third best is to subsidize labor-intensive exports. Where barriers are created by trade policy, preferential liberalization of trade among developing countries may be the only politically practical way of dealing with domestic protectionist lobbies and could create new opportunities for valuable trade. Beyond this, the only other direct action that may be justifiable is the creation of physical and/or institutional infrastructure to facilitate trade, though this should not be done only to facilitate South-South trade. If the prior conditions dictate economically rational expansion of South-South trade channels, such investments will, of course, be justified by the standard project criteria of cost-benefit.

It is important to emphasize how these conclusions fit into the argument that trade among developing countries must serve as a source of growth in the future. Our conclusion is that this argument comes down to a simple proposition: in an environment where developed countries are poor markets, the costs to developing countries of trade-reducing distortions, and of their own barriers to trade with one another, rise. Therefore, action to deal with the policy-created barriers is more important and the economic return to developing countries as a whole is higher than it was before.

RELATED READING

Isaiah Frank, "Reciprocity and trade policy for developing countries," Finance & Development (March 1978).

Helen Hughes, "Inter-Developing Country Trade and Employment," paper presented at International Economic Association, Sixth World Congress on Human Resources, Employment and Development (Mexico City, August 4-9, 1980).

Anne O. Krueger, Growth, Distortions and Patterns of Trade among Many Countries, Princeton Studies in International Finance No. 40 (Princeton, Princeton University Press, 1977).

W. Arthur Lewis, "The Slowing Down of the Engine of Growth," The American Economic Review (September 1980).

Frances Stewart, "The Direction of International Trade: Gains and Losses for the Third World," in A World Divided: The Less Developed Countries in the International Economy, G. K. Helleiner, editor (Cambridge, Cambridge University Press, 1976).

Constantine V. Vaitsos, "Crisis in Regional Economic Cooperation (Integration) among Developing Countries: A Survey," World Development (1978).

United Nations Conference on Trade and Development, Economic Cooperation Among Developing Countries, TD/244 (New York, United Nations, 1979).

Towards a Global System of Trade Preferences Among Developing Countries

NASSAU A. ADAMS

I.

The idea of establishing a global framework of trade preferences and other trade-promoting measures to facilitate the expansion of trade among developing countries received its first clear political expression at the Mexico City Conference on Economic Co-operation among Developing Countries (ECDC) (13-22 September 1976) which, in adopting a comprehensive programme of measures for economic co-operation among developing countries, listed, as the first item under "trade and related measures", the establishment of a "global system of trade preferences among developing countries (GSTP)" with the objective of "promoting the development of national production and mutual trade". The Conference called on the UNCTAD secretariat to undertake the necessary studies on the various aspects of such a system and provided some broad guidelines for such studies.[1]

On the basis of these studies the Fourth Ministerial Meeting of the Group of 77 (Arusha, February 1979) recommended as a long-term objective the establishment of a GSTP, and set out a number of principles which should guide further work on the subject.[2] Subsequently, the matter was discussed at specially convened regional meetings in Africa, Asia and Latin America and at three preparatory meetings of governmental experts held in Geneva under UNCTAD's auspices. The last such meeting, held in July 1982, adopted a set of recommendations setting out the principles, rules and timetable for the negotiations and providing for the establishment of a Negotiating Committee with authority to take all the necessary steps for the establishment of a GSTP. These

From **TRADE AND DEVELOPMENT** UNCTAD Review, Winter 1982 (183-204), reprinted by permisison of the publisher.

recommendations were subsequently endorsed by the Ministerial Meeting of the Group of 77 held in New York in October 1982 and now form the basis for launching the negotiations, which are expected to begin in early 1983.[3]

It should be said at the outset that the GSTP is not a concept that has a ready-made meaning to be found in a dictionary or textbook. Rather, it is a general idea (i.e., the extension of trade preferences among developing countries) that has to be given concrete meaning. And, because a political rather than an academic issue is involved, such concrete meaning must emerge from negotiations and agreement among the governments concerned. Consequently, since much still remains to be determined in the course of the subsequent negotiations, no attempt can be made at the present time to give a clear description of the GSTP on the basis of which its implications could be fully assessed. It is nonetheless possible, in the light of the preparatory work so far and the recommendations recently adopted, to provide some indications of the main lines of thinking concerning the likely features of the GSTP.

Reference may first be made to some of the general principles which will provide the framework for the negotiations.[4] The GSTP is to be open to the participation of all developing countries members of the Group of 77.[5] It is to be negotiated step by step, improved and extended in successive stages, with periodic reviews. It is to be based on the principle of mutuality of advantages in such a way as to benefit equitably all participants, taking into account their various levels of economic and industrial development, the pattern of their external trade and their trade policies and systems. It should not replace but supplement and reinforce present and future subregional, regional and interregional groupings of developing countries, and the concerns and commitments of such groupings should be taken into account in the negotiations. Furthermore, such groupings may participate fully as such in the negotiations if they so desire. The disadvantageous position of the least developed countries should be clearly recognized and concrete preferential measures taken in their favour; in particular, these countries would not be required to make concessions on a reciprocal basis. In principle, all product categories (i.e., both manufactures and commodities in their raw and processed forms) would be covered in the negotiations, as would both tariff and non-tariff concessions. It is also envisaged that participating countries would establish voluntary (non-binding) targets for the expansion of their trade with other developing countries.

The negotiations themselves are to be conducted by rounds of bilateral or plurilateral negotiations between two or more countries (or their economic groupings), and would be based on requests and offers which could involve linear, product-by-product or sectoral approaches or combinations thereof, and could be linked to direct trade measures such as long-term contracts. At the same time, negotiations would proceed on all the outstanding issues on which decisions are needed in order to provide a comprehensive framework for the GSTP and for the implementation of the results of the negotiations.

In general it may be said that the framework as agreed during the preparatory phase puts the stress on flexibility and pragmatism, with minimum resort to a priori rules and pre-determined targets, and with a willingness and desire to get the negotiations started in the belief that it is only in the course of the actual negotiations that all the various problems can be identified and resolved. This flexibility is reflected, for example, in the range of options which participants may explore in respect of negotiating modalities, including linear, product-by-product and sectoral approaches and direct trade measures. Consequently, as matters stand at present the framework for the negotiations is still somewhat open-ended; some general principles have been agreed on but many of the details concerning the rules and modalities are still to be decided in the course of the actual negotiations.

II.

In the past 20 years a number of attempts have been made to institute trade preference schemes among developing countries, mostly at the subregional and regional levels. At the present time, some 70 developing countries in all the major regions of Africa, Asia and Latin America are members of one or another of such groupings. While the scope of these various schemes differs in matters of detail, they all have as their main purpose the reduction or elimination of barriers to trade among the member countries of such schemes. For the most part, the emphasis has been on the reduction of tariffs, though in many cases there are special supplementary arrangements designed to foster trade in specific industrial sectors, often supported by special payments arrangements or similar schemes intended to facilitate the financing of intra-trade. Whatever the doubts about the success of these schemes in achieving all their original objectives,[6] and notwithstanding the many difficulties that they have undoubtedly faced, there is little doubt that they have achieved at least one of their main objectives in contributing to the expansion of trade among their member States.[7]

At the interregional level, a previous attempt has also been made to institute a scheme of preferences among developing countries, i.e., the GATT Protocol relating to Trade Negotiations among Developing Countries, which came into force in 1973 and under which 16 original signatory countries agreed to exchange tariff preferences among themselves. While mutual trade in the products covered by the negotiated concessions remains a small proportion of the total trade of the signatory countries in these products and a tiny fraction of their aggregate trade, it is nonetheless true that mutual trade in the products covered by the negotiated concessions has increased substantially since the entry into force of the Protocol.[8]

The idea of the GSTP differs from earlier attempts at creating trade preferential schemes among developing countries in a number of respects. Perhaps most important is its global scope, intended to encompass the developing countries as a whole in a system of reciprocal trade preferences. While this is the intention, however, it should be noted that inasmuch as the exchange of concessions is to be negotiated by individual countries in bilateral and plurilateral negotiations, the effective participation of individual countries will depend on the extent to which they can negotiate effective trade-promoting concessions with partner countries, and this will only become clear in the light of the evolution of the negotiations themselves.

A second important respect in which the GSTP differs from previous attempts at creating trade preferential arrangements among developing countries is the full acceptance from the outset of the need to cover both tariff and non-tariff concessions in the negotiations. As previously mentioned, most earlier schemes have concentrated on tariff reductions as the basic component of trade liberalization. It is now recognized, however, that tariff liberalization by itself is not likely to provide an effective framework of preferences for the expansion of trade among developing countries, for the reason (among others) that tariff levels and the extent to which tariffs are relied on as trade control measures differ greatly from one country to another, and that in addition these countries make widespread use of non-tariff barriers to trade as instruments of general development policy.

The third important difference reflects the fact that most other schemes, particularly those created at the subregional and regional levels, are based on a common programme of trade liberalization to which all the participating countries are parties. Important exceptions to this general rule are the newly reformulated Latin American Integration Association (ALADI--Asociacion Latinoamericana de Integracion), previously LAFTA (Latin American Free Trade Association), and the GATT Protocol. In the case of the GSTP, however, the intention is not to negotiate a common programme of trade liberalization at the global level but rather to provide a framework within which individual countries can identify trade opportunities and negotiate trade concessions with partner countries under agreed rules and procedures.

An important issue raised concerns the relationship between the GSTP and existing subregional and regional economic integration schemes of developing countries, and more particularly, how to reconcile the main purpose of the GSTP, which is the reduction of barriers to trade among developing countries on a global basis, with the requirement that the GSTP should not replace but rather contribute to strengthening existing subregional and regional integration groupings of these countries.

The first point to be noted in this connection is that the GSTP as at present conceived is a partial preferential arrangement the object of which is not total trade liberalization or the establishment of a free-trade area or customs union. Hence preferences in the global system would be of limited extent, and there will thus be scope for the further extension of additional preferences within subregional and regional groupings. Secondly, it is envisaged that the GSTP would provide explicitly that preferences accorded within existing or future subregional or regional groupings of developing countries need not be extended to other developing countries under any most-favoured-nation (MFN) rule that may eventually be applicable under the GSTP. Thirdly, while it is true that, given the level of trade liberalization already achieved within existing groupings, the extension of preferences by individual members of such groupings to other developing countries will result in an erosion of the levels of such existing preferences, it is also true that such an erosion need not take place if subregional preferences can be deepened pari passu with the introduction of the GSTP. And to the extent that the GSTP could thereby provide an incentive for the progressive deepening of subregional preferences in order to maintain the special character and integrity of such schemes, it could itself even contribute to the strengthening of such schemes.

Furthermore, existing integration groupings are taking or contemplating integration and economic co-operation measures in a number of areas other than tariff liberalization: for example, they are seeking to co-ordinate industrial production plans and policies, transport and communications, and monetary and financial policies. The momentum of subregional integration might, therefore, still be maintained and intensified by more rapid progress at the subregional level in these areas at the same time as intra-group trade preferences are being eroded by the extension of preferences under the GSTP. To the extent that progress in the implementation of the GSTP provides the impetus for such acceleration, it would tend to promote the intensification and strengthening of subregional and regional integration efforts.

The point to stress here is that, if the concept of parallel strengthening is seen in the dynamic sense as linking action at the subregional and regional levels to action at the global level, measures at both levels may in parallel contribute to the achievement of the main objective of closer economic and trade relations among developing countries.

III.

The rationale for the current endeavours to devise a system of special policy measures for stimulating trade among the developing countries should be seen in the light of two basic facts: first, the relatively limited extent to which these countries now trade with each other and their corresponding heavy reliance on the developed countries as trading partners, and secondly, the gloomy prospects for economic growth which now face the major developed industrial countries and which seem likely to persist in the foreseeable future, with the consequence that, unless the developing countries can find alternatives to their continued dependence on these countries as trading partners, their own prospects for growth in the future will also inevitably remain gloomy.

The facts concerning the relatively low share of South–South trade in the trade of the South and the heavy dependence of developing countries on trade with the North are well known and need only be briefly referred to here. South–South trade accounts for only a quarter of the South's total trade, the remaining three–quarters being accounted for by trade with the North. By contrast, over 70 per cent of the total trade of the developed countries represents trade among themselves.

The question whether the low share of South–South trade is "normal" or to be expected in terms of the theory of international trade seems hardly worth pursuing, first, because much of that theory is concerned with explaining the existing or actual pattern of international trade (i.e., it is descriptive rather than prescriptive theory), and secondly, because different theoretical formulations emphasizing different aspects lead to rather different conclusions.[9]

Historically, North–South trade has been the dominant factor in the development of the external trade of the South. The historical forces behind this development are well known. In most cases it was the metropolitan colonial Powers themselves which took the initiatives to develop the external trade of their colonies or client States, the object being to secure for the metropolitan countries low–cost supplies of raw materials and foodstuffs as well as markets for their exports of manufactures. There is no need to enter here into a discussion of the relative benefits to the metropolitan countries and the colonies from this pattern of trade. The important point is that this historical process has left its strong imprint on current North–South trade. This imprint is reflected in the whole infrastructure for external trade which, for the South, is based largely on the North–South axis, characterized by shipping and transport and communications of all kinds originally intended to serve North–South rather than South–South trade, long–established marketing channels with the North, financial networks and currency clearing arrangement dominated by the North–South nexus, and information of all kinds much more readily available about the North than about the South.

It is recognized that there is something of a vicious circle involved here, since while it is true that the existing infrastructure significantly determines the direction of trade, it is also true that the existing trade flows justify the economic cost of the infrastructure, and it may be difficult to contemplate building or developing infrastructure unless the prospects of increased trade flows are fairly well assured. The dilemma is well known and is often encountered in the economics of development, and any programme for expanding or intensifying South–South trade will certainly need to pay particular attention to the question how to build up the necessary infrastructure supporting the expansion of that trade.

There are also other less tangible but equally important institutional aspects of the historical legacy which have a bearing on the issue, such as the use of political connections which most metropolitan Powers are able to retain in their former colonies, often buttressed by the judicious use of foreign aid in order to maintain and strengthen trading links.

The trade policies of both developed and developing countries are of obvious importance in determining the direction and commodity structure of trade. Traditionally, the tariff structures of the developed countries have been based on relatively low tariffs for raw material inputs and non-competing tropical food products, higher tariffs being applied to processed commodities and finished goods, and this tariff structure has facilitated the evolution of the traditional pattern of North-South trade based on the exchange of primary commodities for manufactured goods. In various rounds of tariff negotiations during recent years, significant reductions in the tariff levels of developed countries have been achieved, and these, in conjunction with the introduction of the GSP (generalized system of preferences) have in many cases improved access to the markets of the developed countries for exports of manufactures, and a number of developing countries, particularly the so-called newly industrializing countries, have been able to take advantage of this improvement to expand their exports of manufactures to developed countries. It may be noted, however, that while tariff reductions negotiated among developed countries will inevitably have spill-over effects beneficial to some exports of developing countries, it is hardly to be expected that the goods principally affected will be those of particular interest to developing countries, and hence it is not surprising that tariff reductions have made least impact on those products which are of particular interest to these countries.[10] A more important consideration, however, is the fact that these tariff reductions have been accompanied by a parallel movement in developed countries towards greater reliance on non-tariff barriers to manage trade, and these barriers have had a particularly severe effect on the exports of developing countries.[11]

Broadly, trade policies in the South have been dominated, by two basic factors; first, by a chronic shortage of foreign exchange and the consequential preoccupation with meeting the needs for high priority imports, and secondly, by the desire to protect nascent industries as part of the process of industrialization and development. Owing to these two factors the trade policies of developing countries have been inclined to intensify North-South trade, and to de-emphasize South-South trade.

As a consequence of this foreign exchange scarcity and the balance-of-payments constraints priority has often been accorded in import policies to heavy capital equipment and other industrial inputs essential to sustain the development process, and these are exactly the product categories where dependence on the North as a source of supplies is highest. Grain and other food staples of which developed countries are the principal suppliers also often receive priority in import programmes subjected to severe balance-of-payments constraints. And foreign aid and the various export financing schemes operated by the developed countries often sustain this kind of bias linked to balance-of-payments constraints.

As far as the role of protectionism is concerned, since countries at roughly comparable levels of economic development tend to choose much the same kinds of industries for promotion,[12] protectionism is likely to affect precisely those industries for which developing countries have created production capacities, the products of which they may be in a position to export. The consequential effect is thus to introduce a trade policy bias against trade with developing countries.

Against this must be set the various attempts at promoting regional and subregional economic integration schemes among developing countries based on the lowering of tariffs and other restrictions on their mutual trade. As indicated earlier, these attempts have, notwithstanding the difficulties they have faced, certainly helped to promote trade among the States parties to such schemes and have therefore served as countervailing trade policy measures favouring South-South trade, though clearly their scope has not been wide or far-reaching enough to make a great impact.

The gloomy prospects now facing the industrial countries and thus the world economy have been a subject of growing concern. After more than two decades of almost uninterrupted expansion at an average annual rate of about 5 per cent, the economies of the leading industrial countries began to falter in the early 1970s in the face of rising inflation, the sharp increases in oil prices, the breakdown of the international monetary system and other structural maladjustments, and their growth rates declined substantially. The early 1980s have witnessed an even greater intensification of the crisis, unprecedentedly high interest rates and exchange rate instability clouding all prospects for an early recovery. Observers of the economic scene are therefore now all but unanimous in their prognoses, and while there may be debate as to whether the world now is experiencing the downturn in the Kondratief cycle or whether underlying structural factors have precipitated a permanent slow-down in economic growth, there is little doubt that in the 1980s growth rates in the major industrial countries will be far below those which characterized the 1950s and the 1960s.[13]

This slow-down of economic growth has been accompanied by a corresponding fall in the growth of world trade, the rate of growth in the volume of world trade having fallen from an annual average of 8.5 per cent during 1963-1973 to 4 per cent during 1973-1980, and to zero in 1981.[14] Given the existing pattern of trade dependence, these declines portend very dismal growth prospects for the developing countries, and certainly invite the question whether an alternative pattern based on higher levels of trade interdependence among the developing countries could not be found that would offer an escape from the present situation.[15] It is this possibility which has provided the main impetus for working towards the establishment of a system of trade preferences and other trade-promoting measures that would contribute to exploiting the potential for the expansion of trade among these countries.

IV.

The developing countries[16] are a diverse group, ranging in size from relative economic giants, such as Brazil and India, to tiny islands of insignificant economic size; in income levels from the rich oil States with incomes sometimes above those of the most advanced countries to the poorest least developed countries; in economic and export structures from the Republic of Korea and Singapore, with their relatively highly developed industrial structures and their sophisticated and diversified industrial exports, to the simplest agricultural economies with one-crop exports; in economic performance from those which have been able to average rates of economic growth of 7 per cent and above during the past decade (some 25 developing countries being in this category) to those with average growth rates below zero (10 countries); and in trade regimes from some of the Gulf States, with few or no tariffs or other trade restrictions, to those with high and complex tariff structures as well as wide-ranging quantitative and exchange rate restrictions. This diversity is a source of both strength and weakness in any programme to promote trade expansion--of strength to the extent that it reflects potential complementarities offering opportunities for mutual trade--and of weakness to the extent that it might well be difficult to devise arrangements that would ensure a mutuality of benefits to all participants.

The potential benefits which a participating country may derive from the GSTP will depend on the trade-creating concessions it can obtain in other partner countries, and the ability of each country to negotiate such concessions will depend on the one hand on its ability to identify potential markets in partner countries for its existing or potential export products and on the other on the markets it can offer to those partners for products of interest to them. Clearly, countries with more widely diversified economies and a more diversified export structure will find it easier to identify potential markets in partner countries for which they may wish to negotiate concessions. At the same time, since among developing countries there is much less variation in the commodity structure of imports than in that of exports,[17] there will be much less of a difference among countries in the potential markets which may be offered to trading partners. There is therefore a certain lack of symmetry between the more diversified (and more advanced) developing countries and the simpler (less developed) ones. Thus the scope for negotiating trade-creating concessions as between the more advanced and more diversified developing countries may be very different from the scope for negotiating such concessions between these countries and the less developed and less diversified ones, and hence the modalities and approaches of the negotiations may likewise differ.

Some insight into the relevance to the GSTP negotiations of this diversity among developing countries can be gained from an analysis of the data concerning the pattern of South-South trade. For this purpose, 15 of the more highly industrialized developing countries were selected and their role in South-South trade was studied.[18] The data relate to 1976 and 1979. While the coverage of countries is more comprehensive for the former year (which includes data for 94 developing countries) than the latter (72), they both reflect the same broad features. The data (see table 1), which relate to trade excluding fuels, show that about

23-24 per cent of total exports of the developing countries is
absorbed by other developing countries, and this share is
approximately the same for the 15 more industrialized developing
countries (or the MIDCs) as for the rest. However, while the MIDCs
account for over two-thirds of total South-South exports, they
account for less than half of imports. These more industrialized
countries are therefore as a group major net exporters in the
context of South-South trade. It may also be noted that the bulk
of the MIDCs' imports from the South originate from other MIDCs
(about three-quarters), while between three-fifths and two-thirds
of such imports of all other developing countries also originate in
the MIDCs. Another inference to be drawn from the same data is
that while for the MIDCs' South-South exports are shared
approximately 50:50 between markets in MIDCs and in all other
developing countries, for all other developing countries as a group
markets in the MIDCs account for only a third of their total
South-South exports, with trade among themselves accounting for the
other two-thirds. These data therefore draw attention to the
leading role of the MIDCs in South-South trade, and the somewhat
asymmetrical position of these countries vis-a-vis the others in
this trade.

While there is an obvious merit in distinguishing the MIDCs
for the purpose of analysing the pattern of South-South trade, a
more general approach to such an analysis is possible based on a
grouping of countries by income levels, and for this purpose three
income groups are distinguished: countries with per capita incomes
above $1,000, those with per capita incomes between $500 and
$1,000, and those below $500.

As before, the analysis uses data for 1976 and 1979. For 1976
there are 30 countries in the high-income group, 24 in the
middle-income, and 40 in the low-income group (for 1979 the numbers
are 25, 20 and 27, respectively). It will be seen (table 2) that
in 1976 the 30 high-income countries (out of the 94 developing
countries covered by the data) accounted for two-thirds of all
exports by developing countries to other developing countries, and
for over three-fifths of imports (the figures for 1979 are not very
different). Furthermore, trade among these relatively high-income
developing countries accounted for over 40 per cent of total
South-South trade. At the same time, the bulk of the exports to
the South of both the middle- and low-income countries went to
high-income countries, and conversely the major part of their
imports from the South originated in the high-income countries.[19]
It is therefore evident that in respect of trade among the
developing countries (as in the case for world trade as a whole),
there is a significant element of concentration related to income
levels, with the higher income countries dominating the scene both
as regards trade with each other and as regards the South-South
trade of the countries in the other income groups.

The relative importance of these three income groups in the
commodity structure of South-South trade is illustrated by the data
in table 3. The group of high-income countries accounted for
three-quarters of South-South exports of manufactures and for over
50 per cent of the exports of food and of agricultural raw
materials in the two years considered.[20] As may be expected, the

role of the high-income countries is particularly dominant in respect of trade in manufactures. The table also shows the share of each commodity group in the total South-South exports of the various country groups. Manufactures and food products dominate in the South-South exports of all income groups, the share of manufactures being highest for the high-income countries (over 50 per cent), and the share of food highest for the low-income countries (above 40 per cent).

Table 4 carries the analysis a step further by distinguishing the major sub-groups of manufactures. The group of high-income countries continues to account for the major share of South-South exports of all the sub-groups of manufactures shown. However, as may be expected, it is in the machinery and equipment sector that their share is really dominant, accounting for close to 90 per cent of the total. Correspondingly, machinery and equipment account for a quarter of the total South-South exports of the high-income group, as against 4 to 8 per cent for the other income groups. Hence it is this sector more than any other that distinguishes the high-income countries from the others in terms of the commodity pattern of South-South trade.

The shares of these country groups in total South-South imports of the major commodity groups are shown in table 5. As in the case of exports, the high-income countries account for the highest shares of imports of all commodity groups. As regards imports, however, their share is highest for agricultural raw materials and for ores and minerals.

The significant conclusion that can be drawn from the analysis of the statistical data is that, seen in relation to differences in the levels of economic development of the countries concerned, the pattern of South-South trade presents a virtual mirror image (if in a reduced form) of the pattern of world trade as a whole. The relevance of this finding for the GSTP negotiations should be evident. It suggests that the greatest scope for negotiating concessions will be found among the more economically developed higher-income developing countries, next between these countries and the less developed ones, and that the scope will be smallest among the latter countries.

V.

The tariff structures of most developing countries tend to conform to a pattern: the lowest duties are levied on machinery and equipment and on basic foodstuffs, higher duties on unprocessed raw materials, yet higher duties on processed raw materials, and the highest duties on consumer goods, particularly those regarded as luxury or semi-luxury goods. Within this pattern, however, there is much variation depending on the need to protect local industry, which in turn depends in considerable measure on the stage of development reached and on the types of industries being promoted. The general pattern reflected by this tariff structure is often also buttressed by other complementary trade policy instruments such as licensing and foreign exchange controls. The relatively lenient treatment usually accorded to machinery and equipment in import policies reflects the important role of this product category in investments and development programmes. For basic foodstuffs it reflects the need to contain the cost to the consumer of the wage good. On the other hand, consumer foods, particularly those considered of a semi-luxury or luxury nature, are often considered most readily dispensable in import programmes, both because it is here that import substitution can often most easily be promoted and because, owing to their "non-essential" nature, there is least difficulty in tolerating high prices on the local market.

Given the relatively high protection usually accorded to the non-capital goods sectors of manufacturing in most developing countries, there is clearly much scope for lowering trade barriers in these sectors. Where countries are at roughly similar levels of industrialization, the exchange of concessions in these sectors can be very beneficial; it can have a salutary effect on the efficiency of production and can also be politically feasible given the expansion in intra-industry trade which could result.[21] As between countries at very different levels of development, however, there may be little basis for the exchange of concessions in this sector, for such concessions might hinder the efforts of the less developed countries to establish nascent industries. The situation may be different, however, where import barriers are imposed purely for balance-of-payments purposes (e.g., barriers against various imported consumer items of a "luxury" nature not produced locally), and in such cases there may well be a basis for the less developed countries to extend preferential access to their more developed partners in return for compensating export concessions.

In the case of heavy engineering and other capital goods, where protection is generally low, the negotiating problems would be rather different. The important point here is that a number of developing countries are already becoming internationally competitive producers of such goods and in some cases may even have technologies more appropriate for developing countries. Exports to developing countries have thus been growing fairly substantially in recent years, and while preferential arrangements as such may not be necessary for the continued growth of this trade, they could no doubt help. Developing countries exporters of these goods may therefore have an incentive to grant concessions in other sectors to encourage the continued growth of these exports to the South, with beneficial long-term effects on the economies of all concerned.

Agricultural products are a special case. These are exported widely by a large number of developing countries, both the more developed and the less developed ones. These include basic foodstuffs (e.g., grains, vegetable oils and oilseeds, meat), processed food products, beverages (tea, coffee and cocoa) and agricultural raw materials (e.g., cotton, rubber), and together account for 40 per cent of South-South trade. Where developing countries are already the principal suppliers to world markets (e.g., beverages), there is no scope for trade diversion, and

TABLE 1

Structure of South-South trade [a], 1976 and 1979

Exports from:	Exports to:								
	1976				Per cent [b]	1979			
	All DCs	MIDCs	Others	World		All DCs	MIDCs	Others	World
A. Trade flows ($billion)									
All DCs	20.0	8.5	11.5	87.2	22.9	35.5	16.8	18.7	142.3
MIDCs	13.2	6.2	7.0	55.8	23.6	26.0	13.5	12.5	102.0
Others	6.8	2.3	4.5	31.4	21.6	9.5	3.3	6.2	40.3
B. Shares in South-South exports (per cent)									
All DCs	100	100	100	—	—	100	100	100	—
MIDCs	66	73	61	—	—	73	80	66	—
Others	34	27	39	—	—	27	20	34	—
C. Shares in South-South imports (per cent)									
All DCs	100	42	58	—	—	100	47	53	—
MIDCs	100	47	53	—	—	100	52	48	—
Others	100	34	66	—	—	100	35	65	—

Source: UNCTAD secretariat calculations, based on data for 94 developing countries in 1976 and for 72 developing countries in 1979.

Note. All DCs = all developing countries; MIDCs = 15 more industrialized developing countries identified above; Others = all other developing countries for which data are available.

[a] Excluding trade in fuels.

[b] Share of exports to developing countries in total exports of the group of countries concerned.

South—South preferences can only affect the allocation of supplies
within the South (including domestic suppliers). The role for
South—South preferences is therefore limited. As regards basic
foodstuffs, the overriding consideration is usually to keep down
the cost of imports, and any shift to southern sources of supply
cannot therefore ignore price considerations. Accordingly, efforts
to promote South—South trade in these products must be linked to
measures to expand low—cost production in the South, supported,
where appropriate, by long—term supply and purchase agreements.
Trade in agricultural raw materials, which usually enjoy low duties
where these are required as inputs for industries, could also be
promoted by special trade agreements which could support production
expansion programmes; hence assured markets, rather than tariff
preferences, would seem to be relevant. It is therefore only for
processed food products (and, of course, processed raw materials)
that preferences would seem to be able to play an important role,
and here there should be much scope for the exchange of mutually
beneficial concessions, particularly between the more developed and
the less developed developing countries.

For the relatively more developed of the developing countries,
important possibilities exist for the intensification of
intra—industry trade, i.e., the exchange of goods within broad
industrial categories. This is the kind of trade that has
flourished most vigorously among the industrial countries for the
past two to three decades and indeed has been the most dynamic
component in the growth of world trade during these years.[22] It
has also contributed materially to the growth of South—South trade
in recent years.[23] That the negotiation of trade concessions is
facilitated where these are intended to promote the intensification
of intra—industry trade is now fully recognized, and indeed much of
the success of the various rounds of trade negotiations among the
developed industrial countries in the past years undertaken under
the auspices of the GATT has been due in no small measure to this
aspect of the negotiated concessions. The fact is that domestic
adjustment to trade liberalization is much less painful where
increased foreign competition within an industrial sector is
matched by the opening up of increased export possibilities in the
same sector. As a consequence, the need for painful adjustments
within the sector is reduced and at the same time greater
efficiency and a higher degree of specialization is promoted.
Thus, for the relatively more developed of the developing countries
with more diversified economies it should not only be easier to
identify trade opportunities for their export products for which to
seek trade concessions, but it may be easier as well to grant
concessions, especially where the industries affected can also
expect to benefit from new export opportunities. As demonstrated
by the statistical analysis above, the bulk of existing South—South
trade is already dominated by the more developed and more highly
diversified developing countries, and it is therefore easy to see
how trade concessions negotiated under the GSTP might contribute to
the further expansion of their exports to the South.

For the less developed countries with simpler export
structures, however, the problem is clearly more difficult. Thus,
the scope for negotiating concessions linked to intra—industry

TABLE 2

The network of South-South trade, 1976 and 1979

| | | 1976 | | | | 1979 | | |
Exports from:	All DCs	High income	Middle income	Low income	All DCs	High income	Middle income	Low income
		$ billion				*$ billion*		
All DCs	20.0	13.1	3.7	3.0	35.5	23.5	6.3	5.7
High-income	12.4	8.4	2.5	1.5	22.6	14.5	4.5	3.5
Middle-income	3.8	2.5	0.8	0.5	7.0	5.0	1.2	0.7
Low-income	3.7	2.3	0.4	1.0	6.0	4.0	0.5	1.5
		Per cent				*Per cent*		
All DCs	100.0	65.5	18.5	15.0	100.0	66.2	17.7	16.0
High-income	62.0	42.0	12.5	7.5	63.6	40.8	12.7	19.8
Middle-income	19.0	12.5	0.4	2.5	19.7	14.1	3.4	2.0
Low-income	18.5	11.5	0.2	5.0	17.0	11.3	1.4	4.2

Source: See table 1.

NOTE. Developing countries are grouped according to *per capita* income levels in 1978, as follows: High = above $1,000; Medium = between $500 and $1,000; Low = below $500; All DCs = all developing countries. In the lower half of the table all trade flows are expressed as a percentage of total South-South trade. The data relate to trade flows excluding fuels.

TABLE 3

Commodity structure of South-South exports for countries grouped according to income levels, 1976 and 1979

Country group [a]	Commodity group [b]									
	1976					1979				
	All commodities	Manufacturing	Food	Agricultural raw materials	Ores and minerals	All commodities	Manufacturing	Food	Agricultural raw materials	Ores and minerals
A. Total ($ billion)										
All DCs	20.0	8.5	6.2	2.2	2.0	35.5	16.1	10.1	3.8	3.1
High-income	12.4	6.3	3.2	1.2	0.8	22.5	12.0	5.6	2.0	1.9
Middle-income . . .	3.8	1.2	1.4	0.4	0.8	7.0	2.2	2.2	0.5	0.7
Low-income	3.7	1.0	1.6	0.7	0.4	6.0	1.9	2.3	1.3	0.5
B. Shares in South-South exports of various commodity groups (per cent)										
All DCs	100	100	100	100	100	100	100	100	100	100
High-income	62	74	52	53	40	63	75	55	54	60
Middle-income . . .	19	14	23	17	40	20	14	22	12	25
Low-income	19	12	26	29	20	17	12	23	34	15
C. Commodity structure of country groupings' South-South exports (per cent)										
All DCs	100	42	31	11	10	100	45	28	11	9
High-income	100	51	26	10	6	100	53	25	9	8
Middle-income . . .	100	32	37	11	21	100	31	31	7	10
Low-income	100	27	43	19	11	100	32	38	22	8

Source : See table 1.

NOTE. All data relate to trade excluding fuels.

[a] For definition of country groups see table 2.

[b] Manufacturing = SITC 5 to 8 (less 67 + 61); Food = SITC 0 + 1 + 22 + 4; Agricultural raw materials = SITC 2 less (22 + 27 + 28); Ores and minerals = SITC 27 + 28 + 67 + 68.

TABLE 4

Relative importance of selected commodity groups ᵃ in South-South trade for countries grouped according to income levels, 1976 and 1979

	Country group							
	1976				1979			
Commodity group	All DCs	High Income	Middle income	Low income	All DCs	High income	Middle income	Low income
A. South-South exports ($ billion)								
Chemicals	1.25	0.83	0.30	0.12	2.20	1.53	0.48	0.19
Miscellaneous manufactures	3.85	2.51	0.70	0.63	7.43	4.91	1.34	1.18
Textiles, fibres and clothing	1.88	1.03	0.40	0.45	3.53	1.95	0.79	0.79
Metals and metal manufactures	1.92	0.89	0.62	0.40 ·	3.15	2.22	0.50	0.43
Machinery and equipment	3.42	2.95	0.17	0.30	6.44	5.60	0.34	0.50
B. Share in South-South exports of each commodity group (per cent)								
Chemicals	100	67	24	9	100	70	22	9
Miscellaneous manufactures	100	65	18	16	100	66	18	16
Textiles, fibres and clothing	100	55	21	24	100	55	22	22
Metals and metal manufactures	100	46	33	21	100	70	16	14
Machinery and equipment	100	86	5	9	100	87	5	8
C. Share in each country group's South-South exports (per cent)								
Chemicals	6.3	6.7	8.0	3.1	6.2	6.8	6.8	3.1
Miscellaneous manufactures	19.3	20.2	18.5	16.9	20.9	21.8	19.2	19.6
Textiles, fibres and clothing	9.4	8.3	10.6	12.0	9.9	8.6	11.3	13.1
Metals and metal manufactures	9.6	7.2	16.5	10.8	8.9	9.8	7.2	7.1
Machinery and equipment	17.1	23.7	4.4	8.0	18.1	24.9	4.8	8.4

Source : See table 1.

Note. The commodity groups in terms of SITC, are as follows: Chemicals: 5; miscellaneous manufactures: 6 + 8 less (67 + 68); textiles, fibres and clothing: 26 + 65 + 84; metals and metal manufactures: 67 + 68 + 69; machinery and equipment: 7.

ᵃ Excluding fuels.

73

T A B L E 5

Shares of country groups in total South-South imports [a] of selected commodity groups, 1976 and 1979

(Percentage)

Commodity group	Country group							
	1976				1979			
	All DCs	High income	Middle income	Low income	All DCs	High income	Middle income	Low income
Food	100	64	19	17	100	64	14	22
Agricultural raw materials .	100	80	12	7	100	84	9	7
Ores and metals.	100	74	14	12	100	72	14	14
Manufactured goods. . . .	100	63	23	14	100	61	23	16
of which:								
Chemicals	100	57	26	17	100	51	26	23
Misc. manufactures . . .	100	67	22	11	100	65	20	15
Textiles	100	60	23	17	100	59	20	21
Metal manufactures . . .	100	69	19	12	100	69	18	13
Machinery and equipment . .	100	61	23	15	100	59	26	15

Source : See table 2.

[a] Excluding fuels. For definition of commodity groups see tables 3 and 4.

trade expansion is clearly limited. In exchange for improved
access to their markets for manufactures from the more
industrialized developing countries, these less developed countries
would therefore need, at least for the time being, to seek improved
access for their primary exports. Quite apart from questions which
may be raised concerning the relative merits of trade concessions
for manufactures as against those for primary products (much
discussed in the context of preferential schemes at the subregional
level), there is also the question how easy (or how difficult) it
may be to secure realistic trade concessions for the primary
product exports of these countries. In most cases tariff
concessions will not be very meaningful, either because the primary
products concerned are raw materials for industry and tariffs are
already low, or because as agricultural products they are subject
to special regimes (as was mentioned earlier). For the purpose of
effectively bringing these countries into the framework of the
negotiations some new initiatives would therefore be required, for
example, the negotiation of assured market access linked to
long-term purchase contracts, and perhaps linked as well to special
measures for promoting the related production and exports of these
less developed countries. Concessions might also be negotiated
that would raise the degree of processing of raw materials exported
from these countries. Without some special new initiatives of this
kind it is difficult to see how the less developed of the
developing countries can be effectively brought into the
negotiations, and there is the danger that the GSTP, at least in
the early years, might consist largely of the exchange of
concessions among the more developed of the developing countries.
In view of the importance of preserving the "global" character of
the GSTP, measures should be devised that would forestall this
eventuality.

VI.

What can now be said about the likely impact of the GSTP on
South-South trade, on world trade and development, and on the world
trading system?
As far as South-South trade is concerned, this has been
growing fairly rapidly in recent years, and given the underlying
factors, particularly the continued sluggishness of growth in the
North and the growing number of newly industrializing developing
countries with an ever more diversified range of manufactured
exports, it is likely to continue to grow in the future. The
question is therefore to what extent the exchanges of trade
concessions among developing countries can help promote South-South
trade. As discussed above, there seems fairly wide scope for
exchanging mutually beneficial trade concessions among developing
countries that would stimulate their mutual trade. The greatest
scope undoubtedly exists among the more developed, more
industrialized, of the developing countries for the exchange of

concessions which would be particularly important in promoting the growth of intra-industry trade, and which may be politically acceptable given the particular character of intra-industry trade discussed earlier. As between the more developed and the less developed developing countries, the problems are clearly more difficult for reasons already indicated, but given the increasing demand for various primary commodities in the more industrialized of these countries and their growing ability to export on a competitive basis the more sophisticated engineering and capital goods, it should be possible to devise mechanisms for the exchange of mutually beneficial trade concessions between these countries that would further stimulate their trade with each other.

The question arises as to the possible need to establish negotiating objectives for the GSTP. There are at least two important reasons why such objectives would be in order. First, it would clearly be of important political and psychological value to have some quantitative goals which countries would strive to achieve and which could be used as a yardstick against which to measure actual progress in the negotiations. Second, and perhaps more important, such objectives could be useful for assessing the extent to which individual countries have "contributed" to the negotiations in terms of concessions exchanged, an assessment which may be crucial for deciding on the multilateralization of negotiated concessions under conditions which would assure that a mutuality of advantages and a fair balance of concessions had been achieved.

The argument against establishing negotiating objectives recognizes the obvious complexity of working out meaningful quantitative targets taking account of tariff and non-tariff concessions as well as other trade measures. Thus, while it may be easy enough to set a priori targets for negotiating tariff concessions,[24] it is not evident how such targets could be set for non-tariff concessions, and even less so how these could be combined in order to arrive at overall negotiating objectives. It was in the light of these obvious difficulties that it was decided during the preparatory phase not to recognize, at least for the moment, the need for such objectives. And in the absence of such objectives not much can be said at this stage about the probable impact in quantitative terms of the GSTP on the expansion of trade; the question will therefore have to await actual developments in the negotiations.

So far as the likely impact of the GSTP on world trade and development and on the world economy is concerned, the basic question is how effective the GSTP will be in achieving its primary objective of increasing the autonomous growth and development potential of the developing countries. These countries are still heavily dependent on the North for their trade and development, and while South-South trade has been growing significantly in the past, the potential has not been fully exploited. The argument is that the exchange of preferences and other trade-promotion measures among the developing countries could contribute to the fuller exploitation of this potential for more intensive trade exchanges among them, thereby raising their growth and development beyond levels to which they would otherwise be constrained.[25] This result would clearly have a very positive impact on world trade and development. Developing countries are now an important factor in world trade, providing markets for close to 40 per cent of the exports of manufactures of the developed industrialized countries. Anything that developing countries can do to maintain their own growth rates in the face of the sluggish growth now characterizing the developed countries would therefore provide a welcome impetus to the expansion of the trade and development of developed countries and of the world economy as a whole. Thus, while the exchange of preferences among developing countries may well result in some trade diversion, this should be more than offset by their positive impact on development and trade.[26]

The GSTP and the expansion of trade that is expected to result from its implementation do not imply in any way that developing countries intend to withdraw from the world trading system. On the contrary, they are and certainly will continue to be intimately involved in the wider world trading system. Furthermore, a large number of developing countries are members of the GATT, which provides the institutional and legal framework for the conduct of the bulk of world trade. Developing countries members of GATT will therefore need to obtain the necessary GATT waivers before implementing preferential concessions negotiated under the GSTP, and there is already a general enabling clause in the GATT providing for the granting of such waivers. There are no grounds therefore for thinking that the GSTP implies the setting up of a separate "Third-World Trading System" outside the framework of existing rules. It is rather more modest in its aims of providing a framework for the greater liberalization and promotion of trade among developing countries within the broader framework of the world trading system, and will undoubtedly require for its effective implementation the understanding and sympathy of the major participants in the world trading system as a whole.

NOTES

[1]See TD/B/628, part one, sect. A. The studies in question were duly carried out by the UNCTAD secretariat under its work programme on ECDC, and formed the subject of about 12 documents published between 1979 and 1981.

[2]Arusha Programme for Collective Self-Reliance and Framework for Negotiations, adopted by the Fourth Ministerial Meeting of the Group of 77, held at Arusha (United Republic of Tanzania) from 6 to 16 February 1979, reproduced in Proceedings of the United Nations Conferences on Trade and Development, Fifth session, vol. I, Report and Annexes (United Nations publication, Sales No. E.79.II.D.14), annex VI.

[3]See the Ministerial Declaration on the Global System of Trade Preferences among Developing Countries adopted by the Ministers for Foreign Affairs of the States members of the Group of 77 on 8 October 1982, reproduced in United Nations document A/37/544, annex II.

[4]See the Arusha Programme for Collective Self-Reliance and Framework for Negotiations, Part II A, and the Ministerial Declaration cited in footnote 3 above for the statement of principles.

[5]It may be noted, however, that while the Ministerial Declaration referred to in footnote 3 above states in its paragraph 1 (a) that "the GSTP shall be reserved for the exclusive participation of developing countries members of the Group of 77", the Declaration by the Ministers for Foreign Affairs of the Group of 77 adopted on the same date and reproduced in document A/37/544, annex I, states in part II, paragraph 7, that "the Ministers . . . invited all developing countries to participate fully in the [GSTP]", leaving somewhat open the question of eligibility.

[6]See, e.g., Constantine Vaitsos, "Crisis in economic co-operation (Integration) among developing countries: A survey", World Development, vol. 6, No. 6, June 1978, for an assessment.

[7]Thus the data indicate, that for those groupings that have effectively exchanged tariff preferences, the growth of intra-trade has been greater than the growth of their total trade. (See UNCTAD, Handbook of International Trade and Development Statistics, Supplement 1981, table 1.14.) See also in this connection the conclusions reached in the UNCTAD study "Trade among developing countries by main SITC groups and by regions" (TD/B/C.7/21) (United Nations publication Sales No. E/F.82.II.D.11), p. 8.

[8]See "Review of the preferential arrangements established under the GATT Protocol relating to Trade Negotiations among Developing Countries", Study prepared by Mohamed Hamza at the request of the UNCTAD secretariat (TD/B/C.7/49).

[9]For example, while the Heckscher-Ohlin theory based on the factor proportions argument leads to the expectation of relatively large trade flows between developed and developing countries and much less significant trade flows within these two groups of countries, and Ricardo-type theories based on differences in natural resource endowments lead to no particular expectations about the trade flows between countries at different levels of development, more modern theories based on such ideas as the product cycle or intra-industry trade lead to the expectation of a greater relative importance for trade among countries at similar levels of development. The implications of existing theories for the direction of trade have been extensively examined by Oli Havrylyshyn and Martin Wolf in a study for the World Bank (see their "Trade among Developing Countries: Theory,

Policy Issues and Principal Trends", World Bank Staff Working Papers, No. 479, August 1981), though they do not reach any general conclusion on the subject relevant to the issue under discussion here. They do conclude, however, on the basis of assumptions concerning the relation between trade flows and market size, that the share of South-South trade is greater than could be expected given the share of the South in world incomes.

[10]See A. Olechowski and G. Sampson, "current trade restrictions in the EEC, the United States and Japan", Journal of World Trade Law, vol. 14, No. 3, May/June 1980.

[11]Textiles and fibres are only the most important products of special interest to developing countries that have been particularly affected by such restrictions.

[12]This is evident from the large literature on economic structure and the pattern of development which clearly indicates that there is a definite path by which countries climb the industrial ladder. See in this connection S. Kuznets, "Quantitative aspects of the economic growth of nations: IX. Level and structure of foreign trade: Comparison for recent years", Economic Development and Structural Change, vol. XIII, No. 1, part II, October 1964; N. Adams, "Import structure and economic growth: A comparison of cross-section and time-series data", Economic Development and Structural Change, vol. 15, No. 2, part I, January 1967; and H. Chenery and M. Syrquin, Patterns of Development 1950-70 (London, Oxford University Press (for the World Bank), 1975).

[13]The assessment by the UNCTAD secretariat in its Trade and Development Report, 1981 (TD/B/863/Rev.1) (United Nations publication, Sales No. E.81.II.D.9), p. 4, that the growth of the OECD countries in the 1980s would average 2.5 per cent now seems optimistic.

[14]See GATT, International Trade, 1980/81 and 1981/82.

[15]On this point see W. Arthur Lewis, "The slowing down of the engine of growth", American Economic Review, September 1980, who concludes that in present circumstances it is only by increasing their inter-trade that developing countries can maintain their growth momentum in the years ahead.

[16]Throughout the present article and in the statistical analysis below "developing countries" will be taken to mean countries members of the Group of 77. While this is by no means the only possible definition, its use here reflects the fact that these are the countries which are expected to participate in the GSTP. The expression covers in any event much the same countries as are covered by other definitions.

[17]See S. Kuznets, op. cit., and N. Adams, op. cit.

[18]These are countries whose exports of manufactures exceeded $500 million annually in recent years and which together account for the bulk of exports of manufactures from developing countries. They are: Argentina, Brazil, Colombia, Egypt, India, Indonesia, Malaysia, Mexico, Pakistan, Philippines, Republic of Korea, Singapore, Thailand, Tunisia and Yugoslavia. Romania is not included owing to lack of data.

[19]As before, these data all relate to trade excluding fuels.

[20]For ores and metals the share varies from 40 per cent in 1976 to 60 per cent in 1979, but this fluctuation probably reflects as much the difference in country coverage between the two years as anything else.

[21]For a discussion of this point see below.

[22]See, e.g., S. B. Linder, An Essay on Trade and Transportation (Stockholm, Almqvist and Wicksell, 1961); K. Lancaster, "Intra-industry trade under perfect monopolistic competition", Journal of International Economics, vol. 10, No. 2, 1980; and H. G. Grubel and P. J. Lloyd, Intra-Industry Trade: The Theory and Measurement of International Trade in Differentiated Products (New York, John Wiley and Sons, 1975).

[23]See, e.g., B. Balassa, "Intra-Industry Trade and the Integration of the Developing Countries in the World Economy" in On the Economics of Intra-Industry Trade, edited by Herbert Giersch (Tubingen, J. C. B. Mohr, 1979).

[24]For example, 50 per cent across-the-board tariff cut, or an average tariff cut of 50 per cent on 20 per cent of total imports, etc.

[25]On this point see Arthur Lewis, op. cit.

[26]A parallel could perhaps be drawn here between a GSTP and the EEC, the creation of which undoubtedly contributed to the growth of the EEC economies, resulting in an expansion of their trade with the rest of the world, notwithstanding the obvious element of trade diversion involved.

North-South Trade and Socio-Economic Autonomy: A Peace Formula

WOLFGANG HAGER

The desirability of an increasingly liberal access of manufactured exports of developing countries to markets of the old industrialized countries is one of the few points on which proponents of the new and old international economic order agree--at least in principle. Realists admit that exceptions to the ideal may have to be made in response to pressure groups in Western democracies which force politicians to sacrifice the general interest. Yet it is the duty of all well-intentioned, internationally-minded men to keep protectionist pressures to a minimum.

This paper argues the contrary: that the failure to acknowledge genuine conflicts of interest which pit the privileged rich countries against developing countries, and hence the failure to negotiate a viable order of coexistence, will lead to an increasingly unstable international economic environment and to poisoned political relations.

The welfare case for export-led growth in the developing countries is a dynamic one. Access to rich-country markets enables developing countries to overcome the handicaps of home markets that suffer from insufficient purchasing power: exports as a condition for efficient large-scale production. World market integration, moreover, opens up the cornucopia of the capital, technology and know-how of transnational corporations. Earnings from exports of manufactures constitute a source of foreign exchange, and hence development finance, which is preferred to the often static or erratic income from exports of commodities.

The welfare case for the industrialized countries has both static and dynamic elements. First, these countries are likely to benefit from the world welfare effects of an improved allocation of factors. Secondly, the laws of comparative advantage will push

From **TRADE AND DEVELOPMENT**, UNCTAD Review, Winter 1982, (119-128) reprinted by permission of the publisher.

these countries to higher value-added activities commensurate
with their ample capital and skill endowment. Thirdly, a thriving
third world will provide a needed boost to demand (Brandt Report)[1]
that will offset the stagnation of home demand.

There have always been voices, now muted by the success of
some newly industrializing countries, which point out the
structural consequences of world market integration for developing
countries: distorted development and consumption patterns,
inappropriate levels of capital intensity, etc. Oddly enough, the
misery caused by export-oriented agriculture, from 18th century
Britain to the developing countries now, has not left its
mark on mainstream thinking. Nor is Japan commonly cited as a
prime example of a distorted economy which, with a comparatively
small portion of its GNP devoted to exports, nevertheless has
oriented the whole economy to the production of exportables,
neglecting housing and social infrastructure as well as the service
sector. Yet in the third world, at least, the potential conflict
between world market integration and basic socio-economic autonomy
is recognized.

Few people seem to realize, however, that such a conflict
could arise also in Western Europe. World market integration poses
a threat to the very essence of the socio-economic culture of the
modern welfare State, and it is this threat--even if it is not as
yet recognized--which will increasingly sour North-South relations
while destabilizing the world economy.

To argue this point, a slight re-write of post-war economic
history is in order. Usually, this history is portrayed as a
steady progression towards trade liberalization. Yet until
1958-1959 and the end of exchange controls, Western European
liberalization was largely confined to the continent itself, with
the OEEC encouraged to discriminate against the United States. In
the following years, with tariffs still high, the United States
continued the pattern of complementary trade--agriculture and high
technology--while internationally-minded companies producing the
standard manufactures preferred direct investment to arms-length
exports. By the time tariffs had come down (Kennedy Round), the
dollar was hopelessly overvalued. As a consequence Western
Europe was left without effective competition: Eastern Europe
produced goods which could not find a market at any price. Japan
had a narrow product range and was wholly absorbed in the United
States market. The developing countries seemed permanently trapped
by an insufficiency of capital, infrastructure, manpower skills,
and markets. A tariff structure unfavourable to the "typical"
goods produced in developing countries, and the Cotton Textiles
Arrangement, reinforced this illusion.

In other words, Western Europe enjoyed, collectively, a
(largely) natural protection against the outside world which was no
less effective than the deliberate protectionism practised by
Japan. As a result, not only was Western Europe able to sell its
goods on a cost-plus basis to the rest of the world, but also it
was able to set these costs, allocate resources and distribute
factor rewards in ways which corresponded to its politics and
changing values. Although there were free-trade-like conditions
within the continent, tensions were avoided since these values and

institutions moved roughly in step in the whole region.

In these years of autonomy Western Europe found answers to problems which had occupied domestic and international politics for a century: the class war seemed settled once and for all by a re-distribution of income and the introduction of contractual elements in the labour "market" which narrowed the gap between wage-earners and the middle classes. The continent was unified and integrated economically to the point where armed conflict became unthinkable and the development of a unified "civilian" power as a calm pole in a world of conflict a possibility.

These achievements are now not only taken for granted, but recklessly jeopardized by Europeans with short memories. To the extent that world market integration proceeds, the old income and security bargain with the working class is broken. To the extent that world market integration is resisted, the necessarily underground nature of this resistance leads to national forms of protectionism which threaten the economic, and hence political, unity of Western Europe. These points clearly need amplification.

Our economic history continues with the loss of Western Europe's collective natural protection at the turn of the decade of the 1970s. The dollar was valued realistically, and the United States, pushed by an oil-related mercantilism which is now a pervasive feature of the world economy, sold standard goods, like textiles, to Europe. Eastern Europe equipped itself with modern plants and co-operated with Western transnational corporations to become a presence in world markets. Japan diversified products and markets, capturing significant shares of Europe's home and export markets. Finally, the newly industrializing countries, followed by a host of others likewise bent on industrializing their economy, began their meteoric rise in world export markets for manufactures. Technology transfer, not least through the mediation of transnational corporations, educational advances, and improvements in transport and communications had sharply reduced what had seemed near-insurmountable obstacles for development only a few years earlier.

Deprived of its natural protection--the transient monopoly of advanced forms of industrial production--Western Europe stood revealed as a high-cost economy. It now faced competition throughout the whole range of manufactures: there were few niches left. International organizations, committed to an open-world system, point to the negligible impact, as far as quantities are concerned, of the new competitors.[2] In the short term, however, the impact is likely to be on profits, as firms struggle to maintain market shares by matching competitors' price and/or engaging in capital deepening. This is a costly, but temporarily successful, defence against imports. Yet the labour saving, at the firm level, is nullified at the level of the national economy in societies which pay the idled factor labour a near working wage. The hope, expressed with great confidence by GATT and OECD, is that the idled workers will be re-employed in "viable" activities.

The faith in "upward adjustment" is the single most important reason preventing people from facing the true dilemma. According to this strategy, high-cost European labour is to remain employable by moving it towards high technology production, or towards products belonging to the sophisticated end of traditional sectors. These adjustment strategies, however, find their limits in the structure of final demand.   Consumers will continue to spend their income on   clothes, furniture, TVs and tennis rackets   and consume limited   amounts   of   nuclear   reactors,   jet liners or satellites. Moreover,   as Japan, the   United States, and   Europe are all at the same frontiers   of technology, accelerated adjustment   will lead to instant   overcapacity   rather   than   to   the   long   periods   of technological monopoly rents which,   in earlier times,   allowed   the leaders to recoup R & D costs.   The nuclear power sector, where all are losing money,   provides a modern   example. As regards   the move up-market to sophisticated product   ranges, special steels, quality automobiles, or designer fashions typically constitute no more than a tenth of the total market.   Moreover, these presumed shelters are being   eroded by the   ease with which   the latest design and market information can be transmitted directly to machines   and warehouses around the globe.

It follows that the problem of high cost, high-wage production cannot be sidestepped by   putting one's hopes in   upward adjustment towards technological niches secure from competition.   In fact, the whole notion   is unconsciously   racist.   It   assumes that even the least educated part of   Europe's population is forever destined to make more complex and sophisticated goods than those   which the most mobile and motivated part   of the world's brown population can produce.   The   opposite   is   the   case   and   clearly   a ground for satisfaction.   The problem   lies   in   the—now mutual—influence of different socio-economic cultures, which is itself attributable to market   integration.   That   such   influence   can   be   highly destabilizing in both   economic and political   terms the South   has known for a long time.   And some may think it no more than justice that the   shoe is now   on the other   foot.   Interdependence being a reality,   however,   the   fate of   the rich   countries does touch all others—as OPEC found out.

The   fundamental   point   that   has   been   side-stepped   by the upward-adjustment optimists is that   under conditions of free trade world   labour markets are   de facto integrated.   This follows from Walras's law   which says   that if   one factor   market   and the goods market   are   integrated,   the   second   factor   market is   ipso facto integrated. Of course, national capital markets are not integrated; but the mobility of capital, if only via off-shore markets, is such that the   condition holds in practice.   Nor are goods markets fully integrated;   but to the   extent that they   are, the Walrasian logic applies: European workers compete   directly with workers, in   say, the   third world.   The labour   market is   and will remain for many decades   to   come   in heavy   surplus   overall.   Since   this   is essentially   a free   market, wages   will continue   to be depressed. Local manpower   scarcities, accompanied   by somewhat   higher wages, cannot alter the global market situation.

To the extent that the European worker competes freely in this market,   as implied   under free-trade   conditions,   he   will have to align his productivity wages to some global standard.   If such wage adjustment   does not take place   there will be quantity adjustment: unemployment.   Both these market responses can be observed.

Most   people welcome the   role of foreign   trade as a check on market power within Europe or America, whether it is wielded by unions or by corporations. During the years of autonomy a great many "victories" were chalked up by trade unions in some countries which ultimately damage the earnings and job security of workers. But these are matters of degree. Truly free competition in the world labour market means importing the socio-economic patterns of others: no effective union power at all; a sharply altered income distribution; and the tolerance of large-scale unemployment. (The implicit assumption by adjustment optimists that there is equilibrium in a free exchange between high-cost and low-cost areas of production which maintains something like full employment in the high-cost area is implausible to the point of being disingenuous).

It is important to realize that what is involved in the first instance is a domestic issue of distribution. Clearly, those Europeans and Americans who are working in the sheltered part of the economy, i.e. the majority, have, in the short-term at least, an identity of interest with exporters in the developing countries or in Japan. Their real income increases if they can substitute cheap imports for (more expensive) domestic products. Even in the short term, however, this gain must be offset by the cost of the higher taxes needed to pay for the idled factor labour (including the inflation "tax" implicit in deficit spending by governments), and by the loss of idled or written-off capital stock in which most citizens, via pension funds, etc., have a share. Those are the static losses and gains.

We know from classical economists like Ricardo and Adam Smith (the political economists, not the bloodless abstractions on which today's reductionist models are based) that wages, notably minimum wages, are partly determined by values in society; and partly by what one might call the terms of trade of the labourer with the rest of the economy. The classics thought principally of food as the decisive element in the equation. Today's crucial terms of trade, domestically, are those between the sheltered sector of the economy (which, in addition to food, includes housing and services) and the open sector, i.e. most manufactures.

The sheltered sector in advanced economies is overwhelmingly characterized by contractual arrangements far removed from the market; civil servants, lawyers, bank clerks or farmers claim as an inalienable right the advantages which the worker in the open sector thought he had almost acquired: high wages, short hours, job security, vacations, etc. The worker spends a good part of his income in exchanges with this sheltered sector—he has no choice and has to accept the contractual prices as given. In addition, society imposes a host of conditions on production in the open sector which make it comparatively inefficient: environmental regulations; prohibitions or zoning regulations governing the siting of plants, etc. The United States has accepted the logic of adjustment by reducing the number and scope of such regulations. To the extent that European societies remain true to their values, more of the adjustment cost will fall on industry and the workers.

In other words, trade adjustment invovles not only a marginal reallocation of activities within an otherwise unchanged context, but also a steady yet unmistakable adjustment of society and the polity to the socio-economic practices of successful competitors.

It is not only the welfare State (in the broadest possible interpretation) which is being jeopardized, but free enterprise capitalism which, in democracies, tends to live in symbiosis with the welfare State.

The lowering of cost cannot proceed fast enough and go far enough to maintain the profitability of many industrial enterprises. By postponing costly investment, firms can go on for a remarkably long time producing and matching competitor prices. When adjustment--to new product lines and new production technologies--can no longer be postponed, these firms increasingly face the choice between bankruptcy and rescue by the State. The size of the firm usually determines which of the two solutions is eventually chosen. The State unwillingly acquires (or acquires responsibility for) the commanding heights of modern industry. In other words, Western Europe is stumbling into the State capitalist pattern--defensively and without a clear overall strategy--which is the standard feature of much of its economic environment.

Connected with such systemic responses is a reallocation of national savings and investments which corresponds not to domestically-determined socio-economic priorities, but rather to the mercantilist logic of an integrated world market: investment is channelled to industry by tax concessions, preferential financing and outright subsidies. In part, these supporting measures merely compensate for the fact that the sheltered sector attracts too much investment relatively to the low-profit open sector. But the "ideal" pattern which is being imitated, however badly, is that of Japan: a society geared to the production and (home) consumption of exportables, and a severely underdeveloped, high-cost and inefficient housing and service sector.

These European efforts to channel resources to sectors producing exportables are only part of a world-wide, wasteful scramble by which participants, mercantilists all, seek to subsidize these sectors, at a "static" loss, to reap the dynamic gains of development and to improve their balance-of-payments position. Subsidies to capital, socially regressive fiscal benefits to industry, export subsidies, subsidies to infrastructure and curbs on trade union power are universal phenomena in the Western world, North and South (and of course systemic in Eastern Europe). The caricature of this wasteful mercantilist subsidy race is the shipbuilding industry, which, on a true cost-accounting basis, has yielded negative value added for all but a handful of firms in the world.

We have argued that Europe adjusts to the socio-economic pattern of successful competitors in two fundamental respects: by reversing income and security bargains made with labour; and by drifting into State capitalism, which is, in effect, financial protectionism. There is a third element in the arsenal of policies of competitors, namely trade protectionism. This protectionism allows Japan and the newly industrializing countries to engage in the risky game of world market competition selectively and under controlled conditions, without submitting the whole economy to the uncertain and cumulative effects of adjustment. Western European countries are responding to the logic of the situation by practicing protectionism in their turn--not, to be sure, by way of retaliation, but as a pragmatic step to shore up firms and activities losing out in the mercantilist scramble. Indeed, it would be wrong to speak of "senile industry" protectionism as some sort of mirror image of "infant industry" protectionism. The whole point of the story is that we are dealing with middle-aged industries; or, to put it more technically, that the whole world is working with increasingly similar capital equipment. If anything, nations starting out with green-field plants off the shelf may now enjoy a higher average productivity than nations adding state-of-the art equipment to existing stock (e.g. shipbuilding in the Republic of Korea). And to speak of these core industries, like steel, as declining because they are shedding labour is to endow the linear adjustment model with an inevitability it does not have.

Since the European Community is constrained by some of its members to pursue a conventional liberal trade policy, it falls to the individual nations to deal with real-world problems. Unable by virtue of the Treaty of Rome to take recourse to either tariff or quota protectionism, they take recourse to underground forms of protectionism: technical barriers, national procurement policies, customs harassment, voluntary restriction agreements (sometimes concluded by private industry with official blessing) and, as mentioned above, financial protectionism. The net effect is not only the total erosion of the customs union in all really tough cases, but the erosion of the internal free market. This affects Western Europe as a whole: the free-trade agreements with the European Free Trade Association (EFTA) are equally eroded by the new protectionism.

In other words, a workable free-trade area accounting for two-thirds of the exports of most European countries is being jeopardized for the sake of maintaining free trade with an environment which does not let the market operate either at the border or within its border (where capital is priced and allocated for the purpose of pursing specific development strategies).

Before we turn to the implications of these trends for the third world, let us summarize and sharpen the argument further. The first point is to conceive of economic activity in Europe and the rest of the world not as states of nature which, by marginal adjustment, can be brought into equilibrium, but as man-made patterns, institutions, etc. for the pricing and allocation of factors of production. Europe's distinguishing characteristic is that it does not have a free labour market, and that the uses to which both labour and capital are put are submitted to heavy and costly regulation. By and large the allocation of real capital is decentralized, with a bias, through incentives or pre-emption by the State, towards social infrastructure capital. It is a high-cost area of production; market conditions—competition—and the fiscal and wage effects of distributional bargains reduce the rate of profit, reducing the speed of capital stock rejuvenation and/or channelling savings to the sheltered sector and foreign investment.

In 1981 the combined GDP of EEC and EFTA amounted to some $2,660 billion, and their exports outside Western Europe to $240 billion, i.e. 9 per cent. Imports of manufactures from outside

Western Europe amounted to some $100 billion, or less than 4 per cent of GDP. How can such small magnitudes have the large effects ascribed to them in this article? First, this is an argument about trends. In 1973 manufactured imports into the area from outside Western Europe amounted to $29 billion. Secondly, as argued above, the defensive policies adopted at firm level (i.e. defensive capital deepening or the lowering of cost by non-investment, depending on conditions in the firm and sector concerned when adjustment pressures arise) and at the public policy level (lowering of wage-costs, granting of subsidies) work for a time, as does outright protectionism. Hence the numbers do not reflect the magnitude of the adjustment challenge.

Thirdly, the argument assumes a Galbraithian world of modern capitalism, which requires price and market stability for firms to engage in increasingly costly and long-term investments, and for which oligopoly is the normal and necessary form of organization. The text book teaches us the oligopolies break down either if the number of competing firms increases well above twelve; or if new entrants can produce at substantially lower cost so that the normal sanctions of oligopoly do not work. Europe (and America) is experiencing both challenges at once. (And as experience shows, a market participant with a 5 per cent share selling well below prevailing standards can force the alignment of prices for the remaining 95 per cent).

In this situation of uncertainty, capital will go to places where profits correspond to the risk, e.g. 40 per cent, and hence with a short pay-back period; or will call on the State ex ante or ex post to provide insurance. Similarly, many modern forms of protectionism can be conceived of as a clumsy attempt by the public authorities to force newcomers to observe oligopoly discipline, performing a task previously handled by private enterprise. Yet, as will be argued below, there is no alternative to this method for providing a modicum of order in an integrated world of heterogeneous socio-economic systems.

What is the interest of industrializing developing countries in this situation? To the extent that they increase their shares in the markets of the developed countries, they gain a dynamic source of demand without the need to (fully) pass on productivity advances to domestic labour. This allows high savings ratios which are considered essential for development. There are some diseconomies in the political instability and/or its suppression by force which a policy on these lines requires. The policy also attracts foreign investment. The drain of effective demand and of capital from Western Europe can be considered a net benefit to the developing countries, its dynamic effects mirrored in the industrial stagnation and decline in Europe.

One of the chief drawbacks for developing countries is that the situation just described is unstable and cannot last. While Western European countries, firmly wedded to neo-classical thinking, will drift for years to come towards the socially regressive adjustment measures described above, businessmen and labour, and the despised mechanism of politics, will force ideologically blinded civil servants to act. The initially easy way out, financial protectionism, is being rapidly foreclosed by the budgetary effects of unemployment (which is partially the results of State-subsidized capital deepening). For the developing countries, the net effect of this particular response is a denial of market access (by means of subsidized domestic production) in ways which reduce growth in the rich countries (inflation caused by budget deficits to pay for both unemployment and capital subsidies, with recession as both a policy response and the consequence of dear money in the economy at large).

From the standpoint of governments, outright trade protectionism is a cheaper way out. It is also more in tune with free enterprise capitalism. It provides industry with resources through protectionist rents, not involving direct State interference. It benefits the most efficient firms most, while State rescues are biased towards the least efficient. A look at the firms and countries (the United States, Federal Republic of Germany, Switzerland) which have benefited from the Multifibre Arrangement quickly proves the efficiency of protectionism, so greatly at variance with free-trade dogma.

The chances are, however, that the adoption of protectionist policies willbe as at present--but at an accelerating rate--piecemeal and sudden. Panic protectionism gives the worst of all outcomes to both Europe and the new competitors. First, and perhaps least important for developing countries, panic protectionism will most probably be practised at the national level, increasing the uncertainty and complexity of managing the trade of supplier countries. For Europe the cost is higher, since trade barriers erected against small flows of outside trade often affect much larger amounts of internal European trade. More importantly, panic protectionism carries the risk of hard-to-afford capital stock in an exporting developing country being idled; moreover, it increasingly carries the risk of transmission to the other big market, the United States, as exports surge and price competition in the search for alternative markets triggers the invisible but solid trip-wire of protectionism. Thus, in the late 1970s, the colour TV industry of the Republic of Korea was left working at 20 per cent of capacity after the imposition of a United States quota.

This, then, is the partner for the developing countries' economic development which Western Europe is likely to be under present policies: stagnant, but capable of nullifying some market gains by developing countries with defensive capital deepening; fractious and unpredictable, as individual nations take recourse to quantitative trade restrictions of one kind or another; a poor market for the providers of raw materials, with devastating results for industrial development especially in Latin America; ungenerous in aid and market access for the poorest developing countries.

What are the remedies? The main instrument for greater harmony, to put it at its most abstract, is for developing countries to join, or at least respect, oligopoly discipline when dealing with the markets of rich countries. This means, ideally, earning the same amount of foreign exchange by selling lesser quantities at higher prices, i.e. improving their terms of trade (in manufactures). Recent talks by India and China to limit cut-throat competition in export markets are a step in the right direction.

Part of the remedy are higher exchange rates. Markets are far too imperfect, especially with Japan as part of the adjustment process, to justify relying on exchange rates alone to do the trick by themselves. Even this modest step would require the active collaboration of the most dynamic newly industrializing countries. In order to improve their terms of trade by this route, however, they would have to organize themselves as a group, and be willing to lose quantitative market shares to newcomers to the industrializing process.

A measure with similar effects is to permit free trade unions. With purchasing power of people in the industrialized countries declining or stagnating, and increases of purchasing power in developing countries declining or stagnating, and increases of purchasing power in developing countries kept below growth rates, the relentless growth of productivity worldwide can only result in the kind of underconsumption crisis predicted by Marx, which the mechanism of free wage bargaining helped to avoid. As the scandalously (because of unmet needs) low capital utilization rates worldwide indicate, Say's Law does not operate. The competitive wage cutting to be observed in both North and South can only aggravate the problem. Countries which dare improve domestic purchasing power may see their exports reduced, but will be compensated by more dependable and socially superior domestic sources of growth. This, contrary to popular myth, is how Japan managed to develop. Similarly, in the Republic of Korea (to take just one example) development would not have occurred without the domestic income and growth effect of social reforms in agriculture. In the 19th century European countries stumbled into the provision of basic human needs and adequate purchasing power only under pressure of riots and revolutions. The third world could well shorten the learning process.

In fact, as UNCTAD's <u>Trade and Development Report, 1981</u>[3] points out, as developing countries are faced with an industrialized West growing at just over 2 per cent in the 1980s, and are tied to this growth by South/North growth elasticities of about 1.7, their reliance on demand in the rich countries condemns them to a growth rate of around 4 per cent, well short of the 7 per cent needed to absorb a growing labour force with some rise in real income. As a consequence the conclusion is inevitable: they need to rely on domestic sources of demand and on demand generated by trade among developing countries.

The Report performs a signal service by pointing to the disequilibrium properties of the world economy under present policies, not just as regards growth and employment, but also as regards finance. Apart from those affecting the energy and food sectors, however, it does not explore the disequilibria likely to arise at the sectoral level. Clearly, a juxtaposition of investment plans and/or production assumptions of the participants in the world economy would show a high degree of incompatibility: import substitution, import limitation, and export strategies of each individual country simply do not add up to balance. While the world is far too complex to allow any kind of indicative planning at the sectoral level, some sort of early warning system in the most important capital-intensive and labour-intensive industries is clearly called for. UNIDO is cautiously entering this field. OECD's efforts in this area, whose correct predictions of severe overcapacity in the steel and shipbuiding sectors were not heeded, or the example of Sri Lanka, which built up a textile capacity wildly in excess of the limits of the Multifibre Arrangement, do not suggest that this sort of forecasting is a very effective restraint. Still, after a few expensive mistakes, governments may perhaps be capable of learning the folly of treating their own development strategies as an autonomous given, to be accommodated by an infinitely elastic world market.

The Western world is adhering to neo-classical economic thinking which assumes equilibrium ex ante or relegates disequilibrium to the status of a minor and transitory nuisance. Developing countries should not, however, build their long-term development strategy on what the advanced countries say, but on what they are doing and are likely to do in the future. They should not reject contractual arrangements in world trade (which they rightly clamour for in the case of raw materials) as an illegitimate constraint on their freedom of action, but should maximize stability of access and revenue and minimize self-exploitation.

NOTES

[1]North-South: A Programme for Survival, Report of the Independent Commission on International Development Issues (the Brandt Commission) (London, Pan Books, 1980).

[2]The best known presentation of this view is OECD's The Impact of the Newly Industrialising Countries (Paris, 1981).

[3]United Nations publication, Sales No. E.81.II.D.9.

A Model of Trade and Growth for the Developing World

NORMAN L. HICKS

This paper describes structure, assumptions and projection results of the SIMLINK model. The purpose of this model is to simulate the trade linkages between the developed and developing world. By taking the growth expectations of the OECD countries and the price of petroleum as a starting point, the model estimates the price and volume of a series of commodities important in LDC exports. The export earnings for seven LDC regions are estimated from the commodity projections, and combined with a predetermined estimate of capital inflows to calculate import capacity. A simple growth model for each region then determines the import constrained growth rate for that region.

I. INTRODUCTION AND BACKGROUND

The recent economic events of the past two years have made even more obvious the linkages between the world's economies. Rapid changes in commodity prices, inflation and real growth rates in the developed world have had both favorable and unfavorable impacts on the developing countries. In order to estimate the full range of all these events simultaneously, a model has been developed in the World Bank for analyzing trade linkages and growth prospects for the less developed countries (LDCs) under alternative scenarios of development and inflation in the developed world. This model, called SIMLINK [SIMulated trade LINKages], is not a new theoretical breakthrough, but a combination of existing modeling techniques into a comprehensive system which can furnish inputs for

From **EUROPEAN ECONOMIC REVIEW** 7, 1976, (239-255), reprinted by permission of the publisher.

policy decisions on a timely basis. While comprehensive in nature, the model remains simple enough to be calculated quickly.

In recent years modeling work involving developing countries consisted of parallel, but often unconnected, work along three broad lines: country models, which concentrate on one country and assume the rest of the world as exogenously given; commodity models, which examine the market equilibrium conditions for a single commodity; and world trade models, which use a static share relationship to balance world exports and imports. An effort has been made to combine large econometric models and world trade relationships (Project LINK). This has not proven useful for studies of the developing world, since most of the models are short-term forecasting models of the developed world without the dynamics of the commodity markets and without adequate LDC models. In addition, the LINK system is to unwieldy to provide rapid solutions to policy alternatives. For a fuller discussion of the LINK system, see Ball (1973).

II. THE SIMLINK APPROACH

The approach adopted for SIMLINK is to borrow something from all three of the preceding methodologies, while keeping the level of disaggregation both meaningful and computable. The model might be thought of as being block recursive in the following steps:

(1) -- The rates of growth of output and prices in the developed world (largely the OECD countries) are taken to be exogenously determined and outside the scope of the model. Since the LDC world has little feedback effect on the developed world, this was felt to be a reasonable assumption.

(2) -- Commodity models are developed or adapted for the major primary exports of the developing world to project prices and volumes for these products. While varying in complexity, the emphasis has been to develop models for those commodities of greatest importance to the LDCs.

(3) -- Exports of LDC manufactures and services are projected on the basis of historically estimated elasticities with respect to OECD growth. Prices for these items are projected on the basis of the exogenously forecasted inflation rates in the OECD.

(4) -- The commodity trade volumes and prices so calculated are then translated into export volumes and both import and export prices, for seven LDC groups built up from data for the 40 largest LDCs (excluding OPEC members).

(5) -- A simple growth model is developed for each LDC group which relates growth of imports to growth of output and investment. These models are then solved for the level of growth which equates total imports to total exports and an exogenously specified level of capital inflow.

At the present stage, the model contains 14 commodity models having a total of 79 structural equations, 11 equations for estimating exports of manufactures and services, and seven LDC models having eight equations each. Ignoring definitional equations and identities, the model has a total of 146 structural equations. This makes it easily computable and capable of producing alternative growth scenarios of the developing world on a rapid basis.

The model is estimated from past data generally using ordinary least-squares techniques. The span of data used depends largely on its availability, and the estimated coefficients tend to be based on data ranging from the past six to the past twenty years. The model is largely recursive in nature, although there is some simultaneity in certain parts, mainly related to the individual commodity models.

Section 3 contains a more detailed discussion of the structure of the model, followed by a description of some results obtained from running the model using alternative assumptions.[1]

III. THE MODEL IN DETAIL

3.1 Commodity Models

The model starts with a data base for 40 major LDCs who are not members of the Organization of Petroleum Exporting Countries (OPEC), and who account for approximately 85 percent of World Bank lending. These countries are aggregated together into seven groups: Mineral Producers, South Asia, East Africa (including the low-income areas of Central Africa), Mediterranean, West Africa, East Asia and Latin America. A matrix of export shares in 1972 for 35 primary products, manufactures and services was constructed for these regions. Of the 35 commodities, however, only about 15 account for a substantial share of exports of any one region.[2]

Consequently, commodity models were developed first for the most important commodities. In addition, some exogenous price and volume estimates have been used for a few commodities that are important to the LDCs but for which it proved difficult to construct useful models. These include commodities that in the past have been influenced by U.S. surplus policies (wheat, cotton, tobacco).

It is difficult to summarize in a small space the work done by different researchers on these commodity models. On the supply side, the models assume a distributed lag response to past prices by producers based on biological and information type lags. Other variables introduced often included prices of substitutes, dummy variables for exogenous factors affecting output, and time trends. The general form of the supply equations can be expressed as:

$$Q_j = f(P_{jt-1}, P_{jt-2}, \cdot \cdot \cdot, P_{jt-n}, Y, O_1, O_2, \cdot \cdot \cdot, O_n), \quad (1)$$

where Q is the supply of the jth commodity, P_j is its real prices lagged by an appropriate number of time periods, Y is real OECD GNP in 1963 dollars, and the O's are other variables. In most cases, total supply Q_j is the sum of two or more supply equations estimated on a regional or country basis in order to capture the intrinsically different time lags apparent in various areas of the world. The lagged prices, $P_{jt-2}, \ldots, P_{jt-n}$, were often dropped in favor of simply lagged supply, Q_{jt-1}, thus introducing the assumption of a distributed lag having geometrically declining weights.[3] In some cases, such as rice, where world prices are affected mostly by exports and where a large part of production is not exported, the model deals only with exports rather than total world production. The prices of substitutes were important in only a few commodity models: rice (wheat), tin (aluminum) and fats and oils (other fats and oils).

The price formation or <u>demand</u> side of the models was, generally speaking, estimated in two different ways. In some models, prices were estimated to be a direct function of world supply and demand, giving an equation of the following form:

$$P_j = f(Y, Q, O_1, O_2, \ldots, O_n), \tag{2}$$

where Y is the OECD GNP in contrast 1963 U.S. dollars, Q is the total of either world production or world exports, and the other variables (O_1) often include the prices of substitutes, dummy variables, and the rate of world inflation. An alternative to the simple direct price formation equation (2) above is the slightly more complex stock-adjustment approach. In this approach, the demand vector determines consumption of the commodity in question. Inventories or stocks are defined as current production less current consumption plus stocks from the previous year, and real prices are determined by the level of stocks (which may be expressed as an inverse relationship and/or as a ratio to total production). This three-equation method of determining prices can be summarized as:

$$C_j = f(Y), \tag{3}$$
$$S_j = S_{jt-1} + Q_j - C_j, \tag{4}$$
$$P_j = f(S_j), \tag{5}$$

where C_j stands for consumption and S_j for end year stocks, with only the lagged variables subscripted for time. As before, other variables may be included in the consumption and price equations, although these are not included in the notation above. It can also be readily seen that eqs. (3) to (5) can be reduced to eq. (2) by substitution, so that by using eq. (2) one is merely estimating directly a reduced form of the stock-adjustment model.

The P_j are estimated in terms of real commodity prices, that is, nominal prices deflated by an index of world inflation. Since the supply equations are also related to real, rather than nominal prices, most of the commodity models are found to be neutral in their response to changes in world inflation. In the estimation of certain models, however, the index of world inflation was found to be an important independent variable. This occurred in the

Table 1
Residual commodity model coefficients.

Group	E_y	E_d	s'
Agric – Food	0.5	−0.5	4.0
Agric – Non-food	0.3	−0.3	3.0
Minerals and metals	1.1	−0.4	6.0

Table 2
Income elasticities for imports of manufactured goods from developing countries.

	E_y	t	R^2
Japan/Oceania	2.24	7.4	0.885
Western Europe	2.62	9.9	0.933
North America	5.36	10.9	0.943
Socialist	2.27	6.3	0.849

models for coffee, sugar and rice. In general, the higher the rate
of world inflation, the lower the real prices of these commodities.
This appears to confirm an often stated hypothesis that LDCs suffer
during periods of world inflation because the prices of some of
their exports fail to keep up with other prices, although it fails
to explain why. It should also be pointed out that the lag is
somewhat temporary, and that eventually real prices tend to adjust.
This suggests that perhaps sellers lack perfect vision and fail to
effectively note other world prices, or that sales are made in
advance of production and delivery, and that an acceleration of
inflation rates is generally unexpected.[4]

For primary products not covered by the existing commodity
models, a more general formulation has been used to project volumes
and prices. First, the remaining commodities are aggregated into
three broad classes; food, non-food agriculture and minerals and
metals. The percentage increase in the prices of these 'residual'
commodity groups is estimated using

$$p' = -\frac{y'E_y - s'}{E_d} \qquad (6)$$

where p' is the percentage increase in price for the ith residual
commodity class, y' is the growth rate of OECD real GNP, s' is an
exogenous estimate of the growth rate of supply, and E_y and E_d are
the respective income and price elasticities. The values of the
parameters used in the model for this equation are given in table
1, and are based on estimates provided by the Commodities and
Export Projections Division of the World Bank.

3.2 Manufactured Exports

For manufactured exports from the LDCs, a slightly different
approach is utilized compared to the primary product models. First
of all, since the LDCs have a relatively small share of total
manufactured export trade, we assume that reconciliation of supply
and demand does not occur via the price mechanism. Instead, total
demand for LDC manufactured exports by the OECD and Socialist
countries is allocated among the LDC groups according to shares
based on exogenous initial estimates of the growth of supply. To
estimate demand elasticities, log-log regressions were run between
constant price OECD and Socialist groups GDP and imports by these
groups of manufactures from all LDCs, regardless of source. (The
data for these regressions is based on the U.N. trade data, and
covers the years 1965-72.)[5] As summarized in table 2, these
regressions reveal a fairly high elasticity for import demand by
the developed countries, ranging from 2.2 to 5.4.

The elasticities estimated in table 2 have to be adjusted for
two factors: first, they are for 68 LDCs including Hong Kong,

Taiwan and Singapore, and not for the 40 LDCs used in our sample. Secondly, the exports of manufactures of the LDCs include some exports to other LDCs, while the demand elasticities refer to only imports of the developed world. In order to adjust these elasticities so as to avoid overstating export demand, the export growth for the 40 LDCs, was calculated for the 1965–72 period (12.2 percent per annum) and compared with the OECD import demand growth from all LDCs for the same period (15.7 percent per annum) both in constant prices. The ratio of the two growth rates (0.777) was used to adjust the original elasticities downward.

An estimate of the supply of manufactured exports from the LDCs is used to arrive at the market shares of the exporting regions. These estimates are based on historical growth rates in constant prices for the period 1965–72. For two regions, South Asia and East Africa, political events in the 1970–72 period cause the growth rates of manufactured exports to be very low, so the growth rate for the period 1965–70 is used in its place.

3.3. Service Exports

Exports of services are another very important part of export earnings in LDCs, but often ignored in trade models due to the lack of data on an origin-destination basis. Data for non-factor service exports was obtained from the World Bank's Socio-Economic Data Bank, in current prices for each region for the period 1964–72. It was assumed, once again, that the OECD is the principal source of demand for these services, which includes tourism, travel and shipping services. The results are shown in table 3.[6]

The estimated equations all show good fits with respect to their demand vectors, and all of the income elasticities are significant at the 95 percent confidence level or higher. It is interesting to note the wide differences in elasticities, from 0.45 for South Asia to 1.9 for West Africa. Areas with a highly developed tourism sector seem to have higher elasticities than those without, and this is probably the major factor explaining these regional differences. The 1.9 elasticity for West Africa appears to be unusually high and was probably influenced by the very rapid development of tourism in this region during the past few years. Consequently, this coefficient was lowered to 1.4 for projection purposes in the model.

3.4. Prices and Inflation

An exogenous estimate of the rate of world inflation is given[7] to the model in terms of a general index of international prices.

Table 3

Exports of services.

LDC group	Service exports to total exports	GNP	E	t	R^2
Mineral producers	18.2	W. Europe	1.006	16.09	0.974
South Asia	7.2	Total OECD	0.448	8.54	0.947
East/Central Africa	26.9	Total OECD	1.311	8.55	0.911
Mediterranean	35.9	W. Europe	1.244	15.10	0.970
West Africa	27.2	Total OECD	1.920	15.45	0.971
East Asia	17.8	Japan and N. America	0.959	4.59	0.742
Latin America	23.6	Japan and N. America	1.288	28.89	0.992

This index is used as a current price index for the exports and imports of manufactures and services. The constant price estimates of the commodity models are converted to current price indices using the same general index. By using 1972 weights for exports by commodity type and imports by end-use, a weighted import and export price index is calculated for each of the seven regions. It should be noted that the primary commodity prices enter into both the export and import price indices, since LDC imports include basic foods and intermediate products.

3.5. Regional Growth Models

At this point SIMLINK has produced for each of its seven regional groups a weighted price index for both exports and imports, and a volume index for exports. Capital inflows are given to the model based on exogenous estimates from country analysis of creditworthiness and capital availabilities. The term 'capital' used here is defined as the net transfer of resources from foreign savings, or the so-called 'gap' between imports and exports of goods and non-factor services. This equals, by definition, the gap between investment and domestic savings.

The indices for prices and volumes are used to project export prices, import prices and exports in constant 1967-69 U.S. dollars for each of the regions. The constant dollar exports are adjusted for changes in the terms of trade to produce 'exports-adjusted'. This is necessary so that they reflect true import purchasing power. The adjusted exports (XADJ) for each region are defined as

$$XADJ = (XPI/MPI)X, \tag{7}$$

(all variables are for period t and region i) where X represents exports in constant prices, and MPI and XPI are the relevant regional import and export price indices, respectively. Total import supply or capacity (M_s) is then defined as the sum of XADJ and the available capital inflow or resource gap (RG_a),

$$M_s = XADJ + RG_a. \tag{8}$$

Much discussion has taken place concerning the relationship between imports and growth, and the role of foreign exchange versus other constraints in the developing world.[8] Some authors have contended that there is no relationship, or that increases in imports (particularly those derived from increases in capital inflows) result in lower savings, higher consumption and no appreciable increase in growth [Griffin and Enos (1970)]. Such analyses have tended to examine imports in the aggregate, and their relationship to total GNP. In fact, LDC imports are a very non-homogenous mixture of capital goods, intermediate products and raw materials necessary for the production process, and foodstuffs and other consumer goods that are not related to capital formation and production. The imports of foodstuffs are often inversely correlated with growth, since they often supplement declines in domestic agricultural production. In most of the better country models, imports are disaggregated in some fashion, usually by end-use classes, and related either to sector outputs or some part of GNP expenditure. Following the same approach, a general model of growth and imports was formulated along the following lines. First, industrial production is assumed to be a linear function of total GNP,[9]

$$YIND = a_1 + b_1 GDP \qquad \text{[value added, industry].} \quad (9)$$

Investment is a function of the increment to GDP and lagged investment, on the style of the flexible accelerator where the desired capital stock adjusts with a distributed lag. In this case the implied lag is of the Koyck type, or one having geometrically declining weights,

$$I = a_1 + b_{21}(GDP - GDP_{t-1}) + b_{22}I_{t-1} \qquad \text{[gross investment].} \quad (10)$$

Imports of capital goods are then related linearly to investment, intermediate goods to value added in industry, and imports of fuels and non-factor services to total GDP, or

$$MCAP = a_3 + b_3 I \qquad \text{[imports, capital goods],} \quad (11)$$

$$MINT = a_4 + b_4 YIND \qquad \text{[imports, intermediate products],} \quad (12)$$

$$MFUEL = a_5 + b_5 GDP \qquad \text{[imports, fuels],} \quad (13)$$

$$MSER = a_6 + b_6 GDP \qquad \text{[imports, non-factor services].} \quad (14)$$

Initially, it was proposed that imports of food should be related to private consumption and to agricultural production, and imports of other consumer goods to private consumption expenditures. In almost all cases, however, the results tended to be statistically non-significant or have the 'wrong' signs, since in the case of food it should be expected that food imports vary inversely with food production, but directly with consumption. It appears that both of these import categories are heavily influenced by the level of foreign exchange available for imports. The proxy for foreign exchange availabilities was taken to the actual level of imports of goods, so that the combination of imports of food plus consumer goods was simply related to this variable,[10]

$$MCF = a_7 + b_7 MG. \qquad (15)$$

Total imports of goods are defined as

$$MG = MCAP + MINT + MFUEL + MCF, \qquad (16)$$

and total imports as

$$M_d = MG + MSER, \qquad (17)$$

where the d subscript indicates an estimate of import demand, as opposed to the initial import supply, M.

In the availabilities version of the model an equilibrium condition is enforced such that import demand must equal import supply, or

$$M_d + M_s. \tag{18}$$

The model then solves for that level of GDP that satisfies this equilibrium condition. The predetermined capital flow availability then determines an endogenous level of GDP and GDP growth on an annual basis.

In the requirements version, target growth rates (g) of GDP are specified for each region, or

$$GDP_t = GDP_{t-1}(1 + g). \tag{19}$$

The level of capital inflow necessary or required for this level of GDP is determined as the difference between import demand and import supply,

$$RG_r = M_d - XADJ. \tag{20}$$

Hence the requirements model drops eqs. (8) and (18) from the model and uses (19) and (20) to determine an endogenous capital flow from a predetermined growth level. The additional capital requirements are defined as the difference between the capital available (RG_a) and that required to attain the growth targets (RG_r).

Domestic saving (GDS) can be determined residually from the identity

$$GDS = I - RG. \tag{21}$$

This residual determination of savings is the necessary consequence of the structure of the model which considers foreign exchange, rather than savings, capital or labor, as the binding constraint limiting growth in the developing world. While this is a serious simplification, since the model is being used to project over a period when deteriorating terms of trade and low export volume growth will squeeze foreign exchange earnings, it is considered to be acceptable.

The ex-post calculation of the savings rate allows for the qualitative judgement that such rates are realistic, and that a savings constraint is not binding.

In general, these equations were estimated on the basis of pooled cross-section times series data for the period 1966 to 1971, although the exact time period differs slightly from region to region. The shortness of the time period used is a product of the shortage of data on imports by end-use. The data used here is derived from the United Nations Trade Year-book data, allocated to end-use classes on a two-digit SITC level. The data for individual countries in each region was pooled together for estimates of the region, using the technique of including an individual constant term of each country. This increases the degrees of freedom and offsets the shortness of the observation period. While the R^2 of the estimated equations are low, almost all of the estimated coefficients are significant at the 95 percent level. The low R^2 can be attributed in part to the fact that cross-sectional data is being used. Much higher correlation coefficients are found in the regressions for imports of services, since these are based on straight time series data.[11]

IV. PROJECTION RESULTS

Results for the base case are shown in table 4, in terms of growth rates, 1974-80. The projections for the base case assume:

(1)   OECD growth of about 4.1 percent per annum, 1974-80,[12]
(2)   petroleum price level in constant prices at $9.40 (1974$),
(3)   net capital flows averaging $25 billion per year for the 40 sample countries.

The overall growth rates of export prices is projected at 6.1 percent per annum, somewhat less than the 7.1 percent projected for import prices. This general deterioration of the terms of trade reflects a movement from the historically very high commodity prices of 1974, which has a greater impact on LDC exports than on imports. This deterioration is relatively greater for those regions having a higher percentage of their exports in primary commodities. The overall growth of export volume is projected at 7.1 percent per annum, but this is somewhat unevenly divided between the low-income countries at 5.0 percent and the middle/high-income countries with 7.4 percent. The fall in the terms of trade, combined with a trend for capital flows to grow less rapidly than imports, causes the import growth rate to be substantially lower than the export-volume growth (4.4 versus 7.1). The overall rate of GDP growth consistent with the projected import growth is 4.4 percent for all LDCs, but this is broken down into 2.5 percent for the low-income countries and 4.9 percent for the middle/high. This represents growth substantially below the United Nation Development Decade II (DD-II) targets of 6 percent for the developing world.

In the 'requirements' version of the model, the imports and capital flows necessary to sustain 5 percent growth in the low-income countries and about 6 percent for all LDCs for the 1974-80 period is examined. This implies a growth rate of only about 5.8 percent for the entire decade 1970-80, again somewhat short of the DD-II targets. The gap in terms of the additional capital required for this target growth rate represents an average inflow of $13.0 billion per year, of which $2.0 billion per year would be for the low income countries.[13] It is possible that the total could be higher or lower depending on the basic assumptions used in the model.

Table 4
Base-case projections in terms of growth rates, 1974–80.

	GDP	Imports	Exports adjusted	Export volume	Export prices	Import prices
Low income	2.5	2.9	4.5	5.0	6.3	6.7
South Asia[a]	2.5	3.0	4.7	4.9	6.3	6.5
East Africa[b]	2.4	2.2	4.2	5.6	5.8	7.2
Middle/high income	4.9	4.6	6.4	7.4	6.1	7.2
Mineral producers[c]	4.5	4.2	4.4	4.6	7.0	7.2
Mediterranean[d]	5.4	6.3	7.9	7.2	7.8	7.1
West Africa[e]	4.2	3.9	3.4	5.0	5.4	7.0
East Asia[f]	5.3	5.0	6.2	9.0	4.3	7.1
Latin America[g]	4.8	3.3	6.4	7.6	6.3	7.5
Total	4.4	4.4	6.2	7.1	6.1	7.1

[a]India, Pakistan, Bangladesh, Sri Lanka.
[b]Kenya, Tanzania, Uganda, Ethiopia, Mali, Sudan.
[c]Chile, Bolivia, Jamaica, Liberia, Morocco, Zaire, Zambia.
[d]Egypt, Syria, Tunisia, Greece, Turkey, Yugoslavia.
[e]Cameroon, Ghana, Ivory Coast, Senegal, Sierra Leone.
[f]Korea, Philippines, Thailand, Malaysia.
[g]Argentina, Brazil, Colombia, Dominican Republic, Guatemala, Mexico, Peru, Uruguay.

In table 5 simulations of the model are summarized which use higher and lower OECD growth rates, a lower price of oil and higher LDC exports. In the high OECD growth case the LDCs improve their performance from the 4.4 percent projected in the base case to 5.0 percent while in the low case the growth rate drops to 3.8 percent. Since the corresponding growth rates for the OECD in the high and low cases are 4.7 and 3.5 percent, the implied elasticity between the two growth rates is about 0.9[14] The reduction in growth appears to fall heavily on the low-income countries; their growth rates decline proportionally more between the high and low OECD cases. Since population growth in the low-income countries is about 2.4 percent per annum, the low OECD growth case implies negative per-capita income growth for these countries.

Another possible way in which our base projections may change is in the estimate of the oil price. In case D, a simulation of the model with $7.00 oil is shown.[15] This low oil price results in an increased growth rate over the base case since it increases the purchasing power of export earnings. Lower OPEC demand for LDC exports, however, has a slight offsetting effect, as do the lower earnings of those LDCs in our sample who export small amounts of petroleum. The net result, however, is an increase in the growth of all LDCs, from 4.4 percent in the base case to 4.8 percent but with the major impact falling on the low-income countries. Their growth rates increase from 2.5 go 3.2 percent as opposed to the middle/high-income group which only increase from 4.9 to 5.3 percent. This implies that a $1.00 change in the 1980 real price of oil would raise LDC growth by about 0.17 percentage points. Even if oil prices were to drop to $3.00 or below, the effect would be insufficient to restore 6 percent growth to the LDCs by itself. A simulation of the model with the price of oil dropping immediately to $3.00 in 1976, as opposed to a gradual decline to that level in 1980, produces only a 5.2 percent growth rate for the LDCs. The complete impact of such a decline is difficult to estimate with SIMLINK since the impact of this price decline on the OECD countries is not clear. In addition, the probability of such a price decline occurring is considered highly unlikely, unless it took the form of a price discount or rebate scheme applicable only to the LDCs.

The developing world could be substantially assisted by schemes which would result in a more rapid growth of their exports. As shown in table 5, SIMLINK has been run with two modifications along these lines: an assumption of higher manufactured exports to the OECD and an assumption of greater LDC exports to the OPEC countries.

The higher manufactured exports run (case E) assumes a 17 percent growth rate of manufactured exports versus the 13 percent used in the base case. This would be feasible provided the LDCs would select policies designed to promote exports and the OECD countries would make tariff and other concessions to LDC trade. The effect is to raise the export volume growth from 7.2 percent to 8.2 percent for all LDCs during the 1974-80 period, and the growth rate of GDP from 4.4 to 4.9 percent. The effect, however, is distributed rather unevenly, with the middle/high group receiving most of the benefits since they are already the predominant

exporters of manufactures and have the greatest potential for
expansion. Their growth of exports rises from 7.4 to 8.6 percent,
and their GDP from 4.9 to 5.5 percent, while the low-income group
shows a rise from 5.0 to only 5.3 percent for export volume, and
2.5 to 2.8 percent for GDP.

Another possible way for the developing world to expand its
exports is through expanded trade with the OPEC countries. While
the LDCs are assumed in the base case to have a fixed (5.9 percent)
share of incremental OPEC import demand (excluding military goods),
case F assumes that this will rise to 8.5 percent by 1980. The
result is a substantial increase in export and GDP growth rates for
both LDC income groups. The average growth rate for all LDCs rises
from 4.4 percent in the base case to 4.7 percent in this case.
This is almost as beneficial as the lower oil-price simulation, but
has a greater impact on the low-income countries. The growth rate
of this group rises to 3.3 percent, compared with 2.5 percent in
the base case and 3.2 percent in the low oil-price case. Because
of the proximity of the major OPEC countries to the low-income
areas of South Asia and Africa, increases in OPEC trade have more
impact in these areas than on the middle/high-income areas.

The impact of alternative assumptions on the need for
additional capital to attain the DD-II target, as shown in table
6, tend to reflect a mirror image of the impact on growth rates
shown in table 5.[16] A movement which permits a higher growth rate
naturally reduces the amount of capital necessary to raise that
growth to the 6 percent target. The total required in the base
case is $13 billion per year, an amount in excess of what could be
reasonably expected to come from either official or private
sources. This number is somewhat deceptive, since it involves
$2.0 billion for the low-income countries. Since the
middle/high-income countries achieve a 4.9 percent growth rate in
the base case, the $2 billion annual requirement of the low-income
countries is a more urgent requirement than the $11 billion
requirement of the middle/high group.

The higher OECD growth rate saves the LDCs about $4 billion
per year, and the lower OECD growth rate increases the capital
requirement by about the same amount. The implied trade-off
between capital and OECD growth works out to about a savings of
$6.7 billion in capital requirements for every increase of one
percentage point in the OECD growth rate. The lower oil price
($7.00 in 1980) saves about $3 billion per year, including $500
million annually in the low-income countries. The trade-off here
indicates that a $1.00 drop in the real 1980 price of petroleum
would save about $1.3 billion annually for all LDCs. A one
percentage point increase in the growth rate of manufactures
exports appears to save the LDCs about $750 million annually,
mostly in the middle/high-income group.

Sensitivity tests undertaken with SIMLINK indicate that these
trade-off effects are roughly linear when the variations are not
extreme, and the combined effects are additive. Consequently, the
combined effects of different 'packages' of policy measures can be
deduced by adding together the incremental effects of each
individual policy measure. For instance, the combined effect of
higher manufactured goods exports, high OECD growth and low oil

Table 5
Alternative growth rates of GDP, 1974–80.

Case[a]		Low income	Middle/high income	Total
(A)	Base case	2.5	4.9	4.4
(B)	High OECD growth	3.0	5.5	5.0
(C)	Low OECD growth	2.0	4.4	3.8
(D)	Low oil price	3.2	5.3	4.8
(E)	High manufactured exports	2.8	5.5	4.9
(F)	High OPEC imports	3.3	5.1	4.7

[a]*Base case* (A): OECD growth 4.1 percent, oil price $9.40 (in 1974$), LDC manufactured exports grow at 13 percent per year, LDCs' share of OPEC imports = 5.9 percent. *Sensitivity cases*: Identical to case A except with (B) 4.7 percent OECD growth, (D) oil price dropping to $7.00 by 1980, (E) manufactured exports growing 17 percent per year, (F) OPEC import share rising to 8.5 percent by 1980.

Table 6
Annual average of additional capital requirements, 1975–80 (millions current $).[a]

Case		Low income	Middle/high income	Total
(A)	Base case	2.0	11.0	13.0
(B)	High OECD growth	1.6	7.4	9.0
(C)	Low OECD growth	2.4	14.3	16.7
(D)	Low oil price	1.5	8.4	9.9
(E)	High manufactured exports	1.9	8.1	10.0
(F)	High OPEC imports	1.5	10.0	11.5

[a]Capital requirements shown here are additional to what is presently thought available and based on 40 sample LDCs.

Table 7
Sensitivity of policy instruments and the increase required to raise LDC growth rates by one percentage point.

Policy instrument	Measured in	Amount of change
GNP growth in OECD countries	Average growth rate 1974–80	+1.10
Capital flows to LDCs	Current $ billions/year	+6.7
Price of petroleum	Real 1980 price in 1974 $	−6.00
LDC exports of manufactures	Annual average growth rate	+8.0
LDC share of OPEC imports	Percentage of total OPEC imports in 1980	+8.7

prices would have the cumulative effect of lowering capital requirements by \$10.1 billion (4.0 + 3.1 + 3.0).

There are, of course, multiple combinations of policy changes that could produce the same results, and the variations shown here are merely illustrative. Consequently, the sensitivity of the model to changes in OECD growth rates, capital flows and exports has been recast in terms of the amount necessary to raise the overall growth rate of the LDCs by one percentage point. This is summarized in table 7.

An increase of one percentage point in the LDC overall growth rate can be had by either increasing the OECD growth rate by one percentage point, raising capital flows by \$6.7 billion per year, reducing the price of petroleum by \$6.00 in 1980, increasing the LDC export of manufactures growth rate by 8.0 percentage points, or increasing the LDC share of OPEC imports by 8.7 percentage points. (Capital flows are expressed in current dollars, oil prices in 1974 dollars.) Though these magnitudes are somewhat inexact since they do not consider the distribution of the effects between low- and middle/high-income groups, they nevertheless indicate the scope of trade-offs in policy instruments.

V. CONCLUSIONS

The alternative simulations of the SIMLINK model illustrate the usefulness of the model in analyzing the prospects of the developing world and the impact of alternative policies of the OECD and OPEC countries. The sensitivity illustrations of the model are probably more useful than the actual absolute numbers projected, since the latter are undoubtedly subject to a certain range of error.

One main conclusion of the model appears to be that the slackening of growth in the OECD countries has proven to be more detrimental to the LDCs than the direct effects of the higher price of petroleum. Whether the indirect effects of the higher price of petroleum have caused the lower growth rates in the OECD is, of course, outside the scope of this model. As a consequence, the LDCs are faced with the prospect of growth rates during the 1970s substantially below the level achieved in the previous decade, and below the targets suggested by the United Nations Development Decade II. The deterioration of the situation in the low-income countries is particularly critical, since the prospect for these countries is for little or no increase in per-capita output during the rest of the decade. Policies aimed at expanding LDC exports must be carefully chosen, since they are apt to benefit mostly the middle/high-income group, which has a less severe problem and has greater access to private capital markets. The low-income countries, in addition to having a more severe problem, have far fewer options, and are more dependent on positive policies in the OECD and OPEC countries for relief.

NOTES

[1] A fuller discussion of the model is available in World Bank Staff Working Paper by Hicks (1975).

[2] See IBRD Report no. EC-166/74: "Commodity trade and price trends", August 1974.

[3] For a discussion on the use of the lagged endogenous variable as a transform of the distributed lag equation, see Griliches (1967, p. 16).

[4] For a more detailed description of the actual commodity models, see Hicks (1975).

[5] Manufactures exports are here defined as SITC 5-8 less SITC 68.

[6] Unlike the manufactured export regressions, the non-factor service regressions are done in current prices. In the model, the projected current price service exports are deflated by the implicit GNP deflator of the OECD countries to convert to constant prices.

[7] Basically the International Price Index (IPI) constructed by the staff of the World Bank.

[8] Chenery and Strout (1966), Fei and Ranis (1968), Bruton (1969).

[9] All $\underline{a}$'s are constant terms, and all $\underline{b}$'s are estimated coefficients.

[10] In South Asia and East Africa exogenous estimates of MCF are used, based on a projected increase in foodgrain imports and constant imports of other foods and consumer goods. In the base case, a growth rate of 3.5 percent is used for foodgrain imports in both regions.

[11] Details of the estimated regressions are available from the author.

[12] The projected OECD growth rates used in SIMLINK are derived from Celasun and Pinto (1975).

[13] All capital flow data is expressed in current dollars on an annual average basis for the period 1975-80. The term 'capital' used here means the net transfer of foreign resources or resource cap.

[14] The absolute reduction is on the order of about one to one, but the higher initial growth rate in the LDCs causes the elasticity to be less than one. This result is also sensitive to the distribution of growth among OECD regions.

[15] This assumes a gradual decline to $7.00 (1974 $) by 1980. The effect would be different if the price were to drop immediately to $7.00 in 1976.

[16]The capital requirements described here are additional to what is presently felt to be available, and is based on a sample of the 40 major LDCs. Conversion of these numbers to totals for the entire developing world can be approximated by multiplying by a factor of 1.4

REFERENCES

Ball, R. J., ed., 1974, The international linkage of national economic models (North-Holland, Amsterdam).

Bruton, H. J., 1969, The two-gap approach to aid and development: Comment, American Economic Review 59, 439-446.

Celasun, M. and F. Pinto, 1975, Energey prospects in OECD countries and the possible demand for OPEC oil exports to 1980; The CAP energy models, World Bank Staff Working Paper no. 219 (World Bank, Washington, D.C.).

Chenery, H. B. and A. M. Strout, 1966, Foreign assistance and economie development, American Economic Review 56, 680-733.

Fei, J .C. H. and G. Ranis, 1968, Foreign assistance and economic development: Comment, American Economic Review 58, 897-912.

Griffin, K. G. and J. L. Enos, 1970, Foreign assistance: Objectives and consequences, Economic Development and Cultural Change 18, 313-327.

Griliches, Z., 1967, Distributed lags: A survey, Econometrica 35, 16-49.

Hicks, N. L., 1975, The SIMLINK model of trade and growth for the developing world, World Bank Staff Working Paper no. 220 (World Bank, Washington, D.C.).

Aid or Trade? A Welfare-Theoretic Analysis

DILIP K. GHOSH

In the wake of Prebisch thoughts[1] and later in response to formal UNCTAD recommendations, several ideas have spun off in the exploratory field of policy research directed toward better national and international goals of countries involved in economic welfare maximization. Traditionally, super-economic powers, particularly the United States, have made all-out efforts to (re)construct and develop countries lagging behind in economic growth, and almost without exceptions, aid with different attached strings has been the way to do so. In mid-fifties the United States was quite seriously engaged in what is called 'project-aid' -- which, at best, made piece-meal efforts to turn around in some measure the backwardness of recipient countries. Fifties are over, and so are the objectives of aid programs of that decade. The <u>Kennedy Administration</u> and its fresh look at economic inequalities, lack of developmental opportunities, lopsided or, rather, rickety growth of LDC's, and so on introduced 'program aid' -- (which was, of course, not without pre-set conditions either) -- aiming at a more concerted and harmonious growth of the world economy as a whole. But the <u>United Nations Conference on Trade and Development</u> and the rather recent <u>Declaration of New International Economic Order</u> propose alternatives to aid, -- and these alternatives basically endorse a generalized system of trade preferences. In this paper, therefore, we would like to study the implications of aid -- tying as well as untying -- and then examine the institution of trade through preferences as an <u>equivalent</u> alternative or substitute for aid. Several interesting and useful works have already been done in this area,[2] and so it would be worthwhile to synthesize and unify some of these findings and then extend and generalize it along those lines. In the first section we, therefore, propose to analyze the impact of aid on welfare through some simplistic frameworks, and then compare the costs of conditions usually attached to terms under which aid is used. Some empirical measurement of this cost is also given. In the second section we propose to examine the possibility of an institution of trade through preference as an equivalent alternative to aid and

study the welfare implications thereof through redistribution of
world income. Finally, some general remarks are made as to what
different nations should do in an effort to raise economic welfare
of individual countries and of the world as a whole in this age of
new international economic order.

I. AID & WELFARE

The term 'aid' is intriguing -- and quite misleading, too.
Its connotation in the economic literature -- in theory and in
practice -- ranges from 'give-away' to 'loan' under various
stipulated terms and conditions. If it means just an unconditional
grant, it really is an unilateral transfer of money, goods and/or
real resources from a donor to a recipient country, and in the
framework of international exchange it means then that the
recipient country obviously gains by such a transfer.[3] But aid in
most actual cases has been economic assistance in the form of grant
with specific strings and terms or just long-term[4] loans of various
kinds. United States' aid has been largely tying -- perhaps
because of internal politics or for the motive of increasing
controls over the rate and direction of resource mobilization in
the recipient countries or for indirect expansion of U.S. exports
and so on. Sometimes, it can be observed, it is in the explicit
terms of an aid package that the recipient country is under
obligation to spend at least so much dollars on goods of the donor
country or buy some specific goods from the aid-giving country at
least in the volume of some negotiated level even though those
goods are not the least expensive. First kind of constraint
imposes what can be aptly called 'source-tying distortion' and the
second kind of constraint imposes 'commodity-tying distortion'.
Let us now examine if these varieties of tying aid -- these two
types of distortions -- impose any real cost on the recipient, and
if they do, let us then determine what those costs are. Cost in
this context means the portion of aid which can be reduced along
with elimination of tying strings to leave the beneficiary's
welfare level unchanged. Figure 1 illustrates the effects of aid
with and without ties.

In this diagram horizontal and vertical axes measure,
respectively, units of donor-country and non-donor-country goods,
X_d and X_n. AB measure pre-aid budget line and E denotes pre-aid
equilibrium purchase vector of the recipient country, whose welfare
is defined by $W°$.

Aid in the amount of AD (in terms of X_d - goods) moves the
budget line to FH. Without any constriction whatsoever, the
recipient country's welfare level unambiguously rises because of
aid. But if the recipient becomes bound by the terms of aid to buy
at least AC amount of <u>additional</u> X_d - good, then it would be forced
to choose a point in the post-aid situation in the range of MH, and
it full 'additionality' is required, then recipient country's
post-aid choice range further gets squeezed (NH), and in this case

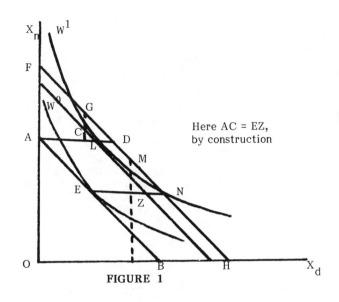

Here AC = EZ,
by construction

FIGURE 1

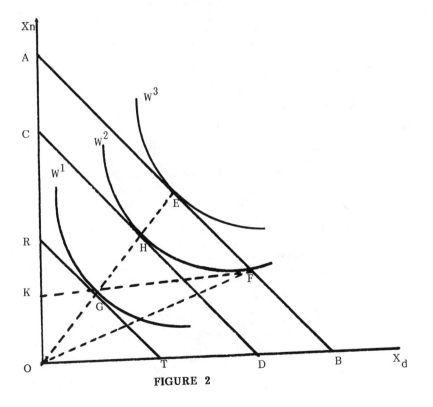

FIGURE 2

the aid-receiving country is forced into a situation of designating non-donor-country goods as non-superior. If the recipient country has to choose the purchase vector N because of full additionality constraint, its welfare index becomes W^1 ($< W^o$, of course), which can be attained with AL amount of foreign aid without the tying constraint. Thus, note that the cost of tying aid is LD. Several other varieties of tying aid, e.g., only at least a predefined fraction or the full (but not additional) amount of foreign aid, can be dealt with in this framework and many interesting conclusions can be derived.

In a slightly modified scenario we can visualize the case where the donor country goods are more expensive than those or quite effective substitutes of those elsewhere, but the recipient country has to, as qualifying condition for aid, purchase those relatively costlier goods from the donor-country. In this case obviously another round of additional cost would arise. The magnitude of such a cost (v) can be measured as follows:[5]

$$ \nu = \Sigma_j \; \theta_j \, t_j \, / \, (1 + t_j) \qquad\qquad (1) $$

where t_j is the ad valorem wedge between the prices of the j-th commodity in the donor-country and the least expensive non-donor-country, and θ_j is the expenditure share of aid on the j-th commodity from the donor country. By use of (1) the estimate of cost of U.S. aid to India is 21.7% by adjusting bias due to the exclusion of certain variables in single equation regression representation.[6]

Now, let us examine source-tying distortion. Figure 2 illustrates this situation and the resulting cost in such case of distortion under the reasonable assumption of homohypallagic welfare functions such as:

(i) $W = \{ a_j \, x_{dj}^{-b_j} + (1-a_j) \, x_{nj}^{-b_j} \}^{-1/b_j}$ for all j,

(ii) $W = A x_{dj}^{\alpha_j} \, x_{nj}^{1-\alpha_j}$ for all j,

which yield Grahamesque homothetic demand structure.

In this diagram horizontal and vertical axes represent effectively the same goods, supplied by the donor and non-donor-countries, respectively. The aid-fed budget line is AB, and without any condition attached to aid, let the optimal purchase vector be denoted by the point E. Now, because of aid-imposed restriction, if (X_d / X_n) has to increase, the recipient country has to move along EB range of the budget line. Under the normal assumption that with respect to the commodity from the non-donor-country the aid-receiving nation faces no constraint on choice, the country concerned ends up at the constrained optional bundle of goods denoted by F, which is just as good as the market H. The cost imposed by the source-tying distortion in this illustrative case is then HE/GE.

A few remarks should be made at this point. On more

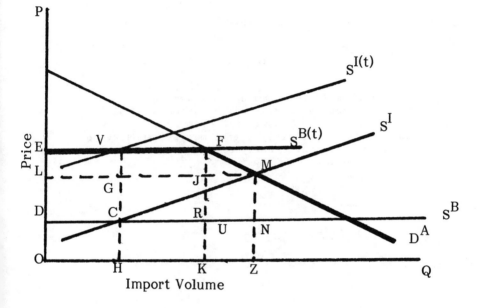

Import Volume

FIGURE 3

reflection one feels that a country is more likely to operate with the maximand welfare functions of the following sorts:

$$\text{(ii)} \quad W = \{\ a_j(x_{dj} - \bar{x}_{dj})^{-b_j} + (1-a_j)(x_{nj} - \bar{x}_{nj})^{-b_j}\ \}^{-1/b_j},$$

$$x_{ij} - \bar{x}_{ij} > 0 \quad \text{for } i = d, n,$$

$$\text{(iii)} \quad W = A\ (x_{dj} - \bar{x}_{dj})^{a_j} (x_{nj} - \bar{x}_{nj})^{1-a_j},$$

$$x_{ij} - \bar{x}_{ij} > 0 \quad \text{for } i = d, n,$$

and most likely to operate with this welfare function:

$$\text{(i)} \quad W = \{\ \Sigma_{h=1}^{H}\ \delta_h\ [\ \Sigma_{j \in h}^{nh}\ B_{hj}\ (x_{hj} - \bar{x}_{hj})^{\rho_h}\ ]^{\rho/\rho_h}\ \}^{1/\rho}$$

These welfare functions[7] are marginally homothetic, and the assumption of these sorts of welfare function increases the welfare loss due to source-tying distortion through minimal 'committed' consumption levels of j-th commodity.

Now, moving explicitly in the multi-commodity world the problem for a recipient country can be set up in the format of a maximization framework as follows:

$$\max\ W = W\ (x_{dj}, x_{nj}), \quad 1 \leq j \leq n$$

sub. to:

$$\text{(α)} \quad \Sigma_j\ (P_{dj}x_{dj} + P_{nj}x_{nj}) \leq F^D + F^A$$

$$\text{(β)} \quad \Sigma_j\ P_{dj}x_{dj} \leq F^A$$

$$\text{(γ)} \quad \Sigma_s\ P_{ds}x_{ds} \leq k \cdot F^A, \quad 0 \leq k \leq 1, \quad s \in \{1,2,\ldots,n\}$$

where F^D and F^A measure, respectively, the amounts of foreign exchange domestically owned and obtained through aid. In the face of any combination of these constraints and/or similar other such constraints or just constraint ( ), the recipient country optimally determines its decision point, and each additional constraint normally[8] imposes some additional excess burden. The United States Department of Commerce as a donor also recognizes this fact of excess cost and it clearly admits:[9]

> of more than $5,000 million in gross grants and credits extended by the United States Government in 1958 all but $300 million "consisted of equivalent transfer from the United States".

Conditional aid thus imposes excess costs on recipients; but does it necessarily help donors? The statistical evidences[10] show that the portion of U.S. aid such as AID contributions to international organizations and assistance to LDC's which have not been rerouted to the United States for direct purchases of U.S. goods and the like have not been irrevocably lost and thus have not increased

deficit in the U.S. balance of payments. To understand this point
we should now relax the hitherto implicitly assumed notion that aid
is used for the purchase of final goods and services. In reality
most of the LDC's receive aid in the form of real resources and
capital equipments and/or for purchase of such items of
intermediate inputs which are used to produce final outputs of
various kinds. That means aid affects technology structure, moves
domestic availability frontier and possibly terms of trade of the
receiving countries, -- thus opening up new vistas and broadening
new contours or horizons of such nations. Reasoning in the
Swedish-Samuelson framework one should compute the Rybczynskin
magnification effects of factor increases induced by foreign
assistance, and it is quite conceivable that apparent drain of
donor's income finds its way back in.

II. TRADE: A SUBSTITUTE FOR AID

In the preceding section we have studied welfare implications
of aid and noted that a dollars worth of aid becomes less than a
dollar to the recipient. Furthermore, it is also observed that an
aid-giving country does not gain as much as it wishes. These facts
coupled with opinions of world organizations and talks and
negotiations by several countries at bilateral and multilateral
levels cry out for institution of trade as a substitute for aid.
Trade through a generalized system of preferences as an effective
expression of international cooperation has been and is being aired
through Multinational Trade Negotiations, the United Nations
Conference on Trade and Development, North-South dialogues, and so
on. The demands of developing countries for differential and
preferential treatment have been quite comprehensively presented in
the Manila Declaration and Programme of Action of the Group of 77.
These preferential treatments relate to a wide spectrum of vital
issues covering concessions interms, structure and conditions for
trade relations with developed countries. The Kennedy Round of
Trade Negotiations (1963-67) have modified the principles of
reciprocity codified in the GATT recognizing 'non-reciprocity' for
LDC's, and later in 1971 we further find, because of such
developments, that the GATT waives the "General Most-Favored-Nation
Treatment" obligation for developed countries for a period of ten
years to the extent needed to grant preferential treatment under
the Generalized System of Preferences as introduced in 1970. The
further series of negotiations relating to trade beginning in 1973
in the Tokyo Round of Multilateral Trade Negotiations corroborate
the merit and necessity of non-reciprocity.

Let us now examine the preferential treatment in theoretical
terms. Within the framework of a general equilibrium analysis, it
has been established[11] that elimination of extreme tariffs is
welfare-augmenting to the tariff-changing country, and Bruno's[12]
gradual reform policy reaffirms the virtues of preferential
treatment of trade. In a multi-commodity two-country trade

structure Ghosh concludes:

> In an economy of gross substitutes optimum tariff rates
> lie within the range of the extreme values of the
> preexisting tariffs. If the preexisting tariff rates are
> all equal, then optimal tariff rates would be the same,
> too. If some of the preexisting tariffs are negative
> while some others are positive, then some sector(s) might
> be optimally tariff-free.

> Elimination of extreme tariff is welfare-augmenting if
> goods are gross substitutes. If goods indexed 1 through
> k are complementary to the n-th good and other goods are
> substitutes for the n-th good, an increase (decrease) in
> the tariff on the n-th sector (t_n) results in an increase
> (decrease) in social welfare if $t_j < t_i$ (j = 1, 2, ...k,
> i not equal to j, n)

One should note the parallel results of Baldwin[13] and Kenen[14]
which can best be summarized as follows:

> In the world of only two countries dealing with only two
> commodities if neither has a tariff, neither should
> impose one; as always, global free trade maximizes world
> welfare. If both countries have tariffs and one will not
> budge, the other can contribute to world welfare by
> cutting its own -- even moving to free trade -- but would
> do better to replace its import tariff by an export
> subsidy equal in size to the first country's tariff. It
> would thereby nullify the first country's tariff,
> installing an efficient substitute for world-wide free
> trade. But in a world of many countries (more than two)
> when tariff rates of some countries are semi-positive and
> those of other countries are semi-negative, one country
> might conceivably trade in tariff-free condition. But
> when tariff rates of all other countries are
> semi-positive, the i-th country cannot maximize world
> welfare by the policy of unilateral free trade -- it must
> impose some import tariff or an export subsidy that must
> be in between the extreme tariff rates of other
> countries.

A close look at these results and the findings on creation of
customs unions, economic integration and trade liberalization point
essentially to the fact that preferential trade structure through
tariff cuts yield the benefits accruing from aid plus something
more. To pursue this point further let us consider the world in a
miniature form consisting of, say, America (A), India (I), and
Britain (B). Assume an initial condition in which America imports
a commodity Q from both India and Britain with nondiscriminatory
tariff barrier. Now if America grants preference to India by a
tariff cut while maintaining the same initial tariff on British
import, India's export earnings normally increases, and in this
case easily one can view the difference between increase in India's

export revenues and its additional costs for increased exports as foreign aid by America to India. It would be worthwhile to examine as to what can be accomplished by this sort of aid through trade. In Figure 3[15] we visualize the effect of preferential tariff cuts -- outcome of aid through trade -- upon economic welfare.

In this diagram D^A, S^I, and S^B curves represent respectively net import demand for Q-goods by America, tariff-free supply of the same goods by India and Britain. $S^{I(t)}$ and $S^{B(t)}$ curves define the supply conditions of the American importable at tariff-ridden prices. If the price is jacked up at OE level for the British goods by the American tariff distortion, India faces the American net import demand denoted by the kinky curve, $EFMD^A$. With existing tariff on its goods India supplies OH units, but if tariff wall is completely demolished for India, India's supply of the American import rises to OZ units. So, aid to India is equal to the area, LMDC,[16] since this area measures increased export revenues accruing to India minus its increase in costs due to increased supply of exports. For the preference-granting country, America, the decrease in income is equal to the area,[17] (LGDC + GJUC - FMJ). Since British elasticity of export supply, as assumed in this diagrammatic case, is infinite, its welfare remains unaffected by American tariff manipulation; so if the gain to India offsets the loss to America, i.e., if in this illustrative case, area FMR minus area RUC is positive, world welfare is increased by the preference-induced trade.[18] So, what we obtain through this entire exercise is the following: because of American tariff-preference to India, India unambiguously gains, Britain does not lose, and world welfare increases. It is obviously a Pareto-superior situation. It simply means it costs less than $100 to U.S. by giving away $100 through trade preferences. AID, the U.S. Treasury, the U.S. Department of Commerce should readily recognize this interesting fact because the clear understanding of this result eliminates lots of misconceptions from the minds of donors and thus enhances the degree of cooperation between the developing and developed countries.

III. SOME REMARKS

We have attempted to establish some results through direct aid and through some indirect aid via tariff preferences. But non-tariff barriers and the effective manipulations thereof are of enormous importance too in the regulation of trade structure and in the change of national and global welfare. Serious efforts[19] have been already made, and it can be shown that by preference structure through removal of non-tariff barriers at appropriate levels of economic welfare can be augmented. One more relevant point should be made at this stage. If analyzed critically, one can see that many of the products of poor nations simply do not enter into rich nations because of the existence of prohibitive transport costs, lack of knowledge of the existence of such goods and sometimes perhaps for lack of taste for such commodities in the foreign countries.

Viewing the transport cost as the real wedge as tariff, it is not difficult to conceptualize that preference structure in the form of trade subsidy can create a case as described through Figure 3. Note that so far onus of trade creation has been placed on the developed countries such as the United States but the real responsibility for creation of new and expansive trade should lie with the LDC's who can gain mostly through such changes. It is both ironic and unfortunate that most of the time these countries seriously lack initiatives in export promotion because of perhaps long-standing inertia, lack of research on foreign needs and taste, cultural rigidities, political stubbornness, and so on. It is imperative that LDC's -- their active business communities and their Governments -- take meaningful interest in world economic relations, their own trade prospects -- short-run as well as long-run -- and move in positive directions for better national lives and global efficiency and economic welfare. Without active participation by rich and poor nations in joint enterprises on dynamic and intertemporal optimization framework, prospect for the New International Economic Order would be at best a rosy dream.

NOTES

[1] See Raul Prebisch, "Commercial Policy in Underdeveloped Countries", American Economic Review, May 1959, pp. 251-73, and for further analysis of Prebisch thoughts, M. June Flanders, "Prebisch on Protectionism: An Evaluation", Economic Journal, June 1964, pp. 305-26.

[2] Of several mimeographed works under the auspices of -nited Nations Conference on Trade and Development at least a few e.g., Jagdish Bhagwati, "The Tying Aid", November 1, 1967, Deepak La, "A Quantitative Analysis of Aid -- Financial Imports of Certain Chemicals into India", December 3, 1968, Mahbub Haq, "Report on Tied Credits: Chile", December 8, 1967, and his "Tied Credits -- A Quantitative Analysis", in John H. Adler, ed., Capital Movements and Economic Development (New York, Macmillan, 1967) should be looked into for more in-depth study in this area.

[3] Wassily Leontief, by presenting a case in Taussig Festschrift volume, Exploration in Economics proves it to the contrary. Note

that in the Leontief model 'inferior-good' phenomenon occurs or what Samuelson calls it is a case in multiple and unstable equilibria.

[4]One can also consider short-term and medium-term cases without prejudicing the perception of the picture or affecting the derived results in the context of long-term credits and loans.

[5]This is basically the same formula developed by M. Haq first in his effort to measure the cost of tied aid for Pakistan, op. cit.

[6]Note different estimates by D. Lal and by J. Bhagwati, op. cit. Their estimates are so much different because of their different representation of economic equations.

[7]In functional representation of welfare indices in eq. (iii) through (i*), the x_{ij}'s measure the minimum "committed" values of consumption levels of x_{ij}'s that consumers must have. These functional forms represent linear expenditure system, modified Cobb-Douglas variety and welfare tree with different branches of modified Strotz-Gorman type. For details on these welfare functions see L.R. Klein and H. Rubin, "A Constant Utility Index of the Cost of Living", Review of Economic Studies, 1948, pp. 84-87, R. Stone, "Linear Expenditure Systems and Demand Analysis: An Application to the Pattern of British Demand", Economic Journal, 1952, pp. 511-27, P. Samuelson, "Some Implications of Linearity", Review of Economic Studies, 1948, pp. 80-90, R.C. Geary, "A Note on Living", Review of Economic Studies, 1950, pp. 65-66, and M. Brown and M. Helen, "The S. Branch Utility Tree: A Generalization of the Linear Expenditure System", Econometrica 1974.

For welfare function such as (i*) or (ii*) the problem of equilibrium (from the standpoint of producer's motive of profit-maximization) and the question of availability of the goods concerned for purpose of consumption might be serious and quite intractable. See D.K. Ghosh, "Market Mechanism and the Maximization Principle", Indian Journal of Economics, Vol. LIX, July 1978. To circumvent such issue it is wise to make use of welfare function such as (iii).

[8]Under different additive welfare functions addition of constraints does not necessarily add further excess costs. See O.A. Davis and A.B. Whinston, "Welfare Economics and The Theory of Second Best", Review of Economic Studies, January 1965.

[9]This quotation is from a U.S. Department of Commerce publication, excerpted in Thomas L. Hutcheson and Richard C. Porter, The Cost of Tying Aid: A Method and Some Colombian Estimates, Princeton Studies in International Finance, No. 30, 1972, p. 8. See also Robert E. Asher, Grants, Loans and Local Currencies (Washington: The Brooking Institution, 1961).

[10]See The Foreign Assistance Program, Annual Report to Congress

(Washington: Government Printing Office, 1968) Lawrence Lynn, Jr., "An Empirical Analysis of U.S. Foreign Economic Aid and the U.S. Balance of Payments, 1954-1963", Ph.D. Dissertation (New Haven: Yale University, 1966).

[11]For details on such issues see Dilip K. Ghosh, "Optimum Tariffs in a Multi-Commodity Framework", Southern Economic Journal, October 1979.

[12]See Michael Bruno, "Market Distortions and Gradual Reforms", Review of Economic Studies, July 1972.

[13]See Robert E. Baldwin, "Customs Unions, Preferential Systems and World Welfare", in M. Connally and A. Swoboda, eds., International Trade and Money (London: George Allen & Unwin, 1973).

[14]Peter B. Kenen, "A Note on Tariff Changes and World Welfare", Quarterly Journal of Economics, December 1974.

[15]This analytical framework heavily draws on Harry G. Johnson, "The Economic Theory of Customs Union", Pakistan Economic Journal, March 1960, pp. 14-32, C.A. Cooper and B.F. Massell, "Towards a General Theory of Customs Unions for Developing Countries", Journal of Political Economy, October 1965, pp. 461-476, R. Blackhurst, "Tariff Preferences for LDC Exports: A Note on Welfare Component of Additional Earnings", Rivista Internazionale di Scienze Economiche e Commerciali, December 1971, pp. 1180-81, J. Pinera, "World Income Redistribution Through Trade", Ph.D. Dissertation (Cambridge: Harvard University, 1974), and R. McCulloch and J. Pinera, "Trade as Aid: The Political Economy of Tariff Preferences for Developing Countries", American Economic Review, December 1977, pp. 959-67.

[16]This area is equal to rectangle OZML (= OZ times OL) minus rectangle OHCD (= OH times OD) minus area HZMC. The difference between the first two rectangles measures increase in export revenue to the preference — receiving nation and the area HZMC measures increase in cost for increase in the volume of exports because of tariff cut.

[17]Here real income loss to the preference-granting country consists of rectangle LGCD (= OH times LD) plus rectangle GJUC (= HK times LD) minus triangle FMJ (= 1/2 KZ times LE).

[18]Here ignoring the loss of tariff revenue we find that as long as the beneficiary gains outweigh the preference-granting country's loss, it is a case of gain for the world, as the third party involved remains unaffected. Introducing income distributions at individual levels, this claim may not hold.

[19]See, for instance, Ingo Walter, "Nontariff Barriers and Export Performance of Developing Countries", American Economic Review, May 1971, pp. 195-205, Robert E. Baldwin, Nontariff Distortions

of International Trade (Washington, D.C.: The Brooking Institution, 1970), and "Nontariff Barriers and the Free Trade Area Option", Banca nazionale del Lavoro Quarterly Review, March 1969.

Aspects of International Trade and Assistance Relating to the Expansion of Employment in the Developing Countries

JULIO A. LARCARTE

I. INTRODUCTION

The Second United Nations Development Decade has been specifically designated as a period in which changes must be made in current trends in the economic development of the various countries of the world -- trends which have led to the existence of an ever widening gap between the developed and the developing countries.

One of the most serious problems which countries will have to face during the forthcoming decade will be that of employment. The level of employment has become an increasingly relevant yardstick for measuring a country's degree of economic development. It is now regarded not simply as a marginal aspect of the growth of per capita income, but as a variable on which specific action must be taken, both because of its relationship with production and because of its far-reaching effects in the social sphere. In recent years, therefore, international oganizations have been laying increasing stress on the importance of employment.

There are certainly very strong grounds for this position, since employment exerts a powerful effect on various levels of the economy. First of all, when the level of employment rises, production must also increase. Since the marginal productivity of labour is positive, the allocation of additional human resources results in an increase in production which, in its turn, contributes to economic growth. Secondly, a decrease in unemployment or underemployment enables new sectors of the population to engage in remunerative activities -- a process which leads to a more equitable distribution of income, which is in fact

From **JOURNAL OF DEVELOPMENT PLANNING**, vol 5, 1972, (115-143), reprinted by permission of the publisher.

another basic objective of the Second Development Decade. Lastly, the very fact of being engaged in productive and remunerative activities makes it possible for those so engaged to establish social values related to man's need to be useful and to devote his energies to the attainment of specific objectives. This is the essential goal which is being sought in relation to employment.

In the developing countries, the problem of employment is particularly serious. The prospects of alleviating the problems of unemployment and underemployment, which are already at very high levels, are bleak, and are worsened by the high rate of population growth in most of these countries. These facts contribute to unfavourable over-all situation of the developing countries in the world economy.

During the First United Nations Development Decade the relative situation of a substantial number of developing countries deteriorated. Although the growth of the gross national product (GNP) of these countries as a whole slightly exceeded the objective of 5 per cent established at that time, individual GNPs vary widely and are in many cases much lower. For example, countries with an annual per capita income of less than $150 attained a mean growth rate of only about 3.8 per cent.

The situation is even more unfavourable if account is taken of annual population growth. The mean average annual increase in the real per capita product in the developing countries was 2.4 per cent, whereas in the developed countries the rates were 3.7 per cent for the market-economy countries and 5.5 per cent for the centrally planned economies. In terms of average levels of real per capita income, these increases were equivalent to $43, $791 and $530 respectively at 1969 prices, which means that in absolute figures the increase in the developing countries was equivalent to 8 per cent of that of the centrally planned economies and 6 per cent of that of the developed market-economy countries.

Since the continuation of this situation can lead only to an increase in tension and social and political instability throughout the world, conditions must be improved during the forthcoming decade. As has already been pointed out, one of the essential objectives to which consideration must be given is employment. This question is all the more important for the developing countries because of their high rates of population growth and the high percentage of young people in their populations.

It is expected that during the period 1970-1980 the labour force in the developing countries will grow at an annual rate of 2.3 per cent, compared with 1 per cent in the developed countries. Even assuming that fertility rates decline to a certain extent as a result of economic development itself, the world population is expected to double or, in other words, to reach approximately 7.5 billion by the year 2000. Of that total, some 6 billion will be in the less developed countries of Africa, Asia and Latin America.

The problem is even more acute because of the population structure in these countries. It has been estimated that 42 per cent of their present population is under 15 years of age, whereas 55 per cent is between 15 and 65. There is thus a need to provide enough jobs for the great mass of the active population and for the young population entering the labour force each year.

This goal cannot be achieved if current trends continue. As part of its World Employment Programme, the International Labour Organisation (ILO) has projected the increases in population and employment in various sectors in the developing countries. According to its estimates for the period 1970-1980, unless appropriate measures are taken, employment will grow less than the labour force and there may also be an increase in underemployment.

In the developing countries of two large regions -- Asia and Africa -- the majority of the population is employed in the rural sector. In these regions agricultural employment accounts for 60 per cent of total employment. It is estimated that by 1980 the rural sector will absorb 30 per cent of new jobs in Asia and 35 per cent in Africa; the industrial sector is expected to provide 30 per cent of new jobs in Asia and 25 per cent in Africa; and in both regions the services sector is expected to absorb 40 per cent of new jobs. The case of Latin America is different, since in that region rural employment accounts for only 25 per cent of total employment and this proportion is not expected to change. It is expected that 40 per cent of new jobs will be provided by the manufacturing and construction sectors and 60 per cent by the services sector.

The above figures obviously take no account of current unemployment and underemployment, since they relate only to persons entering the labour force in the future. This makes the ILO projections of the increase in the labour force and unemployment all the more serious.

The problem of employment does not only mean that unemployment should be eliminated; underemployment, too, is common in the developing countries and its effects on the economy and on society are just as harmful as those of unemployment. The inefficient use of resources implicit in both problems is inadmissible in a world where the majority of the population live in penury and where the growing concept of progress and equality is incompatible with the existence of underprivileged masses.

The issue of unemployment in the developing countries must be solved by the joint efforts of both the developed and the less developed countries. Employment is one of the factors in the gap between the developed and the developing countries, a gap which must be narrowed and if possible eliminated by a joint effort. This is vital if the present situation is not to deteriorate and a serious international economic, social and political crisis is to be avoided. The countries themselves, conscious of their responsibility in the face of world events, have drawn attention to the unavoidable necessity for joint action to solve existing problems. In particular, at the commencement of the Second Development Decade, special emphasis was placed on the common interest of all countries in ensuring the most rapid possible progress of the developing countries; such an objective calls for action by every nation, irrespective of its level of development.

While foreign trade is a key factor in the development strategy of these countries and must be channelled towards the creation of employment and the attainment of economic growth, external assistance is a necessary complement to it. Whatever good effects the measures taken in the sphere of trade may have, it will still be necessary to finance their balance-of-payments deficits to allow for co-operation in development projects, to provide financial and technical support for the trade measures adopted, and in general to supplement internal saving. In the current Development Decade, therefore, external assistance must continue to be an important means of promoting employment and development.

Exports from the developing countries account for high percentages of their national product. Consequently, the multiplier effect of any increase in such exports must be felt on broad sectors of their economies, and particularly on employment. The diversification and stepping up of their exports will thus provide the developing countries with the stimulus they need to increase employment.

The development of world trade has not, however, led to an improvement in the relative position of the developing countries. On the contrary, their share in trade declined steadily during the First United Nations Development Decade and has in general continued to consist mainly of a small number of primary products. Despite the efforts to promote and liberalize world trade, the developing countries are still encountering serious quota and tariff barriers on world markets. These barriers, which are often a violation of the principles advocated and accepted in international forums, have the greatest effect on precisely those products in which the developing countries are most competitive and which would permit more intensive use of their abundant manpower.

Moreover, not only do the developing countries find it difficult to enter markets because of the obstacles referred to above, they also meet competition from products from the developed countries, which in many cases are subsidized to enable them to enter foreign markets. Thus, not only are conditions deteriorating on the international market but misuse of the world's resources is also being encouraged.

The developing countries themselves have sometimes failed to take the measures related to their production and exports without which they cannot hope to achieve the desired improvement in their position.

External assistance can help to promote employment, but during the First Development Decade such assistance not only declined steadily in relation to the gross national product of the developed countries, but it was frequently tied to conditions which did not make for the best use of the resources of the recipient countries, including their manpower. Moreover, there was a sharp drop in the external assistance world trade ratio in the period 1960-1970.

Existing conditions must be improved during the 1970s, for that is the only way in which foreign trade and external assistance can help to solve employment problems in the developing countries. It is the responsibility of both the developing and the developed countries to take appropriate action to ensure that the objectives of the Second United Nations Development Decade do not remain unfulfilled. In that connexion, it must be remembered that, owing to the accelerated growth of world trade in recent years, internal employment has become increasingly dependent on world trade so that the employment trade ratio has become closer and it should be borne in mind that world exports have increased at a faster rate than production.

II. FOREIGN TRADE

Role of Foreign Trade in Promoting Employment in the Developing
Countries

In most developing countries, exports and imports represent
very high percentages of the gross national product. In many
cases, the highest growth rates for the product have gone hand in
hand with high growth rates for exports. Trends in such developing
countries as the Republic of Korea and Mexico are a well-known
example.

However, what is important is not only the increase in
exports, but also the prices obtained for the products exported and
paid for those imported. The terms-of-trade effect is thus an
important variable that influences the growth of the domestic
product. The Centre for Development Planning, Projections and
Policies of the United Nations Secretariat has estimated the effect
of foreign trade on the gross domestic product of various
developing countries, using the terms-of-trade effect.[1] This study
indicates that foreign trade exerts an appreciable effect on the
domestic product, since the growth rates of the former, adjusted by
the terms-of-trade effect, vary considerably.

As to employment, if export earnings increase, this can be
expected to have a multiplier effect on internal economic activity,
which will create a demand for additional manpower.

Despite the importance of foreign trade to the developing
countries, their relative position in this field deteriorated in
the course of the First United Nations Development Decade. In
1960, out of $128.3 billion in total world exports, only some $27
billion were accounted for by exports of the developing countries,
which thus had 21 per cent of the total, despite the fact that they
represented 66 per cent of the world's population. In 1970, the
relative share of the developing countries in world exports
decreased to some 18 per cent of the total, equivalent to $56.4
billion. The per capita exports of the developing countries, which
were equal to only 13.3 per cent of the per capita exports of the
developed countries in 1960, fell to 9.7 per cent of the latter in
1970.

Consequently, trade deficits constitute a serious problem for
the developing countries, and one which will become more serious in
the future. According to the United Nations Conference on Trade
and Development (UNCTAD), with an average annual growth rate of the
gross domestic product of 6.1 per cent, the trade deficit of the
developing countries would be $6.1 billion in 1975 and $5.2 billion
in 1980 (at 1960 prices), on the assumption that the developed
market-economy countries provide the assistance they have stated

they are prepared to grant. If the petroleum-exporting countries are excluded, the deficit will increase to $17.9 billion and $29.8 billion for 1975 and 1980, respectively.

None the less, the industrialized nations keep in operation certain mechanisms which constitute serious obstacles to the trade of the developing countries. Quantitative import restrictions represent a distinctly negative factor in the export picture of the less developed countries, especially when they violate international commitments. Despite countless efforts to eliminate them, these barriers in fact continue to exist in some highly significant economic sectors. Moreover, they are frequently applied in a discriminatory manner, thus aggravating the situation.

These obstacles to trade are of such a nature and are applied in such a way that it is practically impossible to quantify their adverse effects at the world level, but there is absolutely no doubt that they are extremely harmful and are especially prejudicial to the less developed countries. Such restrictions are generally applied to agricultural products and the products of light industry, which are precisely the sectors of major importance for the exports of the less developed countries, as well as the sectors that not only now absorb significant quantities of labour, but also hold out prospects of absorbing more in the future. There is a distinct relationship between the products, that are subject to quantitative import restrictions in the industrialized countries, and those that are totally or partially exempted under the general system of preferences called for by UNCTAD resolution 21 (II) of 26 March 1968.[2]

The customs duties imposed by the developed countries constitute another significant obstacle to the exports of the developing countries. They frequently prevent or hinder the entry of products, which become considerably less competitive because of the higher prices entailed by such duties. It should also be noted that in some cases where customs tariffs are not high, internal taxes are imposed that have the same effect. Likewise, scales of customs duties according to which more duty is paid the greater the degree of processing are still applied in many places and they effectively prevent the import of anything but raw materials. In these circumstances, it is clear that there is still a huge sector of the export economy of the less developed countries which comes up against practically insurmountable customs barriers as soon as attempts are made to export products with any degree of processing.

In addition, the formation of economic blocs by developed countries has unfavourable repercussions on the trade of the developing countries. Expanded markets are created in this way for types of production which, since they are highly protected, no longer need to be competitive at the world level.

Given the objective of promoting employment and the existing distribution of world resources, efforts towards the gradual elimination of barriers should focus, over the short term, on exports from the developing countries of labour-intensive products. The expansion of exports of products of this type would lead to increased employment in developing countries precisely because they are in the best position to compete in the sale of these items.

In the last decade, many efforts have been made to eliminate barriers to world trade; among them, attention should be drawn to the Kennedy Round. However, although the Kennedy Round negotiations dealt with primary products and manufactures, the developing countries did not participate extensively in them. According to an analysis by the secretariat of the General Agreement on Tariffs and Trade (GATT), the tariff rates in force for seven of the nine categories of finished goods for which the developing countries supply more than 10 per cent of total world imports are still higher on the average than those for manufactures as a whole. Moreover, processed agricultural products, the production of which could absorb a considerable quantity of labour, continue to suffer from high tariff and other barriers. Thus, the Kennedy Round negotiations did not provide machinery which would be of enough assistance to promote employment in the developing countries, given the magnitude of the existing problem.

Within the framework of GATT, negotiations between developing countries have been initiated on tariff reductions which are not to be applicable to industrialized countries; in other words, this is a system of preferences between developing countries. As the system is in its infancy, its possible advantages cannot yet be assessed. Nevertheless, it seems clear that it offers fruitful possibilities for the economies of the participating States.

Indeed, the disadvantages faced by the developing countries in competing on the international market with their manufactures would be offset by the margins of preference between these countries to be agreed upon in the negotiations. Support for such a prediction may be found in the fact that other preferential systems set up in recent years have produced similar results.

Of course, if the system of preferences between developing countries is to operate really effectively at the world level, it will have to be considerably expanded. However, if that is to happen, it will also be necessary to bring it into line with the regional economic integration schemes to which many developing countries belong. Despite the substantial benefits offered by such a system in terms of trade and opportunities for access to markets, it would be wise to explore fully the machinery and the political decisions which would help to bring it about.

There is, in addition, the general system of preferences of the industrialized countries in favour of the less developed countries adopted at the second session of UNCTAD, which has been included in the International Development Strategy for the Second United Nations Development Decade. Although priority was to be accorded to a system of this type, it still has not been put into effect by all the developed countries. The European Economic Community and Japan began applying it on 1 July and 1 August 1971, respectively, and Czechoslovakia, Hungary and the United Kingdom of Great Britain and Northern Ireland on 1 January 1972. The United States of America and several other industrialized countries intend to begin applying it during 1972.

The general system of preferences undoubtedly constitutes a step forward in promoting the trade of the developing countries. The main advantages of the system lie in the opportunities for increased access to the markets of the industrialized countries that it holds out to the developing countries. It makes it easier for them to maintain a given level of exports, based on the experience of an earlier period, under existing arrangements, and it also enables the developing countries to increase their exports to those markets, thus expanding their relative share at the expense of the developed countries. While some developing countries are in a better position than others to benefit by the preferences, the placing of a ceiling on the amount that may be exported from any one source makes it possible to ensure a certain share for other countries that may be less able to compete.

Moreover, the general system of preferences marks a step toward a more rational international division of labour. A reduction of the restrictions on the entry of products from the developing countries makes for a restructuring of the more advanced economies so as to channel resources away from the less competitive activities, the products of which will be replaced by the less expensive products of the developing countries, towards those sectors where they may be used more efficiently.

There are, however, grounds for some further reflections on the system. First of all, on the assumption that it remains in force for at least 10 years, an evaluation of its effects on the economies of the developing countries is required. There are not yet sufficient studies on the matter, although some evaluations have been carried out based on the following assumptions: (a) that all tariffs on imports of manufacturers and semi-manufactures from the developing countries are removed; (b) that preferences are granted without limitation and without establishing ceilings; (c) that the cost of expanding manufacturing production in the developing countries will remain constant. On those assumptions, the application of a general system of preferences would result in a 20 per cent increase in exports of manufactures from the developing countries to the developed countries (excluding the socialist countries). This expansion would indicate a figure of $1.5 billion at 1970 trade levels, representing some 3 per cent of the total exports of the developing countries and about 12 per cent of their total net inflow of external aid. Somewhat more than half of this remainder would result from the diversification of exports.

This expansion is relatively small. It is even smaller if some assumptions, which for the present are not actually being met in the systems discussed, are dropped. In reality, not all products are included in the system. The programme of the United States of America, which has not yet been approved, excludes textiles, footwear and petroleum, exports of which are quite important for various developing countries; in addition, these products offer highly encouraging prospects for expansion. The programmes of the European Economic Community and Japan maintain a system of quotas with ceilings and provide for a special treatment of certain sensitive products.

The developing countries would benefit, therefore, by an increase of only about $500 or $600 million annually; and even this increase might be reduced by competition among the developing countries to fill the limited quotas offered under those programmes. Indeed, in view of the fact that the projected reductions of quotas provide only gradual increases over existing flows of trade, it is possible that, in their eagerness to take advantage of quotas with special tariffs, the developing countries might tend to offer their products at lower prices. To the extent that this occurred, a portion of the benefits arising out of the lowering of tariffs in the importing countries would be lost.

The share of imports of manufactures from the developing countries in the total imports of the developed countries varies and is not very large in any case. Thus, in 1968, this figure was 6 per cent for the European Economic Community, 16 per cent for the United States of America, 13 per cent for the United Kingdom and 20 per cent for Japan.

It has been estimated by the European Economic Community that, in the immediate future, only a small number of developing countries will be in a position to gain significant advantages from the general system of preferences. Among those countries are Argentina, Brazil, Egypt, India, Iran, Mexico, Pakistan, Venezuela and Yugoslavia.

The definition of sensitive products, for which smaller preferences are offered, is another important factor to be taken into account in assessing the systems which are currently being or about to be applied. Indeed, existing lists of sensitive products pose considerable limitations, since products so characterized are frequently those that the developed countries are in a position to export competitively over the short term. These lists are identical, in many particulars, with the list of products that the developing countries have asserted to be of special importance for their exports which was presented earlier at a meeting of GATT in connexion with the discussion of quantitative restrictions. In this way, most of the possible benefits of the system of preferences fail to materialize.

Processed agricultural products (Brussels Tariff Nomenclature Nos. 1 to 24) do not benefit from the general system of preferences; a few reductions of customs duties are allowed on some of these items, but that is all. Both under the European Economic Community system and in Japan, processed agricultural products are given preferential treatment in the form of a reduction of customs duties. But an analysis of the lists of these products and of the reductions granted indicates that the latter are not very large; it may therefore be wondered whether they will have any practical effect, bearing in mind past experience with effective customs protection. The system of preferences does not, therefore, provide satisfactory solutions for the developing countries' problems of trade in processed agricultural products. That is to say, it does not cover a whole group of products that it would not be difficult for many of these countries to export in greater quantity.

One point that still needs clarifying is the question of what effects this system will have on the developing countries that were receiving preferential treatment in the markets that are now to be included in the system. Another important limitation of the system is that the decisions on its operation are all taken unilaterally by the importing countries, without the developing countries having any say in the matter. Furthermore, the importing countries reserve the right to invoke escape clauses in connexion with goods imported under the system. Nevertheless, despite its limitations, the general system of preferences is a step towards increasing the exports of developing countries. There is much to be gained from a study of its effects on employment in the industrialized countries, a study which can be started as soon as the necessary statistics become available.

The present system of preferences must not be allowed to divert attention from the liberalization of other imports, those from the developed countries. As far as can be seen from the initial phase of its operations, the system has only encouraged a relative increase and diversification of those imports. Therefore, the introduction of the general system of preferences does not preclude the necessity for a far-reaching liberalization of major export flows from the developing countries; these are mainly food and raw materials, most of which do not come under the system. Only a very few developing countries are in a position to benefit in any real sense from this system; there will be very little change in the situation of the other developing countries, and different solutions will have to be found for them.

One point that should be emphasized is that the developed countries which reduce the barriers to imports from developing countries will really be promoting a better use of their own resources. The imports that come up against barriers in the developed countries are usually products that are more expensive to produce there, so that their manufacture has to be protected. What these countries must do, then, is to restructure their economies and direct their labour force, which is smaller and highly paid than in the developing countries, into activities that are better suited to the advanced technology of the developed countries, thus allowing more imports from the developing countries to enter their markets.

There are as yet very few estimates of the number of workers who would be put out of employment in the industrialized countries. The ILO has, however, estimated the effects that the removal of trade barriers against imports of manufactures from the developing countries and the application of the results of the Kennedy Round would have on labour displacement in European and North American industrialized countries. The data relate to 1964; the estimates are based on a series of assumptions and they have limitations, of which the following are a few: (a) imports of processed agricultural products from the developing countries are excluded, mainly because most of them are subject to quota restrictions; (b) it is assumed that the developing countries can increase production at a constant cost and that the relative shares of the different exporting countries will not change; (c) no consideration is given to the possibility of a drop in the exports of some items parallel to an increase in other exports by the developing countries; (d) there are quota restrictions on some of the exports of manufactures of the developing countries that are considered.

The first and the last of the above limitations are probably the most serious. Processed agricultural products are one of the exports which the developing countries might step up rapidly, as that would have an appreciable effect on employment in those countries. Quota restrictions, on the other hand, are a formidable protective barrier used by the advanced economies, and it is therefore logical to assume that if they were eliminated, the effect on employment in the developing countries would be greater than as indicated by the estimates.

Nevertheless, the projections made by the ILO must be given considerable attention because they give an idea of the magnitude of the problems which a restructuring of their economy would pose for the developed countries. According to the studies that have been carried out, the removal of customs tariffs on imports of manufactures from developing countries and the application of the results of the Kennedy Round would not involve serious problems of unemployment for the developed countries. The results of the Kennedy Round would have almost no effect on employment; the average number of workers rendered jobless, both directly and indirectly, would be about 11,000 in the United States of America and the European Economic Community and a little over 1,000 in the United Kingdom and the European Free Trade Area. The removal of tariffs on imports of manufactures would have a greater, but not too great, effect on employment in the developed countries. In the United States of America, the number thus rendered jobless would be about 42,700; in the European Economic Community, it would be about 30,000; for the United Kingdom it would amount to about 1 per cent of the unemployment figure in 1964.

It may therefore be said that the effect of the above-mentioned measures on employment in the developed countries would not be very great. Furthermore, no account is taken in the estimates of the increased employment which may be expected to result from an increase in exports of capital and other goods from the developed to the developing countries, which would be encouraged by the liberalization of world trade. When a quantified comparison is made between the situation before the restructuring of the economy and after, it may well be that the industrialized countries will be in a better position, in actual figures, afterwards than they were before, as far as employment, production and exports are concerned.

The fact that the estimated labour displacement that would result from the restructuring of the industrialized economies is very small does not mean that the restructuring is not a grave problem which will have to be solved in the near future. It must be borne in mind that the estimates have limitations, due mainly to the exclusion of processed agricultural products and to the inclusion of some items on which there are quota restrictions. Furthermore, a more detailed breakdown of the estimates shows that in some branches of industry, such as textiles, the unemployment problem that would arise if the market was opened to imports from the developing countries is much more serious.

The fact must therefore be faced that the restructuring of the industrialized economies, which is necessary if they are steadily to increase their imports from the less developed countries, is not at all a simple or an easy process. On the contrary, it is not only highly complex in itself, it also involves problems relating to transfers of labour as a result of adjustments in the sectors concerned. Whatever the difficulties and disadvantages of such a process of adjustment may be for the developed countries, it is an adjustment they will have to face in the normal course of their economic development process. Maintaining barriers against imports from countries which can produce the items more efficiently is prejudicial not only to the potential exporters but also to the economy concerned, which is ultimately obliged to pay higher prices for those goods and thus to divert resources from other and perhaps more profitable uses.

Past developments show that technological advance, changes in the patterns of consumption and economic development lead necessarily and continually to transformation and restructuring. In the past, these developments have involved adjustments that have not always been easy. Those which are now the highly developed countries have gone through successive stages of restructuring, as for instance in their cotton and mining industries. Restructuring of this kind is unavoidable; the most rational thing to do is not only to recognize it as a historical fact and a principle, but also to apply this knowledge on the practical plane.

This process, instead of being allowed to take place haphazardly and at a high economic cost -- as it often does -- should be organized at the world level so that there is a smooth adjustment. This would ensure a better utilization of resources through proper planning, which would be facilitated by the fact that the repercussions caused by opening markets to products from developing countries are usually felt in specific branches of production.

It should be emphasized that the restructuring does not always have a negative impact; it ultimately enables the advanced countries to redirect their efforts towards the achievement of specific goals which may even be other than economic and may include, for example, the increase of leisure and of opportunities for cultural and scientific pursuits. Whatever measures the developed countries take to reabsorb their manpower in more productive activities must take account of these new possibilities. Besides establishing retraining and reorientation centres for the purpose of channelling labour into new jobs in the medium or short terms, they can -- even must -- take short-term measures also. In this regard, consideration should be given to the possibility of carrying out infrastructure works, modernizing old installations and building new ones in the field of transport, hospital care, education and recreation. Such work would reflect a trend that has emerged quite recently in the developed countries and that springs from a recognition of the need for a better balance between material ends and spiritual values.

Here, only the industrialized countries can take the initiative, for the developing countries are too short of resources to begin this process of restructuring on a large enough scale to have a world-wide impact. However, once the developed countries have started the process, the effects of it will be felt in the developing countries, which will be induced to give up highly protected activities because they will have gained greater access to external markets. If this task is undertaken and properly planned and co-ordinated at the world level, it will be a big step towards achieving a better international division of labour, with all the benefits that that involves.

The trend of world trade also depends on the policies followed by the developing countries. In their economic growth policies, they are constantly faced with a choice between promoting import substitution or expanding exports, and the alternative they choose depends on the situation in their national economies and on the world markets. When they see a chance of new markets for their products, the developing countries will be less inclined to emphasize activities that require high protective barriers and that are often highly capital-intensive, and more inclined to allocate resources for export promotion. It is precisely the export field that holds out the greatest possibilities of absorbing labour and of utilizing their raw materials. This means that the developing countries must make a very careful choice of the activities they wish to promote, and that they must achieve a level of productivity in the activities selected which will make their products competitive on the world market.

The reduction of high tariff barriers and the promotion of exports will, in turn, improve the capacity of the developing countries to import. On the one hand, new products that will compete with those of the formerly highly protected industries will be allowed to enter the country; on the other, increased exports will earn more foreign exchange, which may be spent on imports. In this way a more rational use of resources, not only by the developing countries but also, as has already been said, by the developed countries, would increase world trade and improve the international division of labour.

If the developing countries wish to make efficient use of the possibilities opened up by the measures they are pressing to have adopted at the world level, they must take the necessary steps to change the present situation of their economies and orient them towards sustained integrated development. They must consider the problem of employment and its relation to foreign trade within the context of a world economic development strategy. They should not place so much emphasis on the creation of short-term employment that they sacrifice long-term economic growth; but if they weigh all these factors in the context of a development programme, they will be led to take measures which will not only increase employment but also create new sources of employment for the future.

Consequently, the promotion of labour-intensive activities, the simplest and most obvious solution to the problem discussed in this paper, is not enough. Development possibilities must be given consideration, which means that due importance must be given to more capital-intensive industries which, by stepping up internal economic activity, will provide many more sources of employment. Otherwise, owing to the rapid development of technology, the gap between the developed and the developing countries will tend to become permanent.

If the developing countries wish to overcome the problems caused by the fluctuating and low levels of their export earnings, they must do everything they can to diversify their economies and their markets. By diversifying their economies, they would put an end to the present, only too frequent situation where concentration on a very restricted range of export commodities means that the entire economy is dependent on world market conditions for those exports. The geographical diversification of their markets would make them less dependent on trade with one or two countries and considerably improve marketing possibilities for their products. Steps cannot be taken in either direction alone; they must be co-ordinated and integrated. The domestic economy must be diversified so as to produce exports that can be sold on many different markets.

This process, which may be facilitated by economic integration, should also lead to specialization in products which make the developing countries more competitive on world markets. Specialization of this kind should encourage the emergence and development of local technologies.

Economic groupings are one of the most powerful instruments for achieving general development objectives, and particularly employment targets, as has been clear from the experience of many developed countries. Although trade between developing countries represents barely 20 per cent of their total exports, there can be no doubt that reciprocal access to each other's markets holds out very promising prospects for the future. What these countries are concentrating on now is making steady progress in diversifying their economies and consequently increasing their export potential; their ability to intensify their reciprocal trade is therefore growing rather slowly. A large proportion of the imports of the least developed countries consists of manufactures from the more advanced countries, which are sometimes subsidized and might just as well be bought from other developing countries. On the other hand, there are good prospects of promoting trade between developing countries, either through the establishment of more efficient marketing machinery (greater availability of trade information, appointment of agents, improvement of transport and communications and so on) or by agreeing on systems of preferential treatment that would facilitate reciprocal trade even in products that, because of their price and/or quality, are not yet competitive on the world market.

If these prospects are to materialize to any satisfactory extent, the developing countries will have to agree on the reciprocal application of many of the principles which they are now pressing the developed countries to apply. The international division of labour may be mentioned as an example. The developing countries will have to admit the validity of this principle in their own sphere and shape their policy in consequence; otherwise, they will be imposing on each other the very same protectionist and inequitable policies that they object to in world trade. The application of these principles runs into practical difficulties when it is unilateral, bilateral or only partial.

The conditions under which the developing countries could jointly envisage reciprocal arrangements to stabilize and to promote their exports are well known. The removal of barriers to their reciprocal trade would give them broader markets; this would enable them to install complex industries with substantial inputs in capital goods which would be uneconomic on the small scale allowed by many developing economies. The international development strategy could thus be applied to all steps connected with the establishment of new labour-intensive industries side by side with new capital-intensive industries. The most advanced form of integration, the common market, brings additional advantages with it; in addition, it is a necessary step towards a better utilization of resources when the economies of a group of countries are to be stimulated. The mobility that is a feature of a common market would be particularly important for labour, as workers could be transferred from sectors suffering from underemployment or unemployment to more productive activities within the same region.

However important it may be for countries to adhere to some form of regional economic grouping, their participation in such a grouping should not cut them off from other countries in a sort of independent regional enclave. On the contrary, in virtue of the principles which the developing countries themselves advocate in international trade, free trade areas or common markets should be established with the idea of their being open to the trade of other countries also, for this is a primary condition for their effectiveness and for the steady growth of export trade.

Trade in Raw Materials and Food-Stuffs

The production of primary products is of prime importance to the developing countries. In addition to constituting the major portion of their exports, such products provide the means of subsistence and employment for great sectors of their population. For that reason, it is essential to solve the problems affecting raw materials production.

The problem of rural overpopulation which affects wide areas will tend to be solved by a lower rate of population growth and by the creation of a greater number of jobs in non-rural sectors. However, since the effects of a slackening off in the population growth rate are felt only over the long term and the foreseeable absorption of manpower into other activities, particularly industry, is not sufficiently high, it is also necessary to increase employment in rural areas. This would also lead to a greater utilization of raw materials and food-stuffs which, together with manpower, are the resources in which developing countries are relatively rich.

Unless domestic demand is big enough to absorb the production increases completely, the prospects for increasing rural employment opportunities through external trade are closely linked to the possibility of finding outlets for primary products on the world market. In view of the fact that the composition of exports cannot be expected to change substantially in the short term, this is a matter on which immediate action needs to be taken, without prejudice to the measures that may be adopted in the manufacturing and services sectors.

Despite the importance for the developing countries of exports of primary products, these exports encounter many obstacles in the international market. Particular mention should be made of the fact that the protection of agricultural activities in the developed countries may make it completely impossible, or at any event extremely difficult, for the products of the developing countries to gain access to the markets of the developed countries. In some instances, while there are no tariff barriers against the entry of particular primary products, quotas are imposed which restrict the volume of such products or internal taxes are applied which produce the same effect as tariffs or tend to limit consumption. Moreover, agricultural products from the developed countries, processed according to advanced techniques and usually highly subsidized, are often sold on the international market, increasing supply, lowering prices and leading to a consequent decline in the export earnings of the developing countries. These factors have not been conducive to a stabilization of the commodity market. Their effect on levels of employment in the developing countries can be gauged from the fact that there are huge areas where more than half the working population is employed in the primary sector. Furthermore, the competition from the man-made materials manufactured in the developed countries has brought down the prices of a number of primary products in the world market.

The prices of a large number of agricultural products fluctuate. Periods of high production, weather, the treatment these products receive on the markets where they are sold, and competition from man-made materials make for unstable markets, and the fluctuations in the export earnings from such products have deleterious effects on the domestic economies of the developing countries. It has been estimated that a variation of 5 per cent in the average price of the export of developing countries is equivalent to their total inflow of public and private capital plus assistance received from external sources. Thus, the instability of their export earnings may negate the effect of other kinds of resources that the developing countries may receive.

The prospects for marketing processed agricultural and mineral products are excellent, provided that there are no tariff or other barriers in the markets for which those products are intended. According to the theory of effective tariff protection, when a product is exempt from duty in its natural state, the imposition of taxes -- even what may appear to be nominal taxes -- has a powerful adverse effect. For instance, if the value added in the initial stages of processing a particular raw material represents a percentage of the value of that raw material equal to the customs duty applied to it, this initial processing stage is protected 100 per cent. In these circumstances, a less developed country needs to make an immense sacrifice in keeping wages and other costs down if it wishes to reach a stage where it can compete in the market of an industrialized country applying such a system to its products. Unless there is a substantial change in this situation, it will be extremely difficult for the developing countries to overcome the existing obstacles, however effective their policies may be.

Since the demand for certain agricultural products is fairly inelastic, the increases in the exports of such products that the removal of restrictions by the industrialized countries might enable the less developed countries to achieve may not, in a number of cases, be as great as could be desired. On the other hand, there are other products -- certain temperate-zone products, for instance -- to which this does not apply; in their case, the existing margins of protection are so great that the only factor preventing a massive increase in supply from the developing countries is precisely the extremely high level of protection that exists.   In either event, however, easier access to the markets of the industrialized countries for semi-processed and fully processed agricultural products would provide a tremendous stimulus to employment in the developing countries.

The conclusion of commodity agreements has for many years been advocated as a means of limiting the wide fluctuations in the market for primary products.   However, although recommendations have repeatedly been made to this effect and negotiations have taken place on numerous occasions, few concrete results have been achieved.   There is currently only a very small number of effective commodity agreements.   In the case of many developing countries, particularly some of the relatively less developed among them, the stabilization of export earnings is of vital significance for their external trade; it is therefore necessary to ensure that the markets for primary products are more highly organized at remunerative price levels.

Finally, a further point arises in connexion with the growing competition from man-made materials, the supply of which in the world market affects the marketing prospects of important primary products and consequently employment in major sectors of the economies of the developing countries.   It is not proposed to eliminate or restrict technical progress, which would obviously be a step backwards in man's development.   However, what can be done is to limit or reduce the excessive incentives to replace natural products by man-made products.   If, for instance, the industrialized countries were to reduce or eliminate the customs duties and non-tariff restrictions that they apply to the various natural products, this would lead to a lowering in the cost of such products in relation to the man-made products with which they are in competition.

Trade In Manufactures

Over the last 20 years there has been a sustained and marked decline in the employment-output ratio in the manufacturing sector throughout the world. Although this trend is more pronounced in the case of heavy industry, the phenomenon also applies to light industry.   The development of technology and the rise in the capital-labour ratio prevent employment from increasing at the same rate as output.   Accordingly, the trend in this sector in relative terms runs directly counter to the aim of increasing employment. The process described cannot be objected to, since it reflects an increase in production efficiency that will free men from the demands of work; however, the fact cannot be overlooked that it will lead to a worsening of the unemployment problem in the less developed countries, in view of their high rates of population growth.

The situation in the developing countries is exacerbated by the fact that the absorption of manpower by industry is sometimes limited by the application of technology evolved by the developed countries which is not fully adapted to national conditions. Wherever this occurs, the efforts of those countries to raise levels of employment will to a large extent be frustrated. Foreign technology must be adapted to the internal resources available; it is also necessary to develop a national technology which will help to increase employment as well as to promote economic growth. Since the creation of technology is a complex process, it is not feasible for the developing countries to create the technology needed for their development in the immediate future. In order to do so, they must have access to the techniques available on the international market. In any event, such techniques should be freely available to all countries, since they are all in some way the product of efforts conducted on a world scale. Yet the current technology market is highly restrictive: the developing countries have to pay high prices, and conditions are usually attached to the transfer and use of technology (for example, they may not export the products to the country selling the technology, or they are bound to buy inputs in specific markets).

The elimination of restriction on the transfer and use of technology is a fundamental prerequisite for the promotion of exports of manufactures from the developing countries. At the present time these exports have to contend both with the limitations imposed by the production capacity of the developing countries themselves and the restrictions arising from the policies of the importing countries. The establishment of the general system of preferences is a step towards the removal of the latter kind of obstacle; but it must have as its complement further action to eliminate the remaining restrictions. Moreover, the developing countries must also improve their trade with each other.

A considerable number of developing countries have followed import substitution policies aimed at the local production of manufactures they previously imported. In its initial stages, an industrialization policy needs to be accompanied by the application of incentives, involving a certain degree of protection. This is just as true now for what are today's developing countries as it was for the present developed countries when they began to industrialize. However, if protection is unduly prolonged and intensified, the protected industries reach a point of relative failure where the dimensions of the domestic market impose a check on their further expansion. The dynamism of such industries disappears once the limits imposed by the domestic market are reached.

In their external trade policies and their efforts to establish and strengthen medium-scale and capital-goods industries, the developing countries must envisage a rationalization of the protection systems they are currently applying. The import substitution policies they have pursued in the past have been based on the existence of strong protection for consumer goods -- the goods that were the easiest to produce to replace imports. Where this protection has been markedly stronger than that granted to the intermediate manufacturing sectors, the attraction of resources to the consumer-goods industries has tended to increase the cost of inputs for the intermediate industries.

In order to promote development and employment, industrial policies must take account of export industries, which escape the limitations of manufacturing for the domestic market. This requires a significant change of approach in general economic policy. This process can clearly not be applied to all industries on an equal basis, since their competitiveness on the world market is not equal; the same phenomenon can be observed in the developed countries, where only a certain number of industries are in a position to go over to the international market. In other words, each developing country has only, at any one time, a particular number of industries that can hope to enter the world market. Even in the case of industries in this category, a combination of efforts by Governments, entrepreneurs and trade unions is required, involving, among other things, a radical change in mentality leading to the abandonment of static situations (which are the product of over-protection) and their replacement by the dynamic approach that is essential if the transition is to be achieved.

There are recent examples of such policies being successfully applied. The developing countries which have registered the greatest increases in exports in recent years are those which took action to promote export industries, making greater use of their plentiful resources, particularly manpower. The strides made by the exports of the Republic of Korea during the 1960s illustrates how some of the present problems of world trade can be overcome by the application of appropriate policies.

The experience of the developing countries which have increased and diversified their exports most rapidly provides a model for the future development of the world economy. If the developed countries restructure their economies to enable them to absorb smoothly the goods which the developing countries are producing in growing quantity and variety and on competitive terms, they will help to expand world trade and increase human well-being without any serious crisis of adjustment. If, on the other hand, they fail in this restructuring, the developing countries will be forced to establish discriminatory systems that favour trade among themselves as against trade with others, which will have the unfavourable effect of dividing the world into separate groups tending towards self-sufficiency.

Although labour is cheaper in the developing countries than in the developed countries, productivity too is usually lower. It is therefore necessary to ensure that this low productivity does not cancel out the effects of lower labour costs. Labour-intensive goods often have to compete with mass-produced goods from other countries. It is therefore clear that all those involved in production -- both management and workers -- must accept their responsibility to produce the output per man required by prevailing conditions in the world market. If they do not, the export drive will fail. There are also certain requirements to be met with regard to quality. Workers must be sufficiently skilled to enable developing countries to specialize in particular goods; they should therefore -- indeed they must -- have some idea of the quality and the level of specialization of the items they are going to export.

The industries that could be developed with substantial inputs of labour have been classified in ascending order of complexity; this might be the order in which they should be encouraged in the developing countries, with growing emphasis being placed on the more capital-intensive industries as the level of economic progress rises:

(a) Industries that require abundant but not highly skilled manpower, simple technology and low inputs of capital: clothing and toy manufacture and artisan-type industries;

(b) Industries that make intensive use of skilled manpower and more complex technology but do not require much capital: electronic goods, optical products, etc.;

(c) Industries that require both manpower and capital: shipbuilding, the manufacture of buses and rolling-stock, etc.

Recently, it has become apparent that goods from the metal-transforming and engineering industries, which are relatively labour-intensive, have great possibilities in the world market. In the case of some of these goods, there are no high barriers against trade and they already form part of the exports of a number of developing countries. Because of the rising cost of labour in developed countries, there has been a tendency for developing countries to take the lead in producing such goods, which range from relatively heavy machinery and transport equipment -- usually exported to other developing countries -- to light manufactures and semi-manufactures -- exported mainly to the developed countries.

In addition to promoting labour-intensive industries, the developing countries must channel resources into the establishment of heavy industries, whose first positive effect may be to supply cheaper inputs for labour-intensive industries. Furthermore, heavy industries will at a later stage help to speed up economic development and will enable the developing countries to participate in world trade in goods produced by increasingly complex technology. Economic blocs composed of the developing countries themselves can provide particularly favourable conditions for the development of such industries.

International Transport and Tourism

The services sector is an important source of employment. The experience of many developing countries has shown that surplus manpower due to population growth which cannot find employment in rural activities is to a large extent absorbed in the services sector.

A substantial amount of manpower is generally concentrated in certain traditional services sectors. Where agricultural and industrial activities do not provide employment for the growing labour force, this surplus labour must be attracted into the services sector, where productivity is sometimes less important than the need to provide employment for the population. On the other hand the very process of economic growth and the expansion of the agricultural and industrial sectors lead to the creation of job opportunities in services linked to those sectors. In the services sector, manpower utilization possibilities are closely linked to the progress of the dynamic sectors of the economy.

Transport and tourism, which are clearly linked to the external sector, are two important sources of employment, and transport is a key factor in shaping and developing a country's trade. Furthermore, the developing of international transport promotes the absorption of manpower, either through the industries producing the necessary goods or through the provision of transport services. The transport sector has still not attained the important position it warrants in the developing countries; they depend heavily on foreign services, thereby spending a substantial amount of their foreign exchange.

The developed countries should co-operate in evolving consultative and negotiating machinery. Such machinery, in which the developing countries would effectively participate, would hold down the steady rise in freight rates, a rise which is mainly to the advantage of the countries owning the means of transport.

The developing countries also require financial and technical assistance, since any progress towards increasing their possibilities of transporting their own exports and imports would lead to increased earnings, in the case of exports, and better use of their foreign exchange resources, in the case of imports. In addition, the industrialized nations can make a valuable contribution by not applying restrictive or discriminatory clauses which specify that goods shall be transported in their own vessels.

In view of the resources required to build up a sizable transport sector, mutual agreements might be a specific means by which the developing countries could attain that objective. Such a procedure would have positive effects on employment in several countries at the same time.

Similar considerations apply in the case of tourism. It has a very important impact on levels of employment since its multiplier effect extends to many different activities, which eventually absorb large amounts of manpower.

The action to be taken by the developed countries lies in the direction of assistance in advertising and promotion, so as to stimulate tourist flows to the developing countries. Specific action might be taken to create conditions conducive to the channelling of tourism to developing countries (lower fares at certain times, more favourable conditions for the introduction into the developed countries of goods from developing countries and so on).

The developing countries for their part could conclude regional agreements to promote the activities connected with tourism. The manpower required for such activities need not always be highly skilled and can therefore be deployed at short notice.

III. EXTERNAL ASSISTANCE

The Role of External Assistance in Creating Employment in the Developing Countries

Although the significance of external trade in the promotion of development and employment is considerably greater than that of external assistance, it is none the less true that this relationship varies considerably according to the level of economic development achieved by a given country.

In the case of those developing countries whose growth rate is relatively high, external trade is a major factor and the role of external assistance is decidedly less important. On the other hand, for many of the relatively less developed countries, external assistance is of capital importance because it not only represents a source of financing which the domestic economy cannot generate but also provides technical assistance, which, directed alike to industry and agriculture as well as to the infrastructure, creates conditions that are essential for development. Admittedly, it is to a large extent a question of degree, but the importance of external assistance cannot be overlooked.

Such assistance should provide the additional financial and technical resources required by projects for the development, training and direction of manpower to the sectors in which it can be used most effectively. For that to be achieved to the fullest extent, the forms that such assistance has taken over the past decade, and especially the financial arrangements, must be changed. Not only has financial assistance been subject to restrictions that frustrated the very purposes for which it was intended, the conditions imposed upon it with the passage of time have led to the creation of a considerable financial problem for the developing countries, whose mounting external indebtedness has increased to the point where, in certain cases, it is an extremely onerous burden for the recipient. In other words, there are two apparently contradictory factors which must be reconciled if the purposes of development assistance are to be achieved, namely, the real need for such assistance in increased amounts on one hand and the growing burden which it represents for the balance of payments of the recipient countries on the other.

External assistance has not increased by any significant extent over the past decade. Although, in terms of the per capita dollar amount received by the developing countries, there has been no reduction of assistance, it has dropped considerably by comparison with the gross national product of the developed States. The proportion of the GNP of the developed market-economy countries devoted to external assistance declined from 0.89 per cent in 1960 to 0.74 per cent in 1969,[3] notwithstanding the stated objective of achieving a level of assistance equivalent to 1 per cent of their GNP. In 1970, the total amount of the net resources received by all the developing regions was some $15,000 million. Given the fact that this figure represents, on the average, 0.70 per cent of the GNP of the developed countries, there is an estimated shortfall of $5,000 million in external assistance in the light of the target of 1 per cent of the GNP.

The downward trend indicated above has been reflected in the per capita amount of aid received by the developing countries, which has remained at $4 per annum throughout the past decade. The freezing of assistance at this figure entails a reduction in practice because it is measured in current dollars, the currency common to the majority of the countries. If the resource flow were measured in constant dollars, the per capita assistance would be seen to have diminished substantially. Thus, in current dollars, the total assistance in 1970 increased 10.7 per cent by comparison with that for the previous year; if measured in real terms, this increase would fall to 7 per cent per annum.

External assistance is a general term which is interpreted in various ways and it may be assumed that closer inspection of the sources of assistance would show that the level of aid was somewhat further removed from the objective of 1 per cent of the GNP of the developed countries. Finally, it should be noted that assistance has declined considerably in relation to the value of world trade, although it might have been supposed that the marked increase in world trade during the past decade would have heralded an equivalent increase in assistance. It is noteworthy that external assistance has been conditioned and deployed under the influence of geographical considerations and that factors alien to its true purposes have thereby been introduced.

In specific cases, therefore, tied aid has not achieved the objectives for which it was designed. If a country accepting the aid binds itself to purchase certain products in specific markets it may be prevented from buying them in other markets where they would be cheaper. In addition, it restricts opportunities for the developing countries themselves to provide such goods. Furthermore, it usually encourages the introduction of technology that is not necessarily the most suitable in view of the financial and human resources available in the recipient country. Such a situation is aggravated where the conditions attached to the financing of the external assistance involve the use of imported inputs as opposed to their locally produced counterparts and therefore exert a doubly negative influence -- on the balance of payments and on the level of internal activity.

An additional factor is that the breakdown of net transfers to the developing countries shows a relative decrease in assistance accompanied by an increase in the flow of private capital, which is obviously made available on more onerous terms. Moreover, as the International Bank for Reconstruction and Development (IBRD) has pointed out, this tendency is reflected in the transfer of a larger share of the financial resources to areas in which there is a rapid rate of growth and this has yet further unfavourable implications for areas that are relatively less developed.

The external assistance provided by the centrally planned economies cannot be estimated in the same way as that from the market-economy countries because the former do not publish equivalent data on the flow of resources. Nevertheless, approximate calculations can be made on the basis of agreements concluded. The commitments assumed by the countries with centrally planned economies amounted to $3,571 million in the period 1961-1965 and to $5,139 million in the period 1966-1970. These figures represent, in the case of the second period, 0.20 per cent of the GNP of those countries, a percentage which falls well short of the target of 1 per cent.

Fundamentally, the external assistance targets set for the developed countries have still not been achieved in quantitative or qualitative terms. The achievement of those targets is an essential counterpart to the objective of increasing domestic saving in the developing countries from 15 per cent to 20 per cent during the current decade.

The External Indebtedness of the Developing Countries

External indebtedness is a serious problem for a great many developing countries. This financial burden is the unavoidable counterpart of the assistance which, in various forms and on various terms, has been channelled to the developing countries over the years. According to the World Bank, the public external indebtedness of 80 developing countries had reached an approximate total of $59 billion by the end of 1969.

In recent years, there has been a strong tendency for the external indebtedness of many countries to increase -- so much so that, in certain cases, transfers of resources from the developed countries have amounted to less than the outflow of debt servicing in the form of interest and amortization payments. During the period 1970-1975, the developing countries will have to make service payments of more than $19.8 billion in respect of their outstanding indebtedness as at the end of 1969 in the amount of $43.4 billion, to bilateral and multilateral official creditors. It is estimated that debt servicing payments to private creditors will amount to nearly $13 billion in respect of an indebtedness of more than $15.5 billion. The latter figure represents an extraordinarily high percentage of the indebtedness, namely, 84 per cent.

This ratio shows that private investment should not be treated, for purposes of calculation, as being on a par with, for example, grants or low-interest loans from intergovernmental bodies. Such investment consists rather in operations of common interest, which are distinct from external assistance proper as it should normally be understood.

Although the degree of external indebtedness varies from one developing country to another, there can be no doubt that it constitutes a serious hindrance to the progress of many of them, in the sense that an excessively high proportion of the foreign exchange inflow is absorbed by amortization and interest payments in respect of external obligations.

As balance-of-payments deficits may be expected to persist in the years to come, consideration should be given to the possibility of restructuring international financial commitments to channel the resources thus liberated into the promotion of development. Indeed, although it might at first sight appear presumptuous even to suggest such a restructuring, the facts surrounding the external indebtedness of the developing countries indicate that, if the current trends continue, a payments crisis will sooner or later occur, whose magnitude and consequences are difficult to predict at the present time.

This last point is closely related to one of the most serious problems facing many developing countries: the mobilization of their domestic savings. Development policies require financing and most of it must come from the developing countries themselves, so as to reduce the degree to which they are dependent on external decisions and policies. It frequently happens, however, that only a small proportion of the domestic savings is brought to bear and it is therefore essential to improve the machinery for mobilizing such savings and deploying them in the financing of national development.

In any event, the problem of external indebtedness remains one of exceptional importance. There is a real need for skillful management of the indebtedness of the developing countries in the context of the Second United Nations Development Decade, because the end result should be the maximum mobilization of financial resources for investment in viable projects which create employment. This requires the integration of external assistance projects with employment plans in the short, and long term and the national planning of development.

Assistance should be channelled primarily towards activities that create employment in the long term. Not only must productive activities and related infrastructure projects be financed, steps must be taken to train and channel the manpower. Assistance for projects involving the education and training of skilled workers is essential in making available the human resources needed to derive the maximum advantage both from the flow of external assistance and from national resources.

The employment situation in the recipient countries will be improved if assistance is directed to the financing of programmes rather than projects, if local costs are financed to the greatest extent possible, if bilateral assistance is limited in favour of multilateral aid, if loans are untied and not made subject to purchases being made in specific markets, if the level of grants rises and if conditions attached to interest and repayment and to grace periods are made more flexible.

IV. CONCLUSIONS

The present international division of labour is not in accordance with the principles set forth in the resolution of the General Assembly of the United Nations proclaiming the Second

United Nations Development Decade. Unemployment and underemployment are an acute problem in the developing countries and unless there is a radical change in this situation there can be no real hope of achieving the targets set with regard to the general improvement of living standards and the equitable distribution of income.

There is no doubt that it is basically for the developing countries themselves to create conditions conducive to the reduction and eventual elimination of the immense wastage of human and material resources involved in unemployment. This task involves a number of different factors -- economic, social, cultural and even political -- whose effects and relative importance vary from one country to another, but which in all cases have a powerful impact on national structures. Yet it cannot be denied -- and this is a fact that has been recognized by the community of nations in international declarations -- that the developed countries share the responsibility for promoting the advancement of the developing world. The problem of employment in the less developed States could be solved by measures applied at the national and international levels by all countries, regardless of the stage of their economic development.

There is a clear and significant relationship between employment and the external sector and this has become more marked during the past decade. It can be assumed that this link will become even stronger in the future because intergovernmental commitments and technological advances are continually creating common interests which draw peoples together.

A fundamental key to the development of employment in the developing countries consists in the rapid expansion of their exports, with particular reference to items that entail the optimum utilization of those resources in respect of which they enjoy a relative advantage, namely, manpower and primary commodities.

The trade policies currently applied at the world level are not structurally such as to resolve the growing problems of unemployment in the developing countries with the rapidity which the principles endorsed by the international community and an elementary feeling of brotherhood would require. The continuation of those policies will rather contribute to the perpetuation of all the essential features of the present situation. The undertaking by the developed countries to respect the standstill commitment regarding import restrictions in respect of the less developed countries has been repeatedly reaffirmed. Nevertheless, that commitment has been ignored on a number of separate occasions, to the consequent detriment of the exporting countries.

Trade restrictions relating to basic commodities, the continuation of subsidies and other forms of agricultural protectionism, the exclusion of agricultural products by means of measures applied by regional groupings, tariff differentials which impede the entry of finished products, the application of quotas; the use of escape clauses and international agreements for the unilateral limitation of trade in certain products, are further devices which, while clearly militating against the rational international division of labour, reduce the export potential of the developing countries and, consequently, their ability to stimulate employment. There can be no justification for such arrangements in relations with the developing countries whose economies so clearly require revitalization in the common interest of the international community. Nor is it a legitimate practice for certain industrialized nations to obtain preferential treatment from certain developing countries in exchange for advantages which they grant to such countries in their own internal markets. Such practices belong to a bygone era. The general system of preferences not only offers a means of promoting the exports of the developing countries, it is also a mechanism which could end the situation described.

Trade problems and the related solutions have been studied intensively at the technical and intergovernmental level. Similarly, rules which would substantially improve the trade position of the developing countries have been in existence for some time and the international community's support of them has been expressed in many forums. Only the most important thing remains to be done, namely, to apply the principles that have been proclaimed.

External assistance, consisting of financing, technical assistance and the transfer of technology, has an important contribution to make to the reduction of unemployment because it provides the financing to complement internal efforts and the means of training manpower. Yet the debts which the developing countries have accumulated on this score have come to represent a heavy burden which is absorbing more and more of the resources that should be devoted to economic development.

Consequently, a new and critical study of the total debt already accumulated and of that resulting from future assistance, together with the conditions applicable to each, should be carried out with a view to adjusting their terms to reconcile two factors: the fulfilment of the commitments assumed and the compelling need to promote economic development by devoting to it an increasing flow of external assistance and internal savings.

It is essential that the action of the developing countries at the international level be better organized, to provide them with the means of making better use of their human and material resources. This could be done in various ways (for example by the adoption of joint policies to strengthen the position of individual primary commodities on the world market, trade preferences, special arrangements for trade promotion, or different types of integration).

The questions of trade and external assistance cannot be divorced from the present acceleration of progress in all spheres at the world level. The legitimate desire of all peoples to improve their living standards calls for new criteria. To the extent that certain commercial and financial practices continue to impede men's efforts to achieve a fuller life through work and production, increasingly vigorous opposition will result and help to produce an atmosphere of frustration and discontent, to the detriment of the development targets established by the international community.

Thanks to economic planning to improve the integration of the world economy and the mobility of manpower, a new pattern for the international division of labour will emerge through trade and external assistance. The intergovernmental machinery for such an undertaking, whose potential contribution to world peace none can deny, is already in place. What is now needed is tangible evidence of the political will to effect changes leading, by a series of sometimes difficult adjustments, to the more rational distribution of activities among the world's peoples and thus to a better utilization of world resources and the ultimate achievement of higher levels of prosperity for all mankind.

NOTES

[1]See World Economic Survey, 1969-1970 (United Nations publication, Sales No. E.71.II.C.1), p. 17.

[2]Proceedings of the United Nations Conference on Trade and Development, Second Session. Volume I: Report and Annexes (United Nations publication, Sales No. E.68.II.D. 14), p. 38.

[3]Among the recipients of this assistance are included some countries of Europe which are normally excluded from the classification "developing countries" in United Nations reports.

Industrial Expansion in Developing Countries and Implications for Trade Policies

JAGDISH N. BHAGWATI

I. INTRODUCTION

The need to keep the markets for manufactures in the developed countries open, in consonance with the spirit of the liberal international economic order underlying the establishment of GATT, is clear today in the developing countries, even though their demands for commodity schemes to regulate international markets for primary products seem to point towards a less liberal international economic order. The reasons for this perception of the importance of open markets in developed countries are essentially threefold.

First, it is widely understood that the process of industrialization cannot be sustained in many developing countries over a very long period by counting on domestic markets alone. Thus the process of import substitution has to give way, at one stage or another, to an outward orientation which permits external markets to sustain industrialization on an ongoing basis.

Secondly, there is a growing awareness that the process of industrialization is both more effective and more efficient with export-promotion rather than import-substituting policies. For "primitive" agricultural and extractive economies, it is admittedly true that the choice between export promotion and import substitution implies, in turn, a choice between specialization in primary products and industrialization. This, however, is no longer the case once industrialization has been initiated, and the question then becomes one of whether the system of foreign trade will bias the industrial sector towards the home market (as in the case of over-valued exchange rates), or whether it will eliminate this bias and restore parity of incentives for the export markets.

From **INDUSTRY AND DEVELOPMENT**, No. 3, 1979 (45-53), reprinted by permission of the publisher.

Under the latter policies, a number of empirical studies now suggest that export, and hence economic, performance is superior, and that industrialization can therefore proceed very rapidly.[1]

Finally, the increased involvement of developing countries in the international capital markets during the 1970s, and the clear need for continuing success in export performance, so as to ensure debt servicing, and for the maintenance of confidence, so as to achieve growing capital inflows, only underline the necessity of an open international economy.[2]

While this paper will focus primarily on the issues raised by the desirability of keeping markets in developed countries open to manufactures of the developing countries, the above-mentioned points also give rise to the following considerations:

(a) Highly successful developing countries, such as Brazil and the Republic of Korea cannot expect to have their markets closed to the manufactured exports of either developed or developing countries. The less developed among the developing countries can properly look upon the most prosperous as virtually developed countries with identical obligations to sustain an open trading system. Similarly, Governments of developed countries that have been absorbing increased developing country exports primarily from the most successful developing countries[3] are under pressure at home, especially from the unions, to seek reciprocal guarantees that the markets of those countries will also be kept open to imports. Therefore, just as the successful developing countries have emulated Japan as well in their export-promoting industrialization, so they will be under the same pressure as Japan to accept their emergence as developed or quasi-developed countries with corresponding obligations;

(b) The importance of trade liberalization among the developing countries, emphasized since the 1950s by eminent economists of various schools of thought but hampered by the generally restrictive trade policies of most of the developing countries, is only further strengthened by the reasons outlined above for an open economy;

(c) Finally, the increasing participation of the centrally planned countries of Eastern Europe in the trade, credit and technology markets of the North (i.e. the developed countries) has implications that are both competitive, hence probably detrimental to developing countries (for example, developing countries and socialist countries of Eastern Europe would bid for the same pool of internationally investible funds), and complementary, hence beneficial. From the latter point of view, still relatively unexplored, joint North-East manufacturing ventures in the South might be considered with the North and East supplying finance and technology, and with export agreements with the countries of the East in accordance with their established practices.[4]

II. ACCESS OF MANUFACTURES TO THE MARKETS OF DEVELOPED COUNTRIES

The question of maintaining assured access to the markets of developed countries has taken on particular urgency with the recent upsurge of protectionist pressures. There is some room for debate whether this upsurge is temporary or of long-term duration. The case for assuming that it may disappear with the restoration of fuller employment rests on the observation that, in the United States at least, the timing of these pressures coincided with a significant rise in unemployment during the 1971-1972 period, when the Burke-Hartke bill, with its remarkable ambition to put a crawling ceiling on all categories of imports, made considerable headway in the United States Congress. On the other hand, the same empirical observation may be used to show that the problem of protectionism is of a long-term nature. It would be indeed unrealistic to expect the problem of stagflation to be solved, at either the theoretical or the policy level, in the near future.

In fact, there are two other arguments that tend to reinforce the conclusion that protectionism is likely to endure as an important political force in developed countries. First, the available evidence suggests that the growth in imports from developing countries into the United States has hardly meant an absolute decline in the output levels of competing domestic industries. Thus, the case for serious injury, in accordance with GATT regulations, hardly exists for the industries that have been demanding protection. It seems as if the problem with low-wage or labour-intensive industries such as textiles, leather products etc. is simply that of secular decline in their employment levels as a reflection of rising wages, capital accumulation and possibly technical change. Complaints about imports therefore consist largely in externalizing rather difficult, secular adjustment problems of industries whose decline is due to factors extraneous to imports. But if this be the case, then protectionist demands are likely to continue, since problems of secular decline are endemic to growing societies. Secondly, as Erik Lundberg of the Swedish Academy of Science has noted in the case of Sweden, demands on the State have tended to multiply outside the United States to the point where the flexibility of hiring and dismissal that substantially open economies need in order to make trade adjustments may no longer be readily available; unions seem to act at times as if on-the-job security is part of the obligations that the modern welfare state must bear towards it citizens.

It is of great importance to the developing countries that the protectionist threats fail, and that the basic framework of a liberal, open international economic order remains intact, thus enabling them to benefit by an expanding world economy without real or threatened trade barriers. In this connection, in recent international discussions basically two alternative approaches have been proposed for the restructuring of the existing GATT framework (as defined by article XIX), and for dealing with matters such as voluntary export restraints (VERs) and the Long-Term Agreement on Textiles, which have been repeatedly applied outside the current framework, and which must therefore, together with article XIX, be viewed as part of the existing order (or disorder) with regard to the access of manufactures of developing countries to the markets of developed countries.⁵

Orderly Marketing Arrangements or Organized Free Trade

One approach favoured by government spokesmen of a number of developed countries and by some writers on the subject, would consist in following the example of the Long-Term Agreement on Textiles and carving up the world trading system into "orderly" markets, with controlled access by developing countries to the markets of developed countries. Such a "system" is a misguided planners' dream. It is noteworthy that the textiles agreement has served to impose very effective entry restrictions on LDCs, while failing to place any restraints on the growth of the import-competing industry in developed countries, thus providing the best available evidence for rejecting such an approach if the interests of both the LDCs and a liberal international order are kept in view.

There is much to be said in favour of an approach that starts from the assumption that trade ought to be allowed to expand in its typically unpredictable manner, without the interference of bureaucrats and politicians, who, unable to foresee the areas in which, and the extent to which, beneficial trade will expand and contract, would tend to encourage selfish bargaining and constraints on trade that would reduce the prospects for rapid expansion of developing country exports. An instructive exercise for spokesmen of developing countries who feel inclined to accept suggestions by developed countries for such a shift in the world trading system would be to calculate the decline that would have occurred in their manufactured exports if the rates of expansion of quotas provided for in the textile agreement had been applicable to all other developing country exports in Standard International Trade Classification (SITC) categories 6 to 9.

Revision of GATT

A far sounder approach would therefore consist in modifying the GATT framework in such a way as to reflect current developments while preserving the original notion that trading rules constitute an order, and that a fair and consistent framework for restricting the use of trade barriers is necessary to enable governments to stand up to special interests calling for protectionism (or, in its euphemistic version, "organized free trade").

The Bhagwati Proposal

An approach along the above-mentioned lines, which takes into account the growing tendency of developed countries to bypass article XIX of GATT has been proposed by this author. The rationale for the specific elements of this proposal is as follows. The threat of protectionists restrictions being applied by importing countries on the grounds of market disruption clearly implies a welfare loss for the exporting countries. The economic welfare of the exporting country will be less than if there were no such threat. If the exporting country reacts in turn by the adoption of optimal policy measures designed to restrict exports and to reduce the likelihood of recourse to VERs or similar constraints related to market disruption, then the welfare loss from the threat of restrictions will be less than if the exporting country took no such action, but there will still be a loss. Moreover, if investment allocations, once introduced, cannot be readjusted without costs, then the presence of adjustment costs will further increase the welfare loss from the threat of trade restraints. Finally, the actual application of trade restraints would inflict a welfare loss on the exporting country in excess of the expected loss from the threat of such restraints at a future date.

From the general theoretical principles outlined above, certain compensatory arrangements would seem to follow. First, there is a case for asking importing developed countries to compensate exporting developing countries faced with threats of trade restraints related to market disruption. The developed countries can reasonably be asked to "buy", by means of compensation payments, the right to demand, for a given product, the application of trade restraints related to market disruption, and to forgo the right to resort to trade restraints on all products not covered by such payments. Thus a list of "restrainable" items can be prepared under multilateral auspices such as GATT, and the inclusion of an item in the list would require compensation payment for threatened exporters incurring corresponding welfare losses. In addition, the actual application of such restraints, by imposing a greater loss, would require further compensation to the adversely affected exporters.

Compensation for potential and actual losses incurred by exporting countries as a result of trade restraints related to market disruption would therefore be the logical outcome of this analysis. The rules governing the compensation process and their implications with regard to the modification of article XIX of GATT and related provisions need to be developed in greater depth. These rules may be defined in a number of ways.

(a) Penalty or compensation for potential restrictions. For the reasons stated above, a list of "items potentially subject to trade restrictions related to market disruption" should be maintained. This list may be described as the list of potentially restrainable items.[6] In order to include an item in the list, the developed countries would be required to pay a "penalty" that could be used to compensate exporting countries subject to welfare loss as a result of the threat of trade restraints on the item;

(b) -- <u>Penalty or compensation for the actual application of trade restraints on potentially restrainable items.</u> As and when trade restraints are actually applied, there should be a further penalty payment for the compensation of exporting countries whose export market interests are prejudiced as a result of the restraints. The penalty so imposed, if it is to reflect the compensation due to the exporting countries, must be less than the actual cost of the trade restraints, taking into account the adjusted sum originally paid for putting the product on the list of potentially restrainable items;

(c) -- <u>Escape clause applicable to the list of potentially restrainable items.</u> While the two preceding rules should, in principle, divide all items into those that are restrainable and those that are not, this is politically unfeasible. There will almost certainly be cases in which unforeseen and politically unmanageable difficulties arise concerning products not already included in the list of potentially restrainable items, and the importing developed country will be unable to avoid responding to political pressures for trade restraints.

An escape clause applicable to items not included in the list would therefore be appropriate. At the same time, since the escape clause should not provide an incentive to avoid the option of including such items in the list of potentially restrainable items, it would be equally appropriate to make the invoking of the clause both more difficult and more costly. Thus, the escape clause should require that the importing developed country be allowed none the less to resort to trade restraints on products not on the list of potentially restrainable items, provided that, on the one hand, it makes a demonstrable case, under multilateral (GATT) auspices, of the existence of serious injury (as under the current provisions of article XIX of GATT), and that, on the other hand, it then makes a considerably larger penalty payment for the compensation of the exporting countries. It would also be necessary in practice to keep a product on the list of restrainable items for a substantial amount of time before permitting recourse to trade restraints in relation to that product. Otherwise, if a period of only a few weeks or months were required, it would be to a country's advantage to wait until the period elapses rather than invoke the proposed escape clause, which involves higher penalties;

(d) -- <u>Automaticity of compensation.</u> The penalty or compensation would be automatic under the preceding rules, rather than representing a mere possibility as is currently the case under article XIX of GATT. This would rule out the use of political pressure to avoid this obligation when resorting to trade restraints;

(e) -- <u>Financial form of compensation.</u> The above rules require financial compensation, in contrast, for example, to the type of compensation currently provided for under article XIX, which takes the form of either the granting of a new tariff concession (on another product) or the withdrawal of a tariff concession by the exporting country. The latter method reflects the tariff-bargaining framework in which GATT rules are enmeshed.

It is basically unsound, since permitting an exporter to raise
retaliatory tariffs as a form of compensation presupposes that such
tariffs are advantageous, whereas in fact they are likely to cause
even more damage through further restraints on trade, and to
disrupt yet another market in seeking redress for the original
market disruption.   The financial form of penalty or compensation
provided for in the rules suggested above is free from these
obvious defects;
    (f) -- Compensation to exporting country.   The preceding
compensation rules may be applied solely to exporting developing
countries, which are the main countries (with the exception of
Japan) to have been seriously affected by the restrictions on
textiles and by VERs.[7] There is in fact a greater willingness, in
the context of the new international economic order, to make
reasonable adjustments on behalf of developing countries through
the framing of new trade regulations.   The financial flows thus
generated are likely to be of far greater significance to
developing countries than to developed countries, taking into
account their respective needs.
    The foregoing set of rules, essentially involving the
compensation of exporting developing countries by importing
developed countries, are not entirely novel in their reference to
the potential use of trade restraints, since the well-established
practice of the binding of tariffs implies waiving the potential
use of restrictions.   With regard to the notion of compensation
itself, there appear to be no obvious precedents.   However, a
partial precedent, which suggests that the preceding proposals are
entirely feasible, concerns the payment by the United States of a
substantial sum of compensation to the Government of Turkey for the
enforcement of the ban on poppy production.   The use of this money
to compensate Turkish farmers would in theory have made it
possible for them to shift to another type of cultivation at no
financial loss.
    In this context, note should be taken of a recent proposal of
Hans Singer for compensatory cash payments to be made by developed
to developing countries for loss of markets arising from unilateral
imposition of trade barriers.   He argues that "developed country
compensation is due to damaged developing country producers."[8]
Interestingly, the Nobel Laureate Jan Tinbergen, in 1962, had also
briefly suggested the desirability of financial compensation to
exporters faced with tariff changes arising from the establishment
of the European Economic Community (EEC).[9]

Preferred Mix of GATT and Developed Country Policy Changes

    The author would prefer a comprehensive change in article XIX
of GATT on firm theoretical foundations, in keeping with GATT's
original philosophy of maintaining open markets, along the lines of
the proposal presented earlier in this paper.[10]
    At the same time, it should be noted that the proposed rules

would be considerably strengthened through the implementation by developed countries of the following two policies, any of which is being gradually extended in scope.

(a) -- To the extent that the response to foreign imports, or to domestic decline due to other reasons, consists in providing domestic adjustment assistance to enable factors of production to retrain and relocate, the need to resort to trade restraints will be correspondingly reduced by making the pressures from the industry for such restraints both less intense and politically less difficult to resist;

(b) -- Elementary principles clearly show that trade restraint, as a means of sustaining the production level of domestic industry, is inferior to the use of a production subsidy, from the standpoint of the importing developed country itself.[11] It is equally obvious that the use of a production subsidy will expand the overall market for the imported item in the developed country, while a tariff, by increasing the consumer price, will reduce it. Therefore, since domestic production must be maintained at a suitable level, the use of a production subsidy by the importing developed country would be preferable, from the standpoint of the exporting developing country, to trade restraints.[12] Thus it would be useful if the overall reform in the field of trade restraints related to market disruption were to include a multilateral agreement by developed countries to use production subsidies rather than tariffs or trade quotas, whenever trade restraints are invoked under the rules specified above. The exceptions to this code could include emergency situations in which an immediate trade quota may be necessary, in which case the quota could be phased out and gradually replaced by a production subsidy on a multilaterally agreed schedule.

III. CONCLUSIONS

An alternative view that requires consideration is that the threat of protectionism is so serious, and the executive authorities' political ability to resist it so strained, that it is best to leave things as they are. Kenneth Dam, the United States lawyer, forcefully advocates this view, contending that recent attempts to change trade rules in the United States have led to an erosion of the principle of free trade. This view would seem to be reinforced from another source. Jan Tumlir of GATT has often spoken recently of the threatened breakdown of the liberal trading order, drawing attention to the numerous attempts at imposing VERs, the firm position adopted by the EEC on renegotiation of the textiles agreement, and the general attitude of spokesmen of developed countries in trade negotiations, who seem to proceed on the assumption that access to the markets of developed countries must be treated by LDCs as a privilege to be negotiated, whereas membership of GATT implies that this is not a privilege, but a right.

If indeed the situation is so fragile, one may well wonder whether, from the vantage-point of the twenty-first century, the post-war period will be seen as a short-lived experiment in restoring free trade in commodities, and whether trade in commodities will have come to be accepted as an area subject to strict regulation by governments through international negotiations and the resulting quotas or price barriers. Viewed from a historical perspective, this possibility cannot be altogether dismissed. Immigration restrictions, for example, are today taken for granted, with human-rights advocates showing a curious absence of any pangs of conscience over the implied loss of the right to live where one chooses. One wonders how many people realize that immigration restrictions are of twentieth-century origin, and that in the nineteenth century great world-wide migrations took place without passports or immigration quotas.

This author is not particularly alarmed by such a prospect materializing in the field of commodity trade. The viewpoint represented by Kenneth Dam and Jan Tumlir seems very pessimistic even as a short-term possibility, and negotiated changes leading to a system incorporating some of the proposals contained in this paper should not be ruled out altogether. The North-South negotiations will be an unspectacular, ongoing process, from which constructive reform will emerge, as always, by means of slow evolutionary change.

NOTES

[1]Among the studies pointing to this conclusion are Bhagwati [1] and Krueger [2], based on a United States National Bureau of Economic Research project on foreign trade regimes and economic development.

[2]On the debts of the developing countries, the annual reports of the World Bank are a good source of information. A useful analysis of their distribution among developing countries and the mix of official and private borrowings defining the debt as of the mid-1970s, with estimates of aid that would be implied by debt write-offs on different conditions, is in Peter Kenen [3].

[3]Thus, between 1965 and 1975, according to estimates made at the World Bank by D. Keesing and associates, the share of East Asian countries in developing country manufactured exports to developed countries rose from 38 to 54 per cent, and that of Latin America (principally Brazil and Mexico) from 14 to 20 per cent. The overall share of developing countries in world manufactured exports, however, appears to have increased from 6.5 per cent in the mid-1960s to around 8.2 per cent in 1973 and 1974.

[4]Such tripartite industrial co-operation was the subject of an
UNCTAD Seminar on Industrial Specialization through Various Forms
of Multilateral Cooperation, Geneva, 2–5 December 1975. See, in
particular, the Chairman's assessment, which forms an annex to
the report of the Seminar, with the present author's synthesis of
the deliberations on the tripartite industrial co-operation
projects. Desai [4], Guy de Lacharriere [5], Thierry de
Montbrial [6] and Berman [7].

[5]For details concerning VERs, the agreement on textiles, etc., see
Bhagwati [8]. A briefer version, omitting some of the relevant
tabular information, appears in Bhagwati [9].

[6]A parallel to this recommendation may be found in the practice of
"binding" tariffs in advance.

[7]VERs have affected Japan seriously. In some cases, such as that
of steel VERs in the United States, the impact was felt
by developed country exporters, and imports were initially
diverted to developing countries, which thereby benefited.

[8]The Singer proposal and that put forward by the present author,
although similar, are different in theoretical approach. For
example, whereas the author's proposal provides a theoretical
basis for paying compensation to Governments of developing
countries, the former proposal suggests that the compensation is
to be paid because Governments of developing countries may have a
fiscal constraint on paying adjustment assistance to developing
country producers. See Joekes, Kaplan and Singer [10].

[9]See Tinbergen [11], which however contains no detailed
theoretical basis for the proposal.

[10]The mechanics of changing article XIX to incorporate the contents
of the Bhagwati proposal have been outlined in Bhagwati [8].

[11]This is one of the important policy prescriptions from the theory
of optimal policy intervention in the presence of non-economic
objectives, arising from the fact that the tariff imposes a
consumption cost by raising prices for consumers, which would be
avoided by a production subsidy, while equally protecting
domestic output. See Bhagwati and Srinivasan [12].

[12]This conclusion would have to be modified, but is not altogether
nullified, if the domestic industry wishes to maintain a certain
share of sales in the domestic market. The optimal policy
intervention in this case, from the developed country's
viewpoint, would be the combination of an import tariff and a
production subsidy.

REFERENCES

1. J. Bhagwati, The Anatomy and Consequences of Exchange Control
    Regimes (Cambridge, Ballinger Publishing Co., 1978).

2. A. O. Krueger, Liberalization Attempts and Consequences
    (Cambridge, Ballinger Publishing Co., 1978).

3. Peter Kenen, "Debt relief as development assistance", in The
    New International Economic Order: The North-South Debate
    (Cambridge, Mass., MIT Press, 1977).

4. Padma Desai, "The transfer of technology to developing
    countries in the framework of tripartite industrial
    cooperation" (TAD/SEM.1.S).

5. Guy de Lacharriere, "The role of East-West cooperation in the
    development of Tripartite Cooperation" (TAD/SEM.1/16).

6. Thierry de Montbrial, "Future prospects for tripartite
    industrial cooperation" (TAD/SEM.1/14).

7. Harold J. Berman, "The legal framework for tripartite
    industrial cooperation" (TAD/SEM.1/3).

8. J. Bhagwati, "Market disruption, export market disruption,
    compensation and GATT reform", World Development, December
    1976.

9. J. Bhagwati, ed., The New International Economic Order: The
    North-South Debate (Cambridge, Mass., MIT Press, 1977).

10. S. Joekes, D. Kaplan and H. W. Singer, "Transformation
    assistance from developed countries to developing
    countries -- an aid to trade expansion", Institute of
    Development Studies Discussion Paper No. 110 (Brighton,
    University of Sussex, April 1977).

11. J. Tinbergen, Shaping the World Economy: Suggestions for an
    International Policy (New York, 20th Century Fund, 1962).

12. J. Bhagwati and T. N. Srinivasan, "Optimal intervention to
    achieve non-economic objectives", Review of Economic Studies,
    January 1969.

Intra-industry Trade and the Expansion, Diversification and Integration of the Trade of the Developing Countries

SAMUEL LAIRD

While intra-industry trade has been mainly noted as a particularity of trade among developed countries, it is also relevant for the expansion of trade among developing countries and for expansion of North-South trade. Intra-industry trade is explained; the results of various studies are examined; and new data show the levels of intra-industry trade among regional economic groupings of countries and for individual selected countries at different stages of development. With some reservations concerning the retained value of the export growth and the distribution of benefits, the effects of expanded intra-industry trade are generally found to be beneficial for both developed and developing countries. In respect of North-South trade it is shown that, as developing countries become more industrialized, their trade with the developed countries is likely to be based on intra-industry specialization, with production and trade being rationalized at the process level, and that whole industries are unlikely to be redeployed to the newly industrializing countries. The tendency towards greater intra-industry specializaton on a North-South basis is also likely to be associated with lower adjustment costs in the North than had been anticipated on the basis of traditional explanations of trade. Country studies and micro-economic studies will be needed to achieve a better understanding of the rationale for and the effects of increased intra-industry trade so that comprehensive and consistent policies can be formulated for its promotion, ensuring the equitable distribution of the benefits and avoiding potential pitfalls.

From **TRADE AND DEVELOPMENT** , UNCTAD Review, No. 3, Winter 1981 (79-101), reprinted by permission of the publisher.

I. INTRODUCTION

The present economic difficulties of the developed countries of the North and the prospects for long-term growth at lower rates than in the past have disposed of notions that economic development in the South can take place as a "spin-off" from economic activity in the North. The lower long-term growth rate and the probable continuation of protectionist pressures as a consequence are likely to work against a "trickle down" of economic growth of the magnitude needed to make a significant impact on economic development in the South. Yet at a time of reduced foreign aid, of growing external indebtedness in the South, and an actual deterioration in the position of the poorer countries, the need for the expansion of international trade is greater than ever.

The basic policy response of the developing countries has been to mount a determined campaign in international forums arguing that the reopening of trade opportunities in the North for the products of export interest to the developing countries through the restructuring of the economies of the developed market-economy countries (DMECs) in particular would be in the mutual interest of both North and South. It has also been pointed out that since the onset of the present economic climate in the DMECs the situation would have been far worse had it not been for the continued rapid growth of trade with the developing countries. While putting forward these "mutual interest" arguments the developing countries have also been looking at other possibilities, in particular co-operation in the South itself, to sustain the momentum of their development.

Both strategies adopted by the developing countries face difficulties. With respect to the protectionist attitudes of the DMECs, particularly vis-a-vis those developing countries which have managed to make some progress through the exports of manufactures, there seems little prospect at the moment of any early reversal of the current trends towards increasing protectionism. With respect to the prospects for greater co-operation within the South, doubts have been expressed about the prospects for the continued growth of trade among developing countries which is at present confined to relatively few of these countries.[1] More seriously, doubts have also been expressed about the usefulness of such trade for the developing countries because of the capital-intensity and import-intensity of such products.[2] To these doubts might also be added concern about the distribution of benefits because of the important role of transnational corporations (TNCs) in such trade.

In respect of both North-South trade and South-South trade on the doubts and concerns about future developments are based in large measure on extrapolations of what has happened in the past. Furthermore, conventional trade theory (i.e. the Heckscher-Ohlin-Samuelson type factor proportions theory) does little to ally these fears. Even the argument that if developing countries gained absolute advantage in all industries they would not have comparative advantage in every sector and North-South exchange could still take place to the mutual benefit of both does little to dispel fears about the time and costs of adjustment in moving towards some long-term optimum. Besides, it is still conceivable that whole industries could be threatened by the appearance of more competitive industries in the developing countries. The same comment applies to Vernon's product cycle or technology-gap theory,[3] which suggests that developing countries gain comparative advantage in the manufacture of new products as the techniques for their production become standardized, while developed countries retain comparative advantage in the manufacture of products embodying new technology. Neither have these theories been particularly useful in predicting how North-South trade would develop, and they are curiously silent about the prospects of trade within the South.

Because these theories are inadequate to explain actual trade patterns, trade economists are increasingly studying the implications of the phenomenon and the underlying theory of intra-industry trade--trade within rather than between industrial sectors. While the phenomenon of intra-industry trade has been recognized for some time,[4] it has mainly received attention by academic economists as a key element in the rapid growth of internal European trade in manufactures.[5] However, recently quite high levels of intra-industry trade have been noted in some economic groupings of developing countries.[6] It has also been shown that one form of intra-industry trade--complementary intra-industry trade--may contribute to the expansion of two-way trade in manufactures between developed and developing countries.[7] New material presented in this article supports earlier findings in relation to intra-industry trade, including associated benefits. It is, for example, suggested that the costs of structural adjustment would be less if a policy of intra-industry specialization were pursued by the developed countries.

Prior to this recent work it had been assumed that the phenomenon of intra-industry trade did not have much bearing on trade between developed and developing countries. Such trade had been assumed to follow the traditional model of inter-sectoral exchanges, such as the exchange of raw materials or agricultural commodities for industrial goods, or of capital equipment for labour-intensive textiles, clothing or footwear. Indeed, for the majority of the developing countries which do not possess a broad industrial base this is probably an accurate description of the interaction of the stage of development and trade. For such countries, the potential for an increased exchange of differentiated products with the developed countries--horizontal intra-industry trade--is less than the potential which exists between developed countries.

However, while it appears to remain true that a larger proportion of the trade between developed and developing countries is of an inter-sectoral nature than in the case of trade between developed countries, this situation is changing in specific cases, reflecting the progressive industrialization of many developing countries. Particularly in the case of those developing countries which have successfully adopted export-oriented industrialization strategies, there is an increasing amount of intra-industry trade between them and developed countries in manufactured and semi-manufactured goods. At present such trade is mainly complementary or vertical, i.e. the exchange of products of adjacent stages of production, but its quantitative significance, its rapid growth, the range of traded products and its potential to be influenced by policy action suggest that, subject to some reservations, it could be an important means of expanding and diversifying exports of manufactures from developing countries in a manner which creates fewer structural pressures on the industries of the developed countries. It may provide new opportunities for expanded trade in complementary products of the same industries. Such an approach could be used to promote export-oriented industrialization by more developing countries, especially the less developed ones where the relatively low labour-costs should provide a basis for initial specialization in complementary labour-intensive processes.

In the past the expansion of intra-industry trade has been associated with specific policy measures and with the formation of regional trading agreements, in the South as well as in the North. Thus, both in respect of North-South trade and intra-area trade, intra-industry trade appears to be capable of being positively influenced by government actions. However, it is not completely clear to what extent or in what manner this trade has been influenced by these policies, nor how the benefits have been distributed. In this regard the article describes the kind of additional information that is required, and further areas to be explored. This material is essential for fleshing out the details of overall trade strategies and specific policy initiatives that would further the expansion of intra-industry trade, while promoting an equitable distribution of the benefits and avoiding some of the potential pitfalls.

II. THE CONCEPT AND MEASUREMENT OF INTRA-INDUSTRY TRADE

Intra-industry trade is the contemporaneous import and export of the products of the same "industry". The corresponding international distribution of the industry or the international rationalization of the production processes of the same industry is described as intra-industry specialization. Intra-industry trade is sometimes called intra-branch trade or intra-sectoral trade, with the virtually identical connotation of simultaneous trade in the products of a particular branch of industry or industrial sector. Intra-product trade is a convenient short-hand expression describing the international exchange of identical products. By contrast, the expression "inter-industry trade" describes the trade of a country, specializing in certain industries or industrial sectors, which exports the products of those industries or sectors and imports the products of other industries or sectors.

Statistically, intra-industry trade may be defined[8] as the value of exports of an industry in one country which is exactly matched by that of the imports of the same industry; in other words, it is the value of the total trade (exports plus imports) of an industry less the absolute difference between the exports and the imports of that industry. It can be expressed as a percentage of the total trade of an industry, yielding the intra-industry trade ratio.[9] When the value of exports of an industry is exactly equal to the value of its imports, the intra-industry trade ratio is 1:1 (100 per cent). When there are exports but not imports, or vice-versa, intra-industry trade is zero. However, when the value of exports is equal to one-half of the value of the imports, or vice-versa, intra-industry trade would be measured at 2-1 (66.6 per cent). Intra-industry trade may be measured for a single industry (at different levels of aggregation) of a single country vis-a-vis that country's trade with a single trading partner, a group or groups of trading partners or the rest of the world. It may then be averaged across groups of industries and/or countries, again vis-a-vis a single trading partner, a group on groups of trading partners or the whole world.

The major economic unit in intra-industry trade is the "industry". An industry's production may be carried out in one or more "plants" or "establishments". Within these production units one or more "processes" may be carried out.[10] Since in most industries, certainly in manufacturing industries, plants generally carry out more than one process, there is often scope for a variety of configurations of production, involving different degrees of vertical integration and employing different technologies. Also, plants within an industry may complement or supplement each other's production in different degrees, adding to the complexity of the make-up of an industry. Thus, an industry's output may comprise homogeneous products, more or less differentiated products or products of vertically adjacent stages of production. It is also possible that single plants in one industry produce, perhaps as a sideline or as joint products, goods which are predominantly made in another industry. However, production statistics relating to an industry, as normally collected, conform to the classification of plants or establishments within an industry according to their predominant activity. There is, therefore, at a certain level of aggregation, a strong but not perfect correlation between commodity statistics, relating to production or trade, and industry statistics, which relate to activities of plants. In fact, it has been found that at the 3 or 4 digit level of the Standard International Trade Classification (SITC) there is a very strong relationship with the International Standard Industrial Classification (ISIC), and this corresponds reasonably to the normal notion of an industry.

This point is made at some length because there is a commonly held notion that, since the amount of intra-industry trade tends to decline as statistical data are increasingly disaggregated, the very idea is rather elusive. However, to the extent to which the concept of an "industry" is valid, intra-industry trade is not merely a statistical curiosity. In any case, it should be noted that, although there is a tendency for intra-industry trade ratios to diminish at lower levels of aggregation (sub-industries or products), in a number of cases the ratios are maintained at a high level down to the narrowest product statistics (i.e. exports and imports of homogeneous or slightly differentiated products).

Regarding the kind of products involved in intra-industry trade, Grubel and Lloyd have identified the following categories:

(a) Homogeneous commodities included in border trade, entrepot trade, seasonal trade, etc.;

(b) Heterogeneous or differentiated commodities which are close substitutes in production, consumption or both; and

(c) Heterogeneous commodities of vertically adjacent or complementary stages or processes of production in the same industrial sector.

In category (a), completely homogeneous goods, a certain amount of intra-industry trade has always taken place with little comment. Most of this can be explained by relaxing the assumptions (e.g. zero transport costs) of the Heckscher-Ohlin theory, i.e. the trade is not explained by the theory but such trade does not weaken the theory because of the assumptions, however unrealistic, which are incorporated. Some examples of classes of trade in homogeneous goods are transactions in:

(i) Bulky or perishable goods for which transport costs may be so high that it is more rational to carry on cross-border trade rather than ship them from a more distant part of the same country (e.g. sand, bricks, cement, fresh dairy products, eggs, etc.);

(ii) Goods which are produced or consumed in different countries at different times, e.g. seasonally produced fruit and vegetables, electricity consumed at different peak periods because of time zone differences, or which are exported under a contractual commitment while domestic production suffers from a shortfall because of lumpy investments.

(iii) Goods which are merely repackaged in an entrepot trade; and

(iv) Goods subject to price distorsions because of tax and/or subsidy arrangements, or due to intervention by governmental or other agencies.

With respect to category (b), heterogeneous or differentiated goods, there could be:

(i) Commodities which have different input requirements but have high elasticities of substitution in consumption;

(ii) Commodities which have similar input requirements but which have different end uses; and

(iii) Commodities which have similar inputs and have similar end uses.

Examples of group (i) might be: furniture made from different materials, such as steel, plastic, timber or cane; textile yarns made from natural or manmade fibres; footwear made of leather, synthetic materials or fabrics; and so on. In these cases, comparative advantage in the production of the inputs (stemming, for example, from the ready availability of natural resources) can explain why countries can be found exchanging processed products within this group.

As to group (ii), there are a number of industries which transform identical inputs into a range of outputs with quite different end uses. For example, the petroleum products industry can produce gasoline or tar, the basic iron and steel industry might produce railway sleepers or heavy plate for shipbuilding. The clothing industry might produce skirts or kilts--although only a Scotsman or a Greek might appreciate the difference! While some of these might be produced as joint products, this is often not possible once production has been adjusted to a certain product mix, or where the cost of change-over to alternative outputs is very high. Thus, intra-industry trade in these commodities is an important exception to traditional trade, but is one in which the main assumptions appear to hold.[11]

Group (iii), similar products produced by similar processes from similar materials, presents the most important challenge to the traditional factor-proportions theories of international trade. To give an example, it would scarcely be plausible to argue that France has a comparative advantage in producing Renault cars, while the Federal Republic of Germany has a comparative advantage in Volkswagens. Other examples of such industries listed by Grubel and Lloyd include processed foods, beverages (alcoholic and non-alcoholic), textiles, clothing, shoes, cars, motor-cycles, bicycles, furniture, tobacco products, appliances, hand-tools, aeroplanes, boats; producer goods such as presses, drills, lathes, cutting-tools, electronic and mechanical data-processing equipment, communications equipment and chemical-processing plants. In most of these industries, evidence of intra-industry trade has been found both within and outside regional trading arrangements, in exchanges between countries at different levels of development and in exchanges between countries with different economic and social systems.

Finally, in category (c), there is another form of intra-industry trade involving the exchange between countries of certain final products of an industry for intermediate products of the same industry, or the exchange of the products of vertically adjacent or complementary stages of production in a multi-stage production process industry, e.g. the importation of copper wire, the export of compressors and the subsequent import of refrigeration equipment.[12] The exchange of finished goods, different parts, components or raw materials used in production may take place as intra-industry trade. This type of exchange is of particular interest in relation to industrial collaboration arrangements, production-sharing, international sub-contracting, off-shore processing, etc. and is relevant to discussions of North-South and East-West trade, as well as to trade within all the major groupings.

The main factors accounting for intra-industry trade in products in category (a) are transport costs, time differentials in production--whether for seasonal reasons or because of lumpy investments--and government-induced distortions. With regard to intra-industry trade in differentiated products--category (b)--the main factor is the existence of economies of scale or specialization. Although the differentiation may require negligible adjustment to the production process, there may be significant savings from specialization arising from uninterrupted production runs, etc., and economies of scale. The basic reasons for the original differentiation may have something to do with the style or characteristics preferred by the main income class in the exporting country.[13] However, government-induced distortions, such as tariffs or subsidies and the existence of natural resource endowments may also be significant, depending on the product. The main factor accounting for complementary intra-industry trade category (c) is that labour cost differentials, associated with the internationally rationalized production processes, are greater than the differentials in labour productivity, but transport considerations, government influences and risk diversification can also be relevant.

Intra-industry trade in the products of categories (a) and (b) is sometimes described as horizontal intra-industry trade, while intra-industry trade in products of category (c) is described as vertical or complementary intra-industry trade.

III. QUANTITATIVE SIGNIFICANCE

Grubel and Lloyd have carried out a review of the results of various studies, including their own. This material, together with the findings of additional studies of East-West trade and trade among groupings of developed and developing countries has been summarized as follows:[14]

   (i)   Both for developed and for developing countries intra-industry trade is growing faster than total trade;

   (ii)   For developed and developing countries which participate in trade groupings, intra-industry trade is growing faster within the groupings than with trading partners outside the groupings;

   (iii) The growth appears to be attributable to trade creation not to trade diversion;

   (iv)   Generally, the higher the degree of industrialization of the trading partners, the higher the level of intra-industry trade;

   (v)   Geographic isolation appears to reduce the potential for the growth of intra-industry trade;

   (vi)   The greater the similarities in the industrial structures of trading partners, the greater the likelihood that their exchanges will take the form of intra-industry trade;[15]

   (vii) Among manufactures, intra-industry trade appears to be growing strongly in the quantitatively important machinery and transport sector.

These findings are generally confirmed by the preliminary results of an extensive review of the trade patterns, covering some 150 groups of manufactures. The review so far covers only manufactures (SITC 5-8), measured at the 3-digit level of the SITC. Results are shown for (i) the developed market-economy countries (DMECs) and developing countries (DCs) as a whole (table 1), (ii) a number of regional trade groupings of DMECs and DCs

TABLE 1

Intra-industry trade ratios of developed market economy and developing countries
in respect of their trade in manufactures within their own trade groupings,
and with other trade groupings

(*Percentages*)

A. TRADE OF DEVELOPED MARKET-ECONOMY COUNTRIES

Year	Trade among DMECs	Trade with developing countries	Trade with socialist countries
1965	54.31	11.91	22.18
1970	60.60	15.76	25.34
1975	63.58	17.27	25.12

B. TRADE OF DEVELOPING COUNTRIES

Year	Trade among developing countries	Trade with DMECs	Trade with socialist countries
1965	21.92	5.17	3.17
1970	29.29	7.76	6.98
1975	28.46	9.23	5.21

Source. Calculations based on information provided by the United Nations Statistical Office Computer Tapes, Series D.

TABLE 2

**Intra-industry trade ratios of selected trade groupings
in respect of their trade in manufactures within their own groupings,
with other groupings and with the rest of the world**

Grouping and year	Intra-group [a]	DMEC (excl. group, where applicable) [b]	Developing countries (excl. group, where applicable) [c]	Socialist countries	Rest of world (excl. group) [d]
EEC					
1962	59.7	48.6	10.3	17.6	55.5
1970	70.1	54.7	12.9	28.7	65.7
1977	74.6	65.0	16.2	29.2	70.4
EFTA					
1962	41.2	44.5	7.3	15.2	48.5
1970	55.7	54.4	8.0	22.4	56.8
1979	59.0	57.4	12.8	25.2	61.0
ECOWAS [e]					
1965	29.6	1.5	1.7	0.1	3.0
1970	37.7	2.5	4.1	neg.	6.3
1975	17.2	1.7	2.9	0.2	5.7
LAFTA [f]					
1965	16.0	5.8	13.6	2.9	10.2
1970	27.1	9.3	16.8	1.9	15.6
1975	29.0	9.2	12.5	2.3	19.0
ANDEAN Group					
1965	10.1	1.9	10.0	3.1	4.0
1970	13.8	2.0	15.1	0.6	4.7
1975	18.2	2.2	12.8	1.3	6.8
CACM					
1965	43.1	1.0	8.2	neg.	17.1
1970	53.2	1.7	23.0	neg.	30.6
1974	50.5	2.5	23.9	0.6	29.6
ASEAN [g]					
1968	30.7	3.0	40.6	5.7	16.4
1973	30.9	15.1	46.2	10.1	28.3
1977	49.0	22.2	38.5	13.7	35.9

Source. As for table 1.

[a] Trade within the regional group shown in the first column e.g. intra-EEC trade, intra-EFTA trade, etc.

[b] For the EEC and EFTA this means trade with DMECs which are not in their own individual groupings. For developing countries it means trade with all DMECs.

[c] For the DC regional groupings this means trade with DCs outside their individual regional groupings. For the EEC and EFTA it means trade with all DCs.

[d] Trade with all countries (DMECs, DCs or SCs) outside the individual trade groupings.

[e] Economic Community of West African States. To achieve consistency of coverage, only the trade of Ghana, Nigeria, Ivory Coast, Mali, Niger, Senegal and Upper Volta is included.

[f] Now ALIDA. To achieve consistency of coverage, only the trade of Argentina, Brazil, Colombia, Mexico, Paraguay, Peru and Venezuela is included.

[g] To achieve consistency of coverage, only the trade of Indonesia, Malaysia, the Philippines, Singapore and Thailand is included.

(table 2), (iii) selected individual countries (table 3).[16] Table 4 gives a breakdown of trade in manufactures for the DMECs and DCs as a whole.

With respect to the broad picture shown by table 1, intra-industry trade can generally be seen to be rising faster than inter-industry trade (shown by increasing intra-industry trade ratios). The trade in manufactures among the DMECs was predominantly intra-industry trade (63.58 per cent), while their trade with the developing and socialist countries is predominantly inter-industry. Since most of their trade in manufactures is carried on among themselves--some $588 billion, out of a total of $761 billion in 1975--their overall trade is predominantly intra-industry trade. The trade of the developing countries, however, is predominantly inter-industry, although their trade with each other has a much higher intra-industry component (28.46 per cent) than that of their trade with the DMECs (9.23 per cent) or the socialist countries (5.21 per cent). Out of the total trade of $148 billion of the DCs in 1975, some $119 billion was contributed by trade with the DMECs, and only $20 billion by total trade in manufactures among the DCs themselves.[17]

Table 2 provides a set of intra-industry trade ratios for a number of regional trade groupings with respect to trade in manufactures within the regional grouping concerned, with other broad groups of countries and with the rest of the world taken as a whole. Again, it is confirmed that intra-industry trade is generally increasing faster than inter-industry trade. It is also clear that intra-industry trade is generally markedly higher within regional economic groupings than in the trade of groups with other broad economic groups or the rest of the world as a whole, and higher levels of intra-industry trade are noted within the more industrialised groups. In fact, intra-industry trade can be seen to predominate in the case of the advanced industrialized country groupings, the EEC and EFTA, in their intra-group trade and in trade with other DMECs. Of the developing countries groupings, only the CACM had reached that situation, and only in respect of intra-group trade, by 1976, but ASEAN has probably now reached that stage in respect of intra-group trade.

The higher rate of growth of trade within trade groupings does not appear to have prejudiced trade with other groupings, since there does not appear to be any diminution of the rate of growth of such trade. This would tend to confirm the finding that the growth of intra-industry trade appears to be attributable to trade creation, not to trade diversion, although it is always difficult to speculate what might have happened had the trade groupings not been formed.

There are a few anomalies in table 2, and these cannot be explained by looking at the raw trade data, e.g. the reduction of the already low intra-industry trade ratios of ECOWAS, within and outside the grouping. In a few other cases, there was a decline in intra-industry trade outside the regional groupings, but from the basic trade data it can be ascertained that this decline was not due to any reduction in trade flows or to any decline in the rate of growth of total trade.

Table 3 provides intra-industry trade ratios for selected

TABLE 3

Intra-industry trade ratios of selected countries
in respect of their trade in manufactures with other countries 1962-1975

(Percentages)

Country	Trade with developed market economy countries		Trade with developing countries		Trade with socialist countries		Total trade	
	1962	*1975*	*1962*	*1975*	*1962*	*1975*	*1962*	*1975*
Industrialized countries								
Australia	17.7	18.5	14.0	21.6	12.9	7.7	22.9	29.4
Canada	30.3	57.7	10.6	20.7	5.9	16.9	33.2	60.6
France	68.4	79.0	7.8	12.5	16.0	29.1	65.6	78.2
Germany, Fed. Rep. of . .	55.2	68.2	7.2	14.6	15.9	19.4	48.8	57.5
Italy	52.7	64.8	8.6	11.3	23.7	25.7	57.4	60.9
Ireland	27.4	58.2	9.4	22.1	2.4	16.8	29.4	59.5
Japan	24.4	38.7	4.5	11.2	7.6	15.5	27.2	26.6
New Zealand , ...	8.0	14.0	6.9	21.4	0.2	6.5	8.4	17.2
United States	52.1	63.9	15.0	28.3	13.3	22.8	46.6	62.3
Other selected countries								
Argentina	3.1	8.9	11.3	29.0	0.5	0.8	4.4	29.3
Brazil	3.7	12.3	6.9	33.7	1.5	4.4	6.0	24.1
Greece	6.4	17.1	15.4	10.5	7.5	15.8	10.0	24.1
Hong Kong	21.8	28.1	22.9	42.5	9.4	22.0	33.6	36.4
India	4.0	11.1	8.2	13.3	1.4	7.6	6.9	24.1
Mexico	12.3	15.5	29.2	41.7	4.4	1.4	15.8	25.2
Pakistan	2.8	7.7	14.8	16.4	5.1	3.4	5.0	11.1
Portugal	15.6	34.2	5.9	17.1	3.7	13.4	24.8	40.6
Rep. of Korea	2.7	32.0	5.2	18.8	0.5	39.3	3.6	36.5
Singapore	2.3	38.0	41.4	60.9	22.1	30.6	74.3	60.5
Spain	17.6	10.5	7.3	13.3	8.3	26.0	23.3	46.4
Sri Lanka	2.3	3.4	0.8	6.5	0.4	0.2	2.0	5.1
Tunisia	4.6	12.0	20.0	10.1	0.8	35.2	6.8	14.9
Yugoslavia	18.2	21.8	5.7	18.8	29.8	44.2	36.5	48.0

Source. As for table 1.

countries with respect to their trade in manufactures with the broad economic groupings of countries and with the rest of the world as a whole for the years 1962 and 1975. The table, together with the underlying trade data, confirms the general findings which have been noted earlier, and again there are anomalies which will need to be explored further. The intra-industry trade ratios have increased in virtually every case and the ratios tend to be higher for the more industrialized countries. It can also be shown that there is some link between the rate of growth of total trade and the rate of growth of intra-industry trade,[18] but other factors (level and diversification of industrialization, the nature of the trading regimes, etc.) are probably also significant and these relationships need further exploration.

The table also reflects some differences in the intra-industry trade ratios of the individual countries which can provide further insights into the pattern of trade flows. For example, among the industrialized countries there are very low intra-industry trade ratios of Australia (29.4 per cent), Japan (26.6 per cent) and New Zealand (17.2 per cent) in respect of their world trade in 1975. These have increased markedly since 1962, mainly because of rapidly growing trade and intra-industry trade with developing countries, probably in the South-East Asian region, although trade with other DMECs is still dominant. This observation lends support to Grubel and Lloyd's finding that geographical isolation tends to be associated with a low volume of intra-industry trade. The relatively high cost of transport to other industrialized markets is bound to reduce the competitiveness in these markets of products which are only slightly differentiated from domestically produced ones.

The most dramatic increases of intra-industry trade among the DMECs are those noted in the case of Canada and Ireland. It seems likely that this trend has much to do with the progressive industrialization of those countries in the period (1962-1975), and with their greater integration with their regions. However, it should be noted that Ireland is also heavily involved in international sub-contracting and much of its intra-industry trade may be vertical, i.e. involving the exchange of products of adjacent stages of production.

No other DMEC listed had as high a value of total trade with the DCs in 1975 as the United States ($35.6 billion) or Japan ($28.7 billion), or such large shares of total trade in manufactures with the DCs--29 per cent in the case of the United States and 44 per cent in the case of Japan. However, Japan's ratio of intra-industry trade with the DCs is the lowest of the DMECs listed, while the United States ratio is the highest. In the Japanese case it is possible that components are exported to developing countries or relatively low-income developed countries for assembly and final export to third markets rather than back to Japan. The United States figure may be higher because of border trade and seasonal trade with Mexico, but is probably also affected by the encouragement given to off-shore processing by the provisions of United States tariff items 806.30 and 807.00 which permit duty to be assessed only on value added abroad.

The mainland European DMECs listed, France, the Federal

Republic of Germany and Italy, have the highest ratios of
intra-industry trade with other DMECs reflecting mainly
intra-European trade, associated with economic integration, but
probably also the comparatively low transport costs. In other
words, they represent the opposite picture to that of Australia,
Japan and New Zealand.

With respect to the remaining selected countries in table 3
there are a number of features about which some speculation may be
useful and also some anomalies which will require further study.
An examination of the intra-industry trade ratios of these
countries vis-a-vis the ratios for their trade with the rest of the
world in 1975 (the final column) suggests higher ratios for those
which are more industrialized, higher ratios for those which are
associated in some kind of regional economic grouping, and higher
ratios for those with export-oriented or relatively open trading
regimes. Many of these countries had higher intra-industry trade
ratios than Australia, Japan or New Zealand. Intra-industry trade
has generally been growing rapidly in the case of the selected
countries. Singapore is an exception to this pattern, although its
intra-industry trade ratios and later figures are now recovering to
the 1962 level. It is possible that the figures reflect a change
in the composition and direction of its trade, associated with
Singapore's transition from a centre for entrepot trade to an
important manufacturer.

With respect to the trade in manufactures of these selected
countries (Argentina-Yugoslavia) with the DMECs, the intra-industry
trade ratios in 1975 were generally higher the greater the degree
of industrialization that had been attained. Singapore and Spain
achieved higher ratios with the DMECs than did Japan, one of the
"remote" industrialized countries. Hong Kong, the Republic of
Korea, Portugal and Yugoslavia also achieved higher ratios with
respect to their trade with the DMECs than did Australia and New
Zealand. In all these cases, trade with the DMECs predominates.
The higher growth rates in total trade with the DMECs also show a
tendency to be associated with high growth rates in intra-industry
trade.

In the case of Greece, the Republic of Korea, Spain, Tunisia
and Yugoslavia, the ratios of intra-industry trade with the DMECs
and the socialist countries in 1975 were higher than the ratios
with respect to their trade with developing countries. Portugal's
intra-industry trade ratio vis-a-vis the DMECs was higher than that
with the DCs which was, in turn, higher than that with the
socialist countries. Of the countries which have higher ratios of
intra-industry trade with the DCs those in regional trade groupings
tend to have the highest ratios. Hong Kong is something of an
exception and will need further investigation. The country with
the greatest amount of trade in manufactures with the socialist
countries is Yugoslavia and it also has the highest intra-industry
trade ratio with these countries. Other countries whose ratios of
intra-industry trade with the socialist countries are higher, are
the Republic of Korea and Tunisia, but the total value and the
proportion of their trade involved are quite small.

While the association which has been noted between high
intra-industry trade ratios, on the one hand, and regional

integration and "remoteness" and/or transport costs, on the other, reinforces the conclusions of earlier studies, the proposition concerning the relationship between intra-industry trade and industrialization is somewhat different. Certainly, intra-industry trade is higher among the industrialized countries, but there also appears to be a relationship between the industrialization process and particularly high rates of growth in intra-industry trade with the DMECs. This is most evident in the cases of the Republic of Korea and Singapore, whose total trade in manufactures with the DMECs grew at a rate some three times faster than their trade with DCs from 1962 to 1975. The intra-industry trade ratios increased from 2.7 per cent in 1962 to 32.0 per cent in 1975 for the Republic of Korea and 2.3 to 38.0 per cent for Singapore. This rapid and basic change in the nature of their trade with the DMECs can also be observed to a lesser degree in the cases of Canada, Ireland, Portugal and Spain.

It is, therefore, possible to suggest that as countries become more industrialized they tend to trade with already industrialized countries (the DMECs) in the way the latter trade with each other. The significance of this observation is that, contrary to the popular myth among entrepreneurs and unions in the DMECs, whole industries are not going to be transferred to the South as the developing countries become more industrialized. Rather, there appears to be greater scope for a two-way expansion of trade based on intra-industry specialization.

A further breakdown of the trade in manufactures, shown in table 4, generally confirms the importance of the machinery and transport equipment sector in terms of its absolute size and higher growth of total trade within and between the broad groups. There is also very rapid growth of total trade and of the share of intra-industry trade in the machinery and transport equipment sector among the DCs.

IV. POLICY IMPLICATIONS

One of the main policy objectives of the developing countries is the expansion and diversification of their exports of manufactures and semi-manufactures. The data examined here suggest that success in achieving this objective will be associated with the attainment of a higher proportion of intra-industry trade. It is also likely that the machinery and transport equipment sector will contain the major growth industries involved in this trade. In the past, such expansion and diversification has been most marked as a consequence of greater regional economic integration after the reduction of trade barriers within regional economic groupings, both developed and developing. The scope for high levels of intra-industry trade will increase as industrialization becomes more advanced. Empirical evidence suggests that this industrialization will involve greater intra-industry specialization in the North and in the South.

TABLE 4

Intra-industry trade ratios for developed market-economy countries and developing countries in respect of their trade in categories of manufactures within their group and with the rest of the world, 1965 and 1975, and changes in total trade, 1965-1975

A. DEVELOPED MARKET-ECONOMY COUNTRIES

	Intra-group trade				Trade with developing countries			
	Trade ratios (%)		Total trade		Trade ratios (%)		Total trade	
			Value	Increase			Value	Increase
SITC	1965	1975	1975 ($ billion)	1965-1957 (Per cent)	1965	1975	1975 ($ billion)	1965-1957 (Per cent)
5 Chemicals.	60.1	67.8	72	496	15.8	16.1	15	499
6 Manufactures classified by material . .	51.7	60.8	167	361	16.9	20.5	37	417
7 Machinery and transport equipment	54.9	64.8	271	512	2.8	13.0	68	676
8 Misc. manufactured articles	54.7	61.3	78	491	26.8	29.6	16	678
5-8 All manufactures .	54.3	63.6	588	452	11.9	17.3	136	555

B. DEVELOPING COUNTRIES

	Intra-group trade				Trade with developed market-economy countries			
	Trade ratios (%)		Total trade		Trade ratios (%)		Total trade	
			Value	Increase			Value	Increase
SITC	1965	1975	1975 ($ billion)	1965-1975 (Per cent)	1965	1975	1975 ($ billion)	1965-1957 (Per cent)
5 Chemicals.	31.5	31.2	2.9	698	8.5	7.5	16	627
6 Manufactures classified by material . .	16.3	22.7	8.3	553	5.7	7.7	36	507
7 Machinery and transport equipment	22.8	32.3	5.9	1 404	2.5	9.1	53	715
8 Misc. manufactured articles	32.2	34.2	2.9	717	9.9	16.2	13	806
5-8 All manufactures .	21.9	28.5	20.1	718	5.2	9.2	119	630

Source. As for table 1.

It is an important finding that the reduction of trade barriers has led to greater intra-industry specialization and not to the elimination of whole industries, as might have been predicted by traditional trade theory. One prediction[19] made in 1966 about prospects for the EEC was that "multilateral reductions in duties will lead to a re-allocation of resources from import-competing to export industries, accompanied by a contradiction in the activity of the former and an expansion of the latter . . . (i.e.) tariff reductions would be accompanied by inter-industry specialization". As it happened, it was the rapid growth of intra-industry trade in Europe that stimulated empirical research and other theoretical work in a reappraisal of earlier trade theory. While it is true that the level of intra-industry trade is greater among the more industrialized countries, it is now clear that intra-industry trade is not merely a phenomenon of the trade of such countries, but that it is becoming a feature of North-South trade and of trade within the South.

The evidence suggests that the trend towards greater intra-industry trade may contribute to the attainment of the trading objectives of the developing countries, since the higher rate of trade expansion with which it is associated is mostly attributable to trade creation, not to trade diversion. Moreover, the costs of structural adjustment in the developed countries may be less than those expected to arise from inter-industry specialization. While these costs may not be zero, they are likely to be considerably reduced because of the increased possibilities for redeployment of capital equipment and labour, as well as reduced labour retraining costs, within an industry, compared with the situation requiring substantial shifts of factors from one industry to another, possibly also involving geographical relocation. Recognition of these effects may help to moderate protectionist pressures against imports from developing countries.

Additional evidence of beneficial effects stemming from intra-industry trade expansion can be derived from the results of simulations with general equilibrium models of international trade and from case studies of certain industries and countries. The simulations show that "the increase in intra-industry trade is associated with increases in aggregate consumption and welfare",[20] and one simulation study claims that there are markedly higher gains from trade liberalization than have been estimated in previous research, the major new feature in the model being the simultaneous introduction of intra-industry specialization and economies of scale.[21] It has also been noted in a broad survey of case studies of <u>vertical</u> intra-industry trade (international sub-contracting/offshore processing—including the operation of export-processing free zones) that "with certain reservations, international subcontracting appears to offer certain specific advantages for developed and developing countries".[22] The survey concludes that, to the extent that international sub-contracting arrangements or other forms of vertical intra-industry trade lead on to long-term gains such as the acquisition of new technology, new skills and management capacity, or to the establishment of backward linkages, this kind of trade represents one way in which

developing countries can participate in and contribute to the
growth of world trade without being perpetually locked into a
pattern of labour-intensive industrial development, although such
production and trade may initially be the basis for offshore
processing in or sub-contracting to the poorer, lower-wage
countries. In the short term, these arrangements would appear to
promote the rapid mobilization of international capital for the
purpose of relieving foreign exchange constraints and creating
employment opportunities.

Some doubts have been expressed about the net beneficial
effects of vertical intra-industry trade on foreign exchange,
employment, regional development and social structures. These
doubts have been partly attributed to the fact that they are based
on results in the short term, whereas many of the gains are of a
longer-term nature.[23] Doubts may also be expressed with respect to
the equity of distribution of the benefits of such trade expansion
because of the amount of intra-firm or related party trade
involved. While there is some controversy about the precise amount
of trade involved and the trends,[24] intra-firm and related party
trade is certainly a substantial part of world trade and, from case
studies, it is known that transnational corporations are heavily
involved in vertical intra-industry trade. The full extent of this
involvement and its effects need further study.

If detailed policy initiatives are to be undertaken in
relation to intra-industry specialization there will be a need to
give greater substance to the overall findings in relation to
intra-industry trade expansion. More information will be required
about the experience of individual countries and regions. In
addition, much more information will be required about the
economics of production at the process level in specific
industries.

In relation to the investigation of the experiences of
individual countries and regions, intra-industry trade needs to be
examined against the overall background of resource availability,
the level of industrial activity and diversification attained and
the policy framework. The reasons for inter-country
and inter-regional differences in levels of intra-industry trade
and the underlying factors need to be explored further. In
examining the costs and benefits associated with expanded
intra-industry trade, and especially some of the arrangements for
the conduct of vertical intra-industry trade, it is important to
assess not merely the increase in exports or export earnings but
rather the retained value or net foreign exchange earnings of
exports.[25] In addition, the extent to which net employment
opportunities are increased, the extent to which technology
transfer or acquisition of labour skills is involved, the costs of
structural adjustment, the effects on regional development and on
social structures would all need to be taken into account and
evaluated in relation to the experiences of the countries being
studied, both in the North and in the South. Allowance would need
to be made for the time flow of costs and benefits, so
that short-term costs could be appropriately offset against
long-term gains, or vice versa. It would also be desirable to make
an assessment of the extent to which expanded intra-industry trade

in its different forms encounters opposition from within the communities of the trading partners. Finally, the question might be put regarding the nature of the dependence or interdependence that builds up between trading partners involved in such trade expansion.

While the level of industrialization has been mentioned as being associated with the level of intra-industry trade, it seems likely that the nature of the foreign trade regimes may also be important. Indeed, overall trade policies or strategies may be more important than specific devices for stimulating intra-industry specialization and trade. Superficially, it would appear from the data in the previous section that the more open economies and the export-oriented developing countries have higher intra-industry trade ratios. If research can establish the importance of the nature of the regime relative to other factors and if it can be shown from the sort of cost/benefit analysis discussed above that there are net long-term gains, then such findings would lend support to the choice of export orientation as a superior industrialization strategy, although this is a very complex question.[26] Certainly, it would seem desirable that any conscious move towards the promotion of intra-industry specialization should be part of a consistent and comprehensive trade and industrialization strategy. On the other hand, the direction of a country's policies and its priorities may change. In this context, specific devices such as export subsidies or export-processing free zones may be useful in promoting the transition to a more open trading regime, in promoting certain social objectives or decentralization, or in offsetting external diseconomies or initial costs. As a general guide, the costs of such schemes, whether used in isolation or as part of a more general strategy, should not exceed the expected flow of future benefits, including any externalities. Similar criteria should also be applied to international sub-contracting and industrial collaboration arrangements which have so far been mainly instrumental in expanding North-South and East-West intra-industry trade, respectively.

Within the North, it would be useful to examine the kind of policies which can foster North-South intra-industry trade and the likely effects of such policies. Should research confirm that there are net welfare gains, then some general guidelines and specific measures for the promotion of intra-industry trade can already be suggested for possible inclusion in a policy package. At the more general level, it would be desirable to achieve consistency between trade policies vis-a-vis, the South and industrial policies. It has been shown that in the last 20 years industrial policies have been increasingly substituted for direct trade restrictions.[27] Such policies could equally be turned towards actively promoting North-South intra-industry trade by facilitating the expansion of intra-industry specialization, including complementary production arrangements.

Certain specific policies immediately suggest themselves as potentially useful for the promotion of intra-industry trade and should be examined in detail. For example, it would be desirable to examine the effects on the potential for expanded intra-industry trade, of the elimination of escalating protection at the later stages of production. At the moment, even when developed countries reduce trade barriers, there tend to be deeper cuts in the barriers against raw materials and intermediate goods, so that the effective rate of protection against finished goods is increased. This protects processors in the developed countries, locking developing countries into their historic role as raw material suppliers to the industrialized nations and hindering the industrial diversification and expansion of the developing countries.[28] It has also been shown that complementary intra-industry trade has been promoted by the use of value-added tariffs such as exist in the offshore assembly provisions of the Netherlands, the Federal Republic of Germany or the United States.[29] The provisions of United States tariff items 806.30 and 807.00 allow for the netting out of domestic components in calculating value for duty and place no restrictions on the extent of foreign processing or the incorporation of foreign components. Trade in goods covered by these items has been growing particularly rapidly, although it was slightly affected in the year in which the United States introduced its scheme in the context of the generalized system of preferences (GSP). In effect, GSP schemes can work in a similar way, and could be further extended by a more liberal application of the rules of origin and the introduction of cumulative treatment to allow without penalizing, processing in or the use of, components from several countries.

It was noted earlier that, for the purpose of formulating policy, more information is also required about the economics of industrial production at the process level. Just as it is important to take account of the economic and policy environment in analysing the different experiences of countries and regions with intra-industry trade, so also is it important to understand the reasons behind the differences in levels of intra-industry trade as between one industry and another. This has implications for trade theory in general and hence for trade policy. At present, the main factors accounting for intra-industry trade are said to be economies of scale and specialization, labour cost/productivity differentials, transport costs, and governmental influences, but, at present, trade theory does not show how these factors interact with each other, with commodity characteristics, and with demand functions. The key to a better understanding is essential to predicting change in production patterns. It should also pave the way for detailed policy-making and possibly negotiations leading towards better policy co-ordination which could influence the rate and manner of adaptation to a more rational and equitable distribution of production.

V. CONCLUSIONS

The material in this article supports the view that "there is much to applaud in intra-industry trade and little to deplore".[30]

The article also shows that it is not merely a phenomenon confined to developed countries, but has also been observed as an increasingly important characteristic of North—South trade and of trade among developing countries. In the context of rising protectionism, it points the way in which trade between developed and developing countries can expand and evolve in a mutually beneficial way after the elimination of trade barriers and the reversal of harmful industrial policies. There is already sufficient evidence to show that the fears of workers and entrepreneurs in the developed countries that more and more sectors are based on a misunderstanding of the interaction of development and trade. In particular, the analysis in this article suggests that as developing countries become more industrialized they will trade more and more with the developed countries in the way in which the developed countries trade among themselves, on the basis of intra—industry specialization. Certain lines of production within industrial sectors may become less competitive, while other lines will have new and expanded trade opportunities. For the present, it is likely that the greatest pressures will be on relatively labour-intensive processes. However, in this context it is important to remember that low-wage countries are low-wage precisely because of their stage of development. Certainly, other low-wage countries will take the place of the more successful developing countries, but so also will technological progress redefine the labour-intensive and capital-intensive processes. As Keynes[31] said in a similar situation "this is only a temporary phase of maladjustment. All this means in the long run is that mankind is solving its economic problems".

While future change and pressures for change may be difficult to identify, many of the changes, expansions and contractions will take place within the same sectors. Thus, it is likely that the adjustment costs may be very much less than if the changes were to take place across sectors. The costs of the retraining and relocation of workers and the extent of social disruption are also likely to be much less. It is also likely that fixed capital will have greater possibilities for transfer to alternative, expanding lines of production than would be the case if adjustments took place across sectors, and this prospect augurs well for a comparatively quick response to positive adjustment policies from both sides of industry.

While these positive findings seem to be confirmed by other research referred to in this article, there are some reservations about the retained value of the extra trade and the distribution of the benefits. Evidence shows that positive action by governments can promote intra—industry trade, but, before a comprehensive and internally consistent policy package can be put together, further information is needed about the experience of individual countries and regions and about the economics of production at the process level in specific industries.

In the context of the formulation of policies and an understanding of the underlying theoretical base, it is a weakness that recognition of the phenomenon of intra—industry trade has not yet given rise to a new generalized theory of international trade.[32] Nevertheless, it is already clear that economists are moving towards some kind of dynamic general equilibrium theory of trade in which economies of scale, technological differences, transport costs, etc. are integrated, rather than assumed away. In such a framework greater emphasis will be given to the economics of production, especially at the process level, and less to the interaction of relative factor endowments with product characteristics. Thus, micro-economic studies may lead to the establishment of an improved theoretical framework without which it is impossible to formulate consistent policies or to make intelligent predictions about the future course of trade.

NOTES

[1] See, for instance, Mahbub ul Haq, "Beyond the slogan of South-South co-operation", World Development, Vol. 8, No. 10, October 1980.

[2] C. F. Diaz-Alejandro, "Some characteristics of recent export expansion in Latin America" in H. Giersch (ed.), The international division of labour: problems and perspectives (Kiel, Institut fur Welwirtschaft, 1974).

[3] R. Vernon (ed.), The technology factor in international trade, (New York, Columbia Press, 1970, for the National Bureau of Economic and Social Research).

[4] See, for instance, B. Ohlin, Interregional and international trade (Cambridge, Mass., 1933).

[5] See, inter alia, P. J. Verdoorn, "The intra-bloc trade of Benelux" in E. A. G. Robinson (ed.) Economic consequences of the size of nations (London, Macmillan, 1960); B. Balassa, "European integration: problems and issues", American Economic Review, Papers and Proceedings, May 1963; H. G. Grubel and P. J. Lloyd, Intra-industry trade (Kiel, Institut fur Weltwirtschaft, 1979).

[6] B. Balassa, "Intra-industry trade and the integration of developing countries in the world economy", in H. Giersch (ed.), On the economics of intra-industry trade (Kiel, Institut fur Weltwirtschaft, 1979).

[7] J. Grunwald, "North-South intra-industry trade: sharing industrial production between developing and developed countries", mimeograph paper prepared for a colloquium on The new international economic order and cultural values, Madrid, 12-14 June 1978.

[8]Grubel and Lloyd, op. cit.

[9]
$$\frac{\sum_{ijk}[(Xijk + Mijk) - (Xijk - Mijk)]}{\sum_{ijk}[Xijk + Mijk]} \quad 100$$

where Xijk = exports of commodity i by country j to country k, and

Mijk = imports of commodity i by country j from country k.

This is Grubel and Lloyd's total trade-weighted average measure, which is also used by the present author in section C below. This measure has a downward bias in each set or subset of industries where exports do not equal imports, and this would affect subsequent averages. However, as noted by Grubel and Lloyd and subsequently by Balassa there is some concern about appropriate weighting techniques to overcome this bias.

[10]The "firm" is the basic decision-making as opposed to production unit. It may be involved in several industries, or in the same industry in several countries, or both. To the extent that intra-industry trade may be intra-firm trade, this relationship will be discussed later.

[11]The absence of joint production is one of the assumptions of the Heckscher-Ohlin theory.

[12]R. G. Gregory and D. S. Tearle, "Product differentiation and international trade flows", Australian Economic Papers, June 1973.

[13]See, for instance, J. Dreze, "Quelques reflexions sereines sur l'adaptation de l'industrie belge au Marche Commun", Comptes rendus des travaux de la Societe Royale d'Economie Politique de Belgique, December 1960, and S. B. Linder, An essay on trade and transformation (New York, John Wiley & Sons, 1961).

[14]"A case study approach to trade-related structural adjustment", Report by the UNCTAD secretariat (TD/B/805/Supp.1).

[15]In other words, the overall result is not merely the consequence of weighting distortions.

[16]The trade of the socialist countries (of Eastern Europe and Asia) (SCs) is not examined, except as a group of trading partners for the DMECs and the DCs, because of the difficulty of obtaining comprehensive data over the time period selected. Data were also hard to obtain for some regional trade groupings, and in some cases only data for a subset of countries were used.

[17]In the table the ratios of intra-industry trade of the DMECs and DCs (Part A of the table) should correspond to the intra-industry trade ratios of the DCs with the DMECs (Part B). The reason why they do not correspond is that, whereas the DMECs have a

comprehensive recording of their trade with the DCs, Part B of the table does not reflect data for all reporting DCs.

[18]The value of the Pearson linear correlation coefficient calculated from observations, weighted by the value of total trade in 1975, was 0.50 (significant at the 99.99 per cent level). The more complex relationship which obviously exists needs to be specified for analysis by multiple regression techniques.

[19]B. Balassa, "Tariff reductions and trade in manufactures", American Economic Review, June 1966.

[20]P. J. Lloyd, "Intra-industry trade, lowering trade barriers and gains from trade", in H. Giersch (ed.) On the economics of intra-industry trade, (Kiel, Institut fur Weltwirtschaft, 1979).

[21]P. Dixon, "Economies of scale, commodity disaggregation and the costs of protection", Australian Economic Papers, Vol. 17, No. 30, June 1978.

[22]"Intra-industry trade and international sub-contracting", Report by the UNCTAD secretariat (TD/B.805/Supp.2).

[23]See the reports of the two UNCTAD Seminars on North-South Complementary Intra-industry Trade held in Mexico in July 1979 and August 1980 (UNCTAD/MD/105 and UNCTAD/MD/111, respectively).

[24]See, for instance, Balassa, op. cit. and G. K. Helleiner and R. Lavergne, "Intra-firm trade and industrial exports to the United States", Oxford Bulletin of Economics and Statistics, November 1979.

[25]For a discussion on the concept of retained value, see D. A. Brodsky and G. P. Sampson, "Retained value and the export performance of developing countries", The Journal of Development Studies, October 1980.

[26]See J. N. Bhagwati and A. O. Krueger, "Exchange control, liberalization and economic development", American Economic Review, Papers and Proceedings, May 1973, for a discussion of export-oriented versus import substitution strategies.

[27]See, for instance, The industrial policies of the developed market-economy countries and their effect on the exports of manufactures and semi-manufactures from the developing countries, Report by the UNCTAD secretariat (TD/230/Supp.1/Rev.1), United Nations publication Sales No. E.79.II.D.13.

[28]G. K. Helleiner, "The new industrial protectionism and the developing countries", Trade and Development: An UNCTAD Review, No. 1, Spring 1979, United Nations publication Sales No. E.79.II.D.8.

[29]J. M. Finger, "Tariff provision for offshore assembly and the exports of developing countries", The Economic Journal, June 1975.

[30]R. Caves, "Intra-industry trade and market structure in industrial countries", Harvard Institute Economic Research Discussion Paper, No. 725, Cambridge, 1979.

[31]J. M. Keynes, "Economic possibilities for our grandchildren", The Nation and Athenaeum, 11 October 1930.

BIBLIOGRAPHY

Balassa, B. "European integration: problems and issues", American Economic Review, Papers and Proceedings, May 1963.

Balassa, B. "Tariff reductions and trade in manufactures", American Economic Review, June 1966.

Balassa B. "Intra-industry trade and the integration of developing countries in the world economy", in H. Giersch (ed.), On the economics of intra-industry trade, Kiel, Institut fur Weltwirtschaft, 1979.

Bhagwati, J. N. and A. O. Krueger, "Exchange control, liberalization and economic development", American Economic Review, Papers and Proceedings, May 1973.

Brodsky, D. A. and G. P. Sampson, "Retained value and the export performance of developing countries", The Journal of Development Studies, October 1980.

Caves, R. "Intra-industry trade and market structure in industrial countries", Harvard Institute Economic Research Discussion Paper, No. 725, Cambridge, 1979.

Commonwealth of Australia, Tariff Board, Annual Report for the year 1969-70, 1970.

Corden, W. M. "Intra-industry trade and factor proportions theory", in H. Giersch (ed.) On the economics of intra-industry trade (Kiel, Institut fur Weltwirtschaft, 1979).

Diaz-Alejandro, C. F., "Some characteristics of recent export expansion in Latin America", in H. Giersch (ed.), The International Division of Labour: Problems and Perspectives (Kiel, Institut fur Weltwirtschaft, 1974).

Dixon, P. "Economies of scale, commodity disaggregation and the costs of protection", Australian Economic Papers, vol. 17. No. 30, June 1978.

Dreze, J. "Quelques reflexions sereines sur l'adaptation de l'industrie belge au Marche Commun", Comptes rendus des travaux de la Societe royale d'economie politique de Belgique, December 1960.

Finger, J. M. "Tariff provisions for offshore assembly and the exports of developing countries", The Economic Journal, June 1975.

Gregory, R. G. and D. S. Tearle, "Product differentiation and international trade flows", Australian Economic Papers, June 1973.

Grubel, H. G. and P. J. Lloyd, Intra-industry trade (London, Macmillan, 1975).

Grunwald, J. "North-South intra-industry trade: sharing industrial production between developing and developed countries", mimeograph paper prepared for a colloquium on The new international economic order and cultural values, Madrid, 12-14 June 1978.

Helleiner, G. K. "The new industrial protectionism and the developing countries", Trade and Development: An UNCTAD Review, No. 1, Spring 1979 (United Nations publication, Sales No. E.79.II.D.8).

Helleiner, G. K. and R. Lavergne, "Intra-firm trade and industrial exports to the United States", Oxford Bulletin of Economics and Statistics, November 1979.

Haq, Mahbub ul, "Beyond the slogan of South-South co-operation", World Development, vol. 8, No. 10, October 1980.

Keynes, J. M., "Economic possibilities for our grandchildren", The Nation and Athenaeum, 11 October 1930.

Linder, S. B., An essay on trade and transformation (New York, John Wiley & Sons, 1961).

Ohlin, B., Interregional and international trade (Cambridge, Mass., 1933).

UNCTAD, "A case study approach to trade-related structural adjustment", Report by the UNCTAD secretariat (TD/B/805/Supp.1).

UNCTAD, "The role of transnational corporations in the marketing and distribution of exports and imports of developing countries", Report by the UNNCY4TAD secretariat (TD/B/C.2/197).

UNCTAD, The industrial policies of the developed market-economy countries and their effect on the exports of manufactures and semi-manufactures from the developing countries, Report by the UNCTAD secretariat (TD/230/Supp.1/Rev.1, United Nations publication, Sales No. E.79.II.D.13).

UNCTAD, Seminar Director's Reports of Seminars on North-South Complementary Intra-industry Trade held in Mexico in July 1979 and August 1980 (UNCTAD/MD/105 and UNCTAD/MD/111, respectively).

Verdoorn, P. J., "The intra-bloc trade of Benelux", in E. A. G. Robinson (ed.) Economic consequences of the size of nations (London, Macmillan, 1960).

Vernon, R. (ed.), The technology factor in international trade, (New York, Columbia Press, 1970 (for the National Bureau of Economic and Social Research)).

The New Industrial Protectionism and the Developing Countries

GERALD K. HELLEINER

The new industrial protectionism of the developed countries poses an important threat to the economic development of the developing countries. It magnifies the distortions to their trade patterns which have already been created by the existing structure of developed country trade barriers, driving them further away from manufacturing activities in which they possess a clear comparative advantage (whether because of resource base or labour-intensity), and towards those in which the trade is "managed" by transnational corporations based in the developed countries. Rather than focussing upon most-favoured nation (MFN) tariff cuts, as the developed countries have been prone to do, or upon achieving "special and differential" treatment in a variety of areas, as the developing countries have sought to do, it is of the greatest importance to arrest this continuing growth of effective discrimination in the structure of trade barriers. The politics as well as the economics of developed countries' trade policy formation and industrial adjustment must be better understood -- and influenced -- if any progress on this front is to be achieved. At the international level, thought should by now be concentrating more on appropriate institutional mechanisms for facilitating international trade "management" after the disappointments of the Tokyo Round.

I. INTRODUCTION

Nation-states have long employed tariffs, non-tariff trade

From **TRADE AND DEVELOPMENT**, UNCTAD Review, Spring, 1979 (15-37), reprinted by permission of the publisher.

barriers, exchange rates, and other trade incentives and disincentives in pursuit of various national objectives. Governmental interventions in the otherwise "free" flow of goods and services across international boundaries have been rationalized in terms of both economic and political objectives. Among the arguments most frequently heard among economists are those couched in terms of the theory of the second-best, the possibility of exercising market power in order to improve the terms of trade, the infant industry argument, and the pursuit of structural changes which are believed to "dynamize" entire economies in the longer-run. Indeed, the qualifications to the general economic case for "free" international trade are so many that, as a recent survey has observed, "by now, any bright graduate student, by choosing his assumptions regarding distortions and policy instruments carefully, can produce a consistent model yielding just about any policy conclusion he favoured at the start. To reach his conclusion, moreover, he need not introduce development targets additional to static efficiency."[1]

It is therefore perhaps remarkable that the weight of orthodox professional economists' opinion and influence is so firmly in favour of "free" trade. As the same survey notes, "In the trade and development literature there has existed for a long time . . . a striking difference between the rigour of formal proofs on the static advantages of free trade, typically involving careful assumptions and caveats, and the impetuous enthusiasm with which most of the professional mainstream advocates free or freer trade policies, on both static and dynamic grounds for all times and places . . . The literature leaps with remarkable ease from the sensible proposition that some trade can potentially make everyone better off, as compared with no trade, to the conviction that more trade is always likely to do just that."[2]

In the post-Second World War period, trade barriers among the world's major trading nations fell markedly through a succession of bargaining rounds under the General Agreement on Tariffs and Trade (GATT). The conventional political wisdom seemed to be in harmony with the conventional economic wisdom of this period: if not "free trade is best", at least "freer trade is better". Even during this period, however, there co-existed an alternative trade policy wisdom in much of Latin America and the newly independent Asian and African countries, which viewed the tenets of free traders' theory with considerable scepticism, and generated policies which either maintained the commercial policy status quo or even increased governmental interventions in international trade.

Widespread governmental "interferences" with international trade in the developing countries have been tolerated by those who regarded them as unwise because of their relatively small overall importance for the world economy. Some of their more costly excesses in this sphere began to be mitigated from the mid-1960s onwards; if there has been a trend at all in these countries in recent years, it has probably been in the direction of classical trade "liberalization" (although it has been somewhat interrupted since 1973). In the industrialized countries, however, where there would seem to have been greater attention paid in the past to the tenets of orthodox economic theory, and where the implications for the world economy are far more serious, the trend is now clearly in the reverse (protectionist) direction.[3]

The new protectionism is highly sector-specific, and therefore cannot at present be described as the product of economic nationalism or neo-mercantilism. The sectors in which it is found are primarily the labour-intensive branches of manufacturing in which developing countries possess a clear comparative advantage. The traditional primary product exports of developing countries are notoriously unstable and uncertain. To a large extent, these instabilities and uncertainties are the product of "natural" influences: the weather and the business cycle. It is especially galling for these countries to face new man-made uncertainties as they seek to diversify into processing and manufacturing for export which, they previously had reason to expect, were less vulnerable to such difficulties. It should go without saying that the impact of sudden trade barriers upon developing economies, where alternative employment possibilities are often limited, is likely to be more severe than that upon developed countries faced with similar restrictions.[4]

While in the long-run these trade barriers merely alter the composition of developing country trade rather than reduce its volume, in the short- to medium-run, the costs which they impose are likely to generate difficulties sufficiently important to affect developed countries' exports to developing countries and the prospects for the latter's repayment of commercial and official debts.[5]

It is easy enough to provide a list of additional and alternative trade policy measures which could be beneficial to the developing countries, and many have done so. It is not even very difficult to achieve ringing declarations and impressive resolutions in which the governments of developed countries solemnly commit themselves to "standstills" or even reductions in trade barriers.[6] It is quite another matter, however, to find specific measures which hold promise of being sufficiently politically acceptable to ensure their actual implementation. The detailed provisions of international agreements may be less important than the day-to-day political realities which must determine governmental actions, for all governments, whether in developing or developed countries, tend to place immediate domestic concerns ahead of their commitments to foreigners. The more difficult analysis of political realities thus needs to be combined with the relatively simple economics of international trade.

On the face of it, the political economy of international trading policy and practice requires much deeper analysis than it has had. Major changes have taken place which cry out for more detailed analysis, investigation and explanation. Actual policy-making, even in the cradles of orthodox thought, has so frequently been so different from that which "should" flow from orthodox analyses that it has become "conventional" for economists to seek explanations for trade policies in terms of "political" analyses. But such studies as they have conducted have been fairly crude, typically employing only the tools they know best: multiple regression analysis. The political economy of international commercial policy and practice remains an intellectually rather underdeveloped area.[7]

The present paper is concerned with the politics and economics of protectionism in the manufacturing sector only. It should not be forgotten, however, that agricultural protectionism in the developed countries is in some sectors -- e.g., sugar, meat and grains -- also extremely costly to many developing countries. It has been estimated that, excluding textiles, roughly one-third of the increased exports which could be generated for developing countries by across-the-board MFN tariff cuts in the Tokyo Round would be in the agricultural sector[8] and non-tariff barriers, particularly the variable levies on agricultural imports into the EEC, severely further restrict the agricultural exports of the developing countries.

There is sometimes an implication in these discussions that, because such a high proportion of developing countries' manufactured exports is concentrated in such a small number of (relatively advanced) countries (80 per cent in 12 countries), market access for manufactures is not of great importance to the majority of developing countries.[9] Nothing could be further from the truth. Apart from the fact that in the long-run every developing country aspires to a more diversified export bundle which includes industrial products, there is no country so poor that even today it is not affected by problems of market access at least for its processed raw materials. In 1975, 40 developing countries exported manufactures to a value of over $100 million.[10] It is true that some countries immediately stand to gain more than others from progress on this front.[11] But that is always true -- it is true of commodity agreements, debt renegotiation, IMF reform and even increases in official development assistance -- and cannot be used as an excuse for lack of concern. In a world of stagnant or slowly expanding export markets, the opportunities for newcomers are especially severely cut back; as the World Bank has recently argued, protectionism in textiles and clothing harms not just the current major exporters of these products but may, rather, exert "the most painful effect . . . in countries that are just emerging as significant exporters of manufactured goods."[12] No doubt the detailed provisions of protectionist arrangements can vary to some degree so as to generate different inter-country distribution of their effects.

Nor must the critics of "export-led" growth be permitted to play down the importance of these questions, on the grounds that "outward orientation" may be harmful to development.[13] The countries whose incomes are constrained and structures affected by market barriers include those with different social and economic systems and different strategies of development.

It is most unlikely that individual developing countries' overall strategies of development could be directed towards greater outward orientation in the consequence of developed countries' trade policies. To the extent that the latter policies have any such overall effect they are bound to continue to be in the reverse direction -- favouring greater "inward orientation" at least as far as production structures (if not factor use) are concerned. But these matters are for independent sovereign governments to determine. Of much greater concern is the nature of the constraints (and opportunities) which the structure of world markets imposes on domestic production and exports; and the factors which influence the distribution of the gains of whatever trade developing countries themselves choose to have. It is by now almost banal to point out that the existing structure of developed country barriers to trade encourages developing countries to export raw materials. Obviously, this has not totally prevented them from exporting manufactures, but it has hindered them from doing so. Now, as will be seen, within the manufacturing sector itself, differential incentives for different types of developing country exports are being created by developed country trading practices. These have been much less noticed, but they are of increasing importance.

II. THE EMERGING STRUCTURE OF DEVELOPED COUNTRIES' TRADE BARRIERS AND ITS IMPACT UPON DEVELOPING COUNTRIES' TRADE

The present tariff structures of the industrialized countries are the product of five GATT tariff bargaining rounds between 1947 and the early 1960s, each of which employed a product-centred reciprocity approach, and the Kennedy Round of the 1960s, which was the first to employ (with some notable exceptions) an across-the-board tariff-cutting formula. It is well known that the limited role of the developing countries in reciprocal GATT bargaining -- a product of their relative economic insignificance -- generated tariff cuts on manufactured products which were biased in favour of the products in which the industrialized countries themselves trade principally with one another, and against those of primary concern to the developing countries. Although the evidence is not as clear, it is also probable that tariffs were cut most on products traded internally by transnational corporations.[14]

A series of econometric investigations of the tariff structures of the United States, Western Europe, Canada and Australia confirm that high rates of tariff protection are today associated with unskilled labour-intensity.[15] These industries are, of course, those in which developing countries are most interested (and transnationals least active). With the introduction of the "linear" tariff cuts of the Kennedy and Tokyo Rounds an opportunity for more balanced treatment for weaker trading partners was retained through resort to "exceptions" in tariff bargaining and, increasingly in recent years, non-tariff barriers (NTB).[16] Non-tariff barriers have multiplied as Japan, the socialist countries of Eastern Europe and the more advanced of the developing countries began significantly to penetrate the industrialized countries' markets in such sectors as textiles, clothing, and footwear;[17] and the world at the same time failed to resume as rapid growth after the 1974-1975 recession as it had enjoyed before.[18]

It is the multiplication of non-tariff barriers in recent

years which has caused the greatest anxiety both to the developing countries and to proponents of a relatively open and stable world trading system. The GATT permits the industrialized countries fairly wide-ranging exceptions to its basic prohibitions on quantitative import restrictions;[19] yet these countries nevertheless now employ many such restrictions in contravention both of the spirit and the letter of the Agreement -- above all, in support of particularly weak industries or sectors. In the main, these weakest industries are those which are most labour-intensive and therefore most vulnerable to the competition of newly industrializing countries.[20] Import quotas, voluntary export restraints, orderly marketing arrangements, countervailing duties, and a wide variety of other formal and informal measures can now be found not only in textiles and garments, but also in footwear, transport equipment, steel, and household appliances; they are under discussion in many more.

The prototype for future international orderly marketing arrangements would seem to be the Arrangement on International Trade in Textiles, the so-called Multi-fibre Arrangements, successor to the previous International Cotton Textile Arrangement, which regulates international trade in textiles. Although it contains some attractive features (required growth rates in the size of quotas, commitments to adjustment programmes, international surveillance), loopholes abound and, as United States commentators have said, "in this case the loopholes are decidedly in favor of the importing countries. Smaller growth rates in restraint levels are explicitly permitted 'in exceptional cases,' and undoubtedly the importing countries will prove to be less than vigorous in honoring their commitments to industrial adjustment in order to facilitate increased imports from developing countries."[21]

The Multi-fibre Arrangement has proved to be "a weapon for retaining and solidifying restrictions and, in some respects, for extending them (even if, as it now seems, it is still too liberal in its formulations to be welcome to some developed countries".[22] There is every justification for developing countries' fear of the extension of this "model" to other major sectors -- footwear, electronics, automobiles -- in which they have, or will shortly acquire, strong comparative advantage.

Emerging non-tariff protectionism in other sectors is already much more sophisticated and complex than heretofore, with a variety of legal weapons, new non-tariff instruments, and governmental arrangements added to the traditional simple instruments ". . . Through an array of esoteric and highly technical manoeuvres, particular industry interests are in a position to undermine overall policy by persistent harassment."[23] The resulting "nightmare of confusion" may be more disruptive to trade than even the import quotas and voluntary export restraints which have attracted so much attention. The complexity of policies and procedures in a variety of countries, particularly those relating to non-tariff barriers, cannot be overemphasized. Moreover, "the complexity is more than a static problem: it is an ever changing, kaleidoscopic kind of complexity that the exporters in developing nations face".[24] This complexity together with the continuing change in its details obviously creates great uncertainty for prospective exporters.

The impact of these new and changing forms of protectionism is discriminatory not only as between products but also as between types of firm. "Institutionally, the larger international trading companies and transnational corporations are much better situated to deal with complexity and a variety of requirements than relatively small-scale exporting entities in developing countries. The trading companies and transnationals operate on a scale that allows specialization in diversity, in information collecting, in management of local and institutional procedures in relation to national and local governments and, where necessary, in location of production facilities to minimize what are perceived to be economically impeding forces. The developing nations do not have large-scale enterprises or trading companies that can operate in this way."[25]

The advantages of the transnationals extend equally to intra-developing country trade, since the trading systems of the developing countries are frequently "impeded by an even more complex and administratively erratic array of border measures and procedures typically found in the developing nations themselves".[26] Moreover, TNCs frequently already have transnational marketing and information networks in place in the developing countries. These uncertainties in the trading arena also have a differential impact upon different actors for another reason. Transnational corporations with a worldwide network of market outlets and sources of supply can view the sudden imposition of particular non-tariff barriers in particular places with much greater equanimity than a national producer who is likely to have a much more specialized trade. These uncertainties are, therefore, likely to have a disproportionately greater adverse impact on independent national exporters.

Effect of Protectionism on Raw Material Processing

It would be misleading to suggest that protectionism's effects upon developing countries are concentrated exclusively in the labour-intensive industrial sectors. For the majority of developing countries, and certainly for the bulk of the poorer ones, the greatest problems created by developed countries' industrial protection are in the raw material processing sectors, which may or may not be labour-intensive as well. This protection, especially in the form of tariff rates which escalate with the level of processing so as to generate very high rates of effective protection for developed countries' early-stage processing industries, is certainly not "new"; but is shows few signs of going away either. Protectionism on raw material processing played an important part in the last two rounds of GATT bargaining. Reduction of tariffs on raw material imports, which is invariably portrayed by the offering countries as a "concession", is frequently designed to lower costs and thereby raise effective

protection for processing. Thus, according to one observer, in the
Dillon round, the probable purpose of the United States tariff
concessions in imported materials (which were running into short
supply within the United States) was "reducing the cost squeeze on
the manufacturing sectors which use them as inputs."[27] In the
Kennedy Round, protection for United States processors was more
straightforward. "The 'exceptions' to the across-the-board cuts on
manufactures were mainly simply processed goods such as wood
products on which LDCs tend to have comparative advantage."[28] Most
recently, it was significant that the European Economic
Commission's (EEC) special tariff reductions on tropical products,
introduced in 1977, were confined to raw materials.[29] Some of
these "concessions", in such cases as coffee and cocoa beans, had
the effect of increasing effective protection for European
processors. In order for such concessions to be most helpful to
developing countries, they must be offered on semi-processed and
processed materials as well as on raw ones.

A variety of economic influences have recently been working to
increase the relative attraction of developing country locations
for raw material processing: widening international wage
differentials, anti-pollution legislation in the industrialized
countries, export incentives or export requirements introduced by
developing countries' governments, altered tariff arrangements
under the generalized system of preferences (GSP) and the Lome
Convention, etc. In addition, the assumption of ownership and/or
control by developing countries' governments has altered the
objective functions of many resource-based enterprises. Despite
the generally slowly rising proportions of raw material exports
from developing countries which are in processed form,[30] trade
barriers in the developed countries remain an important obstacle to
further processing for export. They are particularly likely to
continue to plague the developing countries in those instances in
which they develop their own production, processing and marketing
systems, independently of the transnational corporations which have
traditionally dominated raw materials trade. At present,..."the
structural characteristics of most raw material industries, and
especially the degree of vertical integration prevalent in
them -- from exploration through extraction, concentration,
shipping, smelting, refining and fabrication -- constitute an
important impediment to new entrants and especially to the
establishment of independent systems of production."[31]

Once transnational corporations based in developed countries
do become involved in overseas export-oriented
processing -- overcoming their present distaste for it[32] in
consequence of the changing economic and political
circumstances -- they are likely to become advocates of reduced
trade barriers, and even of improved freight rate differentials,[33]
at least for their own processed products; they may also turn to
advocacy of increased non-tariff barriers against the independent
suppliers against whom they compete. In the immediate future,
outside the Lome Convention, escalated tariffs seem more likely to
be reduced on a commodity-by-commodity basis, as part of a broader
set of agreements with respect to the security of individual
materials supplies[34] than as part of conventional GATT bargaining,

since the beneficiary developing countries typically have little else with which to bargain. The possible means of overcoming existing barriers to the entry of developing countries' enterprises into the processing and distribution sectors of the raw materials industries, in circumstances where this would clearly be economic, deserve much more detailed study than they have so far received. These problems are not less important simply because they are not so new.

Value added tariffs and tariff preferences

Two perhaps more positive innovations in developed countries' tariff structures must also be mentioned in order to complete the picture of their impact upon developing countries' trade. The first is their recent creation or liberalization of "value added tariffs" or "off-shore assembly provisions". Under these provisions, import duties are imposed only upon the foreign value added when domestic materials are sent abroad for processing and subsequently re-imported. The best known tariff provision of this type is that of the United States; under items 806.30 and 807.00 of its tariff schedule, manufactured imports from developing countries, mainly of clothing and electronic components, have been growing at unprecedented rates (32 per cent per year in dutiable value between 1970 and 1977). While this tariff provision is applicable to all foreign trade in the United States case, imports under it from developing countries have risen more quickly than those from developed countries. Obviously, those which have been able to make the best use of these provisions are transnational corporations with productive facilities in a variety of countries linked to one another within a single controlling organization.

The second innovation is the introduction of preferential tariffs for manufactured products from developing countries, as agreed under the terms of the UNCTAD-initiated GSP and authorized under a waiver of the provisions of Article I of the General Agreement (GATT Decision of 25 June 1971 [L/3545]). Unfortunately, by the time that individual developed countries had satisfied all the domestic interests that feared the resulting increased developing country competition, they had to emasculate the GSP with lists of product exceptions, restrictive rules of origin, quotas or ceilings on its use, restrictions on the list of beneficiaries, and safeguard provisions, that a review of the early operations of the GSP[35] concluded that, "Even using the most charitable evaluation criteria leads to a conclusion that the GSP, as it operates today, is insignificant as a new trade policy to benefit the more than 150 developing countries designated as GSP beneficiaries."

The most recent analysis, which takes into account various improvements already made in the GSP shows that while preferential imports from developing countries have grown remarkably during the short period that the scheme has been in operation, there remains

major scope for further improvement by extension of product
coverage and the elimination or liberalization of other constraints
on preferential imports.[37]

Despite the agreed GATT principle of "non-discrimination" and
despite the GSP, the tariff and non-tariff barrier structures
emerging from six rounds of GATT tariff bargaining and other
developments now clearly discriminate against the major
manufactured exports of developing countries. "Non-discrimination"
as understood within the GATT means that the same treatment will be
accorded each exporting country with respect to each individual
traded product. "Discrimination" or "differential" treatment (such
as is found in the GSP) consists of the levying of a different
tariff on the same product depending upon the country of origin.
This is however an inadequate conception of discrimination. The
structure of MFN tariffs and other barriers across products is also
a potential source of inter-country discrimination, when particular
products are associated with particular countries and particular
types of firms. (The special arrangement for textiles and
clothing, and other TNBs, manage to combine both types of
discrimination against developing countries.) It is quite possible
for "preferences" (positive discrimination) in the GATT sense to be
more than offset by negative discrimination in the latter sense.
The discussions in UNCTAD, GATT, and the professional literature on
the subject have probably devoted too much attention to
discrimination in the GATT sense and not enough to discrimination
in the trade barrier structure sense. The latter issue has
recently been discussed under the heading of "special" treatment
for developing countries' products; MFN tariff cuts on products of
special interest to developing countries have been advocated for a
number of years and surfaced again as an issue in the current Tokyo
Round. What has been sufficiently noticed, however, is that while
this discussion of "special" as opposed to "differential" treatment
for developing countries were actually introduced (the GSP), the
degree of discrimination against the manufactured products of
greatest interest to developing countries has continued to
increase.

It is by now fairly predictable how the structure of trade
barriers in the major industrialized countries is likely to evolve.
Trade barriers are likely to continue to be greatest in the sectors
in which the developing countries have the most obvious comparative
advantage and where transnational corporations are least present.
Bhagwati has show that the threat of imposition of trade barriers
is sufficient to generate welfare losses for the exporting
countries since their investment and output decisions must be
affected by the uncertainties which such a threat creates.[37] Thus
a further bias in the productive and trade structure of developing
countries, beyond that created by the already existing trade
barriers is imparted by the bias in the "threat structure"; by
prospects that is, which may never even materialise.

But the developing countries have been expanding their
manufactured exports to the industrialized countries very rapidly
in recent years, while developed countries have been expanding
their imports of manufactures from developing countries at rates
greater than those of their imports from one another.[38] Studies of

the effects of tariff reductions under the GATT Dillon and Kennedy "rounds" have demonstrated that there is some developing country supply response even in products which are "atypical" for them. Thus even though tariff cuts in these two GATT rounds were made primarily for the purpose of the developed countries who were the principal participants in the negotiations, and despite the fact that the cuts were largely for products in which they are not generally considered to have a comparative advantage, developing countries nevertheless were able to take some advantage of them. In both rounds, "...on products which might be called atypical developing country exports (the developed country basket) we observed not only a significant increase of supply from the developing countries, but also a significant response to the marginal incentive of the tariff reductions."[39]

Is all of this talk of protectionism and discrimination therefore overdone? Are those who call attention to it, as some Washington analysts suggest, "crying wolf"? The answer must be a clear "no".

The above-mentioned atypical developing country exports were not those which were the most important to the developing countries or those which were necessarily growing fastest. Developing country manufactured exports to the industrial countries are concentrated in products in which the former have a pronounced comparative advantage and in which their cost advantages are much greater than the marginal additional advantages conferred on some products by these GATT bargaining rounds: their growth has had a substantial momentum of its own which is fuelled by comparative costs.[40] For this reason, the over-all basket of developing country manufactured exports to the industrialized world was probably not significantly affected by the GATT concessions analysed in the above-mentioned studies. Rather, these tariff cuts merely disproportionately (but still minimally) encouraged some exports of atypical products in which the cost differences between rich and poor were presumably not as great as in the typical ones and/or products "dominated by multi-national firms, who switch their global pattern of production in response to marginal signals".[41]

The "twist" in the incentives for developing country manufactured exports which has been imparted by subsequent development is, as has been seen, in the same general direction -- away from those products in which developing countries have the most obvious comparative advantage; and, other things being equal, towards those dominated by multinational firms. This "twist" is now becoming more important. It is the product of both domestic and international political forces, not the least of which is the rise of the transnational corporations which, as has been argued above, are deserving of more careful analysis.[42]

One cannot see the effects of the tariff cuts in the ex post trade data since, as always, it cannot be known what would otherwise have occurred. A demonstration that traditional products are still growing "quickly" is not proof that this has resulted from the tariff cuts. One can obtain a glimpse of the effects of the emerging structure of trade barriers, however, in official forecasts of developing countries' manufactured exports. If the present quantitative restrictions on developed countries' imports of textiles and clothing are strictly applied, and there are few reasons for thinking otherwise[43] the World Bank projects (allowing for a little upgrading of quality) a future real annual growth rate for developing countries' exports of only 5.5 per cent in clothing and 4.5 per cent in textiles (as against 1970-1975 rates of 20.3 per cent and 17.8 per cent respectively![44] During the 1975-1985 period, the Bank projects much more rapid rates of developing country exports growth for chemicals (13.0 per cent), iron and steel (14.5 per cent), and machinery and transport equipment (17.3 per cent). The last-mentioned group is made up largely of electronics products (radio, television, office equipment and calculators, electronic components) which, it says, "are mostly organized by transnational firms" their continued transfer of technology and maintenance of marketing channels, usually through subcontracting arrangements of various kinds, are part of the relatively bright future anticipated for the products.

What "protectionist" barriers do, whether those of a trading partner or one's own, is to alter the composition of output, consumption and trade. Protectionism in the industrialized world need not reduce the role of trade in developing countries but it is likely to alter it. It alters it through the impact which it has upon the structure of incentives, and therefore of trade itself, within the developing countries. The effects of the emerging structure of developed countries' trade barriers are, in their broadest terms, (1) to deflect manufacturing for export in the developing countries away from many of the activities in which they have a clear comparative advantage; and (2) to deflect manufacturing for export away from independent production and marketing systems, and toward those already organized by transnational corporations based in the developed countries.

Developing countries can acquire relatively easy access to OECD markets provided that they deal through the most powerful marketing and producing enterprises; thus, to provide the most dramatic example, it will continue to be easy to gain easy access to OECD markets for electronic components. If, on the other hand, a developing country exporter chooses to "go it alone" in an unskilled labour-intensive industry which is weak and without links in the importing countries -- such as garments or leather products -- he is likely to face trade barriers which are the product of the combined political pressure of labour and domestic capital within that industry.[45] Only if the industrial enterprises in the importing countries turn to international sources of supply and subcontracting are there prospects for tariff cuts (or even "standstills") for developing countries in these industries. Even so, such tariff cuts would probably only be made in circumstances in which firms in the importing countries continue to control the markets.

III. THE NEW PROTECTIONISM AND THE "MANAGMENT" OF INTERNATIONAL TRADE

When in 1972 the Director General of GATT was seeking to launch the present round of multilateral trade negotiations, he called attention to a number of basic changes in international trading relations which had to be "accommodated within a multilateral system of trade which must not insist on rigidly sticking to its traditional character and exigencies".[46] In addition to the emergence of the EEC and Japan, the expansion of the trade of some socialist countries of Eastern Europe with the West, the appearance of the GSP, and the increasing interdependence of national economies, he chose at that time to highlight "the growing importance of the multinational corporation in production and international trade". He would by now certainly want to add to other non-tariff barriers against the exports of the newly industrializing countries, a development which is related to the growth in the trade role of the transnational corporations, both being responses to similar "problems".

Transnational corporations and governments both seek a more "orderly" and predictable economic environment. Where international trade would otherwise constitute a source of disruptions or uncertainties they will both, unless it is obviously too costly to do so, seek to "manage" it in ways which accord with their own perceived interests. As the developed countries have encountered new disruptions and uncertainties in consequence of an unusually deep recession and slow recovery, and the acceleration of technological and structural change in the world economy, their governments are (again) talking of "organizing" free trade and creating "orderly markets".

In calling for increased international "management" of governmental trade policies and actions (through new consultative machinery), Long more recently observed, "...there is a great deal in common between the notions of management of a great commercial enterprise, on the one hand, and the notion of joint responsibility in the handling of the international trading system, on the other. Trade relations today need the same kind of continuous attention, continuous anticipation and assessment of possible crises, continuous consultation to overcome difficulties when they arise. The time is past when international trade could be left to follow its own course or be reviewed only intermittently."[47]

A very substantial and growing proportion of international trade is already managed in more or less the fashion which Long describes by "great commercial enterprises", more usually described as "transnational corporations". The latest report of the United Nations Centre for Transnational Corporations notes that 46 per cent of total United States imports and 45 per cent of total United States exports have been "intra-firm"; comparable data for other countries show intra-firm transactions accounting for 59 per cent of Canadian exports, 29 per cent of Swedish exports and 30 per cent of United Kingdom exports.[48] Such evidence as there is suggests that the proportion of intra-OECD trade which is intra-firm, though international, is rising.

"Organized free trade", "orderly marketing", and international "management" are thus already present in numerous industries with respect to which these phrases have never surfaced in inter-governmental deliberations. This trade is organized and ordered by transnational corporations, which are also responsible for the careful worldwide planning of new investments so that they are geared as much as possible to the best estimates of emerging demand.[49]

There is very wide divergence, however, as between product categories in the degree to which developed countries' imports are so "managed" by private firms.

Evidently the types of products in which the developing countries have the greatest comparative advantage -- with the major exception of electric components -- are found at the bottom end of the ranking of intra-firm trade. This implies that: (1) the markets for many of the manufactured products of developing countries are at present less subject to centralized private "management" than others, and are therefore more unstable and probably more competitive; (2) because of the absence of powerful lobbyists against trade barriers, such as are to be found when transnational corporations are major traders,[50] these markets are peculiarly "vulnerable" to governmental managerial (real "protectionist") efforts.

It would seem that attempts on the part of the governments of developed countries to "manage" the markets for products from developing countries, when they show signs of "disruption", are moving into a relative "management vacuum". Governmental "management" is to provide "order" in those segments of trade where private firms do not. That is obviously not to say that these governments never intervene in industries where their own "great commercial enterprises" are to be found. As in the recent cases of steel, shipbuilding and synthetic fibres, when such large firms, whether private or public, have encountered major difficulties, governments have increasingly sought to assist them through support for rationalization, cartelization, or increased protection.

The state in the developed countries is, in general, becoming more and more involved in a variety of way in the problems of manufacturing industries. Some of this involvement has been designed to encourage new and purportedly dynamic industries, but most is intended to ease the problems of industries which are experiencing economic difficulties. The policy measures now being resorted to extent to the area of trade policy directly, as well as indirectly -- through subsidies, cheap credit, special tax provisions, and the like.

In the international arena, the powerful governments will always seek to influence the weak. The same industrialized countries which are pressuring poorer countries to introduce "voluntary export restraints" on some (manufactured) products are also trying to induce them to provide supply guarantees on others (mainly primary products). These same countries themselves proceed to introduce export restrictions when they require them for domestic political purposes, regardless of their international impact -- as in the cases of soyabeans and scrap metals. In at

TABLE 1

Intra-firm trade as proportion of United States imports :[a] 1975

Lowest shares [b]	Per cent	Highest shares [c]	Per cent
Leather and tanning products	3.7	Plastics and synthetic materials	50.2
Wooden containers	6.5	Paints and allied products	53.5
Miscellaneous textile products	7.3	Primary iron and steel	56.2
Footwear	10.2	Construction and mining machinery	56.3
Apparel	11.7	Machine shop products	56.8
Food products	13.7	General industrial machinery	57.8
		Radio, TV and communications equipment	58.2
		Electrical machinery	58.6
		Engines and turbines	60.1
		Electric industrial equipment	63.0
		Office computing and accounting machinery	72.2
		Farm machinery	76.7
		Motor vehicles and equipment	82.8
		Electric components and accessories	84.7

Source : U.S. Bureau of the Census, Foreign Trade Division.

[a] Proportion of imports originating with parties related by ownership to the extent of 5 per cent equity or more.

[b] Product groups with share under 20 per cent.

[c] Product groups with share over 50 per cent.

least one instance, the United States actually attempted to induce Japan to impose "voluntary import restraints" on particular United States (forest product) exports in pursuit of United States internal policy objectives. All of these pressures are rationalized in the name of "orderly marketing" or "fair trade". When rules and principles are replaced by case-by-case negotiations, the poor can only lose from the resulting inevitable abuses of power and application of discrimination. When governments join private corporations in the unrestrained pursuit of national and sectoral interests, the outcome is bound to be worse both for world welfare and that of the developing countries, than if governments did not intervene at all.

One of the reasons for governmental involvement in "troubled" industries is the limited knowledge of the possible alternatives. Evidently remarkably little is known about the process through which private industry adapts and restructures itself in response to competitive pressures.[51] In what circumstances does it lead to increased firm diversification? increased market concentration? increased internationalization of production? redeployment as opposed to unemployment of labour of different kinds? and so forth:

If the rapid pace of change or the possibly excessive costs of short-term adjustment are deemed too high, in the absence of research which demonstrates the contrary, and in the presence of strong political pressures, then governmental measures to slow down the change or even stop it, are bound to follow. Very rarely indeed does governmental "adjustment assistance" take the form of encouragement to abandon an uncompetitive sector entirely. Among the probable effects of the recent recession and the current general slowdown in growth, together with governmental support for rationalization however, is a further "shakeout" of the less efficient, usually smaller, and less internationally-oriented private firms in "troubled" industries. One recent study found that the declining, rather than infant industries which enjoyed the highest rates of protection in recent years also showed the best (most slowly growing) cost performance.[52] Protectionism is softening the blow for them and for their employees, but the trend towards greater size, greater "transnationalism," and greater governmental involvement with the larger private firms in the developed countries is probably irreversible. "Organized free trade", as understood by governments, then is a euphemism for increased support through protection and a probable licence for increased cartelization. Realistically, it consists of "market-sharing" agreements in favour of aging and inefficient domestic industries at the expense of competitive foreign producers.[53] The stabilization of existing market shares, or even more favourable provision for their regulation, can scarcely be described as any kind of "free" trade. "Whereas in the 1930s cartels on a national and international basis were organized by producers and exporters essentially of their own volition, now they are being organized at the instigation and with the blessing of governments."[54] Developing countries are, of course, not without experience in facing foreign "management" of international markets. But any new thrust towards multiplication of cartels and cartel-like arrangements, now with the express purpose of protecting developed countries' industries primarily against the competitive pressures of new more efficient plants in developing countries, must be strenuously resisted. And in this instance, unlike some others on the New International Economic Order (NIEO) agenda, the developing countries should have the support of the mainstream of the economics profession.

Nor can many economists be pleased with the increasing resort on the part of governments to complex and totally ad hoc other trade arrangements designed to "manage" the problems of troublesome industries more effectively. For instance, the Government of Canada has recently negotiated a duty remission scheme with Volkswagen which provides for reduced duties on imports to Canada of finished Volkswagen automobiles from whatever geographic source, according to a formula which is geared to the Canadian value added in exports of automotive parts by Volkswagen from Canada to any destination. This scheme, according to the Canadian Minister responsible, "represent a first step toward negotiating orders with representatives of other off-shore motor vehicle manufacturers." The same Government had earlier introduced measures to protect domestic manufacturers of televisions sets by allowing them to import a certain number annually of finished television sets free of duty, that number to be proportional to the number built in Canada. GATT regulations have little to say about such firm-specific trade policies, and perhaps it is time they did.

Even those who are generally suspicious of the role of governments in general acknowledge that by now while "there may be too much government at the national level...there may be too little government internationally..."[55] At the international level, "Doctrinal pursuit of the virtues of free markets cannot be meaningful without establishing boundaries for legitimate government action, since governments must act for political reasons. Indeed...there is no virtue in the free market, indeed there is no free market, without fixed rules of all kinds, including those establishing boundaries for government action."[56]

Intergovernmental "management" may be most effective, and most helpful to the developing countries, if it refrains from continual interventions in daily affairs, and instead establishes and maintains agreed rules. The uncertainties created by continued resort to case-by-case approaches in manufactured goods trade could distort and even paralyse decision-making. What may be most required is an increased political commitment to the maintenance of a degree of international "order". This could, of course, be buttressed by international consultative arrangement, information exchanges, and the like, such as abound in the primary product sectors -- under the auspices of FAO, UNCTAD, and the various commodity councils and producers' associations.

Administrative discretion, unpredictable and complex rules and regulations, and ad hoc agreements in international trade all favour the strong traders. The transnational corporations of the developed countries can get along much better in the emerging world of the "new protectionism" than can small and independent firms, particularly those in the developing countries. Rules, norms and codes of conduct protect the weak. The strong can always look after themselves.

The erosion of GATT norms, and the appearance of new <u>ad hoc</u>
practices which bear no relationship to established <u>GATT</u>
principles, must therefore be matters of particular interest to
developing countries, whatever they may think of the GATT as an
institution. If acceptable rules cannot be agreed for the conduct
of international trade, especially in those sectors which are not
at present "managed" by transnational corporations, it will become
ever more difficult to envisage developing country exports which do
not take place under the transnationals' control. It goes without
saying that codes and norms for the "managed trade" and other
activities of the transnationals are themselves of enormous
importance to the developing countries and still remain to be
agreed.

IV. THE TOKYO ROUND AND THE DEVELOPING COUNTRIES

Developing countries were to receive special consideration
under the Tokyo round of GATT bargaining. To this purpose,
analysts have devoted considerable energy to the estimation of the
possible effects of tariff (and other trade barrier) cuts under the
current round of multilateral negotiations upon the exports of
developing countries. The available studies generally conclude
that the developing countries would stand to gain more from
across-the-board MFN tariff reductions than they would lose from
the possible erosion of their existing preferential tariff
margins.[57] These much-quoted results, however, flow from dubious
of unstated political assumptions and do not stand up to careful
scrutiny.

Baldwin and Murray, for instance, assume that MFN tariff cuts
will extend both more widely and more deeply than those at present
available to developing countries under the GSP: 50 per cent cuts
are to be offered on all industrial products other than textiles,
shoes and petroleum; these cuts are to be unrestricted by quotas
and permanent in their application; and they are to be granted to
all countries whether or not they are beneficiaries of the GSP (or,
apparently, signatories to the GATT). With such assumptions how
could their conclusion be otherwise? Unfortunately, they do not
address the political questions. It is not evident why the same
political forces which have generated the limited GSP schemes now
in place and the increasing resort to "safeguard" mechanisms,
orderly marketing arrangements and the like, should now acquiesce
in 50 per cent MFN tariff cuts, much less irreversible ones in a
world in which, as Golt puts it, "formal MFN commitments have by no
means guaranteed to the weaker trading partners, and to the newly
industrialised countries in particular, the full and unfettered
benefits of MFN treatment?"[58] Perhaps there are some reasons why
the peculiar politics of Northern protectionism might generate such
divergent results in response to different negotiating routes, but
they have not yet been stated.

This study itself demonstrates that the elimination of value limits on GSP trade and the extension of the GSP beyond its initial ten years would reverse the results, rendering their postulated MFN tariff cuts, on balance, costly to developing countries. It also notes that "except for the major exporting developing countries, the (postulated) broader product coverage of MFN tariff cuts provides minor trade advantages". The World Bank in its "Prospects for Developing Countries 1978-1985," observes further, that tropical Africa would actually suffer a slight net loss from the Tokyo round's MFN tariff cuts in consequence of erosion of Lome and GSP preference margins (assuming they are renewed).

What stands out from the recent quantifying exercises with respect to the gains from various international trading arrangements for the developing countries is that even the immediate and across-the-board tariff cuts postulated are less important to developing countries' trade prospects than are the continued existence or expansion of the GSP and the offshore assembly (or value added) provisions of the tariff. This can be seen in table 2, which records the most recent estimates of the increased exports of developing countries resulting from various tariff provisions. The estimates with respect to the MFN tariff cuts have here been recalculated, using the original author's methodology, to allow for the prospect that these cuts are now unlikely to reach the 50 per cent or 60 per cent levels postulated earlier; a 40 per cent overall cut, which undoubtedly still overstates the likely actual offers, is here assumed instead.

While too much reliance cannot be placed on estimates of this kind, nevertheless it can reasonably be concluded that, small as the developing countries' gains from the GSP are universally recognised to be, they are of greater consequence in the short-to-medium run than would be the likely gains from MFN tariff cuts. A top relative priority for the developing countries in the near future must therefore be to ensure the extension of the GSP beyond its originally scheduled termination date. Even after some erosion from a successful round of MFN tariff cuts, its estimated value exceeds the estimated gain from the MFN cuts themselves.

Second in relative importance would seem to be the continuation of the value added (or off-shore assembly) provisions in the United States tariff and the extension of similar ones in other countries, where there potential relative importance would presumably be just as great. Noting these apparent priorities is not in any way to deny that the developing countries nevertheless stand to gain something from a successful round of MFN tariff cuts. It is merely to provide a more appropriate context to the international discussion. Both the GSP and the value added tariffs, after all, have encountered some recent political opposition; and there has been relatively little careful assessment of how important these issues are, relative to the attention devoted to MFN tariff cuts under the Tokyo Round. From these various analyses it is quite clear that the developing countries stand to gain from the removal of existing ceiling or safeguard provisions relating to trade barriers on their products; and from the expansion of product coverage of all tariff-cutting schemes relating to their exports, whether under the GSP or the multilateral trade negotiations (MTN). How these results can best

TABLE 2

Estimated effects of different trade arrangements on exports from developing countries to certain developed countries

	Exports to :		
	United States	EEC and Japan	Total
	($ million at 1974-1975 prices)		
Estimated annual increase in exports from developing countries attributable to :			
1. Generalized system of preferences. .	608	504	1 112
(*of which* : manufactures)	(545)	(467)	(1 012)
2. Value-added tariff schemes	416	. . [a]	. . [a]
3. Reduction of 40 per cent in MFN tariffs (excluding oil and textiles) . .	338	564	902
(*of which* : manufactures)	(224)	(255)	(479)

Source : Data in Thomas B. Birnberg, "Economic Effects of Changes in the Trade Relations between the Developed and Less-Developed Countries", Overseas Development Council, Washington, June, 1978, and related calculations by the present author.

[a] Estimate not available.

be obtained in the face of political pressures to the contrary is a matter of diplomatic and political strategy and tactics, not of economics.

Any conclusion that MFN tariff-cutting can work only to the developing countries' advantage must be based, therefore, on political judgements rather than on existing economic analysis.[59] Such judgements need to be made about trade policy formation in the developed countries (most importantly, about the likelihood of GSP improvements and the use of safeguard mechanisms) but also about the inter-country distribution of trade policy effects (GSP beneficiaries versus non-beneficiaries; relatively advanced, versus the poorest, developing countries, and so forth).[60]

While the developing countries do stand to lose disproportionately from a breakdown of accepted rules of trading behaviour and failure to work out new ones, it is not at all evident that they would be very much affected by a failure of the current Tokyo Round to agree upon MFN tariff reductions. If nothing were achieved other than MFN tariff cuts, and most observers believe these are the easiest objectives to achieve, the effect would probably be to increase the "bias" in developed countries' trade barrier structures in favour of products of prime interests to developed countries and transnational corporations;[61] it would be an illusion to think that MFN tariff cuts will be totally across-the-board and non-discriminatory even if they have been described as "linear"; moreover the rollback of a large number of NTB's is not even under discussion.

Two major conclusions emerge from the above analysis:

(1) The developing countries stand to be enormous losers from the multiplication of non-tariff barriers, evasions of accepted international trade conventions, and resort to international trade bullying;

(2) The outcome of the tariff bargaining process among the OECD members in the current GATT round is not, of itself, of great consequence to the developing countries.

It follows that the interests of the developing countries in the GATT stand or fall with its success in re-establishing agreed "rules of the trading game". In particular, in the present context, this must mean, above all, the establishment of internationally agreed procedures with respect to resort to import quotas, voluntary export restraints and orderly marketing arrangements; agreed definitions of such much-abused terms as "market disruption"; agreed provisions for industrial adjustment and international surveillance, etc. In short, their interest lies, above all, in the reform of Article XIX.[62] Even without the preferential treatment which they seek, the developing countries also stand to gain more from the successful negotiation of codes of conduct on NTBs -- countervailing duties (and the export subsidies which give rise to them), government procurement practices, technical standards and customs valuation procedures, all of which are being discussed in the current bargaining round -- than they are likely to derive from MFN tariff cuts. These NTBs, after all, are now being deployed, and are likely to continue to be deployed, disproportionately against them. If these aims cannot be achieved, the developing countries, faced with the continued prospect of trade bullying, have little incentive to co-operate with the GATT in other respects, It might then soon become, in fact, "the rich man's club" which many have long felt it already was in practice. Long has himself recently warned that "if the rich countries refuse to accept for themselves the logic of adjustment and an international division of labour inherent in the present world trading system, they cannot reasonably expect the developing countries to continue to support that system".[63]

Although Golt has observed that too much haste to complete the negotiations may produce the result that "the developing countries will feel, with perhaps some justification, that their pre-occupations will be pushed aside,"[64] he and other informed observers have already abandoned hope of achieving in the current round of GATT bargaining the extra gains for developing countries which were originally promised.[65]

In the longer-run effort at the establishment of new norms, rules, procedures, and codes for a world of increased state trading, intra-firm trade and intergovernmental attempts at "management", one must raise the question of whether the GATT, as it is at present constituted, is an appropriate institution for the purpose. Is it not perhaps time to launch a major new effort to recruit wider membership in an organization which takes broad responsibility for the conduct of world trade? The GATT's signatories number only 84 whereas the IMF's membership is 131 and UNCTAD's is 158. In the Tokyo Round, of "the 78 LDCs officially declared as participants, less than one fourth are actively taking part in the negotiations".[66] An improved constitutional format might also encourage wider forms of international trade co-operation. The GATT machinery is not now well suited, for example, to the negotiation of "deals", such as Bergsten suggests, in which, for example, concessions on commodities (such as supply and price guarantees), are coupled with reduced tariff escalation on processed materials. This need not mean the abandonment of the carefully constructed existing GATT arrangements and precedents. Various alternative possibilities should certainly, however, now be canvassed.

NOTES

[1] Carlos F. Diaz-Alejandro, "Trade Policies and Economic Development", in Peter B. Kenen (ed.), International Trade and Finance, Frontiers for Research (Cambridge University Press), 1975 p. 97.

[2] Ibid., p. 96.

[3] See for example, UNCTAD document "Growing protectionism and the standstill on trade barriers against imports from developing countries." (TD/B/C.2/194); IMF, 29th Annual Report on Exchange Restrictions (Washington) 1978 and Bahram Nowzad "The Resurgence of Protectionism", Finance and Development 15, 3, September 1978, pp. 14-19; Olivier Long "International Trade under Threat: a Constructive Response", The World Economy 1, 3, June 1978, p. 251.

[4] See Tracy Murray and Ingo Walter "Special and Differential Liberalization of Quantitative Restrictions on Imports from Developing Countries" in L. Perez Lorenzo (ed.) Trade Policies towards Developing Countries: The Multinational Trade Negotiations (Bureau for Intergovernmental and International Affairs, Agency for International Development, Washington, D.C.), pp. 50-51, and Jagdish N. Bhagwati, "Market Disruption, Export Market Disruption, Compensation and GATT Reform" in Jagdish N. Bhagwati (ed.) The New International Economic Order: The North-South Debate (M.I.T. Press, Cambridge, USA), pp. 159-191.

[5] It is something of a mystery why the exporting and banking interests of the industrialized countries have not therefore been more effective lobbyists against the new trade barriers.

[6] Such pledges have repeatedly been made -- in GATT, UNCTAD, OECD, and at meetings of Heads of State. (See "Growing protectionism and the standstill on trade barriers against imports from developing countries", op. cit.)

[7] For a discussion on the lack of interdisciplinary research on international economic policy see Fred Bergsten, ed. The Future of the International Economic Order: An Agenda for Research. (1973), p. 82.

[8] See, for example, Thomas B. Birnberg "Economic Effects of Changes in the Trade Relations Between the Developed and Less Developed Countries", (Overseas Development Council, Washington, 1978). William R. Cline; Niboru Kawanabe; Kronsjo; and Thomas Williams, Trade Negotiations in the Tokyo Round: A Quantitative Assessment (Brookings Institution, Washington) 1978. World Bank, Prospects for Developing Countries, 1978-85 (Development Policy Staff, Washington, 1977).

[9]See, for example, UNCTAD, "Recent trends and developments in trade in manufactures and semi-manufactures of developing countries and territories: 1977 Review", TD/B/C.2/190, 1978 and World Bank, World Development Report, 1978 (Washington, D.C.).

[10]World Bank, ibid.

[11]According to one estimate between 67 per cent and 75 per cent of the developing countries' possible export gains in the current multilateral tariff negotiations would accrue to only 10 countries (see Birnberg op. cit.).

[12]World Bank. World Development Report, 1978, op. cit. (p. 18).

[13]See, for example, UNCTAD. "The main issues for UNCTAD in the 1980s," UNCTAD Seminar Programme, Report Series, No. 4, July 1978 (pp. 7-8).

[14]According to Preeg even in the Kennedy Round, "the largest reductions were achieved in industries typified by advanced technology, product innovation, and large, often international firms" (see Ernest Preeg, Traders and Diplomats, An Analysis of the Kennedy Round of Negotiations under the General Agreement on Tariffs and Trade).

[15]See Kym Anderson "The Political Market for Government Assistance to Industries" (Australian National University, 1978, mimeo); David Ball "United States effective tariff's and Labor's share" Journal of Political Economy 75, 2 april 1967 and G.K. Helleiner, "The Political Economy of Canada's Tariff Structure: An Alternative Model" Canadian Journal of Economics 10, 2 May 1977, pp. 318-326; M. Constantopoulos "Labour Protection in Western Europe" European Economic Review 5, 1974, pp. 313-328.

[16]See Helleiner, op. cit., Preeg, op. cit., John Cheh, "United States Concessions in the Kennedy Round and Short-run Labor Adjustment Costs", Journal of International Economics 4, 4 November, 1974, pp. 323-340; James Riedel "Tariff Concessions in the Kennedy Round and the Structure of Protection in West Germany: An Econometric Assessment" Journal of International Economics, May 1977, pp. 134-144. In the Federal Republic of Germany, changes were apparently now in the direction of greater uniformity of protection for all industries, with the result that other "adjustment" policy instruments were deployed to support troubled sectors (Riedel). In the Canadian case, there was not a statistically significant relationship between unskilled labour-intensity and changes in effective tariff protection during the 1960s, although the strong relationship with effective protection levels remained intact. (Helleiner).

[17]The shares of developing countries in developed countries' markets even in these sectors are still, by and large, remarkably small. In textiles and clothing, the sector which has caused the most difficulty, the developing countries' market shares in the

mid-1970s were still only 4 per cent in the United States, 8 per cent in the Federal Republic of Germany, 6 per cent in the United Kingdom, 5 per cent in Canada, 4 per cent in Japan, and 2 per cent in France (World Bank, World Development Report, op. cit. p. 17, 1978) These proportions can obviously be much higher in more narrowly defined product groups.

[18]The likelihood that growth rates in OECD countries will remain lower in the foreseeable future than they had in the period up to the early 1970s provides a powerful rationale for developing countries to expand their trade with one another. Provided that they consciously plan to create the necessary trade infrastructure (credit, transport, insurance, etc. facilities), they may collectively constitute a truly independent engine of growth in the world economy, which would generate stimulatory effects for the economies of the industrialized countries.

[19]These exceptions are authorized under GATT articles, XI, XII, XIX, XX and XXI. For a complete discussion of these "safeguard" provisions, see David Robertson, "Fail Safe Systems for Trade Liberalisation", Thames Essay No. 12 (Trade Policy Research Centre, London), 1977.

[20]Many of the new barriers on labour-intensive products are actually aimed at Japan rather than the developing countries, but the message for the latter is quite clear. Moreover, the harmful impacts upon the developing countries of such barriers as do affect them are likely to be much greater than they are on Japan.

[21]See Tracy Murray and Ingo Walter, "Special and Differential Liberalization of Quantitative Restrictions on Imports from developing countries", op. cit., p. 61.

[22]Sidney Golt "Developing Countries in the GATT System", Thames Essay No. 13 (Trade Policy Research Centre, London, 1978); p. 9; see also UNCTAD "Growing Protectionism and the standstill on trade barriers against imports from developing countries", 1978, op. cit., pp. 10-11.

[23]Harold Malmgren, "Significance of Trade Policies in the World Economic Outlook", The World Economy, 1, 1, October 1977, p. 25.

[24]Harold Malmgren "Trade Policies of the Developed Countries for the Next Decade", in Jagdish Bhagwati, (ed.) The New International Economic Order: The North-South Debate (M.I.T. Press, Cambridge, USA), p. 221.

[25]Harold Malmgren, "Trade Policies of the Developed Countries for the Next Decade", op. cit., pp. 220-221.

[26]Ibid., p. 228.

[27]J.M. Finger, "GATT Tariff Concessions and the Exports of Developing Countries", Economic Journal, 84, September, 1974, p.

573.

[28] J.M. Finger "Effects of the Kennedy Round Tariff Concessions on the Exports of Developing Countries", Economic Journal, 86, March 1976, p. 95.

[29] T.E. Ibrahim, "Developing Countries and the Tokyo Round", Journal of World Trade Law, 1978, 12, 1, pp. 12-13.

[30] Marian Radetzki, "Where Should Developing Countries Minerals Be Processed? The Country View versus the Multinational Company View", World Development, 5, 4, April, 1977 (pp. 325-334); G.K. Helleiner, "Structural Aspects of Third World Trade: Some Trends and Some Prospects". Paper presented to the Twenty-fifth Anniversary Conference of the Institute of Social Studies, the Hague, to be published in Conference Proceedings and a forthcoming issue of the Journal of Development Studies.

[31] Transnational Corporation in World Development: A Re-examination, (United Nations Publication. Sales No. E.78.II.A.5.)

[32] See Marian Radetzki "Where Should Developing Countries Minerals be Processed? The Country view versus the Multinational Company view", op. cit.

[33] See A.J. Yeats, "Do International Transport Costs increase with Fabrication? Some Empirical Evidence", Oxford Economic Papers, 1971, 29, 3, pp. 458-471.

[34] Fred Bergsten, "Access to Supplies and the New International Economic Order" in Jagdish N. Bhagwati (ed.), The New International Economic Order: The North-South Debate (M.I.T. Press, Cambridge, USA) 1977, p. 213.

[35] Tracy Murray, Trade Preferences for Developing Countries (Macmillan, London) 1977, p. 148.

[36] "Review and evaluation of the generalized system of preferences" (TD/232).

[37] Bhagwati, Jagdish "Market Disruption, Export Market Disruption, Compensation and GATT Reform", op. cit., pp. 171, 181-190.

[38] See "Recent Trends and Developments in trade in manufactures and semi-manufactures of developing Countries: 1977 Review," op. cit.

[39] See Finger, "Effects of the Kennedy Round Tariff Concessions on Exports of Developing Countries", op. cit., p. 94.

[40] Kennedy Round tariff reductions apparently did significantly affect developing country exports of "typical" products as well, although many of the key products were "exceptions" on which no

concessions were made.

[41]Finger, "GATT Tariff Concessions and the Exports of Developing Countries, op. cit., pp. 572-573.

[42]Big importing firms have the potential to exert some off-setting influence upon trade policy formation but they have not generally been listened to with nearly as great attention as have the manufacturers and workers in the affected industries. See Helleiner "Transnational Enterprises and the New Political Economy of U.S. Trade Policy" Oxford Economic Papers, 29, 1, March 1977, pp. 102-116 for an attempt at some analysis of this type.

[43]World Bank World Development Report 1978, op. cit., p. 17.

[44]Ibid., pp. 28-29.

[45]Helleiner "Transnational Enterprises and the New Political Economy of U.S. Trade Policy" op. cit.

[46]Long "Towards Better Trade Relations in the 70's" Address to a joint meeting of the Foreign Affairs club and the Trade Policy Research Centre, London, January 24 (mimeo), p. 3.

[47]Long, "International Trade under Threat: a Constructive Response" op. cit., p. 260.

[48]United Nations Transnational Corporations in World Development: A Re-examination, op. cit.

[49]There exists, of course, potential for some competition (and therefore miscalculation) among the transnationals in many sectors, but any resulting "disruptions" are regarded as part of the normal risk of private business; and they are, in any case, as nothing compared to the "disorder" which can arise in consequence of totally unco-ordinated investment and trading decisions which are based upon arbitrary and changing governmental criteria, or upon divergent private information or expectations as to governmental actions.

[50]Transnational corporations will typically be resistant to such protectionism as might interfere with their intra-firm trade since, as the United Nations Report on Transnational Corporations has put it, "the advantages of internationally rationalized production could be greatly reduced, leaving transnational corporations with many useless plants".

[51]Structural adjustment is required in the industries of developed countries today not merely because of the emergence of new low-cost competitors but also because of a variety of other factors: higher energy costs, changing demand patterns, an apparently accelerated pace of technological change, rising domestic labour costs, etc., which, together, according to

virtually all studies, dwarf the former in over-all importance.

[52]Tim Hazeldine, "Protection and Prices, Profits and Productivity in Thirty-three Canadian Manufacturing Industries," Economic Council of Canada, Discussion Paper, No. 110, (Ottawa 1978).

[53]"Growing protectionism and the standstill on trade barriers against imports from developing countries", op. cit., p. 4.

[54]Ibid., p. 4.

[55]Charles P. Kindleberger, "Government and International Trade", Princeton, Essays in International Finance, no. 129, July 1978, p. 17.

[56]Harald Malmgren, "Trade Policies of the Developed Countries for the Next Decade" op. cit., p. 232.

[57]See R. Baldwin and T. Murray, "MFN Tariff Reductions and LDC Benefits under GSP", Economic Journal, 87, 345, March 1977, pp. 30-46, Cline et al., op. cit., and Birnberg op. cit.

[58]Golt, "Developing Countries in the GATT System", op. cit., p. 18.

[59]In a more detailed critique of this "orthodox" view, Ahmad has noted that there is no reason for posing the most-favoured-nation (MFN) tariffs and the generalized system of preferences (GSP) in "either-or" terms. There is a wide variety of mixes of GSP schemes and MFN tariffs which could achieve the same effects. If it really was the objective of the GATT members to do the maximum for developing countries' trade prospects, for instance, it would suffice to accommodate developing countries by retaining existing preferential margins on only 3 per cent of total developed countries' manufactured imports, leaving the other 97 per cent for full MFN tariff-cutting. (See J. Ahmad, "Tokyo Rounds of Tariff Negotiations and the Generalized System of Preferences", Economic Journal, 88, June 1978, p. 294.)

[60]In defence of his view that "It is no longer a question of whether there shall be differential and special treatment. It is now a question of how", Gardner Patterson in his "Comment" in "The New International Economic Order: The North-South Debate", op. cit., pp. 236-259, has provided a useful list of the developing country proposals which have been under discussion in each of the six major negotiating groups of the Tokyo Round. It can serve as a checklist against which to measure the terms of any finally negotiated agreements. It does appear somewhat esoteric, however, to continue to argue the merits of different new schemes for special and differential treatment for developing countries when at the same time the continuing politics of developed countries' trade policies are driving them towards positions of increasing discrimination against developing countries.

[61]While MFN tariff cuts would increase the discrimination as
between products which are protected by NTBs and those which are
not; they might reduce that between some of the products in the
latter category.

[62]The most important of the Baldwin-Murray conclusions, though one
that has not been quoted as much, may have been that non-tariff
barriers "pose a more damaging barrier to developing country
exports than tariff rates" and that "safeguard" measures must be
controlled (see Baldwin and Murray, op. cit.) also Tumlir,
"Emergency Protection against Sharp Increases in Imports" in H.
Corbet and R. Jackson (editors), In Search of New World Economic
Order (Croom Helm) and Robertson, "Fail Safe Systems for Trade
Liberalization", op. cit.) for good surveys of the difficulties
with the present version of GATT's article XIX. In the
discussion of the reform of GATT's "safeguard" provisions, Kenen
(in "Chairman's Concluding Remarks", in Lorenzo L. Perez (ed.),
Trade Policies Towards Developing Countries, the Multilateral
Trade Negotiations, Bureau for Intergovernmental and
International Affairs, Agency for International Development,
Washington D.C., pp. 232-239), has recently persuasively argued
the case for the use of temporary tariff quotas as safeguard
instruments rather than as quantitative restrictions. If imports
above assigned country quotas were temporarily taxed at very high
rates rather than totally prohibited, the resulting trade
distortions would be lessened, the effects would still be
attributable to the "responsible" countries, and the likelihood
of their being phased out would increase.

[63]See Long "International Trade Under Threat", op. cit., p. 254.

[64]See S. Golt "The GATT Negotiations 1973-1979: The Closing Stage"
(British-North American Committee, London), p. 16.

[65]The timetable for the negotiations as it now stands seems to
leave very little chance of working out in detail, or indeed even
in general outline, very much of the "special and differential"
treatment for "the developing countries" which was emphasized in
the Tokyo Declaration. I find it difficult, therefore, to modify
the conclusion which I reached in 1974 that "the problems of
producing a resounding package of benefits for the developing
countries considered as a unified mass may therefore turn out to
be as intractable as ever..." the results in terms of specified
benefits for the developing countries as such may look very
meagre...It now must seem very likely that if any part of these
objectives is to be achieved, it will have to be in the
continuing process of adaptation of the GATT which will follow
the conclusion of the Tokyo Round as such, rather than in the
current negotiations. Even then, the problems will not find easy
or quick solutions. Ibid., pp. 29-30.

[66]Ibrahim "Developing Countries and the Tokyo Round", op. cit., p.
15.

Regulating Technology Imports in Some Developing Countries

DANIEL CHUDNOVSKY

INTRODUCTION

The economic rationale behind government regulations in the market for imported technology in developing countries should be sought mainly in the imperfect features of that market. Recipients of foreign technology have had to deal with suppliers in strong bargaining positions, who have been able to impose a variety of limitations on access to know-how and to charge high prices for making the technology available to firms operating in developing countries.

Although the need for government action was also justified by more general economic and technological consideration, such as the wish to foster the industrialization process and to develop a local technological capacity, it is clear that a basic objective was to help the recipients of technology to strengthen their bargaining position.

Once the case in favour of government action was accepted, specific regulations were adopted and institutional machinery was established in several developing countries.

Some of the results achieved so far are discussed recently in an UNCTAD secretariat report[1] which deals in particular with what has been happening in respect of royalty payments, elimination of restrictive practices and reduction of the duration of contracts. However, in order to shed more light on the impact of government policies in this field, a thorough analysis of the behaviour of suppliers and recipients is called for.

The present article focuses on the market for imported technology by independent firms, i.e. the case where the supplier

From **TRADE AND DEVELOPMENT** , UNCTAD Review, Winter 1981 (133-149), reprinted by permission of the publisher.

has no equity participation in the recipient enterprise.[2] In that imperfect market it has often been assumed that the supply of technology has generally been inelastic to price reductions within a reasonable range. Thus, the monopoly rents enjoyed by technology suppliers might be taxed without affecting supply.

Regarding the demand for foreign technology, it has been assumed that in most cases the recipient firms have a weak bargaining position, because of the peculiarities of the technology market and their lack of technological experience. Recipient firms were thus subject to the monopoly power of suppliers and they would welcome the government intervention as a mean of reducing costs and improving the conditions of importation. Accordingly, private and social interests would seem to coincide and strong support for the government regulations could be expected.

In analysing the behaviour of suppliers and recipients in developing countries where governments have attempted to regulate the market for imported technology, we shall argue that, although some qualifying factors should be taken into account, the available evidence suggests that the monopoly rents enjoyed by technology suppliers might have been reduced without materially affecting the inflow of technology. In this way, the assumption about the elasticity of technology supply, when directed to developing countries, seems not to be too unrealistic. In contrast, the available evidence suggests that it is not realistic to consider that the recipient firms are necessarily interested in reducing the costs of technology imports, especially when they are able to pass on such costs to their customers. Their position seems to be more ambiguous, especially in those frequent cases where transfer of technology agreements have been used mainly as a basic tool for competing with foreign subsidiaries and/or in markets where different varieties of non-price competition are found. We shall argue that, in most cases, the private interest of the recipient firms might differ from the government's objectives and hence the support by the recipient firms of government intervention in the market for imported technology has been more qualified than was originally expected.

Section I highlights the reasons for government action in the market for imported technology and the main results achieved in some developing countries. The supply of technology is discussed in section II. Section III concentrates on the behaviour of recipient firms, and some concluding remarks are made in the last section.

I. GOVERNMENT INTERVENTION IN THE MARKET FOR IMPORTED TECHNOLOGY

A. Establishment of regulatory frameworks

Import substituting industrialization in developing countries has been carried out with heavy reliance on foreign technology. While the local manufacture of consumer and intermediate goods has usually been promoted by tariff protection, capital goods which embody technology have faced low or no import duties and have, in some cases, even been subsidized by overvalued exchange rates. Intangible technology assets (know-how, patents, technical assistance, basic and detailed engineering, etc.) have usually been imported in a basically unregulated manner, with the consequence that the production of a large portion of the goods made locally uses foreign technology and/or foreign trade marks.

Payments for the licensing of foreign technology has risen considerably with the expansion of manufacturing output and it was the pronounced growth of that invisible item in the balance of payments that first attracted government attention to the question of unregulated technology markets in several developing countries in the late 1960s.[3]

In fact, balance-of-payments difficulties were at the origin of attempts by a number of governments to regulate intangible technology imports. This was clearly the case in Colombia, whose Royalties Committee was created in 1967 as a result of a very difficult situation in the balance of payments.

The local manufacture of technology-intensive goods has been undertaken either by foreign-owned firms or by domestic firms relying on licensing agreements. Generally, parent companies are the main technology suppliers of their subsidiaries, and transactions with those subsidiaries (intra-firm transactions) usually have not been carried on at "arm's length" prices. Domestic firms have imported technology in a market whose imperfections are aggravated by the insufficient technological capacity of the purchasers.

Imperfections in the imported technology market became visible when, as a result of a number of studies made on technology,[4] attention came to be concentrated on the restrictive clauses[5] common in licensing agreements and on the long duration of those agreements. It became very clear that the suppliers of technology were using their position in this market in order to impose a variety of limitations on access to technology and on its use, especially when dealing with domestic firms in developing countries.

The growing concern about the level of payments for foreign licences and the need to protect domestic enterprises relying on such technology against the monopoly power of their suppliers were thus at the origin of government intervention in the market. It is important to emphasize, however, that the primary objective of government action was to improve the terms and conditions attaching to imports of intangible technology. The promotion, and eventual protection, of local technological development by government action is an area in which relatively little has been done, and such efforts as have been made in this direction have rarely been co-ordinated with policies for regulating imported technology.

The more industrialized developing countries have established regulatory frameworks for technology transactions. The pioneer example of India, which initiated such controls immediately after independence in 1947, has been followed in Asia by countries like the Republic of Korea, Philippines, Indonesia and Malaysia, although each has pursued its own distinct industrialization strategy. In Africa, only Nigeria has recently established a similar system of control, while Latin America as a region has gone farthest in controlling transfer of technology transactions. Not only do Argentina, Mexico and Brazil have a relatively long experience in regulating technology transfer, but the Andean Pact countries have followed the example of Colombia, one of the members, in enacting such regulations.

A detailed examination of the main features of these transfer of technology regimes is outside the scope of this article. In what follows, the main regulations and some preliminary results obtained in Latin America, India and the Philippines[6] are summarized.[7]

B. Some results

The three areas in which government regulations have produced particularly visible effects are those of the duration of contracts, payments for transfer of technology and restrictive clauses included in agreements relating to transfer of technology.

In contrast to the situation prior to government intervention, where contracts of 10–15 years or of undetermined duration were common,[8] a maximum of five years is now normally allowed. This restriction does not preclude the possibility of renewals, but they are subject to government evaluation and approval.

One of the main purposes of government intervention in the market for imported technology has been to reduce payments for royalties and technical fees to more acceptable levels. In this connection, it is important to note that explicit payments prior to government intervention were very high (between 3 per cent and 10 per cent of the licensed output, depending on countries and industries) and, when combined with a number of implicit costs (like tied purchases of important goods), imposed a heavy burden on the recipient firm and on the balance of payments of the importing country.[9]

In most countries, the competent bodies have been fixing maximum royalty rates, according to the kind of technology and/or to the sector in which the recipient party operates. A ceiling of 5 per cent has often been fixed for the more complex technologies, and much lower rates have been permitted for the licensing of less sophisticated technologies and of trade marks.

The impact of these policies on the level of technology payments is not easy to assess. The correct way to evaluate the evolution of royalty payments would be to relate payments for similar technologies to output in the relevant sectors. If the actual royalty payments are declining as a proportion of the manufacturing output resulting from the application of more or less similar imported technologies, it would be possible to say that the payments should not be fully attributed to government intervention.

The increasing experience of the recipient party in negotiating transfer of technology agreements could certainly play an important role in obtaining better terms and conditions.

Unfortunately, the available information does not make it possible to measure the impact of these policies in an adequate manner. Neither information about the manufacturing output of the licensed enterprise nor a classification of payments for different types of technologies is available. Furthermore, in the royalty payments statistics which are published by developing countries no distinction is made between intra-firm and inter-firm payments.[10]

Despite these deficiencies, some proxy measures can be used for a preliminary analysis. One approach has been to show foreign exchange savings[11] obtained as a result of government intervention in the renegotiation of agreements. In Mexico it has been estimated that between 1973 and 1975 the competent body achieved a saving of $216 million, equivalent to 26 per cent of the value of payments that would have been made in the absence of governmental intervention.[12] Important savings of this kind have also been reported in the Philippines,[13] Colombia,[14] and Venezuela.[15]

Another way of carrying out the analysis is to examine the growth of royalty payments in the period in which regulations governing technology imports were in force with an earlier period during which no such regulations were implemented. As shown in table 1 and, even with a higher dollar inflation in the 1970s, the growth rate of such payments has been lower in the decade of the 1970s than in the 1960s in Argentina, Mexico and Brazil.

Yet another way of measuring the growth of royalty payments is to compare such payments with the total manufacturing output.[16] As shown in table 2, in the four Latin American countries a declining trend is discernible, whereas the trend in India is the other way.

Although these proxy indicators suggest a declining trend in royalty payments in some of the countries enforcing transfer of technology regulations, the issue deserves further examination. In this connection, it is particularly relevant to learn the extent to which the parties have used channels other than royalty payments (e.g. overpricing of inputs provided by technology suppliers) to circumvent government regulations.

The possibilities of using such channels are, to some extent, determined by the clauses of the contract. It would be difficult to overprice the inputs to be provided unless a clause is stipulated in the contract by which the recipient party is obliged to purchase the inputs called for by the contract from a source to be determined by the supplier.

It is for the reason that the action taken regarding royalty payments needs to be assessed jointly with the regulations on restrictive practices provided for in transfer of technology agreements.

The approach followed by developing countries in this field covers far more than the usual anti-competitive behaviour that is dealt with in the regulations in force in developed market-economy countries. The clauses that may negatively affect the economic and technological development of the importing country, even if they do not directly affect competition, are listed in the existing legislation and some of them are declared per se illegal. The

TABLE 1

Growth of transfer of technology payments in selected developing countries

	Period 1	Annual average growth rate (%) (1)	Period 2	Annual average growth rate (%) (2)
Argentina	1965-70	26.9	1971-78	9.6
Brazil	1965-69	20.9	1970-76	16.7
Mexico	1953-68	15.0	1970-79	10.1

Sources. Period 1: UNCTAD, *Major issues arising from the transfer of technology to developing countries...,* **table 12.** Period 2: UNCTAD, *"The implementation of transfer of technology regulations...",* Table 10. In the case of **Mexico** the data for 1979 is from **Dirección General de Inversiones Extranjeras y Transferencia de Tecnología,** *Anuario Estadístico 1980.*

Note. Transfer of technology payments include both intra-firm and inter-firm payments.

restrictive clauses most frequently imposed, such as export limitations, tying clauses, grant-back provisions and those which restrict the use of the technology after the expiration of the agreement, are subject to government review.

Although some practices may be accepted in cases in which the technology transferred is "of special interest to the country"--as in Mexican law--the restrictive clauses previously so common in transfer of technology agreements have been largely eliminated in the countries in question.

As the monitoring system is weak, except in India, and the bodies responsible for supervising technology transfer tend not to co-ordinate their approach with other competent bodies in the government administration, it is difficult to assess the practical results of this action. However, the difference it makes for the contracting parties cannot ignored, as legislative reform has rendered these restrictive practices unenforceable in law. This implies that any attempt by the technology supplier to enforce such practices will either involve coercion or be based on their tacit acceptance by the recipient firms (see section III).

II. THE SUPPLY OF TECHNOLOGY

Government intervention in the market for imported technology in developing countries has been based on the assumption that the monopoly rents enjoyed by technology suppliers could be taxed without affecting the eventual supply. In other words, the supply of technology, when directed to developing countries, was basically supposed to be inelastic to price reductions.

Two main arguments have been put forward in the literature to support such an assumption. First, for the technology suppliers, the developing countries' markets are relatively small as compared to those of the advanced industrial countries in which they are based and to which most innovations are geared. Hence, the markets of developing countries are not usually taken into account when R and D expenditures are planned and, therefore, income obtained in these markets can largely be considered as profits.[17] Secondly, in so far as the transfer of technology, once created, involved basically no extra costs, then any income obtained from its transfer can be considered as pure profit.[18] Although based on different reasoning, this position comes to the same conclusion as the previous one.

In the light of these arguments, the assumption about the inelasticity of technology supply clearly makes sense. However, it is important to take into account some additional factors that make the assumption in question less straightforward.

In contrast to Vaitsos, Teece, after a detailed investigation of 26 transfer of technology projects (mostly involving intra-firm transactions in developed countries), has argued that considerable costs are involved in the transfer of technology. It is, therefore, "quite inappropriate to regard existing technology as something that can be made available to all at zero social cost".[19]

According to the study by Teece, the costs of technology transfer do differ as between one industry and another, and more important, they are inversely related to, among other things, the age of the technology, to the number of firms with similar technologies and to the number of applications that the technology has undergone.

Although the assumption that the transfer of technology involves no extra costs may need to be qualified in the light of the limited evidence presented in the aforementioned study, there is still some ground for arguing that the costs to the licensor are minimal in relation to the income obtained form the use of technology licensed to local firms in developing countries. In this connection, it is important to bear in mind that technologies transferred to these countries are rather old and very much proved in the industrial countries before being actually transferred. In these circumstances, the costs to the tranferor can be considered small not only in relation to the costs involved in creating the technology but also in relation to the income usually obtained from the transfer of such know-how to developing countries. No evidence is shown in the Teece study to contradict this plausible argument. None the less, it can be shown that although the transfer of technology might lead to monopoly rents, it does not mean that the supplying firm will be prepared to reduce its profit margins so easily. In this sense, the private opportunity costs are particularly relevant.

The magnitude of these opportunity costs has little to do with the economics of the generation and transfer of technology. They will mostly depend on the alternatives available to the technology suppliers (e.g. in what other markets the same profit margin can be obtained; what other means exist to exploit its technological assets; what the competitors are doing, etc.) and on the importance of the market in question for the supplying firm.

In any case, as some costs might be involved in the transfer of technology for the licensor and as opportunity costs might be relevant, it makes sense to speak of elasticity of supply of imported technology. The elasticity of supply will probably vary according to the industry concerned, importing countries, the age of the technology and to the marketing strategies of the firms.

The degree of elasticity of technology supply is difficult to measure. One way of estimating it would be to relate the inflow of technology--measured by the number of technology transfer agreements in relevant sectors, or even better by the investments associated with such agreements--to the income obtained by the licensors, e.g. royalty receipts. No evidence is available for a proper estimation and, therefore, only indirect indicators can be used.

If the number of transfer of technology agreements approved or processed by the competent bodies of these countries can be used as a proxy for indicating the inflow of technology,[20] the information available for India, Brazil, Mexico, Argentina, Colombia, Peru and Venezuela shows a relatively stable or growing trend over time in the 1970s.[21] (table 3). This trend has to be seen in context in which the growth of royalty payments has been controlled and where

TABLE 2

Payments for transfer of technology [a] as a percentage of total manufacturing output [b] in selected developing countries, 1970 and 1976

	1970	1976
Argentina	0.82	0.12
Brazil	1.05	0.83
Colombia	0.99	0.35
Mexico	0.90	0.71
India	0.23	0.27

[a] Intra-firm fees and royalties paid by US foreign manufacturing firms—as shown in *Survey of Current Business*, August 1978, and in the *Revised Data Series on US Direct Investment Abroad, 1966-1974* (US Department of Commerce)—were deducted from the total transfer of technology payments as shown in the national sources.

[b] As measured by the value of the contribution of the manufacturing sector to gross domestic product and reported in United Nations, *Yearbook of National Accounts Statistics, 1978* (United Nations publication, Sales No. E.79.XVII.8).

restrictive clauses have been regulated with different degrees of flexibility by the government bodies. These indicators lend some support to the suggestion that monopoly rents enjoyed by technology suppliers might have been taxed without serious prejudice to the inflow of technology.

The reduction of such rents was probably easier when existing contracts were renegotiated than when new contracts were negotiated. This does not mean, of course, that the suppliers have always been willing to accept the regulated conditions and that other means have not been used sometimes (as gentlemen's agreements, see below) to bypass such conditions, especially in the case of new agreements.

It can be argued that this reaction of the supplier has little to do with government regulations of technology transfer and that such reactions have mainly been motivated by the growing relative importance of the markets in these developing countries at a time of recession in their main markets in the industrialized world. If this is the case, then one is in fact saying that the relatively lower opportunity costs of doing business in these developing countries may have compensated for the costs involved in the growing share that these same countries may acquire in the planned R and D activities of the suppliers. There is thus no major effect on the elasticity of supply. If this trend is correct, however, then it can only operate to the advantage of the recipient country, which now may be able to tax the rents enjoyed by suppliers even more.

Another argument frequently advanced is that, as the regulatory activities are mostly carried out in an unco-ordinated manner and with little or no monitoring the suppliers have still some room to exert their monopolistic power without major impediment. Although it is true that a more articulated and efficient system of regulation and control is still needed, the impact of existing regulations on technology suppliers cannot be minimized easily. The mere fact that most of the provisions in which their monopolistic advantages were reflected, i.e., the so-called restrictive clauses, are no longer accepted in those countries, makes it far more difficult for them to benefit from their monopoly position. In cases where the countries in question have foreign exchange control systems or where the approved royalty payments are deductible from local taxes, the extra cost in securing the royalty payments through other means (transfer pricing, use of the unofficial foreign exchange market, etc.) has to be taken into account.

It can be concluded that the actual behaviour of technology suppliers has not been very different from what the arguments mentioned above have suggested. The evidence available is too fragmentary to prove fully that the supply of technology has been inelastic to price reductions, especially in cases of new agreements. However, it clearly reveals that the opposite situation, i.e. an elastic supply, as has sometimes been assumed in business circles in the industrialized countries,[22] is hardly found in those developing countries which have implemented technology transfer regulations.

TABLE 3

The flow of technology transfer agreements [a] in the 1970s

	Year	Number of agreements	Year	Number of agreements
Argentina	1973	129	1979	510
Brazil	1972	1539	1980	2054
Peru	1971-75	90 [b]	1979	145
Colombia.	1967-77	37 [b]	1979	64
Venezuela	1974	108	1978	200
India.	1970	183	1979	267
Mexico			1973-79	1032 [b]

Sources: UNCTAD, "The implementation of transfer of technology regulations...", table 2; INPI, *Relatório de actividades, 1980,* for Brazil; CONITE, *Memoria 1979,* for Peru; and Dirección General de Inversiones Extranjeras y Transferencia de Tecnología, *Anuario Estadístico 1980,* for Mexico.

[a] Argentina, Mexico, Peru, Colombia and India: authorized contracts; Brazil: processed contracts; Venezuela: contracts submitted for approval.

[b] Annual average. For Colombia, technical services agreements are excluded.

III. THE BEHAVIOUR OF RECIPIENT FIRMS

An examination of the behaviour of recipient firms in a government-regulated market for imported technology is particularly relevant to an assessment of the extent to which State intervention in this market has been successful.

If it is assumed that recipient firms were harmed by the exercise of the monopoly power of technology suppliers, it is clear that government action in the imported technology market would have led to tangible results for the firms in question.

If, on the contrary, the private interests of the firms differ from the general objectives of the government policies, a more cautious attitude by recipient firms to government regulations should be expected. In some cases, the terms and conditions approved by the competent authorities might be bypassed by other means, like "gentlemen's agreements". In other cases, recipient firms might object to some of the terms and conditions imposed by the Government, and a tacit acceptance of some restrictive practices should follow.

As regards explicit payments, the extent to which parties are expected to comply with government regulations would not only depend on the government's position in this particular issue but also on the overall institutional framework within which transfer of technology agreements are monitored (for instance, the existence of foreign exchange controls; the requirement of government approval as a condition for the deduction of payments from tax, etc.).

Adequate information about the behaviour of recipient firms is difficult to collect. However, some pieces of evidence in relatively more advanced developing countries about business attitudes towards government action in the market for imported technology that may shed light on this issue are available and are worth examining.

In a study made of a sample of 73 firms in Ecuador, Colombia and Peru in 1975, it was found that half of them favoured stiff regulation of technology transfer agreements and a further 30 per cent favoured at least some regulation. The support for stiff government regulation was higher in Colombia and Peru (59 per cent and 52 per cent, respectively)--where regulations were more thoroughly implemented--than in Ecuador (27 per cent of the firms) and mostly came from privately-owned enterprises.[23]

A study made two years later, in 1977, of the implementation of the metal-working programme in Colombia, also gives some evidence on this point.[24] Forty per cent of the 28 firms included in the sample favoured an active government regulation of the technology market. The remaining firms preferred a passive role to be played by the government in those matters and suggested that regulations should be flexible and exceptions should be contemplated.

The scattered information available concerning Colombia gives the impression that the support of domestic firms for government regulations is more qualified than that which could, a priori, be expected. None the less, some segments of the local business community clearly felt that government intervention was necessary to counteract the practices of technology suppliers.

A recent study in Brazil has indicated that in 1978, out of 46 Brazilian-owned manufacturing firms with transfer of technology agreements, more than half favoured "a more vigorous and selective action from the government, especially in the definition of sectoral policies", while the remaining ones preferred free negotiation without government regulations or intervention.[25] An earlier study in Brazil of the behaviour of recipient firms gives some revealing details on the issue under consideration.[26] The survey covered 49 manufacturing firms (25 of them Brazilian-controlled, including three government enterprises) with transfer of technology agreements in which the competent body (the National Institute of Industrial Property—INPI) had intervened. Although out of 118 contracts submitted to INPI only four were rejected, alterations were required in 22 contracts. Despite the relatively flexible position of the Government in relation to the agreements, 23 out of the 25 Brazilian-controlled firms "indicated implicit °gentlemen's agreement' between them and the supplier as necessary conditions in getting the technology.[27] The "gentlemen's agreements" stipulated what are usually considered to be restrictive practices (confidentiality beyond period of formal agreement, supplier entitled to improvements on technology, purchase of intermediate inputs from supplier, etc.). In some cases these restrictions were accepted implicitly after INPI's rejection of their inclusion in the contract. These practices were not as widespread as before government intervention, but their existence, despite the fact that they were not legally enforceable, was recognized in a number of cases.

The behaviour of recipient enterprises can be better understood when the reasons for entering into a transfer of technology agreement are grasped.

In the course of the research carried out by Mytelka it was found that "51 per cent of the firms gave °brand name' considerations as one of the reasons for licensing, thus implying entry into a °quality segment' of the market in which standards had been set by foreign firms".[28]

According to the study by Fung and Cassiolato referred to above, most Brazilian firms stated that the reasons for undertaking technology change were basically linked to marketing needs. Only a minority of the firms (2 out of 27 Brazilian-controlled firms) considered that a reduction in production costs was the main justification for using foreign technology.

It is also important to take into account that more than half of the firms stated that the product line for which the technology was imported accounted for domestic market shares of 50 per cent or more for the recipient firms and that foreign subsidiaries and domestic firms with licensing agreements were by far the most important competitors in such markets. It is clear that the need for foreign technology has been strongly influenced by sales-oriented considerations in markets in which most participants have relied on foreign technology or on foreign trade marks.

The need for foreign technology in order to ensure a segment of the market for the recipient firm is confirmed in the study by Cruz Filho and Maculan. Nearly 60 per cent of the firms considered that the technology transfer contract was needed for reasons connected with their marketing requirements.

It has also been suggested that an exclusive transfer of technology agreement for the recipient firm is a way of avoiding the entry of the technology supplier through the establishment of a subsidiary which might become a competitor in the market in question.[29] This explanation seems quite plausible in the case of Brazil, which has a very open policy toward the establishment of foreign firms except in some specific sectors, in contrast to the more restrictive approach with respect to technology arrangements.

In the case of India, a small survey of 20 recipient firms with collaboration agreements (only one a foreign subsidiary, the remaining ones mostly firms with purely technical collaboration agreements) gives some information on business attitudes to government regulations.

"With two exceptions, all the firms felt that the restrictions on royalty rates and the limitations on the duration of the agreements were unreasonable."[30] The critical attitude of the firms towards government regulations had led to ways of bypassing the terms and conditions approved by the government, despite the sophisticated system of monitoring agreements which is practised in India. "It was reported that more often than not the Indian firms had to compensate the foreign firms in other ways, by paying a premium on imported equipment, fees such as inspection charges for approving the product and increased commission on sales when the product was exported through the collaborator's marketing channels."[31]

The findings of the Indian study should be treated with caution not only because the Indian Government has combined a flexible approach in the negotiations with a strict monitoring system, but also because—in contrast to Brazil—the policy towards direct foreign investment has been generally more restrictive.

Although the evidence available on the behaviour of recipient firms is scanty, it seems that only in a limited number of cases in which imports were needed for improving their technological capacity have they strongly supported government intervention in the imported technology market. In most cases their position seems to differ from the government's general objectives in this area.

It is possible to suggest some explanations about this divergence between private and social interests that may be considered as a hypothesis for further empirical research.

In so far as technology is not only an input to activities designed to introduce new products, reduce costs or improve quality, but also an element instrumental in securing a share of the output market, the situation of the recipient firm becomes more complex. A recipient firm whose bargaining position may be weak in the input market may well hold a substantial share in the market for the licensed product and be able to pass on to its customers part of the costs associated with technology imports. Therefore, the market power enjoyed by the recipient firm in the market for its products is a basic element to be taken into account.

Where the recipient firm operates in a concentrated product market in which oligopolistic competition prevails, a transfer of technology agreement--often including the licensing of foreign-owned trade marks--becomes an important marketing tool.[32] Such a tool is even more important when the recipient firm has to compete with foreign subsidiaries--which have direct access to the technological assets and trade marks of their parents--in its main product markets.

When the entry of foreign firms is unregulated, or in some cases even encouraged, the possibilities of success for government regulation of technology--where such success is measured in terms of the elimination not only of restrictive clauses in the contracts but also in terms of the actual business practices--are far more limited than in those cases in which the entry of foreign investment is restricted or even excluded.[33]

One of the basic shortcomings of the government-regulated market for imported technology in those developing countries that have been pioneers in this field is that, with the possible exception of India and the original decision 24 of the Andean Group, a restrictive policy on transfer of technology has not been accompanied by a similar policy towards foreign direct investment. But even in those instances in which a comprehensive approach was envisaged in the regulations, as in the case of decision 24, in practice foreign subsidiaries have had more freedom than their domestic counterparts.[34]

IV. CONCLUDING REMARKS

Considerations related to the growing burden of technology remittances in the balance of payments and more general considerations about the technological and economic development of the recipient countries have led to the adoption of specific laws and regulations governing imports of intangible technology in a number of developing countries.

Several studies describing the situation in the imported technology market in developing countries have clearly shown that suppliers have been using their position to impose a variety of limitations on access to technology and to charge high prices for transferring technology. Recipients of technology, owing to their weak bargaining position, have been generally considered to have been harmed. On the basis of this diagnosis, it was suggested that the government intervention could modify the picture and contribute to achieving better terms and conditions for the technology transfer without negatively affecting the inflow of technology.

The first results obtained in a number of developing countries where regulations in this field have been implemented have been encouraging in so far as the narrow objectives of the exercise are concerned. The growth of explicit payments for technology transfer appears to have been more controlled, the duration of the agreements has been reduced and many restrictive clauses have been

eliminated from the texts of contracts. However, more studies are
needed to assess the actual impact of these regulations on payments
and restrictive practices.

An examination of the scarce evidence available about the
behaviour of suppliers and recipients has suggested that the
assumptions on the basis of which government action was taken were
not too far from reality, although the actual picture seems to be
more consistent with the expectations in the case of suppliers than
in that of recipients.

In relation to supply of technology, the available indications
suggest that despite the apparently more reduced rents to be
obtained, technology has continued to flow into the developing
countries which have implemented technology transfer regulations.
It is fair to point out, however, that this flow has been
facilitated by several factors. The growing importance of the
markets in developing countries in the 1970s as a result of the
recession in the main markets in industrialized countries, the
dynamism in the industrialization process in the more advanced
developing countries and the competition between suppliers of
different industrialized countries have also been influential
factors affecting the behaviour of suppliers. At the same time,
the way in which recipients have complied with government
regulations and the inconsistencies in government policies,
especially vis-a-vis foreign investment and foreign technology,
have favoured the reaction of technology suppliers.

As regards technology recipients, among the firms using the
technology transfer agreement as an instrument for improving their
technological capacity in the process of business expansion,
government action seems to have been well received. Government
regulations have helped the recipients in obtaining better terms
and conditions in the agreements. However, since not many firms
seem to have had such an approach in the technology market, support
for government action has been more qualified.

On the part of firms using transfer of technology agreements
as a means of competing with foreign subsidiaries or as a marketing
instrument in order to be able to be active in markets where the
reputation of international licences is highly appreciated,
government regulations seem to be regarded as legal requirements to
be complied with rather than as elements for strengthening their
bargaining position in relation to technology suppliers.

Although the subject deserves much more investigation, it
seems that, to some extent, this divergence between private and
social interests is partly attributable to the contradictory policy
of the government in a number of developing countries. While
attempting to regulate the technology transfer market, governments
have done little to control the activities of foreign subsidiaries
which are receiving the technology flows from their parent
companies. In a more restrictive framework for foreign investment,
government objectives of improving the bargaining position of local
firms in acquiring foreign technology have far more change of being
achieved than in a situation of easy entry and little regulation of
the activities of subsidiaries.

At the same time, since government policy has been
concentrated in the narrowly defined market for technology as an

input, insufficient attention has been paid to the factors influencing the market forces in favour of products made with the use of foreign technology. A more comprehensive policy framework dealing with those factors will not only make it possible to apply a more consistent policy to imports of technology but will also have a bearing on the whole subject of inducing local technological development, which has been mostly treated in a very vague manner in the regulations of technology transfer.

NOTES

[1] See "The implementation of transfer of technology regulations: A preliminary analysis of the experience of Latin America, India and Philippines", Report by the UNCTAD secretariat (TD/B/C.6/55).

[2] Our concern here is mostly with private domestic firms in the manufacturing industries which are mainly oriented towards the internal markets. The behaviour of public enterprises—which are important buyers of technology in developing countries—and imports of technology in socialist countries are beyond the scope of this article.

[3] Some attempts to control royalty payments were made in countries like Brazil or India in the early 1960s, but they were exceptions to the general rule.

[4] Many of these studies are referred to in Major issues arising from the transfer of technology to developing countries. Report by the UNCTAD secretariat (TD/B/AC.11/10/Rev.2), United Nations publication, Sales No. E.75.II.D.2.

[5] Some of the more frequent clauses were grant-back provisions, by which the acquiring party was required to transfer to the supplying enterprise improvements arising from the acquired technology; restrictions on adaptations to the received technology; restrictions on research and on the use of personnel; export restrictions; tying arrangements by which the acquiring party was forced to purchase goods or services from the supplier of technology as a condition for obtaining the technology required; and restrictions operating after expiration of the arrangement.

[6] Because the data are insufficient or because too short a time has elapsed since these regulations were adopted, it is not possible at this time to carry out an analysis of the experience of other countries.

[7]It is important to bear in mind that, although these transfer of technology regulations are alike in many respects, some changes have been taking place not only in their content, but also in the way they are being implemented. In some cases, these changes are due to drastic modifications in overall economic policy, as is the case of Argentina since 1976, while in other cases the changes respond to administrative reorganizations or are a consequence of modifications of policies in related fields.

[8]See UNCTAD, "The implementation of transfer of technology regulations . . .", paras. 105-107, for information about the duration of contracts.

[9]See UNCTAD, Major issues arising from the transfer of technology to developing countries . . .

[10]Information about intra-firm payments by United States firms for technology is available from the statistics collected by the United States and published in Survey of Current Business.

[11]While in the case of a reduction of the price stipulated in existing agreements it makes sense to refer to savings realized through the renegotiation, the stiuation is less clear in the case of new agreements submitted to government approval. In some cases, the parties, following a negotiating tactic, may well adjust the original terms of the contract to give the impression that the government intervention has been successful. In those cases, therefore, the savings are meaningless. Unfortunately, the information available does not make it possible to identify the specific source of the achieved savings.

[12]See A. Nadal Egea, Instrumentos de politica cientifica y tecnologica en Mexico, Mexico City (El Colegio de Mexico, 1977), p. 151.

[13]"Transfer of technology regulations in the Philippines". Study prepared by Lilia R. Bautista at the request of the UNCTAD secretariat (UNCTAD/TT/32).

[14]"Policies relating to technology of the countries of the Andean Pact: their foundatins; a study by the Board of the Cartagena Agreement" (TD/107) and Corr.1 (reproduced in Proceedings of the United Nations Conference on Trade and Development, Third Session, vol. III. Financing and Investment, United Nations publication, Sales No. E.73.II.D.6), para. 38

[15]SIEX, Memoria Annual, 1978, table 13.

[16]Declining ratios of royalty payments in relation to total manufacturing output would reflect lower royalty payments over time only if it is assumed that the manufacturing output resulting from the imported technology is growing at the same or at a higher rate than total manufacturing output. Since technology is usually imported by enterprises with activities in

the most dynamic sectors of the manufacturing industry, this is a reasonable assumption.

[17]H. G. Johnson makes the same point in a different way. "It can be argued, however, that for most of the countries in the world, and especially the less developed countries, the contribution that the opportunity to earn a profit in their markets makes to the encouragement of investment in the creation of new commercial knowledge is negligible, so that any profit they allow to be earned from the command of advanced technology is for them a short-run loss with no compensating long-run gain from the encouragement of technical progress". (H. G. Johnson, "The efficiency and welfare implications of the international corporation" in C. P. Kindleberger (ed.), The International Corporation: A Symposium (Cambridge, Mass. MIT Press, 1970), p. 40.

[18]See C. V. Vaitsos, Intercountry income distribution and transnational enterprises (Oxford, Clarendon Press, 1974).

[19]D. J. Teece, "Technology transfer by multinational firms: The resource cost of transferring technological know-how", The Economic Journal, June 1977, p. 259.

[20]The main difficulties about using the number of agreements as a measure of technology inflow are that, on the one hand, the technological content and the value of the operations involved differ greatly as between agreements and, on the other hand, the finally approved agreements depend on circumstances little related to technology (the efficiency of the competent bodies, the length of the negotiation process, etc.). A better indicator, for instance, the number of agreements submitted for approval, although it does not suffer from the last shortcoming, still covers widely different technologies and investment values.

[21]It is noteworthy that the breakdown of the number of approved contracts in industrial sectors--available for India, for example--does not show any major difference at the sectoral level.

[22]See, for example, Business International, Transfer of technology. A survey of corporate reaction to a proposed Code (Geneva, 1978). In this connection it is worth bearing in mind that the famous cases of Coca Cola and IBM in India arose out of the policies of promoting joint ventures under the Foreign Exchange Regulation Act of 1973 rather than as a result of technology transfer regulations in that country.

[23]L. K. Mytelka, Regional development in a global economy. New Haven and London: Yale University Press, 1979 (pp. 93-94).

[24]M. Mortimore, "La programacion andina y su aplicacion en Colombia: el papel de las empresas transactionales" (Dependencia conjunta CEPAL/CET, Documento de Trabajo N.11, 1978), pp. 51-52.

[25] See M. F. Cruz Filho and A. M. Maculan, "Propriedade industrial e transferencia de tecnologia. Alguns efeitos da legislacao para a empresa nacional", July 1980 (mimeo).

[26] See S. Fung and J. Cassiolate, "The international transfer of technology to Brazil through technology agreements: characteristics of the government control system and the commercial transactions", Massachusetts Institute of Technology, Center for Policy Alternatives, 1976.

[27] Ibid., p. 99.

[28] L. K. Mytelka, op. cit., p. 121.

[29] See A. L. Figueira Barbosa, Propiedade e Quase-Propriedade no Comercio de Tecnologia (Rio de Janeiro, Conselho nacional de desienvolvimento scientifico e tecnologico, 1978), p. 149.

[30] See V. N. Balasubramanyam, International transfer of technology to India (New York: Praeger, 1973), p. 89.

[31] Ibid., p. 90.

[32] See D. Chudnovsky, "Foreign trade markes in developing countries", World Development, vol. 7, No. 7, July 1979, pp. 667-70, on licensing agreements concerning foreign-owned trade marks.

[33] It is noteworthy that one of the outstanding points in the Japanese policy towards technology transfer was to encourage imports while at the same time basically excluding the participation of foreign subsidiaries in the Japanese market.

[34] In the Andean Pact regulations technology payments between parents and subsidiaries were not allowed, but the only control on the subsidiaries was exercised at the time of the investment authorization. Their operations once established in the countries remain largely unregulated by the governments, except in connection with the divestment schemes.

BIBLIOGRAPHY

Balasubramanyam, V. N. International transfer of technology to India. New York, Praeger, 1973.

Business International, Transfer of technology. A survey of corporate reaction to a proposed Code, Geneva, 1978.

Curz Filho, M. F. and Maculan, A. M. "Propriedade Industrial e transferencia de tecnologia. Alguns efeitos da legislacao para a empresa nacional", (mimeo), July 1980.

Chudnovsky, Daniel, "Foreign trade marks in developing countries". World Development, Vol. 7, No. 7, July 1979.

Figueira Barbosa, A. L. Propriedade e Quase-Propriedade no Comercio de Tecnologia, Conselho nacional de desinvolvimento scientifico e tecnologico, Rio de Janeiro, 1978.

Fung, S. and Cassiolato, J. "The international transfer of technology to Brazil through technology agreements: characteristics of the government control system and the commercial transactions", Massachusetts Institute of Technology, Center for Policy Alternatives, 1976.

Johnson, H. "The efficiency and welfare implications of the international corporation", in C. P. Kindleberger (ed.) The International Corporation: A Symposium. Cambridge, Mass. MIT Press, 1970.

Mortimore, M. "La programacion andina y su aplicacion en Colombia: el papel de las empresas transnacionales". Dependencia conjunta CEPAL/CET, Documento de Trabajo N.º 11, 1978.

Mytelka, L. K. Regional development in a global economy. New Haven and London, Yale University Press, 1979.

Teece, D. J. "Technology transfer by multinational firms: The resource cost of transferring technological know-how", The Economic Journal, June 1977.

UNCTAD, Major issues arising from the transfer of technology to developing countries. United Nations publication, Sales No. E.75.II.D.2.

UNCTAD, "The implementation of transfer of technology regulations: A preliminary analysis of the experience of Latin America, India, and Phillipines", 1980 (TD/B/C.6/55).

Vaitsos, C. V. Intercountry income distribution and transnational enterprises. Oxford, Clarendon Press, 1974.

The Negotiations Strategy of Developing Countries in the Field of Trade Liberalization

FABIO R. FIALLO

Never before during the whole post-war period have major structural changes in international economic relations appeared to be more necessary and the time therefore more opportune. The need for such changes has certainly been felt by developing countries for a long time. Indeed, despite serious efforts by these countries during the past few decades, their participation in world production and trade has remained at astonishingly low levels. Developing countries contribute, for instance, less than one-fifth of world exports and less than one-tenth of world manufacturing output, despite the fact that they represent around one-half of mankind. With the current world economic crisis, however, the secular imbalance in international economic relations has been aggravated, and further adverse and destabilizing elements have been introduced in the functioning of the economies not only of these countries but also of the developed countries themselves.

The above considerations have been instrumental in the resolve of the international community, and especially of the developing countries, to bring about a new international economic order. Such resolve has been expressed in a number of fora and these include the United Nations General Assembly particularly at its sixth and seventh special sessions, the second conference of the United Nations Industrial Development Organization and the fourth session of the United Nations Conference on Trade and Development (UNCTAD). The proposed new order aims at providing the conditions for sustained world economic growth by means of bringing about equitable and stable international economic relations and of enhancing the participation of the developing countries in world economic activity to an extent commensurate with their economic potential and with the magnitude of their population.

The establishment of the new order would require a

From **JOURNAL OF WORLD TRADE LAW**, Vol 11, No. 3, May-June 1977, (203-212), reprinted by permisison of the publisher.

reformulation of the overall strategy of developing countries with a view in particular to strengthening their collective self-reliance and to developing effective countervailing power in their relations vis-a-vis developed countries. The new order would further involve a substantial reshaping of trade relations among developing countries, between developing and socialist countries and, last but not least, between developing and developed market economy countries.

Crucial to any significant reshaping of trade relations between developing and developed countries is the liberalization of the conditions of access to the import markets of the latter countries. In fact, a number of tariff and non-tariff obstacles have been imposed in developed countries, particularly with a view to protecting local industries from import competition. Many of the products affected thereby are precisely those on which developing countries are or can be in a position to complete successfully in international markets. The share of developing countries in world output and trade is thereby restricted, and the benefits that these countries could derive from their economic progress are diminished accordingly .

Efforts by developing countries appear therefore necessary for ensuring improved access to the markets of developed countries. What follows constitutes an attempt to discuss the effectiveness of the strategy that has been used in this respect by developing countries, as well as the extent to which a new strategy would seem to be required in the light of the objectives and implications of the proposed new international economic order.

I. THE PRESENT STRATEGY

Developing countries have been active in their quest for improved access to the markets of developed countries particularly since the 1960s when increased recognition was achieved of the importance of securing adequate export outlets. In fact, large developing countries had by then exhausted to a large extent their import-substitution possibilities and, therefore, a most export-oriented development appeared to be necessary for sustaining and accelerating the rates of industrial and overall economic growth. Small developing countries became in turn increasingly aware of the limitations of a purely inward-oriented industrialization in the case of countries with relatively small domestic markets. Serious attention was then given to the institutional framework for international trade relations, as provided principally by the General Agreement on Tariffs and Trade (GATT), as well as to the extent to which such framework had a positive or adverse impact upon the development efforts of developing countries.

The basic elements of the General Agreement, in particular the principles of non-discrimination and reciprocity, were then the subject to a critical examination. By virtue of the principle of non-discrimination, as qualified in the Agreement, developing and developed countries were to receive equal tariff treatment in spite of the disadvantaged position of the former countries in terms of competitiveness in international markets. The principle of non-discrimination was accordingly found to reinforce the imbalance prevailing in international trade relations as between developing and developed countries. As regards the principle of reciprocity, the scope of trade concessions that developing countries can make in reciprocity to concessions granted by developed countries is severely limited by the fact that commercial barriers in the former countries can hardly be lowered without jeopardizing development efforts. Such barriers are actually used in developing countries as a means of fostering the establishment and operation of infant industries and/or as a major source of public revenue to be destined for development purposes. Developing countries are hence bound to obtain meagre concessions from developed countries if such concessions are to be granted on the basis of the principle of non-reciprocity. In the light of these considerations, it was asserted that both principles actually militated against the development endeavours of developing countries and, consequently, contributed to perpetuating the prevailing imbalance in world trade.

The effectiveness of the Agreement was further questioned in terms of the manner in which it had actually operated. A number of commercial obstacles had been imposed by developed countries on products of export interest to developing countries. Such obstacles related _inter alia_ to quantitative restrictions, "voluntary" export restraints, export subsidies and countervailing duties, and safeguard provisions. In some cases, the obstacles were imposed in line with provisions of the Agreement while other cases constituted departures therefrom. Moreover, the trade liberalization negotiations conducted under GATT auspices had hitherto concentrated upon products of particular export interest to developed countries, as compared to products of export interest to developing countries. It was accordingly contended that the Agreement had failed to accommodate and protect the interests of developing countries in a sufficient and adequate manner.

A more equitable international trading framework has been pursued by developing countries by means of a strategy launched in the 1960s aiming at securing preferential, non-reciprocal treatment to be granted by developed countries in the field of tariff and non-tariff liberalization. The strategy constituted a noticeable move by developing countries from the traditional requests for development aid. It was in fact asserted that aid flows were insufficient to compensate fully for the structural bias which prevailed against developing countries in international trade relations which was reinforced by the existing international institutional framework. "Trade rather than aid" was the revolutionary cry of the 1960s and constituted a major step forward in the search for international economic quality. The cry was instrumental to the breakthrough which was involved in the establishment by the international community in 1964 of UNCTAD as a permanent forum to deal with the trade and development problems of developing countries.

Achievements and limitations of the present strategy

The strategy had an immediate impact upon international trade relations. Developed countries agreed to consider granting tariff reductions on a non-reciprocal basis to products of export interest to developing countries, and the first test of the goodwill of the former countries was to be made in the context of the so-called Kennedy Round of trade negotiations. Developed countries also agreed to a standstill on tariff and non-tariff barriers affecting products of export interest to developing countries as well as to the elimination or progressive removal of many such barriers. In addition, Part IV was incorporated into the General Agreement with a view to making the Agreement compatible with preferential tariff treatment to be granted by developed countries to imports originating from developed countries. The GATT principle of non-discrimination was qualified thereby. A further development in this connexion was the agreement of developed countries, reached through negotiation conducted under UNCTAD auspices, to establish a Generalized System of Preferences (GSP) whereby such countries accord, on a preferential basis, duty-free and reduced-tariff treatment to imports from developing countries.

The achievements made as a result of the present strategy, however, have not been free from serious limitations. Negotiations in the Kennedy Round concentrated upon products of which developing countries were not main suppliers, and tariff cuts were particularly important with regard to such products. The benefits secured by developing countries from the Round were constrained thereby. The standstill on the imposition of new trade barriers and on the intensification of existing barriers has not been strictly adhered to by developed countries. Notwithstanding the positive aspects of the GSP, the actual gains derived from the system by developing countries have been very much limited by the narrow product coverage of most of the national schemes of preferences of the different developed countries as well as by a number of restrictive provisions contained in the schemes. Such provisions relate principally to safeguard measures, insufficient tariff cuts, and restrictive rules of origin. The result has been that a large proportion of imports from developing countries fall outside the GSP and hence do not benefit therefrom. Moreover, a new round of multilateral trade negotiations is currently taking place under GATT auspices, but developing countries have already repeatedly expressed disappointment with the actual pace of the negotiations as well as with the meagre nature of the gains that such countries appear to be securing from the exercise.

The limited scope of the above-mentioned achievements could perhaps be best explained by the sufficiently stimulative power of the present strategy, and by the relatively passive role which is implicit for the developing countries. Better market access to imports from developing countries is in fact requested on the grounds of the benefits that the international community as a whole is to derive from equitable and expanded trade relations and on the need for contributing to overcome the grave secular problems of developing countries. Pressures from these countries in this respect generally consist of pledges aimed at demonstrating both the gravity of their problems and the possibility of meeting their claims without necessarily bringing about major disruptions in the developed economies. The stimulus provided thereby to governments of developed countries is not infrequently nullified by active pressures exerted in such countries by local groups opposed to trade liberalization. The groups involved are normally those afraid of being jeopardized by increased import competition. Such pressures are singularly forceful at times, such as the present, when the employment levels in developed countries are not at their highest peak.

The reduced stimulative power of the present strategy and the implicit passive role to be played by developing countries ought in turn to be ascertained in the context of the historical conditions in which the strategy was formulated. In fact, a long political, economic and cultural legacy of dependence relations made it difficult for developing countries to envisage resorting to any means of influencing international relations other than attempting to convince the international community of the gravity of their problems and of the urgent need to overcome them. As pointed out above, the mere fact that such strategy entailed a major departure from the traditional request for development aid constituted _per se_ a revolutionary move. The implicit passive role of developing countries could be justified further by the fact that these countries were then interested mainly in obtaining an incremental participation in world trade -- however important the increment sought may have been -- rather than, as in the present circumstances, in bringing about a new international economic order.

II. A NEW STRATEGY

To the extent that the proposed new order aims at a substantially different pattern of world trading relations, an appropriate strategy of developing countries in the field of trade liberalization would inevitably have to involve a more active and forceful role on the part of such countries. A new strategy would further need to be stimulative enough to persuade developed countries to carry out the requested changes in their commercial policies. Using the jargon of international politics, the formulation of an appropriate new strategy could be secured by a move from a debate-type to a game-type of strategy. A debate strategy essentially aims at convincing the counterparts, at obtaining their consensus, and this is precisely the case with regard to the present strategy. A game strategy would in turn seek to secure a desirable behaviour on the part of the partners, and this is sought by means of providing the partners with appropriate incentives and disincentives according to established rules of conduct.

Developing countries do possess means of carrying forward a game strategy in the field of trade liberalization, suitable for their endeavours of bringing about a new international economic order. For instance, many of their natural resources are important for the smooth functioning of the economies of developed countries. Such importance is shown, in particular, by the so-called OPEC experience and by the growing expressed concern of developed countries in securing sufficient and stable supplies of raw materials from developing countries. In addition, in spite of the relatively low levels of their total and per capita incomes, developing countries taken together represent major outlets for goods produced in developed countries. Access to the import markets of developing countries could therefore become a non-negligible bargaining instrument in the negotiation of tariff and non-tariff reductions in developed countries. Under a new strategy, the conditions of access to supplies and markets of developing countries could be laid down in such a way as to treat individual developed countries according to whether and to what extent their respective import markets are accessible to the former countries. Major stimuli for undertaking trade liberalization could be provided thereby to developed countries, and such stimuli would likely be seconded by local groups in developed countries interested in securing good access to the supplies and/or import markets of developing countries.

Possible Elements of a New Strategy

The implementation of a new strategy could be undertaken by means of a differentiated imposition by developing countries, vis-a-vis individual developed countries, of export and import duties and quantitative restrictions. Export and import duties and restrictions imposed in developing countries could accordingly consist of two different components: one fixed component which would be applied, as is traditionally the case, irrespective of the destination of the exports or the source of the imports affected; and one variable component, imposable on individual developed countries according to how stringent are the commercial policies of the developed country in question. Exports to and imports from developed countries granting easy access would accordingly be subject to lower variable components than those destined to and originating from restrictive developed countries. Variable components would of course be imposed only on goods of export or import interest to developing countries, namely goods which such countries are keen on purchasing or selling.
    The exercise suggested above would constitute a new qualification to the GATT principle of non-discrimination and may be considered to involve a system based upon reverse preferences.[1] The new qualification would represent a step ahead with regard to the move which led to the introduction of Part IV in the General Agreement. The basic difference is that the new qualification

would enable developing countries to play an active and decisive role in the process of trade liberalization, while under the existing qualification the active role is played merely by developed countries.

In addition to duties and restrictions, a new strategy could involve the use of the so-called packaged deals, whereby sets of goods of export or import interest to developed countries would be exchanged against sets of goods of export interest to developing countries. The magnitude and composition of the former sets could be made dependent upon the magnitude and composition of the latter. Developed countries would thereby feel encouraged to acquire large magnitudes of goods of export interest to developing countries so as to correspondingly secure large sale and purchase magnitudes of goods of export or import interest to themselves.

A new strategy along the above lines would have both corrective and preventive effects. It would in fact tend to correct the imbalance which prevails in the present international trade relations to the detriment of the interests of developing countries. The preventive effects would in turn relate to the discouragement that such strategy would provide with regard to the imposition of further restrictions by developed countries. The preventive power becomes particularly useful at moments, such as the present one, when developed countries may be tempted to resort to further commercial restrictions as a handy means of coping with unemployment and related problems in their own economies.

The proposed strategy could also serve to discourage developed countries from transferring their inflation to developing countries via increased export prices. Such discouragement would occur if variable components were determined, and packaged deals concluded, taking into account not only trade barriers but also prices of imports from developed countries. The suggested system would further serve to stimulate trade among developing countries to the extent that intra-trade would not be subject to variable components and, therefore, duties and restrictions affecting intra-trade would normally be lower than those affecting trade with developed countries.

Policy-Co-ordination and Distribution of Benefits Among Developing Countries

The formulation of a new strategy along the lines suggested above would require careful discussions among developing countries aimed at co-ordinating positions and at ensuring that all such countries can derive substantial benefits therefrom. In this connexion, account would have to be taken of the fact that any classification of developed countries in terms of the stringency of their respective commercial policies is likely to vary according to which developing country undertakes the classification: each developing country is likely to work out a different classification on the basis of which particular goods are of export interest to such country and of how restrictive the import policies of the various developed countries are with respect to such set of goods. The classification is also likely to depend upon whether commercial agreements, particularly of a preferential nature, exist as between developed countries and the developing country in question.

Any policy co-ordination would therefore need to allow each developing country to have a high degree of freedom in determining and imposing commercial policy measures and particularly variable components. Appropriate rules of origin would further need to be devised by developing countries with a view to avoiding the possibility of policy measures being circumvented. In addition, in the determination of potential benefits, account would have to be taken of the special situation and problems of the least developed countries as well as of the possibility of the strategy's having some side effects such as those related to industrial relocation and trade reorientation.

Discussions on these matters could be envisaged as among groups of developing countries. The group discussions could relate, for instance, to suppliers of similar manufactures and semi-manufactures, to developing countries interested in exporting to the same developed countries, to developing countries importing similar products, to developing countries importing mainly from the same developed countries, and to developing countries forming part of the same regional or sub-regional groups. Countries are likely to form part of more than one of such groups, and the decisions reached through such discussions could be consolidated and co-ordinated and elaborated further perhaps by means of discussions among the developing countries as a whole.

The foregoing endeavours would certainly constitute a more complicated exercise than the traditional request for preferential concessions to be granted by developed countries. Negotiations relating to trade liberalization, however, have reached a stage where general good-will declarations will inevitably have to be superseded by action aimed at securing concrete results. Such action is to entail a complex and sophisticated negotiation strategy. Complexity is therefore likely to be observed in the case of any future strategy and not only as regards that suggested above.

Institutional Implications of a New Strategy

The formulation of a new strategy along the lines suggested above would involve a major modification of the existing legal and institutional framework for international trade relations. The existing framework is basically determined by the General Agreement and therefore the aforementioned modification would need to be undertaken bearing particularly in mind the existence of the Agreement. Serious consideration should be given in this respect to whether and to what extent an adequate modification of the framework for international trade relations could be achieved in

the context of the General Agreement. GATT is far from embracing
all the trading partners of the international community. Its
membership amounts to only 83 countries, as opposed to 146 of the
United Nations. In fact, many socialist and developing countries
do not form part of the Agreement. It is difficult to conceive how
the basis for a lasting pattern of world trade could be laid down
without the active participation of the whole international
community.

It would accordingly seem worthwhile to give consideration to
the possibility of establishing a new trade framework of a
substantially larger nature than GATT, not only in terms of
membership but also in terms of issues and problems covered. In
spite of its great importance, trade liberalization is but one
dimension of the proposed new international economic order. Other
important dimensions relate inter alia to improvement of the supply
capability of developing countries, development financing and
related issues, terms and modalities of the transfer of technology
to developing countries, and policies vis-a-vis transnational
corporations. These dimensions are deeply intertwined, and an
appropriate consideration and negotiations thereon could be best
undertaken in the context of a forum concerned with all such
issues.

III. CONCLUSIONS

The establishment of a new international economic order is to
involve a reorientation of world economic activity aimed
particularly at enabling developing countries fully to develop
their potentialities and at ensuring a substantial expansion of
their participation in world production and trade. For the
achievement of these objectives, major progress will need to be
made inter alia in the liberalization of tariff and non-tariff
barriers imposed by developed countries on products of export
interest to developing countries. The strategy presently followed
by the latter countries in the field of trade liberalization is
essentially based upon requests to developed countries for
preferential, non-reciprocal treatment. This strategy would seem
to have insufficient stimulative power and has not yet produced the
results expected.

A more effective strategy on the part of developing countries
appears therefore to be necessary for the establishment of a new
international economic order. A new strategy could attempt to
match the interests of developing countries in respect to trade
liberalization with the interests of developed countries in respect
of access to supplies and to the import markets of the former
countries. The strategy would seek a more active and persuasive
role for developing countries in international commercial
relations, and its formulation and operation is likely to entail
complex and delicate negotiations. The exercise might accordingly
constitute a sound opportunity to test both the resolve of

developing countries to bring about a new trade pattern and the realization by developed countries of the inevitable need for effectively sharing responsibilities with developing countries as regards international decision making.   Such resolve and realization are in the final analysis the sole means of building up lasting and stable world trading relations.

NOTES

[1]Such reverse preferences, however, would be totally different from, and would have nothing to do with, the so-called reverse preferences that some developing countries had to accord to certain developed countries (for instance, in the context of the Yaounde Convention).

Export Subsidies in Developing Countries and the GATT

LORENZO L. PEREZ

I. INTRODUCTION

The object of this paper is to analyse the use of export subsidies and countervailing duties currently under discussion in the multilateral trade negotiations, and to consider the possibility of differential treatment in this area for developing countries. This is an important topic because subsidies are first-best policy instruments for developing countries' governments to correct for a number of distortions and externalities in their domestic and foreign markets. The existing GATT rules do not recognize these special conditions in the case of developing countries and for this reason many of the current subsidy practices of developing countries violate those rules.

Under the GATT auspices a new round of multilateral trade negotiations (MTN) were launched in Tokyo in September 1973. These negotiations are considered particularly important not only to maintain the movement towards a more open trading system but also to provide the necessary counterweight to the widespread protectionist tendencies accentuated by the world economic recession. The previous round of negotiations, the "Kennedy Round," led to substantial tariff reductions on industrial goods but these mainly benefitted developed countries. Sensitive labor-intensive products whose trade had potential implications for domestic employment in the developed economies were substantially left out of the negotiations. These labor-intensive products in many instances happened to be the ones that developing countries could most easily export. The degree of tariff escalation on processed primary products was scarcely reduced and in some cases

From **JOURNAL OF WORLD TRADE LAW**, Vol 10, No. 6, Nov.-Dec. 1976, (529-545), reprinted by permission of the publisher.

was increased.

II. POSITION OF THE DEVELOPING COUNTRIES ON NON-TARIFF TRADE MEASURES

The developed countries in the Tokyo Declaration, recognizing the special interests of developing countries, agreed to secure additional benefits for the international trade of developing countries so as to achieve a substantial increase in their foreign exchange earnings, export diversification and an acceleration in the rate of growth of their exports. Since developing countries are producing an increased variety of industrial products for export, these new multilateral trade negotiations will be of more interest to them.[1]

Despite the Tokyo Declaration, this round of negotiations is viewed with some skepticism by developing countries because the easiest trade barriers to liberalize, tariffs, probably now play a more limited role in the overall determination of trade patterns. As a result of past reductions in tariff barriers non-tariff barriers have increased in importance and in many instances are now far more important than tariff barriers in determining trade performance. Non-tariff barriers such as quantitative restrictions, standards restrictions, subsidies and countervailing duties, seriously affect exports of developing countries.

The developing countries have asked for differential treatment in any new rules that are negotiated on non-tariff trade measures. They want differential treatment because the non-tariff barriers of developed countries significantly constrain their trade and compound the economic disadvantages that result from their low levels of development. At the same time developing countries claim they might be forced to use nontariff barriers more than developed countries to take into account their structural economic problems. For these reasons developing countries want flexible international rules governing the use of non-tariff barriers which would exempt them from strict rules. They argue that strict rules would interfere with their development requirements. Developed countries seem to be willing to make some exceptions for developing countries but only to the extent that there is some real economic need. However, agreement between developed and developing countries of what constitutes economic need might not be easily achieved. In addition, developed countries will probably ask for some reciprocity if they exempt developing countries from obligations in the area of non-tariff barriers.

One of the areas of the non-tariff barrier negotiations where the developing countries have shown significant interest is in the area of export subsidies and countervailing duties negotiations. The developing countries have been using a wide variety of export subsidies in their export promotion programs and are quite concerned about possible limitations that might be imposed on their use by new international agreements.

A number of reasons have been put forth by the developing countries to justify the establishment of export subsidy programs: (a) Export subsidies are a means of offsetting the disadvantages faced by the export sector due to the high levels of protection existing in the country which place exporters at a competitive disadvantage. The high levels of protection are usually accompanied by overvalued exchange rates which might aid the exports of primary commodities but might penalize the export of manufactured products. A devaluation might not be considered an appropriate solution because of the inelasticity of foreign demand for its primary commodity exports and the corresponding domestic repercussions. Multiple exchange rates might not be acceptable internationally, leaving a combination of export taxes and export subsidies as the only solution; (b) Even in instances when the distortions created by policies of import substitution are not that significant, export promotion programs are sometimes organized to increase the overall import capacity in industries where developing countries feel they could have a comparative advantage in the future; (c) Subsidies are also used to offset certain disadvantages that exporting industries in developing countries might face such as inferior infrastructure, limited financing facilities, low skill levels, etc. (d) Otherwise, export promotion programs are selected for individual key industries because of their strategic importance. Key industries might need to expand production levels to achieve economics of scale, with additional sales in foreign markets seen as achieving this purpose. It is also argued that certain industries might be at the verge of breaking into foreign markets and they might accomplish this with some government help. It is not argued here that all these reasons are valid. They are presented to illustrate the reasons usually forwarded by developing countries for the use of subsidies.

III. FORMS OF EXPORT SUBSIDIES

Export subsidies have taken many forms including measures exempting exporters from indirect and direct taxes, government-subsidized provisions for export credit and, in some cases, cash subsidies. For example, the Colombian government has been promoting minor exports through a program which includes exchange rate provisions, fiscal incentives, import-export schemes, special credit facilities, regional trade agreements and other institutional agreements.[2] Among the fiscal incentives used for the promotion of minor exports are tax credit certificates (CAT for Certificado de Abono Tributario) which have been used in the amount of 15 per cent of the value of exports for all exports excluding coffee, petroleum, and raw hides.[3] The CAT's, which are freely negotiable, can be used to pay at face value income, sales, and import taxes one year after they are issued. Brazilian exporters have also received export subsidies in the form of tax credits for corporate income taxes. In addition, a wide system of indirect tax rebates is used in Brazil which in some cases might constitute an overrebate of the original taxes.

Before proceeding to the next section of the paper and a discussion of the GATT rules on export subsidies along with proposals for differential treatment, we should define what we mean by export subsidies. We broadly define a subsidy as any government revenue and expenditure measure that affects the return on an economic activity. Under this definition a subsidy would be positive if it encouraged an economic activity or negative if it discourages an economic activity, whether in domestic or foreign markets. We will be mostly concerned with positive subsidies. If a subsidy encourages export sales we consider it a positive export subsidy. Under this definition an export subsidy can exist even if the subsidy measure also encourages domestic sales and was originally set up to encourage domestic activity. This definition of export subsidy is similar to the one apparently used in the monitoring of countervailing duty cases in the United States.[4]

Section I discusses the current GATT rules on export subsidies. Section II presents conclusions of trade and welfare theory under the presence of domestic distortions and their implications for export subsidy programs. Finally Section III uses some of these conclusions to offer suggestions for differential treatment for developing countries.

Section I. GATT Rules on Export Subsidies and Countervailing Duties

The text of the GATT contains no definition of a subsidy but some inferences can be derived from some substantive provisions that have subsequently been made. For example, it can be inferred that a subsidy exists when a practice creates a cost to the government using it[5] (this is even a wider definition than the one adopted above) or when there is remission of direct taxes[6] or in the use of multiple exchange rates.[7]

While Article VI of the GATT, refers, _inter alia_, to subsidies and stipulates the specific conditions under which countervailing duties may be imposed, the major provisions dealing with the export subsidies in the GATT are included in Article XVI.[8] Article XVI (1) obliges the contracting parties to report their trade subsidy programs and to participate on request in consultation on these subsidies if it is determined that serious prejudice to the interests of another contracting party or parties is caused by these programs. Article XVI (2) states that the granting of export subsidies may have harmful effects on other contracting parties, both importing and exporting countries, causing disturbance in their normal commercial interests. Notable for its absence is any discussion of whether such actions are ever justified. Article XVI implicitly assumes that as long as no serious prejudice is caused to other countries, contracting parties are free to use subsidy programs. In fact most GATT members have not subscribed to the

Declaration giving effect to article XVI and feel free to apply any subsidies they consider appropriate to their needs. Article XVI (3) suggests that the contracting parties should seek to avoid the use of subsidies on the export of primary products. However, the drafters of this provision implicitly recognized that some countries were going to subsidize primary product exports. For this reason, they also stated that primary product exports should only be subsidized as long as such subsidies did not result in a disproportionate share of world trade. The implication is that an export subsidy should not be allowed if it gives an exporter a disproportionate share of world trade.

This wording was included to provide some restrictions on primary product subsidies, while allowing subsidies to assist new exports of developing countries and to maintain some of the subsidy programs of developed countries. Interpretative notes added later confirmed that fulfilment of this provision should not preclude any country from establishing an export trade in a particular product even if it had no exports of the product beforehand. Another note stipulated that Article XVI (3) would not apply to primary product price stabilization programs as long as they had provisions allowing export prices to go below and above domestic prices.

Article XVI (4) asked contracting parties to cease granting either directly or indirectly any form of subsidy on the export of any product other than a primary product which resulted in the sale of such product for export at a price lower than the comparable price charged for the like product to buyers in the domestic market. Few countries have accepted Paragraph four and it has remained one of GATT's gray areas. Acceptance was supposed to be achieved by 1958 but agreements at the OEEC achieved reductions in the use of export subsidies and reduced the pressure on GATT members to reach agreement on the elimination of subsidies. However, negotiations in 1960 led to an agreement among certain GATT members to prohibit certain specific export subsidies.[9] At this time there was some talk justifying export subsidies for developing countries because of their overvalued exchange rates. The practical effect of this agreement is that governments used subsidies which did not necessarily create price differentials, and supported producers irrespective of whether the output was sold in domestic or foreign markets.

The 1960 Declaration has been looked upon as the most practical way of dealing with this problem and it is the way the negotiations on export subsidies and countervailing duties will probably move. In the negotiation of the Declaration the emphasis was on prohibiting certain kinds of subsidy practices. The Declaration did not include any discussion of when subsidy programs are justified on economic grounds.

In addition, tax rebates on indirect taxes, as well as "drawback" of import duties, have become accepted under GATT rules, but not rebates for direct taxes nor rebates on "tax occultes" (Tax on inputs not directly incorporated in the export products). The latter remains an open issue. Countries differ in their acceptance of indirect tax rebates in their countervailing duty administration. Legal practice in some countries and some international precedents created in international courts have only tended to accept the rebates of indirect taxes of inputs that can be physically identified in the product in question. However, a more meaningful economic practice would be to allow the drawback of any indirect tax on a product's input whose cost is reflected in the selling price. This is obviously an issue which affects both developed and developing countries. What kinds of rules are finally universally accepted regarding "tax occultes" is very important and it could make a very large difference in the sizes of export subsidies that are estimated for purposes of imposing countervailing duties.

Countries which rely more on direct taxes have argued that this practice discriminates against them. Johnson and Krauss have maintained that in the long run it does not make any difference what type of border tax adjustment the government uses, whether direct taxes based on the origin principle or indirect taxes based on the destination principle. However, this assumes factor price flexibility and competitive conditions which are not very realistic assumptions even in the long run in any realistic situations.[10]

Section II. Prescriptions of Trade and Welfare Theory Under the Presence of Domestic Distortions

Recent contributions by a number of authors have been concerned with prescriptions of optimum trade policy in the presence of domestic distortions which eliminate some of the properties of the perfectly competitive model.[11] These theoretical results support the economic case for the use of export subsidies to promote some industries' exports and have relevance for the current GATT negotiations.

One of the principal propositions of this analysis is that when there is a domestic distortion in the economy or there exists economic externalities affecting international trade, an optimum subsidy (or a tax-cum-subsidy equivalent) is necessarily superior to a tariff. This is because the subsidy hits the cause of the distortion while the tariff only treats the effects.[12] At the same time, if protection is adopted as a means of correcting domestic distortions, not only will the result be that economic welfare will fall short of the maximum obtainable, but economic welfare may even be reduced below what it would be under a policy of free trade. This would be the case if, when correcting one distortion with another, a greater distortion was established in the relative prices of the traded and non-traded goods, leading to greater misallocation of resources.[13] The exception to this general conclusion is when a country has some monopoly power in international markets and through the use of a tariff can change its terms of trade, i.e. the optimum tariff case.

One case of the superiority of a tax-cum-subsidy equivalent over measures of protection to correct domestic distortions is that of <u>production externalities</u>. If there is an economic externality in the operation of one firm within an industry, the theoretically justified government action is direct government help to subsidize the activity where the externality lies. For example, there might be some positive economic externalities in the training of the labor force in a new import-competing industry since not all the benefits of such training might accrue to the firm financing the training. In such a case, private firms might be hesitant to make a worthwhile investment from a social point of view. This situation calls for a government subsidy to finance the training of labor rather than trade protection in the form of tariffs or quotas which add another distortion on the consumption side through the resulting increase in domestic price of the protected product. A logical corollary to this proposition is that if there are some economic externalities involved in breaking into new markets whether they are part of the domestic or foreign economy, the proper government policy in helping new firms is a subsidy which directly corrects for the distortion. One example of this situation would be when an exporting firm from a developing countries have to incur high initial marketing costs to establish adequate selling channels and/or establish a good reputation with retailers and consumers abroad regarding supply accessibility and quality reliability. Once a firm from a developing country accomplishes this recognition it is possible for other firms with the capacity to make the original investment since they would lose part of the foreign markets to their competitors. Some government aid would break the impasse so that the original investment is made.

A second case that calls for a government subsidy rather than a tariff or other measures of trade protection is when there is factor immobility and/or downward price rigidity which might create serious unemployment in some areas of a country. Rather than protecting these industries through tariffs the optimum policy for the government is to directly intervene to correct the source of the distortion, e.g. give aid for workers to move out of an area to another where there are employment opportunities. If part of the output of the firms hiring these workers is sold abroad the question arises whether these are justifiable exports from an international viewpoint.

A third case is one which involves binding non-economic constraints such as political constraints to maximize employment or how government's revenue should be raised. Bhagwati and Srinivasan have shown that if the binding non-economic constraint relates to the level of employment of a factor of production in a sector, the optimal policy is to use a factor tax-cum subsidy that directly taxes (subsidies) the employment of the factor in the sector where its employment must be lowered (raised) to the constrained level.[14] This case would have implications for international rules regarding the use of subsidies if part of the output of these industries is exported or if foreign exports to these markets have to compete with these domestic subsidized firms.

The trade and welfare literature has advanced to the point that a rigorous ranking of optimum government policies can be made depending on the type of distortion that a government faces.[15] Regarding the ranking of optimum government policies in the cases of economic distortions of interest for the trade problems of developing countries, Bhagwati reached the following conclusions:[16]

(a) in the case of pure production externality, the first best policy instrument is a production tax-cum-subsidy. The second best is either a tariff (trade subsidy) or factor tax-cum-subsidy.[17]

(b) in the case of non-operation on the efficient production possibility curve such as in the case of a factor market imperfection where, for example wage differentials exist, the first best policy is a factor-tax-cum-subsidy. The second best is a production tax-cum-subsidy.

(c) in the case of a production level as a constraint, the first best policy is a production tax-cum-subsidy and the second best is either a tariff (trade subsidy) or a factor tax-cum-subsidy.

(d) finally, in the case of a constraint where the use of factor of production has to be maximized in a sector (e.g. labor), the first best is a factor tax-cum-subsidy and the second best is a production tax-cum-subsidy.

These theoretical results clearly support the economic case for the promotion of specific industries which face the economic distortions or externalities discussed above. These distortions or externalities can appear in principle in developing and developed countries alike, however, the conditions for their existence are more likely to be present in developing countries. For this reason, we use these theoretical arguments to make the case for differential treatment for developing countries. This is not to argue that some of these conditions might not prevail in some developed countries. In those instances the same case could also be made for allowing developed countries to use export subsidies.

The decision to give differential treatment to developing countries is a value judgement which reflects the political will of trading countries. Proposing the differential treatment on these economic grounds has the advantage of implementing a political objective in a way that promotes a more efficient allocation of world resources. However, policy-makers certainly face a difficult task in applying these principles because specific situations are seldom clearcut theoretical cases of one distortion calling for a specific optimum policy. And even if what should be done is clear, it is often politically impossible, forcing the policy maker to adopt third, fourth, or fifth best solutions instead. In addition, it is very difficult to measure the magnitude of the distortion and hence to measure the needed subsidy.

Nevertheless, in developing new international rules concerning the use of export subsidies, these theoretical results can provide guidelines for the establishment of differential treatment to developing countries which are economically efficient from a world point of view. We argue below that importing countries with industries being affected by subsidized imports should take into consideration how appropriate are the subsidy programs for the developing countries from an economic point of view when considering retaliatory measures. Specific suggestions are discussed in the next section.

Section III. Suggestions for Differential Treatment of Developing
Countries as Regards Subsidies and Countervailing Duties

From the discussions of the previous sections it is clear that
developing countries are going to be increasing their manufactured
exports in the years ahead as they expand their industrial
capacities. The developing countries have been promoting their
exports through subsidy programs which do not necessarily comply
with the GATT rules and it is unlikely that they will voluntarily
change their practices. No developing country signed the 1960
Declaration on Article XVI: 4 and it is unlikely that they would
accept new subsidy rules unless some provisions are made for their
economic needs.

On the other hand, the pressure exerted on the developed
countries' governments by their domestic industries to retaliate
against subsidized imports has increased substantially in recent
years. This is especially true in the United States. Developed
countries have used different measures to protect their domestic
industries. The United States has assessed additional duties when
imports are found to be subsidized by foreign governments. There
has been a significant increase of countervailing duty cases
against imports from developing countries in the last two years in
the United States. With the new time constraints recently
established for the administration of countervailing duty cases by
the Trade Act of 1974, the cases will have to proceed faster,
eliminating the option that the U.S. Treasury previously had of
indefinitely delaying a final determination on countervailing duty
cases. Unless some new international agreement is reached on the
use of export subsidies, countervailing duty cases can be expected
to be a source of serious friction at least between the U.S. and
developing countries as well as between developed countries
themselves.

If the past negotiations on the use of export subsidies are
any indications for how the current GATT negotiations will proceed,
one could expect that the negotiations will follow the lines of
agreeing on acceptable and nonacceptable subsidy practices. This
is admittedly the path of least resistance since negotiators could
reach agreement on the kind of subsidy practices which would be
acceptable or not, rather than trying to agree on circumstances
under which a subsidy would be acceptable on efficiency and/or
political grounds. Which subsidy practices will be prohibited or
accepted will be mostly a function of the political and economic
value of the existing programs of the negotiating countries and how
much domestic flexibility they have in eliminating some of these
programs or changing them to meet the new rules.

Negotiations based on the technique of drawing lists of
acceptable and nonacceptable subsidy practices have the
disadvantage from an economic viewpoint that the same kind of
export subsidy could in some cases be totally justified while in
others be totally unjustified. For example, as a general rule it
might not be economically justifiable to subsidize manufactured
exports; but the same kind of subsidy might be economically sound

for some specific industries.

Nevertheless, it seems likely that if any progress is going to be made in the subsidy negotiations, the negotiations will follow the path of agreeing on acceptable or prohibited practices in the spirit of the 1960 Declaration. For this reason we will assume this framework in the discussion in this section. Differential treatment in this context, which takes into account the theoretical prescriptions discussed in the previous section, could allow developing countries to use otherwise prohibited subsidy practices if certain conditions are fulfilled. This paper recommends differential treatment in export subsidies for developing countries which directly ties the provisions concerning countervailing duties in Article VI to Article XVI. Countervailing duties are a logical recourse of importing countries if, after the consultations called under Article XVI, exporting countries do not change their subsidy programs. Our proposal for differential treatment for developing countries also includes guidelines for the imposition of countervailing duties.

The discussion of differential treatment is presented in two parts. The first part consists of a discussion of the economic rationale on ground of global efficiency justifying the use of export subsidies by developing countries. The second part modifies the first, recognizing that subsidy programs which might be economically efficient from a world point of view might cause economic losses to particular importing countries. The proposals are adjusted to take into account the economic and political constraints that importing countries would have in accepting these losses.

Economic Rationale for the Use of Export Subsidies in Developing Countries

No distinction should be made in principle between export subsidies which apply to primary product exports and those which apply to manufactured product exports. In considering whether governments should be allowed to subsidize export sales or not, the same kind of general principles could apply for differential treatment of developing countries regardless of whether the export is of a primary or a manufactured product.

In addition the rationale of the language of Article XVI (4), which calls for countries to stop subsidies of manufactured exports if they result in dual prices between foreign and domestic markets, does not reflect current economic situations. A subsidy program can affect equally the domestic and export market while still having an impact on the exporting industry. For this reason the dual price criterion might not be very useful today for subsidy negotiations. In the case of developing countries, government action might be necessary to take into account the existence of economic externalities or distortions that could affect domestic and export sales. There might also be instances in which the economic activity being subsidized involves only export sales and the dual price criterion is completely irrelevant.[18]

We can also distinguish two kinds of conditions in developing countries which might call for differential treatment: macroeconomic and microeconomic conditions.

Under macroeconomic conditions the situation might be one of an overvalued exchange rate accompanied by a highly protectionistic system affecting most of the sectors of the economy. The competitiveness of the export sector is hurt by the currency overvaluation because it has to purchase its inputs at prices higher than world prices and because in general the sector operates in an inefficient way due to the protection which it receives. The most desirable policy under these circumstances would be a devaluation accompanied by a reduction in the levels of protection and the imposition of export taxes on major exports facing inelastic demand conditions.

Many developing countries find it very difficult to follow these policies because of the undesirable domestic consequences of a devaluation and the difficulties of imposing an export tax on their major export commodities. Under these circumstances an across-the-board export subsidy could be the most appropriate policy in the short-run to offset the negative effects of the exchange rate overvaluation and the protection-induced distortions which lead producers to sell more in the domestic market.[19] The practical problem in this prescription is determining the equilibrium exchange rate for the calculation of the appropriate subsidy rate.[20]

However, this kind of across-the-board subsidy can only be defended as a temporary measure. Countries using this policy should use the time earned this way to gradually devalue while at the same time reducing the subsidy.[21] In fact, given the limited financial resources that developing countries have and the relative success that some developing countries have had with crawling pegs, a uniform export subsidy program might be harder to implement than a straight devaluation program.

The theoretical propositions in Section II can be used to establish guidelines for microeconomic conditions. Three general cases can be distinguished:[22]

(a) _Infant-industry case._ As discussed in Section II the optimum government policy in the case of a production externality is a production tax-cum-subsidy where the producers receive a subsidy to finance the activity where the externality lies. This is an argument for a temporary subsidization and for a subsidy rate that will be sufficient to correct for the externality. Such an approach, however, calls for selective subsidization since it is unlikely that all the industries in a developing country are infant industries in international markets. There are serious administrative problems with the selective application of the infant industry criterion since government officials will probably be subject to political and economic pressures from industrialists trying to get infant industry treatment. Little can probably be done to avoid this problem, except that agreeing on internationally accepted rules on infant industry criterion would strengthen the position of government officials.

Strictly speaking, the only way of determining if an industry is an infant industry is through a specific analysis of the industry in question. There is no generally accepted method of identifying infant industries but one can use a number of general measures of economic or industrial activity as indicators of the relative stage of industrial development, i.e. relative infancy of the industry. Such indicators could include shares of production which is exported, the share of import markets abroad or some combination of these. For the degree of acceptable subsidy rates, some rate ranges could be agreed upon based on the industrialization experience of developing countries. Such rate ranges would have to be flexible enough to take into account a country's special situation.

(b) Economic Distortions which do not permit a country to operate on the efficient points of its production possibility curve: Immobility of Factors of Production. This situation could arise in a country where there exists an underdeveloped region which is suitable for increased economic activity but because of the lack of infrastructure investment, labor and capital, the private rate of return is too low to encourage the needed investment. At the same time it might be very costly for the government to invest in the infrastructure without some assurance that private investment and economic production would occur simultaneously with the government development program. To break the deadlock, it will pay the governments to subsidize firms' sales for a period of time until the region develops sufficiently so that factors of production move easily into the area. The measurement problem is again a difficult one in this instance. However, the issue has to be faced since it is a scenario that frequently arises in regional development problems in poor countries.

(c) Non-economic Constraints. Some developing countries have non-economic constraints regarding the kind of taxes they use to raise government revenue. For example, governments may use payroll taxes rather than indirect taxes to finance large social programs (e.g. social security programs or public housing programs). These governments give tax rebates to the firms selling abroad to offset any competitive disadvantage they might suffer as a result of the existence of these programs financed by payroll taxes. If the purpose of giving rebates for indirect taxes is to avoid placing firms at a competitive disadvantage, it is also appropriate to allow rebates for these kinds of indirect taxes. The contrary position would be to argue that these programs should be financed through more conventional taxes and importing countries do not necessarily have to accept these kinds of policies which could be heavily abused. However, it might cause unnecessary equity problems for developing countries to design their fiscal policies along the lines of the existing GATT rules.

Differential Treatment Suggestions taking into consideration the
Constraints of Importing Countries

It is very unlikely that importing countries would fully agree that
the above-mentioned economic conditions completely justify the use
of subsidies to the extent necessary to full correct for these
conditions. It is conceivable that some of these
distortion-correcting subsidies might be income maximizing from a
global point of view but be less than income maximizing from the
point of view of a particular importing country. There is also a
fairly strong mercantilistic tone in the basic tenants of most
countries' trade policies, e.g. imports are bad, exports are good,
with the consumer interest being largely ignored. In addition, it
is not unreasonable to look with some suspicion at proposals to
allow the use of subsidies by developing countries. Developing
countries frequently have subsidy programs which exceed by
substantial margins the level which could be justified on economic
grounds. For these reasons, proposals for differential treatment
for developing countries based on the economic rationale discussed
above, which have any change of acceptance, could not include the
use of subsidies to the full extent necessary to obtain an optimum
allocation of resources from the world point of view.

Taking these practical constraints into account we can suggest
the following procedures for implementing a differential treatment
program for developing countries in the subsidy area.

(1) As a general principle developing countries should be
allowed to use otherwise prohibited subsidies under a revised
Article XVI if they can make an economic case for the use of
subsidies under some of the conditions discussed in section III-A.
An international review of such economic cases could be made under
GATT auspices and at that time developing countries would have to
submit an estimate of the duration of the subsidy programs and when
and how they expect the economic externalities to be internalized
by the exporting firms or the distortions eliminated.

(2) In addition to the acceptance of the general principle
that developing countries can use these subsidy programs under a
revised Article XVI, it should also be agreed that subsidized
imports would be allowed to come unchallenged into developing
countries markets up to a certain percentage of the developed
country's total import market. This agreement would in fact
constitute a revision of Article VI. The fact that developing
countries exports would be allowed to grow up to a certain level of
the import market of a developed country provides (a) time for the
developing countries to adjust to macroeconomic distortions or (b)
allows for part of the microeconomic externalities to be
internalized by private exporters. In this way developing
countries to some extent will be placed on an equal footing with
exporters from developed countries. As long as the developing
countries do not gain an unreasonable share of the market it can be
presumed that the subsidy is achieving the desired results. This
proposal could, however, be restrictive if the permitted market
share level is set too low and the developing countries are not

allowed to capture their potential share of the market. But as long as the import market share is set high enough to allow the firms to develop and become competitive without government aid, the developing countries' firms can always maintain or improve their share of the market once the subsidy program is eliminated.

(3) After the trigger level is met, importing countries could be entitled to impose countervailing duties on subsidized imports if injury is caused to their industries. The proposal could be even further refined to stipulate a stricter injury criterion in the case of subsidized imports from developing countries. Of course, if the developing countries cannot make the economic justification for their subsidy programs, importing countries would not have to wait until after the trigger level is passed before considering the imposition of countervailing duties.

The acceptance of such a proposal by the United States would mean that it would be ready to accept some limitations in the imposition of countervailing duties with respect to the use of the trigger level and acceptance of an injury criterion for its countervailing duty law. For most other developed countries the proposal would imply the acceptance of a trigger level.

If the importing country's industry suffering competition from subsidized imports is heavily protected, the argument can be made that the subsidies are correcting for the distortions created by the protection. In this case, the proposal of this paper would be on even stronger grounds as long as the protection given by the importing country to its industry is not justified on economic rationale similar to the one discussed in this paper. Paradoxically it is likely that these industries would generate the most resistance to such proposals.

IV. CONCLUDING COMMENTS

The proposals discussed in this paper for differential treatment for developing countries are based on standard economic analysis. They would involve changes in both the GATT rules with regard to the use of export subsidies and domestic trade laws. In this sense they are very ambitious but if presented in the context of the multilateral trade negotiations, the required changes might not be impossible.

The proposals do not only require changes in developed countries laws but they would also require developing countries to be more selective in their use of export subsidy programs. It would not be surprising if these proposals would be unacceptable to many developing countries which want carte blanche to use subsidies indiscriminately to promote their exports. But this request for unlimited power to use export subsidies might not be in the LDC's best interests.

A very strong case can be made to the effect that developing countries could increase their economic growth possibilities by liberalizing their trade regimes which would reduce substantially the need for excessive export subsidy programs. In addition, the mood in developed countries is not in favour of allowing developing countries to continue these practices without some agreed rules.

Both the policy flexibility of developed and developing countries will be limited if these rules or other similar ones are adopted for differential treatment for developing countries. However, they would help to achieve international consensus in an area of trade relations where potential friction and misunderstandings are frequent.

BIBLIOGRAPHY

Balassa, Bela and Associates: The Structure of Protection in Developing Countries, 1971.

Bhagwati, J. and Ramaswani V.K.: "Domestic Distortions, Tariffs and the Theory of Optimum Subsidy," Journal of Political Economy, February 1963.

Bhagwati, J.: "The General Theory of Distortions and Welfare," in J. Ghagwati et. al. Balance of Payments and Growth, 1971.

Chenery, Hollis and Hughes, Helen, Prospects for Partnership: Industrialization and Trade Policies in the 1970s (1974).

Dam, Kenneth, The GATT Law and International Economic Organization, 1970.

Floyd, J.E., "The Overvaluation of the Dollar: A note on the International Price Mechanism," American Economic Review, Volume LV, 1965, pp. 95-107.

Guido, Robert, and Morrone, Michael F.: "The Michelin Decision: A Possible New Direction for U.S. Countervailing Duty Law," Law and Policy in International Business, Vol. 6, No. 1, Winter 1974.

Johnson, Harry, "Optimal trade Intervention in the Presence of Domestic Distortions," In H. Johnson, Aspects of the Theory of Tariffs, 1972.

Johnson, Harry and Krauss, Mel: "Border Taxes, Border Tax Adjustments, Comparative Advantage, and the Balance of Payments," in Further Essays in Monetary Economics (1972).

Kemp, M. and Nagishi, T.: "Domestic Distortions, Tariffs, and the Theory of Optimum Subsidy," Journal of Political Economy, November 1969.

Marks, Matthew and Malgren, Harald: "Negotiating Non-tariff Distortions to Trade," Law and Policy in International Business. Vol. 7, No. 2, Spring 1975.

Rom, Michael, "GATT, Export Subsidies, and Developing Countries," Journal of World Trade Law, 1968.

Teigeiro, Jose D., and Elson, R. Anthony: "The Exports Promotion System and the Growth of minor Exports in Colombia," International Monetary Fund Staff Papers, July 1973, Vol. 20, No. 2, pp. 419-470.

NOTES

[1]During the last ten years a large number of developing countries have shifted from an import substitution development policy to one which gives more emphasis to export promotion. Originally only a few developing countries had a vigorous export promotion program -- Hong Kong, Taiwan, Korea, Israel, Singapore -- which were considered special cases because of higher levels of skills and access to capital facilities. More recently larger countries have joined this group like Brazil and Mexico and their rate of growth of exports equals that of the first group. See Chenery and Hugher (1974), Table 1-2.

[2]Jose D. Teigeiro and R. Anthony Elson (1973).

[3]Ibid.

[4]See Guido and Morrone (1974) for a discussion of the Michelin case which illustrates this approach.

[5]GATT, Basic Instruments and Selected Documents, Ninth Supplement, page 191.

[6]Ibid.

[7]Ibid, p. 192.

[8]For an excellent analysis of the GATT which cover both the legal and economic aspects see Dam (1970). Rom (1968) also review the GATT subsidy rules with regard to developing countries.

[9]In the "Declaration Giving Effect of the Provisions of Article XVI:4" of GATT, November 19, 1960, (Basic Instruments and Selected Documents, Ninth Supplement pp. 186-187) a number of government practices were prohibited. This declaration was signed by 17 developed countries. The practices were:

1. Currency retention schemes or any similar practices which involves a bonus on exports or re-exports;
2. The provision by governments of direct subsidies to exporters;
3. The remission, calculated in relation to exports, of direct taxes or social welfare charges on industrial or commercial enterprises;
4. The exemption, in respect of exported goods, of charges or taxes other than charges in connection with importation or indirect taxes levied at one or several stages on the same good if sold for internal consumption; or the payment in respect of exported goods of amounts exceeding those effectively levied at one or several stages on these goods in the form of indirect taxes or of charges in connection with importation as in both forms;
5. In respect of deliveries by governments or governmental

agencies or imported raw materials for export business on different terms than for domestic business, the charging of prices below world prices;

6. In respect of government export credit guarantees, the charging of premiums at rates which are manifestly inadequate to cover the long-term operating cost and losses to the credit insurance institutions;

7. The grant by governments (or special institutions controlled by governments) of export credits at rates below those which they have to pay in order to obtain the funds so employed;

8. The government bearing all or part of the costs incurred by exporters in obtaining credit.

[10]H. Johnson and M. Krauss (1972) argue this point.

[11]J. Bhagwati and V.K. Ramaswani (1963); H. Johnson (1972); M. Kemp and T. Nagishi (1969); and J. Bhagwati (1971).

[12]J. Bhagwati and V.K. Ramaswani (1963).

[13]H. Johnson (1972).

[14]See J. Bhagwati (1971), p. 78 for a discussion of this result.

[15]J. Bhagwati (1971) summarizes this literature and organizes the major results.

[16]Ibid, pp. 79-80.

[17]We limit the discussion to only the first and second best policies. See Bhagwati (1971) for a complete ranking.

[18]The dual price criterion is not very meaningful either, as a criterion to identify the existence of subsidized exports from developed countries.

[19]Rom (1968) already discussed this case. He recommended that an export subsidy should be allowed as long as it results in sales prices which do not undercut world market prices.

[20]See Floyd (1965) for an attempt to measure the degree of disequilibrium of exchange rate changes and Balassa and Associates (1971) for the methodology in measuring export bias which takes into account exchange rate overvaluation.

[21]Even during the recent period of flexible exchange rates most developing countries have continue to have their currencies pegged to the currencies of their major trading partners. The subsidy program could be used to gain time while devaluing vis-a-vis the currency of its major trading partner.

[22]No claim is made here that these are the only cases; they only seem to be the most important ones.

Import Controls and Exports in Developing Countries

I. M. D. LITTLE

The use of import controls by developing countries is enshrined in multilateral trade agreements and is supported by an influential body of literature and thought which has emerged since 1945. This article contains a brief critical assessment of the main aspects of the theoretical debate and practical experience with controls. On the basis of recent research and analysis, the author offers the view that poor export performance and inefficient production for domestic markets can be directly related to the excessive use of trade controls by developing countries.

Imports, and to a lesser extent exports, have been controlled by almost all developing countries since World War II. Yet the evidence indicates what theory suggests, that the more open the economy the higher is income and the better the growth rate. But reliance on controls persists. Why? In this article I shall examine the legacy of the intellectual case for import controls which was first made in the 1940s, and which still influences both the debate and the policy-making of today. I will then discuss the drawbacks of controls in the light of new analysis which contradicts the still widely accepted thesis that open trade between inequal partners damages the poorer partner.

For some countries in Latin America, controls were introduced in the depression of the 1930s or during World War II, because of worsening terms of trade. But almost invariably the controls instituted by developing countries since World War II have been the result of a balance of payments (BOP) crisis brought on by increased pending for development. Of course, World War II also left most Western industrialized countries with an almost complete array of import and exchange controls. But within a decade the import controls and most exchange controls in the developed countries had been dismantled. Why did the developing world

From **FINANCE AND DEVELOPMENT**, March, 1982 (20-23), reprinted by permission of the publisher.

intensify import controls long after the extreme dislocations caused by the war had vanished?

My impression is that this reliance arose mainly from the conviction among leaders of opinion and policymakers in the Third World that a poor country could not develop and manage its foreign trade and payments without controls. Of course, all controls protect, and sometimes protect absolutely. But there are several reasons among them the timing of the controls, and the fact that the countries instituting these controls had few industries to protect anyway) that lead us to believe the primary motive to have been BOP management -- not protection.

Furthermore, an intellectual heritage has probably played an important role in maintaining the control system, as the new intelligentsia, taught by the development economists of the 1940s and 1950s, rose in support of the system. In many semi-industrialized countries this has resulted in a strong meeting of the minds of intellectuals, businessmen, and bureaucrats.

I. THE CASE FOR CONTROLS

The rationale for poor countries to control imports was developed in the 1950s, mainly by Hans Singer and Raul Prebisch. Briefly, Singers's thesis was that developing countries had not got much out of international investment and trade -- above all, not much industrialization. There were dark hints that these countries might have got less than nothing out of it, as foreign trade diverted activities away from industrialization, which would have played a catalytic role in development. Singer also promoted the thesis of a secular worsening in the terms of trade of the developing countries, basing his argument on a United Nations document, Relating Prices of Exports and Imports of Underdeveloped Countries, published by the Department of Economic Affairs in 1949. Singer presented this thesis as an "indisputable fact,: and explained it essentially by an ever-increasing degree of monopoly (with labor sharing in it) in the production of manufactured goods. However, he drew no inference for BOP management.

Prebisch, and the Economic Commission for Latin America headed by him, emphasized the same worsening in the terms of trade of developing countries from 1949 onward. This thesis became enshrined in the United Nations Conference on Trade and Development (UNCTAD), and in repeated pronouncements by many development economists. The peaks in commodity prices during the Korean War, the subsequent decreases in prices followed by recovery after the early 1960s, the historically high levels of today, and the fact that all the scholarly work I know of denies any long-run trend, has probably still not fully exorcised the myth created by the 1949 UN study (which was based on the United Kingdom's terms of trade from 1876 to 1946).

To the argument of declining terms of trade was added the view that the demand for exports from developing countries would inevitably be sluggish compared with their own demand for imports -- especially, of course, if domestic demand were to be steered toward investment goods for development. To this was added the acceptable argument that the price elasticity for exports was very low (at least for developing countries taken together). Thus, exports of developing countries were determined by external forces not under their control, and this was also true of aggregate capital imports. Therefore, the level of imports was also determined. The conclusion was that their own import controls and other restrictions did not restrict trade but served only to control the pattern of imports in the interest of development. Also, with the declining terms of trade, BOP trouble would be endemic, and frequent devaluation and inflation would result. Moreover, devaluation would further worsen the terms of trade in the face of an inelastic foreign demand.

However, even if we accept the elasticity assumptions, it still does not add up to a case. Export taxes could be used to prevent devaluation from reducing export proceeds. Luxury taxes could prevent low priority imports. If industrialization needed a special push, this could be achieved by tariffs or, better still, by subsidies which would not discriminate against exports. Finally, it is probably an illusion that the reduction of consumption associated with price rises that result from controls is less inflationary than price rises resulting from other policies.

The argument could thus be fully convincing only to those who had acquired faith in planning -- and by "planning" I mean here trying to manipulate quantities with some end in view, with prices as a byproduct rather than vice versa. To express a disbelief in planning, at least for developing countries, in the 1950s, was a confession of confusion or worse. In Europe, Thomas Balogh and Gunnar Myrdal were among the conspicuously successful teachers of the need for controls and planning and of the view that trade between unequal partners might damage the poorer partner.

The emphasis on quantities was also connected with "structuralism." This seemed to involve the belief that a country's structure of production, and of imports and exports, was not only inappropriate but also unchangeable, except in the long run by investment, which must be controlled in order to produce eventually a more desireable structure. As far as trade and its effects on the proper pattern of production is concerned, structuralism essentially implied pessimism about the capacity of developing countries to expand exports. Export pessimism, together with the fact that most developing countries had only a tiny capital goods industry, led to the view that growth in the typical developing country was limited by foreign exchange and not by savings (which logically required the view that savings could not be transformed into investment).

Structuralism may have been conceived in Latin America, but the principles behind the Second and Third Development Plans in India were also essentially structuralist. Export pessimism, India's relative lack of minerals, and its desire to become independent of aid led structurally to the conclusion that anything needed for growth must be made at home. There was no choice! Consequently, plans based on this reasoning must be optimal. It also followed that relative prices and most other key concepts of traditional economics were irrelevant. The argument was logical, but hopelessly wrong.

Quite a few of the undesirable extravagances of the resultant import substitution policies had been recognized by Prebisch by 1964. These recognized drawbacks included capital intensity, low value added at international prices (but not value subtracted!), loss of scale, lack of competition, and the growth of "inessential" production behind the barriers to trade. There was, however, no recognition of the effect of protection on exports, nor that the developing countries' falling share of world trade was due either to this effect or to lagging agricultural production. The idea of the long-term decline in the terms of trade was still being advanced, and policies of import substitution were still favored. No distinction was drawn between protection by controls and by tariffs. The philosophy was still one of controlled trade. Neither then nor since has UNCTAD favored free trade -- not even for industrialized countries. For how then could the developed countries grant preferences? Any reciprocity was and has remained anathema and a part of the asymmetry argument -- what was bad for the developed was good for the developing world.

II. CHALLENGING CONTROLS

In the 1960s the great majority of developing countries were married to control systems and high protection (as indeed they still are, although to a lesser extent). Thus, it is to the challenge to the controlled-trade establishment that we must now turn. On a theoretical plane the seeds were sown by 1963 by J. Bhagwati and V. K. Ramaswami, among others. At the more influential applied level it did not acquire real force until 1970, when the extraordinary average heights and variability of effective protection were exposed in a book by Ian Little, Tibor Scitovsky, and Maurice Scott, and in another by Bela Balassa, et al (see the related reading list). The former work also discussed the inhibiting effects of general control regimes (which had spread from simple import controls). Both books laid some stress on promoting rather than protecting industry so as to achieve, as far as possible, neutrality between the domestic market and exports. The Little-Scitovsky-Scott volume also discussed how a transition to more liberal trade, which would be more favorable to exports, might be made, and suggested that it would be very difficult to justify effective subsidization of industry, whether directly or by tariffs, of more than 20 per cent.

More recently there has been a massive ten-country study of trade regimes guided by Jagdish Bhagwati and Anne Krueger (yet to be published). Brazil, Chile, Colombia, Egypt, Ghana, India, Israel, the Philippines, the Republic of Korea, and Turkey were the countries covered between 1950 and 1972. The study found that the open or relatively open countries grew faster -- faster than when they were less open and faster than the chronically "closed." Brazil, Israel, and Korea performed best of the group. The main reasons given for superior performance were as follows. Exports proved to be highly responsive to the reduction or elimination of the bias against them. The partly consequential increase in imports reduced the chaos in the pattern of import substitution incentives and ensured a freer flow of inputs, with production benefits resulting from greater capacity utilization and a reduction in required stocks. The greater value of exports also made it easier to borrow. In some countries, especially in Korea, more direct foreign investment was attracted to the relatively labor-intensive export sector.

I would put rather more stress than Bhagwati does in his summary volume on the supposition that exports are simply good business for the country. Social (that is, shadow priced) profits and savings are higher on exports than on import substitutes at the margin. That restrictive regimes result in more investment in capital-intensive sectors and plants is empirically clear for a number of countries both within and outside the Bhagwati-Krueger ten. This also has implications for spreading the benefits of growth, as well as for growth itself.

Krueger, in her summary volume, deals primarily with the conditions under which liberalization attempts have been made. Twenty-two liberalization efforts are reported for the ten countries between 1950 and 1972. All involved packages. Devaluation was combined with import liberalization, deflation, reduction of tariffs, and export subsidies, in varying degrees. Most efforts were made in periods of economic crisis, usually in a situation in which the government had committed itself to an overvalued exchange rate, and in which there was a loss of reserves or debt rescheduling. Many efforts included attempts at stabilization.

Of course, if a simple devaluation is to be effective, inflation has to be stopped. It was the consequent deflationary measures, and the foreign (International Monetary Fund or World Bank) involvement, which often made these attempts unpopular, and resulted in a reversal. It must be remembered that the Fund norm was then a fixed exchange rate. But a floating rate, or a sliding peg, was used in several countries on and off.

The reasons for failure to liberalize are divergent. Either the effective devaluation was inadequate, or the bias against exports was not removed or was not much reduced (as in India and the Philippines), so that exports did not respond sufficiently. Inflation and a fixed rate continued or was reimposed (Chile under Allende). There was insufficient political and intellectual commitment (India, Chile), or an actual reversal for political reasons (Ghana), or bad monsoon luck (India again). Needless to say, manufacturers require some expectation of continuing profitability for exports if they are to invest for export production, make products designed for export, and spend money on a marketing organization. Only in a few countries was the government commitment to the change of policy sufficient for this expectation.

But although failure was frequent, there was progress among the ten. The Bhagwati-Krueger phase analysis suggests an increasing degree of liberalization after the mid-1960s and comes down in favor of an export promotion strategy. (Oddly enough, Bhagwati means by "export promotion" a strategy that is neutral between the domestic and export markets.)

III. EXPORT STRATEGIES

Further relevant evidence is added by Balassa in a preliminary report on his World Bank studies of exports in developing countries, where he discusses Argentina, Brazil, Chile, Colombia, India, Israel, Korea, Mexico, Singapore, Taiwan, and Yugoslavia. More material is provided by two chapters (by Maurice Scott and myself) in a new book on Taiwan. A few major points which seem to me to emerge from including a few more countries, and even more recent information, in the review are as follows:

*Of the above, only Korea, Singapore, and Taiwan have created virtually free trade regimes for exports. In these countries exporters can buy not only imports but also domestic inputs at world prices. Singapore and Taiwan are now as free trading as most developed countries. Korea and Taiwan also have free labor markets, barely affected by trade unions or labor legislation. These three countries sustained gross national product growth rates of about 10 percent for as much as a decade prior to 1973 -- a performance shared only by Hong Kong, Israel, and Japan.

*Although Israel is fully liberalized, tariffs still result in a significant bias against exports. None of the other countries mentioned are fully liberalized, and none have created the free trade regimes for exports of Korea, Singapore, and Taiwan (and, of course, Hong Kong). All, however, have made some effort at export promotion. The staggering export performance of Hong Kong, Korea, Singapore, and Taiwan is well known. However, the manufactured exports of Argentina, Brazil, and Colombia have also grown very fast, at about 30 percent per annum in 1967-73, but from very low levels. As a consequence, the proportion of manufactured output exported remains very low: in 1973 the ratios were 3.6 per cent, 4.4 per cent, and 7.5 percent, respectively, compared with 49.9 per cent for Taiwan and 40.5 percent for Korea.

*The highly open economies of Hong Kong, Korea, and Taiwan all weathered the world recession of 1974-75 very well, despite their extreme dependence on imported energy. Korea's growth rate never dipped below 8.3 percent. Hong Kong's and Taiwan's were brought below 3 percent, but they recovered to rates of 16.2 percent and 11.9 percent in 1976. Despite continued sluggish world demand, and increasing protection in many industrialized countries -- some of it specifically directed against these three economies -- the U.S. dollar value of the exports of the three rose by 39.4 percent, 56.2 percent, and 52.2 percent in 1976.

One thing at least is certain. The more labor-intensive manufactures of the now semi-industrialized countries need no protection or subsidization. Of course, it will still be argued that the least industrialized countries need considerable promotion of manufactures, if not protection, to get going. This may be true. But need it be very heavy? And need it be protective rather than promotional?

Of course, liberalization and reduced protection cannot achieve all the miracles it has produced for the four Asian countries discussed. It is obvious that the speed of the consequential changes in industrialized countries has some limit. But the fact that there is this limit to the degree of market penetration that will be permitted at any one time by the industrialized countries (and a limit to the size even of their markets) should not be regarded as a reason to continue with a policy bias in favor of import substitution. There are still gains to be made by all countries, even if only a few more miracles can be expected.

The developed countries still produce a very high proportion of the labor-intensive manufactures they consume. Clothing imports from the developing countries account for little more than 5 percent of consumption in the developed world. The range of labor-intensive goods for which there has been any significant market penetration is still quite limited. Yet for 15 years manufactured exports from developing countries have increased at the rate of 15 per cent per annum. With reasonable goodwill on the part of the developed countries, and appropriate policies on the part of the developing countries, this rate of growth could be maintained for a very long time. The growth of exports from Hong Kong, Korea, Singapore, and Taiwan is certain to slow down greatly because at present they export such a high proportion of their output; hence, the growth rate of exports must soon approach the countries' overall growth rate, which is unlikely to exceed 10 per cent. In this situation there should be room for sales of comparable goods by other developing countries. It must be remembered that these countries now play a role that is far from small in markets for manufactured exports (the _growth_ of exports from them in 1976 was worth about $7 billion).

Furthermore, developing countries trade little with each other. Such trade is greatly inhibited by their own import substitution policies. This has been of secondary importance because the market in developing countries is so much smaller than the market in the developed world, but its importance is increasing as markets in developing countries for tradeable items are growing faster than those in developed countries. Preferential regional trading arrangements are very much a second-best option, and they are also very difficult to negotiate. Policies of general liberalization and reduced protection can be of far greater benefit and cost much less in terms of scarce administrative talent. Yet organized and controlled regional trading remains the conventional wisdom of leaders of the developing world when trade among themselves is under discussion.

I have discussed mainly manufactured goods, but it seems also likely that considerable gains could result from more intratrade in agricultural products and even minerals, although this seems to have been studied relatively little. Furthermore, there is little doubt that liberal trade regimes would help even if exports did not increase greatly. All the benefits arising from greater use of the price mechanism -- the reduction in administration, in delays, in stocks, in corruption, and the increase in competition -- occur anyway.

IV. TRANSFER OF TECHNOLOGY

In the 1970s there have been renewed attacks on trade and foreign investment, much of it stemming from England. The focus is now more on the evils of inappropriate technology and its inappropriate products, on multinationals, and, indeed, on the transfer of capital in any form -- including aid. It is related to the increased emphasis on income distribution and poverty. But trade is involved. It is claimed that trade has harmed the poor in developing countries. If there were no trade, none of the other alleged evils could result. If the conclusion that no trade should occur is too extreme, nevertheless trade and the transfer of technology should be carefully controlled, just as it has been for 25 years, only, I suppose, on a broader scale and more effectively (see, for example, Singer, 1971, Keith Griffin, 1974, and Paul Streeten, Finance & Development, September 1977).

How is it, then, that the developing countries have grown so fast as a group, that is by 5.6 percent in 1960-65 and by 6.0 percent in 1965-73? Within these averages, half a dozen countries have grown, without special benefit from ample mineral resources, at rates which would have been deemed inconceivable 20 years ago. The industrialized countries do not grow as fast, nor the centrally planned economies either. None but Japan has ever achieved even half the growth rates of the half dozen developing countries with the best performance. Even Japan's high growth was for nearly a hundred years based primarily on foreign technology, designed for countries with higher wage levels than Japan.

I suggest that the basic reason is plain. Such rapid growth can only be the result of catching up by importing relatively inappropriate technology. The result is technical change. Yet Keith Griffin has recently advanced the theory that growth in developing countries has come predominantly from increases in the amount of labor and capital and not from technical change. Not only are the supporting figures and analysis inadequate but the conclusion flies in the face of common sense. No one can be against making technology more appropriate -- that is, more labor intensive -- but this should not blind one to the fact that foreign technology can and has produced miracles. These benefits are found not only in the agricultural and industrial spheres but also in advances in public health and life expectancy. We can all agree that the poor in developing countries have not benefited from growth as much as desirable. But the claim that the mass of the poor have not benefited at all is rhetoric. Even in Brazil, where inequality has increased with fast growth, it is clear that the poorest 40 percent of the population has benefits. Most observers will also agree that they would have benefited more if development had been more labor intensive. I am convinced that with appropriate and open policies on the part of the developing countries, more labor- intensive development would have resulted.

In the open and fast growing Asian economies, the standard of living of the relatively poor has been revolutionized in a period of 15 years. If one wants to look for millions who have scarcely benefited, or even lost out in the postwar period, there can be little doubt that one would find them most easily in the slow-growing, low-trading countries, principally in South Asia and the Sahel. To attribute this primarily to foreign technology is the greatest absurdity. The attack, mainly Western-inspired, on the transfer of technology, and on one of its modes of transfer -- the multinational firm -- has gone much too far, and threatens the poor.

However, I do not think that these recent arguments for import and technology controls have much effect on leaders in the developing world, as they violate common sense. Even the hatred and fear of the multinationals, and the feeling of being "dominated," seem to be dying down, as developing countries come to realize their strength. Many countries in Latin America are trying to struggle out of the trap of having established an excessively inwardlooking industrial structure. The problem is that change takes many years if it is to be relatively painless for all. At the same time, potential exporters need confidence that exports will remain profitable, and this, in turn, means confidence that a government committed to change will remain in power. The tragedy is that elsewhere, especially in Africa, a number of countries seem to be falling into the old trap of anything goes provided it is capital-intensive import substitution.

RELATED READING LIST

H. W. Singer, "The Distribution of Gains Between Investing and Borrowing Countries," American Economic Review, Papers and Proceedings, May 1950.

J. Bhagwati and V. K. Ramaswami, "Domestic Distortions, Tariffs and the Theory of Optimum Subsidy," Journal of Political Economy, February 1963.

Toward a New Trade Policy for Development, United Nations, 1964.

D. B. Keesing, "Outward Looking Policies and Economic Development," Economic Journal, June 1967.

Ian Little, T. Scitovsky, and M. F. G. Scott, Industrialization and Trade in Some Developing Countries, Oxford University Press, 1970.

B. Balassa, et al. The Structure of Protection in Developing Countries, Johns Hopkins Press, 1971.

K. Griffin, "The International Transmission of Inequality," World Development, Vol. 2, No. 3, March 1974.

"The Distribution of Gains Revisited," IDS, May 1971, published in H. Singer, The Strategy of International Development, International Arts and Sciences Press, New York, 1975.

"Export Incentives and Export Performance in Developing Countries," World Bank Staff Working Paper No. 248, January 1977.

J. Bhagwati, Anatomy and Consequences of Trade Control Regimes (National Bureau of Economic Research, New York, forthcoming).

Anne O. Krueger, Synthesis, (National Bureau of Economic Research, New York, forthcoming).

Walter Galenson (editor), The Economic Development of Taiwan (Cornell University Press, forthcoming).

Policy Issues in the Fields of Trade, Finance and Money and Their Relationship to Structural Changes at the Global Level

UNCTAD SECRETARIAT

I. INTRODUCTION

There has been a presumption that international development strategies concerned with the development of developing countries could be treated independently of broader developments at the global level. Implicit in this view has been the notion that the development of developing countries could be accommodated within the framework of a steadily expanding world economy. Thus, special measures in favour of developing countries were seen as temporary exemptions from the "rules of the game", granted only for the purpose of speeding up the process of "graduation" of these countries to full partnership in the global system.

The first and second United Nations Development Decades[1] broadly reflected this conceptual framework. The international measures, mostly in the form of aspirational targets, ranging from the provision of official development assistance to trade preferences, were meant to improve the international environment for developing countries largely within the context of the existing international economic order.

In the event, the basic objectives of the International Development Strategy for the Second United Nations Development Decade did not materialize. For one thing, developed countries, as a group, failed to fulfil the role that the Strategy envisaged for them, perhaps partly because the measures expected of them were not perceived by their public and their policy-makers as being essential elements of their own foreign economic policy or domestic development. For another, the underlying assumptions regarding a steadily growing world economy have been largely invalidated by the

From **PROCEEDINGS OF THE UN'S CONFERENCE ON TRADE AND DEVELOPMENT,** 1981, (35-45), reprinted by permission of the publisher.

serious economic crisis that has dominated the decade of the 1970s. Underlying this crisis are shifts in the domestic structures of the major industrial countries as well as shifts in the distribution of economic power among them. These structural shifts have placed increasing pressures upon the international economic system, which now appears ill-equipped to provide an effective mechanism for reconciling conflicting national objectives.

Two major conclusions emerge from the experience of the 1970s. First, the development issue cannot be isolated from those basic to the operation of the world economy. Indeed, the rapid development of developing countries can best be promoted within a policy framework encompassing the entire world economy and having among its objectives the restructuring of the world economy for global development. Secondly, a successful global development strategy presupposes reconciliation of conflicting national objectives. Given the derailment of the entire international economy, the resolution of these conflicts can no longer be entrusted to consultations among a few States only or to separate and largely unco-ordinated international examination of issues in the fields of trade, payments, finance and development; rather, it would require a broad overview of the management of the world economy on the basis of internationally agreed objectives and with the effective participation of all States.

These conclusions have far-reaching implications for the preparation of the International Development Strategy for the 1980s and the interrelationship between development objectives and structural changes on a world scale.[2] But they also have implications regarding the manner in which policies affecting the world economy are to be assessed. In particular, effective management of the world economy would require that problems in the areas of trade, payments and finance should be considered together and in the context of their interdependence and relationship to development. The past two sessions of the United Nations Conference on Trade and Development stressed the need for considering these interrelated problems in such a broader framework. In response to this, the Trade and Development Board has included this issue in its agenda as a regular review item. In order to assist the Board to carry out this mandate more effectively, it is suggested that a high-level advisory group be established which would examine the problems relating to the management of the world economy, especially in the interrelated fields of trade, payments, finance and development, and make recommendations for consideration by the Board, particularly at its ministerial sessions, regarding action that may be required to bring actual policies into closer harmony with the requirements of structural change in the world economy and the development of developing countries.

II. GLOBAL DEVELOPMENT AND STRUCTURAL CHANGE

The present report is concerned essentially with problems of the management of the international economy and with the relationships between short-term policies and longer-term development objectives, particularly the objective of promoting structural change. It thus complements the report that focuses on the long-term aspects of the restructuring of the global economy.[3] The links between global development, structural change, international development objectives and economic management are complex. It would appear useful, therefore, to explicitly outline the analytical and normative framework within which they are approached in the present report.

It is taken as accepted that a fundamental goal of the international community is the eradication of the present overwhelming disparities among and within countries with respect to per capita consumption levels and quality of life. It is further presumed that this goal is to be achieved by increasing the productive capacity of the poorer groups in the world community within a context of global development -- a process which will involve a more equitable decision-making process at the international level.

While there appears to be a general consensus on the fundamental goal of global development, there is not as yet agreement as to how progress towards this objective it to be advanced. Nevertheless, the debate regarding the management of the world economy would be placed on a firmer basis if the underlying goal were clearly understood and kept in the forefront by all parties concerned.

Global development implies, by definition, continuous structural changes on a world-wide basis. Yet, not all patterns of structural changes yield a form of global development that satisfies the fundamental goal mentioned above. The set of structural changes that meet this condition must, among other things, provide for an accelerated pace of development of the developing regions.

The development of the developing regions, in turn, implies that their domestic production structures would become more highly evolved and internally integrated. They would attain the capability of producing a much wider range of products and, in general, their economies would be less heavily concentrated in particular sectors. At the same time their income levels would increase in relation to the world average and their consumption patterns would alter as a consequence.

This structural transformation of the domestic economies of the developing regions would be reflected in the level and composition of their demand for imports from the rest of the world and in their relative competitiveness in world markets for more highly processed goods. The present trade patterns whereby the developing regions for the most part export primary commodities to the industrialized regions and import manufactured goods in turn would be replaced by a more balanced composition, in particular with growing exports of manufactures from developing countries. The current pattern of trade among industrialized countries, which is characterized by intra-branch specialization, would come to predominate throughout the world economy.

The indicated changes in the pattern of international economic relations obviously imply that structural changes in the domestic economies of the existing industrialized regions will be required. Indeed, any viable international development strategy will need to be based on the recognition that the development process includes not only increased productive capacities in the developing regions but also corresponding structural changes in the developed regions.

The link between short-term economic management and development objectives at the global level

At the global level, development objectives have been expressed in the form of aspirational targets. On the other hand the structure of the world economy has been shaped mainly as a result of policy decisions by those industrialized countries that have come to play a major role in the management of the world economy. The conditions required for consistency between global development objectives and the national policies and objectives of major economies are indeed very stringent and, as the post-war experience has amply demonstrated, it is most unlikely that these conditions can be met within the current framework of international co-operation. It follows that a viable strategy for global development must provide mechanisms for ensuring that economic policies devoted to immediate problems are fully consistent with the longer-term development objectives.

The lack of an explicit treatment of linkages between current policy issues and long-term development objectives is one of the major shortcomings in international economic co-operation. The existing dichotomy between long-term development objectives on the one hand and short-term policies on the other results not only in an increased sense of frustration but also in an inefficient management of the world economy. Indeed, the short-term horizon implied in policy decisions devoted to immediate problems often compromises their success.

Interrelationship of problems in the areas of trade, payments, finance and development

The framework of international economic relations is based on rules and regulations that are usually embodied in multilateral agreements of covenants. The set of these rules define the parameters of the international economy system.[4]

An international economic system may be said to be in a state of dynamic equilibrium when it permits reconciliation of national objectives in a manner that permits all countries to make full use of their productive capacity and growth potential. For example, for developed countries a system that required departures from high levels of employment in order to achieve external balance would be deemed unsatisfactory. Likewise, developing countries would regard as inadequate a system that failed to provide the external environment needed for the attainment of otherwise domestically feasible growth rates. In other words, the system must be fully consonant with the requirements of a dynamic world economy; in particular, it should be able to accommodate the world-wide structural shifts in the allocation of investment, industrialization and trade flows that are implied by the process of development.

When the international economic system is in equilibrium, its management is limited to assuring that the rules of the game are observed. For a number of reasons, this task may be entrusted to multilateral organizations each specializing in one of the distinct albeit interrelated components of the system, namely, trade, payments and finance. On the other hand, when the system experiences strains of fundamental disequilibrium this largely compartmentalized approach to the management of the international economy bears a number of risks. Since the various elements of the trading, monetary and financial systems are closely intertwined, the success of changes in the rules and procedures in one area will depend on complementary measures and changes in the other areas. Changes in the rules and procedures adopted separately in the several spheres should, in the final analysis, be regarded as part of a co-ordinated over-all settlement of the tensions in the international economy. It is in the nature of the case that some elements of that settlement will appeal most to some countries, other elements to others. There is a danger that if each measure were acted upon by itself, countries might feel free to accept or reject the various component parts one by one instead of taking a view of the entire settlement as a whole. This in turn could lead to an unbalanced outcome.

As is explained below, the international economy is in fact operating under severe stresses. It follows, therefore, that present arrangements and prospective changes in the spheres of trade, money and finance must be assessed in the context of a comprehensive approach and must be viewed in terms of the requirements for economic expansion and structural changes in the world as a whole.

III. LESSONS OF THE POST-WAR ERA FOR THE WORLD ECONOMY

The interrelated character of the world economy was in the minds of those responsible for the post-war effort to fashion a new and viable system of international trade, payments and lending.

This effort was undertaken to avoid a recurrence of the interwar experience in which unemployment, trade and payments restrictions, currency uncertainty and the collapse of the international credit system each reinforced the other in depressing output and arresting growth.

The system established in the aftermath of the Second World War was intended to encourage a cumulative process making for world expansion. This was to be accomplished by complementary action on several fronts; the dismantling of trade barriers and payments restrictions; the maintenance of orderly exchange rates and the prevention of disruptive capital movements; the provision of credit facilities for payments adjustments and the resumption of investment flows into developing countries.

The International Monetary Fund (IMF) and the International Bank for Reconstruction and Development (IBRD), which emerged from the Bretton Woods Conference, and later on the General Agreement on Tariffs and Trade (GATT),[5] embodied the rules and procedures of the post-war international economic system.

The post-war system was remarkably successful in its basic objectives, namely the attainments of high levels of employment in the industrialized countries and the expansion of world trade and output. This success, which was cumulative in character, was accompanied by progressive liberalization of world trade and payments, the avoidance, by and large, of competitive undervaluations and the expansion of international investment.

The system had, however, a number of important limitations. In the first instance, the universality of membership originally envisaged for the Bretton Woods institution failed to materialize. Partly because of the inherent difficulties in accommodating economies with centrally planned systems into essentially a liberal and market-oriented framework and partly because of the general political climate prevailing at that time, the socialist countries of Eastern Europe and China did not join. In fact, the former organized themselves into a system of mutual economic co-operation, the Council for Mutual Economic Assistance (CMEA), on the basis of rules and procedures that reflected the centrally planned character of their economies. A further serious limitation was that the system was not geared to tackle the special trade and financial problems of developing countries. In a sense, the international discussions relating to the development of developing countries may be seen as originating from the strong feeling of these countries that the development issue should be treated as an integral part of the management of the world economy and that the rules governing international economic relations should take explicitly into account their special problems.

The fact that the remarkable expansion of world trade and output took place in the framework of the rules of the game enshrined in the Articles of Agreement of the Bretton Woods institutions and in the General Agreement on Tariffs and Trade may lead to the conclusion that the latter were a necessary and sufficient condition for the former. Whether the rules of the game were necessary in view of the market-oriented character of the major industrial countries participating in the system remains a matter for conjecture. What can be said with some certainty is

that these rules prevailed during the period of expansion of world
trade and output. But the element of growth were not provided by
the rules themselves. The thrust of the post-war growth is to be
found in the sharply unequal distribution of economic power among
the industrial countries and the willingness of the major
industrial Power to underpin the system -- in terms of maintaining
the key currency, opening its markets, providing capital and
technology and extending financial aid -- and thus make it possible
for the other industrial countries to proceed with relative ease
with the reconstruction and development of their economies.

The shifting balance of economic power and structural changes

The most significant feature of the evolution of the world
economy in the post-war era is the transition from the monopolar
situation which existed among the developed market-economy
countries immediately after the war to the multipolar conditions of
today.
The aftermath of the war placed the United States of America
in the position of the single major supplier of capital and
technology to Western Europe and Japan. The role of the dollar as
the major reserve currency enabled the United States to become a
net exporter of capital and goods while maintaining, mainly on
account of military and security expenditures, a deficit on current
account. The foreign economic policy of the United States provided
all necessary ingredients for stimulating the growth of the other
industrial countries. The induced structural changes in the latter
led to a rapid increase in productivity which, coupled with the
added stimulus to demand supplies by the external position of the
United States, led in turn to rapid shifts in the relative economic
position among the industrial countries. A sensitive indicator of
the shifts in productivity which took place is the balance of trade
of machinery and transport equipment for the United States. Thus,
over the decade 1955-1965 the trade surplus of the United States
with Western Europe as a share of its total exports in this
category fell from 55 per cent to 30 per cent and with Japan from
73 per cent to 20 per cent.
The changes in economic balance are also reflected in the
broader economic aggregated of gross domestic product and total
trade. For example, in 1950 the major reserve currency countries,
namely, the United States and the United Kingdom, accounted for
approximately 50 per cent of total exports of the developed
market-economy countries, whereas by 1970 this figure had fallen to
30 per cent. Rates of growth of GDP, in real terms, also reflect
these shifts, with Western Europe and Japan growing at average
annual rates of 4.4 and 8.4 per cent respectively during the period
1950-1976, while the corresponding figure for the United States was
only 3.5 per cent.
The socialist countries of Eastern Europe have also
experienced impressive gains during the post-war period. Taken as

a group, these countries achieved an average annual rate of growth in national production of 7.7 per cent during the period 1950–1976. While the economic transactions of this group with the rest of the world have increased steadily and at impressive rates since the mid-1950s, the level achieved fell far short of that which would have been observed if the institutional framework were more elastic. In dealing with the need for a reformed system, it is fitting that the measures taken should be of a character that makes it possible to envisage a greater degree of economic co-operation among groups with different economic and social systems.[6]

The developing countries, taken as a group, have grown somewhat faster than the developed market-economy countries and achieved a growth rate of GDP in real terms in the neighbourhood of 5 per cent per annum during the period 1950–1976, although on a per capita basis the gap in standard of living has increased. A number of developing countries which have either abundant natural resources or relatively sophisticated infrastructure experienced significant inflows of capital and technology and succeeded in pursuing an export-oriented development path which bears some similarities with that followed by several countries in Western Europe and by Japan. The overwhelming majority of developing countries, however, were not in a position to avail themselves of the opportunities opened to the industrial or industrializing countries and their role in international economic co-operation has remained, by and large, that of the provider of raw materials in exchange for manufactured goods. In the absence of a scheme to strengthen commodity markets and adequate provision of concessional finance, these countries have found it increasingly difficult to meet the requirements of even minimal development plans.

The shifting of the economic balance was associated with profound changes in the areas of trade, finance and payments. With regard to trade, it is noteworthy that its impressive expansion was associated with pronounced changes in its composition. While in the earlier periods exports of manufactured goods were sustained largely by their exchange against commodities, the post-war era was characterized by increasing trade of a variety of manufactures with one another. An immediate consequence of the phenomenon was the over-all growth of trade ceased to be constrained by the volume of commodities that primary producers in developed and developing countries were able to export. Thus, while the volume of world trade in commodities less than doubled, the volume of manufactures nearly tripled between the years 1960 and 1971. Moreover, the post-war trade in manufactures was a reflection more of technology factors and intrabranch specialization among the trading partners than of relative factor endowments. An important exception to this was the exports of manufactures from developing countries which, by and large, consisted of labour-intensive or resource-intensive goods. This distinction perhaps helps to explain, to some extent, the asymmetrical treatment of manufactures by developed and developing countries in multilateral exercises for tariff cuts. In the case of the former, the manufacturers saw the possibilities of further gains in freer trade. But for this to be feasible they had to agree on product specialization or differentiation and inter-penetration of national markets. The prospects of mutually beneficial tariff cuts are evident and this explains the relative ease with which most of these products were the subject of trade liberalization. In the latter case, however -- labour-intensive or resource-intensive exports -- there was little scope for a bargain to be effected between industrial and developing countries on the basis of reciprocal advantage.

Perhaps even more impressive than the expansion of trade was the striking movement towards the internationalization of production which materialized through massive transfers of long-term capital, mainly in the form of direct investment. In 1971, the total value of "international production"[7] was placed at $330 billion, as compared to $310 billion of total world exports. This phenomenon has had far-reaching implications for the management of the world economy. First, the emerging new financial and production decision centres transcend national governmental surveillance. Secondly, an important part of international trade, about one third, reflected exports by foreign affiliates. Thirdly, about 20 to 25 per cent of exports of major industrial countries consisted of intracompany transactions.[8] As a result, the efficacy of policy instruments in influencing real and monetary variables, as well as the balance of payments, was reduced.

The movement towards internationalization was also evident in the monetary field. The spectacular growth of highly mobile short-term capital in the past 15 years has had a profound influence on both national economies and the working of the international system. On the one hand, these markets provide an important source of funds for countries which experience payments deficits and for a number of reasons wish to finance rather than suppress them. On the other hand, the highly liquid character of the assets renders the market unstable. Sudden changes in market perceptions which trigger massive movements of capital are by no means infrequent. Governments have found it difficult to amass the necessary resources to stave off a speculative run on their currencies. As a result, Governments are often obliged to tailor their policies to market perceptions even at the risk of compromising national objectives and priorities.

The emergence of structural disequilibria and the crisis

The shift in the balance of economic power that was brought about by the post-war pattern of growth and structural changes placed the international economic system under increasing strains. By the mid-1960s, it became apparent that the margin for reconciling conflicting objectives through the growth process was indeed very limited. Conflicts in the field of trade, especially with regard to agricultural products, increased, and in Western Europe there was widespread concern about the tendency towards internationalization of production under the leadership of American multinational corporations.

In the monetary area, the conflicts became even more serious.

Major industrial countries Western Europe and Japan, whose industries are relatively export-oriented, profited from the overvaluation of the dollar and succeeded in increasing their share of world trade and establishing a comfortable payments surplus. Continuation of this situation meant, however, that these countries would continue to be prepared to "finance" the growing deficit on current account of the main reserve centre by accumulating dollar reserves whose eventual conversion into gold was becoming increasingly problematic. On the whole, the stand that these countries took was somewhat ambivalent. On the one hand, they stressed the need for the United States to take measures to strengthen its current account position and thus help avoid world inflationary pressures which, in their view, would stem from a weakening dollar. On the other hand, they were reluctant and often unwilling to take measures themselves, mainly through appreciation of their currencies, which inter alia might reduce payment imbalanced by weakening their own trade and current account position.

For the main reserve centre the problems were equally pressing. The overvaluation of the dollar had significantly weakened its competitive position and key industries were losing ground to foreign competitors (including subsidiaries of United States companies operating abroad) even in the domestic market. At the same time, the role of the dollar as the main reserve currency required that it remain stable in its relation to gold. In the face of the dilemma between the need to meet national priorities and goals and the requirements of the dollar as an international reserve asset, the Government remained indecisive until August 1971.

The measures announced by the United States Government in August 1971[9] had far-reaching implications for the international economic system. Not only did they seal the fate of the Bretton Woods system but they drove home the clear message that the United States was no longer prepared to underpin the viability of an international monetary system at the cost of its national priorities and requirements. Henceforth, the dollar would have the same freedom of exchange-rate changes as other currencies in order to adjust imbalances in external accounts. This meant that the management of the system as well as the costs and responsibilities accompanying it had to be shared with other countries.

Managing the economy under crisis conditions

The immediate response of the international community to the monetary crisis was the establishment of the IMF Committee on Reform of the International Monetary System and Related Issues (Committee of Twenty) which was entrusted with the task of working out the blueprint of a new international monetary system. While the Committee did recognize that the question of monetary reform was intimately related to problems in the areas of trade and development finance, its working assumption was that the rules prevailing in these areas were, broadly speaking, satisfactory.

The reformed monetary system was expected to work hand-in-hand with a liberal (that is, an open and non-discriminatory) trading system. The Committee did not, and perhaps could not, fully anticipate the rising wave of protectionist policies that came to challenge the foundations of the trading system in later years. Nor did the Committee consider it necessary to take into account the need for reform in the commodity area. Here again, the Committee implicitly assumed that the process of growth would continue to be based on abundant supplies of raw materials, at relatively low prices. Fluctuations in commodity prices were seen as posing some balance-of-payments problems to the producing nations but those were to be dealt with in the context of an improved compensatory financing facility.

In the area of finance, the Committee explicitly recognized the need for policies to underpin the functioning of the monetary system. In fact, one of the key issues to which it addressed itself was the proposal for establishing a link between the creation of special drawing rights (SDRs) and additional development finance for developing countries. The relationship between the functioning of the international monetary system on the one hand and capital movements on the other hand was also recognized, but the Committee stopped short of considering measures to harness the operations of private capital markets in respect of both the creation of international credit and short-term capital movements. To be sure, the Committee could not have anticipated the phenomenal growth of private capital markets that payments imbalances in later years brought about. In the event, the functioning of the international monetary system in general and the adjustment process in particular came to depend upon market perceptions about the effectiveness of national policies and the differential economic performance of Governments.

The negotiations for a reformed international monetary system proved to be difficult. Views differed on fundamental aspects of the reform between the main reserve currency country and the others, between surplus and deficit countries and between developed and developing countries. The trade-offs that were offered in the reform exercise were not adequate to reconcile conflicting interests. In retrospect, it appears that the probability of reaching a consensus would have been higher if the reform exercise had encompassed the broader question of restructuring the international economic system with specific measures in the areas of trade, finance and development. For example, Governments that did not consider a particular proposal in the monetary field to be in their interest could have been induced to accept it had they been offered adequate compensatory changes in other spheres.

The unusual constellation of forces that shocked the world economy in the period 1972-1974[10] led the international community to abandon its efforts for a fundamental reform of the international monetary system. In completing its work in 1974, the IMF Committee of Twenty sketched out the basic objectives of a reformed international monetary system, which were to be achieved in an evolutionary manner as world economic conditions improved.[11]

Thus ended the first and only genuine attempt to introduce fundamental reform in one of the key areas of international economic relations.

The response of Governments to the economic crisis was on the whole defensive. Attention was focused on the immediate problems that the crisis posed. At the same time, there was also widespread feeling that the problems at hand had their roots in deep-seated structural factors. Led by developing countries, the international community acknowledged the need to establish a new international economic order. The Programme of Action on the Establishment of a New International Economic Order launched at the sixth special session of the General Assembly and further elaborated at the seventh special session[12] gave a powerful impetus to negotiations relating to the development of developing countries. Perhaps more important than the measures proposed was the fundamental change in the framework in which the development issue was viewed. For the first time, development issues were seen to be an integral part of the broader question of the management of the world economy. Development brings along structural changes not only in the domestic economies but also in the international economic system. Conversely, the latter affects in a profound way the potential of development and its pattern. There was, of course, nothing new in this. The novelty lay in the realization that the post-war development of developing countries had rendered them an important economic force in the world economy and that those countries, when acting in unison, could effectively challenge the international system of production, distribution and pricing. In a deeper sense, the challenge of the 1970s was to bring the decision-making process regarding the working of an international economic system into line with the shifting balance of economic power. This is an issue of paramount importance to the stability of the world economy: a system that resists adapting its rules to changing economic realities and its decision-making to shifting balances of economic power is bound to be inherently unstable; and, conversely, an elastic system that allows itself to evolve in line with changing economic realities has a high probability of succeeding in reconciling conflicting objectives through balanced and stable growth.[13]

For a number of complex reasons the international community did not address the question of the management of the world economy in a broader context. Faced with immediate and serious problems, it focused on selected issues which, at the time, appeared to be the most pressing. Among these issues, the ones that stand out as more important from the point of view of the management of the system are the following: exchange rate policies; international financial intermediation and the question of external indebtedness; the multilateral trade negotiations; and the Integrated Programme for Commodities.[14] The role of transnational corporations in the world economy has also received attention from the international community. Certain aspects are being dealt with in ongoing negotiations related to restrictive business practices and the code of conduct for the transfer of technology. It is further envisaged that the code of conduct of transnational corporations currently under negotiation will encompass a number of these issues.[15]

The major feature of the monetary gradualism that was adopted after the completion of the work of the Committee of Twenty was the system of flexible exchange rates.[16] The proponents of the scheme argued that flexible exchange rates could provide an effective and nearly automatic mechanism for balance-of-payments adjustment. In addition, and perhaps more importantly, it was argued that this regime accorded individual economies a significant degree of insulation from world trends and thus conferred upon Governments a high degree of autonomy in pursuing national stabilization policies. The latter point was particularly attractive given the shaken confidence in the effectiveness of a collectively managed and co-ordinated international system. Thus flexible exchange rates were seen to provide both maximum benefits derived from an open economy and minimum surrender of autonomy in respect of national economic policies.

Events proved these expectations to be ill-founded. Changes in exchange rates affected expenditures and trade flows, if at all, with a time lag of one or even two years, and offsetting forces operating in the interim period often had a perverse effect on the balance of payments and the domestic economy. Moreover, exchange rate flexibility could not be effective in the absence of policy changes in the area of capital markets. With high mobility in the capital markets allowed to persist, exchange rate policies could be easily offset by speculative capital movements which, in turn, precipitate further changes in exchange rates -- often in the wrong direction.

Apart from these factors, exchange rate flexibility could not be relied upon to effect the required shifts in expenditures and production when the response of real factors to changes in relative prices is limited, owing to structural and institutional rigidities. This posed serious problems to all countries whether in a surplus or a deficit position. The former were reluctant to let appreciation of their currencies erode their export competitive position, weaken profit margins in the trading sector and reduce levels of economic activity. For the deficit countries, depreciation of currencies led, more often than not, to accentuation of inflationary pressures which in turn rendered the attainment of structural adjustments even more problematic.

In order to cushion the impact of exchange rate changes on their domestic economies and trade positions, developed countries have increasingly resorted to protectionism in the form of import restrictions or export subsidies. This not only subverted the adjustment process but placed additional strains on the trading system.

The outcome of all these forces was that the flexible exchange rate regime led to currency instability, which in turn resulted in a cumulative disequilibrating process with depreciating countries caught in a self-reinforcing process exhibiting high rates of unemployment and inflation and surplus countries enjoying low inflation rates and increasing surpluses but at lower levels of economic activity.

The disenchantment of Governments with the flexible exchange rate regime has become apparent in recent months. The members of the European Economic Community have recently laid the foundations of a regional monetary system centred around stable parities among their currencies. In November 1978, the United States Government reversed its earlier position and, in co-operation with other major industrial countries, took a series of measures to arrest the declining trend of the dollar's external value. Both initiatives mark a departure from the earlier approach, and their ultimate success would very much depend on effective co-ordination of national macro-economic policies -- a condition that the introduction of floating exchange rates was to minimize.

In the period 1974-1978 the problems in the area of finance were frequently the subject of headlines in the international press. Yet the international community did surprisingly little in this area. The view of capital market countries that the financial intermediation between surplus and deficit economies might best be left to the private sector prevailed and the international community limited itself to the adoption of ad hoc measures designed to supplement the operations of private capital markets. Additional balance-of-payments facilities were established and the scope of existing ones was expanded with a view to improving the recycling of funds especially in respect of countries with limited access to capital markets. The financial intermediation worked remarkably well and played a major counter-cyclical role. But it was by no means faultless. The distribution of funds was extremely skewed, reflecting both market perceptions regarding creditworthiness and virtual stagnation of flows of concessional finance. As a result, the recycling process largely bypassed the low-income developing countries and particularly the least developed countries, which, in the event, bore a disproportionate burden of adjustment through cutting back their development programmes.

The longer-term stability of the financial system rested on a series of assumptions regarding developments in related areas. The recycling process was seen as one of a short-term nature and it was envisaged that debt repayments could be effected through increased export earnings induced by the recovery of the world economy, strengthening of commodity markets and improved access to markets. When the events of recent years cast doubt on the validity of these assumptions, the question of the stability of the financial system came to the forefront. The international community found itself unable to agree on measures to deal with this issue on a broad front and focused its attention on measures to alleviate the debt burden of the poorer developing countries and on the establishment of international rules and procedures for the reorganization of the debts of individual countries seeking such reorganization.[17] Notwithstanding the positive contribution that implementation of these measures would bring about, the problem is far from over. At stake is not merely stability in the financial area but the foundation of the existing rules in the fields of trade and payments.

The international community, and in particular the developed market-economy countries, gave priority attention to measures designed to safeguard the functioning of the trading system as reflected in GATT. An open and non-discriminatory trading system was seen not only as a powerful instrument for promoting international specialization and efficiency but as a pre-condition to the functioning of the monetary and financial system.

The launching of the multilateral trade negotiations within GATT was to further liberalize the trading system. These prolonged, complex and difficult negotiations, which are not yet fully completed, have been taking place under conditions of rising protectionism. By repeated "trade pledges" the OECD countries sought to discourage protectionist pressures and to highlight the risks of trade warfare that might ensue if restrictive trade policies were to become widespread. Nevertheless, protectionist measures by developed countries increased at an accelerated pace. Apart from the traditional trade limiting measures, new and complex forms, often evading GATT rules, were developed, such as "orderly marketing arrangements", "trigger price" mechanisms and "rationalization schemes".

The strain placed upon the balance of payments by the unsatisfactory adjustment process and higher levels of unemployment has undoubtedly contributed to the protectionist climate prevailing in most developed countries. Protectionist policies themselves, on the other hand, have introduced elements of inefficiency in the allocation of resources and thus tended to aggravate further the precarious conditions prevailing in the factor markets and the general price levels, and they have also made difficult the adjustment process in the partner countries.

Vigorous recovery can, no doubt, contribute to breaking this vicious circle, but it will not eliminate protectionist policies. It should be recalled that protectionism was on the rise when the OECD economies were operating on near full employment levels. One of the more important sources of this phenomenon is the increasing shift in emphasis in many OECD countries towards problems of economic security and equity in income distribution. At the same time, there have been pressures on the pricing mechanism stemming from structural factors as well as a narrowing in the spread of interindustry wage differentials.[18] Such factors have resulted in a reduced role being played by prices in the allocation of resources among sectors. These phenomena are at the root of the resistance in developed countries to maintaining access to their markets for the growing variety of manufactured goods exported by those developing countries that have broadly followed the development pattern of Japan in the post-war period.

The conclusion that emerges from the above is that, as in the case of the malfunctioning of the exchange rate system, the fundamental problem in the trading area lies in the inconsistency between the market-oriented rules of the game and the reduced role of market prices in determining allocation of resources within domestic economies. The case for revision of the rules of the trading system rests precisely on this inconsistency. While nothing concrete can be said at this stage regarding the broader framework of a viable trading system, it is clear that it would have to deal not only with commercial policies but also with questions relating to investment decisions and the allocative mechanism on a global scale.

An issue which is intimately related to the trading system and which came to be the focal point of the North-South dialogue is the need for strengthening the international commodity markets. While the international community agreed that the strengthening of these markets and the stabilization of the prices of primary commodities would greatly enhance the functioning of the international economic system and would confer benefits to both producing and consuming countries, the negotiations concerning the specific aspects of the Integrated Programme for Commodities have proved rather difficult. The agreement on the fundamental elements of the common fund represents a major breakthrough in this area and will no doubt provide stimulus to the conclusion of individual commodity agreements as well as to the completion of the other elements of the programme.[20]

It is noteworthy that of all major global issues regarding the shaping of the international economic system, the Integrated Programme for Commodities stands out as the only case in which structural changes in the market forces and in the decision-making process are involved. This is not unrelated to the fact that the negotiations have been carried out with the participation of all countries, with the developing countries being given the opportunity of full and active participation.

As was noted earlier, there is a growing awareness that the pendulum has swung too far towards reliance upon automatic market force to restore balanced conditions in the fields of money, finance and trade. There is already evidence that Governments of developed market-economy countries are intervening more agressively in these areas. This, of course, gives additional significance to the need for co-ordination of government policies.

Review of the macro-economic policies of its members from the point of view of their mutual consistency has been a regular feature of the work of OECD. Since 1975, the co-ordination of these policies has been carried out in the context of annual meetings of the heads of State or Government of the seven major OECD countries. While these meetings have made an invaluable contribution to the understanding of the problems involved, it is a matter of record that the strategy set forth in the meetings did not fully materialize. As the strategy was concluded at the highest political level, the outcome cannot be attributed to insufficient commitment. The question that arises, then, is whether the fault might not lie in basic inadequacies of the traditional macro-economic policies in dealing with the structural problems that the summit meetings have acknowledged to exist in the economies of the major industrial countries. This possibility raises two further issues: first, in dealing with structural problems it is necessary to define explicitly the longer-term targets and to devise a package of short-term policies that is fully consistent with these objectives;[21] secondly, long-term structural changes cannot by meaningfully assessed in the absence of a global framework which would ensure consistency of objectives and requirements.

IV. TOWARDS EFFECTIVE ARRANGEMENTS FOR INTERNATIONAL ECONOMIC CO-OPERATION

The major conclusion that emerges from the experience of the past is that the management of the economy in a multipolar world has failed, on the whole, to provide a credible strategy for global development. On the other hand, the problems facing the international community are novel and their solution would require novel mechanisms. Such mechanisms will have to evolve in practice

In considering possible alternatives for action in the future, the past experiences provides some useful insights, which are summarized below:

(a) While the interrelationship of problems in the areas of trade, money, finance and development are fully acknowledged, policy measures in each of these areas are taken, by necessity, in separate forums. In dealing with each one of these issues the assumptions made about developments or policies in the other areas have more often than not turned out to be unrealistic. An overview of the problems involved and alternative solutions in these interrelated areas would greatly facilitate the task of negotiating policy measures in each of these areas in a manner that would ensure consistency.

(b) Viable agreements require that the decision-making process reflect the economic interests of all the parties involved. Negotiations on global issues with limited participation have not had a credible record of achievement.

(c) There is a need to ensure consistency between the principles and rules governing the international economic system, on the one hand, and the changing character of the national economies, on the other. The present rules of the game appear to be based on assumptions about the functioning of national economies that are no longer valid, even in the case of major market-economy countries.

(d) In view of the persistence of structural and institutional rigidities in the national economies, the functioning of the international economic system may require less reliance upon market forces and more active involvement of Governments.

(e) The reconciliation of conflicting national economic objectives cannot be effected in a context of slow growth and structural disequilibria; it appears to require an agreed plan of action for restructuring the world economy and reducing the gaps in standards of living between countries through world growth and development.

(f) If a longer-term programme of action can be agreed, the co-ordination of short-term policies would be easier, since the latter would have to be considered in the light of their consistency with internationally agreed norms and long-term objectives.

An important question that arises from the above is that the international economy is unlikely to break away from the vicious circle of instability, recession, inflation and payments disequilibria without planned structural changes. The latter would require large investments on a world-wide scale which under current conditions cannot be spearheaded by the private sector or by a single country. It would need collective action by the entire international community. Such action would lower the threshold of uncertainty under which individual governments and markets are not operating and would set the stage for a cumulative process of global development.

The development of developing countries should be the focal point for such action. The investment requirements of these countries far exceed the resources that can be obtained through the existing channels. New mechanisms of resource transfers may be envisaged that would provide developing countries with the resources required, on appropriate terms and conditions, in order to accelerate their development process.[22] This would not only serve to stimulate the levels of world demand in the short run but would provide a reliable guide for the establishment of complementary industries in the developed countries.[23]

The Role of UNCTAD

The need for international co-operation to ensure that co-ordinated policy actions are taken at the global level in the interrelated areas of trade, payments, finance and development has been recognized and stressed in UNCTAD. This item has been on the agenda of the Trade and Development Board for several years and it has been the subject of discussion both in the Board and at the third and fourth sessions of the Conference.

At its third session the Conference adopted resolution 84 (III) in which, inter alia, trade and finance spheres should be resolved in a co-ordinated manner, taking into account their interdependence, with the full participation of developing and developed countries, and requested the Secretary-General of UNCTAD to consult the Managing Director of IMF and the Director-General of GATT and to report to the Board with a view to enabling it to consider the ways in which this co-ordination could be effected.[24]

At its fourth session the Conference, in resolution 90 (IV), stated that among the main tasks performed by UNCTAD has been the reviewing, on a continuous basis, of the interrelated problems in the field of international trade and related areas of international economic co-operation with a view to ensuring an effective contribution, including recommendations, by UNCTAD to the co-ordinated solution of such problems.[25]

The Trade and Development Board, which has considered this issue on a continuous basis, has also addressed itself to the question of appropriate institutional arrangements within UNCTAD with a view to enabling it to carry out its mandate more effectively. At the first part of the fourteenth session, a draft resolution entitled "Interdependence of problems of trade, development finance and the international monetary system" was submitted by a number of countries on behalf of States members of the African Group. In paragraphs 3-5, the draft resolution called for the establishment of a high-level standing committee of the Trade and Development Board which would be entrusted with the study, review and formulation of recommendations concerning issues of particular interest to developing countries in the international trade, development finance and monetary spheres and would undertake consultations with parallel bodies in GATT and IMF with a view to facilitating co-ordination and co-operation with those bodies.[26]

Although the Board has not as yet taken action on that draft resolution, it adopted, on 23 October 1976, resolution 144 (XIV), in which it requested the Secretary-General of UNCTAD to keep under continuous review, (with the assistance of high-level experts appointed by Governments as appropriate, and in consultation with the Director-General of GATT and the executive heads of appropriate financial institutions), and to formulate recommendations for consideration and appropriate action by the Board. In pursuance of that resolution, the Secretary-General of UNCTAD convened a meeting of intergovernmental experts in June 1978, and he reported on their deliberations to the Trade and Development Board at its eighteenth session.[27]

In the light of the experience gained thus far, the question arises whether the task of the Trade and Development Board in dealing with the interrelated issues of trade, money and finance might not be enhanced by further improvements in the preparatory arrangements. In this connexion, the Conference may wish to consider the establishment of a high-level advisory group which will (a) examine the problems relating to the management of the world economy, especially policies in the fields of trade, payments and finance and their relationship to development, (b) assess the consistency of those policies with the longer-term development objectives and especially the development of developing countries, and (c) recommend for consideration concerted measures in those areas that would promote structural changes in the world economy and thus provide a favourable environment for sustained development at the global level. The reports of the advisory group would be submitted for consideration and necessary action to the Trade and Development Board, particularly at its ministerial sessions.

In order to be able to carry out its task effectively, the advisory group should be balanced both geographically and in terms of specialization in trade, development, monetary and financial matters. The members of the group, numbering perhaps 24 or so, could be nominated by the Secretary-General of UNCTAD in consultation with Governments and, in view of the importance of the tasks entrusted to them, their appointments could be confirmed by the Trade and Development Board. The heads of relevant international organizations or their representatives would participate in the meetings and could submit contributions or documentation for consideration by the group. The group, which would normally meet every six months, could be authorized to invite eminent persons and specialists to appear before it and give their views on particular agenda items. It could also be authorized to establish small working or study groups to examine in depth specific and technical problems that may arise. In general, the principles regarding the group's composition and work should be such as to ensure that its deliberations and reports to the Trade and Development Board would be well prepared, innovative and representative of the views expressed internationally and would carry conviction with member States.

Such a high-level group would enable the Trade and Development Board, especially at its ministerial sessions, to take political decisions that would lead to significant improvement in the functioning of the world economy and help make the international economic system truly supportive of the development of developing countries. If the Conference endorses the need for such new global modalities of co-operation and establishes the institutional mechanism to give it operational meaning, then the fifth session of the Conference could prove to be a turning-point in the search for effective forms of international co-operation.

NOTES

[1] General Assembly resolution 1710 (XVI) of 19 December 1961 and 2626 (XXV) of 24 October 1970.

[2] These issues are explored in document TD/224, reproduced in the present volume.

[3] Ibid.

[4] The international economic system is not necessarily a global one. The world economy may comprise, as in fact it does, several international systems which come into contact with each other in the framework of ad hoc arrangements.

[5] The General Agreement on Tariffs and Trade emerged as an interim arrangement for commercial policies in the aftermath of failure to ratify the establishment of an International Trade Organization. The latter was envisaged as a necessary complement to IBRD and IMF. The Havana Charter, which was drawn up in 1948, adopted in article 1 the following objectives:

"1. To assure a large and steadily growing volume of real income and effective demand, to increase the production, consumption and exchange of goods, and thus to contribute to a balanced and expanding world economy.

"2. To foster and assist industrial and general economic development, particularly of those countries which are still in the early stages of industrial development, and to encourage the international flow of capital for productive investment.

"3. To further the enjoyment by all countries, on equal terms, of access to the markets, products and productive facilities which are needed for their economic prosperity and development.

"4. To promote on a reciprocal and mutually advantageous basis the reduction of tariffs and other barriers to trade and the elimination of discriminatory treatment in international commerce.

"5. To enable countries, by increasing the opportunities for their trade and economic development, to abstain from measures which would disrupt world commerce, reduce productive employment or retard economic progress.

"6. To facilitate through the promotion of mutual understanding, consultation and co-operation the solution of problems relating to international trade in the fields of employment, economic development, commercial policy, business practices and commodity policy.

[See United Nations Conference on Trade and Employment, Havana, Cuba, 21 November 1947-24 March 1948, Final Act and Related Documents (E/CONF.2/78).]

[6] For a discussion of the problems involved in and the opportunities offered by expansion of economic relations among countries having different social and economic systems, see document TD/243, reproduced in the present volume.

[7] Defined as the output of enterprises owned or controlled by parent organizations outside the producing country.

[8] Taking into account only majority-owned affiliates.

[9] The domestic measures included a short-term freeze on rents, wages and prices followed by guidelines, cuts in government spending and taxes, and investment incentives biased in favour of domestic suppliers. At the same time, a 10 per cent surcharge on about 50 per cent of imports was imposed. Finally, the gold convertibility of the dollar was suspended.

[10] For an account of these events, see "Report of the Group of High-level Government Experts on the effects of the world inflationary phenomenon on the development process" (Official Records of the Trade and Development Board, Eighteenth Session, Annexes, agenda item 5, document TD/B/704).

[11] This issue is discussed in document TD/233, in the present volume.

[12] General Assembly resolutions 3202 (S-VI) of 1 May 1974 and 3362 (S-VII) of 16 September 1975.

[13]This, of course, has to remain a hopeful conjecture since the world economy has not as yet experienced the working of such an elastic system. Throughout human history the question of redressing imbalances between the relative weights in decision-making on the one hand and economic power or potential of nations on the other has not been resolved through peaceful means.

[14]See Conference resolution 93 I(V) of 30 May 1976.

[15]These were not the only issues of global significance but they appear to have been the ones on which global attention was focused.

[16]For a discussion of developments in the monetary field, see document TD/233, reproduced in the present volume.

[17]For a review of these measures, see document TD/234/Add.1, reproduced in the present volume.

[18]For a discussion of the effects of structural factors, including oligopolistic market structures, see Official Records on the Trade and Development Board, Eighteenth Session Annexes, agenda item 5 document TD/B/704.

[19]See "Report of the United Nations Negotiating Conference on a Common Fund under the Integrated Programme for Commodities on its third session (12 to 19 March 1979) (TD/IPC/CF/CONF/19), para. 12.

[20]Progress on this issue is reviewed in documents TD/228 and ADD. 1. reproduced in the present volume.

[21]This, of course, presupposes the working out of an indicative and perspective plan.

[22]See document TD/235, reproduced in the present volume.

[23]See document TD/230, reproduced in the present volume; and The industrial policies of the developed market economy countries and their effect on the exports of manufactures and semi-manufactures from the developing countries (United Nations publication, Sales No. 79.II.D.13).

[24]Conference resolution 84 (III), para. 7.

[25]Conference resolution 90 (IV), sect. I, para. 1 (a) (iii).

[26]TD/B/L.360 (Official Records of the General Assembly, Twenty-ninth Session, Supplement No. 15 (A/9615/Rev.1)), annex II.

[27]See Official Records of the Trade and Development Board, Eighteenth Session, Annexes, agenda item 2, document TD/B/712.

Planned Changes in Foreign Trade and Payments

DEPARTMENT OF ECONOMIC AND SOCIAL AFFAIRS,
THE UNITED NATIONS

The programmes of output and investment planned by developing countries, which were discussed in earlier chapters of the present study, have been strongly influenced by the contributions planned or expected from foreign trade. As indicated in chapter II, in establishing targets for agricultural output and industrial production, countries have taken into account the potential of both exportation and import substitution. Similarly, as discussed in chapter I, the investment targets of most developing countries are linked in part to the expected or required inflow of external resources or, to put it differently, the excess of imports over exports of goods and services.

In many developing countries in which exports account for a large proportion of the productive activity, understandably, a great deal of stress has been laid on the need for securing growing outlets for exports. But even in other developing countries, the search for remunerative export outlets is a major theme, particularly for giving impetus to industrialization. Increased export earnings, generally supplemented by a net inflow of finance from abroad, have also been sought by developing countries to enhance their capacity to import, especially to import the goods that are crucial for stepping up the tempo of development, such as machinery, basic metals, fertilizer and fuel.

From **JOURNAL OF DEVELOPMENT PLANNING,** No.11, 1977 (43-139), reprinted by permission of the publisher.

I. PLANNED INCREASES IN TOTAL EXPORTS AND TOTAL IMPORTS

By and large, developing countries have posted a substantial increase in their total exports during the latter part of the 1970s. As may be seen from table 39, almost two fifths of the countries for which it has been possible to obtain reasonably comparable information (13 out of 35 countries) have planned to increase the quantum of their exports of goods and services, excluding receipts of factor income, annually by 10 per cent or more. The corresponding target amounts to 7 per cent or more but less than 10 per cent in a little more than two fifths of the countries (15 out of 35) and to less than 7 per cent in the remaining one fifth of the countries (7 out of 35).[1] The average age of the annual increases planned by all of the countries listed in the table is about 8.5 per cent, which is substantially higher than the average annual increase of a little more than 7 per cent specified for the developing countries as a whole in the International Development Strategy for the Second United Nations Development Decade.

A broad association is discernible between the planned rate of growth of gross domestic product and the planned rate of increase in the quantum of total exports. Thus, a majority of the countries that have planned to expand their gross domestic product at a relatively high annual rate (8 per cent or more) have postulated a double-digit annual increase in the quantum of their total exports. The countries that have planned a relatively moderate annual expansion of their gross domestic product (6 per cent or more but less than 8 per cent) have set a target for annual increase in total exports that is also comparatively moderate (on the average 8-9 per cent). Similarly, in countries that have indicated a relatively low planned annual rate of growth of gross domestic product (less than 6 per cent), the target for annual increase in total exports is also relatively low (on the average about 7 per cent).

Of the 35 countries that have specified targets for total exports, some idea about their planned expansion of total imports can be obtained for only 32 of them. One fourth of the countries (8 out of 32) have projected an annual increase of 10 per cent or more in their quantum of imports during the latter part of the 1970s. In nearly one third of the countries (10 out of 32), the planned annual increase is 7 per cent or more but less than 10 per cent. In the remaining countries -- more than two fifths of the total number (14 out of 32) -- the corresponding target amounts to less than 7 per cent. The average of the annual increases in total imports planned by the 32 countries is about 7.5 per cent, compared with the indicative average of a little less than 7 per cent specified for the developing countries as a whole in the International Development Strategy.

Although some association can be seen between the planned increase in total imports and the planned expansion of gross domestic product, the association appears to be weaker than that between the planned increases in total exports and gross domestic

TABLE 1. Planned Increases in Quantum of Exports and Imports of Goods and Services (Excluding Factor Income) From Base Year to Final Year of Plan

Country[b]	Percentage annual rate of increase		Planned elasticity in relation to gross domestic product[e]	
	Exports	Imports	Exports	Imports
Countries indicating a planned annual rate of growth of gross domestic product of 8 per cent or more				
Iran[d]	58.0	60.0	2.24	2.32
Botswana[e, f]	23.0	11.4	1.63	0.81
Jordan	22.7	7.3	1.96	0.62
Algeria	10.2	21.0	0.91	1.88
Brazil[d,f]	20.1	...	2.00	...
Ecuador	16.4	8.7	1.66	0.88
Democratic Yemen[f]	15.2[g]	3.8	1.63[g]	0.40
Nigeria	5.0	19.8	0.53	2.08
Malawi	9.2	7.5	1.07	0.87
Malaysia	8.4	8.1	1.00	0.96
Venezuela	1.4	1.4	0.17	0.17
Kenya	7.3	6.7	0.94	0.84
Countries indicating a planned annual rate of growth of gross domestic product of 6 per cent or more but less than 8 per cent				
Bolivia	13.0	7.5	1.69	0.97
Argentina	19.5	13.1	2.60	1.75
Costa Rica	9.6	7.8	1.28	1.04
Dominican Republic	6.0	5.1	0.80	0.68
Guatemala	7.0	2.9	0.93	0.39
Indonesia[d, f]	10.5	19.0	1.40	2.53
Morocco	10.0	8.0	1.33	1.07
Mali	8.1	9.4	1.11	1.29
Panama[h]	7.2	6.7	1.03	0.96
Philippines	10.0	9.6	1.43	1.37
El Salvador	7.0	7.6	1.05	1.13
Nicaragua	9.1	5.9	1.36	0.88
Chile	6.9	6.2	1.05	0.94
Mauritius[f]	8.0	...	1.23	...
Peru	15.6	5.6	2.40	0.86
Sierra Leone	8.2	4.7	1.32	0.76

TABLE 1. (continued)

Country[b]	Percentage annual rate of increase		Planned elasticity in relation to gross domestic product[c]	
	Exports	Imports	Exports	Imports
Countries indicating a planned annual rate of growth of gross domestic product of less than 6 per cent				
India	7.6 [f]	3.6 [i]	1.33 [f]	0.63 [i]
Bangladesh	7.3	...	1.33	...
Afghanistan[f]	4.6	3.9	0.92	0.78
Barbados	7.7	6.0	1.64	1.28
Burma[d]	6.6	14.7	1.47	3.27
Uruguay	9.7	15.1	2.55	3.97
Madagascar	3.9	2.1	1.22	0.66

Source: See table 1.

[a] For base year and final year of plan, see table 1. However, the base year for the following countries differs: Bangladesh, 1969/70; Indonesia, 1974/75; Panama, 1976; Peru, 1975.

[b] Countries are listed in descending order of their planned annual rate of growth of gross domestic product.

[c] Ratio of planned change in quantum of exports or imports to planned change in gross domestic product in constant prices. For differences in underlying concepts and in definitions of gross domestic product, see foot-notes to table 1.

[d] Calculated on the basis of data in current prices.

[e] Base year data in 1972 prices, final year data in 1973 prices.

[f] Merchandise trade only.

[g] Including re-exports.

[h] Including petroleum imports and re-exports.

[i] Merchandise imports plus net service payments.

product. Thus, while a number of countries that have set a
comparatively high target for expansion of gross domestic product
have -- not surprisingly -- postulated a comparatively high rate of
increase in total imports, some other countries that have planned a
relatively moderate or even low rate of expansion of gross domestic
product also have postulated a comparatively high annual increase
in total imports. The high rates of increase in imports envisaged
by such countries as Algeria, Indonesia, Iran and Nigeria are in
large part a reflection of the economic power accumulated by these
countries in recent years by virtue of their buoyant earnings from
export of petroleum. In contrast, the high rates of increase in
imports envisaged by such countries as Burma and Uruguay imply that
a substantial increase is anticipated in the net flow of financial
resources from abroad to finance the growing trade deficit.

An important conclusion revealed by the targets assembled in
table 39 is that, in general, developing countries are seeking to
enhance their self-reliance. Thus, nearly three fourths of the
countries (23 out of 32) have stipulated their total exports to
increase faster than their total imports. The target for annual
increase in total exports exceeds the corresponding target for
total imports by 10 percentage points or more for Botswana,
Democratic Yemen, Jordan and Peru; for Argentina, Bolivia, Ecuador,
Guatemala and Nicaragua, this differential is in the range of 3-8
percentage points.

In their search for enhanced self-reliance, developing
countries have revealed two dominating tendencies in their current
plans: to have their exports expand faster than their gross
domestic product and their imports increase contrariwise. To
demonstrate this point, the percentage increases planned in exports
and imports have been related in the last two columns of table 39
with the percentage increases planned in gross domestic product. A
figure of greater or smaller than 1 in these two columns shows
whether exports or imports have been posited as increasing,
respectively, faster or slower than gross domestic product. It can
be readily judged that in nearly four fifths of the countries (27
out of 35) the planned elasticity of total exports in respect to
gross domestic product exceeds the figure of 1 and that in nearly
three fifths of the countries for which it has been possible to
make such an estimate (19 out of 32) the planned elasticity of
total imports in respect of gross domestic product is less than 1.

It follows as a corollary from the two dominating tendencies
just mentioned that the share of total exports in gross domestic
product is generally posited as rising, whereas the corresponding
share of total imports is posited as declining in a majority of
developing countries. As may be seen from table 2 , a very sharp
annual increase in the share of total exports has been envisaged in
Botswana and Jordan, and a moderately sharp increase in Barbados
and Argentina, followed at some distance by Bolivia, Indonesia and
Uruguay and then by Costa Rica, Nicaragua and Sierra Leone. At the
other extreme, the two prominent countries that have planned a
decline in the share of total exports in gross domestic product in
real terms are Nigeria and Venezuela, both major exporters of
petroleum, for whom apparently it is the increase in the price of
their main export rather than the increase in export volume that

shapes the expansion of their total export earnings.

In general, then, the importance of exports, which is already great, is expected to become still greater during the latter part of the 1970s in developing countries. In Barbados and Botswana, for example, total exports are expected to account for 73 per cent and 64 per cent, respectively, of their gross domestic product in the final year of their current plans; the corresponding proportion amounts to nearly 52 per cent in Algeria, to over 40 per cent in Jordan, Malaysia and Panama, and to 25 per cent or more but less than 40 per cent in Costa Rica, Kenya, Nicaragua, Nigeria, Sierra Leone and Venezuela. India is by far the extreme example of a country in which, despite the increase postulated, the share of exports in gross domestic product is expected to be only 5 per cent in the final year of the current plan. The two other examples of a country in which the share of exports is similarly expected to be small -- 8 per cent or less -- are Afghanistan and Bangladesh.

The pervasive role played by the export trade in the progress of developing countries which, as just noted, is envisaged by these countries as growing still further in the years immediately ahead, raises important policy issues. Undoubtedly, developing countries need to make vigorous efforts to promote their exports; the policies they intend to pursue in this regard are touched on in the next section of the present chapter. However, their efforts will yield meaningful results only if their products find a hospitable economic environment abroad. This is one critical area, therefore, in which the success of their development thrusts hinges on the role that needs to be played by the world community in general: by developed countries through the provision of outlets for the goods exported by developing countries and by developing countries through expansion of mutually beneficial trade among themselves.

The counterpart of the importance of exports to the progress of developing countries is to be seen in the fact that, notwithstanding the decline postulated by many countries, most developing countries envisage total imports as amounting to a substantial proportion (see table 2). To meet their burgeoning requirements for machinery, heavy equipment and other goods that are crucial for stepping up the tempo of production, developing countries are seeking not only an increase in export earnings (with which to pay for increased imports) but also a shift in the composition of imports in favour of producer goods. This aspect is dealt with in a subsequent section.

II. TARGETS AND POLICIES FOR MERCHANDISE EXPORTS

Since merchandise items predominate in the foreign trade of developing countries, the generalizations emerging from the targets relating to total exports of goods and services apply with little or no modification to the targets set by these countries for expansion of their merchandise exports. Thus, as may be seen from table 41, most countries have planned to expand their merchandise

TABLE 2. Planned Changes in Percentage Shares of Exports and Imports of Goods and Services (Excluding Factor Income) in Gross Domestic Product from Base Year to Final Year of Plan

Country[b]	Exports			Imports		
	Base year	Final year	Average annual change	Base year	Final year	Average annual change
Countries indicating a planned annual rate of growth of gross domestic product of 8 per cent or more						
Botswana[c, d]	41.5	63.8	4.5	54.1	46.3	−1.3
Jordan	25.2	40.5	3.1	73.6	60.6	−2.6
Algeria	53.3	51.5	−0.4	35.9	50.3	3.6
Nigeria	45.6	37.0	−1.7	15.1	23.5	1.7
Malawi	23.3	24.0	0.1	31.2	29.7	−0.3
Malaysia	40.8	40.8	−	27.9	27.6	−0.1
Venezuela	34.2	28.2	−1.5	22.2	18.3	−1.0
Kenya	28.1	27.0	−0.2	31.6	29.4	−0.4
Countries indicating a planned annual rate of growth of gross domestic product of 6 per cent or more but less than 8 per cent						
Bolivia	16.6	21.2	0.9	22.3	22.1	−
Argentina	8.9	13.5	1.2	6.4	7.8	0.4
Costa Rica	32.5	36.5	0.7	39.2	39.9	0.1
Dominican Republic	23.2	20.1	−0.3	25.0	20.0	−0.5
Guatemala	19.9	19.5	−0.1	17.6	14.2	−0.7
Indonesia[c, e]	16.9	20.8	0.8	19.9	21.9	0.4
Morocco	15.0	16.5	0.4	20.0	20.5	0.1
Mali	22.3	23.5	0.2	27.5	31.2	0.6
Panama	41.8	41.5	−0.1	52.5	50.8	−0.4
El Salvador	24.3	24.5	−	27.3	28.3	0.2
Nicaragua	30.8	34.4	0.7	39.4	37.9	−0.3
Chile	17.8	18.1	0.1	14.9	14.7	−
Sierra Leone	30.8	33.8	0.6	40.7	37.7	−0.6

TABLE 2. (continued)

Country[b]	Exports			Imports		
	Base year	Final year	Average annual change	Base year	Final year	Average annual change
Countries indicating a planned annual rate of growth of gross domestic product of less than 6 per cent						
India	4.0[c]	4.4[c]	0.1[c]	5.1[f]	4.6[f]	0.1[f]
Bangladesh	7.3	8.1	0.2	...	...	...
Afghanistan[e]	7.4	6.4	−0.2	5.8	4.9	−0.2
Barbados	63.4	73.1	1.9	79.5	84.9	1.1
Uruguay	12.0	15.9	0.8	10.9	18.3	1.5
Madagascar	16.9	17.5	0.1	20.3	19.2	−0.2

Source: See table 1.

[a] Calculated from data in constant prices. For base year and final year of plan, see table 1. However, the base year for the following countries differs: Bangladesh, 1969/70; Panama and Venezuela, 1976.

For differences in underlying concepts and in definition of gross domestic product, see foot-note to table 1.

[b] Countries are listed in descending order of their planned annual rate of growth of gross domestic product.

[c] Merchandise trade only.

[d] Base year data in 1972 prices; final year data in 1973 prices.

[e] Calculated from data in current prices.

[f] Merchandise imports plus net service payments.

exports at a substantial rate. Indeed, the average of the annual
increases planned by these countries in their merchandise exports
amounts to just about the same magnitude as the average of the
annual increases planned in their total exports of goods and
services -- namely, 8.5 per cent.

Among the countries that have planned to increase their
merchandise exports at a relatively high annual rate -- 10 per cent
or more -- are Algeria, Ecuador, Iran and Nigeria, which are major
exporters of petroleum, as well as Jordan and Morocco, whose major
export item is phosphate. In all of the six countries just
mentioned, the planned rate of increase in the export of their
major commodity exceeds the planned rate for all merchandise
exports. At the other end of the scale, the countries that have
planned to expand their merchandise exports at a comparatively low
annual rate -- less than 7 per cent -- include El Salvador,
Guatemala and Kenya, whose major export commodity is coffee; all of
these three countries expect their coffee exports to lag behind the
planned annual rate of increase in their total merchandise exports
which itself is quite low (less than 5 per cent). Panama, too, has
postulated a comparatively low annual rate of increase in its
merchandise exports, and its main export item, bananas, is slated
to increase in line with all merchandise exports. Among the
countries listed in table 3 , the lowest annual rate of increase in
merchandise exports, 1.4 per cent, has been planned by Venezuela.
This is because the exports of petroleum and petroleum products,
which account for more than four fifths of the country's
merchandise exports, are deliberately postulated as declining in
volume. It may also be recalled in this connexion that, as
indicated earlier in chapter I, Venezuela has planned to contract
its mining output during the second half of the 1970s (see table
3). The export pattern postulated by Venezuela is thus in marked
contrast to the corresponding pattern envisaged by such other
petroleum-exporting countries as Algeria, Ecuador, Iran and
Nigeria.

A substantial number of developing countries have specified
targets for increase in the export of their major traded items,
which have traditionally figured prominently in their export trade,
as well as for newer or non-traditional items, which are now
gathering some significance. It can be seen from the data
assembled in table 3   that, in the majority of developing
countries, important shifts in the composition of exports have been
envisaged as taking place during the latter part of the 1970s. Not
only has a reduced dependence on the main traditional exports been
planned in most countries, but a considerable reshuffling in the
order and importance of leading export items has also been
foreseen.

Thus, for example, Costa Rica and El Salvador have planned a
slower rate of increase in what were their three major exports just
prior to the time period of the country's current plan than in
their total merchandise exports: bananas, coffee and meat in Costa
Rica; and coffee, cotton and sugar in El Salvador. Similarly,
Malaysia has projected that three out of its four top
exports -- rubber, tin and wood -- will increase more slowly than
total merchandise exports. In Guatemala, Malawi and Nicaragua, a

TABLE 3. Planned Increase in Quantum of Merchandise Exports from Base Year to Final Year of Plan

Country[b]	Major export items prior to plan period	Percentage annual rate of increase					Non-traditional items	All merchandise
		Major items						
		Item 1	Item 2	Item 3	Item 4			
Countries indicating a planned annual rate of growth of gross domestic product of 8 per cent or more								
Iran[c]	Petroleum, petroleum products	60.6						59.0
Botswana	Non-ferrous ores, meat	...	5.8				...	...
Jordan	Crude fertilizer, vegetables, cement, fruits and nuts	43.5	...	...	...		...	27.6
Algeria	Petroleum, wine	10.4	...	...	...		30.0	10.2
Ecuador	Petroleum, bananas, coffee, cocoa	37.5	3.4	2.7	...		...	16.8
Nigeria[c]	Petroleum, cocoa	10.5	...	...	...		...	10.3
Malawi	Tobacco, tea, ground-nuts, cotton	3.0	3.5	...	...		...	9.3
Malaysia	Crude rubber, palm oil, tin, wood (rough)	5.9	15.9	0.3	6.3		18.9	8.4[d]
Venezuela	Petroleum, petroleum products	0.5					30.4	1.4
Kenya	Coffee, tea, petroleum products, vegetable materials	—	10.7	...	...		...	5.6

TABLE 3. (continued)

| Country[b] | Major export items prior to plan period | Percentage annual rate of increase | | | | | |
| | | Major items | | | | Non-traditional items | All merchandise |
		Item 1	Item 2	Item 3	Item 4		
Countries indicating a planned annual rate of growth of gross domestic product of 6 per cent or more but less than 8 per cent							
Bolivia	Non-ferrous ores, petroleum products	...	38.8				
Argentina	Meat, cereals, machinery and transport equipment, wool	18.0	14.7	...	...	39.7	...
Costa Rica	Bananas, coffee, meat, sugar	5.1	2.0	8.6	12.1	19.0	9.1
Guatemala	Coffee, cotton, sugar, bananas	2.2	−8.9	14.5	5.7	21.1	4.2
Morocco	Crude fertilizer, fruits and nuts, vegetables, non-ferrous ores	12.7	4.9	3.9	12.9	19.3	10.5
Mali	Cotton, live animals, groundnuts (and oil), fish	13.8	3.2	16.6	...	...	8.1
Panama[e]	Bananas, petroleum products, fish	6.6	...	...		31.7	6.6
Philippines	Sugar, non-ferrous ores, wood (rough), copra	7.5	11.0	25.9	7.0	25.0	10.0
El Salvador	Coffee, cotton, sugar, non-cotton textiles	4.0	3.3	2.9	...	10.7	7.0
Nicaragua	Cotton, meat, coffee, sugar	4.4	8.2	12.2	24.0	8.2	8.7
Mauritius	Sugar	2.7				39.0[c]	8.0

TABLE 3. (continued)

Country[b]	Major export items prior to plan period	Percentage annual rate of increase				Non-traditional items	All merchandise
		Major items					
		Item 1	Item 2	Item 3	Item 4		
Countries indicating a planned annual rate of growth of gross domestic product of 6 per cent or more but less than 8 per cent (continued)							
Peru	Fish meal, copper, sugar, zinc	9.8	...	1.1	...	...	...
Sierra Leone	Diamonds, iron ore, coffee, cocoa	-0.7	-3.6	...	...	24.7	8.2
Countries indicating a planned annual rate of growth of gross domestic product of less than 6 per cent							
India	Jute products, engineering goods, cotton textiles, tea	—	16.7	6.4	1.4	12.1 [f]	7.6
Bangladesh	Jute products, jute (raw)	7.3	4.0	...	...	...	7.3
Uruguay	Meat, wool, animal skins, rice	5.1	...	...	6.4	...	10.0

Source: See table 1.

a For base year and final year of plan, see table 1. However, the base year for the following countries differs: Bangladesh, 1969/70; Guatemala, 1976; Panama, 1976; Peru, 1975; Uruguay, 1970.

The most important export item (or in some cases groups of items) for each country according to their value in the period just before the plan, are listed on the left, up to a maximum of four. When less than four items are listed, this signifies that those listed already accounted for over 80 per cent of the country's total merchandise exports. The planned rates of increase for the items shown in the table appear to the right, under the appropriately numbered column. Non-traditional exports comprise typically manufactured or processed goods not previously exported in significant quantities, or products that appear to have good prospects for expanded export sales with the right promotional policies.

c Calculated on the basis of data in current prices.
d Exports of goods and services, excluding factor income.
e Includes re-exports of petroleum and products.
f Does not include any engineering goods for which the target rate is shown separately.

311

similar pattern is evident with regard to each of the country's top
two export items: coffee and cotton in Guatemala, tobacco and tea
in Malawi, cotton and meat in Nicaragua. Sierra Leone expects its
two major exports -- diamonds and iron ore -- to decline in volume.
Bangladesh projects that exports of raw jute will increase
substantially more slowly than total merchandise exports. As the
country's top export item, apart from the cases already mentioned,
jute products in India, tobacco in Malawi, rubber in Malaysia,
sugar in Mauritius and the Philippines and meat in Uruguay are
expected to trail well behind the advance in total merchandise
exports. In Kenya, a stagnation in export of coffee, the country's
top traded commodity, is envisaged.

In respect of the envisaged changes in the relative importance
in quantum terms among the major export items, it may be noted that
petroleum is expected to gain still further in Algeria, Ecuador,
Iran and Nigeria. Similarly, gains have been postulated for
phosphate in Jordan and Morocco, and for cotton in Mali; while jute
products (in contrast to raw jute) in Bangladesh and bananas in
Panama are expected to hold their own.

The top two commodities in Costa Rica, bananas and coffee,
would lose to the next two items in order of importance, meat and
sugar. Similarly, the current plans expect coffee and cotton to
fall in relative terms in favour of sugar and bananas in Guatemala;
jute products in favour of engineering goods and cotton textiles in
India; coffee in favour of tea in Kenya; rubber and tin in favour
of palm oil and wood in Malaysia; cotton and live animals in favour
of groundnuts and ground-nut oil in Mali; sugar in favour of
non-ferrous ores and wood in the Philippines.

Many developing countries, irrespective of the planned trends
in their major items of export, have planned to increase
non-traditional exports at an exceptionally high rate, surpassing
20 per cent a year or even 30 per cent in Algeria, Argentina,
Mauritius, Panama and Venezuela. It should, of course, also be
noted that often such high rates are simply a reflection of the
fact that non-traditional exports are to increase from a rather
small base. Naturally, non-traditional exports differ from country
to country, but they are mainly manufactured goods and processed
raw materials that were not exported in the past in significant
quantities by the countries concerned. The non-traditional exports
also include items that, while exported in the past, seemed capable
of significant expansion with the help of appropriate promotional
policies.

In trying to expand and diversify exports, countries have
resorted to a variety of measures. Experience has shown that
usually export promotion involves the use of several policy
instruments at the same time. At a global level, the main policy
thrusts have involved efforts to give more edge to schemes of
economic integration among interested countries and, especially in
Latin America and to an extent in Asia, to bring exchange-rate
policy to the aid of export promotion. Argentina and Brazil have
articulated the need to strengthen the functioning of the Latin
American Free Trade Area. The export programmes concerning
manufactures, in particular of Costa Rica, El Salvador, Guatemala
and Nicaragua, have emphasized the need for a more dynamic Central

American Common Market. Bolivia, Ecuador, Peru and Venezuela have stressed their mutually beneficial links through the Andean Pact, especially in terms of the importance of so-called complementarity agreements for increasing exports. Malaysia and the Philippines have looked to the Association of South-East Asian Nations as a means of increasing their trade through selective trade liberalization, regional industrial projects and complementarity agreements. Iran has looked to marketing opportunities for its industrial goods in the Persian Gulf region. The normalization of trade relations between India and what is now Bangladesh has offered important opportunities for trade -- initially, for instance, in raw jute and freshwater fish. In Africa, too, the importance and existing scope for co-operation with neighbouring countries has been explicitly recognized by many countries, among them Botswana, Kenya, Malawi, Mali and Nigeria.

As to exchange-rate policy, Argentina and the Philippines offer examples of countries that have articulated the need for an exchange rate that helps to expand exports. Bolivia, to the same end, has given consideration to allowing its exchange rate to be determined freely by market forces. Brazil and Chile have decided to maintain flexible exchange rates during the plan period; this would involve frequent, small, adjustments designed to reduce the uncertainties that exporters face when cost-price relations change substantially in times of rapid domestic inflation. Bangladesh, in establishing a uniform rate of exchange for raw jute and jute products, has hoped to improve the competitiveness in export markets of its raw jute.

Among many other measures of export promotion, a number may be mentioned by way of illustration. Thus, Mauritius and the Philippines have stressed the importance of special export processing zones whereby the Governments can extend a wide range of tax and other concessions and offer other forms of help to domestic and especially foreign concerns that establish themselves for production for export. Prominent among the countries that are focusing their efforts on better market information for exporters and improved training in international marketing are Chile, Costa Rica, the Philippines, Somalia and Venezuela. Those attempting to get their products better known and promoted abroad include Brazil, India, Iran, Kenya, Madagascar and Morocco. Kenya and Malaysia have stressed research into new uses for some of their traditional products. Iran's export-promotion programme includes the granting of export credit, while Venezuela's programme calls for an increase in the resources at the disposal of the export-financing fund. Virtually every country has outlined proposals for some special fiscal measure, tax, import duty or similar concessions, or changes in the system of concessions now in force. Thus Kenya intends to reform the import duty drawback system, the old system being considered too biased in favour of import-substituting industries. In Argentina, a special system of reimbursements designed to stabilize the real income of exporters has been proposed. In many instances, the proposed reforms have been prompted by the need for a more efficient promotion of particular exports, normally of the non-traditional kind, either by restricting concessions to such exports or by granting an extra margin of advantage to designated product categories.

Leading petroleum-exporting countries, such as Algeria, Iran, Nigeria and Venezuela, have planned investments in industries with an export potential that would be financed out of public funds derived from export proceeds of crude petroleum. Primarily geared to developing new export products, based on crude petroleum as an input, these efforts are also essentially special cases of a more general category of policy measures that has been emphasized in current plans. This category of measures is basically concerned with increasing the supply of exportable products, be they traditional agricultural products or newer processed commodities, or traditional as well as completely new manufactured goods. In some countries, exports do not necessarily always offer the most lucrative outlet for the producer, especially when a buoyant home market for the product exists. Increasing supply for export -- at competitive prices and of the right quality -- in the face of competing domestic demand is therefore a particularly important policy issue. It is of acute concern in India, for instance, which has stressed the need to step up production of the goods that can find a ready world market.

III. TARGETS AND POLICIES FOR MERCHANDISE IMPORTS

As in the case of exports, for the reason mentioned earlier, the broad generalizations regarding targets for merchandise imports do not differ significantly from those relating to targets for all imports of goods and services. The average of the annual increases planned by developing countries in their merchandise imports during the latter part of the 1970s, as may be seen from table 42, is approximately of the same order as the corresponding average of the increases planned in their total imports of goods and services -- namely, 7.5 per cent. The development thrusts planned by developing countries have in general called for not only a substantial increase in the volume of merchandise imports but also significant shifts in the composition of imports.

Few developing countries have been in a position in which foreign exchange was not scarce. Indeed, the careful management of available foreign exchange through close scrutiny of import needs -- even when strong efforts are made to increase earnings through expanded exports -- continues to be a central feature of policy in most developing countries. The focus of measures designed to conserve foreign exchange has typically been on consumer goods, partly because many such imports have been regarded as low-priority luxury goods but more importantly because import-substitution efforts in the industrial arena have tended to be concentrated in consumer-goods industries. The latter still remains the primary thrust in many African countries and some Asian countries -- for example, Afghanistan, Bangladesh, Burma and Nepal -- and continues to be important in most of East Asia as well. India, which has already gone a long way towards reducing consumer imports to very low levels through both controls and import-substitution, has sought to concentrate such efforts now on petroleum and petroleum products, fertilizer and machinery. In many Latin American countries the traditional approach whereby almost any product for which there existed the technical capacity for domestic production could receive government backing has been abandoned in favour of a selective approach. The present effort is based on considerations of long-run viability, and there is a preference for products that do not need very high effective protection to succeed. In such countries as Argentina and Brazil, the emphasis has shifted towards import-substitution in certain capital-goods industries and strategic intermediate goods. However, import-substitution in agriculture has also been given a prominent place, notably in Chile and Venezuela, while some countries, such as Nicaragua and Panama, continue to emphasize consumer manufactures.

As a result of these various developments, the familiar trend whereby imports of consumer goods trail behind total imports is expected to hold in current plans (see table 4). Of the 16 countries that have indicated the expected trends in the major categories of imports, only Malawi and the Philippines expect imports of consumer goods to increase faster than all merchandise imports. Consumer imports have been postulated as rising particularly slowly in relation to all merchandise imports in Argentina, El Salvador and Sierra Leone. In contrast, imports of intermediate goods -- parts, components, semi-manufactures, fuels, raw materials and other inputs for industry or agriculture -- are expected to expand more rapidly than total imports in the majority of countries. Exceptions are Algeria, Argentina, Bangladesh, El Salvador, Jordan, the Philippines and Uruguay, where the fast rates of increase in imports of capital goods to build up new productive capacity has taken precedence over imports of intermediate goods. In some of these exceptional cases, the imports of intermediate goods may be excepted to increase sharply once the new capacity is commissioned. Thus, for example, Bangladesh foresees a sharp increase in the output of consumer goods -- requiring stepped up intermediate imports -- at the end of the current plan period, when major investments undertaken in the plan would have been completed. Uruguay, while planning a very rapid increase in investment, and therefore in imports of capital goods, is not expecting output to rise very quickly in the plan period itself; hence the need for imports of intermediate goods during the plan period is estimated to be comparatively low. In Argentina, in contrast, the high rate of increase in imports of capital goods and the relatively low rate of increase in imports of intermediate goods follows from the new emphasis on replacing imports of such strategic items as steel, aluminium, paper, cellulose and chemicals with domestically produced substitutes. Algeria has planned an especially high level of investment. While its capacity to produce capital goods is limited, it can economize on its imports of intermediate goods because of its own resource endowments, which provide important inputs for industry.

In general, largely because of the substantial increase planned in investment while the capacity to produce capital goods

TABLE 4. Planned Annual Rate of Increase in Quantum of Merchandise from Base Year to Final Year of Plan

(Percentage)

Country[b]	Total[c]	Consumer goods[c]	Intermediate goods[c]	Capital goods[c]
Countries indicating a planned annual rate of growth of gross domestic product of 8 per cent or more				
Iran	60.0[d]	...	...	...
Jordan	8.1	7.0	5.5	17.2
Algeria	19.3	11.4	18.7	24.5
Ecuador	8.7	...	...	...
Democratic Yemen	3.6	...	...	...
Nigeria[d]	33.9	29.9	35.1	37.1
Malawi	7.2	8.0	7.7	6.5
Venezuela	4.9	3.2	7.1	3.5
Kenya	7.5	6.8	8.0	7.0
domestic product of 6 per cent or more but less than 8 per cent				
Argentina	11.1	2.5	9.3	19.8
Costa Rica	7.9	4.5	9.2	9.3
Morocco	8.2	7.2	9.7	8.2
Mali	8.7	2.8	11.2	21.0
Panama[e]	6.5	...	...	13.8
Philippines	9.6	11.6	7.8	16.5
El Salvador	7.7	3.8	6.4	13.4
Nicaragua[f]	6.3	3.1	5.9	9.1
Sierra Leone	4.8	−4.9	10.6	16.4
domestic product of less than 6 per cent				
India	7.6[g]	...	...	...
Bangladesh[d, h]	6.7	4.0	3.5	11.9
Afghanistan	3.9[e]	...	...	...
Barbados	5.7	...	...	...
Uruguay	7.6	7.4	5.3	13.6

Source: See table 1.

[a] For the base year and final year of plan, see table 1. However, the base year differs for the following countries: Bangladesh, 1973/74; Panama, 1976; Uruguay, 1970.

[b] Countries are listed in descending order of their planned annual rate of growth of gross domestic product.

[c] The definition is normally that of the country and may differ slightly from country to country.

[d] Calculated from data in current prices.

[e] Total includes imports of petroleum for re-export.

[f] Some imports that are not classified by end-use are included in total imports but not in individual categories specified in the table.

[g] Based on data that do not include a provision for imports of food grains but including some provision for higher prices of imported petroleum and petroleum products.

[h] Excluding food grains.

is limited as yet, the rate of increase planned for imports of capital goods exceeds -- in many countries, very substantially -- that for imports of all goods. Among the countries listed in table 4 , only Kenya, Malawi and Morocco anticipate that imports of capital goods will increase more slowly than total imports. Kenya and Malawi have planned a relatively small increase in investment. Although Morocco postulates a rapid rate of increase for investment, a large part of it is intended for building and construction, which would be undertaken by using domestically produced goods to a substantial extent.

As a result of the planned changes in various categories of imports, most countries foresee a decrease in the share of consumer goods in total imports. In several countries, the share is expected to be relatively small in the final year of the current plan. In Argentina, this share is expected to remain a mere 2 per cent. India also anticipates a very small share, although precise data in a comparable form are not available. In Uruguay, it is expected to be only about 9 per cent. In 10 other countries, as may be seen from table 5 , the share of consumer goods in total merchandise imports is postulated at less than a quarter of all imports. Only Jordan, Mali and Morocco, of the 17 countries for which the relevant data are shown in that table, expect to import more than a third of their total merchandise items in the form of consumer goods. Over-all, it is projected that the immediate-goods category will remain the largest of the three categories of imports. This is so for 10 countries, although the divergence in this respect from country to country is very wide, with the shares ranging from over 50 per cent in Argentina, Kenya, Nicaragua, the Philippines and Uruguay, to a low of less than 30 per cent in Jordan, Mali, Morocco and Nigeria. However, the capital-goods category, if the latest planned increases were realized, would represent a sizable proportion of merchandise imports -- at least one third of the total in Algeria, Bangladesh, El Salvador, Indonesia, Mali, Malawi, Morocco, Nigeria, Panama, Uruguay and Venezuela. In virtually all countries, substantial changes have also been planned within each of these three broad categories of imports.

While developing countries generally face a shortage of foreign exchange, for some countries the shortage that they might have had has been much eased by the surge in petroleum income, or, in a few cases, by other exceptional developments -- for example, the surge in Botswana's mineral exports. Such developments have made it possible for these countries to contemplate the relaxation or total removal of import controls and the elimination or reduction of tariffs, as ways of increasing the efficiency of domestic production, streamlining administration or keeping down the cost of living. More generally, however, the need for keeping a close check on total import demand, while striving to increase the over-all capacity to increase imports, and for canalizing available foreign exchange to the most important economic uses remains paramount.

In their efforts to limit dispensable items and to ensure the flow of indispensable items, countries have generally looked to the traditional battery of policy weapons, foremost among them being

TABLE 5. Planned Change in the Percentage Share of Major Categories of Imported Goods in Total Merchandise Imports from Base Year to Final Year of Plan and Planned Share in Final Year

Country[b]	Consumer goods[c]		Intermediate goods		Capital goods	
	Average annual change	Final year of plan	Average annual change	Final year of plan	Average annual change	Final year of plan
Countries indicating a planned annual rate of growth of gross domestic product of 8 per cent or more						
Jordan	−0.7	67.3	−0.4	15.7	1.1	17.0
Algeria	−1.3	15.5	−0.3	42.8	1.6	41.7
Nigeria[d]	−1.1	31.8	0.2	28.2	0.9	40.0
Malawi	0.1	23.7	0.1	40.7	−0.2	35.6
Venezuela	—	15.5	1.2	46.4	−1.2	38.1
Kenya	−0.2	23.1	0.3	57.6	−0.1	19.3
Countries indicating a planned annual rate of growth of gross domestic product of 6 per cent or more but less than 8 per cent						
Argentina	—	2.1	−2.0	70.4	2.0	27.5
Costa Rica	−1.0	23.0	0.6	46.1	0.4	31.0
Indonesia	−3.1	16.6	2.4	49.0	0.6	34.0
Morocco	−0.3	38.0	0.3	24.0	—	38.1
Mali	−3.0	36.6	0.3	26.7	2.7	36.7
Panama[e]	...	...	...	...	2.0	43.0
Philippines	0.2	10.2	−1.6	68.2	1.4	21.6
El Salvador	−1.2	22.6	−0.7	38.9	1.9	38.5
Nicaragua[f]	−0.7	20.7	−0.1	52.3	0.6	25.4
Sierra Leone	−3.9	31.2	2.3	48.6	1.6	20.2
Countries indicating a planned annual rate of growth of gross domestic product of less than 6 per cent						
Bangladesh[d, g]	−0.4	21.8	−1.0	36.2	1.4	42.0
Uruguay	—	8.7	−2.1	56.9	2.1	34.4

Source: See table 1.

the licensing of imports, or control through quotas, tariffs, limited foreign exchange allocations and restrictions on credit availability for certain imports. But even while continuing to emphasize restrictive measures, many countries have tried to streamline the system of import controls and further attune it to the needs of the economy. The stress on efficiency and greater selectivity where import-substitution is concerned has, for instance, called for experiments with methods that save imports without unduly increasing industrial costs and that also allow enterprises relatively easy access to essential imports. Some countries have expressed interest in market mechanisms to achieve this -- through adjustment of exchange rates, for example -- while at the same time signalling their attention to be more selective in exempting imports of intermediate and capital goods from taxation.

IV. TARGETS AND POLICIES FOR SERVICE ITEMS

In developing countries, generally, international transactions involving service items remain on balance an important charge on their export earnings. Partly because of the rapid increase planned in international trade of merchandise, most developing countries expect to continue encountering, in the latter part of the 1970s, deficits in regard to international transport, shipping and insurance or re-insurance. Deficits are also expected to continue in regard to such items as consultants' and patent fees, or other miscellaneous services. At the same time, the aim is to economize on as many service payments as possible by developing a domestic capacity. A number of developing countries also envisage efforts to build up a capacity to provide other countries with some of these services, especially shipping and other transport. Promotion of tourism from abroad has attracted considerable attention as a way of covering a part of the country's requirements of foreign exchange.

The measures specified by countries with regard to international transport and shipping include efforts to improve and expand the operations of the Eastern Africa National Shipping Line, which is jointly owned by Kenya and some of its neighbouring countries, or of the operations of the Malaysian International Shipping Corporation. Argentina has planned an increase in the share of goods shipped to and from the country under its national flag from 23 per cent to 34 per cent during the plan, in line with its longer-term objective of raising this total to about 50 per cent. India, which has also accorded a high priority to shipping, foresees the development of facilities for servicing ships in its harbours and an increase in its own mercantile fleet from 4.8 million to 8.6 million gross registered tons during the five-year span of its current plan. Venezuela has planned to reduce its international transport costs by 4 per cent per year by promoting its national shipping line, as well as by improved management.

Guatemala has expressed hopes of strengthening the links within
Central America in order to enhance its bargaining position to
negotiate international transport contracts. The Philippines
expects to be able to promote the same ends through the newly
created Shippers' Council. Democratic Yemen anticipates that
following the reopening of the Suez Canal, additional earnings will
materialize from more ships using the services of the port of Aden
and from additional earnings on re-export. In other areas of
transport, Malawi and Nigeria have proposed measures to reduce the
operating deficits of their international railway and airline
operations, respectively, through more appropriate rate structures
and better management through stepped-up training.

Several countries have specified targets for attracting
foreign tourists. As may be seen from table 44, which depicts the
targets set by 15 countries, a substantial annual increase in
earnings of foreign exchange from tourist traffic is envisaged.
Although the magnitude of the planned annual increase varies from
7.5 per cent in India to 24 per cent in Morocco, the target amounts
to about 15 per cent or more in as many as two thirds of the
countries listed in the table. Barbados, which is heavily
dependent on tourist trade, expects a comparatively modest annual
increase -- 11 per cent -- in its receipts of foreign exchange from
tourism; but even so, tourism is expected to contribute the
equivalent of 80 per cent of merchandise exports in the final year
of the country's plan. In Kenya and Jordan, whose economies are
also substantially dependent on the flow of tourists from abroad,
earnings of foreign exchange from tourism in the final year of
their plans are expected to equal 33 per cent and 25 per cent,
respectively, of their merchandise exports. At the other end of
the scale, in Malaysia, even though the specified rate of yearly
increase is high (22 per cent), receipts from tourism are
expected to be just about the equivalent of 2 per cent of the
country's merchandise exports. The corresponding figures for
Ecuador and India are also low: 3 per cent and 2 per cent,
respectively.

As part of their efforts to increase tourist traffic and
earnings, developing countries have planned a wide-ranging set
of measures. Many countries have focused attention on improving
transport facilities to handle arrivals from abroad, especially
improvements in airports, both for handling aircraft and
passengers; among these countries are Afghanistan, Barbados, Kenya
and Nepal. Mauritius, for its part, faced with high air fares to
major countries that contain much of its potential tourist
clientele, has indicated that it would require air carriers to
promote cheaper package holidays in order to help step up tourist
interest in the island. Afghanistan, Bolivia and Botswana have
emphasized improvements in road transport to step up tourism, while
some countries have stressed the need for improving internal
transport in general for tourists. Among these countries is
India, which has laid much stress on improving facilities for
tourists in places of local or regional importance; its measures
include, apart from transport, beautification of tourist
attractions, provision of water, toilet facilities and electricity,
and, as the centre-piece, accomodation for middle-income tourists.

TABLE 6. Planned Expansion of Receipts from Tourism from Base Year to Final Year of Plan

Country[b]	Percentage annual rate of increase in receipts	Receipts as a percentage of merchandise exports in final year of plan
Countries indicating a planned annual rate of growth of gross domestic product of 8 per cent or more		
Jordan	14.9	25
Ecuador	20.0[c]	3
Malawi	15.0	5
Malaysia	22.0	2
Kenya	16.0	33
Countries indicating a planned annual rate of growth of gross domestic product of 6 per cent or more but less than 8 per cent		
Bolivia	20.0[c]	9
Costa Rica	15.0	15
Guatemala	20.0	16
Morocco	24.0	. . .
Mauritius	15.5	10
Sierra Leone	13.4	10
Countries indicating a planned annual rate of growth of gross domestic product of less than 6 per cent		
India	7.5	2
Afghanistan	12.3	. . .
Barbados	11.0	80
Uruguay	9.0[c]	. . .

Source: See table 1.

[a] For base year and final year of plan, see table 1. Data refer generally to tourist receipts as defined for balance-of-payments purposes. For Costa Rica, Jordan, Guatemala and Sierra Leone, data refer to receipts from tourism and other travel. Receipts are generally on a gross basis, except for Morocco and Sierra Leone, where they are net of corresponding expenditures by nationals abroad. All data are in current prices, except for Bolivia, Costa Rica, Ecuador and Sierra Leone, where they are in constant prices.

[b] Countries are listed in descending order of their planned annual rate of growth of gross domestic product.

[c] Based on expected number of tourist arrivals, irrespective of length of stay. These figures provide only a rough order of magnitude of expected increases in tourist receipts.

This policy, moreover, serves the aim of decentralizing tourism, an idea also at the heart of Kenya's tourist policy. Kenya is considering various efforts to disperse tourists. These include promotion of the attractions of areas outside the traditional tourist centres, as well as provision of more hotel beds outside such places. At the same time, policy would also focus on the critically important task of conserving the environment on which the wildlife of the country depends -- an attraction on which, in turn, the tourist industry was largely founded.

By means of the efforts contemplated, several developing countries envisage some improvement in their balance of transactions in services, excluding flows of factor income. Among the countries that have indicated a quantitative estimate of their expectations in this regard, as is evident from table 7 , six countries had a surplus in the base year of their plan, while 13 others had a deficit, which was substantial in some cases. Five of those six countries -- Argentina, Barbados, Costa Rica, Kenya and Panama -- expect to continue enjoying a surplus in the final year of the plan, with Costa Rica and Kenya expecting the surplus to increase faster than their merchandise exports. Argentina and Costa Rica envisage the surplus as relatively small: 3 and 8 per cent of their merchandise exports, respectively. In contrast, Barbados, Kenya and Panama expect the surplus to become quite large, predominantly by means of earnings from tourism in Barbados and Kenya and of the direct and indirect earnings of the Panama Canal, which provides a shipping route between the Atlantic and the Pacific Oceans. Only Mauritius, among the six countries that started their current plans with a surplus in the balance of transactions in services, has postulated a corresponding deficit by the final year of the plan.

Among the 13 countries starting their current development plans with a deficit in the balance of transactions in services, the deficit as a percentage of merchandise exports is expected to diminish in five countries -- namely, Botswana, Ecuador, Guatemala, India and Sierra Leone -- remain unchanged in Chile, and turn into a surplus in Jordan. In the remaining six countries -- the deficit as a proportion of exports is expected to worsen.[2] Thus, for about half of the countries that started with a deficit, it can be said that some easing of the burden, leading to release of foreign exchange for other important uses, has been visualized.

Many developing countries have also given attention to the possibility of reducing the burden of the net payments that they usually have to make on account of factor income. For example, the need to examine carefully offers of economic aid from abroad has been stressed in a number of current plans, including those of Bangladesh and India. In Iran, whose plan has emphasized similar considerations in respect of commercial loans, a stated objective is to pay back in advance the loans incurred on unfavourable terms in the past. Similarly, a number of countries have indicated their intention to exercise stricter control in the matter of encouraging investments from abroad in order to ensure that the outflow of profits and interest does not offset the value of the investment. However, the limitations in this regard are often severe, since foreign capital will not normally come without what are considered to be adequate arrangements for the remittance of interest and dividends. The Philippines has stressed this very point in its announced policy of liberalizing the arrangements in effect before the commencement of the current plan.

As the combined result of the past inflows of capital and of the inflows envisaged during the current plan period, about half of developing countries expect net factor income payments to absorb a larger proportion of their earnings from merchandise exports by the end of the current plan than at its outset. Thus, of the 17 countries for which it has been possible to obtain relevant information, this pattern is reflected in the plans of nine countries (see table 7). Prominent among these nine countries are Botswana, Ecuador and Malawi. Among the six countries that expect net payments of factor income as a percentage of merchandise exports to decline, the conspicuous examples of a substantial decline -- 4 percentage points or more from the base year to the final year of the country's current plan -- are offered by Argentina, India, Nigeria and Panama; but whereas Argentina, India and Nigeria expect net payments of factor income to absorb 7 per cent or less of their merchandise export earnings, the corresponding figure is expected to be as much as 50 per cent in Panama. Venezuela expects to continue recording a net inflow of factor income from abroad, while the expectation in Jordan is that its payments and receipts of factor income would be virtually equal.[3]

V. TARGETS AND OVER-ALL BALANCE OF PAYMENTS

As indicated earlier, nearly three fourths of developing countries have planned to increase their total exports faster than their total imports. Thus, a widespread aim is to achieve some improvement in the balance of payments by the final year of current plan. Although efforts are planned in respect of trade in both merchandise and service items, much of the improvement is expected to stem from shifts in merchandise trade, which bulks large in total exports or imports.

The targets established by developing countries for their overall balance of payments on current account for the latter part of the 1970s are shown in table 8 . It is evident that a particularly sharp improvement in the balance has been planned by Botswana and Jordan. Although both of these countries expect to have a deficit in the balance (including factor income) in the final year of their plans, the deficit as a percentage of the country's gross domestic product is expected to decline steeply. Similarly, a significant reduction in the deficit is planned by Ecuador, Nicaragua and Sierra Leone. India has estimated its deficit in the final year of the current plan to be equivalent to a mere 0.6 per cent of the country's gross domestic product. Iran has calculated that the relatively small deficit recorded by it in the base year of its current plan would turn into a relatively

TABLE 7. Balance of Transactions in Service Items in Base Year and Final Year of Plan

(Percentage of merchandise exports)

Country[b]	Balance of transactions in service items, excluding factor income[c]		Net payments of factor income[c]	
	Base year	Final year	Base year	Final year
Countries indicating a planned annual rate of growth of gross domestic product of 8 per cent or more				
Botswana	−38	−14	−18	−24
Jordan	−14	9	20	—
Ecuador	−17	−11	−18	−21
Nigeria	− 9	−14	−14	− 7
Malawi	−19	−21	−11	−16
Malaysia	...	...	− 6	− 8
Venezuela	− 6	− 8	5	4
Kenya	27	53	− 8	−10
domestic product of 6 per cent or more but less than 8 per cent				
Bolivia	−26 d	−31 d	...	...
Argentina	4	3	−11	− 7
Costa Rica	7	8	−13	−16
Guatemala	− 7	− 2	− 8	− 6
Indonesia	−11	−16	...	...
Panama	106	83	−57	−50
Philippines	...	...	−15	−14
Nicaragua	−16	−24	...	...
Chile	− 2 e	− 2 e	...	...
Mauritius	7	− 3	1	− 3
Sierra Leone	− 3	− 1	− 5	− 7
domestic product of less than 6 per cent				
India	−28	− 3	−11	− 6
Barbados	141	139	−12	−13

Source: See table 1.

ᵃ For base year and final year of plan, see table 1. However, for Panama and Venezuela, the base year refers to 1976.

ᵇ Countries are listed in descending order of their planned annual rate of growth of gross domestic product.

ᶜ Minus sign indicates deficit in the balance or net outflow of payments; no sign indicates surplus in the balance or net inflow of receipts.

Since the data on merchandise imports are generally inclusive of insurance and freight charges, the balance of transactions in service items is understated to that extent for most countries. Exceptions are Guatemala, Nicaragua and Venezuela, where the deficit is calculated on the basis of more detailed information.

Data are in current prices except for Bolivia, Costa Rica, Ecuador, Panama, Sierra Leone and Venezuela, where they are in constant prices, normally of the plan base year. For Botswana, data for the base year are in 1972 prices; those for the final year in 1973 prices.

ᵈ Including net factor income payments.

ᵉ Including net transfers.

TABLE 8. Planned Change in the Balance of Payments on Current Account from Base Year to Final Year of Plan

(Percentage of gross domestic product)

Country[b]	Balance, excluding factor income			Balance, including factor income		
	Base year	Final year	Average annual change	Base year	Final year	Average annual change
Countries indicating a planned annual rate of growth of gross domestic product of 8 per cent or more						
Iran	. . .	. . .	. . .	− 1.7	12.6	2.9
Botswana[c]	− 29.1	8.3	6.2	− 39.5	− 7.1	5.4
Jordan	− 48.4	− 20.1	5.7	− 45.5	− 20.1	5.1
Algeria	17.4	1.2	− 4.1	. . .	. . .	. . .
Ecuador	. . .	. . .	. . .	− 8.2	− 4.3	0.8
Nigeria	30.5	13.5	− 5.4	24.5	11.8	− 2.5
Malawi	− 7.9	− 5.7	0.4	− 12.1	− 10.3	0.4
Malaysia	12.8	13.2	0.1	10.6	9.9	− 0.1
Venezuela	12.0	9.9	− 0.5	. . .	. . .	. . .
Kenya	− 3.6	− 2.4	0.2	− 4.9	− 6.2	− 0.2
Countries indicating a planned annual rate of growth of gross domestic product of 6 per cent or more but less than 8 per cent						
Bolivia	− 5.7	− 0.9	1.0	− 8.1	− 5.4	0.5
Argentina	2.5	5.7	0.8	1.5	5.1	0.9
Costa Rica	− 6.7	− 3.4	0.5	− 9.4	− 7.3	0.4
Dominican Republic	− 1.8	0.1	0.2	. . .	. . .	. . .
Guatemala	2.3	5.3	0.6	1.3	4.7	0.7
Indonesia[d]	− 3.0	− 1.1	0.4	− 7.4	− 5.2	0.4
Morocco	− 5.1	− 4.0	0.3	. . .	. . .	. . .
Mali	− 5.2	− 7.7	0.4	− 6.4	− 13.0	− 1.1
Panama	− 10.7	− 9.3	0.3	− 15.5	− 14.9	0.1
Philippines	. . .	. . .	. . .	0.7	4.4	0.9
El Salvador	− 3.0	− 3.8	− 0.2	− 2.5	− 3.7	− 0.2
Nicaragua	− 8.6	− 3.5	1.0	− 12.6	− 9.1	0.7
Chile	2.9	3.4	0.1	. . .	. . .	. . .
Mauritius	9.5	− 8.6	− 3.0	. . .	. . .	. . .
Sierra Leone	− 9.9	− 3.9	1.2	− 11.3	− 5.5	1.2

TABLE 8. (continued)

Country[b]	Balance, excluding factor income			Balance, including factor income		
	Base year	Final year	Average annual change	Base year	Final year	Average annual change[d]
Countries indicating a planned annual rate of growth of gross domestic product of less than 6 per cent						
India	− 1.1	− 0.2	0.2	− 1.6	− 0.6	0.2
Barbados	−16.1	−11.8	0.9	. . .	. . .	. . .
Uruguay	1.1	− 2.4	−0.7	. . .	. . .	. . .
Madagascar	− 3.4	− 1.7	0.3	− 4.2	. . .	. . .

Source: See table 1.
a For base year and final year of plan, see table 1. However, for Panama and Venezuela, the base year refers to 1976.
b Countries are listed in descending order of their planned annual rate of growth of gross domestic product.
c Base year data in 1972 prices; final year data in 1973 prices.
d Calculated from data in current prices.

large surplus by the end of the plan. Argentina, Guatemala and the
Philippines, which started their current plans with a surplus in
their balance of payments on current account, expect the surplus to
become significantly larger by the end of the plan.

Although the dominating tendency is clearly to seek some
improvement in the balance of payments in relation to the country's
gross domestic product -- a reduction in the deficit or, in a
number of countries, an increase in the surplus -- there are a few
prominent examples of countries that expect a relative
deterioration in the balance. Such is the case, for example, in
Nigeria and Venezuela, which have postulated a decline -- indeed, a
sharp one in Nigeria -- in their surplus on external account in
relation to gross domestic product. These two petroleum-exporting
countries, in other words, intend to reduce the rate at which they
have been accumulating foreign assets. Mali, by contrast,
anticipates a sizable increase in the deficit on external
account -- that is, in the net inflow of external finance.

The search for improvement in the balance of payments on
current account, if successful, would ease the problems of
developing countries to an extent. But most of these countries
would still be critically dependent on net flows of finances from
abroad to accelerate their economic and social progress. While the
data summarized in table 9 cover only 18 countries, the number is
large enough to attest that a substantial proportion of the imports
of goods and services of a substantial majority of developing
countries would be financed by a net inflow of external finances.
Even in India, where the target for the deficit in the balance of
payments on current account in the final year of the current plan
amounts to no more than 0.6 per cent of gross domestic product, the
net inflow of finances from abroad is expected to pay for 14 per
cent of imports of goods and services in that very year.[4]

VI. ECONOMIC AND TECHNICAL CO-OPERATION WITH OTHER DEVELOPING COUNTRIES

The need for strengthening economic and technical co-operation
with neighbouring countries, as well as with developing countries
on other continents, has been mentioned by many developing
countries in their plans for the latter part of the 1970s.
Countries that have been associated in long-established free trade
areas, customs unions and similar groupings have stressed such
co-operation in particular.

At the same time, some members of the older groupings have
expressed the need for, and their own willingness to contribute to,
a better and more dynamic functioning of the relevant groupings.
For example, Argentina and Brazil have emphasized the role of the
Latin American Free Trade Area. Similarly, several of the
countries that are members of the Andean Pact have stressed the
importance of maintaining and extending their links as a
prerequisite to successful development, especially

TABLE 9. Planned Change in Net Flow of External Finances as Percentage of Imports of Goods and Non-factor Services from Base Year to Final Year of Plan

Country[b]	Base year	Final year
Countries indicating a planned annual rate of growth of gross domestic product of 8 per cent or more		
Botswana[c]	73	15
Jordan	62	33
Nigeria	−162	−50
Malawi	39	35
Malaysia	−38	−36
Kenya	16	21
Countries indicating a planned annual rate of growth of gross domestic product of 6 per cent or more but less than 8 per cent		
Bolivia	36	24
Argentina	−23	−65
Costa Rica	24	18
Guatemala	− 7	−33
Indonesia[d]	37	24
Mali	23	42
Panama	30	29
El Salvador	9	13
Nicaragua	32	24
Sierra Leone	28	15
Countries indicating a planned annual rate of growth of gross domestic product of less than 6 per cent		
India[e]	31	14
Madagascar	21	f

Source: See table 1.

[a] For base year and final year of plan, see table 1. However, for the following country the base year differs: Panama, 1976.

Net inflow of external finances equals excess of imports over exports of goods and services, including factor income. Minus sign indicates net outflow.

[b] Countries are listed in descending order of their planned annual rate of growth of gross domestic product.

[c] Base year data in 1972 prices; final year data in 1973 prices.

[d] Calculated from data in current prices.

[e] Net inflow as a percentage of imports of goods and net trade in services.

[f] Target not available because plan does not indicate figure for net factor payments for final year of plan. The target for net inflow of finances estimated as excess of imports over exports of goods and services, excluding factor income, is equivalent to 9 per cent of imports; the corresponding figure for the base year is 17 per cent.

industrialization; many of the same points, though in a rather different institutional setting, have been made by several countries that are members of the Central American Common Market. In Kenya, the focus of co-operation has been on the East African Community, with its trade arrangements and many joint institutions and services. With the Community facing severe internal strains, Kenya's policy has centred on efforts to hold it together and revive it; to that end, it has declared its readiness to accept certain sacrifices, such as the bearing of a relatively greater burden of certain costs of Community services. In West Asia, Jordan has called for the rationalization of trade through, among other measures, the enforcement of the articles of the Arab Common Market Agreement, and has stressed in general the importance of co-operation with Arab countries.

In respect of newer groupings for co-operation in trade and development among developing countries, Nigeria has indicated support for the recently established Economic Community of West African States. Malaysia has stressed the importance of economic co-operation among developing countries and has planned to intensify its efforts to foster greater collaboration at the international, regional and subregional levels. Malaysia and the Philippines have paid considerable attention to their membership in the Association of South-East Asian Nations as a way to promote co-operation in trade, industry and other ventures, including the possible creation of various joint services. In their plans, both countries have restated their interest in the agreements that have been reached for proceeding with trade liberalization on a selective basis, with industrial complementation and subregional allocation of some new industrial enterprises in the public sector. Through the medium of an expert group, projects initially mooted for industrial co-operation -- such as those involving the production of urea, superphosphates, soda ash and diesel engines -- would be examined to ascertain their feasibility.

In respect of a geographically wider form of co-operation, the Philippines has stressed the importance of tariff concessions exclusively among the developing countries -- in addition to any general liberalization that might be achieved through universal multilateral negotiations. Intercountry discussions on this subject were initially held in 1971 and led to a protocol under which 16 countries, including the Philippines, were to grant each other preferential tariff concessions on products covering more than 300 headings in the Brussels Tariff Nomenclature. The draft protocol embodying the agreements was in the process of ratification in the countries concerned, including Brazil, Chile, India and Uruguay, at the time when their current development plans were in preparation.

Examples of a different form of co-operation among countries, involving in this case common efforts in respect of specific regions or areas that lie next to or straddle national frontiers, include those undertaken through the River Niger Commission, the Senegal River Basin Office, the Lake Chad Basin Commission, the Parana River co-operative venture for water control and power generation, involving Argentina and Paraguay, the schemes of El Salvador and Venezuela for co-operation with neighbouring countries for the purpose of developing frontier regions, or the Bangladesh-India Joint Rivers Commission. A relatively new form of co-operation that has received considerable attention, especially in the plans of major petroleum-producing countries -- including Iran, Nigeria and Venezuela -- involves joint industrial projects both within and outside a regional co-operation framework, whereby the finances, technology, raw materials and markets of the co-operating countries are exploited to mutual advantage. In the more traditional field of transport, many countries have indicated their intention to participate in schemes designed to improve links with each other, by developing air, road, rail, water, pipeline and telecommunication links and by simplifying border formalities for both cargo and passengers. The simplification of border formalities is of particular interest to such land-locked countries as Botswana, Malawi and Mali in Africa, Afghanistan and Nepal in Asia, and Bolivia in Latin America.

Scientific and technical co-operation among developing countries, including mutual assistance in training, co-ordination of research and the promotion of joint ventures in research (including socio-economic research) and technology, are all given some emphasis in many current plans. Venezuela, for instance, has expressed its support for co-operative efforts within the framework of the Latin American Economic System, a central objective of which is to sponsor regional joint ventures based on advanced technology, some of it developed within the region. Co-operation in technological matters is also an inherent part of the aims of the Andean and Central American economic groupings, and has received attention in many current plans in the context of industrial development measures. Elsewhere, considerable emphasis is given to this aspect of co-operation by, among others, Iran, Kenya, Malaysia and Nigeria. The Malaysian plan has also enumerated the many regional technical co-operative measures that are under way and are to receive continued support, covering such areas as fisheries and aquaculture, population planning, tax and development administration and the teaching of science and mathematics. Malaysia has also expressed its willingness to continue to expand the provision of places and scholarships for nationals of other developing countries to train in Malaysian institutions under the auspices of the Colombo Plan or the Islamic Conference, as well as under bilateral schemes of technical co-operation. Many countries are now offering scholarships and training places to nationals from other developing countries; several have expressed their intentions in this regard in their current plans, among them Algeria, Bangladesh, India and Nigeria.

A number of developing countries -- for example, Iran and Nigeria -- have also expressed their willingness to provide economic aid in the form of grants or loans to other developing countries. Venezuela anticipates stepping up its assistance in the future, especially to countries in Central America and the Caribbean; its plan has provided for a level of transfers to other countries reaching almost $900 million by 1980, as against $155 million in 1976, both figures being expressed in constant 1975 dollars. Iran, Nigeria and Venezuela have also expressed their intentions to help petroleum-importing developing countries meet their petroleum needs or to contribute towards the cost of such imports. Among traditional givers of aid to neighbouring developing countries, India, which itself is a net recipient of aid, has indicated its intention to continue providing capital assistance in addition to technical aid.

The growing co-operation among developing countries in commercial, financial and technological matters is indeed of great importance. While such co-operation could help significantly to spur their economic and social progress, much would still depend on the trading and other economic links of these countries with the rest of the world. The present chapter has focused attention on the targets and policies indicated by developing countries for foreign trade and payments in the latter part of the 1970s. Their expectations with regard to external finance, though implicit in the foregoing discussion, are examined more systematically in the next chapter.

NOTES

[1]For a few countries, in the absence of corresponding information on service transactions, the targets shown in table 1 refer to merchandise trade only. However, since merchandise items usually bulk large in the total exports or imports of developing countries, the target rates of increase in merchandise trade of these countries can be taken as an adequate indicator of the planned expansion of their total trade. It should also be noted that for some countries the trade targets are wholly or partially in current prices. While in such cases the precise magnitude of the planned change in the quantum of trade is not known, the broad generalizations put forward in the text above in terms of ranges of the planned change appear to be valid.

[2]It should be noted, however, that the data for Bolivia, unlike those for other countries listed in table 7 , are net of factor income payments.

[3]This statement is based on data excluding remittances of Jordanians working abroad. In Jordan, the practice is to treat such remittances as receipts of factor income from abroad. However, in order to keep intercountry comparisons as valid as possible, such remittances have been excluded from the data for Jordan shown in the present study.

[4]It should be noted that the estimates shown in table 8 are derived from data in constant prices, usually in prices of the base year of plans. If prices of exports and imports vary greatly from those recorded in the base year, changes in the flow of finances over the plan period would turn out to be significantly

different from those envisaged at the time of the plan's
preparation.

Exports in the New World Environment: The Case of Latin America

BAREND A. de VRIES

Exports have played a crucial role in the economic growth of Latin America. The countries that fared best in the recent crisis were those which had succeeded in diversifying their domestic economies and their exports -- on the basis of earlier industrialization efforts -- and which continued to encourage their export trade. Similarly, if they are to cope successfully with the complications of the present and future external position, deriving from the higher cost of oil, increased external indebtedness, and the pressure of available capital resources, it will be indispensable for exports to keep up or regain their momentum.

    The present article analyses the conditions that would make it possible for the Latin American countries to maintain a viable balance of payments in a context of growth: more specifically, the conditions that would enable them, by the end of the present decade, to increase their exports at an annual rate of 9 per cent or more, their imports at a lower rate and their product by 7 per cent per annum. The aspects analyses include, among others, the evolution of external markets (both those of the industrialized countries and those of the region); the role of exports of agricultural and mining products; the diversification of industrial exports; exchange policy and export incentives; and import substitution projects.

From **CEPAL REVIEW,** 1977, (93-113), reprinted by permission of the pub - lisher, The U.N. Publications, N.Y.

I. INTRODUCTION

Over the past ten years most Latin American countries have, to an increasing extent, pursued measures to expand and diversify their exports. These outward-oriented policies, together with a generally favourable external environment, made possible unexpectedly high export growth rates in 1968-1973. This export growth greatly enhanced the economic strength of the Latin American countries. It increased their creditworthiness for substantially higher external borrowing, which in turn helped to finance larger investments in industry, mining and infrastructure; and it substantially improved their capacity for adjusting to the adverse effects on their external financial position of the 1974-1975 recession in the industrial countries.

Continuation of export growth and diversification will be important for the development prospects of the Latin American countries over the next 5-10 years, as well as for their ability to adjust to the changes in external price, demand and supply relationships which have occurred since 1973 and to obtain adequate amounts of external financing. At the same time, however, the changes in the external environments may be putting pressures on the outward-oriented policies adopted in the late sixties. International conditions for the supply of capital and for export growth may be less favourable than they were in the early seventies.

This paper seeks to assess the role that continued export growth must play in Latin America's development and to discuss how export policies can best be adapted to the changes both in external and in domestic conditions which have taken place since 1973.

First, the paper focuses on developments in 1971-1975, with special emphasis on those features which are likely to have a bearing on the pattern and level of future growth. What were the factors behind the export acceleration? What role did exports play in enabling countries to adjust to the 1974-1975 recession, and how did manufactured exports fare during that time?

Secondly, it considers the role of exports and export policies in Latin America's growth during the next 5-10 years. What minimal export growth rates must be achieved in order to maintain a viable external position? Can these rates be realized? What are the factors which could cause a slow-down of the growth of industrial exports and a change in export composition? What do these factors imply for export policies, what are the pressures on these policies and what will be the case for special incentive measures? Will Latin American be able to maintain some degree of stability in its external payments position and cope with the effects of fluctuations in external demand?

Thirdly, it considers some aspects of the role of intra-regional trade in recent and prospective export development. How was intra-regional trade affected by the acceleration in exports, and what contribution can regional markets make to export growth and the countries' ability to cope with fluctuations in the demand of the major industrial nations?

II. DEVELOPMENTS IN 1971-1975

(a) Export acceleration

Table 1 summarizes the major elements in the GDP, balance of payments and external debt of ten Latin American countries,[2] which account from 83 per cent of total GDP of Latin America and the Caribbean, 73 per cent of exports (excluding those of the oil exporters, Venezuela, Ecuador and Trinidad and Tobago) and 89 per cent of external debt (again excluding these oil exporters). Major characteristics of growth trends in the first three years, 1971-1973 (i.e., those preceding the increase in oil prices and the OECD recession) are:

(i) Growth in GDP, exports and especially manufactured exports reached high levels not achieved in previous years. In 1973 GDP growth averaged over 8 per cent for the ten countries, and manufactured exports increased by 31.3 per cent in real terms. These growth parameters reflect the progressive integration of major Latin American countries into the world economy (trade, investment and finance);

(ii) As GDP growth accelerated, the ratio between imports and GDP remained stable and the resources gap dwindled to less than 0.5 per cent of GDP, or barely more than 1 thousand million dollars in 1973;

(iii) Terms of trade improved by more than 8 per cent in these three years, despite the sharp increase in import prices associated with the higher oil prices and world inflation.

The acceleration of export growth was most marked for manufactured exports. Those of LAFTA[3] increased by an average annual rate of 39.8 per cent (in current dollars), with rates for the four countries shown in table 2 ranging from 34.5 per cent for Argentina to 52.2 per cent for Brazil. This growth reached a peak in 1973, when it amounted to 31 per cent in real terms for the ten countries shown in table 1, covering a broad range of items such as light and heavy consumer goods, machinery and electrical equipment. Many of these items started from a zero or very small base in 1968 and reached substantial amounts in 1973. Annex table 7 shows twenty-six such export items for Brazil, some of which increased to almost 100 million dollars by 1973. Similar observations can be made for Argentina, Colombia and Mexico (see Annex tables 8, 9 and 10).

The major factors underlying the acceleration of manufactured exports were:

(i) Major Latin American countries had significantly changed their foreign exchange rate policies (especially Brazil and Colombia, which introduced flexible exchange rates in 1968) and/or

Table 1

GROWTH, BALANCE OF PAYMENTS AND DEBT: ARGENTINA, BOLIVIA, BRAZIL, CHILE, COLOMBIA, DOMINICAN REPUBLIC, GUATEMALA, JAMAICA, MEXICO, PERU

	Estimated actual				
	1971	1972	1973	1974	1975
Macro-economic parameters					
G.D.P. growth	7.9	7.6	8.3	7.5	2.9
Export growth	3.1	7.9	5.7	1.1	-1.5
(Manufactured export growth)	16.5	20.7	31.3	8.3	4.1
Ratios					
Resource gap/G.D.P. (%)	1.4	1.1	0.5	2.6	2.8
Investment/G.D.P. (%)	20.8	21.7	21.1	23.8	21.9
Domestic savings/investment (%)	93.3	95.1	97.8	89.1	87.3
Incremental capital output	2.4	2.7	2.6	2.8	8.3
Imports/G.D.P. (%)	10.3	10.1	9.9	11.5	10.5
Marginal savings (%)	25.4	40.2	18.2	26.9	-40.0
Terms of trade (1967-69 = 100)					
Export price index	109.4	119.9	158.0	208.5	108.0
Import price index	110.8	121.0	147.6	197.2	215.2
Terms of trade index	98.8	99.1	107.0	105.7	96.7
Balance of payments (Millions of dollars)					
Exports (goods + non-financial services)	12 913.5	15 261.6	21 247.2	28 364.3	27 879.2
Imports (goods + non-financial services)	14 921.2	17 062.3	22 287.4	36 860.6	37 948.1
Resource balance	*-2 007.7*	*-1 800.7*	*-1 040.2*	*-8 496.3*	*-10 068.9*
Other services (net)	-1 594.0	-1 878.4	-2 371.6	-3 022.8	-4 248.0
Interest (net)	-1 165.5	-1 372.3	-1 856.7	-2 296.6	-3 543.9
Balance on current account	*-3 601.7*	*-3 679.1*	*-3 411.8*	*-11 519.1*	*-14 316.9*
Amortization	-2 438.0	-2 944.5	-3 786.2	-3 980.6	-4 309.1
Capital required	*6 039.7*	*6 623.6*	*7 198.0*	*15 499.7*	*18 626.0*
Financing (Millions of dollars)					
Official sources (gross)	1 136.6	1 371.8	1 708.3	2 126.9	2 633.4
(net)	*690.1*	*937.0*	*1 165.9*	*1 446.6*	*1 786.0*
Multilateral	425.0	505.9	576.7	769.9	841.8
Bilateral	265.1	431.1	589.2	676.7	944.2
Private sources (gross)	3 409.8	6 118.3	7 432.5	11 221.9	11 837.4
(net)	*1 418.3*	*3 609.6*	*4 187.7*	*7 931.6*	*8 375.7*
Suppliers	142.0	249.9	458.6	831.4	919.0
Financial	1 230.0	3 316.8	3 823.1	6 500.9	7 322.6
Bonds	85.1	184.6	19.5	38.4	204.7
Others	-38.8	-141.7	-113.5	560.9	-70.6
Direct investment	574.8	677.3	1 662.1	1 544.0	2 122.9
Other capital n.e.s.	893.3	1 179.0	-581.5	-223.7	-299.7
Reserve change (- = increase)	25.2	-2 722.8	-3 023.4	830.6	2 331.9
External debt (Millions of dollars)					
Debt outstanding + Disbursement total	*17 659.8*	*22 746.6*	*28 819.9*	*37 870.3*	*47 900.0*
Debt service	3 603.5	4 316.8	5 642.9	6 277.2	7 853.0
Amortization	-2 438.0	-2 944.5	-3 786.2	-3 980.6	-4 309.1
(Official)	446.5	434.8	542.4	680.3	847.4
(Private)	1 991.5	2 508.7	3 244.8	3 290.3	3 461.7
Interest	-1 165.5	-1 372.3	-1 856.7	-2 296.6	-3 543.9
(Official)	295.4	325.3	410.1	511.1	673.4
(Private)	870.1	1 047.0	1 446.6	1 785.4	2 870.5
Debt service ratio (%)	27.9	28.3	26.6	22.1	28.2

Table 1

GROWTH, BALANCE OF PAYMENTS AND DEBT: ARGENTINA, BOLIVIA, BRAZIL, CHILE, COLOMBIA,
DOMINICAN REPUBLIC, GUATEMALA, JAMAICA, MEXICO, PERU

			Projections		
	1976	1977	1978	1979	1980
Macro-economic parameters					
G.D.P. growth	3.7	5.2	6.0	6.5	6.9
Export growth	8.7	9.2	10.0	8.7	9.0
(Manufactured export growth)	12.4	11.5	12.5	12.9	13.0
Ratios					
Resource gap/G.D.P. (%)	1.5	0.7	0.3	-0.1	-0.3
Investment/G.D.P. (%)	20.3	21.6	22.1	22.4	22.8
Domestic savings/investment (%)	92.9	96.6	98.8	100.4	101.2
Incremental capital output	5.9	3.9	3.6	3.4	3.2
Imports/G.D.P. (%)	9.3	8.8	8.8	8.7	8.7
Marginal savings (%)	13.7	61.6	37.2	30.7	30.8
Terms of trade (1967-69 = 100)					
Export price index	218.8	234.8	257.0	276.3	296.3
Import price index	232.0	251.1	270.4	289.5	308.9
Terms of trade index	94.3	93.5	95.0	95.4	96.1
Balance of payments (Millions of dollars)					
Exports (goods + non-financial services)	31 869.0	37 336.5	44 934.8	52 520.0	61 509.3
Imports (goods + non-financial services)	37 699.3	40 649.2	46 248.0	52 017.0	59 669.9
Resource balance	*-5 830.3*	*-3 312.7*	*-1 313.2*	*503.0*	*1 839.4*
Other services (net)	-5 595.8	-6 366.9	-7 123.9	-8 004.3	-8 629.5
Interest (net)	-4 857.2	-5 571.7	-6 141.0	-6 622.1	-7 006.0
Balance on current account	*-11 426.1*	*-9 679.6*	*-8 437.1*	*-7 501.3*	*-6 790.1*
Amortization	-5 144.0	-6 916.6	-8 842.9	10 248.8	-11 426.7
Capital required	*16 570.1*	*16 596.2*	*17 280.0*	*17 750.1*	*18 216.8*
Financing (Millions of dollars)					
Official sources (gross)	2 848.0	3 020.5	3 288.7	3 572.7	3 854.6
(net)	*1 761.9*	*1 807.2*	*2 074.8*	*2 231.1*	*2 326.1*
Multilateral	1 195.3	1 362.8	1 626.7	1 817.7	1 956.2
Bilateral	566.6	444.4	448.1	413.4	369.9
Private sources (gross)	10 671.3	11 597.2	11 698.4	12 351.7	12 548.4
(net)	*6 614.4*	*5 893.9*	*4 069.8*	*3 447.5*	*2 651.2*
Suppliers	1 144.5	1 284.7	1 351.9	1 331.2	1 365.9
Financial	5 288.4	4 551.9	2 658.5	2 111.3	1 289.6
Bonds	245.5	124.8	128.5	75.8	67.4
Others	-64.0	-67.6	-69.1	-70.9	-71.8
Direct investment	2 138.6	2 493.7	3 001.4	3 294.0	3 455.7
Other capital n.e.s.	-508.1	-55.5	151.3	28.5	144.7
Reserve change (- = increase)	1 420.3	-459.8	-859.9	-1 496.9	-1 786.7
External debt (Millions of dollars)					
Debt outstanding + Disbursement total	*56 489.0*	*64 422.4*	*70 926.0*	*76 902.4*	*82 229.1*
Debt service	10 001.2	12 488.3	14 983.9	16 870.9	18 432.7
Amortization	-5 144.0	-6 916.6	-8 842.9	-10 248.8	-11 426.7
(Official)	1 086.1	1 213.3	1 214.0	1 341.6	1 528.5
(Private)	4 056.9	5 703.3	7 628.0	8 904.2	9 897.2
Interest	-4 857.2	-5 571.7	-6 141.0	-6 622.1	-7 006.0
(Official)	761.6	833.9	934.2	1 079.9	1 247.4
(Private)	4 095.6	4 737.8	5 206.8	5 542.2	5 758.6
Debt service ratio (%)	31.4	33.4	33.3	32.1	30.0

Source. Based on IBRD staff estimates, July 1976.

adopted effective export incentive measures;[4]

(ii) Their industrial production and marketing capacity had reached a stage where they were able to achieve significant export growth. A substantial part of their export production and marketing was organized with the assistance of transnational companies.[5] In fact, exports increased most to countries where these companies provided access to extensive marketing and retailing facilities (see section 3);

(iii) Market conditions were favourable, partly because of good business conditions prevailing simultaneously in the United States and the other OECD countries, and partly because of the effects of import liberalization and preferential tariff arrangements;

(iv) Country shares in import markets were still relatively low at the start of the period.

Latin American countries had to adjust to the increase in oil prices and the subsequent 1974-1975 recession, especially those which were not self-sufficient in oil and which, through diversification of manufactured exports to industrial countries, had become more integrated with the world economy. Notable example are Brazil, Chile and Uruguay. Although the movements of prices for major commodities, especially agricultural, were not strictly parallel in the most recent cyclical downturn -- with weather conditions even causing increases for some (e.g., sugar and coffee) -- , demand for manufactured exports did generally decline or decelerate.

At the end of 1973 most of the countries were in a relatively strong position to cope with the adverse impact of the OECD recession:

(i) Exports had been rising dynamically and, in fact, the year-to-year increases in export earnings covered a substantial portion of total service payments on external debt (for example, in 1974 the increase in Brazil's exports of goods and services was equivalent to 73 per cent of its total debt service, while for the ten-country group the figure was even larger: 113 per cent);

(ii) The debt service ration was relatively low -- 22 per cent for the ten-country group in 1974 compared with 28 per cent in 1971. Although total debt rose sharply in 1974 and terms generally hardened in 1975, the increase in service payments lagged behind, and in fact these payments declined in relation to export earnings. Hence, countries were in a strong position to utilize the large amounts of private credits available for financing imports and investments while taking the necessary short- and long-term adjustment measures;

(iii) Imports were at a sufficiently high level in relation to GDP for some compression to be achieved without severely endangering longer-term growth.

In the first phases of the 1974-1975 adjustment process imports did, however, increase faster than GDP in most countries -- notable exceptions being Chile and Colombia. External capital facilitated the maintenance of import levels and hence made the adjustment process more gradual than it could have been otherwise. Between 1973 and 1975 import payments rose by 16 thousand million dollars for the 10-country group (or by 70 per

Table 2

EXPORTS TO LAFTA AS PERCENTAGE OF EXPORTS TO ALL DESTINATIONS
FOR TOTAL LAFTA, ARGENTINA, BRAZIL, COLOMBIA AND MEXICO

(1968 and 1973)

| | Exports to LAFTA (%) | | o/o change in share | Average annual growth of exports |
	1968	1973		(1968-1973)
LAFTA				
Manufactured products	35.7	26.8	-24.9	39.8
Basic and miscellaneous manufactures	32.2	20.4	-36.6	40.5
Chemicals	27.1	39.3	45.0	21.2
Machinery and transport equipment	58.4	34.1	-41.6	54.0
ARGENTINA				
Manufactured products	47.3	53.3	12.7	34.5
Basic chemicals	34.7	38.0	9.5	38.0
Chemicals	35.5	50.7	42.8	13.6
Machinery and transport equipment	71.0	77.4	9.0	48.0
Miscellaneous manufactures	68.3	37.9	-45.5	32.8
BRAZIL				
Manufactured products	45.6	25.9	-43.2	52.2
Basic manufactures	44.1	18.5	-58.0	47.8
Chemicals	14.1	24.1	70.9	32.3
Machinery and transport equipment	70.4	49.2	-30.1	49.2
Miscellaneous manufactures	37.0	14.8	-60.0	111.2

	Exports to LAFTA (%)			Average annual growth of exports
	1968	1973	% change in share	(1968-1973)
COLOMBIA				
Manufactured products	28.0	22.2	-20.7	41.9
Basic manufactures	19.3	12.2	-36.8	41.7
Chemicals	51.3	60.7	18.3	42.5
Machinery and transport equipment	55.7	62.7	16.8	34.5
Miscellaneous manufactures	28.5	21.6	-24.2	78.5
MEXICO				
Manufactured products	18.3	11.4	-37.7	37.3
Basic manufactures	9.5	4.7	-50.5	26.8
Chemicals	21.1	25.0	18.5	19.8
Machinery and transport equipment	24.3	9.7	-60.1	66.3
Miscellaneous manufactures	27.0	12.8	-52.6	20.1

Source: Based on United Nations *Commodity Trade Statistics* (1968-1973).

Note: SITC nomenclature.

(5 to 8 excluding 68) Manufactured products.

(5) Chemicals: chemical elements, compounds, dyes, perfume, fertilizers, plastics, pesticides.

(6 excluding 68) Basic manufactures: leather, rubber articles, wood and cork manufactures, veneers, plywood, paper, textile yarn (natural and synthetic), cement, glass, iron and steel, metal tools and structures.

(68) Non-ferrous metals: silver, platinum, aluminum, copper, nickel, lead, zinc manufactures.

(7) Machinery and transport equipment: boilers, steam engines, aircraft engines, turbines, harvesting and threshing machinery, tractors, office machines, metal-work machines, industrial machinery, pumps, appliances, telecommunications, electric machines and tools, railway vehicles, road motor-vehicles, aircraft, ships.

(8) Miscellaneous manufactures: lighting fixtures, furniture, travel goods, clothing, footwear, professional, scientific and controlling instruments, musical instruments, printed matter, articles of artificial plastic, toys, jewelry, works of art, artisanry.

cent), the resource gap increased from 1 thousand million dollars to 10 thousand million (or 2.8 per cent of GDP) and external debt climbed from 29 thousand million to 48 thousand million dollars.

A notable feature of the capital inflow was the increased importance of private credits. The net inflow of capital from private sources doubled between 1973 and 1975 to 8.4 thousand million dollars. The share of private credits in total external debt increased from less than 49 per cent in 1970 to 71 per cent in 1975.

Up to 1974 the growth of external debt was roughly in line with the growth of exports. In 1967-1970 external debt increased by 12.6 per cent per annum while export earnings rose by 12.2 per cent. As the growth rate of exports accelerated in 1971-1974, so did that of external debt -- 29 per cent per annum for exports as against 23.5 per cent for external debt.[6] In 1974-1975 external capital was used in part to help offset the adverse balance-of-payments effects of the recession. External debt increased more rapidly than exports, i.e., on average by 29.1 per cent per annum as against an export growth rate of 15.7 per cent. In addition, in 1975 private credit terms hardened markedly.

(b) Manufactured exports in the 1974-1975 recession

Some observations on the behaviour of manufactured exports in the two recession years, even if incomplete and tentative, are useful for understanding the issues confronting countries in their export strategy.

First, in real terms exports decelerated markedly. Table 1 shows real growth rates of manufactured exports of 31.3 per cent in 1973, 8.2 per cent in 1974, and 4.2 per cent in 1975. In current dollars exports increased by 53.9 per cent in 1974 and 7.2 per cent in 1975.[7] While the 1974 and 1975 growth rates are clearly more favourable than those achieved for traditional staple products, they are much lower than the 1971-1973 rates, and the experience of some countries suggests that certain manufactured exports also suffered considerably, in terms both of volume and of prices. In Colombia, for example, the increase in volume in 1975 was more than offset by the decline in unit values; non-traditional agricultural exports did better than manufactured goods. In Brazil, while unit prices of total exports rose by 0.7 per cent, prices of manufactured exports declined by 6 per cent in 1975 (as against a 44 per cent increase in 1974) and prices of semi-processed goods[8] fell by 18 per cent. Export prices of capital goods -- a rapidly growing category -- decreased by 5 per cent (as against an increase of 21 per cent in capital goods import prices). In General, exports of the more 'traditional' items (shoes, textiles, wood products) did not do well -- these also tend to have the larger market shares in the United States. Those produced and marketed by the transnationals (automotive products and machinery) generally did better than other exports.

Policies affecting general price competitiveness clearly had an effect on the behaviour of manufactured exports in these recession years. This is apparent from a comparison between Chile and Uruguay, on the one hand, with Mexico and Peru on the other. In Chile -- where real devaluation of 37 per cent occurred in 1974-1975 -- manufactured exports increased from 226 million dollars in 1973 to 675 million in 1975. Continuation of this growth trend, even at a slower pace, would significantly alter and enhance Chile's development pattern and prospects. Likewise, changes in Uruguay's policies (exchange rate flexibility, export subsidies and import liberalization) made it possible for non-traditional exports to expand by 50 per cent in 1975, thereby offsetting the decline in exports of meat and wool tops caused by EEC restrictions and other adverse market conditions. (Non-traditional exports as a percentage of the total increased from 18 per cent in 1973 to 45 per cent in 1975.) On the other hand, in Peru and Mexico, countries which continued to apply a fixed-rate policy in an inflationary environment, such exports suffered relatively large decreases in volume (14.7 per cent for Mexico in 1975 and 27.9 per cent for Peru). And Mexico's share of United States imports tended to decline in both years.

The conclusions emerging from these preliminary observations are:

(i) General policy measures, especially concerning exchange rates (but also investment policies in the private sector) were important in achieving export growth in the adverse conditions of 1974 and 1975;

(ii) Manufactured exports, while faring better than most staples, were adversely affected by the recession. Some sub-categories did better than others, but in general industrial exports slowed down markedly and prices of many products declined. In some countries the performance of non-traditional agricultural exports was more satisfactory than that of manufactured goods. In these circumstances general incentive measures -- affecting a broad range of exports -- would seem to be more desirable than measures focusing on selected items.

III. FUTURE EXPORT GROWTH

(a) Main characteristics of growth

The projections in table 1 for the group of 10 Latin American countries sum up those prepared for the individual countries on the basis of uniform assumptions about the external environment (e.g., demand in industrial countries, prices of raw material exports, international inflation). Country growth rates reflect growth potentials and strategy, investment and export plans and policies, and the necessary adjustments in the balance of payments during the projection period. The projections bring out certain key issues to be considered in an export development policy:

(i) Exports have become a leading sector in relation to Latin America's growth. And they are fundamental for maintaining a country's ability to obtain and service adequate amounts of external capital. The scenario presented in table 1 assumes that real growth of total exports can reach 8-10 per cent per annum -- reflecting growth of all major categories (agricultural, mineral and manufacturing); manufactured exports would increase by 10-15 per cent per annum, a good growth rate, but below the super-growth levels (23 per cent) achieved in the early seventies. Terms of trade are projected to improve only marginally for the remainder of the decade. Export growth lower than the projects would depress GDP growth because of the direct impact of the export sector on the economy, and the reduced foreign exchange available for importing investment goods; capital inflows would also be adversely affected, with the consequent aggravation of the cut in external resources;

(ii) The projection assumes that imports can be reduced from 11 per cent of GDP in 1974 and 1975 to less than 9 per cent by the late seventies (as compared with 10 per cent in 1971-1973; in 1974 imports were somewhat inflated by inventory building in some countries). A decline in the import ratio would seem to be feasible, given the possibilities of adjusting to the new external environment (which in some countries has already entailed some real devaluation of the exchange rate) and the plans for import substitution projects, especially in Brazil (e.g., capital goods, fertilizers and steel). Combining policies which will reduce imports with those which will permit a resumption of vigorous export growth may prove to be a difficult task in certain cases;

(iii) Overall GDP growth would accelerate to 6-7 per cent. Significantly lower growth rates would not be compatible with the objective of improving the levels of living of the lowest income groups;

(iv) The external resource gap would decline progressively (from 2.8 per cent in 1975) and turn into a small surplus after 1979. This turn-around, if achieved and sustained, would, of course, be the most important single factor in containing the build-up of external debt. Interest on debt outstanding has risen substantially in the last few years because of both the hardening of terms and the higher level of debt -- and is expected to remain a substantial charge on available resources (3.5 thousand million dollars in 1975 and 7 thousand million in 1980). In all, the build-up of external debt would decelerate in relation to export earnings -- 12 per cent per annum growth in debt in 1975-1980 as against 18 per cent in export earnings.

Balance-of-payments and growth prospects are, of course, highly sensitive to increases in petroleum and mineral production. Without substantial new oil production, countries that are now self-sufficient in oil, or nearly so, would have to step up their imports considerably. Moreover, in most countries other than the petroleum exporters, increased exports of mineral products will be fundamental for the maintenance of the growth momentum achieved in the past decade. This is true, for example, for Peru and Colombia

(phosphate, coal, nickel, copper, and petrochemical developments).
These projects will require substantial external capital
investments, many of which will not bear fruit until well into the
eighties. In Brazil both major agricultural export increases
(e.g., soya beans) and mineral exports (e.g., iron ore) are key
elements in the export growth scenario. Besides Brazil,
agricultural exports will play a key role in Argentina, Uruguay,
Paraguay, and Colombia. Mineral and agricultural products are
essential in supplementing the potential growth of manufactured
exports.

The projections present one possible scenario for the
medium-term growth of the major Latin American countries. They
should definitely not be regarded as a forecast, and, as will be
clear from the discussion in the subsequent sub-sections, several
comments should be made on them which can be briefly summarized as
follows:

(i) The real growth rate for total exports -- 9 per cent or
more per annum in 1978-1980 -- is well above the performance in
1971-1973 (when the average was 5.6 per cent). This improvement is
related primarily to exports of staples, both agricultural and
mineral, in an environment of marginally improving terms of trade;

(ii) Manufactured export growth is projected at what must be
regarded as a moderate level (averaging 12.8 per cent for 1978-1980
in real terms). The rate of growth of imports in the most
important market for Latin American exports, the OECD countries,
would reach 15 per cent, assuming a GDP growth rate of 5 per cent
and an income-elasticity of 3. Latin American manufactured exports
would exceed the 15 per cent growth rate if they continued to
increase their share in total OECD imports, mainly by displacing
supplies from such developed countries as Italy and Japan, an
achievement which would exempt Latin American exports from being
affected by import restrictions in industrial countries;

(iii) Vigorous export promotion policies would require that
countries, in adjusting their imports, should refrain from direct
controls and maintain a flexible, 'realistic' exchange rate policy,
and confine import substitution to economically justifiable
projects. Such policies need not imply higher import levels than
those envisaged in table 1, but the attainment of high growth rates
for manufactured exports could easily entail levels of imports
above those envisaged in the projections;

(iv) It is conceivable therefore that the
growth-cum-adjustment policies would result in higher levels of
both exports and imports. In these circumstances the resource
gap -- and hence the accumulation of new debt -- could continue to
decline progressively in the late seventies. At the same time, GDP
growth would come closer to the 8 per cent rate which is more
compatible with the creation of sufficient employment opportunities
than the 7 per cent rate envisaged for 1980 in table 1.

(b) External factors determining export growth

Crucial external factors are GDP growth rates in customer countries, income-elasticities of demand for imports in these countries, liberalization of import tariffs and restrictions, and shares of less developed countries' (LDCs') products in importing markets.

Given the uncertainties surrounding any forecast dependent on as many variables as affect LDC exports, and the poor record of most past projections and forecasts, it is futile to claim precision for the projections underlying table 1. Certain identifiable changes in the major factors pinpoint several of the policy features of interest to LDC export growth.

Official projections suggest that the growth of industrial markets in the late seventies would be about the same as the favourable 1971-1973 record.[9] Yet one can have doubts as to the realism of these projections for planning industrial export policies. The industrial countries are still suffering from higher unemployment and inflation rates than they experienced in the early seventies. While inflation at present is lower than in the previous 12 months, concern with reducing it further continues to be a central element in the policies of major industrial countries. This concern can hardly be considered a passing phenomenon, as the persistence of inflation may, in fact, be influenced by deep-seated structural, institutional and social factors. In such an environment, attempts to hold back inflation may dampen growth performance.

Even at a somewhat reduced rate of expansion the OECD market would remain a major growth factor for Latin American exports, because of its large size and the relatively high income-elasticity of imports.[10]

Concern with unemployment is bound to make industrial countries more sensitive to increases in imports of labour-intensive products as well as of other products where imports offer severe competition to existing domestic industries, even if the demonstrable employment effects of further import liberalization are small. This may be particularly relevant for the products whose exports grew most rapidly in 1967-1973, and in which market shares have increased substantially (viz, clothing, textiles, wood and leather products, electrical machinery[11]). A relatively small group of products (clothing, textiles and electrical machinery) alone make up close to one-half of total LDC manufactured exports; for these products, import market shares in the major customer countries (United States and Japan) can no longer be regarded as small. On the other hand, a more basic consideration is the share of LDC imports in the total market of the developed countries. These total market shares are still very modest for the majority of products, although for some of the most rapidly growing LDC export products they have increased in the last decade.[12] Moreover, LDC exports have progressively displaced imports from developed countries in a dynamic process of adaptation to shifting comparative advantage. Total market shares of LDCs are as yet negligible for non-electrical machinery and other capital goods -- products which could form the spearhead of the new export growth phase of key LDCs.[13]

In the sixties and early seventies, LDC exports benefited considerably from the Kennedy Round of liberalization of import tariffs and restrictions.[14] In the future the effects of further trade liberalization may well be slower, in particular, in those categories in which LDC exports in the past 10 years enjoyed the most spectacular growth. On the other hand, to the extent that they displace imports from industrial countries, Latin American exports will not suffer from the effects of import restrictions. Cline and Associates, in a Brookings Institution study, conclude that the present Tokyo Round may result in 60 per cent cuts in tariffs and non-tariff agricultural trade barriers which would probably increase exports of the developing countries 2.5 by thousand million and 0.5 thousand million dollars, respectively (in 1974 values), raising their annual non-oil export earnings by somewhat more than 3 per cent. Although politically unlikely, a similar liberalization of textiles would add another 2.3 thousand million dollars in export gains, raising the total gains from import liberalization to approximately 6 per cent of non-oil exports.[15]

A 3-6 per cent effect -- and 3 per cent would seem more certain than 6 per cent -- is only a fraction of the year-to-year total export increase projected for the major Latin American countries in table 1. On the other hand, the liberalization effect, excluding textiles, computed by Cline and Associates, is equivalent to one entire year's growth (12 per cent) as projected for total LDC manufactured exports. Absence of renewed import restriction on the part of industrial countries in the 1974-1975 recession augurs well for the continuance of relatively liberal import policies.

The major conclusions which emerge are: (i) continuing manufactured export growth need not be significantly slowed down by restrictive policies in the industrial countries; and (ii) dynamic growth of manufactured exports will need to be accompanied by continuing diversification to incorporate new items -- especially those in which even the major LDCs (Brazil, Korea, Taiwan) are still in the early stages of development.[16] These new exports -- capital goods, nonelectrical machinery and other technologically more complicated products -- will necessitate the opening-up of new lines of production, both for import substitution and for export. Once the LDCs manage to enter the markets for these new products, the potential for further growth is very substantial. Given their present industrial structure, several LDCs should b able to embark upon these new production lines -- Brazil and Korea are good examples of countries already preparing themselves for this new phase.

c) Domestic Factors

    The favourable turn in the trade and exchange policies of Brazil and Colombia initiated in 1968 has since been followed by similar action on the part of Argentina, Chile and Uruguay. Mexico also introduced export incentive measures. Will these policies continue in the face of changing external conditions? On the one hand, since these conditions may, in some respects, be less favourable to export growth than they were in the early seventies, and since competition among LDCs can be expected to intensify in several product lines, export industries in LDCs will press for the continuation of outward-looking policies. They will be supported by those concerned with overall growth and creditworthiness. Without clear continuity in policies, export industries will hesitate to make the substantial investments needs to maintain the forward momentum of the past decade.[17]

    On the other hand, the changes in external environment may exert pressures on the maintenance of outward-looking policies, especially flexible exchange rates, in various ways. The control of inflation has become a much more difficult task than in the sixties and early seventies. In the wake of the 1974-1975 recession most Latin American countries will reduce their balance-of-payments deficits, in part because the net inflow of external capital is bound to recede. Hence, the balance of payments will not exert the same contractive effect as it has in the last two years. At the same time, prospects are that external inflation -- the rate at which import prices, especially for capital goods, are rising -- will proceed at 5-10 per cent per year.

    In this environment -- and most Latin American countries have themselves inflation rates of 20 per cent or more -- continued exchange rate flexibility is the cornerstone of a successful export policy. but this flexibility cannot be taken for granted. When the government encounters increasing difficulties in containing inflation, and external factors exert an inflationary pressure, the exchange rate adjustments themselves may come to be regarded as part of the forces feeding into the process of continued price inflation. In this respect various exchange rate adjustments -- mini-devaluations, crawling-peg, managed free rates -- have the same disadvantages as universal indexing. Although they are necessary as a defence against the ill effects of (accelerating) inflation on the balance of payments, fitting them into a programme of containing or reducing inflation will cause steady strain. A commitment to maintain and improve the competitiveness of industry -- and its integration into world markets -- is needed to ensure the continuance of exchange rate flexibility.

    The adjustments to the changes in the external environment are putting flexible exchange rate policies under pressure in several other ways.

    Reductions in imports have, in some countries, been achieved through increases in direct restrictions, heavier deposit requirements or higher tariffs. The import cost increases effected outside the exchange rate system indirectly put exports at a disadvantage (e.g., in the case of Brazil).

Recovery of major export commodity prices (e.g., those of coffee and copper) will make the overall balance-of-payments case for rate adjustments less apparent. Yet given high domestic inflation rates, adjustments continue to be necessary if manufactured exports are to be competitive.

Greater emphasis on resource-based export developments may divert attention from the need for exchange rate flexibility. The economic case for the mineral and other resource-based export projects has been strengthened by external price changes and, in the case of oil importers, by the greater foreign exchange requirements associated with the higher cost of oil. These projects are less dependent on domestic labour and input costs -- in effect they have more of an 'enclave' nature -- and hence, the case in favour of exchange rate flexibility seems less evident than it is for manufactured exports.

The next phase of industrialization -- and in fact also of export diversification -- in certain countries, e.g., Brazil, Argentina and Mexico, may involve substantial investment in capital goods industries and other technologically more complicated products. Initially these industries may be primarily oriented toward the domestic market, and they may therefore be less concerned with the continuation of present export-oriented policies.

(d) Defence Against Recession: How Stable is the Growth Path?

The growth profile given in table 1 does not envisage fluctuations in export demand, prices and volumes. The 1973 oil crisis and the ensuing 1974-1975 recession brought major changes in export prospects, price structures, creditworthiness and investment strategies. While Latin America was in a strong position to make the necessary adjustments, and is now resuming a more vigorous growth trend, it may not be so well fortified to face another recession should one strike in the next 3-5 years. Even after the recovery envisaged in the next few years, the countries represented in table 1 would, in combination, be in a weaker position than they were in 1973:

(i) External debt service would be higher in relation to exports (and the year-to-year increases in exports), and hence countries would be less able to obtain private compensatory financing;

(ii) Imports would be lower in relation to GDP and hence less 'compressible', i.e., import reductions might more quickly affect growth;

(iii) Reserves might be lower in relation to imports.

Clearly, if growth rates were to exceed the levels envisaged in table 1, Latin America would be in a stronger position to withstand the adverse impact of external recessions. Continued vigorous growth and internal diversification are the most essential ways of combating external fluctuations. At the same time, closer linkage with the more rapidly growing customer markets will help to mitigate the effects of recessions. Normally, one would expect that faster growth will make it easier to cope with external fluctuations. Trade with more rapidly growing countries may be subject to severe reductions or decelerations than trade with slower-growing groupings subject to recessions. It has already been observed that the OECD market will continue to be a major factor in the export growth of Latin America, particularly if the region continues to replace imports from other industrial countries. On the present world scene it would seem that OPEC and the Latin American region itself are among the more rapidly growing groups and hence should be important export markets. The next section explores to what extent regional trade can contribute to the growth and stability of Latin American exports. This paper leaves aside the question of expanding trade with the non-Latin OPEC countries.

IV. INTRA-REGIONAL EXPORTS

The regional arrangements -- LAFTA, the Central American Common Market, the Caribbean Free Trade Association and the Andean Group -- have attracted a great deal of attention over the years. The first two of these, at least, exerted considerable influence in the sixties. The liberalization measures of the Andean Group, however, did have an initial impact in the early seventies: but further encouragement of trade -- and investment -- must await the resolution of crucial issues in the treatment of foreign investment, and agreements on the level of the common external tariff and regional industrial programming. The Andean Group will have to find common ground, in the interest of all, among the divergent economic philosophies of its members. The prospects are that progress will be slow at best -- and that it will need to be encouraged by a shared political concern. Yet, even if slow, it could make, eventually, a significant contribution to the development of its members. Only in combination can they begin to form a market of sufficient use for the technologically more complicated industries which constitute the cornerstone of the next major phase of LDC export development.[18]

With growth rates for Latin America projected some 40-50 per cent above those for the OECD, exports to the region should necessarily assume a special place in any country's strategy. What has happened in respect of intra-regional exports, especially of manufactured goods, and what can realistically be done to encourage them?

Table 3

LAFTA, ARGENTINA, BRAZIL, COLOMBIA AND MEXICO: DIRECTION OF MANUFACTURED EXPORTS, 1968 AND 1973

SITC (5-8)-68		1968			
	LAFTA (%)	Argentina (%)	Brazil (%)	Colombia (%)	Mexico (%)
World total	100.00	100.00	100.00	100.00	100.00
I. To developed economics	56.0	45.8	48.5	49.7	72.3
U.S.A.	38.2	25.7	27.3	26.4	62.7
Western Europe [a]	14.2	18.3	17.9	18.1	6.9
Other Developed Economies [b]	3.6	1.8	3.3	5.2	2.7
II. To developing economies	42.2	50.9	50.4	49.8	27.5
LAFTA [c]	35.7	47.3	45.6	28.0	18.3
– Andean Group [d]	–	23.9	8.8	19.9	11.5
CACM [e]	–	0.3	–	4.4	5.0
Caribbean area [f]	–	0.1	–	–	–
Other developing economies [g]	6.5[h]	3.2	4.8[h]	17.4[i]	4.2[i]
III. Centrally planned economies [j]	1.3	3.4	1.1	0.5	0.2

Source: U.N. Commodity Trade Statistics (1968-1973).
UNCTAD International Trade & Development Statistics, 1976.

[a]Mainly EEC and EFTA countries.
[b]Includes Canada, Japan, Israel, Australia, New Zealand and other developed economies of Asia and Africa.
[c]Latin American Free Trade Association: Argentina, Bolivia, Brazil, Chile, Colombia, Ecuador, Mexico, Paraguay, Peru, Uruguay, Venezuela.

Table 3

LAFTA, ARGENTINA, BRAZIL, COLOMBIA AND MEXICO: DIRECTION OF MANUFACTURED EXPORTS, 1968 AND 1973

SITC (5-8)-68	1973				
	LAFTA (%) of world total	Argentina (%) of world total	Brazil (%) of world total	Colombia (%) of world total	Mexico (%) of world total
World total	100.00	100.00	100.00	100.00	100.00
I. *To developed economies*	59.8	37.6	63.0	59.7	80.3
U.S.A.	36.0	17.3	25.9	27.3	66.9
Western Europe [a]	16.7	15.8	25.8	19.9	8.9
Other Developed Economies [b]	6.8	4.5	11.3	12.5	4.5
II. *To developing economies*	36.7	57.9	34.9	39.9	19.2
LAFTA [c]	26.8	53.3	25.9	22.2	11.4
— Andean Group [d]	—	26.3	11.4	18.3	7.0
CACM [e]	—	1.0	0.7	3.7	3.9
Caribbean area [f]	—	0.2	0.6	4.1	1.3
Other developing economies [g]	9.6 [h]	3.4	7.7	9.9	2.6
III. *Centrally planned economies* [j]	2.6	4.5	2.1	0.4	0.5

[d]Andean Group: Bolivia, Chile, Colombia, Ecuador, Peru, Venezuela.
[e]Central American Common Market: Costa Rica, El Salvador, Guatemala, Honduras, Nicaragua.
[f]Caribbean: Antigua, Bahamas, Barbados, Dominican Republic, Haiti, Jamaica, Netherlands Antilles, Trinidad and Tobago, etc.
[g]All developing economies of Asia, Africa, Europe and Oceania.
[h]Includes CACM and the Caribbean.
[i] Includes the Caribbean.
[j] Includes Socialist countries of Eastern Europe and Asia.

(a) Regional Export Trends 1968-1973

While exports of manufactured goods to all destinations, as well as exports to the region, increased rapidly, the latter generally tended to lag behind those to industrial countries. Hence, while in 1962-1968 Latin American intra-regional exports grew more rapidly than exports to all destinations, the situation was reversed in 1968-1973:

Latin American Manufactured Exports[19]
(Annual Growth rates)

	To All Destinations	To Latin America
1962-67	31.9	34.1
1967-68	21.2	22.7
1968-73	39.8	32.0

The percentage of Latin American manufactured exports that went to LAFTA tended to shrink in 1968-1973; for LAFTA exports in the aggregate, it declined from 35.7 per cent in 1968 to 26.8 per cent in 1973.[20] From the data presented, it appears that the drop in LAFTA shares during this period occurred in the exports pertaining to the major industrial commodity categories, the main exception being exports of chemicals.[21]

(i) Brasil's manufactured exports grew most rapidly (52.2 per cent average annual growth in current dollars compared with 39.8 per cent for total LAFTA exports), while the proportions it exported to LAFTA fell most (by 43.2 per cent compared with 24.9 per cent for total LAFTA manufactured exports)[22] (see table 2);

(ii) For the three largest countries, which also have relatively more developed industrial structures (Argentina, Brazil and Mexico), exports of machinery and automotive equipment grew relatively faster than other sub-groups, with the exception of 'miscellaneous' exports from Brazil and Colombia;

(iii) For the machinery and automotive equipment group, and for miscellaneous products, the faster was the growth of exports to all destinations, the sharper tended to be the decline in the shares going to LAFTA.

There are two noteworthy exceptions where the proportions exported to the region increased: Brazilian exports of motor vehicles (the LAFTA share increased from 61.8 per cent in 1968 to 87.1 per cent in 1973), and Colombian exports of machinery and transport equipment to LAFTA and to the Andean Group (the LAFTA share increasing from 55.7 per cent to 62.7 per cent). The proportion of Colombia's non-coffee exports (agricultural and manufactured) destined to the Andean Group also rose from 11.6 per cent to 15.2 per cent.[23]

As can be expected, intra-regional trade is most important where location and geography favour trade with neighbouring countries. About one-half of Argentina's manufactured exports goes to LAFTA -- and this share even increased in the period for all manufactures and for three of the four sub-groups.[24] On the other hand, the proportion of Mexican exports going to LAFTA is small, and it declined from 18 per cent to 11 per cent.

(b)   What Prospects for the Future?

Even after noting the exceptions, and they are important, the conclusion remains that the pull of trade with an increasingly integrated world market was stronger than the pull exerted by demand within the region. Perhaps one should say that given the dynamic increase in manufactured exports to the industrial countries, it is amazing that intra-regional exports performed as well as they did. It is possible that in the two recession years, 1974 and 1975, the shares of exports going to LAFTA increased somewhat, as demand in the region suffered declines less steep than those in the industrial countries. Nevertheless, over the next several years the forces pulling Latin American into a broader world market are likely to remain strong, especially if the relatively more developed Latin American countries succeed in entering industrial country markets for machinery and other technologically more complicated products. Interdependence with the industrial countries will also be enhanced by the development of resource-based exports, which, as has been noted, are expected to be important for certain countries (e.g., Peru and Colombia.)[25]

Given the close interdependence with the rest of the world, there is clear need for adequate compensatory financing mechanisms to help offset the effects of external fluctuations and recessions. These mechanisms will make it possible to develop export production along the most economic lines -- and without undue subsidization burdens or intra-regional protection. Yet, given the imperfections which are likely to remain in any system of compensatory arrangements, it would seem desirable that regional export measures supplement the extra-regional forces which have exerted themselves strongly since the late sixties. These measures must necessarily be different in nature in different countries, allowing for considerable variations in the importance of exports to the region. In 1973, Argentina exported 56 per cent of its manufactured goods to LAFTA and Central America, compared with a corresponding figure of 15 per cent for Mexico.

The development of exports will necessarily have to exploit the considerable differences in natural endowments existing among some countries. Agricultural and food exports may, therefore, be at least as important as manufactured exports in increasing intra-regional trade, as is evident from the experience of Colombia, which significantly enlarged its percentage of non-coffee agricultural exports to the Andean sub-region. Once again, this point stresses the importance of adopting incentive measures in relation to a broad range of items, both agricultural commodities and manufactures.

A further measure needed to boost intra-regional exports is a strengthening of the complementarity of export production. This will call for close sub-regional co-operation in the location of production of intermediate goods, machinery and transport equipment, especially among the middle-sized countries. Hence special importance attaches to the efforts at co-ordination of investment in certain key industries within the Andean sub-region. Assuming it is carried out without excessive intra-regional protection, industrial co-ordination of this kind may, at least over the longer term, make an important contribution to export development. To be successful, this type of industrial co-operation will require direct assistance from national governments and international finance, both public and private, in addition to receiving the necessary price incentives.

NOTES

[1]Paper prepared for the Seminar on Export Promotion Policies held under the joint sponsorship of CEPAL, the International Bank for Reconstruction and Development (IBRD) and the United Nations Development Programme (UNDP), at Santiago, Chile, 5 to 7 November 1976. The views expressed are not necessarily those of the World Bank, of which the author is a staff member.

In revising an earlier version of this paper the author benefited from comments formulated at the Seminar, especially those made by Dr. Raul Prebisch, Dragoslav Avramovic and Bela Balassa. Mr. Steven Foley and Mr. Guillermo Marmol provided research assistance and Mrs. Michaela H. Rubin editorial assistance.

[2]Argentina, Bolivia, Brazil, Chile, Colombia, Dominican Republic, Guatemala, Jamaica, Mexico and Peru.

[3]Latin American Free-Trade Association: Argentina, Bolivia, Brazil, Chile, Colombia, Ecuador, Mexico, Paraguay, Peru, Uruguay and Venezuela.

[4]'Exchange rate flexibility' in this paper means a policy of adjusting exchange rates, frequently if necessary, to the pace of domestic inflation, maintaining as a minimum the real purchasing power parity and permitting the exchange rate to play a central role in resource allocation. (Generally characterized by Phase IV of the National Bureau of Economic Research (NBER) project: see Jagdish N. Bhagwati and Anne O. Krueger, "Exchange control, liberalization and economic development", American Economic Review, Vol. LXIII, No. 2, May 1973). Brazil is one of several countries which relied on a mixture of exchange rate, fiscal and

credit measures to stimulate exports. "When we incorporate our measure of the incentives into the discussion of the evolution of the real exchange rate for manufactured exports over time, we see that the various incentive instruments have more than offset any decline in the real exchange rate since late 1964 . . . While exchange rate policy since 1968 has been used to stabilize real exporter remuneration, fiscal policy has been the instrument by which such remuneration has been increased." (William G. Tyler, Manufactured Export Expansion and Industrialization in Brazil, Tuebingen, 1976, p. 222.

[5]See G. K. Helleiner, "Manufactured exports from less developed countries and multinational firms", The Economic Journal, Vol. 83, No. 329, March 1973. Tyler, (op. cit., page 148) states that multinational firms accounted for 43 per cent of all manufactured exports of Brazil in 1969. Foreign firms were most important for the machinery and transport equipment category, in which they undertook 76 per cent of all 1969 exports.

[6]The figures in this sentence and in the previous one are for a group of 18 countries: Argentina, Bolivia, Brazil, Chile, Colombia, Costa Rica, Dominican Republic, El Salvador, Guatemala, Guyana, Honduras, Jamaica, Mexico, Nicaragua, Panama, Paraguay, Peru and Uruguay. The 1971-1974 data for the 10-country group in table 1 would show increases of 29.5 per cent per annum in exports and 29.0 per cent in external debt.

[7]These percentages are for a group of 5 countries: Brazil, Chile, Colombia, Mexico and Peru.

[8]Including, among others, cocoa butter (20 per cent), soybean oil (31 per cent), castor oil (31 per cent), pig iron (24 per cent), and wood pulp (27 per cent).

[9]The growth rates of the recovery years, 1976 and 1977, are most likely to turn out higher than those of the recession years, 1974 and 1975. For the intermediate-term outlook a comparison between 1978-1980 and 1971-1973 is more meaningful. For these years the actual figures and those projected by OECD are:

	1971-1973	1978-1980	1981-1985
United States	4.3	4.8	4.6
Japan	8.7	6.8	6.4
Western Europe	4.2	4.8	4.6
OECD total	5.1	5.1	4.9

[10]Based on an analysis of data of manufactured exports from Hong Kong and on studies of the United States and West German markets by M. E. Kreinin and Hans H. Glismann). Donges nd Riedel point to an income-elasticity of about 3. (See Jeurgen B. Donges and James Riedel. The Expansion of Manufactured Exports in Developing Countries: An Empirical Assessment of Supply and

Demand Issues, Kiel Institute of World Economics, Working Paper No. 49, June 1976, pp. 38-39.)

[11]In the United States import market LDC shares have increased significantly for several commodities:

	1967	1974
Clothing	40	74
Travel goods and handbags	33	68
Wood and cork manufactures	38	55
Electrical machinery	10	45
Textiles	40	45
Leather and leather products	24	43

(See Donald B. Keesing and Phi Anh Plesch, "Industrial Countries' Manufactured Imports from Develpoing Countries", IBRD (mimeographed text), May 5, 1976, table 6.)

[12]LAFTA's manufactured exports to the developed countries amounted to 2 thousand million dollars in 1973, compared with a total market for manufactured goods in the developed countries of close to 2 billion dollars ($2,000,000,000,000).

[13]The relatively small total market shares of LDCs and the role of country substitution (imports from LDCs displacing those from developed countries) are emphasized in Juergen B. Donges and James Riedel, op. cit.

[14]Cf. J. M. Finger, "Effects of the Kennedy Round tariff concessions", The Economic Journal, Vol. 86, No. 341, March 1976. This article also points out that the success of manufactured exports from LDCs resulting from the tariff cuts suggests that LDCs benefit from general (most-favoured-nation) tariff reductions, and that a system of general preferences may not be to their advantage in the long run. This conclusion is also stated in the Brookings Institution study quoted below.

[15]William R. Cline, Noboru Kawanabe, T.O.M. Kransjo and Thomas Williams, Trade, welfare and employment: Effects of multilateral trade negotiations in the Tokyo Round, Brookings Institution draft, chapter 7, "Trade negotiations and the less-developed countries".

[16]The importance of flexibility in exports is stressed by Hollis B. Chenery in "The Structuralist Approach to Development Policy", The American Economic Review, Vol. 6, No. 2, May 1975, page 314.

[17]Outward-looking policies are 'good' for export growth but not necessarily for other objectives, e.g., increasing the lowest incomes and improving income distribution. The consequences of outward-looking policies for employment and real wages are not discussed here. Some of the different views on these policies are mentioned in P. P. Streeten, "Trade strategies for

development: Some themes for the seventies", World Development, June 1973.

[18]The difficult problems and issues confronting the smaller economies of Central America and the Carribbean are not considered in this paper. Questions of capital transfers to small countries are discussed in Barend A. de Vries, "Development aid to small countries", in Percy Selwyn (ed.), Development Policy in Small Countries, London, Croom Held, Ltd., and Sussex, Institute of Development Studies, 1975.

[19]Data for 1962-1967 and 1967-1968 from Hollis B. Chenery and Helen Hughes, "Industrialization and trade trends: Some issues for the 1970s", in Helen Hughes (ed.), Prospects for Partnership, Industrialization and Trade Policies in the 1970's, IBRD and the Johns Hopkins University Press, 1973, tables 1-5. Data for 1968-1973 for LAFTA countries only: table 2 in the present article and Annex table 1.

[20]Table 2 and Annex tables 1 to 6 give data for all manufactured exports and major SITC sub-groups for LAFTA as a whole, Argentina, Brazil, Colombia and Mexico. Annex table 5 presents data on Colombian exports to the Andean sub-region. The direction of manufactured exports is shown for LAFTA and for Argentina, Brazil, Colombia and Mexico in table 3.

[21]Chemicals make up the smallest of the 4 sub-groups studies -- accounting for 1.6 per cent of total exports in 1968 and 2.0 per cent in 1973. LDC exports of chemicals to industrial countries tended to lag behind other LDC manufactured exports: imports of chemicals of fifteen industrial countries from LDCs showed an increase of 15.4 per cent per annum in 1967-1973 as against 30.0 per cent for all manufactures. Similarly, the share of United States imports of chemicals and compounds from LDCs declined from 31 per cent in 1967 to 19 per cent in 1973 and 21 per cent in 1974, as against an increase for miscellaneous manufactures from 19.5 per cent in 1967 to 26.6 per cent in 1973, and 32.3 per cent in 1974 (see Keesing and Plesch, op. cit., tables 3 and 6).

[22]Tyler (op. cit., p. 270) also observes that LAFTA's importance as a determining force and stimulant of Brazilian manufactured exports has been curtailed since 1967.

[23]Of Colombia's exports to the Anden Group in 1974 only 10 per cent was covered by the liberalization programme (information from F. Thoumi, based on unpublished Incomex data).

[24]A closer inspection of Argentina's exports indicates that for several of the most rapidly growing items, the LAFTA share actually did decline -- as in the case of similar categories in the other countries -- e.g., paper and paper-board, textile yarn and thread, agricultural machinery and machines n.e.s., non-electrical. It is also worth while to note that even in Argentina the share of miscellaneous exports to LAFTA decreased

sharply (see Annex table 2).

[25]The integration of Latin America into the world economy is the special focus of <u>Latin America, A Broader World Role</u>, by Adalbert Krieger Vasena and Javier Pazos, London, 1973.

Annex

Table 1

EXPORTS FROM LAFTA COUNTRIES TO THE LAFTA REGION[a]

SITC classification	SITC code	Composition of exports to all destinations (millions of dollars)		Composition of exports to all destinations (%)	
		1968	1973	1968	1973
Total exports	0,1,2,3,4,5,6,7,8	10 390	22 150	100.00	100.00
I. Manufactured goods	5,6,7,8,-68	675	3 595	6.5	16.2
(1) Basic and miscellaneous manufactures	6,8,-68	380	2 080	3.7	9.4
(2) Chemicals	5	170	445	1.6	2.0
(3) Machinery and transport equipment	7	125	1 070	1.2	4.8
II. Non-manufactured goods	0,1,2,3,4,68	9 710	18 190	93.5	82.1
(1) Food items	0+1+22+4	3 890	8 600	37.4	38.8
(2) Agricultural raw materials	2-(22+27+28)	910	1 180	8.8	5.3
(3) Crude fertilizers and minerals, metalliferous ores and metal scrap	27+28	750	1 510	7.2	6.8
(4) Mineral fuels, lubricants and related materials	3	3 010	5 660	29.0	25.6
(5) Non-ferrous metals	68	1 150	1 240	11.1	5.6

Source: Based on U N Commodity Trade Statistics (1968-1973);
UNCTAD International Trade and Development Statistics (1976).

[a]LAFTA: Argentina, Bolivia, Brazil, Chile, Colombia, Ecuador, Mexico, Paraguay, Peru, Uruguay, Venezuela.

Table 1

EXPORTS FROM LAFTA COUNTRIES TO THE LAFTA REGION[a]

classification	Composition of exports to LAFTA (%)		Exports to LAFTA as percentage of total, by categories		Average annual growth of exports to LAFTA		Average annual growth of total exports	
	1968	1973	1968	1973	1968-1973	1970-1973	1968-1973	1970-1973
exports	100.00	100.00	9.7	10.8	19.0	23.1	16.4	20.5
Manufactured goods	24.0	40.1	35.7	26.8	32.0	31.6	39.8	43.3
(1) Basic and miscellaneous manufactures	12.0	17.6	32.2	20.4	28.2	28.3	40.5	44.8
(2) Chemicals	4.6	7.3	27.1	39.3	30.6	33.9	21.2	25.5
(3) Machinery and transport equipment	7.2	15.2	58.4	34.1	38.0	34.5	54.0	51.5
Non-manufactured goods	75.7	58.6	7.9	7.8	13.0	17.9	13.4	17.0
(1) Food items	37.1	29.5	9.6	8.3	13.6	19.6	17.2	20.1
(2) Agricultural raw materials	13.4	6.0	14.8	12.3	1.5	-1.3	5.3	9.5
(3) Crude fertilizers and metalliferous ores and scrap	1.2	2.0	1.6	3.1	31.3	20.5	15.0	11.8
(4) Mineral fuels, lubricants and related materials	16.3	16.8	5.5	7.2	19.7	37.8	13.5	22.7
(5) Non-ferrous metals	7.7	4.4	6.8	8.5	6.1	0.0	1.5	-1.1

EXPORTS FROM ARGENTINA TO LAFTA[a]

SITC classification	SITC code	Composition of exports to all destinations (thousands of dollars)		Composition of exports to all destinations (%)	
		1968	1973	1968	1973
Total exports	0,1,2,3,4,5,6,7,8,9	1 367 865	3 266 003	100.00	100.00
I. *Manufactured goods*	5+6+7+8-68	165 923	730 103	12.1	22.4
(1) Chemicals	5	49 929	94 496	3.7	2.9
(2) Basic manufactures, excluding non-ferrous metals	6-68	57 711	288 060	4.2	8.8
(a) Leather	611	17 155	97 551	1.3	3.0
(b) Paper and paperboard	641	660	11 200	0.1	0.3
(c) Textile yarn and thread	651	513	14 538	0.04	0.5
(d) Iron and steel shapes	673	14 285	71 582	1.0	2.2
(3) Machinery and transport equipment	7	35 842	254 944	2.6	7.8
(a) Agricultural machinery	712	2 357	21 832	0.2	0.7
(b) Office machines	714	11 690	32 274	0.9	1.0
(c) Machinery n.e.s., non-electrical	719	4 191	41 643	0.3	1.3
(d) Electrical machinery, n.e.s.	729	1 446	10 895	0.1	0.3
(e) Road motor vehicles	732	4 294	86 719	0.3	2.7
(4) Miscellaneous manufactured goods	8	22 441	92 603	1.6	2.8
(a) Clothing, not of fur	841	2 514	13 061	0.2	0.4
(b) Fur clothing, etc.	842	1 264	14 911	0.1	0.5
(c) Footwear	851	176	20 284	0.01	0.6
(d) Printed matter	892	15 251	24 373	1.1	0.8
II. *Residual*	0+1+2+3+4+68+9	1 201 942	2 535 900	87.9	77.6
(a) Meat, fresh, chilled	011	204 948	639 902	15.0	19.6
(b) Wheat, etc., unmilled	041	139 085	273 775	10.2	8.4
(c) Cereals, n.e.s., unmilled	045	45 687	200 488	3.3	6.1
(d) Sugar and honey	061	17 858	102 958	1.3	3.2
(e) Wool and animal hair	262	111 296	188 202	8.1	5.8

Source: Based on U N *Commodity Trade Statistics.*

[a]LAFTA: Argentina, Bolivia, Brazil, Chile, Colombia, Ecuador, Mexico, Paraguay, Peru, Uruguay, Venezuela.

EXPORTS FROM ARGENTINA TO LAFTA[a]

classification	Composition of exports to LAFTA (%)		Exports to LAFTA as percentage of total, by categories		Average annual growth of exports to LAFTA		Average annual growth of total exports	
	1968	1973	1968	1973	1968-1973	1970-1973	1968-1973	1970-1973
exports	100.00	100.00	24.7	24.4	18.7	29.5	19.0	22.5
Manufactured goods	23.2	48.8	47.3	53.3	37.7	34.0	34.5	43.7
Chemicals	5.2	6.0	35.5	50.7	22.0	20.5	13.6	19.6
Basic manufactures, excluding non-ferrous metals	5.9	13.7	34.7	38.0	40.5	43.1	38.0	49.3
(a) Leather	0.04	0.5	0.7	4.4	108.0	231.0	41.5	40.5
(b) Paper and paperboard	0.1	0.8	68.6	57.6	70.0	68.0	76.0	101.0
(c) Textile yarn and thread	0.05	0.5	31.8	25.4	86.7	61.2	95.0	138.0
(d) Iron and steel shapes	1.2	3.7	28.2	41.6	49.4	60.2	38.1	65.3
Machinery and transport equipment	7.5	24.8	71.0	77.4	50.5	59.0	48.0	45.5
(a) Agricultural machinery	0.7	2.4	96.1	86.8	53.0	53.5	58.0	60.6
(b) Office machines	1.4	2.2	40.3	53.4	29.6	17.7	22.5	16.4
(c) Machinery n.e.s, non-electrical	1.1	4.1	88.1	78.4	54.0	55.0	58.5	50.2
(d) Electrical machinery, n.e.s.	0.4	0.8	86.5	59.2	38.9	37.0	49.8	58.0
(e) Road motor vehicles	1.1	9.9	88.3	90.6	83.5	107.6	82.5	109.0
Miscellaneous manufactured goods	4.5	4.3	68.3	37.2	17.6	24.0	32.8	35.1
(a) Clothing, not of fur	–	0.1	–	3.4	–	26.5	39.0	49.0
(b) Fur clothing, etc.	–	–	–	–	–	–	63.0	8.3
(c) Footwear	–	–	–	0.6	–	–		
(d) Printed matter	3.7	2.5	81.5	81.3	9.8	17.4	9.9	17.6
Residual	76.8	51.2	21.6	16.1	9.7	18.5	16.1	18.5
(a) Meat, fresh, chilled	3.9	4.3	6.5	5.4	21.0	29.6	25.6	28.0
(b) Wheat, etc., unmilled	28.0	16.9	68.1	49.2	7.3	22.8	14.5	29.6
(c) Cereals, n.e.s., unmilled	0.7	3.6	5.0	14.2	65.5	70.0	34.3	24.5
(d) Sugar and honey	0.6	2.0	10.4	15.5	54.2	103.1	42.0	83.0
(e) Wool and animal hair	3.5	1.2	10.7	5.2	(2.0)	(11.0)	11.1	28.5

EXPORTS FROM BRAZIL TO LAFTA[a]

SITC classification	SITC code	Composition of exports to all destinations (thousands of dollars)		Composition of exports to all destinations (%)	
		1968	1973	1968	1973
Total exports	0,1,2,3,4,5,6,7,8,9	1 881 316	6 199 192	100.00	100.00
I. Manufactured exports	(5-8)-68	152 680	1 216 918	8.1	19.6
(1) Chemicals	5	27 052	109 726	1.4	1.8
(2) Basic manufactures, excluding non-ferrous metals	6-68	79 912	557 664	4.3	9.0
(3) Machinery and transport equipment	7	41 096	303 842	2.2	4.9
(a) Electrical and non-electrical machinery	71+72	37 321	219 472	2.0	3.5
(b) Road motor vehicles	732	972	61 687	0.1	1.0
(4) Miscellaneous manufactured goods	8	4 622	245 685	0.3	4.0
(a) Clothing	84	462	88 682	0.02	1.4
(b) Footwear	851	450	93 478	0.02	1.5
II. Other exports	(0-4)+9+68	1 728 636	4 982 274	91.9	80.4
(1) Food and live animals	0	1 212 595	3 053 096	64.5	49.2
(2) Beverages and tobacco	1	20 476	65 949	1.1	1.1
(3) Crude materials excluding fuels	2	431 010	1 453 806	22.9	23.5
(4) Mineral fuels, etc.	3	638	83 564	0.03	1.4
(5) Animal and vegetable oils and fats	4	51 881	194 278	2.8	3.1
(6) Goods not classified by kind	9	11 612	119 829	0.6	1.9
(7) Non-ferrous metals	68	421	11 804	0.02	0.2

Source: Based on U N Commodity Trade Statistics.
[a]LAFTA: Argentina, Bolivia, Brazil, Chile, Colombia, Ecuador, Mexico, Paraguay, Peru, Uruguay, Venezuela.

EXPORTS FROM BRAZIL TO LAFTA [a]

classification	Composition of exports to LAFTA (%)		Exports to LAFTA as percentage of total, by categories		Average annual growth of exports to LAFTA		Average annual growth of total exports	
	1968	1973	1968	1973	1968-1973	1970-1973	1968-1973	1970-1973
exports	100.00	100.00	10.3	9.0	23.5	22.5	27.0	31.5
Manufactured exports	36.1	56.6	45.6	25.9	35.2	30.2	52.2	49.8
Chemicals	2.0	4.7	14.1	24.1	47.3	45.0	32.3	41.5
Basic manufactures, excluding non-ferrous metals	18.2	18.5	44.1	18.5	23.9	15.9	47.8	39.8
Machinery and transport equipment	15.0	26.8	70.4	49.2	38.9	33.2	49.2	46.1
(a) Electrical and non-electrical machinery	14.6	18.1	75.7	46.1	29.0	20.2	42.5	38.7
(b) Road motor vehicles	0.3	8.4	61.8	87.1	138.8	112.4	129.2	86.6
Miscellaneous manufactured goods	0.9	6.5	37.0	14.8	85.0	94.0	111.2	120.8
(a) Clothing	–	3.2	–	20.2	–	197.3	186.2	208.8
(b) Footwear	–	0.1	–	0.5	–	–	190.7	124.4
Other exports	63.9	43.4	7.1	4.9	14.4	14.9	23.7	28.0
Food and live animals	31.6	16.6	5.0	3.0	8.8	8.2	20.2	24.4
Beverages and tobacco	0.5	1.3	4.9	10.7	47.5	60.1	26.3	24.2
Crude materials, excluding fuels	29.8	17.4	13.4	6.7	11.0	12.6	27.5	31.8
Mineral fuels, etc.	0.2	3.3	61.9	21.9	115.1	109.1	165.1	73.5
Animal and vegetable oils and fats	0.3	1.8	1.0	5.0	79.2	90.5	30.2	42.1
Goods not classified by kind	1.4	2.3	23.7	10.9	36.5	8.7	58.0	67.5
Non-ferrous metals	0.1	0.8	50.6	34.4	80.0	9.6	95.0	27.4

EXPORTS FROM COLOMBIA TO LAFTA[a]

SITC classification	SITC code	Composition of exports to all destinations (thousands of dollars)		Composition of exports to all destinations (%)	
		1968	1973	1968	1973
Total exports	0,1,2,3,4,5,6,7,8,9	558 278	1 175 512	100.00	100.00
Non-coffee exports	(0-9)-07	206 804	577 584	37.0	49.1
I. *Manufactured goods*	(5-8)-68	53 334	307 311	9.6	26.1
(1) Chemicals	5	8 621	35 647	1.5	3.0
(2) Basic manufactures, excluding non-ferrous metals	6-68	35 921	205 464	6.4	17.5
(a) Leather, dressed fur . . .	61	3 510	18 502	0.6	1.6
(b) Textile yarn, fabrics	65	9 304	54 250	1.7	4.6
(3) Machinery and transport equipment	7	4 166	17 719	0.8	1.5
(a) Machinery, electrical and non-electrical	71+72	3 907	14 903	0.7	1.3
(4) Miscellaneous manufactured goods	8	4 639	48 482	0.8	4.1
(a) Clothing	84	515	19 221	0.1	1.6
II. *Other exports*	(0-4)+9+68-07	153 470	270 273	27.4	23.0
(a) Meat and preparations	01	1 471	40 945	0.3	3.5
(b) Fish and preparations	03	3 195	10 685	0.6	0.9
(c) Cut flowers, foliage	292.7	277	8 415	0.1	0.7

Source: Based on U N *Commodity Trade Statistics.*

[a]LAFTA: Argentina, Bolivia, Brazil, Chile, Colombia, Ecuador, Mexico, Paraguay, Peru, Uruguay, Venezuela.

Annex

Table 4

EXPORTS FROM COLOMBIA TO LAFTA[a]

classification	Composition of exports to LAFTA (%)		Exports to LAFTA as percentage of total, by categories		Average annual growth of exports to LAFTA		Average annual growth of total exports	
	1968	1973	1968	1973	1968-1973	1970-1973	1968-1973	1970-1973
exports	100.00	100.00	6.1	9.5	27.0	6.7	16.1	17.6
	88.6	92.2	14.6	17.8	27.8	15.9	22.8	29.8
Manufactured goods	43.7	61.1	28.0	22.2	35.5	58.5	41.9	73.8
Chemicals	12.9	19.4	51.3	60.7	38.0	51.5	42.5	60.0
Basic manufactures, excluding non-ferrous metals	20.3	22.4	19.3	12.2	29.2	62.7	41.7	76.0
(a) Leather, dressed fur . . .	0.3	–	3.3	–	–	--	39.7	48.2
(b) Textile yarn, fabrics	3.4	3.6	12.4	7.5	28.8	70.0	42.3	62.0
Machinery and transport equipment	6.6	9.9	53.7	62.7	37.8	55.5	34.5	47.0
(a) Machinery, electrical and non-electrical	6.6	7.9	57.2	59.2	31.7	50.0	30.7	45.0
Miscellaneous manufactured goods	3.8	9.4	28.5	21.6	51.2	68.0	78.5	97.5
(a) Clothing	0.3	2.3	21.6	13.2	87.0		106.5	160.0
Other exports	44.9	31.1	10.0	12.7	17.8	(11.0)	12.0	9.4
(a) Meat and preparations	3.4	5.7	79.5	15.4	40.0	103.6	94.0	105.5
(b) Fish and preparations	–	–	–	–	–	–	27.2	30.3
(c) Cut flowers, foliage	–	–	–	–	–	–	97.5	105.0

366

Table 5

EXPORTS FROM COLOMBIA TO THE ANDEAN GROUP[a]

SITC classification	SITC code	Composition of exports to all destinations (thousands of dollars)		Composition of exports to all destinations (%)	
		1968	1973	1968	1973
Total exports	0,1,2,3,4,5,6,7,8,9	558 278	1 175 512	100.00	100.00
Non-coffee exports	(0-9)-07	206 804	577 584	37.0	49.1
I. Manufactured goods	(5-8)-68	53 334	307 311	9.6	26.1
(1) Chemicals	5	8 621	35 647	1.5	3.0
(2) Basic manufactures, excluding non-ferrous metals	6-68	35 921	205 464	6.4	17.5
(a) Leather, dressed fur ...	61	3 510	18 502	0.6	1.6
(b) Textile yarn, fabrics	65	9 304	54 250	1.7	4.6
(3) Machinery and transport equipment	7	4 166	17 719	0.8	1.5
(a) Machinery electrical and non-electrical	71+72	3 907	14 903	0.7	1.3
(4) Miscellaneous manufactured goods	8	4 639	48 482	0.8	4.1
(a) Clothing	84	515	19 221	0.1	1.6
II. Other exports	(0+4)+9+68-07	153 470	270 273	27.4	23.0
(a) Meat and preparations	01	1 471	40 945	0.3	3.5
(b) Fish and preparations	03	3 195	10 685	0.6	0.9
(c) Cut flowers, foliage	292.7	277	8 415	0.1	0.7

Source: Based on U N Commodity Trade Statistics (1968-1973).
[a]Andean Group: Bolivia, Chile, Colombia, Ecuador, Peru, Venezuela.

EXPORTS FROM COLOMBIA TO THE ANDEAN GROUP

classification	Composition of exports to the Andean Group (%)		Exports to the Andean Group as percentage of total by categories		Average annual growth of exports to the Andean Group		Average annual growth of total exports	
	1968	1973	1968	1973	1968-1973	1970-1973	1968-1973	1970-1973
exports	100.00	100.00	4.3	7.5	29.6	12.1	16.1	17.6
exports	99.5	99.8	11.6	15.2	29.6	12.4	22.8	29.8
Manufactured goods	44.2	63.8	19.9	18.3	39.5	56.7	41.9	73.8
Chemicals	13.4	17.6	37.2	43.4	36.9	38.2	42.5	60.0
Basic manufactures, excluding non-ferrous metals	17.7	25.5	11.8	10.9	39.5	75.7	41.7	76.0
(a) Leather, dressed fur . . .	–	–	–	–	–	–	39.7	48.2
(b) Textile yarn, fabrics	3.3	3.6	8.6	5.8	31.3	114.2	42.3	62.0
Machinery and transport equipment	8.7	11.5	50.1	57.0	37.1	52.5	34.5	47.0
(a) Machinery electrical and non-electrical	8.7	8.9	53.4	52.5	30.3	45.8	30.7	45.0
Miscellaneous manufactured goods	4.4	9.2	22.7	16.8	50.7	67.5	78.5	97.5
(a) Clothing	–	2.0	–	9.4	–	–	106.5	160.0
Other exports	55.3	36.0	8.7	11.7	19.0	(11.6)	12.0	9.4
(a) Meat and preparations	4.9	7.1	79.5	15.4	40.2	107.2	94.0	105.5
(b) Fish and preparations	–	–	–	–	–	–	27.2	30.3
(c) Cut flowers, foliage	–	–	–	–	–	–	97.5	105.0

EXPORTS FROM MEXICO TO LAFTA[a]

SITC classification	SITC code	Composition of exports to all destinations (thousands of dollars)		Composition of exports to all destinations (%)	
		1968	1973	1968	1973
Total exports	0,1,2,3,4,5.6,7,8,9	1 110 152	2 631 496	100.00	100.00
I. Manufactured goods	(5-8)-68	225 597	1 102 871	20.3	41.9
(1) Chemicals	5	68 516	168 973	6.2	6.4
(2) Basic manufactures, excluding non-ferrous metals	6-68	83 362	274 190	7.5	10.4
(a) Textile yarn and thread	651	15 375	67 349	1.4	2.6
(b) Cotton fabrics, woven	652	2 027	43 628	0.2	1.7
(c) Glassware	665	5 646	17 526	0.5	0.7
(3) Machinery and transport equipment	7	36 427	463 658	3.3	17.6
(a) Machinery non-electrical	71	19 798	199 477	1.8	7.6
(b) Electrical machinery	72	8 573	136 013	0.8	5.2
(c) Road motor vehicles	732	3 223	97 068	0.3	3.7
(4) Miscellaneous manufactured goods	8	37 301	196 050	3.4	7.5
(a) Clothing	841	4 648	67 144	0.4	2.6
II. Other exports	(0-4)+9+68	1 083 938	1 528 625	79.7	58.1
(a) Live animals	001	26 214	91 317	2.4	3.5
(b) Vegetables, etc., fresh, preserved	054	44 669	178 985	4.0	6.8
(c) Coffee	071	69 260	168 731	6.2	6.4
(d) Cotton	263	122 398	166 454	11.0	6.3
(e) Silver, platinum	681	73 125	186 336	6.6	7.1
(f) Copper	682	11 452	41 662	1.0	1.6

Source: Based on U N Commodity Trade Statistics.
[a]LAFTA: Argentina. Bolivia, Brazil, Chile, Colombia, Ecuador, Mexico, Paraguay, Peru, Uruguay, Venezuela.

EXPORTS FROM MEXICO TO LAFTA[a]

classification	Composition of exports to LAFTA (%)		Exports to LAFTA as percentage of total, by categories		Average annual growth of exports to LAFTA		Average annual growth of total exports	
	1968	1973	1968	1973	1968-1973	1970-1973	1968-1973	1970-1973
exports	100.00	100.00	5.6	6.6	22.6	23.2	18.8	29.8
Manufactured goods	66.0	72.4	18.3	11.4	24.9	21.5	37.3	41.2
Chemicals	23.1	24.4	21.1	25.0	24.0	24.6	19.8	19.9
Basic manufactures, excluding non-ferrous metals	12.6	7.5	9.5	4.7	10.5	5.4	26.8	37.1
(a) Textile yarn and thread	0.2	0.1	0.8	0.2	–	(30.0)	34.3	60.6
(b) Cotton fabrics, woven	–	–	–	–	–	–	84.2	116.6
(c) Glassware	0.8	0.3	9.0	3.4	–	(21.5)	25.3	30.2
Machinery and transport equipment	14.1	26.0	24.3	9.7	38.5	25.8	66.3	53.3
(a) Machinery non-electrical	7.6	16.2	23.9	14.0	42.8	15.9	58.5	59.6
(b) Electrical machinery	4.9	5.4	36.0	6.8	24.6	45.2	73.3	35.7
(c) Road motor vehicles	0.3	2.9	6.2	5.2	92.0	69.2	97.6	80.0
Miscellaneous manufactured goods	16.1	14.5	27.0	12.8	20.1	21.1	20.1	21.1
(a) Clothing	–	0.1	–	–	–	–	70.5	95.0
Other exports	32.7	27.4	2.3	3.1	18.4	28.2	11.5	23.5
(a) Live animals	0.2	–	0.4	–	–	–	28.3	43.5
(b) Vegetables, etc., fresh, preserved	0.8	2.4	1.1	2.3	58.2	150.5	32.0	50.7
(c) Coffee	–	0.3	–	0.3	–	–	19.5	31.4
(d) Cotton	7.9	7.9	4.0	8.2	22.9	36.9	6.3	26.0
(e) Silver, platinum	0.3	0.5	0.3	0.4	30.0	–	20.5	86.5
(f) Copper	1.4	1.8	7.6	7.7	29.7	33.6	29.4	59.4

DYNAMIC MANUFACTURED EXPORTS OF BRAZIL

(Thousands of dollars)

SITC	PRODUCT	1968	1973
897	Goldsmiths' and silversmiths' wares, including jewellery	594	10 631
892	Printed matter	–	11 356
851	Footwear	450	93 478
842	Fur, fur clothing, etc.	–	5 610
841	Clothing, not of fur	462	83 072
831	Travel goods, handbags	–	8 280
821	Furniture	502	10 297
732	Road motor-vehicles,	972	61 687
724	Telecommunications equipment	734	46 191
722	Electric power machinery, switchgear	913	11 337
717	Textile and leather machinery	2 542	14 616
714.2	Accounting machines and computers	833	4 960
712	Agricultural machinery	566	9 229
711.5	Internal combustion engines, other than for aircraft	111	8 645

Annex

Table 7

SITC	PRODUCT	1968	1973
673	Iron and steel shapes	2 682	19 185
671	Pig-iron	5 656	47 235
665	Glassware	–	2 076
661	Cement	267	3 536
656	Textile and other made-up articles, n.e.s.	1 116	21 589
654	Lace, ribbons, tulle, etc.	–	1 813
653	Woven textiles, non-cotton	7 301	42 586
652	Cotton fabrics, woven	1 831	53 946
651	Textile yarn and thread	2 727	97 522
641	Paper and paperboard	–	23 883
629	Rubber articles, n.e.s.	553	6 362
581	Plastic materials	318	5 991
561	Fertilizers, manufactured	–	2 279

DYNAMIC MANUFACTURED EXPORTS OF ARGENTINA

(Thousands of dollars)

SITC	PRODUCT	1968	1973
851	Footwear	176	20 284
842	Fur, fur clothing, etc.	1 264	14 911
841	Clothing, not of fur	2 514	13 061
732	Road motor-vehicles	4 294	86 719
719.9	Machine parts, accessories, n.e.s.	842	7 385
719.6	Non-electrical machines, n.e.s.	1 076	9 812
719.2	Pumps, centrifuges	593	11 540
718	Machines for special industries	662	16 342
714.2	Accounting machines, computers	5 302	19 483
712	Agricultural machinery	2 357	21 832
674	Iron or steel universals, plates, sheets	371	24 977
673	Iron and steel shapes	14 285	71 582
651	Textiles, yarn and thread	513	14 538
611	Leather	17 155	97 551

Table 9

DYNAMIC MANUFACTURED EXPORTS OF COLOMBIA

(Thousands of dollars)

SITC	PRODUCT	1968	1973
841	Clothing, not of fur	515	19 213
673	Iron and steel shapes	–	5 708
667	Pearls, precious and semi-precious stones	1 467	86 622
652	Cotton fabrics, woven	5 076	24 175
651	Textile yarn and thread	3 693	19 988
611	Leather	3 410	17 117
292	Cut flowers	277	8 415

DYNAMIC MANUFACTURED EXPORTS OF MEXICO

SITC	PRODUCT	1968	1973
714.2	Accounting machines, computers	396	29 330
711.5	Internal combustion engines, other than for aircraft	1 996	31 291
673	Iron and steel shapes	–	9 189
652.1	Grey woven cotton fabrics, unbleached, not mercerized	1 617	28 822
652.2	Woven cotton fabrics, bleached, dyed, mercerized, printed or otherwise finished	410	14 806
651.3	Grey cotton yarn (unbleached), not put up for retail sale	5 536	26 315
642	Articles of paper	1 127	10 260
631	Veneers, plywood, etc., n.e.s.	2 053	10 356
513.3	Inorganic acids	609	24 935

Annex
Table 10

DYNAMIC MANUFACTURED EXPORTS OF MEXICO

SITC	PRODUCT	1968	1973
897.1	Goldsmiths' and silversmiths' wares, including jewellery	1 783	12 408
894	Toys, sporting goods, etc.	2 889	24 464
891	Sound recorders and reproducers	2 115	13 505
862	Photographic and cinematographic supplies	–	7 790
841	Clothing, not of fur	4 648	67 144
734	Aircraft	1 492	23 218
732	Road motor-vehicles	3 223	97 068
724	Telecommunications equipment	3 771	83 912
722.2	Electrical apparatus for making and breaking or for protecting electrical circuits (switchgear, etc.)	2 178	33 479
719.9	Machine parts, accessories n.e.s.	12 124	109 302

PART II
STATISTICAL
INFORMATION
AND SOURCES

I. BIBLIOGRAPHY OF INFORMATION SOURCES

Main purpose of this section is to provide a current bibliography of data sources and statistical data for various indicators of international development, as they relate to international trade with special reference to the developing countries. An attempt is made to provide the reader with an overview of global trends, based on an analysis of the country data, as it is sometimes difficult to form any such general impression when faced with a general body of highly detailed data.

BIBLIOGRAPHY OF DATA SOURCES

AFRICAN STATISTICAL YEARBOOK, UN

Presents data arranged on a country basis for 44 African countries for the years 1965-1978. Available statistics for each country are presented in 48 tables: population; national accounts; agriculture, forestry, and fishing industry; transport and communications; foreign trade; prices; finance; and social statistics: education and medical facilities.

ASIAN INDUSTRIAL DEVELOPMENT NEWS, UN, Sales no. E.74.II.F.16

In four parts: (a) brief reports on the ninth session of the Asian Industrial Development Council and twenty-sixth session of the Committee on Industry and Natural Resources; (b) articles on multinationals and the transfer of know-how, acquisition of technology for manufacturing agro-equipment, fuller utilization of industrial capacity; (c) report of Asian Plan of Action on the Human Environment; and (d) statistical information on plywood, transformers, and transmission cables.

Banks, Arthur S., et al., eds.
ECONOMIC HANDBOOK OF THE WORLD: 1981. New York; London; Sydney
and Tokyo: McGraw-Hill Books for State University of New York
at Binghamton, Center for Social Analysis, 1981.

Descriptions, in alphabetical order, of all the world's independent
states and a small number of non-independent but economically
significant areas (such as Hong Kong). Data are current as of
1 July 1980 whenever possible. Summary statistics for each country
include: area, population, monetary unit, Gross National Product
per capita, international reserves (1979 year end), external
public debt, exports, imports, government revenue, government
expenditure, and consumer prices. Principal economic institutions,
financial institutions, and international memberships are listed
at the end of each description.

BULLETIN OF LABOUR STATISTICS. Quarterly, with supplement 8
times per year. Approx. 150 p.

Quarterly report, with supplements in intervening months, on
employment, unemployment, hours of work, wages, and consumer
prices, for 130-150 countries and territories. Covers total,
nonagricultural, and manufacturing employment; total unemployment
and rate; average nonagricultural and manufacturing hours of
work per week, and earnings per hour, day, week, or month; and
food and aggregate consumer price indexes.

COMPENDIUM OF SOCIAL STATISTICS, 1977. 1980, UN, Sales No. E-F.
80.XVII.6.

Contains a collection of statistical and other data aimed at
describing social conditions and social change in the world.
In four parts. Part 1 includes estimates and projections for
the world, macroregions, and regions. Part 2 comprises data
for countries or areas that represent key series describing social
conditions and social change. Part 3 consists of general
statistical series for countries or areas. Part 4 is devoted
to information for cities or urban agglomerations. Includes
a total of 151 tables, covering population, health, nutrition,
education, conditions of work, housing and environmental
conditions, etc. Provides an overall view of the world social
situation and future trends.

DEMOGRAPHIC YEARBOOK, 1978. (ST-ESA-STAT-SER.R-7) 1979, UN,
Sales No. E-F.79.XIII.I.

--Vol. 1. viii, 463 p. This volume contains the general tables
giving a world summary of basic demographic statistics, followed
by tables presenting statistics on the size distribution and
trends in population, natality, fetal mortality, infant and
maternal mortality, general mortality, nuptiality, and divorce.
Data are also shown by urban/rural residence in many of the tables.
--Vol. 2: Historical supplement.

DEVELOPMENT FORUM BUSINESS EDITION. DESI/DOP, UN, Palais des Nations, CH-1211 Geneva 10, Switzerland. 24 times a yr. 16 p.

A tabloid-size paper, published jointly by the United Nations Department of Information's Divison for Economic and Social Information and the World Bank. Presents articles on all aspects of the development work of the United Nations, with emphasis on specific development problems encountered by the business community. Contains notices referring to goods and works to be procured through international competitive bidding for projects assisted by the World Bank and the International Development Association (IDA). It also includes a Supplement of the World Bank, entitled "Monthly Operational Summary", and a similar supplement of the Inter-American Development Bank (IDB), once a month, which provide information about projects contemplated for financing by the World Bank and IDB, respectively.

DEVELOPMENT FORUM GENERAL EDITION

A tabloid-size paper, published jointly by the United Nations Department of Public Information's Division for Economic and Social Information and the World Bank, having as objective the effective mobilization of public opinion in support of a number of major causes to which the United Nations is committed. Presents articles reporting on the activities of various UN agencies concerned with development and social issues (health, education, nutrition, women in development). Includes a forum for nongovernmental organizations (NGO's) and book reviews.

DEVELOPMENT AND INTERNATIONAL ECONOMIC CO-OPERATION: LONG-TERM TRENDS IN ECONOMIC DEVELOPMENT. Report of the Secretary-General. Monograph. May 26, 1982.

Report analyzing world economic development trends, 1960's-81, with projections to 2000 based on the UN 1980 International Development Strategy, and on alternative low and medium economic growth assumptions. Presents data on GDP, foreign trade, investment, savings, income, population and labor force, housing, education, food and energy supply/demand, and other economic and social indicators.

DIRECTORY OF INTERNATIONAL STATISTICS: VOLUME 1. 1982 Series. Sales No. E.81.XVII.6

Vol. 1 of a 2-volume directory of international statistical time series compiled by 18 UN agencies and selected other IGO's. Lists statistical publications, and machine-readable data bases of economic and social statistics, by organization and detailed subject category. Also includes bibliography and descriptions of recurring publications, and technical descriptions of economic/social data bases.

VOLUME 2: INTERNATIONAL TABLES. Sales No. E.82.XVII.6, Vol. II

Presents analytical summary of major income and product accounts for approximately 160 countries, by country and world region.

ECONOMIC AND SOCIAL PROGRESS IN LATIN AMERICA: 1980-81 REPORT. 1981, IDB.

Provides a comprehensive survey of the Latin America economy since 1970, with particular emphasis on 1980 and 1981. Part One is a regional analysis of general economic trends, the external sector, the financing of development from internal and external sources, regional economic integration, and social development trends (women in the economic development of Latin America). Part Two contains country summaries of socioeconomic trends for 24 States members of IDB. Statistical appendix includes data on population, national accounts, public finance, balance of payments, primary commodity exports, external public debt, and hydrocarbons.

ECONOMIC AND SOCIAL SURVEY OF ASIA AND THE PACIFIC, 1977. The International Economic Crises and Developing Asia and the Pacific. 1978, UN, Sales No. E.78.II.F.1.

In two parts: (a) review of recent economic developments and emerging policy issues in the ESCAP region, 1976-1977; and (b) the impacts of the international economic crises of the first half of the 1970's upon selected developing economies in the ESCAP region and the market and policy response thereto. Topics discussed include: the food crisis; the breakdown of the international monetary system; fluctuations in the international market economy comprising the primary commodities export boom, the associated inflation and the subsequent recession, and, finally the sharp rise in the price of petroleum.

ECONOMIC AND SOCIAL SURVEY OF ASIA AND THE PACIFIC, 1979. Regional Development Strategy for the 1980's. 1981, UN, Sales No. E.80.II.F.1.

Analyzes recent economic and social development in the UN ESCAP region, as well as related international developments. Focuses on economic and social policy issues and broad development strategies. In two parts: (a) recent economic developments, 1978-1979, covering the second oil price shock economic performance of the developing countries of the ESCAP region, inflation, and external trade and payments; and (b) findings of a two-year study dealing with regional developmental strategies, covering economic growth, policies for full employment and equity, energy, technology, implementation systems, international trade, shipping, international resource transfers, and intraregional cooperation.

ECONOMIC SURVEY OF ASIA AND THE FAR EAST, 1973. 234 p. (also issued as Economic Bulletin for Asia and the Far East, vol. 24, no. 4), 1974, UN, Sales No. E.74.II.F.1.

Contains a general summary followed by Part One, which covers: education and employment--the nature of the problem; population, labor force and structure of employment and underemployment in the ECAFE [ESCAP] region; the role of location--assumptions underlying the education policies of developing countries in the ECAFE region; momentum and direction of expansion of education; structuring the flow of workers into the modern science of education for self employment--the traditional and informal sectors; and the search for new policies--a review of current thinking. Part Two covers: current economic developments--recent economic developments and emerging policy issues in the ECAFE region, 1972/73; and current economic developments and policies in 28 countries of the ECAFE region.

ECONOMIC SURVEY OF LATIN AMERICA. Series.

Series of preliminary annual reports analyzing recent economic trends in individual Latin American countries. Each report presents detailed economic indicators, including GDP by sector, agricultural and industrial production by commodity, foreign trade, public and private sector finances, and prices. Also includes selected data on employment and earnings.

THE ECONOMIST. THE WORLD IN FIGURES. Third edition. New York: Facts on File, Inc., 1980.

Compendium of figures on economic, demographic, and sociopolitical aspects of over 200 countries of the world. The first part is a world section with information on population, national income, production, energy, transportation, trade, tourism, and finance. The second part is organized by country (grouped by main region), containing statistics on location, land, climate, time, measurement systems, currency, people, resources, production, finance and external trade, and politics and the economy. The data, from many sources, cover through 1976. Country name and "special focus" indices.

FACTS OF THE WORLD BANK. Monthly (current issues).

A compilation of figures on World Bank lending, giving cumulative amounts and amounts for the current fiscal year of commitments by number of projects and by sector, as well as for each country by region. Also gives figures on sales of parts of Bank loans and IDA credits and on World Bank borrowings by currency of issue, original and outstanding amounts, and number of issues.

IMF SURVEY. Biweekly.

Biweekly report on international financial and economic conditions; IMF activities; selected topics relating to exchange rates, international reserves, and foreign trade; and economic performance of individual countries and world areas.

MAIN ECONOMIC INDICATORS: HISTORICAL STATISTICS, 1960-1979. 1980, OECD, Sales No. 2750 UU-31 80 20 3.

Bilingual: E-F. Replaces previous editions. Base year for all indicators is 1970. Arranged in chapters by country, the tables cover the period 1960 to 1979, and are followed by short notes describing some major characteristics of the series, and, where applicable, indicating breaks in continuity. Note: Supplements the monthly bulletin Main Economic Indicators.

MONTHLY BULLETIN OF STATISTICS. Monthly.

Monthly report presenting detailed economic data including production, prices, and trade; and summary population data; by country, with selected aggregates for world areas and economic groupings, or total world. Covers population size and vital statistics; employment; industrial production, including energy and major commodities; construction activity; internal and external trade; passenger and freight traffic; manufacturing wages; commodity and consumer prices; and money and banking. Each issue includes special tables, usually on topics covered on a regular basis but presenting data at different levels of aggregation and for different time periods. Special tables are described and indexed in IIS as they appear.

POPULATION AND VITAL STATISTICS REPORT. Quarterly.

Quarterly report on world population, births, total and infant deaths, and birth and death rates, by country and territorial possession, as of cover date. Also shows UN population estimates for total world and each world region.

QUARTERLY BULLETIN OF STATISTICS FOR ASIA AND THE PACIFIC. Quarterly.

Quarterly report presenting detailed monthly and quarterly data on social and economic indicators for 38 ESCAP member countries. Includes data on population; births and deaths; employment; agricultural and industrial production; construction; transportation; foreign trade quantity, value, and direction; prices; wages; and domestic and international financial activity.

1978 REPORT ON THE WORLD SOCIAL SITUATION. 1979, UN, Sales No. E.79.IV.1.

Deals with the global issues of population trends and employment; growth and distribution of income and private consumption; the production and distribution of social services; and changing social concerns. A supplement reviews the patterns of recent governmental expenditures for social services in developing countries, developed market economies, and centrally planned economies.

STATISTICAL INDICATORS FOR ASIA AND THE PACIFIC. Quarterly.

Quarterly report presenting selected economic and demographic indicators for 26 Asian and Pacific countries. Covers, for most countries, population size, birth and death rates, family planning methods, industrial and agricultural production, construction, transport, retail trade, foreign trade, prices, money supply, currency exchange rate, and GDP.

STATISTICAL YEARBOOK, 1979/80. 1981, UN, Sales No. E/F.81.XVII.1.

A comprehensive compendium of the most important internationally comparable data needed for the analysis of socioeconomic development at the world, regional and national levels. Includes tables (200) grouped in two sections: (a) world summary by regions (17 tables); and (b) remaining tables of country-by-country data, arranged in chapters: population; manpower; agriculture; forestry; fishing; industrial production; mining and quarrying; manufacturing; construction; development assistance; wholesale and retail trade; external trade; international tourism; transport; communications; national accounts; wages and prices; consumption; finance; energy; health; housing; science and technology; and culture. For this first time, this issue contains three new tables on industrial property: patents, industrial designs, and trademarks and service marks. Note: This issue is a special biennial edition, covering data through mid-1980, and in some cases for 1980 complete.

STATISTICAL YEARBOOK FOR ASIA AND THE PACIFIC, 1978. 1979, UN, Sales No. E-F.79.II.F.4.

Eleventh issue. Contains statistical indicators for the ESCAP region and statistics for period up to 1978 available at the end of 1978 for 34 countries and territories members of ESCAP, arranged by country, covering, where available: population; manpower; national accounts; agriculture, forestry, and fishing; industry; consumption; transport and communication; internal and external trade; wages, prices, and household expenditures; finance; and social statistics.

STATISTICAL YEARBOOK FOR LATIN AMERICA, 1979. 1981, UN, Sales No. E/S.80.II.G.4.

In two parts. Part 1 presents indicators of economic and social development in Latin America for 1960, 1965, 1970 and 1975-1978, including: population; demographic characteristics; employment and occupational structure; income distribution; living levels; consumption and nutrition; health; education; housing; global economic growth; agricultural activities; mining and energy resources; manufacturing; productivity; investment; saving; public financial resources; public expenditure; structure of exports and imports; intra-regional trade; transport services; tourist services; and external financing. Part 2 contains historical series in absolute figures for the years 1960, 1965 and 1970-1978 on population; national accounts; domestic prices; balance of payments; external indebtedness; external trade; natural resources and production of goods; infrastructure services; employment; and social conditions.

SURVEY OF ECONOMIC AND SOCIAL CONDITIONS IN AFRICA, 1980-81 AND OUTLOOK FOR 1981-82: SUMMARY

Examines growth in GDP, agricultural and industrial production, trade and balance of payments, resource flows, energy production/consumption, and selected other economic indicators, 1979-80, with outlook for 1981-82 and trends from 1960's.

TECHNICAL DATA SHEETS

Provides up-to-date information about projects as they are approved for World Bank and IDA financing. In addition to a description of the project, its total cost, and the amount of Bank financing, each technical data sheet describes the goods and services that must be provided for the project's implementation and gives the address of the project's implementing organization. On the average, 250 such sheets will be issued annually. Requests for sample copies are to be addressed to: Publications Distribution Unit, World Bank, 1818 H St., N.W., Washington, D.C. 20433, U.S.A.

UNESCO STATISTICAL YEARBOOK, 1978-79, 1266 p. 1980, UNESCO.

Composite: E/F/S (introductory texts). Presents statistical and other information for 206 countries on education; science and technology; libraries; museums and related institutions; theater and other dramatic arts; book production; newspapers and other periodicals; film and cinema; radio broadcasting; and television. In this edition, the summary tables relating to culture and communications, previously given in the introduction to each of the corresponding chapters, have been grouped together in a separate chapter.

World Bank. ANNUAL REPORT, 1982. 1982, WBG.

Presents summary and background of the activities of the World Bank Group during the fiscal year ended 30 June 1982, covering: the International Bank for Reconstruction and Development (IBRD); the International Development Association (IDA); and the International Finance Corporation (IFC). Chapters cover: brief review of Bank operations in fiscal 1982; a global perspective of the economic situation; Bank policies, activities and finances for fiscal 1982; 1982 regional perspectives; and Executive Directors. Lists projects approved for IBRD and IDA assistance in fiscal 1982 by sector, region and purpose. Also reviews trends in lending by sector for 1980-82 and includes statistical annex.

WORLD BANK COUNTRY STUDIES. Series.

Series of studies, prepared by World Bank staff, on development issues and policies, and economic conditions in individual developing countries. Studies may focus on specific economic sectors or issues, or on general economic performance of the country as a whole.

The World Bank.
WORLD DEVELOPMENT REPORT, 1978. August 1978.

First volume in a series of annual reports designed to provide a comprehensive, continuing assessment of global development issues. After an overview of development in the past 25 years, the report discusses current policy issues and projected developments in areas of the international economy that influence the prospects of developing countries. Analyzes the problems confronting policy makers in developing countries, which differ in degree and in kind, affecting the choice of appropriate policy instruments, and recognizes that development strategies need to give equal prominence to two goals: accelerating economic growth and reducing poverty. Reviews development priorities for low-income Asia, sub-Saharan Africa, and middle-income developing countries.

The World Bank.
WORLD DEVELOPMENT REPORT, 1979. Washington, D.C.

Second in a series of annual reports designed to assess global development issues. Focuses on development in the middle income countries, with particular emphasis on policy choices for industrialization and urbanization. Part one assesses recent trends and prospects to 1990 and discusses capital flows, and energy. Part two focuses upon structural change and development policy relevant to employment, the balance between agriculture and industry, and urban growth. Part three reviews development experiences and issues in three groups of middle income countries: semi-industrialized nations; mineral primary-producing countries; and predominantly agricultural primary-producing countries. Maintains that progress toward expanding employment and reducing poverty in developing countries lies not only in internal policy choices but also in a liberal environment for international trade and capital flows.

The World Bank.
WORLD DEVELOPMENT REPORT, 1980. New York: Oxford University Press for the World Bank, 1980.

Third in a series of annual reports. Parts one examines economic policy choices facing both developing and developed countries and their implications for national and regional growth. Projects, to the year 2000 but particularly to the mid to late 1980's, growth estimates for oil-importing and oil-exporting developing countries; and analyzes the fundamental issues of energy, trade, and capital flows. Part two focuses on the links between poverty, growth, and human development. It examines the impact of

education, health, nutrition, and fertility on poverty; reviews
some practical lessons in implementing human development programs;
and discusses the trade-offs between growth and poverty and the
allocation of resources between human development and other
activities. Stresses the views that growth does not obviate
the need for human development and that direct measures to reduce
poverty do not obviate the need for economic expansion. Concludes
that world growth prospects have deteriorated in the past year,
but higher oil prices have impoved the outlook [for the first
half of the 1980's] for the fifth of the developing world's
population that lives in oil-exporting countries; however, the
four-fifths that live in oil-importing countries will experience
slower growth for the first half of the decade. Includes a
statistical appendix to part one; a bibliographical note; and
a very lengthy annex of World Development Indicators.

The World Bank.
WORLD DEVELOPMENT REPORT, 1981. New York: Oxford University
Press for the World Bank, 1981.

With the major focus on the international context of development,
examines past trends and future prospects for international trade,
energy, and capital flows and the effects of these on developing
countries. Presents two scenarios for the 1980's, one predicting
higher growth rates than in the 1970's and one lower. Analyzes
national adjustments to the international economy, presenting
in-depth case studies. Concludes that countries pursuing
outward-oriented policies adjusted more easily to external shocks.
Contends that whichever scenario prevails, income differentials
will increase between the industrial and developing countries.
Low income countries have fewer options and less flexibility
of adjustment, therefore requiring continued aid from the more
affluent countries. Advocates policies to channel increased
resources to alleviate poverty.

The World Bank.
WORLD DEVELOPMENT REPORT, 1982.

The Report this year focuses on agriculture and food security.
As in previous years there is also a section on global prospects
and international issues, as well as the statistical annex of
World Development indicators.

The World Bank.
WORLD TABLES 1980: FROM THE DATA FILES OF THE WORLD BANK. Second
edition. Baltimore and London: Johns Hopkins University Press
for the World Bank, 1980.

A broad range of internationally comparable statistical information
drawn from the World Bank data files. Includes historical time
series for individual countries in absolute numbers for most
of the basic economic indicators for selected years (1950-77
when available); also presents derived economic indicators for
selected periods of years and demographic and social data for

selected years. Although the number of social indicators is fewer than those in the 1976 edition the quality of the data has been improved through the use of more uniform definitions and concepts, greater attention to population statistics, and better statistics on balance of payments and central government finance. Includes an index of country coverage.

WORLD ECONOMIC OUTLOOK: A SURVEY BY THE STAFF OF THE INTERNATIONAL MONETARY FUND. 1980, IMF.

An in-depth forecast of the world economy in 1980 and a preliminary summary for 1981. Chapters discuss: a profile of current situation and short-term prospects; global perspectives for adjustment and financing; industrial countries; developing countries--oil-exporting and non-oil groups; and key policy issues. Appendixes include country and regional surveys; technical notes on the world oil situation, estimated impact of fiscal balances in selected industrial countries, and monetary policy and inflation; and statistical tables.

WORLD ECONOMIC OUTLOOK: A SURVEY BY THE STAFF OF THE INTERNATIONAL MONETARY FUND. [1982 ed.] 1982, IMF.

A comprehensive analysis of economic developments, policies, and prospects through June 1981 for industrial, oil exporting and non-oil developing countries. It highlights persistent imbalances in the world economy, high inflation, rising unemployment, excessive rates of real interest, and unstable exchange rates. Appendix A includes supplementary notes providing information on selected topics in greater depth or detail than in the main body of the report: country and regional surveys; medium-term scenarios; fiscal development; monetary and exchange rate development; world oil situation; growth and inflation in non-oil developing countries; developments in trade policy; and commodity price developments and prospects. Appendix B presents statistical tables on: domestic economic activity and prices; international trade; balance of payments; external debt; medium-term projections; and country tables.

The World Bank.
WORLD BANK ATLAS. Fourteenth edition. 1979. Annual.

Presents estimates of gross national product (GNP) per capita (1977), GNP per capita growth rates (1970-77), and population (mid-1977), with population growth rates (1970-77) for countries with populations of one million or more in three global maps; a computer-generated map shows GNP per capita (1977) by major regions. Six regional maps give the same data for 184 countries and territories, as well as preliminary data for 1978. The base years 1976-78 have been used for the conversion of GNP for both 1977 and 1978. A Technical Note explains in detail the methodology used.

The World Bank.
WORLD DEVELOPMENT INDICATORS. June 1979. 71 pages.

A volume of statistics prepared in conjunction with and
constituting the Annex to the World Development Report, 1979
to provide information of general relevance about the main features
of economic and social development, reporting data for a total
of 125 countries whose population exceeds one million. Countries
are grouped in five categories and ranked by their 1977 per capita
gross national product (GNP) levels. The volume contains 24
tables covering some 110 economic and social indicators. The
choice of indicators has been based on data being available for
a large number of countries, the availability of historical series
to allow the measurement of growth and change, and on the relevance
of data to the principal processes of development.

The World Bank.
WORLD ECONOMIC AND SOCIAL INDICATORS. Quarterly (current issues).

Presents most recent available data on trade, commodity prices,
consumer prices, debt and capital flows, industrial production,
as well as social indicators and select annual data (by countries
where applicable). Each issue contains an article on topics
of current importance. Strategies for improving the access to
education of the disadvantaged rural poor by serving areas out
of range of existing schools are discussed and programs in four
projects financed by the World Bank are described.

WORLD ECONOMIC OUTLOOK: A SURVEY BY THE STAFF OF THE INTERNATIONAL
MONETARY FUND. Annual. April 1982. (Occasional Paper No. 9)

Annual report on economic performance of major industrial and
oil exporting and non-oil developing countries, 1970's-81 and
forecast 1982-83, with some projections to 1986. Includes analysis
of economic indicators for selected industrial countries, world
economic groupings, and world areas, primarily for IMF member
countries. Covers domestic economic activity, including prices,
GNP, and employment; international trade; balance of payments;
and foreign debt. Also includes financial indicators for selected
industrial countries, including government budget surpluses and
deficits, savings, money supply, and interest rates.

WORLD ECONOMIC SURVEY. 1978, UN, Sales No. E.78.II.C.1.

Provides an overview of salient developments in the world economy
in 1977 and the outlook for 1978. Focuses on policy needs for
improving the tempo of world production and trade. Examines
in detail the course of production and trade and related variables
in the developing economies, the developed market economies,
and the centrally planned economies.

WORLD ECONOMIC SURVEY 1979-80. 1980, UN, Sales No. E.80.II.C.2.

A survey of current world economic conditions and trends, with chapters on salient features and policy implications; the growth of world output, 1979-80; the accelerating pace of inflation; world trade and international payments; world economic outlook, 1980-1985; and adjustment policies in developing countries. Annexes cover external factors and growth in developing countries--the experience of the 1970's; supply and price of petroleum in 1979 and 1980; and prospective supply and demand for oil.

YEARBOOK OF NATIONAL ACCOUNTS STATISTICS, 1980. Annual. 1982.

Annual report presenting national income and product account balances for approximately 170 countries, and for world areas and economic groupings, selected years 1970-79, often with comparisons to 1960 and 1965. Data are compiled in accordance with the UN System of National Accounts (SNA) for market economies, and the System of Material Product Balances (MPS) for centrally planned economies. SNA data include GDP final consumption expenditures by type; production, income/outlay, and capital formation accounts, by institutional sector; and production by type of activity. MPS data include material and financial balances, manpower and resources, and national wealth and capital assets.

STATISTICAL NEWSLETTER. Quarterly.

Quarterly newsletter on ESCAP statistical programs and activities, and major statistical developments in ESCAP countries. Includes brief descriptions of meetings, working groups, upcoming international statistical training programs, and regional advisory services; and an annotated bibliography of recent ESCAP and UN statistical publications.

1976 FAO TRADE YEARBOOK. Vol. 30. FAO Statistics Series, no. 8. Rome: Food and Agriculture Organization; distributed by Unipub, New York, 1977.

Annual summation of world trade in agricultural products for the calendar year 1976. The 182 tables provide information on: trade index numbers for the aggregate agricultural and aggregate food products; quantities and values of trade for agricultural products and requisites; and present value summaries by Standard International Trade Classification divisions for selected countries. Data acquired for national publications of the respective governments and/or FAO questionnaires. This edition is shorter than previous editions due to the reduction of the General and Commodity Notes.

HANDBOOK OF INTERNATIONAL TRADE AND DEVELOPMENT STATISTICS, 1979. New York: United Nations, 1979.

Compilation of data drawn from existing international and national sources related to world trade and development. Tables, covering various time periods since 1950, with countries and territories classified: according to economic type and geographic area, developed market economies, socialist countries of Asia, and developing countries and territories. In eight parts: value of world trade by regions and countries 1950-78; volume, unit value, and terms of trade index numbers by regions, commodity prices, and consumer price indices, networks of world trade; exports and imports for individual countries by commodity structure, major exports of developing countries, and LDC imports of manufactured goods and imports from LDC's of semi-manufactured goods; balance of payments, financial resource flows, and external indebtedness of LDC's; basic indicators of development; special studies; and shipping statistics.

WORLD DEBT TABLES. December 28, 1979.

A compilation of data on the external public and publicly guaranteed debt of 96 developing countries, 1972-78 from the World Bank Debtor Reporting System (DRS). Volume I contains five parts. Parts A, C, and D describe the nature, content, and coverage of the data. Part B gives a review of external debt of 96 countries through 1978. Part E contains statistical tables supporting the review given in Part B. Volume II contains tables on external public debt outstanding, commitments, disbursements, service payments, and net borrowing of 96 developing countries, by country and category of lender, 1972-85.

FOREIGN TRADE STATISTICS OF ASIA AND THE PACIFIC. UN, 1977.

Detailed regional commodity trade statistics (imports and exports) for the calendar year 1974 of the countries and territories of the region (18) which reported to the UN Economic and Social Commission for Asia and the Pacific (ESCAP). Data are reported by sections and groups of the Standard International Trade Classification. Revised (SITC), in matrix form.

HANDBOOK OF INTERNATIONAL TRADE AND DEVELOPMENT STATISTICS: SUPPLEMENT 1980. UN, 1981, Sales No. E/F.80.II.D.10.

Provides, on an interim basis, a revised and updated version of the Handbook of International Trade and Development Statistics, 1979. It is planned to issue the Handbook in its entirety for the next session of UNCTAD, tentatively scheduled for 1983, in seven parts: (a) value of world trade by regions and countries, 1950, 1960, 1970-1979; (b) volume, unit value, and terms of trade index numbers by regions; commodity prices; consumer price indexes; (c) network of world trade--summary by selected regions of origin and destination and structure of exports and imports by selected commodity groups; (d) exports and imports for individual countries by commodity structure, and major exports of developing countries by leading exporters; (e) balance of payments, financial resource flows and external indebtedness of developing countries.

BALANCE OF PAYMENTS YEARBOOK: VOL. 31. Ed. by Werner Danneman and Arie C. Bouter. IMF, 1980.

Each monthly issue of the yearbook consists of a booklet containing annual, half-yearly, or quarterly balance of payments data in the form of an analytic presentation for those countries that have provided new data during the preceding month. Notes and additional tables to complete each country section of the Year book will not be published until the annual issue is prepared at the end of the year. Note: a subscription covers eleven monthly booklets and a copy of the annual issue. In addition, each subscriber will receive a copy of a supplement giving a world summary of international transactions within a framework of categories of transactions, which are then analyzed by country.

DIRECTORY OF UNITED NATIONS INFORMATION SYSTEMS.   IOB for UN, 1980.

Vol. 1: Information Systems and Data Bases. This volume gives particulars of United Nations family organizations and their information systems, together with the practical details, such as the address to contact for information, the conditions of access, the type of services that can be obtained. Details are provided on where to obtain bibliographies, indexes and other publications which are frequently available in several languages. The information systems covered include libraries, referral centres, clearing-houses, data banks, statistical information systems and other data collections, computerized or manual.
Vol. 2: Information Sources in Countries. Gives information by country, to facilitate contact between users and organizations' systems and services. More than 2,500 addresses in 167 countries are given. The addresses include organizations' offices, centres contributing information or serving as contact points to the various systems, and depository libraries where the publications or organizations can be found. Information is given on the publications and papers of the different organizations held in depository libraries and in United Nations Information Centres, and on the related services provided.

COMMODITY TRADE STATISTICS. Series.

Series of annual reports on foreign trade on individual countries with the rest of world, by country, world area and economic grouping; by SITC 1- to 4-digit commodity. Each report covers imports, exports, and sometimes re-exports, by country, for 1 or several countries. Data sources: National government records. Format and data presentation: (a) Index and explanatory notes; (b) 2-3 import/export tables arranged by SITC classification, repeated for each country covered in report. All tables show trade values in US$ and, frequently, quantities traded. All tables show country of origin or destination for each commodity group.

II. STATISTICAL TABLES AND FIGURES

This section focuses attention on some of the major economic and social indicators from a global and developing country perspective. It's aim is to highlight some generalizations made in the first part of this book as pointers to needed policies. The limited extent to which statistical information is cited in this book is solely for illustrative purposes. Most of the statistical information in the following pages have been reproduced from the following sources:

WORLD TABLES 1980: FROM THE DATA FILES OF THE WORLD BANK, Baltimore: Johns Hopkins University Press for the World Bank, 1980, (Reprinted by permission of the World Bank and Johns Hopkins University Press).

WORLD ECONOMIC AND SOCIAL INDICATORS, October 1978. Report No. 700/78/04. Washington, D.C.: WORLD BANK.

GLOBAL INDICATORS

TABLE 1. SOCIAL INDICATORS BY INCOME GROUP OF COUNTRIES

(ADJUSTED COUNTRY GROUP AVERAGES)

INDICATOR	DEVELOPING COUNTRIES EXCLUDING CAPITAL SURPLUS OIL EXPORTERS								
	LOW INCOME			LOWER MIDDLE INCOME			INTERMEDIATE MIDDLE INCOME		
	1960	1970	MOST RECENT ESTIMATE	1960	1970	MOST RECENT ESTIMATE	1960	1970	MOST RECENT ESTIMATE
GNP PER CAPITA (IN CURRENT US $)	67.4	107.4	162.0	136.1	239.6	398.6	225.6	410.9	817.9
POPULATION									
GROWTH RATE (%) - TOTAL	2.2	2.4	2.4	2.7	2.7	2.6	2.7	2.7	2.5
- URBAN	5.3	4.7	4.7	4.7	4.4	9.8	5.4	4.9	5.1
URBAN POPULATION (% OF TOTAL)	10.4	14.0	14.8	17.7	21.6	26.1	33.7	41.4	46.1
VITAL STATISTICS									
CRUDE BIRTH RATE (PER 1000)	47.5	46.9	45.2	47.1	45.5	42.6	44.6	41.2	38.2
CRUDE DEATH RATE (PER 1000)	26.1	21.7	18.2	21.4	16.1	12.7	18.6	13.5	11.1
GROSS REPRODUCTION RATE	2.9	3.1	3.1	3.4	3.2	3.3	3.0	2.8	2.6
EMPLOYMENT AND INCOME									
DEPENDENCY RATIO - AGE	0.8	0.9	0.9	0.9	0.9	0.9	0.9	0.9	0.9
- ECONOMIC	1.0	1.1	1.1	1.3	1.4	1.4	1.6	1.6	1.5
LABOR FORCE IN AGRICULTURE (% OF TOTAL)	65.4	62.0	59.3	70.4	65.9	62.5	62.8	54.5	47.0
UNEMPLOYED (% OF LABOR FORCE)	4.7	4.0	3.1	6.3	8.4	5.3	6.1	6.0	5.8
INCOME RECEIVED BY - HIGHEST 5%	24.5	23.3	20.3	25.1	23.1	25.5	31.5	27.0	19.3
- LOWEST 20%	4.6	5.1	6.5	4.8	4.9	4.8	4.4	3.9	5.7
HEALTH AND NUTRITION									
DEATH RATE (PER 1000) AGES 1-4 YEARS	43.6	33.0	33.0	9.3	6.8	7.5	8.5	3.6	2.7
INFANT MORTALITY RATE (PER 1000)	129.0	121.3	102.8	84.6	79.9	58.4	88.6	65.8	55.0
LIFE EXPECTANCY AT BIRTH (YRS)	39.2	43.8	46.0	45.0	50.8	53.2	51.1	57.0	59.1
POPULATION PER - PHYSICIAN	21790.7	15219.9	13235.9	16767.4	11977.3	10586.0	3299.7	2549.2	2412.7
- NURSING PERSON	8472.3	5215.0	4830.9	4078.2	1921.9	1683.8	3394.0	2205.1	1502.1
- HOSPITAL BED	1386.7	1267.8	1236.2	1037.6	815.3	793.1	721.8	629.2	507.1
PER CAPITA PER DAY SUPPLY OF:									
CALORIES (% OF REQUIREMENTS)	89.8	91.5	94.5	85.1	93.3	102.3	94.4	101.8	103.9
PROTEIN (GRMS) - TOTAL	50.5	51.6	53.9	47.4	53.0	56.9	54.4	58.7	60.6
- FROM ANIMALS & PULSES	14.9	14.4	16.4	17.7	18.1	18.8	21.8	22.1	23.0
EDUCATION									
ADJ. ENROLLMENT RATIOS - PRIMARY	37.4	48.4	59.0	60.7	74.0	92.7	77.8	95.3	99.9
- SECONDARY	4.8	10.3	13.9	4.8	12.7	22.6	14.5	26.7	29.4
FEMALE ENROLLMENT RATIO (PRIMARY)	34.6	39.0	43.3	45.6	75.0	77.5	65.8	87.8	87.6
ADULT LITERACY RATE (%)	24.4	32.0	33.8	41.0	60.0	63.0	49.8	57.8	62.3

TABLE 1. Social Indicators by Income Group of Countries (Continued).

DEVELOPING COUNTRIES EXCLUDING CAPITAL SURPLUS OIL EXPORTERS (ADJUSTED COUNTRY GROUP AVERAGES)

INDICATOR	LOW INCOME 1960	1970	MOST RECENT ESTIMATE	LOWER MIDDLE INCOME 1960	1970	MOST RECENT ESTIMATE	INTERMEDIATE MIDDLE INCOME 1960	1970	MOST RECENT ESTIMATE
HOUSING									
PERSONS PER ROOM – URBAN	2.5	2.0	2.8	2.6	2.5	2.2	2.3	2.2	1.6
OCCUPIED DWELLINGS WITHOUT WATER	62.2	69.8	..	68.7	64.6	67.8	74.6	64.2	58.9
ACCESS TO ELECTRICITY (%) – ALL	..	..	..	17.3	23.3	40.4	28.4	49.6	71.9
– RURAL	..	..	..	..	..	..	5.6	26.7	34.1
CONSUMPTION									
RADIO RECEIVERS (PER 1000 POP.)	4.5	14.4	23.1	11.9	62.3	70.4	48.8	96.2	102.6
PASSENGER CARS (PER 1000 POP.)	1.3	2.5	3.0	3.0	6.5	8.6	4.2	7.5	11.1
ENERGY (KG COAL/YR PER CAPITA)	62.0	83.4	104.8	99.6	220.1	265.2	258.7	489.2	586.2
NEWSPRINT (KG/YR PER CAPITA)	0.2	0.4	0.3	0.6	0.8	0.8	1.1	1.8	2.4

INDICATOR	DEV'G CTRIES. EXCL. CAP. SURP. OIL EXP. UPPER MIDDLE INCOME 1960	1970	MOST RECENT EST.	CAP. SURP. OIL EXP. HIGH INCOME 1960	1970	MOST RECENT EST.	CAP. SURP. OIL EXP. 1960	1970	MOST RECENT EST.	INDUSTRIALIZED COUNTRIES 1960	1970	MOST RECENT EST.
GNP PER CAPITA (IN CURRENT US $)	401.2	817.1	1648.7	689.4	1564.2	2911.1	1054.3	2858.9	5710.5	1417.4	3096.8	5297.7
POPULATION												
GROWTH RATE (%) – TOTAL	1.6	1.3	1.5	2.1	3.1	2.9	4.5	2.4	2.7	0.9	0.9	0.9
– URBAN	3.3	3.4	2.8	4.5	3.9	3.5	..	5.8	6.8	1.6	1.3	1.3
URBAN POPULATION (% OF TOTAL)	43.4	51.1	53.1	63.0	82.1	88.6	24.6	20.0	39.0	66.1	70.5	73.8
VITAL STATISTICS												
CRUDE BIRTH RATE (PER 1000)	26.2	28.5	20.8	41.7	37.4	33.6	48.3	49.4	45.0	21.3	20.0	18.7
CRUDE DEATH RATE (PER 1000)	10.4	9.1	8.9	9.6	8.3	8.0	21.2	22.8	14.7	9.7	9.0	8.8
GROSS REPRODUCTION RATE	1.7	1.8	1.8	2.3	2.5	1.8	..	3.5	3.3	1.3	1.3	1.2

TABLE 1. Social Indicators by Income Group of Countries (Continued)

(ADJUSTED COUNTRY GROUP AVERAGES)

INDICATOR	DEV'G CTRIES. EXCL. CAP. SURP. OIL EXP. UPPER MIDDLE INCOME			CAP. SURP. OIL EXP. HIGH INCOME			CAP. SURP. OIL EXP.			INDUSTRIALIZED COUNTRIES		
	1960	1970	MOST RECENT EST.	1960	1970	MOST RECENT EST.	1960	1970	MOST RECENT EST.	1960	1970	MOST RECENT EST.
EMPLOYMENT AND INCOME:												
DEPENDENCY RATIO - AGE	0.7	0.7	0.6	0.8	0.6	0.6	0.9	0.9	0.9	0.5	0.6	0.4
- ECONOMIC	1.3	1.7	1.6	1.2	1.2	1.2	1.8	1.7	1.7	0.9	0.9	0.8
LABOR FORCE IN AGRICULTURE (% OF TOTAL)	48.5	42.5	36.3	26.1	17.8	21.0	54.7	44.5	29.0	19.8	13.2	10.0
UNEMPLOYED (% OF LABOR FORCE)	7.4	3.3	4.0	9.0	5.4	5.1	7.4	2.0	3.0	2.1	1.5	1.9
INCOME RECEIVED BY - HIGHEST 5%	32.5	28.2	21.3	18.9	16.1	..	13.3	..	..	19.3	14.0	15.5
- LOWEST 20%	4.2	3.8	4.7	5.8	6.6	..	10.1	..	..	4.2	7.0	5.7
HEALTH AND NUTRITION												
DEATH RATE (PER 1000) AGES 1-4 YEARS	4.8	2.9	1.9	..	1.3	..	..	3.6	3.6	1.2	0.9	0.8
INFANT MORTALITY RATE (PER 1000)	74.4	51.3	37.9	44.9	27.8	23.2	..	134.3	80.3	27.9	17.0	15.0
LIFE EXPECTANCY AT BIRTH (YRS)	64.6	67.3	68.4	66.2	64.0	68.2	45.4	44.9	52.9	69.5	71.4	72.5
POPULATION PER - PHYSICIAN	1625.8	967.5	718.2	1117.5	888.9	756.0	9833.7	6323.4	1260.0	895.2	825.6	656.0
- NURSING PERSON	1690.7	1279.6	1028.5	1165.0	605.9	683.5	5140.0	2856.8	460.0	279.6	194.6	167.1
- HOSPITAL BED	209.9	180.4	185.8	170.0	162.5	170.0	1093.2	727.5	230.0	96.1	86.0	81.9
PER CAPITA PER DAY SUPPLY OF:												
CALORIES (% OF REQUIREMENTS)	104.5	114.4	111.5	106.3	107.2	113.6	83.9	90.3	104.9	118.7	118.7	119.5
PROTEIN (GRMS) - TOTAL	75.5	84.9	77.8	78.5	79.2	89.9	53.6	57.0	65.1	90.3	94.1	94.8
- FROM ANIMALS & PULSES	27.0	29.0	27.5	33.0	40.1	48.0	11.0	14.8	18.2	49.7	55.0	54.9
EDUCATION												
ADJ. ENROLLMENT RATIOS - PRIMARY	94.6	97.9	95.7	104.4	120.1	107.6	18.2	47.1	145.0	106.7	104.3	103.3
- SECONDARY	22.7	36.6	46.7	18.1	40.1	46.2	3.1	12.4	47.0	59.5	79.1	79.8
FEMALE ENROLLMENT RATIO (PRIMARY)	89.7	87.9	86.1	100.2	100.0	102.0	3.5	31.6	40.4	111.4	104.6	104.0
ADULT LITERACY RATE (%)	51.4	67.8	66.1	81.8	86.2	87.2	25.2	17.1	..	98.0	99.0	99.0
HOUSING												
PERSONS PER ROOM - URBAN	1.4	1.2	..	1.1	..	..	..	1.9	..	0.8	0.7	0.9
OCCUPIED DWELLINGS WITHOUT WATER	59.1	75.3	67.1	57.1	20.0	..	..	69.0	..	7.2	3.1	4.3
ACCESS TO ELECTRICITY (%) - ALL	50.6	47.4	59.8	79.3	91.0	..	..	24.0	..	97.3	98.9	99.1
- RURAL	26.9	..	..	57.0	58.0	..	..	..	..	91.4	95.2	94.8
CONSUMPTION												
RADIO RECEIVERS (PER 1000 POP.)	76.3	137.2	200.4	170.7	174.3	185.6	13.8	17.5	18.4	277.1	359.4	379.3
PASSENGER CARS (PER 1000 POP.)	11.2	29.2	42.3	14.1	41.3	54.4	7.6	16.6	113.7	90.7	233.3	266.5
ENERGY (KG COAL/YR PER CAPITA)	676.2	1426.1	1618.7	798.4	1755.1	2467.6	302.5	1003.1	1419.4	2624.7	4575.2	4997.3
NEWSPRINT (KG/YR PER CAPITA)	1.4	1.9	2.3	3.5	8.7	6.6	0.2	0.2	0.1	16.4	22.3	22.2

TABLE 2. SOCIAL INDICATORS BY GEOGRAPHIC AREAS (DEVELOPING COUNTRIES)

(ADJUSTED COUNTRY GROUP AVERAGES)

INDICATOR	EUROPE			LATIN AMERICA & CARIBBEAN			N. AFRICA & MIDDLE EAST		
	1960	1970	MOST RECENT ESTIMATE	1960	1970	MOST RECENT ESTIMATE	1960	1970	MOST RECENT ESTIMATE
GNP PER CAPITA (IN CURRENT US $)	496.6	1018.0	2070.3	362.0	626.8	1015.6	307.7	579.0	1290.3
POPULATION									
GROWTH RATE (%) - TOTAL	1.0	0.8	0.9	2.5	2.7	2.6	2.7	2.9	3.0
- URBAN	3.8	2.8	2.1	4.2	4.1	4.2	6.4	4.5	5.1
URBAN POPULATION (% OF TOTAL)	32.1	40.7	38.7	48.3	54.3	58.5	33.8	39.6	44.3
VITAL STATISTICS									
CRUDE BIRTH RATE (PER 1000)	23.3	20.5	19.2	40.9	39.0	36.8	48.3	47.2	45.7
CRUDE DEATH RATE (PER 1000)	10.5	9.0	9.0	14.1	10.9	9.2	22.6	18.0	15.3
GROSS REPRODUCTION RATE	1.4	1.3	1.3	2.7	2.6	2.6	2.3	3.4	3.4
EMPLOYMENT AND INCOME									
DEPENDENCY RATIO - AGE	0.6	0.6	0.4	0.9	1.0	0.9	0.9	1.0	1.0
- ECONOMIC	1.0	1.1	1.0	1.6	1.5	1.7	1.6	2.0	1.9
LABOR FORCE IN AGRICULTURE (% OF TOTAL)	47.9	31.8	27.4	48.3	41.0	36.9	52.6	43.4	42.9
UNEMPLOYED (% OF LABOR FORCE)	3.0	4.0	6.0	7.6	6.2	8.8	6.3	3.4	4.1
INCOME RECEIVED BY - HIGHEST 5%	21.8	24.5	25.0	37.1	30.4	31.7	24.0	25.0	21.0
- LOWEST 20%	5.4	3.9	3.9	3.9	3.5	2.0	4.4	4.2	5.2
HEALTH AND NUTRITION									
DEATH RATE (PER 1000) AGES 1-4 YEARS	4.7	2.8	1.7	10.6	7.7	6.6	..	6.0	..
INFANT MORTALITY RATE (PER 1000)	60.4	39.7	34.5	77.4	67.3	56.2	127.8	111.6	97.8
LIFE EXPECTANCY AT BIRTH (YRS)	65.8	68.6	69.1	55.8	60.6	62.5	45.5	50.3	52.8
POPULATION PER - PHYSICIAN	1004.0	821.3	694.4	2058.1	1866.8	1796.9	5690.8	5760.2	4724.7
- NURSING PERSON	1343.2	653.9	339.2	4542.1	3389.5	2804.5	3286.6	2564.7	2383.1
- HOSPITAL BED	190.5	168.0	170.5	444.1	392.1	405.6	670.8	661.6	700.0
PER CAPITA PER DAY SUPPLY OF:									
CALORIES (% OF REQUIREMENTS)	109.3	118.0	118.0	97.6	103.2	105.5	80.9	91.0	96.0
PROTEIN (GRMS) - TOTAL	85.9	90.7	90.0	63.7	59.8	60.7	54.5	58.3	63.1
- FROM ANIMALS & PULSES	27.0	29.0	33.0	29.0	28.0	28.2	17.5	15.0	15.6
EDUCATION									
ADJ. ENROLLMENT RATIOS - PRIMARY	105.0	102.1	104.3	85.0	101.7	105.1	51.5	75.6	80.5
- SECONDARY	25.5	50.5	49.2	15.0	27.6	36.0	10.3	20.4	22.2
FEMALE ENROLLMENT RATIO (PRIMARY)	98.9	99.4	100.4	85.6	98.3	98.1	30.8	50.2	52.3
ADULT LITERACY RATE (%)	64.9	75.0	88.2	61.4	74.6	75.7	17.7	26.9	40.6
HOUSING									
PERSONS PER ROOM - URBAN	1.4	1.5	1.4	1.9	1.3	2.1	1.8	2.3	3.0
OCCUPIED DWELLINGS WITHOUT WATER	67.0	63.3	59.5	65.5	67.0	66.4	62.2	77.1	90.5
ACCESS TO ELECTRICITY (%) - ALL	51.4		57.9	44.4	54.2	53.1	40.1	31.0	39.1

TABLE 2. Social Indicators by Geographic Areas (Developing Countries), Continued

(ADJUSTED COUNTRY GROUP AVERAGES)

INDICATOR	AFRICA SOUTH OF SAHARA			SOUTH ASIA			EAST ASIA AND PACIFIC		
	1960	1970	MOST RECENT ESTIMATE	1960	1970	MOST RECENT ESTIMATE	1960	1970	MOST RECENT ESTIMATE
GNP PER CAPITA (IN CURRENT US $)	94.9	137.0	207.4	54.1	88.2	131.4	141.8	290.0	568.3
POPULATION									
GROWTH RATE (%) – TOTAL	2.2	2.4	2.6	2.2	2.6	2.1	3.0	2.8	2.3
– URBAN	5.6	6.0	6.0	5.2	4.1	4.3	5.4	5.0	5.2
URBAN POPULATION (% OF TOTAL)	9.1	12.5	13.5	7.8	9.8	12.4	28.1	27.1	38.1
VITAL STATISTICS									
CRUDE BIRTH RATE (PER 1000)	48.8	48.1	47.1	47.4	45.8	45.1	42.3	40.7	32.0
CRUDE DEATH RATE (PER 1000)	26.7	23.7	21.2	26.4	21.4	17.3	19.2	12.4	8.7
GROSS REPRODUCTION RATE	2.9	3.1	3.0	3.2	3.0	2.9	3.0	2.5	2.3
EMPLOYMENT AND INCOME									
DEPENDENCY RATIO – AGE	0.9	0.9	0.9	0.8	0.8	0.8	0.9	0.9	0.7
– ECONOMIC	1.1	1.1	1.1	1.5	1.4	1.2	1.4	1.4	1.3
LABOR FORCE IN AGRICULTURE (% OF TOTAL)	79.8	75.0	73.1	61.8	60.8	63.0	67.9	59.5	48.4
UNEMPLOYED (% OF LABOR FORCE)	5.1	4.6	5.1	..	..	11.0	5.1	5.1	4.1
INCOME RECEIVED BY – HIGHEST 5%	28.2	26.4	25.7	24.6	23.2	18.6	22.7	20.5	19.8
– LOWEST 20%	5.2	3.9	5.7	4.6	5.2	7.8	5.5	5.8	6.6
HEALTH AND NUTRITION									
DEATH RATE (PER 1000) AGES 1-4 YEARS	..	..	..	..	..	..	..	3.4	2.0
INFANT MORTALITY RATE (PER 1000)	153.9	129.6	127.5	136.2	124.3	104.0	61.2	31.1	27.4
LIFE EXPECTANCY AT BIRTH (YRS)	36.9	41.5	43.4	40.6	45.2	48.1	52.5	59.1	61.6
POPULATION PER – PHYSICIAN	31866.1	24906.5	21616.5	9920.9	8519.2	7412.6	3429.3	2268.9	2208.9
– NURSING PERSON	4558.4	3088.7	2496.5	14566.1	9168.1	8339.3	3096.6	1935.5	1465.5
– HOSPITAL BED	1234.7	819.9	799.9	2885.8	1998.5	1908.0	1270.8	921.7	662.1
PER CAPITA PER DAY SUPPLY OF:									
CALORIES (% OF REQUIREMENTS)	89.6	90.7	91.9	89.1	97.6	96.0	90.0	99.4	106.5
PROTEIN (GRMS) – TOTAL	56.6	59.0	60.6	47.8	53.2	50.8	48.1	53.4	55.6
– FROM ANIMALS & PULSES	19.2	19.8	23.1	15.0	16.0	15.5	19.0	22.1	22.1
EDUCATION									
ADJ. ENROLLMENT RATIOS – PRIMARY	27.7	42.4	50.0	36.9	47.9	55.2	95.0	105.7	110.0
– SECONDARY	1.9	5.6	6.9	9.1	15.5	20.0	17.3	26.9	51.1
FEMALE ENROLLMENT RATIO (PRIMARY)	21.7	37.4	43.2	22.2	53.8	44.5	83.5	102.0	104.7
ADULT LITERACY RATE (%)	9.8	17.4	18.4	16.0	20.0	21.0	47.7	66.4	72.6
HOUSING									
PERSONS PER ROOM – URBAN	2.7	2.4	1.7	..	..	..	2.5	2.3	..
OCCUPIED DWELLINGS WITHOUT WATER – URBAN	..	..	..	..	..	..	83.7	69.5	60.3
ACCESS TO ELECTRICITY (%) – ALL	..	..	..	..	..	..	22.6	40.7	50.5
– RURAL	..	..	..	..	..	..	12.0	20.1	23.4

GLOBAL INDICATORS

TABLE 3. COMPARATIVE SOCIAL INDICATORS FOR DEVELOPING COUNTRIES (BY GEOGRAPHIC AREA AND COUNTRY)

AREA AND COUNTRY	POPULATION & VITAL STATISTICS				EMPLOYMENT AND INCOME			HEALTH & NUTRITION			(MOST RECENT ESTIMATE) EDUCATION		
	POP. GROWTH RATE % (65-75)	URBAN POP. % OF TOTAL	CRUDE BIRTH RATE (/000)	CRUDE DEATH RATE (/000)	LABOR IN AGR. % OF TOTAL	INCOME RECD BY HIGHEST 5% HH	INCOME RECD BY LOWEST 20% HH	LIFE EXPECT. YRS AT BIRTH	CALORIE SUPPLY %/CAP RECD.	PROTEIN SUPPLY GR/DAY /CAP	PRIMARY SCHOOL ENROLL RATIO %	FEMALE ENROLL. RATIO PRIMARY	ADULT LITERACY RATE % OF TOTAL
EUROPE:													
CYPRUS	0.6	42.2	22.2	6.8	34.0	12.1	7.9	71.4	113.0	86.0	71.0	72.0	85.0
GREECE	0.6	64.8	15.4	9.4	34.0	18.7	6.3	71.8	132.0	102.0	106.0	104.0	82.0
MALTA	0.2	94.3	17.5	9.0	6.0	..	..	69.6	114.0	89.0	109.0	109.0	87.0
PORTUGAL	0.3	28.8	19.2	10.5	32.5	56.3	7.3	68.7	118.0	85.0	116.0	94.0	70.0
ROMANIA	1.2	43.0	19.7	9.3	36.0	..	..	69.1	118.0	90.0	109.0	109.0	98.0
SPAIN	1.0	59.1	19.5	8.3	23.0	18.5	6.0	72.1	135.0	94.1	115.0	115.0	94.0
TURKEY	2.6	42.6	39.4	12.5	52.5	28.0	3.5	56.6	113.0	75.7	104.0	94.0	55.0
YUGOSLAVIA	0.9	38.7	18.2	9.2	39.0	25.1	6.6	68.0	137.0	97.5	97.0	93.0	85.0
ALL COUNTRIES - MEDIAN	0.8	42.8	19.4	9.3	34.0	18.6	6.5	69.4	118.0	89.5	107.5	99.0	85.0
LATIN AMERICA & CARIBBEAN													
ARGENTINA	1.4	80.0	21.8	8.8	15.0	21.4	5.6	68.3	129.0	107.1	108.0	109.0	93.0
BAHAMAS	3.6	57.9	22.4	5.7	7.0	20.7	3.4	66.7	100.0	87.0	135.0	..	93.0
BARBADOS	0.4	3.7	21.6	8.9	18.0	19.8	6.8	69.1	133.0	82.5	117.0	116.0	97.0
BOLIVIA	2.7	34.0	44.0	19.1	65.0	36.0	4.0	46.8	77.0	48.5	74.0	65.0	40.0
BRAZIL	2.9	59.1	37.1	8.8	37.8	35.0	3.0	61.4	105.0	62.1	90.0	90.0	64.0
CHILE	1.9	83.0	27.9	9.2	19.0	31.0	4.8	62.6	116.0	78.3	119.0	118.0	90.0
COLOMBIA	2.8	70.0	40.6	8.8	39.0	27.2	5.2	60.9	94.0	47.0	105.0	108.0	81.0
COSTA RICA	2.8	40.6	31.0	5.8	36.4	22.8	5.4	69.1	113.0	60.8	109.0	109.0	89.0
DOMINICAN REPUBLIC	2.9	45.9	45.8	11.0	53.8	26.3	4.3	57.8	98.0	45.4	104.0	105.0	51.0
ECUADOR	3.4	41.6	41.8	9.5	43.5	..	..	59.6	93.0	47.4	102.0	100.0	69.0
EL SALVADOR	3.4	39.4	42.2	11.1	55.0	38.0	2.0	65.0	84.0	50.3	75.2	69.0	63.0
GRENADA	1.0	..	27.4	6.8	30.8	..	..	..	89.0	57.0	99.0	..	85.0
GUATEMALA	3.2	37.3	42.8	13.7	56.0	35.0	5.0	54.1	91.0	52.8	62.0	56.0	47.0
GUYANA	2.1	40.0	32.4	5.9	30.9	18.8	4.3	67.9	104.0	58.0	114.0	114.0	85.0
HAITI	1.6	23.1	35.8	16.3	77.0	..	..	50.0	90.0	39.0	70.0	37.0	20.0
HONDURAS	2.7	31.4	49.3	14.6	60.3	28.0	2.5	53.5	90.0	56.0	90.0	88.0	53.0
JAMAICA	1.7	37.1	32.2	7.1	26.9	30.2	2.2	69.5	118.0	68.9	111.0	112.0	86.0
MEXICO	3.5	63.3	42.0	8.6	41.0	27.9	3.4	64.7	117.0	66.9	112.0	109.0	76.0
NICARAGUA	3.6	48.0	48.3	13.9	48.0	42.4	3.1	52.9	105.0	68.4	85.0	87.0	57.0
PANAMA	3.2	49.6	36.2	7.1	30.0	22.2	4.6	66.5	105.0	61.0	124.0	120.0	82.2

TABLE 3. COMPARATIVE SOCIAL INDICATORS FOR DEVELOPING COUNTRIES (BY GEOGRAPHIC AREA AND COUNTRY)   Continued

AREA AND COUNTRY	POP. GROWTH RATE % (65-75)	URBAN POP. % OF TOTAL	CRUDE BIRTH RATE (/000)	CRUDE DEATH RATE (/000)	LABOR IN AGR. % OF TOTAL	INCOME RECD BY HIGHEST 5% HH	INCOME RECD BY LOWEST 20% HH	LIFE EXPECT. YRS AT BIRTH	CALORIE SUPPLY %/CAP REQD.	PROTEIN SUPPLY GR/DAY /CAP	PRIMARY SCHOOL ENROLL RATIO %	FEMALE ENROLL. RATIO PRIMARY	ADULT LITERACY RATE % OF TOTAL
PARAGUAY	2.6	37.4	39.8	8.9	49.0	30.0	4.0	61.9	118.0	74.5	106.0	102.0	81.0
PERU	2.9	55.3	41.0	11.9	40.0	28.8	3.1	55.7	100.0	61.7	111.0	106.0	72.0
TRINIDAD & TOBAGO	1.0	25.1	27.3	5.9	13.5	..	..	69.5	114.0	66.0	111.0	111.0	90.0
URUGUAY	0.4	80.6	20.4	9.3	13.2	19.0	4.4	69.8	116.0	98.1	95.0	94.0	94.0
VENEZUELA	3.3	75.7	36.1	7.0	21.0	21.8	3.6	66.4	98.0	63.1	96.0	96.0	82.0
ALL COUNTRIES - MEDIAN	2.7	43.7	36.2	8.9	37.8	27.9	4.0	63.0	104.0	61.7	105.0	105.0	81.0
NORTH AFRICA & MIDDLE EAST													
ALGERIA	3.3	39.9	48.7	15.4	42.8	..	..	53.3	88.0	57.2	77.0	72.0	35.0
BAHRAIN	3.3	78.1	49.6	18.7	..	..	..	44.5	..	..	..	..	..
EGYPT	2.4	44.6	37.8	14.0	43.9	21.0	5.2	52.4	113.0	70.7	72.0	55.0	40.0
IRAN	2.9	43.0	45.3	15.6	41.0	29.7	5.0	51.0	98.0	56.0	90.0	67.0	50.0
IRAQ	3.3	62.0	48.1	14.6	51.0	35.1	2.1	52.7	101.0	60.4	93.0	63.0	26.0
JORDAN	3.4	42.0	47.6	14.7	19.0	..	..	53.2	90.0	65.0	83.0	77.0	62.0
KUWAIT	7.7	88.0	45.4	..	2.0	..	..	64.0	..	..	90.0	86.0	55.0
LEBANON	2.8	60.1	39.8	9.9	17.8	26.0	4.0	63.3	101.0	67.9	132.0	125.0	68.0
LIBYA	4.2	30.5	45.0	14.7	19.5	13.3	10.1	52.9	117.0	62.0	145.0	135.0	27.0
MOROCCO	2.4	40.1	46.2	15.7	50.0	20.0	4.0	53.0	108.0	70.5	61.0	44.0	28.0
OMAN	3.1	5.0	49.6	18.7	48.0	..	..	47.0	..	..	44.0	..	20.0
QATAR	10.5	85.0	50.2	24.4	..	..	..	..	..	..	112.0	..	21.0
SAUDI ARABIA	1.9	17.9	45.4	15.4	61.0	17.0	5.0	42.0	86.0	56.0	34.0	27.0	15.0
SYRIAN ARAB REP.	3.1	46.2	40.0	13.8	49.9	..	..	56.0	104.0	66.7	102.0	81.0	40.0
TUNISIA	2.3	47.0	..	..	37.4	..	..	54.1	102.0	67.4	95.0	75.0	55.0
UNITED ARAB EMIRATES	13.1	80.0	..	..	..	..	..	..	..	..	75.0	..	21.0
YEMEN ARAB REP.	1.7	7.0	49.6	20.6	73.0	..	..	37.0	83.0	58.3	25.0	6.0	10.0
YEMEN PEOP. DEM. REP.	3.1	35.3	49.6	20.6	42.9	..	..	44.8	84.0	57.0	78.0	48.0	27.1
ALL COUNTRIES - MEDIAN	3.1	43.8	46.9	15.6	42.9	21.0	4.0	52.8	101.0	62.0	83.0	70.5	28.0
AFRICA SOUTH OF SAHARA													
BENIN PEOP. REP.	2.7	13.5	49.9	23.0	47.5	31.4	5.5	41.8	87.0	56.0	44.0	28.0	20.0
BOTSWANA	2.1	10.7	45.6	23.0	83.0	28.1	1.6	43.5	85.0	65.0	85.0	93.0	25.0
BURUNDI	2.0	3.7	48.0	24.7	86.0	..	..	39.0	99.0	62.0	23.0	17.0	10.0
CAMEROON	1.9	28.5	40.4	22.0	82.0	..	..	41.0	102.0	59.0	111.0	97.0	6.0
CENTRAL AFRICAN EMPIRE	2.2	35.9	43.4	22.5	91.0	..	..	41.0	102.0	49.0	79.0	53.0	15.0

(MOST RECENT ESTIMATE)

TABLE 3. COMPARATIVE SOCIAL INDICATORS FOR DEVELOPING COUNTRIES (BY GEOGRAPHIC AREA AND COUNTRY) Continued *(MOST RECENT ESTIMATE)*

AREA AND COUNTRY	POPULATION & VITAL STATISTICS				EMPLOYMENT AND INCOME			HEALTH & NUTRITION			EDUCATION		
	POP. GROWTH RATE % (65-75)	URBAN POP. % OF TOTAL	CRUDE BIRTH RATE (/000)	CRUDE DEATH RATE (/000)	LABOR IN AGR. % OF TOTAL	INCOME RECD BY HIGHEST 5% HH	INCOME RECD BY LOWEST 20% HH	LIFE EXPECT. YRS AT BIRTH	CALORIE SUPPLY %/CAP REQD.	PROTEIN SUPPLY GR/DAY /CAP	PRIMARY SCHOOL ENROLL RATIO %	FEMALE ENROLL. RATIO PRIMARY	ADULT LITERACY RATE % OF TOTAL
CHAD	2.0	13.9	44.0	24.0	90.0	21.5	7.7	38.5	75.0	60.2	37.0	20.0	15.0
CONGO PEOP. REP.	2.3	38.0	45.1	20.8	56.0	:	:	43.5	98.0	44.0	153.0	140.0	50.0
EQUATORIAL GUINEA	1.3	:	:	:	:	:	:	:	:	:	:	:	:
ETHIOPIA	2.5	11.2	49.4	25.8	85.0	:	:	41.0	82.0	58.9	23.0	14.0	7.0
GABON	1.5	32.0	32.2	22.2	58.0	45.3	3.2	41.0	98.0	49.3	199.0	197.0	12.0
GAMBIA	2.3	14.0	43.3	24.1	79.6	:	:	40.0	98.0	64.0	32.0	21.0	10.0
GHANA	2.6	32.4	48.8	21.9	52.0	:	:	43.5	101.0	53.4	60.0	53.0	25.0
GUINEA	2.8	19.5	44.6	22.9	84.1	:	:	41.0	84.0	42.7	28.0	:	7.0
IVORY COAST	4.1	34.3	45.6	20.6	80.0	30.9	9.0	43.5	113.0	64.5	86.0	64.0	20.0
KENYA	3.4	13.0	48.7	16.0	84.0	20.2	3.9	50.0	91.0	59.6	109.0	101.0	40.0
LESOTHO	2.2	3.1	39.0	19.7	90.0	61.7	5.5	46.0	109.0	67.6	121.0	144.0	40.0
LIBERIA	3.3	27.6	43.6	20.7	72.0	41.0	5.2	43.5	87.0	39.0	62.0	44.0	15.0
MADAGASCAR	2.9	14.5	50.2	21.1	83.0	29.5	5.7	43.5	105.0	57.0	85.0	80.0	40.0
MALAWI	2.5	6.4	47.7	23.7	86.0	:	:	41.0	103.0	68.4	61.0	48.0	25.0
MALI	2.2	13.4	50.1	25.9	88.7	:	:	38.1	75.0	64.0	22.0	16.0	10.0
MAURITANIA	2.6	23.1	44.8	24.9	85.0	:	:	38.5	81.0	63.2	17.0	9.0	10.0
MAURITIUS	1.4	48.3	25.1	7.8	30.3	31.0	4.5	65.5	108.0	55.8	80.0	78.0	80.0
MOZAMBIQUE	2.2	55.0	43.3	21.4	73.0	:	:	41.0	94.0	41.0	46.0	:	:
NIGER	2.7	9.4	52.2	25.5	91.0	23.0	6.0	38.5	78.0	62.1	17.0	12.0	5.0
NIGERIA	2.5	26.0	49.3	22.7	62.0	:	:	41.0	88.0	46.3	49.0	39.0	25.0
RWANDA	2.8	3.8	50.0	23.6	93.0	:	:	41.0	90.0	51.3	58.0	54.0	23.0
SENEGAL	2.7	38.8	47.6	23.9	73.0	36.8	3.2	40.0	97.0	67.1	43.0	33.0	10.0
SIERRA LEONE	2.3	15.0	44.7	20.7	73.0	36.2	1.1	43.5	97.0	50.9	35.0	28.0	15.0
SOMALIA	2.4	28.3	47.2	21.7	77.0	:	:	41.0	79.0	55.1	58.0	41.0	50.0
SUDAN	2.2	13.2	47.8	17.5	66.5	20.9	5.1	48.6	88.0	60.4	40.0	27.0	15.0
SWAZILAND	3.2	14.3	49.0	21.8	83.0	:	:	43.5	89.0	:	103.0	102.0	50.0
TANZANIA	2.8	7.3	47.0	20.1	83.1	33.5	2.3	44.5	86.0	47.1	57.0	46.0	49.0
TOGO	2.7	15.0	50.6	23.3	75.0	:	:	41.0	96.0	52.1	98.0	68.0	12.0
UGANDA	3.1	8.4	45.2	15.9	86.0	20.0	6.2	50.0	90.0	54.0	44.0	43.0	25.0
UPPER VOLTA	2.2	12.1	48.5	25.8	89.0	:	:	38.0	78.0	59.2	14.0	11.0	7.0
ZAIRE	2.7	26.4	45.2	20.5	77.0	:	:	43.5	85.0	32.0	88.0	87.0	15.0
ZAMBIA	2.9	36.3	51.5	20.3	52.0	23.0	3.8	44.5	89.0	58.8	88.0	86.0	43.0
ALL COUNTRIES-MEDIAN	2.5	14.8	47.4	22.1	82.5	30.9	4.5	41.0	90.0	57.0	58.0	47.0	15.0

TABLE 3. COMPARATIVE SOCIAL INDICATORS FOR DEVELOPING COUNTRIES (BY GEOGRAPHIC AREA AND COUNTRY)

Continued

AREA AND COUNTRY	POPULATION & VITAL STATISTICS				EMPLOYMENT AND INCOME			HEALTH & NUTRITION			EDUCATION (MOST RECENT ESTIMATE)		
	POP. GROWTH RATE % (65-75)	URBAN POP. % TOTAL	CRUDE BIRTH RATE (/000)	CRUDE DEATH RATE (/000)	LABOR IN AGR. % OF TOTAL	INCOME RECD BY HIGHEST 5% HH	INCOME RECD BY LOWEST 20% HH	LIFE EXPECT. YRS AT BIRTH	CALORIE SUPPLY % CAP REQ.	PROTEIN SUPPLY GR/DAY /CAP	PRIMARY SCHOOL ENROLL RATIO %	FEMALE ENROLL. RATIO PRIMARY	ADULT LITERACY RATE % OF TOTAL
SOUTH ASIA													
AFGHANISTAN	2.2	14.3	51.4	30.7	52.9	..	..	40.3	83.0	61.5	23.0	7.0	14.0
BANGLADESH	2.3	8.8	49.5	28.1	78.0	16.7	7.9	45.0	93.0	58.5	73.0	51.0	23.0
BURMA	2.2	22.3	39.5	15.8	67.8	14.6	8.0	50.1	103.0	58.0	85.0	81.0	67.0
INDIA	2.2	20.6	37.0	17.0	69.0	25.0	4.7	49.5	89.0	48.0	65.0	52.0	36.0
NEPAL	2.1	4.8	42.9	20.3	94.4	..	..	43.6	95.0	50.0	59.0	10.0	19.2
PAKISTAN	2.9	26.0	47.4	16.5	54.8	17.3	8.4	49.8	93.0	54.0	51.0	31.0	21.0
SRI LANKA	2.0	24.3	28.2	7.9	55.0	18.6	7.3	67.8	97.0	48.0	77.0	77.0	78.1
ALL COUNTRIES-MEDIAN	2.2	20.6	42.9	17.0	67.8	17.3	7.9	49.5	93.0	54.0	65.0	51.0	23.0
EAST ASIA & PACIFIC													
CHINA REP.	2.6	51.1	23.0	4.7	35.0	13.3	8.8	68.6	111.0	68.0	104.0	..	82.0
FIJI	2.2	38.5	25.0	4.3	43.3	19.0	5.1	70.0	..	..	111.0	110.0	75.0
INDONESIA	2.3	18.2	42.9	16.9	69.0	33.7	6.8	48.1	98.0	43.8	81.0	75.0	62.0
KOREA	2.1	48.5	28.8	8.9	44.6	18.1	7.2	68.0	115.0	75.7	109.0	109.0	92.0
LAO P.D.R.	2.7	15.0	44.6	22.8	85.0	..	..	40.4	94.0	58.0	57.0	47.0	20.0
MALAYSIA	2.7	30.2	31.7	6.7	45.2	28.3	3.5	59.4	115.0	56.5	93.0	91.0	60.0
PAPUA NEW GUINEA	2.5	12.9	40.6	17.1	83.0	..	..	47.7	98.0	48.2	59.0	44.0	31.0
PHILIPPINES	2.9	29.8	43.8	10.5	52.6	28.8	5.5	58.5	87.0	50.0	105.0	103.0	87.0
SINGAPORE	1.7	90.2	21.2	5.2	2.8	..	..	89.5	122.0	74.7	111.0	108.0	75.0
THAILAND	3.1	16.5	37.6	9.1	76.0	22.0	5.6	58.0	107.0	50.0	78.0	75.0	82.0
VIET NAM	2.6	21.5	36.9	6.7	67.0	..	..	58.0	100.0	52.7	91.0	..	97.8
WESTERN SAMOA	1.9	..	36.9	8.9	52.6	..	..	58.5	103.5	53.6	93.0	91.0	75.0
ALL COUNTRIES-MEDIAN	2.6	29.8	36.9	8.9	52.6	22.0	5.6	58.5	103.5	53.6	93.0	91.0	75.0

COMPARATIVE ECONOMIC DATA
TABLE 4. Selected Economic Development Indicators: Population and Production
(Average annual real growth rates)

Income group/ region/country	Population				Gross domestic product				GDP per capita			
	1950-60	1960-65	1965-70	1970-77	1950-60	1960-65	1965-70	1970-77	1950-60	1960-65	1965-70	1970-77
Developing countries	2.2	2.4	2.5	2.4	4.9	5.6	6.4	5.7	2.7	3.1	3.8	3.2
Capital-surplus oil-exporting countries	2.3	3.2	3.7	4.1	..	..	11.0	6.7	..	..	7.2	3.0
Industrialized countries	1.2	1.2	0.9	0.8	3.8++	5.3	4.9	3.2	2.5++	4.0	4.0	2.4
Centrally planned economies	1.7	1.8	1.6	1.4	..	6.2+	7.7+	6.0+	..	4.8+	6.7+	5.6+
A. Developing countries by income group												
Low income	2.0	2.4	2.4	2.2	3.8	3.8	5.3	4.0	1.8	1.4	2.8	1.7
Middle income	2.4	2.5	2.5	2.5	5.3	6.1	6.6	6.0	2.8	3.5	4.0	3.4
B. Developing countries by region												
Africa south of Sahara	2.3	2.5	2.5	2.7	3.6	5.0	4.9	3.7	1.3	2.4	2.3	0.9
Middle East and North Africa	2.4	2.6	2.7	2.7	5.1	6.4	9.4	7.1	2.6	3.7	6.5	4.3
East Asia and Pacific	2.4	2.6	2.5	2.2	5.2	5.5	8.0	8.0	2.8	2.8	5.4	5.7
South Asia	1.9	2.4	2.4	2.2	3.8	4.3	4.9	3.2	1.8	1.9	2.4	1.0
Latin America and the Caribbean	2.8	2.8	2.7	2.7	5.3	5.2	6.1	6.2	2.4	2.3	3.3	3.4
Southern Europe	1.5	1.4	1.4	1.5	6.1	7.5	6.5	5.3	4.5	6.0	5.0	3.8
C. Developing countries by region and country												
Africa south of Sahara												
Angola	1.6	1.5	1.6	2.3	..	5.9	3.2	-9.4	..	4.3	1.6	-11.5
Benin	2.2	2.5	2.7	2.9	..	3.1	2.7	2.7	..	0.6	0.0	-0.1
Botswana	1.7	1.9	1.9	1.9	2.9	4.2	9.8	15.7	1.2	2.2	7.8	13.5
Burundi	2.0	2.3	2.4	1.9	-1.3	2.8	5.8	2.3	-3.2	0.5	3.3	0.4
Cameroon	1.4	1.7	1.9	2.2	1.7	2.9	7.3	3.4	0.3	1.2	5.3	1.2
Cape Verde	3.1	3.1	2.7	2.1	..	..	4.0	3.0	..	..	1.3	0.9
Central African Republic	1.4	2.2	2.2	2.2	2.6	0.5	3.5	3.1	1.1	-1.7	1.3	-0.9
Chad	1.4	1.8	1.9	2.2	..	0.5	1.6	1.2	..	-1.3	-0.3	-0.9
Comores	3.0	3.2	3.3	3.8	..	9.5	3.2	-1.5	..	6.1	-0.1	-5.2
Congo, People's Republic of the	1.6	2.1	2.2	2.5	1.1	2.7	3.4	3.9	-0.5	0.6	1.2	1.4
Equatorial Guinea	1.5	1.7	1.9	2.2	..	13.8	2.0	-3.0	..	11.8	0.1	-5.0
Ethiopia	2.1	2.3	2.4	2.5	3.9	5.1	3.7	2.6	1.7	2.7	1.2	0.1

TABLE 4. COMPARATIVE ECONOMIC DATA (Continued)

Income group/ region/country	Population				Gross domestic product				GDP per capita			
	1950-60	1960-65	1965-70	1970-77	1950-60	1960-65	1965-70	1970-77	1950-60	1960-65	1965-70	1970-77
Gambia, The	2.0	3.3	3.2	3.1	1.3	5.2	4.3	8.2	-0.7	1.9	1.1	4.9
Ghana	4.5	2.7	2.1	3.0	4.1	3.3	2.5	0.4	-0.4	0.6	0.4	-2.5
Guinea	2.2	2.7	3.0	3.0	…	3.9	3.0	5.4	…	1.2	0.0	2.4
Guinea-Bissau	0.2	-1.1	-0.2	1.6	…	…	…	…	…	…	…	…
Ivory Coast	2.1	3.7	3.8	6.0	3.6	10.1	7.4	6.5	1.5	6.1	3.5	0.5
Kenya	3.3	3.4	3.5	3.8	4.0	3.6	8.8	4.8	0.7	0.2	4.9	1.0
Lesotho	1.5	1.8	2.2	2.4	4.4	8.7	2.1	8.0	2.8	6.7	-0.1	5.5
Liberia	2.8	3.1	3.2	3.4	10.5	3.1	6.4	2.7	7.4	0.0	3.1	-0.6
Madagascar	1.8	2.1	2.3	2.5	2.3	1.4	4.9	-0.7	0.5	-0.7	2.5	-3.2
Malawi	2.4	2.7	2.9	3.1	…	3.3	4.5	6.3	…	0.6	1.5	3.1
Mali	2.1	2.5	2.4	2.5	3.2	3.2	2.9	4.7	1.0	0.7	0.5	2.1
Mauritania	2.2	2.5	2.6	2.7	…	9.9	4.0	2.2	…	7.2	2.0	-0.5
Mauritius	3.3	2.7	1.9	1.3	0.1	5.4	-0.3	8.2	-3.0	2.7	-2.2	6.8
Mozambique	1.4	2.1	2.3	2.5	3.1	2.3	8.3	-3.7	1.7	0.2	5.9	-6.1
Namibia	…	2.4	2.6	2.8	…	…	…	…	…	…	…	…
Niger	2.3	4.0	2.7	2.8	…	6.6	-0.3	1.2	…	2.5	-2.9	-1.5
Nigeria	2.4	2.5	2.5	2.6	4.1	5.3	4.5	6.0	1.6	2.7	1.9	3.3
Réunion	…	3.3	2.5	1.8	…	…	…	…	…	…	…	…
Rhodesia	4.1	4.2	3.7	3.3	…	3.2	6.1	3.2	…	-0.9	2.4	-0.1
Rwanda	2.3	2.5	2.7	2.9	1.0	-2.9	8.5	5.2	-1.2	-5.3	5.6	2.2
Senegal	2.2	2.4	2.5	2.6	…	3.6	1.3	2.8	…	1.1	-1.2	0.2
Sierra Leone	1.8	2.1	2.3	2.5	3.6	4.3	3.9	1.5	1.8	2.1	1.6	-1.0
Somalia	2.0	2.4	2.5	2.3	12.8	-0.5	3.4	1.2	10.6	-2.8	0.9	-1.1
South Africa	3.0	2.5	2.7	2.7	2.9	6.6	5.9	4.0	-0.1	4.0	3.1	1.2
Sudan	1.9	2.2	2.4	2.6	5.5	1.5	1.3	5.4	3.5	-0.7	-1.0	2.7
Swaziland	2.0	2.3	2.1	2.5	8.4	13.6	6.3	6.2	6.3	11.0	4.1	3.7
Tanzania, United Republic of	2.2	2.6	2.8	3.0	6.0	5.2	5.9	5.2	3.7	2.6	3.1	2.1
Togo	2.2	2.7	2.7	2.6	1.3	8.4	6.7	4.0	-0.9	5.6	3.9	1.4
Uganda	2.8	3.8	3.7	3.0	3.3	5.7	5.9	0.5	0.5	1.8	2.2	-2.4
Upper Volta	1.9	1.6	1.6	1.6	1.6	2.7	3.3	0.5	-0.3	1.0	1.6	-1.0
Zaire	2.3	1.9	2.1	2.7	3.4	3.7	4.3	1.0	1.1	1.7	2.2	-1.7
Zambia	2.4	2.8	2.9	3.0	5.6	5.4	2.8	2.8	3.1	2.6	-0.1	-0.2

TABLE 4. COMPARATIVE ECONOMIC DATA (Continued)

Income group/ region/country	Population				Gross domestic product				GDP per capita			
	1950-60	1960-65	1965-70	1970-77	1950-60	1960-65	1965-70	1970-77	1950-60	1960-65	1965-70	1970-77
C. Developing countries by region and country (cont.)												
Middle East and North Africa												
Algeria	2.1	2.0	3.7	3.2	0.5	0.8	8.1	5.4	4.4	-1.2	4.2	2.2
Bahrain	3.5	4.2	2.9	7.1	...	...	...	10.7ᵈ	...	...	...	3.2ᵈ
Egypt, Arab Republic of	2.4	2.5	2.1	2.1	3.3	7.6	3.2	6.4	0.9	4.9	1.1	4.2
Iran	2.5	2.7	2.8	3.0	5.9	9.2	12.6	7.4	3.3	6.3	9.5	4.3
Iraq	2.8	3.1	3.2	3.4	9.9	7.7	4.1	8.1ᵉ	6.9	4.5	0.9	4.7ᵉ
Jordan	3.2	3.0	3.2	3.3	...	...	...	7.0ᶠ	...	...	...	3.6ᶠ
Lebanon	2.6	3.0	2.8	2.5	...	...	...	...	...	...	...	...
Morocco	2.7	2.5	2.9	2.7	2.0	4.2	5.7	6.4	-0.7	1.7	2.8	3.6
Syrian Arab Republic	2.7	3.1	3.3	3.3	...	8.8	5.6	9.6	...	5.4	2.3	6.2
Tunisia	1.8	1.9	2.1	2.0	...	5.2ᶜ	4.9	8.5	...	3.3ᶜ	2.8	6.4
Yemen, Arab Republic of	2.0	2.1	1.5	1.9	...	...	...	8.4	...	...	...	6.4
Yemen, People's Democratic Republic of	1.9	1.9	1.9	1.9	...	...	...	6.8ᵈ	...	...	...	4.8ᵈ
East Asia and Pacific												
Fiji	3.1	3.3	2.3	1.8	2.8	3.7	7.4	5.0	-0.3	0.3	5.0	3.1
Hong Kong	4.5	3.7	1.3	2.0	9.2	11.7	8.0	8.0	4.5	7.7	6.6	5.9
Indonesia	2.1	2.2	2.2	1.8	4.0	1.6	7.5	8.0	1.9	-0.6	5.2	6.1
Korea, Republic of	2.0	2.6	2.2	2.0	5.1	6.7	10.3	9.9	3.1	4.0	7.9	7.8
Malaysia	2.5	2.9	2.9	2.7	3.6	6.8	5.9	7.8	1.0	3.7	2.9	4.9
Papua New Guinea	1.8	2.3	2.4	2.4	4.8	6.4	5.7	5.0	2.9	4.0	3.3	2.5
Philippines	2.7	3.0	3.1	2.7	6.5	5.2	5.2	6.3	3.6	2.2	2.1	3.5
Singapore	4.8	2.8	2.0	1.6	...	5.5	13.0	8.6	...	2.6	10.7	6.9
Solomon Islands	2.6	2.6	2.6	3.5	10.7	3.7	2.5	5.4	7.9	1.1	-0.1	1.8
Taiwan	3.5	3.0	2.4	2.0	7.6	8.9	9.2	7.7	4.0	5.8	6.7	5.6
Thailand	2.8	3.0	3.1	2.9	5.7	7.4	8.4	7.1	2.8	4.2	5.1	4.0
South Asia												
Afghanistan	1.5	2.2	2.2	2.2	...	1.7	2.3	4.5	...	-0.4	0.2	2.2
Bangladesh	2.4	2.8	3.0	2.5	...	4.6	3.4	2.3	...	1.8	0.4	-0.1

TABLE 4. COMPARATIVE ECONOMIC DATA (Continued)

Income group/region/country	Population 1950-60	1960-65	1965-70	1970-77	Gross domestic product 1950-60	1960-65	1965-70	1970-77	GDP per capita 1950-60	1960-65	1965-70	1970-77
Bhutan	..	1.9	2.1	2.3	..	..	..	..	..	..	..	..
Burma	1.9	2.1	2.2	2.2	6.3	4.4	2.3	3.6	4.3	2.2	0.1	1.4
India	1.9	2.3	2.4	2.1	3.8	4.0	5.0	3.1	1.9	1.7	2.6	1.0
Nepal	1.2	1.9	2.2	2.2	2.4	2.7	2.2	2.6	1.2	0.8	0.0	0.4
Pakistan	2.3	2.7	2.9	3.1	2.4	7.2	6.9	3.8	0.1	4.4	3.8	0.7
Sri Lanka	2.6	2.5	2.3	1.7	3.9	4.0	5.8	2.9	1.3	1.5	3.4	1.1
Latin America and the Caribbean												
Argentina	1.9	1.5	1.4	1.3	2.8	3.6	4.5	2.8	0.9	2.0	3.1	1.5
Bahamas	3.6	4.8	4.4	2.7	..	..	..	..	..	..	..	..
Barbados	0.9	0.3	0.3	0.5	5.9	4.5	7.9	2.0	4.9	4.1	7.6	1.4
Belize	3.1	2.8	2.8	0.9	..	..	..	6.0	..	..	..	5.0
Bolivia	2.1	2.5	2.6	2.7	..	5.0	4.8	5.9	..	2.5	2.1	3.1
Brazil	3.1	2.9	2.9	2.9	6.9	4.0	8.0	9.9	3.7	1.1	5.0	6.8
Chile	2.2	2.3	1.9	1.7	4.0	4.9	3.6	0.1	1.8	2.6	1.7	-1.6
Colombia	3.1	3.3	2.8	2.1	4.6	4.7	5.9	5.7	1.5	1.4	2.9	3.6
Costa Rica	3.7	3.7	3.2	2.5	..	5.3	6.9	6.0	..	1.5	3.6	3.3
Dominican Republic	2.9	2.9	2.9	3.0	5.8	4.6	6.6	8.0	2.8	1.6	3.6	4.9
Ecuador	2.9	3.0	3.0	3.0	..	..	5.8	9.2	..	..	2.7	6.0
El Salvador	2.8	3.4	3.5	3.1	4.4	6.7	4.3	5.3	1.5	3.2	0.7	2.1
Honduras	3.3	3.5	2.8	3.3	3.1	4.9	4.2	3.2	-0.2	1.4	1.4	-0.1
Jamaica	1.5	1.6	1.2	1.7	8.1	3.7	5.1	0.0	6.5	2.1	3.9	-1.7
Mexico	3.2	3.3	3.3	3.3	5.6	7.4	6.8	4.9	2.4	3.9	3.5	1.5
Netherlands Antilles	1.7	1.7	1.4	1.2	..	..	..	..	..	..	..	..
Nicaragua	2.9	3.0	3.0	3.3	5.2	10.4	4.1	5.8	2.2	7.2	1.1	2.4
Panama	2.9	3.1	3.1	3.1	4.9	7.9	7.8	3.5	1.9	4.7	4.6	0.4
Paraguay	2.6	2.6	2.7	2.9	2.7	4.5	4.3	7.0	0.1	1.9	1.6	4.0
Peru	2.6	2.9	2.9	2.8	4.9	7.1	4.3	4.5	2.2	4.1	1.4	1.7
Puerto Rico	0.6	1.6	1.3	1.2	5.3	8.1	7.0	3.6	4.7	6.5	5.6	0.7
Trinidad and Tobago	2.8	3.0	1.1	1.2	..	4.7	3.3	2.2	..	1.8	2.2	1.0
Uruguay	1.1	1.2	1.0	0.2	1.7	0.6	1.9	1.6	0.3	-0.6	1.0	1.3
Venezuela	4.0	3.6	3.3	3.4	8.0	7.4	4.9	5.6	3.8	3.7	1.6	2.2

TABLE 4. COMPARATIVE ECONOMIC DATA (Continued)

Income group/ region/country	Population				Gross domestic product				GDP per capita			
	1950-60	1960-65	1965-70	1970-77	1950-60	1960-65	1965-70	1970-77	1950-60	1960-65	1965-70	1970-77
C. Developing countries by region and country (cont.)												
Southern Europe												
Cyprus	1.5	0.6	0.8	0.7	4.0	3.7	8.1	1.0	2.5	3.0	7.2	0.3
Greece	1.0	0.5	0.6	0.7	6.0	7.7	7.2	4.6	5.0	7.2	6.6	3.9
Israel	5.3	3.9	3.0	2.8	11.3	9.8	8.7	5.0	5.6	5.6	5.5	2.2
Malta	0.5	-0.6	0.5	0.3	3.3	0.3	9.0	11.4	2.7	0.9	8.5	11.1
Portugal	0.7	0.2	-0.2	0.8	4.1	6.4	6.4	4.6	3.4	6.1	6.6	3.7
Spain	0.8	1.0	1.1	1.0	6.2	8.0	6.3	4.7	5.3	7.5	5.1	3.6
Turkey	2.8	2.5	2.5	2.5	6.3	5.3	6.3	7.3	3.4	2.8	3.7	4.6
Yugoslavia	1.2	1.1	0.9	0.9	5.6	6.6	6.2	6.2	4.4	5.4	5.2	5.2
D. Capital-surplus oil-exporting countries												
Kuwait	6.2	11.1	9.6	6.2	...	4.7[b]	5.7	-0.1	...	-5.8	-3.5	-6.0
Libyan Arab Republic	2.7	3.8	4.2	4.1	...	...	...	...	...	...	...	...
Oman	2.0	2.5	2.7	3.2	...	5.7	39.7	6.8	...	3.2	36.0	3.5
Qatar	2.4	7.1	6.9	10.3	...	...	...	...	...	...	...	...
Saudi Arabia	2.0	2.5	2.8	3.0	...	...	9.1	12.7	...	...	6.1	9.4
United Arab Emirates	2.4	9.3	13.7	16.7	...	...	...	12.5[f]	...	...	...	-2.1[f]
E. Industrialized countries												
Australia	2.3	2.0	1.9	1.7	4.7[i]	5.3	6.2	3.3	2.3[i]	3.2	4.2	1.6
Austria	0.2	0.6	0.5	0.2	5.6	4.3	5.1	4.0	5.4	3.7	4.6	3.8
Belgium	0.6	0.7	0.4	0.3	3.1[i]	5.2	4.8	3.7	2.5[i]	4.5	4.4	3.4
Canada	2.7	1.9	1.7	1.2	4.0[i]	5.8	4.8	4.7	1.3[i]	3.8	3.0	3.4
Denmark	0.7	0.8	0.7	0.4	3.6[j]	5.1	4.5	2.8	2.9[j]	4.3	3.7	2.4
Finland	1.0	0.6	0.2	0.4	4.9	5.0	5.1	3.4	3.9	4.4	4.9	3.0
France	0.9	1.3	0.8	0.7	4.8	5.9	5.3	3.8	3.8	4.5	4.5	3.1
Germany, Federal Republic of	1.0	1.3	0.6	0.2	7.3[j]	4.8	4.5	2.4	6.3[j]	3.5	3.9	2.2
Iceland	2.1	1.8	1.2	1.3	...	7.1	1.1	4.6	...	5.2	-0.2	3.2
Ireland	-0.5	0.3	0.5	1.2	...	4.0	5.3	3.4	...	3.7	4.7	2.3
Italy	0.7	0.7	0.7	0.7	5.5[g]	5.0	6.1	2.9	4.8[g]	4.3	5.4	2.2

TABLE 4. COMPARATIVE ECONOMIC DATA (Continued)

Income group/ region/country	Population				Gross domestic product				GDP per capita			
	1950-60	1960-65	1965-70	1970-77	1950-60	1960-65	1965-70	1970-77	1950-60	1960-65	1965-70	1970-77
Japan	1.3	1.0	1.1	1.2	8.0[i]	10.1	12.4	5.0	6.6[i]	9.0	11.2	3.7
Luxembourg	0.6	1.1	0.4	0.8	..	3.3	3.6	2.3	..	2.2	3.2	1.5
Netherlands, The	1.3	1.4	1.2	0.9	4.7	4.9	5.7	3.2	3.3	3.5	4.4	2.3
New Zealand	2.2	2.1	1.4	1.7	..	5.0	2.6	2.9	..	2.9	1.2	1.2
Norway	0.9	0.8	0.8	0.6	3.4[i]	5.1	4.8	4.8	2.5[i]	4.3	3.9	4.1
Sweden	0.6	0.7	0.8	0.4	3.4	5.3	3.9	1.7	2.7	4.6	3.1	1.3
Switzerland	1.3	2.1	1.1	0.2	4.6	5.2	4.2	0.2	3.2	3.0	3.1	0.0
United Kingdom	0.4	0.7	0.3	0.1	2.8	3.2	2.5	1.9	2.3	2.4	2.2	1.7
United States	1.7	1.5	1.1	0.8	3.3	4.7	3.2	2.8	1.5	3.2	2.1	1.9
F. Centrally planned economies[k]												
Albania	2.8	3.0	2.8	2.5	..	..	..	..	..	..	..	..
Bulgaria	0.8	0.8	0.7	0.6	..	7.0	8.6	7.5	..	6.2	7.8	6.9
China	1.9	2.0	1.8	1.6	..	..	..	..	..	..	..	..
Cuba	2.6	2.1	1.9	1.6	..	..	..	..	..	..	..	..
Czechoslovakia	1.0	0.7	0.3	0.7	..	..	6.6[a]	5.2	..	..	6.3[a]	4.5
German Democratic Republic	-0.6	-0.3	0.0	-0.2	..	2.7[l]	5.5[l]	5.1[l]	..	5.9	5.5	5.3
Hungary	0.7	0.3	0.4	0.4	..	4.5	6.8	6.2	..	4.2	6.4	5.8
Korea, Democratic People's Republic of	0.8	2.8	2.8	2.6	..	..	..	..	..	..	..	..
Mongolia	2.2	2.8	3.1	3.0	..	..	..	..	..	..	..	..
Poland	1.8	1.3	0.6	1.0	..	6.0	6.0	8.7	..	4.6	5.4	7.6
Romania	1.2	0.7	1.4	0.9	..	8.8	7.7	10.7	..	8.0	6.2	10.1[m]
Union of Soviet Socialist Republics	1.8	1.5	1.0	0.9	..	6.6	8.2	6.1	..	5.0	7.1	5.5[m]

+ Weighted average of the country growth rates; GDP in US dollars were used as weights; these are not strictly comparable to other group averages.   ++ 1955-60.   a. 1966-70.   b. 1967-70.

differences in national accounting system   l. Based on NMP index (1960=100) constructed from 1975 constant price series.   m. 1970-76.

TABLE 4. COMPARATIVE ECONOMIC DATA (Continued)

| | Gross production | | | | | | | |
| | Agriculture | | | | Manufacturing | | | |
	1950-60	1960-65	1965-70	1970-77	1950-60	1960-65	1965-70	1970-77
Developing countries	3.9	2.6	3.4	2.7	4.9	7.6	7.5	7.4
Capital-surplus oil-exporting countries	..	..	2.2	4.4	..	..	..	..
Industrialized countries	2.3+	2.0	2.2	2.1	6.1+	5.9	5.8	2.8
Centrally planned economies	..	..	3.2+	2.4+	..	8.0+	8.3+	7.4+
A. Developing countries by income group								
Low income	..	1.6	4.1	2.2	..	8.4	3.3	5.2
Middle income	4.5	3.1	3.0	3.0	4.7	7.5	7.9	7.2
B. Developing countries by region								
Africa south of Sahara	4.8	2.6	2.4	1.3	..	8.3	6.0	5.6
Middle East and North Africa	..	1.3	3.6	2.8	..	10.0	6.9	12.1
East Asia and Pacific	4.8	4.6	3.4	4.1	..	4.8	11.9	11.6
South Asia	3.2	1.1	4.7	2.1	6.4	8.8	3.5	4.3
Latin America and the Caribbean	..	3.5	2.8	3.3	4.0	5.6	6.7	5.8
Southern Europe	4.4	3.2	3.2	3.1	8.4	11.4	9.3	6.1
C. Developing countries by region and country								
Africa south of Sahara								
Angola	..	3.2	2.0	-3.4	..	..	..	..
Benin	3.3	1.9	5.2	1.5	..	..	..	..
Botswana	..	2.4	0.4	4.5	..	..	..	..
Burundi	-1.5	1.7	1.7	2.0	..	..	..	..
Cameroon	3.7	7.2	4.4	1.8	..	..	10.7*	6.2
Cape Verde	..	..	..	..	..	..	..	..
Central African Republic	..	-1.2	3.3	2.1	..	4.1	8.1	6.0
Chad	..	0.9	-0.3	0.2	..	..	2.0[b]	5.7
Comoros	..	..	..	..	..	..	..	..
Congo, People's Republic of the	..	0.0	2.9	2.8	..	3.4	7.7	2.3
Equatorial Guinea	..	4.8[c]	-3.1	-4.9	..	..	..	..
Ethiopia	4.1	1.8	1.9	-0.1	..	..	..	..
Gabon	..	3.2[c]	1.9	1.3	..	..	..	..

TABLE II COMPARATIVE ECONOMIC DATA (Continued)

| | Gross production | | | | | | | |
| | Agriculture | | | | Manufacturing | | | |
	1950-60	1960-65	1965-70	1970-77	1950-60	1960-65	1965-70	1970-77
Gambia, The	0.4	7.1	-0.3	1.7	...	3.1	8.9	4.3
Ghana	7.0	3.5	3.8	-0.4	4.0	10.8	12.5	-1.9
Guinea	2.7	1.9	3.5	0.0	...	...	...	...
Guinea-Bissau	...	...	...	...	...	...	...	...
Ivory Coast	9.3	11.3	3.7	4.5	...	14.2	8.0	7.5
Kenya	4.7	2.9	1.1	3.0	...	...	...	...
Lesotho	...	0.1	1.5	2.0	...	...	...	...
Liberia	2.6	3.0	3.0	2.3	...	...	14.1	5.5
Madagascar	3.9	4.1	1.6	2.7	...	...	...	1.2
Malawi	...	3.8	3.4	3.8	...	...	...	10.6
Mali	1.8	2.3	3.2	2.7	...	...	4.0	9.2
Mauritania	...	3.4	2.2	-3.3	...	...	35.1	2.9
Mauritius	...	3.1	-1.4	2.6	...	...	...	...
Mozambique	...	0.8	4.4	-1.6	...	...	...	...
Namibia	...	...	...	...	...	...	...	...
Niger	5.5	5.2	0.6	0.4	...	14.6	8.8	8.6
Nigeria	5.1	2.1	1.7	1.7	...	11.1	10.4	8.1
Réunion	...	...	...	...	...	...	...	...
Rhodesia	...	2.9	0.0	3.9	5.0	6.2	7.5	3.8
Rwanda	...	-1.6	8.4	3.6	...	...	...	...
Senegal	4.8	4.1	-4.5	5.0	...	0.4	1.2	8.2
Sierra Leone	0.3	4.7	2.2	2.0	...	...	2.7	3.6
Somalia	...	2.7	1.9	0.0	...	...	...	...
South Africa	4.1	1.5	3.9	2.2	5.0	8.4	6.7	3.2
Sudan	-0.4	5.4	6.0	2.3	...	...	...	...
Swaziland	...	4.6	7.0	3.6	...	17.1[c]	21.9	7.3
Tanzania, United Republic of	6.9	2.9	3.0	1.2	...	...	...	...
Togo	9.3	31.3	1.4	-5.5	...	...	6.7	11.3
Uganda	6.9	1.4	4.2	0.8	...	...	...	...
Upper Volta	-0.2	7.2	2.2	1.6	...	...	3.8[b]	7.1
Zaire	1.0	-2.2	2.3	1.9	...	...	0.3	1.1
Zambia	...	1.2	1.9	4.7	...	12.1	8.6	1.7

TABLE 4. COMPARATIVE ECONOMIC DATA (Continued)

| | Gross production | | | | | | | |
| | Agriculture | | | | Manufacturing | | | |
	1950-60	1960-65	1965-70	1970-77	1950-60	1960-65	1965-70	1970-77
C. Developing countries by region and country (cont.)								
Middle East and North Africa								
Algeria	-0.5	-2.2	4.1	0.4	..	..	..	..
Bahrain	..	..	1.6	4.0	..	..	..	..
Egypt, Arab Republic of	3.4	3.6	3.5	0.7	..	20.0	3.8	6.3
Iran	2.1	2.7	4.1	4.2	8.8	9.5	13.4	16.0
Iraq	1.5	4.0	4.0	-2.3	..	..	..	..
Jordan	..	20.7	-15.3	-1.6	..	..	..	..
Lebanon	5.0	9.1	0.7	-0.5	..	..	..	..
Morocco	3.0	5.1	4.1	-2.0	5.2	3.3	5.8	6.5
Syrian Arab Republic	2.1	10.8	-1.7	9.8	6.3	9.2	4.8	8.3
Tunisia	4.5	3.6	-0.5	5.6	..	2.9	4.8	5.6
Yemen, Arab Republic of	..	1.2	-4.3	3.1	..	..	..	..
Yemen, People's Democratic Republic of	..	2.6	1.2	3.8	..	..	..	..
East Asia and Pacific								
Fiji	..	11.2^c	3.3	-0.4	..	..	5.4	3.0
Hong Kong	..	0.9	-0.3	-10.3	..	12.4	18.6	4.0
Indonesia	2.0	3.9	3.3	3.1	..	1.0	7.9	12.5
Korea, Republic of	5.5	6.3	3.1	4.9	16.4	13.9	25.6	23.5
Malaysia	0.9	5.2	6.4	4.3	..	..	11.5	12.6
Papua New Guinea	..	4.2	2.8	3.1	9.7^g	..	..	..
Philippines	3.3	2.8	3.2	5.8	..	6.2	4.4	5.2
Singapore	..	1.4	15.8	1.0	..	7.7	15.8	11.2
Solomon Islands	..	1.4	0.9	1.9	..	..	..	..
Taiwan	4.8	4.8	2.9	3.1	15.4	13.6	21.0	13.3
Thailand	3.8	6.6	3.1	4.7	6.4	10.8	10.2	11.8
South Asia								
Afghanistan	..	1.6	1.0	4.0	..	..	8.0	9.3
Bangladesh	..	3.1	3.1	1.8	..	5.8	7.4	5.7

TABLE 4. COMPARATIVE ECONOMIC DATA (Continued)

	Gross production							
	Agriculture				Manufacturing			
	1950-60	1960-65	1965-70	1970-77	1950-60	1960-65	1965-70	1970-77
Bhutan	2.5	..	..	..	..	..	..	..
Burma	3.2	3.1	3.1	1.6	6.6	5.6	1.7	4.4
India	..	0.5	4.9	2.1	..	9.0	2.8	4.6
Nepal	..	0.9	1.7	1.2	..	..	..	..
Pakistan	..	4.6	5.9	2.6	..	12.1	9.4	2.6
Sri Lanka	2.3	3.0	2.1	2.4	-0.9	6.1	5.6	2.7
Latin America and the Carribean								
Argentina	..	3.0	3.0	3.3	0.4	3.9	6.1	3.0
Bahamas	..	..	..	..	..	..	..	..
Barbados	..	3.6	-2.5	-2.7	..	..	1.6*	6.5
Belize	..	13.7	5.4	2.6	..	..	..	..
Bolivia	..	4.1	4.2	4.4	1.3	7.0	3.4	7.1
Brazil	4.5	3.2	2.7	4.4	9.1	3.7	10.4	9.6
Chile	2.9	2.2	2.5	1.7	5.7	6.7	1.5	-4.4
Colombia	..	2.8	3.6	3.9	6.5	5.7	6.2	6.5
Costa Rica	..	3.4	5.6	3.5	..	9.2	8.0	8.1
Dominican Republic	..	-2.7	3.0	2.0	5.0	1.5	11.4	8.8
Ecuador	..	5.8	0.4	3.5	..	..	7.2	10.6
El Salvador	..	2.9	5.3	3.3	5.7	17.0	5.0	8.3
Honduras	..	4.5	-1.3	1.3	7.0	3.0	4.9	5.6
Jamaica	2.9	3.2	2.0	1.1	..	7.6	3.0	0.6
Mexico	5.4	5.9	3.1	2.1	7.0	9.6	8.4	5.9
Netherlands Antilles	..	1.2	1.2	..	..	..	..	..
Nicaragua	1.1	13.0	0.5	9.7	10.7	12.6	..	..
Panama	..	4.3	0.5	5.0	..	..	9.6	1.2
Paraguay	..	4.9	2.4	3.5	..	3.5	5.9	3.1
Peru	3.6	2.4	2.3	4.6	7.3	9.7	6.7	5.8
Puerto Rico	..	2.8	..	0.7	..	..	..	..
Trinidad and Tobago	..	2.8	1.4	-0.5	..	..	6.1	-1.1
Uruguay	0.3	2.3	3.1	0.4	3.2	1.0	2.4	2.7
Venezuela	..	5.6	5.7	2.2	13.0	9.5	3.6	5.6

TABLE 4. COMPARATIVE ECONOMIC DATA (Continued)

| | Gross production | | | | | | | |
| | Agriculture | | | | Manufacturing | | | |
	1950-60	1960-65	1965-70	1970-77	1950-60	1960-65	1965-70	1970-77
C. Developing countries by region and country (cont.)								
Southern Europe								
Cyprus	3.8	7.7	5.4	0.8	:	2.5	10.1	1.4
Greece	4.7	6.5	2.4	3.8	7.9	7.9	8.7	7.7
Israel	12.0	8.1	5.8	4.9	11.6	13.6	11.6	6.1
Malta	:	2.7	6.7	0.4	:	:	:	:
Portugal	2.1	3.7	1.1	-1.1	6.7	8.7	8.9	1.2
Spain	2.9	2.6	3.3	3.4	8.8	12.6	10.1	7.9
Turkey	4.7	2.9	4.0	3.7	8.6	12.7	11.6	10.1
Yugoslavia	6.2	2.5	3.1	4.6	10.4	11.7	6.1	8.2
D. Capital-surplus oil-exporting countries								
Kuwait	:	:	3.0	1.5	:	:	:	:
Libyan Arab Republic	3.9	7.2	-2.0	11.4	:	:	:	:
Oman	:	:	2.8	2.1	:	:	:	:
Qatar	:	:	:	:	:	:	:	:
Saudi Arabia	:	2.8	2.9	2.8	:	:	11.9	4.0
United Arab Emirates	:	:	:	:	:	:	:	:
E. Industrialized countries								
Australia	3.8	0.5	3.6	1.9	6.3	6.1	4.9	1.3
Austria	4.7	0.7	3.6	1.9	7.5	4.5	6.4	3.3
Belgium	1.3	0.7	4.3	0.9	4.1	6.3	6.0	2.6
Canada	2.5	5.0	-1.2	2.8	3.5	6.3	4.9	3.7
Denmark	1.5	0.8	-1.1	1.2	3.5	6.9	4.6	1.8
Finland	3.4	2.4	1.4	1.4	6.4	6.2	7.5	3.3
France	3.2	2.7	1.6	1.3	6.8	5.5	9.6	2.8
Germany, Federal Republic of	3.3	0.8	3.7	0.4	9.8	5.7	6.5	1.6
Iceland	:	:	:	3.2	:	:	:	:
Ireland	2.2	0.3	3.2	3.9	3.0	6.6	7.1	4.1
Italy	2.2	3.0	2.4	1.0	9.3	6.3	7.3	3.0

TABLE 4. COMPARATIVE ECONOMIC DATA (Continued)

	Gross production							
	Agriculture				Manufacturing			
	1950-60	1960-65	1965-70	1970-77	1950-60	1960-65	1965-70	1970-77
Japan	2.4	3.2	3.3	2.1	18.3	11.5	16.3	2.9
Luxembourg	1.3	0.7	4.5	0.9	4.4	1.8	4.5	0.0
Netherlands, The	2.9	0.1	6.6	3.0	5.9	6.2	7.4	2.1
New Zealand	3.0	3.0	2.2	1.0	..	..	..	..
Norway	0.6	-0.8	0.8	1.6	4.8	5.8	4.2	2.2
Sweden	-0.2	0.3	0.7	2.5	3.0	7.4	4.9	2.0
Switzerland	1.1	-0.9	2.5	1.9	6.0	5.1	5.8	-1.0
United Kingdom	2.7	3.1	1.1	0.8	3.5	3.4	3.0	0.5
United States	1.8	1.7	1.5	3.1	3.4	6.3	3.8	3.3
F. Centrally planned economies								
Albania	..	..	4.2	3.4	..	..	..	..
Bulgaria	..	..	1.5	1.6	..	11.0	11.0	8.4
China	..	..	2.5	3.0	..	..	..	..
Cuba	..	..	4.0	0.0	..	..	..	..
Czechoslovakia	..	..	3.8	2.9	..	4.5	6.8	6.7
German Democratic Republic	..	..	1.2	3.6	..	5.7	6.4	6.3
Hungary	..	..	2.7	3.7	..	7.7	5.9	6.2
Korea, Democratic People's Republic of	..	..	2.1	6.7	..	..	..	..
Mongolia	..	..	-2.0	2.3	..	..	..	..
Poland	..	..	1.6	1.3	..	8.7	8.9	10.7
Romania	..	..	-0.4	6.9	..	..	..	..
Union of Soviet Socialist Republics	..	..	4.1	1.8	..	8.4	8.6	7.2

c. 1961-65. d. 1973-77. e. 1970-75. f. 1972-77. g. 1951-60. h. 1962-65. i. 1952-60. j. 1953-60. k. GDP data are not strictly comparable to those of other countries

TABLE 5 Capital Flows and Debt of the Oil-importing Developing Countries : Low-income and Middle-income, 1975–90

(billions of current dollars)

Item	Low-income					Middle-income				
	1975	1977	1980	1985	1990	1975	1977	1980	1985	1990
Current account deficit before interest payments[a]	4.8	1.4	8.8	16.0	26.8	28.1	15.3	33.9	27.4	25.5
Interest payments	0.6	0.7	1.2	2.6	5.3	6.1	7.4	17.1	32.3	56.7
Changes in reserves and short-term debt	0.4	3.0	−0.9	0.7	1.0	−9.5	7.0	−3.5	6.1	22.5
Total to be financed	5.9	5.1	9.1	19.4	33.0	24.7	29.7	47.4	65.8	94.7
Financed by medium- and long-term capital										
From public sources	5.4	4.7	8.3	18.5	31.4	7.1	8.5	13.4	22.6	35.2
From private sources	0.5	0.4	0.8	0.9	1.7	17.6	21.2	34.0	43.2	59.5
Private direct investment	0.2	0.2	0.3	0.6	1.0	4.0	3.7	6.2	9.0	15.4
Private loans	0.3	0.3	0.5	0.2	0.7	13.6	17.5	27.9	34.2	44.1
Total net capital flows										
Current dollars	5.9	5.1	9.1	19.4	33.0	24.7	29.7	47.4	65.8	94.7
Constant 1977 dollars	6.6	5.1	6.5	9.6	12.2	27.7	29.7	33.6	32.5	35.0
Outstanding medium- and long-term debt										
Public sources	24.4	32.0	44.8	89.4	172.2	33.3	45.5	55.6	123.5	224.9
Private sources	3.1	3.3	0.8	3.6	9.3	69.5	105.6	186.3	339.8	549.2
Total debt										
Current dollars	27.5	35.3	45.6	93.0	181.5	102.8	151.1	241.9	463.3	774.1
Constant 1977 dollars	30.9	35.3	32.3	46.0	67.0	115.5	151.1	171.2	229.0	285.9
Debt service										
Interest payments	0.6	0.7	1.2	2.6	5.3	6.1	7.4	17.1	32.3	56.7
Debt amortization	1.2	1.3	2.2	3.7	6.0	11.5	17.6	26.4	61.3	108.3
Interest payments as percentage of GNP	0.4	0.4	0.4	0.5	0.6	1.0	0.9	1.3	1.3	1.4
Price deflator	89.2	100.0	141.3	202.3	270.8	89.3	100.0	141.3	202.3	270.8

Source: High-case projections of *World Development Report, 1980.*
a. Excludes official transfers.

TABLE 6. Developing Countries: Structure of Production, 1975 and 1990
(Percentages of gross domestic product, at 1975 prices)

	Agriculture		Industry[a]		Services	
	1975	1990	1975	1990	1975	1990
Low Income Countries	41	30	23	28	36	42
Africa	41	33	17	20	42	47
Asia	41	30	24	29	35	41
Middle Income Countries	15	10	38	41	48	49
East Asia and Pacific	22	12	31	39	47	49
Latin America and Caribbean	12	9	36	40	52	51
Middle East and North Africa	12	8	51	50	37	42
Sub-Saharan Africa	22	17	37	37	41	46
Southern Europe	15	11	36	39	49	50
All Developing Countries	19	14	35	39	46	47

Note: Sectoral shares may not add to 100 percent, due to rounding.

[a]Industrial production in all tables in this report refers to value added in manufacturing, mining, construction and public utilities.

417

TABLE 7. Trade in Manufactures Among Developing Countries, 1976

From	Destination of Manufactured Exports (percentage of total)						Total Manufactured Exports Traded Among Developing Countries (billion current US dollars)
To	East and South Asia	Latin America and Caribbean	Middle East and North Africa	Other Africa	Southern Europe	All Developing Countries	
East and South Asia	26.6[b]	2.3	11.8	5.5	1.3	47.6	9.0
Latin America and Caribbean	0.4	13.9	0.3	1.0	0.6	16.1	3.1
Middle East and North Africa[a]	0.9	0.2	7.6[b]	0.2	0.4	9.3	1.8
Other Africa	0.4	0.4	0.5	3.0	0.5	4.8	0.9
Southern Europe	2.4	4.9	7.2	5.0	2.8	21.2	4.2
All Developing Countries	30.7	21.7	27.4	14.6	5.6	100.0	19.0

Note: Capital surplus oil exporters are included with developing countries in this table, while trade in manufactures excludes SITC 9. Totals may not add due to rounding.

[a] Includes the capital surplus oil exporters; excludes Algeria and Morocco which are counted in "Other Africa".

[b] Includes substantial re-exports of goods manufactured elsewhere.

Sources: Computed from United Nations Yearbook of International Trade Statistics, 1977, Vol. 1, Table B (New York: United Nations, UN Statistical Office), and United Nations Commodity Trade Statistics, Series D (New York: United Nations, UN Statistical Office) for individual countries.

418

TABLE 8. Regional Structure of Imports of Developing Regions

(Percentage of total imports of goods into each region, based on 1970 prices)

Region	Agriculture	Resources[a]	Light industry	Machinery and equipment	Materials	Invisibles	Subtotals	
							Agriculture and resources	Manufacturing
Latin America (medium-income)								
1970	10.6	13.1	6.7	37.2	13.6	18.1	23.7	57.5
2000	5.0	17.1	6.4	46.6	11.3	13.5	22.1	64.4
Latin America (low-income)								
1970	11.7	8.4	11.9	37.0	13.2	17.6	20.1	62.1
2000	6.1	1.5	12.6	51.3	14.5	14.0	7.6	78.4
Middle East								
1970	13.9	11.8	12.2	40.0	12.8	9.3	25.7	65.0
2000	7.3	2.1	14.2	47.5	22.7	6.2	9.4	84.4
Asia (low-income)								
1970	21.1	11.6	15.6	31.8	12.2	7.9	32.7	59.6
2000	14.6	13.7	15.6	35.4	13.8	6.9	28.3	64.8
Africa (arid)								
1970	21.0	9.0	15.0	31.3	13.3	10.6	30.0	59.6
2000	13.1	3.1	26.8	30.1	18.2	18.7	16.2	75.1
Africa (tropical)								
1970	13.4	9.7	15.6	37.8	13.2	10.2	23.1	66.6
2000	9.9	7.4	25.3	33.2	14.1	10.1	17.3	72.6

[a] Including services and transportation.

419

TABLE 9. Shares of Regions in World Exports of Goods

(Percentage in 1970 prices)

Region	Year	Scenario[a]	Agriculture	Mineral resources	Light industry	Machinery and equipment	Materials	Invisibles[b]	Total exports
Developed market economies[c]	1970		46.0	43.5	75.2	83.9	85.0	75.0	68.7
	2000	X	47.5	16.4	69.6	73.2	77.4	76.3	64.7
	2000	M	41.4	16.4	66.7	73.2	77.6	74.1	63.2
Centrally planned economies	1970		10.5	12.4	7.5	13.0	6.4	0	9.3
	2000	X	9.8	6.2	9.1	20.2	8.6	0	12.0
	2000	M	8.5	6.2	8.6	20.1	8.5	0	11.7
Developing market economies	1970		32.7	39.3	12.8	1.5	5.1	12.3	16.2
	2000	X	31.6	75.0	13.8	2.7	7.1	11.9	17.2
	2000	M	40.5	75.0	17.4	2.7	7.1	14.4	19.1
Latin America	1970		12.7	10.8	1.2	0.4	1.7	6.2	5.1
	2000	X	12.9	15.6	1.9	0.9	2.7	5.7	4.6
	2000	M	24.0	15.6	2.2	0.9	2.7	7.0	5.5
Asia and the Middle East	1970		12.9	23.8	9.9	1.0	2.6	4.5	8.5
	2000	X	12.1	51.9	11.2	1.7	3.9	4.6	11.0
	2000	M	10.7	52.1	14.4	1.8	3.9	5.6	11.9
Africa (non-oil)	1970		7.1	4.8	1.7	0.1	0.8	1.6	2.5
	2000	X	6.6	7.5	0.7	0.1	0.5	1.6	1.8
	2000	M	5.8	7.4	0.8	0.1	0.5	1.8	1.8

[a] For 2000, X and M indicate names of two scenarios with different assumptions. Scenario M is analysed in the balance-of-payments section.

[b] Including services and transportation.
[c] Not including medium-income regions.

TABLE 10. Shares of Regions in World Imports

(Percentage in 1970 prices)

Region	Year	Scenario[a]	Agriculture	Mineral resources	Light industry	Machinery and equipment	Materials	Invisibles[b]
Developed market economies[c]	1970		63.5	70.6	70.5	63.2	63.8	79.0
	2000	X	43.1	56.0	59.4	45.8	44.5	62.5
	2000	M	43.0	55.8	60.1	47.2	45.8	62.4
Developing market economies	1970		15.3	10.7	16.2	18.8	20.4	13.9
	2000	X	39.4	19.3	22.2	34.0	39.6	27.0
	2000	M	39.4	19.4	20.9	33.5	37.8	27.0
Latin America	1970		3.5	3.5	3.7	6.4	7.0	7.0
	2000	X	7.5	8.2	4.4	12.0	8.9	12.5
	2000	M	8.0	8.2	4.1	10.7	8.1	12.7
Asia and the Middle East	1970		9.3	5.7	9.4	9.3	10.0	5.0
	2000	X	28.6	10.3	15.1	22.0	28.4	12.7
	2000	M	28.3	10.3	14.3	21.3	27.6	12.6
Africa (non-oil)	1970		2.4	1.5	3.1	3.0	3.4	2.0
	2000	X	3.2	0.9	2.7	1.7	2.3	1.8
	2000	M	3.2	0.9	2.5	1.6	2.1	1.7

[a] X and M indicate names of two scenarios with different assumptions. Scenario M is analysed in the balance-of-payments section.
[b] Including services and transportation.
[c] Not including medium-income regions.

TABLE 11. Growth of Merchandise exports, by Product Category and Country Group, 1960–77 and 1977–90

(average annual percentage growth rates, 1977 prices)

Product category	1960–77			1977–90[a]		
	World	*Industrialized countries*	*Developing countries*	*World*	*Industrialized countries*	*Developing countries*
Fuels and energy	6.4	4.4	6.6	1.8	3.3	3.0
Other primary products	4.5	5.6	3.3	3.8	4.0	3.6
Food and beverages	4.6	6.3	2.8	4.1	4.3	3.9
Nonfood agricultural products	4.7	6.0	3.2	2.8	2.9	2.2
Minerals and nonferrous metals	4.1	3.6	5.2	4.1	4.0	3.8
Manufactures	8.9	8.8	12.3	6.8	6.5	9.7
Machinery and transport equipment	9.6	9.6	16.8	7.2	6.8	14.2
Other manufactures	8.3	8.0	11.3	6.5	6.2	7.7
Total merchandise[b]	7.2	7.7	6.0	5.4	5.9	6.0

Sources: World Bank; UN, *Yearbook of International Trade Statistics*, various issues; UNCTAD, *Handbook of International Trade and Development Statistics*, various issues.
a. High-case projections.
b. Excludes gold.

TABLE 12. Regional Structure of Exports of Developing Regions

(Percentage of total exports from each region, based on 1970 prices)

Region	Agriculture	Resources[a]	Light industry	Machinery and equipment	Materials[b]	Invisibles[c]	Subtotals Agriculture and resources	Manufacturing
Latin America (medium-income)								
1970	49.4	18.1	3.8	3.4	4.0	21.4	67.5	11.2
2000	21.6	34.9	9.0	11.1	8.6	14.7	56.5	28.7
Latin America (low-income)								
1970	31.6	52.0	2.3	0.7	2.4	10.9	83.6	5.4
2000	17.0	56.0	6.5	2.2	7.6	10.7	73.0	16.3
Middle East								
1970	8.6	84.7	1.2	0.5	0.7	4.3	93.8	2.4
2000	1.9	88.0	4.4	1.6	2.3	1.8	89.9	8.3
Asia (low-income)								
1970	40.3	11.2	26.9	6.5	5.3	9.9	51.5	38.7
2000	16.6	9.3	44.0	13.2	8.7	8.2	25.9	63.9
Africa (arid)								
1970	47.2	14.2	17.2	3.4	5.4	12.6	61.4	26.0
2000	36.3	9.8	23.2	4.0	8.8	17.9	46.1	36.0
Africa (tropical)								
1970	46.7	37.5	5.3	1.0	2.4	7.1	84.2	8.7
2000	23.2	62.8	3.7	0.7	2.3	7.3	86.0	6.7

[a] Resources in this and other tables relating to foreign trade include exports of petroleum, refining products and primary metals.
[b] Materials (manufactured) in this and other tables relating to foreign trade exclude exports of petroleum-refining products and primary metals.
[c] Including services and transportation.

423

TABLE 13. External Capital Requirements, Developing Countries, 1976, 1985 and 1990

(Billions of current dollars)

	Low-income countries			Middle-income countries			Developing countries as a whole		
	1976	1985	1990	1976	1985	1990	1976	1985	1990
Net imports	3	19	29	24	75	91	26	94	119
(Imports of non-factor goods and services)	(26)	(90)	(146)	(275)	(889)	(1 539)	(301)	(979)	(1 685)
Less: (Exports of non-factor goods and services)	(24)	(71)	(118)	(251)	(814)	(1 448)	(275)	(885)	(1 566)
Interest on medium-term and long-term loans	1	4	6	9	40	73	10	44	79
Repayment of principal	2	8	11	18	115	214	20	122	225
Increase of reserves	3	2	4	5	21	42	8	23	46
Total to be financed	8	32	50	56	251	419	64	283	469
Net factor income, excluding interest on medium-term and long-term loans	(.)	1	2	5	21	32	5	21	33
Government grants and concessionary loans (gross amounts)	5	19	32	9	23	33	15	42	65
Medium-term and long-term loans on market conditions (gross amounts)	4	9	12	45	179	309	49	188	321
Direct investment and other capital (net amounts)	−1	2	3	−5	23	38	−6	25	41
Private transfers (net)	(.)	1	1	2	5	8	3	7	9
Total capital received	8	32	50	56	251	419	64	283	469
At 1975 prices	8	15	17	54	118	147	62	133	165

Source: World Bank, *World Development Report, 1979* (New York, Oxford University Press, 1979).

NOTE: The mean annual inflation rate taken for the period 1975–1990 is 7.2 per cent.

PART III
RESOURCE
BIBLIOGRAPHY

This bibliography is entirely restricted to publications in English language and covers the literature since 1970. In a bibliography of this nature, it is essential that the material be as contemporary as possible, while at the same time it was thought desirable to provide a balanced weight of materials discussed over the last decade.

With respect to classification of the material, a bibliographic subject index by item number has been provided at the end of this section.

First part of this bibliography entitled, DEVELOPMENT (GENERAL) has been classified for the general reader, according to the following categories. This classification is arbitrary, however, much cross indexing has been done in the bibliographic subject index following this section of the book.

A. Problems, Issues and Trends;
B. Analytical Methods;
C. Strategies and Policies; and
D. Country Studies.

Many of the annotations in this section have been compiled from the Journal of Economic Literature, World Bank Publications, IMF-IBRD Joint Library Periodicals, Finance and Development, U.N. Documents and Publisher's Book Promotion Pamphlets.

I. BOOKS

DEVELOPMENT (GENERAL)

01   Abraham, M. Francis
A B   PERSPECTIVES ON MODERNIZATION: TOWARD A GENERAL THEORY
      OF THIRD WORLD DEVELOPMENT
      Washington, D.C.:   University Press of America, 1980.

02   Adelman, Irma and Morris, Cynthia Taft
B   ECONOMIC GROWTH AND SOCIAL EQUITY IN DEVELOPING COUNTRIES
      Stanford, Calif.: Stanford University Press, 1973.

      A quantitative investigation of the interactions among
      economic   growth,   political   participation,   and   the
      distribution of income in noncommunist developing nations.
      The study is based on data (presented in the earlier
      study, Society, politics, and economic development) from
      74 countries which is given in the form of 48 qualitative
      measures of the [countries] social, economic, and political
      characteristics, and it includes the use of discriminant
      analysis in an examination of the forces tending to
      increase political participation and the use of a stepwise
      analysis   of   variance   technique   in   analyzing   the
      distribution of income.

03   Albin, Peter S.
A B   PROGRESS WITHOUT POVERTY; SOCIALLY RESPONSIBLE ECONOMIC
      GROWTH
      New York: Basic Books, 1978.

      Examines   the   relationship   among   important   social
      tendencies, growth processes, and growth policies and
      argues for the return of the growth economy, with the
      caveat   that   social   objectives   and   policy   directions   be

reformulated to avert ecological disaster and to improve economic welfare. Using a dualistic imbalance framework, explores the style and impact of unbalanced growth in modern industrial capitalism, focusing on educational policy, income distribution, and the control of technology, poverty, and urban decay. Concludes with policy recommendations for a program of social and technical advance that is geared to the intelligent management of a growth economy and the renovation of its distributive mechanisms. An appendix presents a dualistic-imbalance model of modern industrial growth.

04   Alexander, Robert J.
A B C   A NEW DEVELOPMENT STRATEGY
        Maryknoll, N.Y.: Orbis Books, 1976.

Focusing on the demand side of the development equation, this monograph concerns itself with an economic development strategy of import substitution where industries are established to manufacture products for which a home market has already been created by imports. Analyzing the effect on development of this assured demand, and exploring the limit to which this strategy can be used, the author, looks in detail at the prerequisites for the use of this method (substantial imports and protection for newly created industries) and discusses the priorities for private and public investment in this phase. Contends that this process provides a basis for developing countries to decide which projects should be undertaken first and which can be postponed until later.

05   Alvarez, Francisco Casanova
A C   NEW HORIZONS FOR THE THIRD WORLD
        Washington, D.C.: Public Affairs Press, 1976.

Presents the factors leading to approval of the Charter of Economic Rights and Duties of States by the United Nations General Assembly on 12 December 1974. Shows that the charter, with the main objective of overcoming the injustice prevailing in economic relations between nations and [elimination of] the dependence of Third World countries on industrial nations, owes its origin and adoption to President Luis Echeverria of Mexico. Argues that the developing nations remain essentially colonized and dependent entities of the industrialized world. Concludes that the future world will be less unjust and less ridden with anxiety, more secure and better able to care for its own if we respect the principles of the charter.

06   Anell, Lars and Nygren, Birgitta
A B C   THE DEVELOPING COUNTRIES AND THE WORLD ECONOMIC ORDER
        New York: St. Marin's Press, 1980.

Explores the possible form, functioning, and enforcement
of a New International Economic Order (NIEO). Provides
an account of the demands of developing countries for
a better allocation of the world's resources and considers
the early cooperation between developing and developed
countries, particularly resolutions passed at various
U.N. General Assembly sessions. Also analyzes and comments
on the central NIEO demands. Among the possible actions
the authors suggest developing countries could take are:
(1) force industrialized countries to increase the flow
and quality of aid by threatening trade discrimination;
(2) establish a list of honest consultancy firms and
a file of information on technology procurement; and
(3) feel free to steal patents from big corporations
and make use of copyrights without compensation.

07   Angelopoulos, Angelos T.
A C   FOR A NEW POLICY OF INTERNATIONAL DEVELOPMENT
        New York: Praeger, 1977.

08   Angelopoulos, Angelos T.
A C   THE THIRD WORLD AND THE RICH COUNTRIES;
        PROSPECTS FOR THE YEAR 2000
        Translated by N. Constantinidis and C. R. Corner
New York: Praeger, 1972.

An examination and projection of the gap in incomes between
the developed and underdeveloped countries of the world.
The author brings data on and discusses the indicators
of poverty, the population explosion in the developing
world, the main causes of economic backwardness, the
"myth" of development aid, the need for a new international
development strategy, various strategies of development
financing, precipitating factors in the emergence of
the Third World, economic growth and forecasts of world
income in the year 2000, and the possibilities of China
becoming the spokesman for the Third World.

09   Arkhurst, Frederick S., ed.
B C D   AFRICA IN THE SEVENTIES AND EIGHTIES;
        ISSUES IN DEVELOPMENT
        New York and London: Praeger in cooperation with the
        Adlai Stevenson Institute of International Affairs, 1970.

Eleven experts in various fields express their views
in a symposium "Africa in the 1980's" which met in Chicago
in early 1969 under the auspices of the Adlai Stevenson
Institute of International Affairs. The purpose...was
to attempt to draw a portrait of Africa in the 1980's
on the basis of the experience of the past decade and,
also, on the basis of current trends in the area of
politics, economic development, population, agriculture,
trade, education and law - all viewed as composite and
interactive factors in the development process.

10   Arndt, H. W., et al.
A B C   THE WORLD ECONOMIC CRISIS: A COMMONWEALTH PERSPECTIVE
        London: Commonwealth Secretariat, 1980.

        Report of a group of experts from Commonwealth countries
        on obstacles to structural change and sustained economic
        growth, with recommendations for specific measures by
        which developed and developing countries might act to
        reduce or eliminate such constraints. Focuses on the
        implications of the world economic crises - inflation,
        slowdown of economic growth, and staggering disequilibria
        in balance of payments - for the developing countries
        of the Third World. Stresses the need for collective
        action in view of the interdependence of the world economy.

11   Bairoch, Paul
A C D   THE ECONOMIC DEVELOPMENT OF THE THIRD WORLD SINCE 1900
        Translated from the fourth French edition by Cynthia
        Postan
        Berkeley: University of California Press, 1975.

        The author covers a wide range of factors important to
        development, namely population, agriculture, extractive
        industry, manufacturing industry, foreign trade, education,
        urbanization, the labor force and employment, and
        macroeconomic data. Particular attention is devoted
        to the development of agriculture. Comparison is drawn
        between the economic progress of Third World countries
        and developed countries at a similar stage of
        industrialization. Twenty-four countries were selected
        for the analysis, representing 80 percent of the population
        of the Third World. These include seven countries from
        each of Africa, Latin-America, and Asia respectively,
        and three countries from the Middle East.

12   Bairoch, Paul and Levy-Leboyer, Maurice, eds.
A B   DISPARITIES IN ECONOMIC DEVELOPMENT SINCE THE INDUSTRIAL
        REVOLUTION
        New York: St. Martin's Press, 1981.

        Collection of thirty-five previously unpublished essays
        presented at the 7th International Economic History
        Congress in Edinburgh in August 1978. Main theme deals
        with disparities in economic development. Concerns
        differences in income at micro-regional and international
        levels. In four parts: (1) discussing economic
        disparities among nations (two papers on international
        disparities: ten on the Third World and five on the
        developed world); (2) covering regional economic
        disparities (eight essays on northern, western, and central
        Europe; three on France; two on Southern Europe and one
        on the Third World); (3) detailing relations between
        regional and national disparities (two papers); and (4)
        discussing the methodological aspects of measurement
        of economic disparities (two papers).

13   Baldwin, Robert E.
B C   ECONOMIC DEVELOPMENT AND GROWTH
        New York, London, Sydney and Toronto: John Wiley and
        Sons, Inc., 1972.

        This short text seeks to provide "an analysis of economic
        development that in terms of breadth and sophistication
        lies between the usual elementary and advanced approaches
        to the development topic." It is organized around three
        themes, i.e., what the nature of growth problem is, what
        the main theories of growth and development are, and
        what the main policy issues facing less developed countries
        are. Therefore, the chapters deal with the characteristics
        of poverty, various classical development theories
        relatively more recent contributions to development theory,
        national and sectoral policies for growth, and issues
        in the financing of development.

14   Bauer, P.T.
B C   DISSENT ON DEVELOPMENT.   STUDIES AND DEBATES IN DEVELOPMENT
        ECONOMICS
        Cambridge, Mass.: Harvard University Press, 1972.

        A collection of previously published articles, essays,
        and book reviews, some of which have been rewritten and
        expanded, dealing with various theoretical and empirical
        issues in economic development. Part One ("Ideology
        and Experience") examines general problems of concept
        method, analysis, historical experience and policy in
        economic development, such as the vicious circle of
        poverty, the widening gap, central planning, foreign
        aid, Marxism, etc. Part Two ("Case Studies") features
        five of the author's studies on developing countries,
        particularly Nigeria and India. Part Three ("Review
        Articles") brings book reviews on such well known books
        as W. Arthur Lewis' The Theory of Economic Growth, Benjamin
        Higgins' Economic Development, Walt W. Rostow's The Stages
        of Economic Growth, Thomas Balogh's The Economics of
        Poverty. and other volumes by Gunnar Myrdal, John Pincus,
        Harry G. Johnson, E.A.G. Robinson, B.K. Madan and Jagdish
        Bhagwati.

15   Bauer, P.T.
A B   EQUALITY, THE THIRD WORLD AND ECONOMIC DELUSION
        Cambridge, Mass.: Harvard University Press, 1981.

        Critique of methods and finding of contemporary economics,
        particularly development economics, arguing that there
        is a hiatus between accepted opinion and evident reality.
        All but four chapters are extended and/or revised versions
        of previously published articles. In the three parts:
        equality, the West and the Third World, and the state
        of economics. Criticizes economics and especially
        development economics for disregard of personal qualities

and social and political arrangements as determinants
of economic achievement and for ignoring the role of
external contracts in extending markets. Notes that
the benefits of mathematical economics have been bought
at the cost of an uncritical attitude, which has led
to inappropriate use and in some cases to an emphasis
on form rather than substance.

16   Berry, Leonard and Kates, Robert W., eds.
A C   MAKING THE MOST OF THE LEAST
         New York: Holmes and Meier Publishers, 1979.

The poverty faced by Third World countries today seriously
challenges the stability of the world order. The
contributors look torward the restructuring of the present
economic order by establishing "harmonious linkages"
between the industrialized and nonindustrialized worlds.
A welcome addition to the literature on economic
development.

17   Bhatt, V. V.
A B C   DEVELOPMENT PERSPECTIVES: PROBLEM, STRATEGY AND POLICIES
         Oxford; New York: Sydney and Toronto: Pergamon Press,
         1980.

Discusses the dynamics of the socioeconomic system in
terms of the cumulative and cyclical changes in economic
institutions, ideologies, and technology. Stresses the
importance of: upgrading traditional technology and
adapting modern technology to given situations; the
financial system, since it affects savings and shapes
the pattern of resource allocation; and upgrading of
agricultural organization and technology. Sets forth
as necessary for the development process: the stability
of the international currencey and the international
monetary system, which the author proposes be linked
to prices of primary products; the shaping of the
international monetary-financial-trade system to be
consistent with LDC's development strategy; and viewing
the process of socioeconomic development as an integral
part of nation-building and of building the international
community.

18   Brown, Lester R.
A C   THE GLOBAL ECONOMIC PROSPECT: NEW SOURCES OF ECONOMIC
         STRESS
         Worldwatch Paper no. 20
         Washington, D.C.: Worldwatch Institute; New York, 1978.

Considers the relationship between the expanding global
economy and the earth's natural systems. Discusses the
increase in fuel costs, suggesting that the world is
running out of cheap energy; diminishing returns in grain
production and to fertilizer use; overfishing; global

inflation; capital shortages; unemployment; and the changing growth prospect. Concludes that future economic policies must shift from growth to sustainability; not advocating abandonment of growth as a goal, but with concern for carrying capacities of biological system. Fisheries, forests, grasslands, and croplands, require development of alternative energy sources and population policies consistent with resource availability.

19   Chenery, Hollis and Syrquin, Moises
A B C   PATTERNS OF DEVELOPMENT, 1950-1970
        Assisted by Hazel Elkington
        New York and London: Oxford University Press, 1975.

Examines principal changes in economic structure that normally accompany economic growth, focusing on resource mobilization and allocation, particularly those aspects needed to sustain further growth. These aspects are treated in a uniform econometric framework to provide a consistent description of a number of interrelated types of structural change and also to identify systematic differences in development patterns among countries that are following different development strategies. The major aim of the research is to separate the effects of universal factors affecting all countries from particular characteristics. The authors use data for 101 countries in the period 1950 to 1970. Countries are grouped into three categories: large country, balanced allocation; small country, industry specialization. Chapter 5 compares the results obtained from time-series data with those observed from cross-sectional data. Results are obtained from regression techniques, where income level and population are treated as exogenous variables. The demographic variables show how the movement of population from rural to urban areas and lowering of the birth rate and death rate have influenced demand and supply of labor. A technical appendix discusses the methods used, the problems encountered, and all the regression equations specified in this study.

20   Chenery, Hollis B., et al., eds.
A B C   STUDIES IN DEVELOPMENT PLANNING
        Cambridge, Mass.: Harvard University Press, 1971.

Attempts to bring together the contributors' varied backgrounds in both field work and the use of quantitative techniques and show how modern methods can be used in operational development planning.

21   Chodak, Szymon
A B   SOCIETAL DEVELOPMENT: FIVE APPROACHES WITH CONCLUSIONS
        FROM COMPARATIVE ANALYSIS
        New York: Oxford University Press, 1973.

A sociologist analyzes the development and change of societies using five different conceptual approaches, attempting to view the processes of development in society from a multidimensional synthesizing perspective. These five approaches are called: "Evolutionary Theories," "Development - The Growing Societal Systemness," "Development and Innovation in the Search for Security," "Economic and Political Development," and "Modernization." The author gives references to the societal development which has taken place in various parts of the world and under different political systems.

22   Colman, David and Nixson, Frederick
A B C   ECONOMICS OF CHANGE IN LESS DEVELOPED COUNTRIES
        New York: Wiley, Halsted Press, 1978.

Analyzes the changes that are occurring in the less-developed countries (LDC's); considers the problems generated by change; and examines the agents of change. Emphasizes the internal (rather than the international) aspects of development and focuses on economic inequality within LDC's and the impact on the development process in agriculture and industry of different income distributions. Although recognizing the impact of transnational corporations on the nature and characteristics of development within the LDC's, the authors argue that it is the LDC government that is responsible for the economic policies pursued. Also outlines the concepts and measurement of development, and reviews the literature on economic theorizing about development. A final chapter discusses inflation and migration in LDC's. Authors note that too often policy recommendations ignore political acceptability and recommend that the economist should cooperate with the political scientist in the study of inflation and with the sociologist in the study of rural urban migration.

23   Corbet, Hugh and Jackson, Robert, eds.
A B C   IN SEARCH OF A NEW WORLD ECONOMIC ORDER
        New York and Toronto: Wiley, Halsted Press, 1974.

Focuses on the reform of the international commercial systems for further liberalizations of world trade. Papers are grouped into four categories: (1) introduction, (2) general factors affecting negotiations, (3) outside issues of significance, (4) issues on the agenda.

24   Fields, Gary S.
A B C D   POVERTY, INEQUALITY, AND DEVELOPMENT
          New York and London: Cambridge University Press, 1980.

Focuses on the distributional aspects of economic development and explores the impact of the rate and type of growth on poverty and inequality in poor countries. Findings show that in general growth reduces poverty, but a high aggregate growth rate is neither necessary nor sufficient for reducing absolute poverty or relative inequality. Uses case studies of distribution and development in Costa Rica, Sri Lanka, India, Brazil, the Phillippines, and Taiwan to examine which combinations of circumstances and policies led to differential performance. Concludes that a commitment to developing to help the poor does not guarantee progress, but it helps a great deal. In its absence, the flow of resources to the haves, with only some trickle down to the have-nots, will be perpetuated.

25   Finger, J. M.
A B D   INDUSTRIAL COUNTRY POLICY AND ADJUSTMENT TO IMPORTS FROM DEVELOPING COUNTRIES
World Bank Staff Working Paper no. 470, July 1981.

A background study for World Development Report 1981. Reviews and interprets recent analyses of the policies established by industrial countries in response to increasing imports from developing countries.

26   Finger, Nachum
A C D   THE IMPACT OF GOVERNMENT SUBSIDIES ON INDUSTRIAL MANAGEMENT: THE ISRAELI EXPERIENCE
New York: Praeger, 1971.

27   Fitzgerald, E. V.
A B   PUBLIC SECTOR INVESTMENT PLANNING FOR DEVELOPING COUNTRIES
New York: Holmes and Meier, 1978.

28   Florence, P. Sargant
A B C   ECONOMICS AND SOCIOLOGY OF INDUSTRY: A REALISTIC ANALYSIS OF DEVELOPMENT
Baltimore, Md.: Johns Hopkins University Press, 1969.

29   Frank, Andre Gunder
A B C   CRISIS IN THE THIRD WORLD
New York: Holmes and Meier, 1981.

30   Frank, Andre Gunder
A B   DEPENDENT ACCUMULATION AND UNDERDEVELOPMENT
New York and London: Monthly Review Press, 1979.

Explains underdevelopment by an analysis of the production and exchange relations of dependence. Distinguishes the three main stages or periods in this world embracing process of capital accumulation and capitalist development: mercantilist (1500-1770), industrial capitalist (1770-1870), and imperialist (1870-1930). Analyzes each period in terms of history, trade relations between the metropolis and the periphery, and transformation of the modes or relations of production, and the development of underdevelopment in the principal regions of Asia, Africa, and the Americas.

31   Frank, Charles R., Jr., and Webb, Richard C., eds.
A B D   INCOME DISTRIBUTION AND GROWTH IN THE LESS-DEVELOPED COUNTRIES
         Washington, D.C.: Brookings Institution, 1977.

Fourteen previously unpublished essays representing part of the results of a project undertaken jointly by the Brookings Institution and the Woodrow Wilson School of Public and International Affairs at Princeton University, dealing with the relation between income distribution and economic growth in the developing countries. The first two articles present an overview of income distribution policy and discuss the causes of growth and income distribution in LDC's, respectively. The next nine examine the relation between income distribution and different economic policies and factors, including: industrialization, education, population, wage, fiscal, agricultural, public works, health and urban land policies.

32   Gant, George F.
A B   DEVELOPMENT ADMINISTRATION - CONCEPTS, GOALS, METHODS
        Madison, Wisconsin: The University of Wisconsin Press, 1979.

Growth and modernization in the less developed countries (LDC's) during the past three decades has frequently depended upon the state's ability to plan and manage a range of developmental activities. Gant's study of development administration looks at some of the issues that could be of concern to managers in LDC's: in particular, coordination, budgeting, the selection of personnel, training, etc. He also delves into the administrative side of certain specific governmental concerns, such as family planning and education, drawing on examples from a number of Asian countries. This is not a book which goes into much technical detail. Nor does it tell one how to design an efficient administrative setup. Primarily for the general reader interested in an overview of these topics.

33   Garbacz, Christopher
A B D   INDUSTRIAL POLARIZATION UNDER ECONOMIC INTEGRATION IN LATIN AMERICA
        Austin, Texas: Bureau of Business Research, Graduate School of Business, The University of Texas, 1971.

The author discusses the problem of increased disparities in the levels of regional economic development that tend

to come about as a result of economic integration. The
political and economic implications of industrial
polarization are studies within the context and experience
of the Central American Common Market and the Latin
American Free Trade Association. Finally, the author
considers the problem in the light of the planned Latin
American Common Market, discussing the various measures
that could be taken as well as the implications for the
future.

34   Garzouzi, Eva
A B C   ECONOMIC   GROWTH   AND   DEVELOPMENT: THE   LESS   DEVELOPED
COUNTRIES
New York: Vantage Press, 1972.

Essays to consolidate into one readable text the whole
of the economics of growth and development. Part I
discusses the meaning and theories of economic development,
outlines historical patterns of development, and summarizes
the impact of capital, agriculture, industry, monetary
and fiscal policies, international trade, and foreign
aid on economic growth. Part II presents comparative
analyses of developing regions, including Latin America,
the Middle East and North Africa, Africa south of the
Sahara, and Southeast Asia.

35   Geithman, David T., ed.
A B C D FISCAL POLICY FOR INDUSTRIALIZATION AND DEVELOPMENT IN
LATIN AMERICA
Gainesville: University Presses of Florida.

Collection of 10 previously unpublished papers (and related
comments) presented at the Twenty-First Annual Latin
American Conference held in February 1971. Central theme
of the conference was the analysis and evaluation of
the interaction among fiscal problems, fiscal tools,
and fiscal systems in the industrializing economies of
Latin America.

36   Ghai, D. P.
A B C   THE BASIC-NEEDS APPROACH TO DEVELOPMENT: SOME ISSUES
REGARDING CONCEPTS AND METHODOLOGY
ILO, Geneva, 1977.

Contains five papers which discuss issues which arise
in the formulation of criteria and approaches for the
promotion of employment and the satisfaction of the basic
needs of a country's population. Presents the first
results of the research and conceptual work initiated
by the ILO to help countries implement the basic
needs-oriented strategy recommended by the World Employment
Conference in 1976.

37   Gianaris, Nicholas V.
A B C   ECONOMIC DEVELOPMENT: THOUGHT AND PROBLEMS
         North Quincy, Mass.:   Christopher Publishing House, 1978.

         Part one examines the process of development, the
         historical perspective, mathematical models, and modern
         theories of development;   part two considers domestic
         problems of development, specifically land and other
         natural resources, human resources (particularly the
         role of education), capital formation and technological
         change, the allocation of resources, and the role of
         government and planning;   part three discusses the
         international aspects of development (foreign trade,
         aid, investment, and multinationals) and current issues
         such as environmental problems, the status of women,
         income inequalities, and discrimination.

38   Giersch, Herbert, ed.
A B C D INTERNATIONAL ECONOMIC DEVELOPMENT AND RESOURCE TRANSFER:
         WORKSHOP 1978
         Tubingen, Germany: J. C. B. Mohr, 1979.

         Twenty-four previously unpublished papers from a workshop
         held in June 1978 at the Institut fur Weltwirtschaft,
         Kiel University.   Contributions organized under ten
         headings: Rural Industrialization, Employment and Economic
         Development;   Choice of Techniques and Industries for
         Growth and Employment; Agricultural Patterns and Policies
         in Developing Countries;   Hypotheses for the Commodity
         Composition of East-West Trade; The Relationship Between
         the Domestic and International Sectors in Economic
         Development; Patterns of Trade in Services and Knowledge;
         Changes in Industrial Interdependencies and Final Demand
         in Economic Development; Public Aid for Investment in
         Manufacturing Industries;   Institutional and Economic
         Criteria for the Choice of Technology in Developing
         Countries; and Problems of Measuring the Production and
         Absorption of Technologies in Developing Countries.

39   Gierst, Friedrich and Matthews, Stuart R.
A B C   GUIDELINES FOR CONTRACTING FOR INDUSTRIAL PROJECTS IN
         DEVELOPING COUNTRIES
         New York: United Nations Publications, 1975.

         Designed to serve public and private organizations in
         developing countries as a guide in preparing contracts
         concerned with industrial investment projects.   Examines
         various stages involved in the preparation of an industrial
         project and discusses the basic types of contacts involved
         (i.e. those with financial institutions, with consultants
         and with contractors).

40   Gill, Richard T.
A B C   ECONOMIC DEVELOPMENT: PAST AND PRESENT

Third Edition.   Foundations of Modern Economics.
Englewood Cliffs, N.J.:   Prentice-Hall, 1973.

Third edition of an introductory textbook with revisions
of the discussions. The Green Revolution, two-gap analysis
of foreign aid, Denison-Jorgenson-Griliches studies of
factors affecting United States economic growth and
Leibenstein's "X-efficiency" concept have been added.
Statistical tables have been updated to include figures
on Chinese economic growth. Six chapters cover: 1)
General factors in economic development, 2) Theories
of development, 3) Beginnings of development in advanced
countries, 4) Growth of the American economy, 5) Problems
of underdeveloped countries, and 6) Development in China
and India.

41   Goulet, Denis
A B C   THE CRUEL CHOICE: A NEW CONCEPT IN THE THEORY OF
          DEVELOPMENT
          Cambridge, Mass.:   Center for the Study of Development
          and Social Change, Atheneum, 1971.

This work is intended to probe moral dilemmas faced by
economic and social development. Its central concern
is that philosophical conceptions about the "good life"
and the "good society" should be of more profound
importance in assessing alternative paths to development
than economic, political, or technological questions.
The theoretical analysis is based on two concepts:
"vulnerability" and "existence rationality." Vulnerability
is defined as exposure to forces that can not be
controlled, and is expressed in the failure of many
low-income countries to attain their development goals,
as well as in manifestations of mass alienation in certain
societies where prosperity has already been achieved.
Existence rationality denotes those strategies used by
all societies to possess information and to make practical
choices designed to assure survival and satisfy their
needs for esteem and freedom. These strategies vary
with a country's needs and are conditioned by numerous
constraints.

42   Griffin, Keith
A B C   INTERNATIONAL INEQUALITY AND NATIONAL POVERTY
          New York: Holms & Meier, 1978.

Nine essays, seven previously published between 1970
and 1978. Challenges the classical assumption that
unrestricted international intercourse will reduce
inequality and poverty. Argues that forces creating
inequality are automatic, and not due to malevolence
of developed nations or corporations, but that the motor
of change in the contemporary world economy is technical
innovation. Since the advances tend to be concentrated

in the developed countries where they are applicable to their technology, rich countries are able to extract supra-normal profits and rents from the poor countries through trade. The high level of factor earnings in rich countries attract the most valuable financial and human resources of the poor countries through induced international migration. Divided into two parts, part one deals with international inequality and discusses: the international transmission of inequality; multinational corporations; foreign capital, domestic savings, and economic development; emigration, and the New International Economic Order. The essays in part two focus on national poverty, discussing the facts of poverty in the Third World, analyzing models of development, and assessing the Chinese system of incentives.

43   Griffin, Keith B. and Enos, John L.
A B C   PLANNING DEVELOPMENT
        Reading, Mass.; Don Mills, Ontario; Sydney; London; and
        Manila: Addison-Wesley, 1971.

Part of a series intended to serve as guidebooks on development economics, this book deals with practical problems of planning and economic policy in underdeveloped countries. Consists of four parts: 1) the role of planning, 2) quantitative planning techniques, 3) sector policies, and 4) planning in practice with reference to Chile, Columbia, Ghana, India, Pakistan and Turkey.

44   Hagen, Everett E.
A B C   THE ECONOMICS OF DEVELOPMENT
        Revised Edition. The Irwin Series in Economics.
        Homewood, Ill.: Irwin, 1975.

Revised edition with two new chapters added, one dealing with the earth's stock of minerals and economic growth, and the other on the relationships between economic growth and the distribution of income. Chapters on population and economic planning have been extensively revised, with the former focusing on the relationship of food supply to continued world growth. Additional changes include: reorganization of the discussion of growth theories; a considerably augmented discussion of entrepreneurhsip; and a reorganization of the chapters on import substitution versus export expansion and external finance.

45   Helleiner, G. K., ed.
B C   A WORLD DIVIDED: THE LESS DEVELOPED COUNTRIES IN THE
        INTERNATIONAL ECONOMY
        Perspectives on Development, no. 5
        New York; London and Melbourne: Cambridge University
        Press, 1976.

Twelve papers discussing the new policies and instruments needed if the interests of poor nations are to be met. Within the realm of trade, consideration is given to the possibility of increased cooperation through: supply management schemes; bargaining capacity and power; closer ties with other less developed countries; and the development of alternative marketing channels and joint sales efforts. Relations between the less developed countries and transnational firms is then considered with special attention given to the factors affecting the bargaining position of the countries. Issues in international finance and monetary policy are: the borrowing of Eurodollars by less developed countries, internationally agreed upon principles for an honorable debt default, and interests of less developed countries in a new international monetary order. Another paper considers means by which a self-reliant but poor country can seek to conduct its economic affairs in the face of a most inhospitable and uncertain international environment. The concluding paper considers the implication of the new mood in the less developed countries for future international organisation.

46   Hermassi, Elbaki
A C D   THE THIRD WORLD REASSESSED
            Berkeley: University of California Press, 1980.

47   Horowitz, Irving Louis, ed.
A B C   EQUITY, INCOME, AND POLICY: COMPARATIVE STUDIES IN THREE
            WORLDS OF DEVELOPMENT
            New York and London: Praeger, 1977.

Ten previously unpublished papers by sociologists and economists on the multiple ideologies of development and the drive toward equity congruent with different social systems. Six essays address the problems of the "First World," i.e. those types of societies dominated by a free market and an open society, where the main problem would seem to be how to maintain growth and development while providing distributive justice. Two papers look at the "Second World" of socialism; these assume the central role of state power as imposing its will to produce equity. The remaining papers consider the Third World, examining in particular income distribution in Tanzania and economic equality and social class in general.

48   Jalan, Bimal
A B C   ESSAYS IN DEVELOPMENT POLICY
            Delhi: S. G. Wasani for Macmillan of India, 1975.

A common theme of the 11 essays (some previously published) is the explicit reference to political philosophies involved in the choices of means and objectives of development and social change. Essays include: discussion of self-reliance objectives; trade and industrialization policies; distribution of income; the project evaluation manual of Professors Little and Mirrlees; UNIDO guidelines for project evaluation; criteria for determination of appropriate terms of aid assistance; the definition and assessment of performance in developing countries; the history of the United Nations Capital Development Fund, the World Bank, and the International Development Association; and an analysis of the principal recommendations of the Pearson Commission Report (1969).

49   Jumper, Sidney R.; Bell, Thomas L. and Ralston, Bruce A.
B C   ECONOMIC GROWTH AND DISPARITIES: A WORLD VIEW
        Englewood Cliffs, N.J.: Prentice-Hall, 1980.

The authors emphasize understanding of real world differences in levels of human development, rather than sophisticated analytical procedures. In seven parts: geographical concepts; the factors influencing variations in levels of development; world food supplies; minerals; factors affecting intensity of manufacturing development; the service industries; and a summary of the role of geographers in facing these development problems.

50   Kahn, Herman
A B C   WORLD ECONOMIC DEVELOPMENT: 1979 AND BEYOND
        With the Hudson Institute.
        Boulder: Westview Press, 1979.

Examines economic prospects focusing on the period 1978-2000, and particularly the earlier part of the period. In two parts, part one presents the general historical framework, concepts, and perspectives on economic growth and cultural change. Part two examines the major trends and problems of the real world, focusing on the elements of change and continuity in both the advanced and developing economies. Rejects attempts by some to stop the world and argues for and suggests strategies for rapid worldwide economic growth, for Third World industrialization, and for the use of advanced (or at least appropriate) technology.

51   Kasdan, Alan R.
A B C   THE THIRD WORLD: A NEW FOCUS FOR DEVELOPMENT
        Cambridge, Mass.: Schenkman Publishing, 1973.

52   Kindleberger, Charles P. and Herrick, Bruce
B   ECONOMIC DEVELOPMENT
        Third Edition. Economics Handbook Series.
        New York; London; Paris and Tokyo: McGraw-Hill, 1977.

Textbook that survey[s] the present panorama of international poverty, the applications to it of economic analysis, and the policies for improvement that the analysis implies. This edition which has been completely rewritten and updated, includes new chapters on: population, urbanization, collective international action, employment, income distribution, and the theories of economic development.

53   Leipziger, Danny M., ed.
A B C   BASIC NEEDS AND DEVELOPMENT
        Foreword by Paul P. Streeten
        Cambridge, Mass.: Qelgeschlager, Gunn & Hain, 1981.

Five previously unpublished essays discuss the potential contribution of the basic needs approach to developmental theory and practice. Michael J. Crosswell gives his views in two essays on a development planning approach and on growth, poverty alleviation, and foreign assistance. Maureen A. Lewis discusses sectional aspects of the linkages among population, nutrition, and health. Danny M. Leipziger writes about policy issues and the basic human needs approach. Martha de Melo presents a case study of Sri Lanka focusing on the effects of alternative approaches to basic human needs. The authors are all economists.

54   Leontief, Wassily, et al.
A B C   THE FUTURE OF THE WORLD ECONOMY: A UNITED NATIONS STUDY
        New York: Oxford University Press, 1977.

Investigates the interrelationships between future world economic growth and availability of natural resources, pollution, and the impact of environmental policies. Includes a set of alternative projections of the demographic, economic, and environmental states of the world in the years 1980, 1990, and 2000 with a comparison with the world economy of 1970. Constructs a multiregional input-output economic model of the world economy. Investigates some of the main problems of economic growth and development in the world as a whole, with special accent on problems encountered by the developing countries. The findings include: (1) target rates of growth of gross product in the developing regions...are not sufficient to start closing the income gap between the developing and the developed countries; (2) the principal limits to sustained economic growth and accelerated development are political, social and institutional in character rather than physical; (3) the necessary increased food production is technically feasible, but dependent on drastically favorable public policy measure; (4) pollution is not an unmanageable problem.

55   Lin, Ching-Yuan
A C D   DEVELOPING COUNTRIES IN A TURBULENT WORLD: PATTERNS
         OF ADJUSTMENT SINCE THE OIL CRISIS
         New York: Praeger, 1981.

         Examines national authorities' policy reactions to changes
         in the world economy since 1973, to determine whether
         differences in national economic performances can be
         explained in terms of differences in their policy
         reactions.   Investigates global patterns of absorption,
         production, and adjustment since the oil crisis; global
         expenditure flows before and after the crisis; and
         international bank transactions and world trade.   Reviews
         the experiences of developing countries during the period,
         focusing on non-oil countries.   Finds that collectively
         the non-oil developing countries experienced a much milder
         contraction of domestic demand and real ouput than the
         more developed countries after the disturbances in 1973-75,
         although individual experiences varied; however, inflation
         remains persistent.   Argues that most developing countries
         did not pursue demand management policies early enough
         to counteract sharp changes in external demand.

56   Madhava, K. B., ed.
A B C D INTERNATIONAL DEVELOPMENT, 1969:   CHALLENGES TO PREVALENT
         IDEAS ON DEVELOPMENT
         Dobbs Ferry: Oceana for Society for International
         Development, 1970.

         Contains the proceedings of the 11th World Conference
         of the Society for International Development held in
         1969 in New Delhi.   The theme "Challenges to Prevalent
         Ideas on Development" was carried out through roundtable
         discussions centering on: the redefinition of goals;
         foreign   aid;   manpower,   education,   and   development;
         population communication; social communication; political
         and social-cultural requisites; and challenges to theorists
         and strategists.

57   May, Brian
A C D   THE THIRD WORLD CALAMITY
         London and Boston: Routledge & Kegan Paul, 1981.

         Assessment of social conditions, politics, economics,
         and cultural barriers in the Third World, with particular
         reference to India, Iran, and Nigeria.   Contends that
         the "chronic socio-economic stagnation" that characterizes
         these countries is not attributable to Western imperialism,
         maintaining   that   fundamental   change   in   Third   World
         countries was and is blocked by psychological and cultural
         facts.   Compares relevant factors in Europe and in the
         three countries to show the constraints that block
         significant socioeconomic change.

58   McGreevey, William Paul, ed.
A B C   THIRD-WORLD POVERTY: NEW STRATEGIES FOR MEASURING
            DEVELOPMENT PROGRESS
            Lexington, Mass.:   Heath, Lexington Books, 1980.

Five previously unpublished papers on the problems of measuring progress in alleviating poverty in the Third World, originally part of a series of seminars (1976-79) sponsored by the Agency for International Development. Editor McGreevey reviews the development progress from both a human capital and poverty alleviation standpoint; Gary S. Fields looks at absolute-poverty measures (i.e., those not depending on income distribution considerations); Harry J. Bruton considers the use of available employment and unemployment data in assessing government poverty policy, and G. Edward Schuh and Robert L. Thompson discuss measures of agricultural progress and government commitment to agricultural development.   The fifth paper by Nancy Birdsall is a summary of discussion in two seminars on time-use surveys and networks of social support in LDC's. The authors find in part that: (1) existing data are inadequate to judge progress; (2) the best data gathering method is multipurpose household surveys; and (3) networks of social support are important (and unmeasured) means of income transfer between households.

59   McHale, John and McHale, Magda C.
A B C   BASIC HUMAN NEEDS: A FRAMEWORK FOR ACTION
            New Brunswick, N.J.:   Rutgers University, Transaction
            Books, 1978.

60   Meadows, Dennis L., ed.
A B C   ALTERNATIVES TO GROWTH--I: A SEARCH FOR SUBSTAINABLE
            FUTURES: PAPERS ADAPTED FROM ENTRIES TO THE 1975 GEORGE
            AND CYNTHIA MITCHELL PRIZE AND FROM PRESENTATIONS BEFORE
            THE 1975 ALTERNATIVES TO GROWTH CONFERENCE, HELD AT
            THE WOODLANDS, TEXAS
            Cambridge, Mass.: Lippincott, Ballinger, 1977.

Seventeen previously unpublished interdisciplinary papers on the transition from growth to a steady-state society, i.e., a society with a constant stock of physical wealth and a constant stock of people.   In four parts: the relation between population and food or energy; economic alternatives; the rationales, mechanisms, and implications of various long-term planning proposals; and analysis of the determinants, nature, and implications of current paradigms, norms, laws, and religion.

61   Melady Thomas Patrick and Suhartono, R. B.
A B   DEVELOPMENT -- LESSONS FOR THE FUTURE
            Maryknoll, New York: Orbis Books, 1973.

Investigation of what determines, economically, which
countries are developing, based on examination of
characteristics of nations agreed to be undergoing this
experience. The study examines such facets of development
as the nonhomogeneity of the developing countries; factors
affecting economic growth, the sectoral aspect of growth
(industry and agriculture), measurements of the phenomenon,
and the applicability of economic theory in this work;
and the effects of economic development on man and his
role in society.

62   Morawetz, David
A B D   TWENTY-FIVE YEARS OF ECONOMIC DEVELOPMENT, 1950 TO 1975
Johns Hopkins University Press for IBRD, 1977.

Assesses development programs of developing countries
and global development targets adopted by international
organizations over the past 25 years. Chapters cover:
a) changing objectives of development; b) growth in GNP
per capita, population and the gap between rich and poor
countries; c) reduction of poverty, including employment,
income distribution, basic needs, nutrition, health,
housing and education; d) self-reliance and economic
independence; and e) conclusions, hypotheses, and
questions.

63   Morgan, Theodore
B C   ECONOMIC DEVELOPMENT: CONCEPT AND STRATEGY
New York and London: Harper & Row, 1975.

Textbook in economic development with emphasis on policy,
its appropriate definition, its targets, and its
improvement of application. Diverts focus from GNP and
average income growth rates and into issues such as income
distribution, nutrition, disease, climate, and population
increases and their effects on development. Surveys
existing theoretical literature. Discusses development
planning and the importance of the statistical foundation
of decision-making, and planning techniques such as
cost-benefit analysis. Provides sporadic data for
less-developed countries, mostly for the post-World War
II period, on various national variables.

64   Ramati, Yohanan, ed.
A B C   ECONOMIC GROWTH IN DEVELOPING COUNTRIES--MATERIAL AND
HUMAN RESOURCES: PROCEEDINGS OF THE SEVENTH REHOVOT
CONFERENCE
Praeger Special Studies in International Economics and
Development
New York and London: Praeger in cooperation with the
Continuation Committee of the Rehovot Conference, 1975.

Collection of 49 papers presented in September 1973.
The papers are grouped into five sections following the

structure of the conference. Part I includes papers
setting the framework to analyze natural and human
resources as factors in development and problems of
planning and the quality of life. Part II includes papers
on resources, technology, and income distribution. Part
III deals with external constraints on development. Part
IV examines planning and implementation. Part V contains
the very brief closing addresses by Simon Kuznets and
Abba Eban. Participants included 99 experts and policy
makers for developing countries in Africa, Latin America,
and Southeast Asia.

65   Rubinson, Richard, ed.
A B   DYNAMICS OF WORLD DEVELOPMENT
       Political Economy of the World-System Annuals, vol. 4
       Beverly Hills and London: Sage, 1981.

Twelve previously unpublished papers, almost all by
sociologists, presented at the Fourth Annual Political
Economy of the World-System conference at Johns Hopkins
University, June 1980. Papers are based on the assumption
that the world's history is the history of capitalist
accumulation; and that capitalist development is the
development of a single...modern world-system. Papers
cover: development in peripheral areas; development
in semiperipheral states; development and state
organization; cycles and trends of world system
development; theooretical issues; and dynamics of
development of the world economy.

66   Sachs, Ignacy
A C   THE DISCOVERY OF THE THIRD WORLD
       Cambridge, Mass., and London: M. I. T. Press, 1976.

Focusing on a redefinition of development theory, discusses
the role of ethnocentrism and domination by European
and Western ideas in such areas as science, technology,
and economics. Argues that discussions regarding economic
development strategies attempt to apply Western theories
and ignore the fact that Third World growth, unlike
capital-intensive European growth, must be based on the
use of labor. Proposes a general development theory to
bridge the gap between European theory and Third World
practice and discusses problems such as economic surplus
and economic aid. Recommends that the U.N. assess Western
nations and funnel the money to Third World nations on
a "no-strings" basis.

67   Shafei, Mohamed Z.
A B   THREE LECTURES ON ECONOMIC DEVELOPMENT
       Beirut, Lebanon: Beirut Arab University, 1970.

The first lecture focuses on the characteristics of
developing countries. The second traces the process

of economic development in the U.A.R. (Egypt) since 1952. The third is on the foreign assistance needs of developing countries.

68   Singer, H. W.
A C   THE STRATEGY OF INTERNATIONAL DEVELOPMENT: ESSAYS IN
        THE ECONOMICS OF BACKWARDNESS
        Edited by Sir Alec Cairncross and Mohinder Puri
        White Plains, N.Y.:   International Arts and Sciences
        Press, 1975.

A collection of 13 papers by the author, all published in past years, dealing with some of the central problems of economic development and development policy. Papers cover such issues as gains distribution among borrowing and investing countries, dualism, international aid, trade and development, employment problems, income distribution, science and technology transfers, etc. Introduction to the author's work and career by editor Sir Alec Cairncross.

69   Singer, Hans W. and Ansari, Javed A.
A   RICH AND POOR COUNTRIES
        Baltimore and London: Johns Hopkins University Press,
        1977.

Examines the changes that are required if the relationship between rich and poor countries is to make a more effective contribution to the development of the poor countries. Part one describes the structure of international economy and the nature of development process. Part two discusses the importance of the international trade sector to development in the poorer countries and reviews the trade policies of the rich and poor countries. Part three deals with the role of aid in the development process; and part four is concerned with international factor movement. Stresses the need for the formulation of an international development strategy...by the rich countries (both old and new), providing assistance in an increasing flow of resources through trade, aid capital and the transfer of skills and technology to the poor countries. Argues that such a strategy first must provide for some discrimination in international trade in favor of poor countries to provide more resources and secondly to enable the importation of more appropriate technologies.

70   Spiegelglas, Stephen and Welsh, Charles J., eds.
A B   ECONOMIC DEVELOPMENT;   CHALLENGE AND PROMISE
        Englewood Cliffs, N.J.:   Prentice-Hall, 1970.

A collection of 33 reprinted readings, each representing an outstanding contribution, controversial issue, or synthesis of ideas in economic development. Major sections

include: an   introduction;   nature   and   techniques   of
planning;   strategy   and   policy;   and   trade   or   aid.   The
selection   of   topics   in   these   sections   reflects   recent
increased   emphasis   on   practical   development   problems,
particularly   on   human   resources   development   and   the   need
to   create   exportable   manufactured   goods.   A   matrix   showing
how   each   selection   fits   into   the   scheme   and   sequence
of   the   seven   widely   used   development   textbooks   is   included.

71   T. N. Srinivasan
A B C D DEVELOPMENT, POVERTY, AND BASIC HUMAN NEEDS: SOME ISSUES
         World Bank Reprint Series, 76
         IBRD, 1977.

Reprinted   from   Food   Research   Institute   Studies,   vol.
XVI,   no.   2   (1977),   pp.   11-28.   Deals   with   the   raising
of   standard   of   living   of   the   poorest   sections   of   the
population   in   developing   countries.   Discusses   aid
problems,   distributional   aspects   of   economic   growth,
employment goals, and the new perceptions of development.

72   Stein, Leslie
A C D   ECONOMIC REALITIES IN POOR COUNTRIES
         Sydney, London and Singapore: Angus and Robertson, 1972.

This   book   surveys   the   problems   of   growth   faced   by   the
developing   countries   of   the   world.   The   first   part   of
the   book   describes   the   economic   and   social   characteristics
of   Third   World   countries   and   presents   some   theories   of
development,   including   Baran's   Marxian   view,   W. W. Rostow's
non-Marxist   alternative,   balanced   growth   theory,   and
Myrdal's   view   which   considers   non-economic   as   well   as
economic   factors   of   growth.   Succeeding   chapters   discuss
population   growth,   problems   of   education,   the   role   of
agriculture   and   industrial   development,   obstacles   to
trade,   and   government   plans   which   have   been   used   in
developing   countries.   Designed   for   use   as   a   text   or
for the layman.

73   Streeten, Paul
A B D   DEVELOPMENT PERSPECTIVES
         New York: St. Martin's Press, 1981.

A   combination   of   17   previously   published   articles   and
7   new   chapters,   in   five   parts: concepts,   values,   and
methods   in   development   analysis;   development   strategies;
transnational   corporations;   the   change   in   emphasis   from
the   growth   approach   to   the   basic   needs   approach;   and
two   miscellaneous   chapters   on   taxation   and   on   Gunnar
Myrdal.   Newly   written   chapters   cover: the   results   of
development   strategies   for   the   poor,   alternatives   in
development,   the   New   International   Economic   Order,   the
basic   needs   approach,   human   rights   and   basic   needs,   the

search for a basic-needs yardstick (with Norman Hicks), and transnational corporations and basic needs.

74   Thomson, W. Scott, ed.
A C   THE THIRD WORLD: PREMISES OF U.S. POLICY
       San Francisco: Institute for Contemporary Studies, 1978.

75   Tinbergen, Jan
A B   THE DESIGN OF DEVELOPMENT
       The Johns Hopkins University Press, 1958.

       Formulates a coherent government policy to further development objectives and outlines methods to stimulate private investments.

76   Todaro, Michael P.
A B C ECONOMIC DEVELOPMENT IN THE THIRD WORLD: AN INTRODUCTION TO PROBLEMS AND POLICIES IN A GLOBAL PERSPECTIVE
       London and New York: Longman, 1977.

       In four parts: Part one discusses the nature of underdevelopment and its various manifestations in the Third World, and parts two and three focus on major development problems and policies, both domestic (growth, income distribution, population, unemployment, education, and migration) and international (trade, balance of payments, and foreign investment). The last part reviews the possibilities and prospects for Third World development.

77   Todaro, Michael P.
A B   DEVELOPMENT PLANNING: MODELS AND METHODS
       Series of undergraduate teaching works in economics, Volume V.
       London, Nairobi, and New York: Oxford University Press, 1971.

       This is the last in a series of undergraduate teaching works in economics developed at Makere University, Uganda. This book is an introduction to development planning, with emphasis on plan formulation rather than implementation.

78   United Nations Department of Economic and Social Affairs
       THE INTERNATIONAL DEVELOPMENT STRATEGY: FIRST OVER-ALL REVIEW AND APPRAISAL OF ISSUES AND POLICIES. REPORT OF THE SECRETARY-GENERAL
       New York: United Nations, 1973.

       Deals with the issues and policies in the field of economic and social development...of prime concern in the first two years of the Second United Nations Development Decade. Emphasis is upon changes in the following areas: priorities of objectives, techniques of production, trade and aid relationships, and the external environment in which economic and social development takes place.

79   United Nations Department of Economic and Social Affairs
A C SHAPING ACCELERATED DEVELOPMENT AND INTERNATIONAL CHANGES
     New York: United Nations Publications, 1980.

Contains views and recommendations of the UN Committee for Development Planning relating to the international development strategy for a third UN development decade. Chapters cover general premises and basic objectives; priority areas for action; means and implementation; and key goals and needed changes.

80   United Nations Department of Economic and Social Affairs
A C DEVELOPMENT IN THE 1980'S: APPROACH TO A NEW STRATEGY;
     VIEWS AND RECOMMENDATIONS OF THE COMMITTEE FOR DEVELOPMENT
     PLANNING
     New York: United Nations Publications, 1978.

Reviews development issues for the 1980's with a discussion of the current situation and preliminary comments relating to a development strategy for the 1980's. Discusses economic cooperation among developing countries, covering trade, economic integration and other arrangements for economic cooperation.

81   United Nations Industrial Development Organization
A B C INDUSTRIALIZATION FOR NEW DEVELOPMENT NEEDS
      New York: United Nations Publication, 1974.

Emphasizes the reshaping of industrial development in the light of new development needs that the pervasive problems of unemployment, maldistribution of income, and poverty in general have brought to the fore in the developing countries.

82   UNRSID
A B C THE QUEST FOR A UNIFIED APPROACH TO DEVELOPMENT
      UNRSID: 1980.

Provides background information on UNRSID's efforts to formulate a unified approach to development analysis and planning, an approach which would bring together all the different aspects of development into a set of feasible objectives and policy approaches. Chapters cover: styles of development--definitions and criteria; strategies; the findings of the Expert Group; an assessment by Marshall Wolfe, former Chief of the Social Development Division of UN ECLA; and an annex containing the final report on the project by the UN Commission for Social Development, covering questions of diagnosis, monitoring, indicators, and planning and capicitation.

83   Uri, Pierre
A B C   DEVELOPMENT WITHOUT DEPENDENCE
          New York: Praeger for the Atlantic Institute for
          International Affairs, 1976.

          Monograph on foreign aid. Contends that the aid programs
          of the 1950's and 1960's were lopsided and failed to
          address the needs of the truly poor. According to Bundy,
          the author argues that although effective transfer of
          resources and skill remains a vital part of the need...such
          nation-to-nation aid...can only help to foster the very
          feelings of dependence...that are the deepest grievance
          of the developing world. Discusses control of population
          growth, the role and necessary scale of official foreign
          aid, stabilization of the raw materials market so as
          to assist consumers and producers alike, and the types
          of industries the developing countries should strive
          to build as a part of a rational world division of labor.
          Examines the control and regulation of multinational
          corporations and, focusing on Latin America, the extent
          to which regional cooperation can be developed. Recommends
          that development planning be based on future population
          growth and distribution.

84   Varma, Baidya Nath
A B C   THE SOCIOLOGY AND POLITICS OF DEVELOPMENT: A THEORETICAL
          STUDY
          International Library of Sociology Series
          London and Boston: Routledge & Kegan Paul, 1980.

          The author critically examines theories of development
          and presents his own theory. Considers general criteria
          used for evaluating the modernization process; describes
          a model for a general paradigm of modernization; surveys
          other models encompassing ideological, social scientific,
          anthropological and activistic theories; and discusses
          theoretical problems of planning and national
          reconstruction. Summarizes views of theorists in various
          social science disciplines and features of modernization
          in terms of guidance provided for economic, political,
          educational, and bureaucratic decision-making in a
          developing country. Concludes that both the socialist
          and capitalist systems of modernization are viable models
          for Third World countries.

85   Vogeler, Ingolf and De Souza, Anthony R., eds.
A C   DIALECTICS OF THIRD WORLD DEVELOPMENT
          Montclair: Allanheld, Osmun, 1980.

          Collection of previously published (some revised) papers
          designed for use by students of economics, political
          science, and development. Representing a variety of
          ideas and arguments relevant to Third World
          underdevelopment, the readings discuss climate and

resources,   cultural   traditions,   European   colonialism
(i.e.,   plantation   agriculture),   population,   tourism,
and   imperialism.   An   appendix   provides   "awareness"
exercises.

86   Wallman, Sandra, ed.
A B   PERCEPTIONS OF DEVELOPMENT
        New York: Cambridge University Press, 1977.

87   Ward, Richard J.
A C   DEVELOPMENT ISSUES FOR THE 1970'S
        New York and London: Dunellen, 1973.

An assessment of key issues and problems which emerged
from the Decade of Development and which will continue
to absorb the attention of students of development in
the present decade. The author, former Chief of Planning
of the U.S. Agency for International Development, presents
much data which has not been previously released and
which is unavailable elsewhere. The book is divided
into three parts: "Food and Human Welfare," "Development
Problems for This Decade," and "Planning Programs and
Strategies." The chapters specifically discuss such
issues as labor absorption in agriculture, means of
population control, the burden of debt service, the role
of foreign aid, big-push development, etc.

88   Waterston, Albert
A B   DEVELOPMENT PLANNING; LESSONS OF EXPERIENCE
        The Johns Hopkins University Press, 1979.

Analyzes the success of the development planning experience
in over 100 countries in Asia, Africa, Europe, and the
Americas. In two parts. Part 1 describes and analyzes
the problems associated with the implementation of planning
programs, the provision of basic data, the role of national
budget, and administrative obstacles. Part 2 contains
an extensive and comparative discussion of the experience
of the countries under review in setting up organizations
and   administrative   procedures   for   preparing   and
implementing development projects; the distribution of
planning functions, types of central planning agencies,
and subnational regional and local planning bodies.

89   Watts, Nita, ed.
A B   ECONOMIES OF THE WORLD
        New York: Oxford University Press.

The purpose of this new series is to provide a brief
review of economic development during the post-war period
in each of a number of countries which are of obvious
importance in the world economy, or interesting because
of peculiarities of their economic structure or experience,
or   illustrative   of   widespread   economic   development

problems. The series will be of interest to economists in universities, and in business and government.

90   Wilber, Charles K., ed.
A B   THE POLITICAL ECONOMY OF DEVELOPMENT AND UNDERDEVELOPMENT
        New York: Random House, 1973.

Emphasis in approach and content is on political economy in the sense of attempting to incorporate such noneconomic influences as social structures, political systems, and cultural values as well as such factors as technological change and the distribution of income and wealth. Readings are radical in that they are willing to question and evaluate the most basic institutions and values of society. Divided into eight groups concerned with methodological problems, historical perspective, trade and imperialism, agricultural and industrial institutions and strategies, comparative models of development, the human cost of development, and indications for the future.

91   Worsley, Peter
A C   THE THIRD WORLD
        Chicago: University of Chicago Press, 1972.

92   Wriggins, W. Howards and Adler-Karlsson, Gunnar
A C   REDUCING GLOBAL INEQUALITIES
        New York: McGraw-Hill, 1978.

Two papers, plus an introduction on the role that developing countries themselves take to reduce the gap between rich nations and poor and to eliminate mass poverty within their own societies. W. Howard Wriggins, U.S. ambassador to Sri Lanka and formerly professor of political science at Columbia University, analyzes the various bargaining strategies open to developing countries such as developing commodity or regional coalitions, or a variety of threats to developed countries. The future is likely to see continued efforts at coalition building, but also periodic outbreaks of irregular violence against local opponents, neighbors, or Northern centers of power.

93   Zuvekas, Clarence, Jr.
A B C   ECONOMIC DEVELOPMENT: AN INTRODUCTION
        New York: St. Martin's Press, 1979.

Text written from an interdisciplinary perspective stressing policy and empirical findings rather than an overall development theory. Aims at balance between theory and policy, including historical development and empirical evidence. After discussing the terminology of and the obstacles to development, the author examines population growth, trade and development, and the role of government. Also covers: the problems of agriculture

and industry, income distribution, employment, mobilization
of domestic and foreign savings, manipulation of trade
to the advantage of the developing country, and with
the limits to growth controversy. Presumes acquaintance
with basic macro and micro theory.

INTERNATIONAL TRADE AND THIRD WORLD DEVELOPMENT

94   Abbott, George C.
INTERNATIONAL INDEBTEDNESS AND THE DEVELOPING COUNTRIES
White Plains, NY: M. E. Sharpe, 1979.

95   Agrawal, Chandra P.
EXPORT METHODS AND SERVICES IN INDIA
International Publications Service, 1972.

96   Ahmad, Jaleel
IMPORT SUBSTITUTION: TRADE AND DEVELOPMENT
Greenwich, Conn.: JAI Press, 1978.

Analyzes the process of import substitution, stressing
motivations of countries that undertake import substitution
policies, the structural effects on outputs, factor
rewards, and the consequences for the locus of production
in the international economy. Also discusses approaches
to measurement of import substitution, the problems
encountered in import substitution and the analytical
relationship of import substitution to trade theory.
Argues that any new economic order must actively seek
to allocate a larger share of industrial production to
the LDC's as cumulative changes in production structures,
helped by previous import substitution policies, lead
them into the capability of producing increasingly complex
manufactures. Concludes that, although import substitution
policies may be criticized for a number of shortcomings,
such policies occupy a central place in the hierarchy
of policy options, and the benefits of import substitution
policies can be enhanced and the drawbacks reduced by
appropriate subsidiary policies.

97   Akrasonee, Narongchai
TRADE AND EMPLOYMENT IN ASIA AND THE PACIFIC
UH Press, 1977.

98   Alcock, F.
TRADE AND TRAVEL IN SOUTH AMERICA
Gordon Press, 1976.

99   Ananaba, Wogu
THE TRADE UNION MOVEMENT IN AFRICA: PROMISE AND
PERFORMANCE
New York: St. Martin's Press, 1979.

Focuses on the development and organization of trade
unions in Africa since 1961, but includes brief discussions
of events during the periods from 1939-45 and 1945-60.
Part one surveys the general trade union situation by
country in West, Eastern, Central, Southern, and North
Africa; presents case studies of Lesotho and Liberia;
and examines the continental trade union organizations
of the African Regional Organization (AFRO), the
All-African Trade Union Federation (AATUF), the African
Trade Union Confederation (ATUC), and the Organisation
of Trade Union Unity (OATUU). Part two assesses union
activities, problems, and prospects, finding that
fragmentation, maladministration, indiscipline, abuse
of office and undemocratic procedures are still the order
of the day; and that law and politics, which violate
international labour standards abound in most African
states; and that bona fide unions have ceased to exist
in many countries.

100   Anderson, Dole A.
MARKETING AND DEVELOPMENT: THE THAILAND EXPERIENCE
East Lansing, MI: Michigan State University, 1970.

Studies the growth of the national market for consumer
goods in Thailand. Part one reviews the Thai ecological
matrix: history, geography, religion, education, and
other characteristics unique to its society. Part two
examines the marketing structure and the development
of the national market particularly through transportation
improvements.

101   Anderson, Kym and Baldwin, Robert E.
THE POLITICAL MARKET FOR PROTECTION IN INDUSTRIAL
COUNTRIES: EMPIRICAL EVIDENCE
Working Paper No. 492; Washington, D.C.: World Bank,
1981.

This report is part of an inquiry being undertaken by
the World Bank in conjunction with scholars from twelve
industrial countries into the penetration of the markets
of industrial countries by exports of manufactures from
developing countries.

102   Andersson, Jan Otto
STUDIES IN THE THEORY OF UNEQUAL EXCHANGE BETWEEN NATIONS
Abo, Finland: Abo Akademi, 1976.

Focuses on three questions in the theory of international
trade: when is exchange between two countries "unequal"?
can one nation exploit another? and when are the terms
of trade adverse to a nation or group of nations?
Discusses the concept of exploitation, three concepts
of unequal exchange, and the law of value. Sets forth
and criticizes Arghiri Emmanuel's theory of unequal

exchange and then works out a modified Emmanuelian model. In his chapter on the consequences of nonequivalent exchange, the author finds that due to great differences in labour-productivity and labour-equipment ratios in agriculture, there may well exist an objective basis for antagonism between the workers in the developed and underdeveloped countries.

103   Arellano, Richard G. and Allen, Alexandra
       EXPORT POTENTIAL: MEXICO SPECIAL RESEARCH STUDY
       International Marketing, 1979.

104   Ariff, K. A. Mohamed
       EXPORT TRADE AND THE WEST MALAYSIAN ECONOMY -- AN ENQUIRY
       INTO THE ECONOMIC IMPLICATIONS OF EXPORT STABILITY
       Kuala Lumpur: Faculty of Economics and Administration,
       University of Malaya, 1972.

       A case-study of foreign trade and commodity instability
       as exemplified by the West Malayan economy. The author
       studies supply and demand for that country's exports,
       the short-term effects and long-term implications of
       export instability, the use of commodity control schemes,
       and various policy issues related to the instability
       problem.

105   Baer, Werner and Gillis, Malcolm, eds.
       EXPORT DIVERSIFICATION AND THE NEW PROTECTIONISM: THE
       EXPERIENCES OF LATIN AMERICA
       Champaign: University of Illinois, Bureau of Economic
       and Business Research and National Bureau of Economic
       Research, 1981.

       Twelve previously unpublished papers presented at a
       conference in Sao Paulo, Brazil, 23-26 March 1980. Focus
       is on trade relations between Latin America and the
       advanced industrial countries, particularly the United
       States. Also examines the opportunities for and
       constraints upon intra-Latin American trade. Covers
       empirical and theoretical perspectives of current issues
       and problems likely to be of significance during the
       rest of the 1980's. These issues include: Latin American
       development policies and their impact on the region's
       position in the international economy; primary exports;
       reactions to external shocks; external disequilibrium
       in Brazil; Colombia's participation in the Andean Group;
       comparative development and trade strategies of East
       Asian superexporters and Latin American countries;
       reactions of developing countries to Latin America's
       export drive; recent U.S. responses to dumping and export
       subsidies by foreign giants; and Latin America's increasing
       external indebtedness.

106   Balassa, Bela
A C   INDUSTRIAL   PROSPECTS   AND   POLIOCIES   IN   THE   DEVELOPED
       COUNTRIES
       World Bank Staff Working Paper No. 453, April 1981.

       Addresses the allegations that increases in the import
       of manufactured goods from developing countries adversely
       affect the industrial sector in the developed countries
       and that growing protectionism in the developed countries
       has made it necessary for developing countries to turn
       to domestic markets or to trade among themselves in order
       to sell their manufactured goods. Argues that trade
       with the developing countries actually benefits the
       developed countries, that rates of industrial protection
       should be lowered, and that an international safeguard
       code should be instituted to smooth the process of
       adjustment to freer trade in the developed countries.

107   Balassa, Bela
       THE "NEW PROTECTIONISM"AND THE INTERNATIONAL ECONOMY
       Reprinted   from   JOURNAL   OF   WORLD   TRADE   LAW   12
       (1978):409-436.

       Examines the recent emergence of the "new protectionism."
       Considers the beneficial effects of postwar trade
       liberalization and appraises the adverse effect of
       protective measures after the oil crisis and the 1974-75
       world recession. Makes recommendations for developed
       countries to raise rates of economic growth and apply
       measures of adjustment instead of restricting imports,
       while emphasizing the need for an International Code
       of Good Conduct. The paper was presented at the Seminar
       on the Role of World Trade in the Present Economic
       Situation, Milan, March 31, 1978.

108   Balassa, Bela and others
       THE STRUCTURE OF PROTECTION IN DEVELOPING COUNTRIES
       The John Hopkins University Press, 1971.

       Presents criteria for evaluating the system of protection,
       applying them to seven countries on the basis of a common
       methodology and providing guidelines for policy
       formulation. Estimates are given for primary activities
       and for manufacturing, for import substitution and export
       industries, as well as for major commodity groups, with
       separate consideration of the interindustry structure
       of protection, the extent of import protection and the
       bias against exports. Some tentative calculations are
       also provided on the economic loss due to protection
       and an appraisal of the effects of protection on export
       performance and economic growth.

109   Balassa, Bela
       A "STAGES" APPROACH TO COMPARATIVE ADVANTAGE

May 1977.

Examines intercountry differences in export structure
with a view to indicating the changing pattern of
comparative advantage in the process of economic
development. Empirical estimates show that these
differences are largely explained by differences in
physical and human capital endowments, resulting in changes
in the export structure as physical and human capital
is accumulated.

110   Balassa, Bela
        INTRA-INDUSTRY TRADE AND THE INTEGRATION OF DEVELOPING
        COUNTRIES IN THE WORLD ECONOMY
        January 1979.

Reviews the experience of the Latin American Free Trade
Association and the Central American Common Market with
intra-industry trade in manufacturing, entailing the
exchange of differentiated products, and considers the
welfare effects of this trade. Also examines
intra-industry specialization between developed and
developing countries, involving the importation of
labor-intensive product varieties and parts, components,
and accessories into the former group of countries from
the latter. Recommends policy measures to encourage
intra-industry specialization, including regional
integration and multilateral trade liberalization. Revised
version of a paper presented at the Conference on
Intra-Industry Trade at the Institute fur Weltwirtschaft,
Kiel, December 7-8, 1978.

111   Balassa, Bela
        EXPORTS AND ECONOMIC GROWTH: FURTHER EVIDENCE
        Reprinted from JOURNAL OF DEVELOPMENT ECONOMICS 5
        (1978):181-189.

Indicates the existence of a positive relationship between
exports and economic growth in a group of 11 developing
countries that have already established an industrial
base.   This result is shown for manufactured as well
as for total exports; in the case of the latter, adjustment
has further been made for domestic and foreign investment
and for increases in the labor force.   The paper was
prepared in the framework of the research project,
"Development Strategies in Semi-Industrial Countries"
(Ref. No. 670-01), now completed.

112   Balassa, Bela and Sharpston, Michael J.
        EXPORT SUBSIDIES BY DEVELOPING COUNTRIES: ISSUES OF
        POLICY
        Reprinted from COMMERCIAL POLICY ISSUES (November
        1977):13-50.

Considers quesions of import protection and export

subsidies in light of their international acceptability and in the framework of optimal trade policies. Also reviews attitudes in developing nations toward export subsidies applied by developing countries and analyzes international rules with suggestions for modifying them.

113   Balassa, Bela
EXPORT INCENTIVES AND EXPORT PERFORMANCE IN DEVELOPING COUNTRIES: A COMPARATIVE ANALYSIS
Reprinted from WELTWIRSCHAFTLICHES ARCHIV 114 (1978):24-61.

Evaluates export incentives and their effects on exports and economic performance in 11 developing countries classified in four groups, depending on the timing and extent of their export promotion efforts, for the period 1966-73. Also considers future growth possibilities for exports by developing countries and makes recommendations for an "ideal" system of incentives for exports and for resource allocation in general. The paper was prepared in the framework of the research project, "Development Strategies in Semi-Industrial Countries" (Ref. No. 670-01), now completed.

114   Balassa, Bela
ADJUSTMENT TO EXTERNAL SHOCKS IN DEVELOPING ECONOMIES
World Bank Staff Working Paper No. 472, July 1981.

A background study for World Development Report 1981. Analyzes adjustments to external shocks, in the form of changes in the terms of trade and the slowdown in foreign export demand, in twenty-eight developing economies, classified according to the character of external shocks, the level of industrial development, and the policies applied.

115   Balassa, Bela, et al.
WORLD TRADE: CONSTRAINTS AND OPPORTUNITIES IN THE 80'S
Atlantic Papers, no. 36. Paris: Atlantic Institute for International Affairs, 1979.

Four papers, most originally prepared for the Spring 1978 Conference in Geneva organized by the International Chamber of Commerce, the European Management Forum, and the Europa Consortium of Newspapers. In the introductory paper, Carl-Henrik Winqwist asks "Is Protection Unavoidable?" and argues for an open world economy. Martin Wassell discusses the historical and regulatory background to the Multilateral Trade Negotiations; Sidney Golt and William Eberle preview the constraints, opportunities, and issues of the 1980's. In the extended final paper, previously published in the September 1978 issue of the Journal of International Trade Law, Bela Balassa evaluates the "new protectionism" and discusses policy options for long-term growth.

116   Baldwin, Robert E.
       FOREIGN TRADE REGIMES AND ECONOMIC DEVELOPMENT: THE
       PHILIPPINES. A special Conference Series on Foreign
       Trade Regimes and Economic Development, Vol. V.
       New York: National Bureau of Economic Research;
       distributed by Columbia Universisty Press, New York and
       London, 1975.

       Describes and analyzes both the trade and payments policies
       and fiscal and monetary policies followed by the
       Philippines during the past 25 years. Attempts to quantify
       the differential levels of protection these combined
       policies offered to various sectors of the economy. Also
       examines the effects of different exchange-control methods
       and various development policies on industrial allocation
       of resources, the distribution of income, and the rate
       of growth of the economy. Finds that the economy possesses
       favorable basic conditions for growth; notes, however,
       that: (1) "the main driving forces for sustaining
       development will have to come from the internal economic
       interactions among the various sectors"; (2) development
       policy should focus on export production and high
       employment in light manufactures and services in the
       industrial sector; and (3) the government must exercise
       a greater degree of fiscal and monetary discipline.
       Related trade data provided.

117   Baldwin, Robert E. and Richardson, David J.
       INTERNATIONAL TRADE AND FINANCE READINGS
       Little 1981.

118   Bale, Malcolm D. and Lutz, Ernst
       TRADE RESTRICTIONS AND INTERNATIONAL PRICE INSTABILITY
       October 1978.

       Evaluates the effects of international trade disortions
       on world price instability in an equilibrium model of
       two countries and one commodity. Different cases of
       trade intervention are presented and the conditions stated
       under which price instability is increased, decreased,
       or left unchanged.

119   Banerji, Ranadev
       THE DEVELOPMENT IMPACT OF BARTER IN DEVELOPING COUNTRIES:
       THE CASE OF INDIA 205 p., fig., tables (Technical Studies;
       "Document" Series)
       OECD 1977.

       Discusses the impact of international barter in bilateral
       trade and payments agreements on the economies of
       developing countries, specifically India. Chapters cover:
       (a) introduction; (b) characteristics of India's bilateral
       trade agreements and their barter content; (c) Indian
       economy and the background to bilateralism; (d) impact
       of bilateral trading agreements on India's foreign trade;

(e) trade diversion and trade creation under barter-like agreements; (f) economic assistance to India through bilateral trade agreements--the East European approach to aid; (g) the impact of barter-like trade on India's economy; and (h) concluding remarks.

120   Bates, Robert H. and Lofchie, Michael F., eds.
AGRICULTURAL DEVELOPMENT IN AFRICA: ISSUES OF PUBLIC POLICY Praeger Speical Studies--Praeger Scientific.
New York: Praeger, 1980.

Eleven papers drawn from a colloquium on African rural development at the University of California, Los Angeles, in the spring of 1978. Central themes are the importance of price and market responsiveness and the specific conditions under which African rural producers are likely to react to price incentives and market opportunities. Part one consists of three "general studies" on the history of long-distance trade and marketing in tropical Africa, on the failure of African governments to use price incentives as a means of promoting increased production, and on the disirability of small-farmer strategies toward the production of export crops. Part two consists of country case studies illustrating the views in part one. The papers in part three consider special topics--the functioning of agricultural markets, the economic impact of traditional forms of communal land tenure, and the implications of risk aversion among peasantries.

121   Behrman, Jere R.
FOREIGN TRADE REGIMES AND ECONOMIC DEVELOPMENT A Special Conference Series on Foreign Trade Regimes and Economic Development, Vol. 8.
New York: National Bureau of Economic Research; distributed by Columbia University Press, New York and London, 1976.

Examines the relations between international economic policies and macroeconomic goals in Chile, including: growth, external position and the degree of national autonomy, stability in real and nominal terms, resource allocation and the distribution of control over income and other resources. The author's major findings include: (1) attempts at exchange control and import substitution in Chile antedate World War II; (2) decisions over time to alter foreign-sector policies have been strongly influenced by external developments, however, most recent shifts have been motivated by internal political changes and policy considerations; (3) responses of the domestic price level to devaluations have been substantial and immediate; (4) general-equilibrium analysis suggests that the impact of devaluation on the balance of payments and on employment is much less positive than suggested by partial equlibrium analysis; (5) variations in domestic resource costs are large, both between and within sectors;

(6) in the short-run, tightened quantitative restictions have been more successful than devaluations; and (7) evidence does not support either polar position, namely, that exchange control accelerates development or that liberalization quickens development. Data mainly for 1946-72.

122   Bennathan, Esra and Walter, A.A.
PORT PRICING AND INVESTMENT POLICY FOR DEVELOPING COUNTRIES
Oxford University Press, 1979.

Seeks to develop a set of principles of cost-based prices which can be used to plan port tariffs and to suggest practical ways of introducing tariff schedules to improve the allocation of resources and financial performance. Argues that efficient port operation requires that the authorities levy prices which closely follow marginal costs. This implies that, when demand for port facilities is very high, tariffs should be raised by using a congestion levy; when demand is low, promotional two-part tariffs should be charged.

123   Berendsen, B.S.M.
REGIONAL MODELS OF TRADE AND DEVELOPMENT, Studies in Development and Planning, Vol. 7.
Leiden and Boston: Martinus Nijhoff Social Sciences Division, 1978.

Studies the effect of integration and coordination policies among developing countries on the structure of intra- and extra-regional trade. Reviews the theoretical literature on multi-country, multi-sector models for economic development, regional integration, and foreign trade of developing countries; develops new approaches for the regional framework; and presents statistical exercises for the closed econometric multi-country, multi-sector model for the region of Southeast Asian Nations. Some conclusions are that (1) the theory of comparative costs applies to developing as well as to developed countries; (2) export-promotion is generally superior to import substitution as a trade strategy, but are situations where import-substitution should be supported; (3) regional economic policy should aim at intersectoral specialization; (4) benefits for developing countries involve increased regional trade in food items, expanded trade in intermediate imports, and improvement in balance-of-payments deficits. An appendix offers trade flow matrices.

124   Bhagwati, Jagdish N.
FOREIGN TRADE REGIMES AND ECONOMIC DEVELOPMENT: ANATOMY AND CONSEQUENCES OF EXCHANGE CONTROL REGIMES, A Special Conference Series on Foreign Trade Regimes and Economic Development, Vol. 11.
National Bureau of Economic Research, Studies in

International Economic Relations. New York: NBER; Cambridge, Mass.: Lippinscott, Ballinger, 1978.

Designed as a partial synthesis of major findings of the project, "a guide to certain key contributions in the country studies." One of two summary volumes, which examine the anatomy of exchange control, the relationship between different types of exchange control regimes and economic efficiency, and transition to less restrictive regimes. Focusing on the first two areas examined by the project (the previously published synthesis volume by Anne Krueger addresses the third area), this summary investigates the patterns and sequences of regimes and their consequences for such items as exchange control and illegal transactions, allocative efficiency, saving, and export performance. Results seem "to come down in favor of the export-promoting trade strategy."

125   Bhagwaiti, Jagdish N. and Srinivasan, T.N.
FOREIGN TRADE REGIMES AND ECONOMIC DEVELOPMENT INDIA. A Special Conference Series on Foreign Trade Regimes and Economic Development, Vol. 6.
New York: National Bureau of Economic Research; distributed by Columbia University Press, New York and London, 1975.

Examines India's foreign trade regime's interaction with domestic policies and objectives between 1950 and 1970, assessing its efficiency and growth. Discusses the anatomy of exchange control, focusing on 1956-66 and examines 1966-70 with emphasis on the "liberalization episode," beginning with devaluation in June 1966. The last part investigates the growth effects of the foreign trade regime throughout the entire period. Finds that "India's foreign trade regime, in conjunction with domestic licensing policies in the industrial sector, led to economic inefficiencies and impaired her economic performance." Concludes that analysis of the devaluation-cum-liberalization package of 1966 shows that an improved liberalization policy could be successful and is necessary to stimulate increased efficiency and faster growth. Includes tables of related macroeconomic data.

126   Bhagwati, Jagdish N. and Srinivasan, T.N.
TRADE POLICY AND DEVELOPMENT, reprinted from International Economic Policy: Theory and Evidence, Rudiger Dornbusch and Jacob A. Frenkel, eds.
Baltimore and London: The Johns Hopkins University Press, 1978.

Focuses principally on the trade policies of developing countries, in regard to the optimal methods of utilizing available trade opportunities and on how those trade opportunities ought to be defined. Two subjects of recent

interest are considered--the theoretical and policy issues
raised by the problem of market disruption-related threats
of trade restriction on imports of manufactures by
developing countries, and the recent demand by developing
countries, as part of the New International Economic
Order (NIEO), for commodity agreements.

127   Bhagwati, Jagdish N. and Padma, Desai
A C D   INDIA: PLANNING FOR INDUSTRIALIZATION: INDUSTRIALIZATION
        AND TRADE POLITICS SINCE 1951
        New York: Oxford University Press, 1979.

128   Bhagwati, J.N.
        TRADE, BALANCE OF PAYMENTS AND GROWTH
        Elseruei, 1971.

129   Bhagwati, Jagdish
        INTERNATIONAL TRADE: SELECTED READINGS
        MIT Press, 1981.

130   Bhagwati, Jagdish and Srinivason, T.N.
        FOREIGN TRADE REGIMES AND ECONOMIC DEVELOPMENT: INDIA
        Columbia University Press, 1975.

131   Bhattacharya, Anindya K.
        FOREIGN TRADE AND INTERNATIONAL DEVELOPMENT
        Lexington, Mass.; Toronto and London: Heath, Lexington
        Books, 1976.

        An examination of the political basis of economic doctrines
        governing the interrelationship between foreign trade
        and international development of non-oil-producing
        countries (LDC's). Examines the domestic political
        conflicts of interest in developing trade within the
        LDC's and in the international area, the economic
        efficiency basis of LDC trade demands, and the equity
        of redistributionist LDC trade demands. Data on trade,
        capital flows, and commodity prices, selected years 1960
        to 1974, derived from U.N. publications.

132   Blackhurst, Richard; Marian, Nicolas and Tumlir, Jan
        ADJUSTMENT, TRADE AND GROWTH IN DEVELOPED AND DEVELOPING
        COUNTRIES, Gatt Studies in International Trade, No. 6.
        Geneva: General Agreement on Tariffs and Trade, 1978.

        Consisting og two chapters and a conclusion, this monograph
        focuses on specific obstacles in the area of adjustment
        and trade. Surveys long-term and recent changes in the
        growth and trade of developing countries and examines
        selected problems affecting the trade structure and
        economic activity in developed countries. Assumes that
        "protectionism is a short-run and ultimately self-defeating
        alternative to the needed adjustment" and that "adjustment

to change is a necessary condition of economic growth."
Analyzes situations in developed countries related to
(1) inflation and investment, (2) uncertainty in
international economic relations, (3) deterioration of
the allocative mechanism, and (4) labor market
developments. A primary conclusion is that obstacles
to adjustment "turn out in the end to be essentially
political." Appendices give statistical tables and notes
on definitions and data sources.

133   Blackhurst, Richard; Marian, Nicolas and Tumlir, Jan
TRADE LIBERALIZATION, PROTECTIONISM AND INTERDEPENDENCE,
GATT Studies in International Trade, No. 5.
Geneva: General Agreement on Tariffs and Trade, 1977.

Reviews the main trends in production and trade over
the long run and outlines the case for further trade
liberalization, emphasizing the contribution of
liberalization to efficiency, growth, and its impact
on macroeconomic stability. Also deals with the economic
and political aspects of the current protectionist
pressures. Finds that despite the gains to be had from
further liberalization of trade, it is unlikely that
protectionist pressures will of themselves begin soon
to wane. Concludes that the original and essential
function of governments has been, and continues to be,
the reduction of uncertainty; protection introduces an
arbitrary external element, which is inherently
destabilizing to the process of economic activity.

134   Boltho, Andrea
FOREIGN TRADE CRITERIA IN SOCIALIST ECONOMIES
Cambridge University Press, 1970.

135   Bradford, Colin L., Jr., et al.
NEW DIRECTIONS IN DEVELOPMENT: LATIN AMERICA, EXPORT
CREDIT, POPULATION GROWTH, AND U.S. ATTITUDES
New York: Praeger, 1974.

136   Brafman, Morris and Schimel, David
TRADE FOR FREEDOM
Shengold 1975.

137   Cappi, Carlo; Fletcher, Lehman; Norton, Roger D.; Pomareda,
Carlos and Wainer, Molly
A MODEL OF AGRICULTURAL PRODUCTION AND TRADE IN CENTRAL
AMERICA, reprinted from Economic Integration in Central
America, eds. William R. Cline and Enrique Delgado.
Washington, D.C.: Brookings Institution, 1978.

Based on the earlier CHAC model for Mexico, the model
describes production by crop, food processing activities,
international trade, consumption demands, and price
formation for the five countries of the Central American

Common Market (Costa Rica, El Salvador, Guatemala, Honduras, and Nicaragua). Its purpose is to assess benefits and costs of expanded agricultural trade within the region and with the rest of the world.

138   Center for Strategic and International Studies, ed.
       WORLD TRADE COMPETITION: WESTERN COUNTRIES AND THIRD
       WORLD MARKETS
       New York: Praeger, 1981.

       Six previously unpublished papers examine the extent to which U.S. market shares have been lost to United States competitors in the industrialized countries, particularly Germany, France, and Japan. Reviews the export experience of some key U.S. trading partners in the markets of the developing Third World and discusses the outlook in the 1980s for trade competition in manufactured goods.

139   Chaudhuri, K.N.
       THE TRADING WORLD OF ASIA AND THE ENGLISH EAST INDIA
       COMPANY: 1660-1760
       Cambridge University Press, 1978.

       Comprehensive history of the English East India Company during the period 1660 to 1760, an analysis of economic life in those Asian countries in which the Company traded, and a glimpse into the general difficulties involved in long-distance trade in pre-Industrial Revolution societies. Uses systems analysis and the formulation of a decision and operational model to collect and analyze the data drawn from the records of Company officials and the Company's account books on the total volume and value of trade, prices, currency values, transport costs, and other economic variables. Extensive appendices provide the time-series analysis, statistical tables, the trading model, and a list and glossary of Indian textile types.

140   Chenery, Hollis B. and Keesing, Donald B.
       THE CHANGING COMPOSITION OF DEVELOPING COUNTRY EXPORTS
       January, 1979.

       Explores trends in exports and the influences that have shaped export growth in developing countries since 1960 together with the prospects for further expansion, with particular emphasis on manufactured exports which grew twice as fast as total exports from 1960-75. Analyzes relationships between initial economic structure, trade policies, and manufactured export performance in different groups of developing countries. Notes that increased exports of developing countries combined with poor economic performance in the developed countries have triggered rising protectionism in the latter, and suggests that special measures may have to be considered to provide opportunities for those developing countries that are

not yet successful exporters of manufactures but need
to be so to facilitate their growth.

141   Cogham, David
THE ECONOMICS OF INTERNATIONAL TRADE
Cambridge: Woodhead-Faulkner in association with Lloyds
Bank, 1979.

An introductory text on the principles of international
trade and payments and the recent facts on Britain's
position in the world economy, which discusses the
advanatages of free trade and the concept of and the
nature of problems with balance of payments, and which
empirically investigates the foreign trade and balance
of payments of the U.K. It also describes the
international economic environment. It concludes: that
the general key question in the revival of world trade
is when and at what rate the economic growth of the
developed market economies will be resumed, that the
trend towards international interdependence will continue,
and that as a result the U.K.'s trade as a proportion
of GDP will increase. Suitable for students and those
requiring a knowledge of British overseas trade.

142   Dodoni, Rene, et al.
WORLD TRADE FLOWS. INTEGRATIONAL STRUCTURE AND CONDITIONAL
FORECASTS. Two Volumes. CENTER FOR ECONOMIC RESEARCH,
SWISS FEDERAL INSTITUTE OF TECHNOLOGY, RESEARCH MONOGRAPHS,
NEW SERIES, Vol. 5.
Zurich; Schulthess Polygrpahischer Verlag AG, 1971.

Volume I analyzes the structural features of the present
world trade system and reviews the history of regional
economic integration among less-developed countries,
in Latin America, Africa, and Asia. The study uses
Leontief-type models to illustrate the relations between
economic development and trade and to present some findings
on the quantitative relationship between GNP growth rates
and the trade gaps of individual countries participating
in world trade. Volume II contains the statistical data
on which the findings of Volume I are based.

143   Cosway, R.
TRADE AND INVESTMENT IN TAIWAN: THE LEGAL AND ENVIRONMENT
IN THE REPUBLIC OF CHINA
International Scholastic Book Service, 1980.

144   De Sa Torre, Jose
EXPORTS OF MANUFACTURED GOODS FROM DEVELOPING COUNTRIES:
MARKETING FACTORS AND THE ROLE OF FOREIGN ENTERPRISE
Arno, 1976.

145   de Milo, Jaime and Robinson, Sherman
TRADE ADJUSTMENT POLICIES AND INCOME DISTRIBUTION IN

THREE ARCHETYPE DEVELOPING ECONOMIES
World Bank, 1980.

146   Desai, Padma
       IMPORT SUBSTITUTION IN THE INDIAN ECONOMY, 1951-63.
       Delhi: Hindustan, 1972.

       A statistical   analysis   of   the   pattern   of   import
       substitution in the manufacturing sector during India's
       three Five Year Plans of the period 1951-1963. Provides
       detailed data for 169 items in three major groups of
       industries, consumer goods, intermediates, and capital
       goods.   In   addition,   discusses   various   concepts   and
       alternative measures of import substitution.

147   de Vries, Barend A.
       THE EXPORT EXPERIENCE OF DEVELOPING COUNTRIES
       World Bank Staff Occasional Papers, No. 3.   The Johns
       Hopkins University Press, 1967.

148   de Vries, Barend A., et al.
       EXPORT PROMOTION POLICIES
       January 1979.

       Presents   summaries   of   studies   on   the   promotion   of
       nontraditional (manufactured) exports, along with comments,
       presented   at   a   Joint   IBRD/ECLA/UNDP   Conference,   held
       in Santiago, Chile, November 1976.   Deals with general
       aspects of industrial and trade incentive policies and
       of manufactured export growth, and with the experience
       of   four   Latin   American   countries   (Argentina,   Brazil,
       Colombia,   and   Mexico)   and   four   countries   outside   the
       region (India, Israel, Republic of Korea, and Yugoslavia).
       The   studies   were   supported   by   the   research   project,
       "Promotion of Nontraditional Exports" (Ref. No. 671-10),
       now completed.

149   Diaz, Ramon P.
       THE LONG-RUN TERMS OF PRIMARY-PRODUCING COUNTRIES.
       London and Menlo Park, Calif.: Tonbridge for International
       Institute for Economic Research, 1973.

       A thorough re-examination of the literature, key concepts,
       approaches,   and   empirical   studies   which   surround   the
       controversy over the long-run behavior of the developing
       countries' terms of trade.   The author argues that any
       deterioration in these terms of trade is merely a
       reflection of the fact that many developing countries
       are neither producing efficiently nor are they allowing
       for   domestic   resource   allocation.   He   believes   that
       adequate   development   policies   coupled   by   trade
       liberalization on the part of all countries will succeed
       in counter-balancing any terms-of-trade deterioration.

150   Diaz-Alejandro, Carlos F.
       FOREIGN TRADE REGIMES AND ECONOMIC DEVELOPMENT: COLOMBIA,
       A Special Conferecne Series on Foreign Trade Regimes
       and Economic Development, Vol. IX.
       New York and London: National Bureau of Economic Research.
       Distributed by Columbia University Press, 1976.

       Analysis of Colombian foreign trade and payment system
       in relation to development over the period 1950-1972.
       The study begins with a review of the major trends in
       Colombian foreign trade and payments with some discussion
       of events before and after the period 1950-72.   Next
       is a description of the commodity composition of major
       exports and a discussion of policy instruments used to
       encourage them.   Merchandise imports and different policy
       instruments used to repress and manipulate the demand
       for imports are examined in detail.   Also examined are
       the Colombian efforts during 1965-66 to eliminate
       administrative controls over imports and other
       transactions.   And lastly, there is a review of major
       economic trends between 1967 and 1973 and a discussion
       of the possible effects of further liberalization on
       efficiency, growth, income distribution, employment,
       stability, and national autonomy.

151   Dixit, Avinash and Norman, Victor
       THEORY OF INTERNATIONAL TRADE A DUAL GENERAL EQULIBRIUM
       APPROACH
       Cambridge University Press, New York, 1980.

       There have been no major breakthroughs in international
       economics for some time but conceptual refinements and
       improvements in technique continue.   Dixit and Norman
       have produce a useful and fairly up-to-date textbook
       for graduate students which reflects the current
       preoccupation with the general equilibrium approach and
       contains enough symbols to satisfy those who like their
       economics well buttered with convexities and other
       mathematical bric-a-brac.

152   Donaldson, T.H.
       LENDING IN INTERRNATIONAL COMMERCIAL BANKING
       John Wiley & Sons, New York, 1979.

       These two books are part of a series on international
       banking designed to explain how basic international banking
       functions are performed.   Both are written by experienced
       London commercial bankers.   The Hudson volume deals with
       the technical aspects of international money and foreign
       exchange dealing and includes arithmetic examples of
       selected transactions.   The Donaldson volume is concerned
       with the lending function--how banks analyze international
       credits and how such lending differs from domestic
       operations.

153   Dutta, Amita
        INTERNATIONAL MIGRATION, TRADE, AND REAL INCOME.   A CASE
        STUDY OF CEYLON, 1920-38
        Calcutta: World Press Private, Ltd.   for   Indian Council
        of Social Science Research, 1973.

        Based on the author's doctoral dissertation, the book
        is a study of the importance of the interaction between
        international   labor   migration   and   trade;   and   the
        relationship between that country's trade patterns and
        growth and its international labor flow.   The 1920-38
        period is used as a case study.   There is an analysis
        of the economics of migration, the conditions of the
        economy during the period, Ceylon's income and export
        supply functions, foreign demand for exports, the migration
        function, and various effects on the domestic economy
        and foreign trade of labor migration.   Material in three
        of the book's seven chapters has been previously published.

154   El Mallakh, Ragael
        KUWAIT: TRADE   AND   INVESTMENT,   Westview   Special   Studies
        in International Economics and Business.
        Boulder, Colo.:   Westview Press, 1979.

        Describes Kuwait's economic characteristics and social
        infrastructure, economic growth in the 1970's, its banking
        and monetary system, marketing operations, and bilateral
        and multilateral arrangements.   Assesses investment trends
        and   opportunities   and   considers   the   impact   of   Kuwait's
        capital-surplus funds on the region, Europe, and the
        United   States.   The   author   is   Professor   of   Economics
        at the University of Colorado, Boulder.   Lengthy appendices
        provide   additional   statistical   and   factual   information
        on ministries and agencies, laws and regulations, licensing
        procedures, and trade.

155   Feder, Gershon
        ON EXPORTS AND ECONOMIC GROWTH
        World Bank Staff Working Paper No. 508.   February 1982.

        An analytical framework is developed to analyze the sources
        of   growth   during   the   period   1964-73   for   a   group   of
        semi-industrialized   developing   countries.   Discusses
        the relationship between export performance and economic
        growth and concludes that growth can be generated not
        only by increases in the aggregate levels of labor and
        capital but also by the reallocation of existing resources
        from   the   less-efficient   nonexport   sector   to   the
        higher-productivity export sector.

156   Findlay, Ronald
        INTERNATIONAL   TRADE   AND   DEVELOPMENT   THEORY,   Columbia
        Studies in Economics No. 7.
        New York and London: Columbia University Press, 1973

A contribution to the theory of international trade and economic development. First examines economic growth within the context of both a closed and an open dual economy, thus constituting a set of variations on a theme by Lewis' that are intended to extend his original vision of the development process by specifying a number of alternative structural patterns for his generic modern sector, each of which is an idealization of some particular type of developing economy. The author then turns to the role of comparative advantage in non-dualistic growing economies. Finally, he discusses some influential ideas about the persistence of "structural" disequilibrium in developing economies as a result of inflexibility in the allocation of resources in response to changes in relative prices. Five of the book's eleven chapters have been previously published elsewhere.

157   Frank, Charles R.
FOREIGN TRADE AND DOMESTIC AID
Brookings, 1977.

158   Frank, Charles R., Jr.; Kim, Kwang Suk and Westphal, Larry E.
FOREIGN TRADE REGIMES AND ECONOMIC DEVELOPMENT: SOUTH KOREA
New York: National Bureau of Economic Research; distributed by Columbia University Press, New York and London, 1975.
Examines the relationship between trade and exchange rate policies and the rapid growth of South Korean output and trade. Stresses the exchange rate regimes, liberalization of trade, foreign aid, and their effects on resource allocation and growth. Argues that, although foreign assistance has been important to South Korean rapid economic growth, its economic policies have played a major role in ensuring the effective use of foreign resources while increasing the domestic contribution to the process of growth. Points out that South Korea has followed a policy of export promotion instead of import substitution and has adjusted the exchange rate frequently and dramatically. Contains data on GNP, exports, imports, prices, etc., for 1953-72.

159   Frank, Charles R., Jr., et al.
ASSISTING DEVELOPING COUNTRIES: PROBLEMS OF DEBTS, BURDEN-SHARING, JOBS AND TRADE
New York: Praeger, 1972.

160   Frank, Isiah
THE "GRADUATION" ISSUE IN TRADE POLICY TOWARD LDC'S
Working Paper No. 334; Washington, D.C.: World Bank, 1979.

A background study for World Development Report, 1979.

Starts from the premise that developed and developing
countries have a common interest in maintaining a
reasonably open international trading system based on
agreed rules and constraints on national behavior. Under
the present system, developing countries are accorded
certain forms of preferential treatment, but as a country's
development progresses, arrangements for "graduating"
selected countries into the developed group should be
devised, otherwise the system will be weakened. Explores
the issues at stake for developing countries and suggests
how "graduation" might be handled in the General Agreement
on Tariffs and Trade (GATT).

161   Franko, Lawrence G.
A SURVEY OF THE IMPACT OF MANUFACTURED EXPORTS FROM
INDUSTRIALIZING COUNTRIES IN ASIA AND LATIN AMERICA:
MUST EXPORT-ORIENTED GROWTH BE DISRUPTIVE?
Washington, D.C.: National Planning Association Committee
on Changing International Realities, 1979.

Examines the growth and composition of manufactured exports
from developing economies to OECD countries and their
sectoral and macroeconomic effects on the United States
and other OECD countries. Assesses the degree to which
barriers to trade adopted by some OECD countries have
led the more advanced LDC exporting nation to direct
their exports disproportionately to a few open, developed
markets, such as the United States, and considers actual
and potential policy responses of the advanced
industrialized countries to the LDC export thrust.
Discusses the preconditions for lowering barriers to
trade under GATT guidelines and for satisfying the LDC
desire for export-led development. Finds that despite
the growth of LDC exports, the aggregate job displacement
impact in advanced-country employment has been minimal.

162   Garlick, Peter C.
AFRICAN TRADERS AND ECONOMIC DEVELOPMENT IN GHANA
New York: Oxford University Press, 1971.

163   Gibson, Charles R.
FOREIGN TRADE IN THE ECONOMIC DEVELOPMENT OF SMALL NATIONS:
THE CASE OF ECUADOR
New York: Praeger, 1971.

164   Gillion, C. and O'Neil, M. J.
AN INPUT-OUTPUT MODEL OF STRUCTURAL DEVELOPMENT
Wellington: Reserve Bank of New Zealand, 1978.

Introduces a medium-term econometric input-output model
of the New Zealand economy and employs it to project
the size and configuration of the economy in 1986.
Describes basic features of the model, discusses the
forecasts of the exogenous and policy variables, and

examines several alternative exogenous forecasts and their impact on projections. Notes that the model is chiefly concerned with supply side and does not incorporate considerations of the timing and feasibility of the growth path.

165   Girgis, Maurice
INDUSTRIALIZATION AND TRADE PATTERNS IN EGYPT
Tubingen: J. C. B. Mohr (Paul Siebeck), 1977.

Examines the impact on industrialization and employment of the import substitution (IIS) policy of the Egyptian government since 1950. Discusses the major characteristics of the industrial sector and its growth, focusing on the period 1950-70; analyzes both qualitatively and quantitatively the relative contributions of import substitution, export expansion, and domestic demand to industrial output and employment; reviews foreign exchange and tariff policies and assesses their impact on balance of payments; estimates the nominal and effective rates of protection by sector and by industry; tests and confirms the hypothesis that domestic trade and industrialization policies led to sub-optimal allocation of resources; and describes the volume, composition, and direction of the foreign trade section, inquiring into the causes of Egypt's lagging exports. A major argument is that import substitution added to the economy's productive capacity, which in turn increased output and employment in the short run. In the long run, however, the negative aspects of IIS [e.g., excessive use of exchange controls, distorted resource allocation, stifled export expansion, contributions to capacity underutilization, and inflation] outweigh its positive contributions.

166   Grossack, Irvin Millman
THE INTERNATIONAL ECONOMY AND THE NATIONAL INTEREST
Bloomington and London: Indiana University Press, 1979.

Critically assesses established trade and investment theory, arguing that it is irrelevant to the postwar international economy, and proposes an alternative theory that integrates international trade and investment into a single model. Redefines international trade as "transnational transactions" that occur when citizens or organizations of different nationalities transact business, regardless of their locations; this view suggests that indirect foreign investment (or foreign loans) is simply another type of trade, while direct foreign investment enables new types of trade. The emphasis throughout is the economic welfare of the individual nation. The approach in non-mathematical.

167   Grotewold, Andreas
THE REGIONAL THEORY OF WORLD TRADE
Grove City, PA: Ptolemy Press, 1979.

168   Hansen, Harald
       THE DEVELOPING COUNTRIES AND INTERNATIONAL SHIPPING
       Working Paper No. 502; Washington, D.C.:   World Bank,
       1981.

       Considers whether developing countries can benefit from
       investments in international shipping and discusses the
       circumstances under which such investment might be
       favorable.

169   Hanson, John R., II
       TRADE IN TRANSITION: EXPORTS FROM THE THIRD WORLD,
       1840-1900
       New York; London; Toronto and Sydney: Harcourt Brace
       Jovanovich, Academic Press, 1980.

       Reexamines the historical relationship between the less
       developed nations and the international economy during
       the nineteenth century, based upon examination of the
       statistical data on the network of international trade.
       Adopts the point of view of the less developed countries
       in presenting comprehensive statistics on the composition
       of exports for 40 to 91 countries for several benchmark
       dates between 1840 and 1900 on both a
       commodity-by-commodity and region-by-region basis; also
       presents new data concerning the magnitude of exports
       in relation to national or regional output in the
       developing nations during the Victorian era.   Finds,
       contrary to widely-accepted accounts, that exports of
       the LDC's expanded along with the rest of world trade
       to about 1860 and most LDC's had entered the network
       of trade by that date; by 1880, the rate of growth of
       LDC exports declined however, as British demand for LDC
       products slackened.   Demand for LDC exports in other
       Western European and North American countries did not
       increase fast enough to offset losses in the British
       market, and supply conditions within the LDC's themselves
       diminished.   Suggests that trade was just one, and perhaps
       not even the major, potential contributor to economic
       development and argues that consequently the claims that
       the potential gains from trade were stolen from the LDC's
       by the advanced nations becomes less plausible.   Further
       concludes that the spectacular expansion of the world
       economy during the nineteenth centry was probably
       insufficient to improve the prospects for most of the
       millions of people living in Asia, Africa, and Latin
       America to enjoy the fruits of export-led economic
       development, even in the absence of exploitative behavior
       by advanced nations.

170   Hansen, Roger
       BEYOND THE NORTH-SOUTH STALEMATE
       New York; London; Montreal and Paris: McGraw-Hill, 1979.

Examines the major North-South issues of global politics in the 1970's and outlines the necessary changes for political reform in state behavior in the international system in order to move beyond stalement in the 1980's. Part one is an introduction; part two focuses on the problems and perspectives of the North-South split since the early 1970's; part three examines in detail the evolution of the South and the North as diplomatic entities and the domestic constraints of their capacity to act as cohesive units in the 1980's; part four considers three modal sets of northern policy responses to present southern demands, focusing on northern initiatives and cost-benefit calculations; part five sets forth substantive and procedural goals, strategies, and policies for improved North-South relations in the 1980's. Suggests that priority considerations be given to issues such as food production and distribution, energy production and distribution, and population stabilization, and that the Southern Perspective be included among the primary factors in Northern proposals.

171   Hartland-Thunberg, Penelope
TRADING BLOCS, U.S. EXPORTS, AND WORLD TRADE
Boulder, CO: Westview Press, 1980.

Focusing on U.S.-European relations, examines the impact of trading blocs on U.S. exports and world trade. Notes that thus far pointing out that the only truly effective bloc has been the EEC. Two-thirds of the book consists of statistical and information annexes, which include three papers on (1) trade blocs in Latin America by Wilbur F. Monroe, (2) economic organizations in Africa by Tamburai M'ndange-Pfupfu, and (3) ASEAN by George J. Vicksnins.

172   Havrylyshyn, Oli and Wolf, Martin
TRADE AMONG DEVELOPING COUNTRIES: THEORY, POLICY ISSUES, AND PRINCIPAL TRENDS
Working Paper No. 479; Washington, D.C.: World Bank, 1981.

A background study for World Development Report 1981. Presents the results of empirical work on trade among developing countries. Based on data derived from a sample of thirty-three developing countries that account for about 60 percent of developing countries' exports to one another.

173   Hay, Alan M. and Smith, Robert H. T.
INTERREGIONAL TRADE AND MONEY FLOWS IN NIGERIA, 1964
New York: Oxford University Press, 1970.

174   Helleiner, G. K.
INTERNATIONAL TRADE AND ECONOMIC DEVELOPMENT
Baltimore, MD: Penguin Books, 1972.

175   Helleiner, Gerald K.
         INTRA-FIRM TRADE AND THE DEVELOPING COUNTRIES
         New York: St. Martin's Press, 1981.

176   Hewett, E. A.
         FOREIGN TRADE PRICES IN THE COUNCIL FOR MUTUAL ECONOMIC
         ASSISTANCE
         Cambridge University Press, 1974.

177   Hicks, George L. and McNicoll, Geoffrey
         TRADE AND GROWTH IN THE PHILIPPINES: AN OPEN DUAL ECONOMY
         Cornell University Press, 1971.

178   Hillman, Jimmye S. and Schmitz, Andrew, eds.
         INTERNATIONAL TRADE AND AGRICULTURE: THEORY AND POLICY
         Boulder, CO: Westview Press, 1979.

         Thirteen papers first presented at the Symposium on
         International Trade and Agriculture held at Tucson,
         Arizona, in April 1977. Focuses on major topics of trade
         and commerce policy as they relate to agriculture.   In
         four parts: (1) general theory and policy; (2) gains
         from   trade: theory   reexamined;   (3)   analyses   of
         agricultural trade problems; and (4) research and research
         needs.   An introduction by the editor Jimmye S. Hillman
         reviews the issues discussed.

179   Hogendorn, Jan S.
         NIGERIAN GROUNDNUT EXPORTS: ORIGINS AND EARLY DEVELOPMENT
         Zaria: Ahmadu   Bello   University   Press;   Ibadan: Oxford
         University Press Nigeria, 1978.

         Traces the development of the Nigerian groundnut (peanut)
         industry from the time of military pacification of Northern
         Nigeria in 1907 to the outbreak of the First World War.
         Discusses the role of the railroad to the north in opening
         up   the   export   of   groundnuts   to   Europe   (particularly
         Germany) and ultimately foiling British plans to establish
         a cotton industry.   Emphasizes the entrepreneurial acumen
         of Hausa traders and farmers in adapting to changing profit
         opportunities in the face of the customary view of the
         Hausa people as lacking in economic initiative.   Argues
         that study supports formalist school view that rational
         economic responses to standard economic incentives often
         permeate the behaviour of many so-called primitve peoples.

180   Holbik, Karel and Swan, Philip L.
         TRADE AND INDUSTRIALIZATION IN THE CENTRAL AMERICAN COMMON
         MARKET: THE FIRST DECADE
         University of Texas, 1972.

181   Holzman, Franklyn D.
         FOREIGN TRADE UNDER CENTRAL PLANNING
         Harvard University Press, 1974.

182   Hong, Wontack and Krueger, Anne O., eds.
TRADE AND DEVELOPMENT IN KOREA: PROCEEDINGS OF A
CONFERENCE HELD BY THE KOREA DEVELOPMENT INSTITUTE
Seoul: Korea Development Institute, 1975.

Nine papers presented at the Third Korea Development
Institute International Symposium on Trade and Development
in Korea held in 1974. The economic growth of Korea
in the period 1962-73 is examined in two papers in the
context of her export strategy as well as a discussion
on the changing components of the balance of payments.
Five papers investigate the determinants of Korean
comparative advantage, examining: factor supply and
factor intensity of trade; employment generated by exports;
the roles of government and multinational corporations
in export growth, using the electroncis industry as a
case study; growth rates of productivity for export and
import-substituting industries; and the way in which
the exporting countries of the Far East have increased
their share of overseas markets. The final papers examine
the optimality of the policies adopted for export
promotion.

183   Hong, Wontack and Krause, Lawrence B., eds.
TRADE AND GROWTH OF THE ADVANCED DEVELOPING COUNTRIES
IN THE PACIFIC BASIN: PAPERS AND PROCEEDINGS OF THE
ELEVENTH PACIFIC TRADE AND DEVELOPMENT CONFERENCE
Seoul: Korea Development Institute; distributed by the
University Press of Hawaii, Honolulu, 1981.

Fifteen previously unpublished papers and comments analyze
the differences in the rapid growth of Korea, Taiwan,
Hong Kong, and Singapore through export expansion during
the 1960's and 1970's. Examines the problems confronting
each country, particularly control of domestic inflation,
maintenance of high levels of investment and
balance-of-payments equilibrium, and adjustment in
industrial structures. The editors find that the studies
demonstrate the merits of an export-oriented growth
strategy, although there are still serious problems.

184   Hong, Wontack
TRADE, DISTORTIONS, AND EMPLOYMENT GROWTH IN KOREA
Seoul: Korea Development Institute, 1979.

Analyzes the impact of export promotion on employment
growth in Korea, 1910-77; reviews economic policies and
development plans, particularly those relevant to trade,
for the period 1953-77; examines preferential direct
and indirect tax policies, tariff and non-tariff import
restrictions, and loan allocation policies; analyzes
factor market distortions; and investigates the employment
implications of trade and subsidy policies. A primary

conclusion is that the effect of export promotion on employment in Korea was a rapid growth in total employment in the 1960's, a relatively full employment since about 1970, and a change in the sectoral distribution of employment [from the farm to the manufacturing sector]. Part of the Korea modernization study, a joint undertaking by the Korea Development Institute and Harvard Institute for International Development.

185   Helleiner, Gerald K.
INTRA-FIRM TRADE AND THE DEVELOPING COUNTRIES
New York: St. Martin's Press, 1981.

Discusses the importance of intra-firm trade and the role of transnational corporations in the evolution of post-World War II international trade in the developing countries. Emphasizing that a high proportion of international trade takes place within firms, the author analyzes data on intra-firm trade in developing countries and on U.S intra-firm imports. Discusses intra-firm trade, structural adjustment, and trade policy in general and its influence on U.S. trade policy. Argues that the structure of trade barriers (both tariff and non-tariff) may be systematically related to the importance of intra-firm trade. Proposes further directions for research on the empirical relationship between intra-firm trade or the transnational corporation and the formation of different national trade policies.

186   Helpman, Elhanan and Razin, Assaf
A THEORY OF INTERNATIONAL TRADE UNDER UNCERTAINTY
New York and London: Harcourt Brace Jovanovich, Academic Press, 1978.

Develops an integrated general equilibrium framework for the analysis of international trade in goods and in financial capital flows under uncertainty. Provides relevant background material on the deterministic theory of international trade and the theory of economic decision-making under uncertainty. Includes a critical survey of the literature of international trade under uncertainty. Develops the basic model and applies it to problems in commerical policy, in gains from trade, and in the efficient intervention in financial capital markets. Suggest dynamic extensions to the model.

187   Holbrik, Karel and Swan, Philip L.
TRADE AND INDUSTRIALIZATION IN THE CENTRAL AMERICAN COMMON MARKET: THE FIRST DECADE
Austin, Texas: Bureau of Business Research, University of Texas, 1972.

A study of the historical development, institutional framework, and trade and industrial achievements of the

Central American Common Market during the 1960's. The author believes that the future growth of interregional trade is a function of the development of new lines of production as well as the solving of the political problems brought about by the 1969 war between Honduras and El Salvador.

188   Hudec, Robert E.
THE GATT LEGAL SYSTEM AND WORLD TRADE DIPLOMACY
New York and London: Praeger, 1975.

Examines the legal operations of GATT from 1948 to 1975 from the perspective of current failing following earlier successes, focusing on its historical procedure for third-party dispute settlement. The book contains five parts: Part I gives a preliminary veiw of the GATT legal design by examining the GATT/ITO negotiating history; Part II deals with the development of the GATT legal system during the years 1948-58; Part III includes seven case studies illustrating the major aspects of the GATT legal system in the period to 1958; Part IV examines the causes and effects of the legal breakdown during the period 1958-75; and Part V consists of nine appendices including a compilation of complaints through 1974 as well as additional cases.

189   Hughes, Helen, ed.
PROSPECTS FOR PARTNERSHIP: INDUSTRIALIZATION AND TRADE POLICIES IN THE 1970'S
Baltimore: Johns Hopkins University Press, 1973.

Papers presented and summary of discussions at a seminar of international economists at the World Bank, October 1972, focusing on the demand aspects and trade adjustment problems inherent in the increasing volume of manufactured product exports from developing countries.

190   Indian Society of Agricultural Economics
SEMINAR ON EMERGING PROBLEMS OF MARKETING OF AGRICULTURAL COMMODITIES
Bombay: Author, 1972.

Contains 18 selected papers, the inaugural address, and the proceedings of the seminar conducted by the Indian Society of Agricultural Economics in collaboration with the Directorate of Marketing and Inspections (of the government of India) in February, 1971.   Also includes a special lecture to the seminar participants by the late Professor D. R. Gadgil. The main themes of the discussions concerned: 1) the identification of emerging problems in agricultural marketing, 2) the role of the Directorate of Marketing and Inspection in agricultural marketing development, 3) empirical studies on marketing, margins, price spread, etc., 4) recent policy decisions in marketing, support prices, procurement, etc., 5) the role of forward trading and comparative efficiency of different trading agencies, and 6) research problems in marketing in the changed context.

191   Ingham, Barbara
TROPICAL EXPORTS AND ECONOMIC DEVELOPMENT: NEW PERSPECTIVES ON PRODUCER RESPONSE IN THREE LOW-INCOME COUNTRIES
New York: St. Martin's Press, 1981.

Examines the empirical evidence surrounding the role of cocoa exports in the economic development of Ghana at the turn-of-the-century and compares Ghanaian experience with that of Nigeria and New Guinea. Compares and contrasts an approach based on an understanding of the decision-making processes of peasant entrepreneurs and of their social system with Hla Myint's dynamic "vent of surplus" theory of growth and change and with neoclassical comparative static views. Finds that a perspective that acknowledges that activity is prompted primarily by a desire for prestige, power and security manifested in increased wealth [land] is more consonant with the historical evidence for tropical export growth than a perspective that argues that activity is prompted primarily by a desire for enhanced consumption of goods and services. Argues that uneven levels of economic activity arising from constraints on access to markets ought to be emphasized in theories of relative underdevelopment and suggests, on the basis of the evidence, that theories of growth and change should give an important place to human attitudes toward risk-taking and money-making, and to savings and the accumulation of capital.

192   International Trade Centre
THE CREATION AND MANAGEMENT OF JOINT EXPORT MARKETING GROUPS
Geneva: Author; distributed by Unipub, NY, 1973.

Analyzes the benefits of an export marketing consortium as well as providing guidelines for its creation and management. Based on case histories of ten export consortia, with stress placed on successful formulas and solutions in developing countries. Finds that a relatively short period is needed for newly formed consortia to penetrate new markets and that government support is needed during their formation and development in developing countries.

193   Islam, Nurul
FOREIGN TRADE AND ECONOMIC CONTROLS IN DEVELOPMENT: THE CASE OF UNITED PAKISTAN
New Haven: Yale University Press, 1981.

Analysis of trade and exchange controls in Pakistan, emphasizing the differing perceptions and priorities of policy makers during the periods 1947-58, when the controls were introduced, and 1958-70, when the movement was started to dismantle controls and place greater reliance on the price mechanism and private enterprise. Discusses the employment and income distribution aspects of economic controls and policy making, detailing the nature, magnitude, and problems of regional inequality and imbalance in development between East and West Pakistan, which was a major factor in the break-up of United Pakistan. Examines the impact of controls on savings, capital accumulation, and productivity growth. Concludes that Pakistan's experience demonstrates that unequal ownership of assets and unequal distribution of economic and political power results in distributing the benefits of economic progress to those who have higher initial income and assets. Moreover, argues that in a mixed economy, neither an unhindered price mechanism nor a total system of controls is successful in practice. Also comments that the inability to develop adequate institutions that would have permitted a greater role for indirect policy measures both put more emphasis on direct controls and inhibited their working.

194   ITC UNCTAD/GATT
THE SCOPE FOR INCREASED TRADE BETWEEN DEVELOPING COUNTRIES
IN VEGETABLE OILS AND OTHER OILSEED PRODUCTS
ITC UNCTAD/GATT, 1981.

Discusses overall trade trends in oils and fats in the 1970's; import structure; trade policies and practices; import prospects to 1985; potential for developing country trade. Provdes comments and data on supply, demand and market prospects in 15 countries; and gives notes on production, export structure and trends of seven major export developing countries. Also gives notes on trade in oil meals.

195   ITC UNCTAD/GATT
EXPORT FINANCING FOR DEVELOPING COUNTRIES
ITC UNCTAD/GATT, 1977.

Handbook on export financing, with particular references to developing country needs. Deals with the categories of short-, medium- and long-term export financing schemes; and outlines types of government assistance in export financing.

196   ITC UNCTAD/GATT
THE MARKET FOR TOOLS FROM DEVELOPING COUNTRIES
ITC UNCTAD/GATT, 1980.

A market study on hand tools and interchangeable tools,

blades and tips for machine tools and handheld
power-operated tools in the U.S.A., Federal Republic
of Germany, Japan, Sweden, India, Singapore, Venezuela,
Kenya and Tanzania. Gives comments and data on world
trade, general market requirements, distribution network,
trade practices, marketing; and for each country covers
domestic production, foreign trade, quality and technical
requirements, packaging, delivery and payment terms,
distribution network, prices and import duties; also
gives marketing advice to developing country suppliers
and lists selected importers and dealers.

197   Jainarain, Iserdeo
       TRADE AND UNDERDEVELOPMENT: A STUDY OF THE SMALL CARIBBEAN
       COUNTRIES AND LARGE MULTINATIONAL CORPORATIONS
       Georgetown: University of Guyana, Institute of Development
       Studies, 1976.

198   Johnston, R. J.
       THE WORLD TRADE SYSTEM: SOME ENQUIRIES INTO ITS SPATIAL
       STRUCTURE
       New York: St. Martin's Press, 1976.

       Investigates the major patterns of international trade
       by applying concepts and methods already shown to be
       successful in the study of systems at other spatial scales.
       Emphasizing general rather than particular trade flows,
       a very general model is used to sketch the major features
       of the world trade system as a space-economy. Includes
       indices for 1960 of the degree of commodity specialization
       of each country, analyses designed to suggest types of
       country by the nature of the goods they trade and the
       degree of trade-partner specialization and choice, a
       discussion of individual commodity flow patterns, and
       a description of world trade data. The author views
       the world trade system as the product of international
       capitalism, where each country's role is primarily
       determined, with some exceptions, by its initial
       comparative advantage.

199   Kassalow, Everett M. and Damachi, Ukandi G., eds.
       THE ROLE OF TRADE UNIONS IN DEVELOPING SOCIETIES
       Geneva: International Institute for Labour Studies,
       1978.

       Seven essays, one of which has been previously published
       elsewhere, on labor and politics in seven developing
       economies. Authors and articles include: U. G. Damachi
       on trade unions and development in Ghana; Pang Eng Fong
       and Leonard Cheng on inudstrial relations in Singapore;
       Chris Jecchinis on trade unions and development in Greece;
       Henry Landsberger and Tim McDaniel on hypermobilization
       in Chile, 1970-73; Elias T. Ramos on trade unions in
       the Philippines ; J. Douglas Muir and John L. Brown on

the role of government in collective bargaining in Kenya; and George Ogle on labor-government-mangement relations in South Korea.

200   Keesing, Donald B.
WORLD TRADE AND OUTPUT OF MANUFACTURES: STRUCTURAL TRENDS AND DEVELOPING COUNTRIES' EXPORTS
Working Paper No. 316; Washington, D.C.: World Bank, 1979.

Analyzes major trends in world trade and the changing structural features of manufactured exports of developing countries, which increased at rates around 15 percent per year from 1960-76, and how they relate to world manufacturing ouput and markets, which have expanded much more slowly. Numerous relationships are explored. The paper is a revised version of a background study for the World Development Report, 1978 using narrower defintions of developing countries.

201   Keesing, Donald B.
TRADE POLICY FOR DEVELOPING COUNTRIES
Working Paper No. 353; Washington, D.C.: World Bank, 1979.

A background study for World Development Report, 1979. States that trade policy must deal with strategic choices, economy-wide management (including exchange-rate policy), and incentives. Part I discusses trade policy for purposes of industrial development; Part II examines relationships of trade policy with social and political systems and goals, for example, its effects on poverty, and how it interacts with repression or redistribution; Part III explores ways to achieve a successful transition from an unsatisfactory to a desirable trade policy regime.

202   Keesing, Donald B. and Wolf, Martin
TEXTILE QUOTAS IN DEVELOPING COUNTRIES
London: Trade Policy Research Centre, 1980.

Focuses on restrictions on international trade in textiles and clothing proceedings from the 1973-74 multi-fibre arrangement (MFA), which provides protection to textile producers and clothing manufacturers in industrial countries against the competition of imports from developing countries. Examines the economic effects in the developing countries; in so far as developed countries are discussed, covers only United States, and the European Community; reviews the case for protection; and discusses renegotiation prosepcts of the MFA at the time of its renewal in 1981. Concludes that abandonment of the system of managed trade is most unlikely.

203   Kenen, Peter B.
       INTERNATIONAL TRADE AND FINANCE
       Cambridge University Press, 1976.

204   King, Timothy
       MEXICO: INDUSTRIALIZATION AND TRADE POLICIES SINCE 1940
       New York: Oxford University Press, 1970.

       Outlines the main features of Mexican development in
       the first two chapters and analyzes the framework,
       instruments, and impact of industrialization policy in
       the last four. Shows that growth in manufacturing ouput
       is the most important contributor to growth in total
       output; it is possible, however, that in comparing Mexico
       with less successful countries following the same pattern
       of industrial development, the most distinctive features
       of her economic success have been her agricultural and
       financial policies and performance.

205   Knudsen, Odin and Parnes, Andrew
       TRADE INSTABILITY AND ECONOMIC DEVELOPMENT: AN EMPIRICAL
       STUDY
       Lexington, Mass.; Toronto and London: Heath, Lexington
       Books, 1975.

       Examines the causes and effects of export instability.
       Seeks to explain the intercountry differences in
       instability by analyzing the type of goods traded, the
       degree of commodity concentration, and the direction
       of trade flow. Uses time-series data for 53 countries
       for the period 1958 to 1968. The first part of the
       analysis is concerned with eliminating the trend in
       time-series data and deriving an index of instability,
       which is used as the dependent variable. The authors
       then develop a theory of the effects of trade instability
       in terms of uncertainty.

206   Krauss, Melvyn B.
       THE NEW PROTECTIONISM: THE WELFARE STATE AND INTERNATIONAL
       TRADE
       New York: New York University Press for the International
       Center for Economic Policy Studies, 1978.

       Focuses upon the relationship between welfare state
       policies and international trade and argues that the
       welfare state both depends upon economic growth to support
       it and reduces economic growth through its pursuit of
       economic security and the redistribution of income from
       capital to labor. Reviews the traditional issues of
       free trade versus protectionism.

207   Kreinin, Mordechai E.
       TRADE RELATIONS OF THE EEC: AN EMPIRICAL INVESTIGATION
       New York and London: Praeger, 1974.

A bringing together of several empirical studies (most previously published, but presently revised) which are reasonably independent. Each investigates a particular aspect of the European Economic Community's (EEC) trade with the outside world. Seven chapters describe recent developments in EEC commercial relations, present a theoretical review of the effects of regional integration on international trade flows, estimate annual trade creation and diversion for 1967-68 and 1969-70, investigate tariff preferences granted by French Africa to the EEC and by the EEC to the Associated African States and to southern European countries, and assess the effect of EEC enlargement on both international trade flows and the General System of Preferences accorded by the EEC to the developing nations. Numerous tables giving data on trade for 1959-70.

208   Krueger, Anne O.
FOREIGN TRADE REGIMES AND ECONOMIC DEVELOPMENT: LIBERALIZATION ATTEMPTS AND CONSEQUENCES
Cambridge, Mass.: Lippincott, Ballinger for National Bureau of Economic Research, 1978.

Synthesis based on the nine country studies of this series, the author examines for developing countries how initial conditions of the exchange control regime affect the economic impact of currency devaluation and discusses the differing effects of devaluation under exchange control as opposed to convertibility. Comments on questions related to the effects of successful devaluation and export performance on economic growth and analyzes the effects of differing exchange policies on the trade and payments regime as well as growth strategy and performance. Finds that: (1) the quantitative restriction regimes were often far more protective than the governments imposing them knew or intended and (2) a stable government bias towards exports is most favorable for economic growth.

209   Krueger, Anne O.
GROWTH, DISTORTIONS, AND PATTERNS OF TRADE AMONG MANY COUNTRIES
Princeton, NJ: Princeton University, Department of Economics, International Finance Section, 1977.

Explores the way in which the factor-proportions explanation of trade may be stated as a testable hypothesis or series of hypotheses. Introduces a simple model of comparative advantage under the usual competitive assumptions, amends it to incorporate the existence of a primary commodity or agricultural sector, and examines the implications for empirical work. Pays particular attention to methods of identifying the impact of distortions in the goods and factor markets on the pattern of trade and factor proportions in export and import-competing industries.

210   Krueger, Anne O., et al.
       TRADE AND EMPLOYMENT IN DEVELOPING COUNTRIES
       Chicago and London: University of Chicago Press, 1981.

       First of three volumes, presenting eleven papers tackling
       the basic question of what links exist, if any, between
       the policies of a developing country toward international
       trade and the ability to create enough employment.
       Includes ten country studies (Brazil, Chile, Colombia,
       Indonesia, Ivory Coast, Pakistan, South Korea, Thailand,
       Tunisia, and Uruguay).   Using a common framework papers
       trace the major characteristics of trade and payments
       regimes which influence the commodity composition of
       trade and the factor proportions in traded goods
       industries.   Concludes that with reasonably open markets
       abroad, export-oriented policies have been and/or could
       have been more favorable than import substitution policies
       in expanding employment in developing countries.

211   Kuyvenhoven, Arie
       PLANNING WITH THE SEMI-INPUT-OUTPUT METHOD: WITH EMPIRICAL
       APPLICATIONS IN NIGERIA
       Leiden; Boston and London: Martinus Nijhoff Social
       Sciences Division, 1978.

       Comprehensive exposition of the nature, techniques, and
       use of the semi-input-output method, an approach for
       solving the related problems of efficiency in production
       and international trade through the right choice of sectors
       and projects to be developed, emphasizing the role of
       a country's comparative advantage for investment decisions.
       Compapres method with the Little-Mirrlees approaches
       and discusses its applicability both at the sector and
       project level.   Notes that in contrast to traditional
       input-output analyses which is primarily suuited to ex
       post analyses, this method is suitable for ex ante resource
       allocation decisions about capacity creation; further
       it emphasizes the complementarity between expansions
       in the national and international sectors.   Presents
       results of an economy-wide application using Nigerian
       data for 54 existing sectors and 48 new manufacturing
       activities, carried out at both market and accounting
       prices, and taking effects of trade limitations into
       account.

212   Lal, Deepak
       INDIAN EXPORT INCENTIVES
       Washington, D.C.:   World Bank Reprint Series, No. 105

       Analyzes Indian export incentives within the framework
       of piecemeal second-best welfare economics, taking the
       extant import control system as a binding constraint.
       Provides a condensed account of recent Indian export
       incentives together with some quantitative estimates

(based on firm level data for some engineering goods exporters) of their likely effects on feasible second-best welfare levels.

213   Lee, Eddy, ed.
EXPORT-LED INDUSTRIALISATION AND DEVELOPMENT
Geneva: International Labour Organization, 1981.

Seven previously unpublished studies on the economic change which has occurred in Asia during the last two decades. Papers describe the economic growth achieved in South Korea, Taiwan, Singapore, and Hong Kong through phenomenal rates of growth of labor-intensive manufactured exports, and examine Indonesia and the Philippines, where export-led industrial growth has not occurred. One paper discusses the role of the general trading companies in Japan's export-led industrialization. Emphasizes the factors responsible for successful export-led industrialization and the prospects for other developing countries.

214   Leith, J. Clark
FOREIGN TRADE REGIMES AND ECONOMIC DEVELOPMENT: GHANA
New York and London: National Bureau of Economic Research; distributed by Colombia University Press, NY, 1974.

Examination of Ghana's system of exchange control and the attempted liberalization during its first 15 years of independence (1957-72). Reviews the evolution of the restrictive system and the workings of the instruments brought to bear on the foreign sector and discusses the allocative and growth effects, with attention paid to the capital market and input intensities. Explores the steps to liberalization, including details of the initial devaluation. Finds that the experience with exchange and import controls have not been happy.

215   Leppo, Matti
REGULARITIES OF SECTORAL CHANGES IN ECONOMIC ACTIVITY: A STUDY ON THE OUTPUT AND INPUT SHARES OF PRIMARY PRODUCTION, TRANSFORMING INDUSTRIES AND SERVICES IN GROWING ECONOMIES
Helsinki: Suomalainen Tiedeakatemia, 1980.

Examines empirical regularities of sectoral shares of economic activity in growing economies. Reviews the history of the classification of economic activity by sectors and discusses a number of propositions concerning expected changes among sectors in a developing economy and examines statistics used by Simon Kuznets and available from various international and other agencies. Concludes with a discussion of the factors underlying these changes, including consumer demand, public sector activity, and international developments.

216   Levich, Richard M. and Wihlborg, Clas G.
       EXCHANGE RISK AND EXPOSURE: CURRENT DEVELOPMENTS IN
       INTERNATIONAL FINANCIAL MANAGEMENT
       Lexington, MA: D. C. Heath and Co., 1980.

       Papers and commentary presented at a conference at New
       York University in February 1979 organized around the
       question: does the currency of denomination matter in
       international business operation? The papers bring
       together key themes of extensive recent academic writing
       on various aspects of exchange risk under floating
       currencies and the effects of uncertainty on international
       firms. Of advanced academic interest.

217   Lewis, Stephen R., Jr.
       PAKISTAN: INDUSTRIALIZATION AND TRADE POLICIES
       London, New York and Karachi: Oxford University Press,
       1970.

       Analysis of the structure and performance of the
       manufacturing sector, with focus on economic policy making.
       Concludes that the time is somewhat overdue for Pakistan
       to begin emphasizing a structure of relative prices within
       manufacturing, and between manufacturing and agriculture,
       that will induce manufacturers and potential investors
       in manufacturing industry to adopt technologies and to
       improve productivity to a degree more consistent with
       Pakistan's real resource availabilities.

218   Library of Congress, Congressional Research Service
       WHAT SHOULD BE THE FUTURE DIRECTION OF THE FOREIGN POLICY
       OF THE UNITED STATES? PURSUANT TO PUBLIC LAW 88-246
       U.S. Senate, 96th Congress, 1st Session.
       Washington, D.C.: U.S.G.P.O., 1979.

       Reference material for the 1979-80 national high school
       debate. Contains a large number of reprints of general
       and specific articles that examine the foreign policy
       considerations for debate on United States' position
       on trade policy, sale of weapons internationally, and
       foreign assistance to totalitarian states. Also includes
       a bibliography and a guide to securing material and
       publication for the debate.

219   Lin, Ching-Yuan
       INDUSTRIALIZATION IN TAIWAN, 1946-72: TRADE AND IMPORT
       SUBSTITUTION POLICIES FOR DEVELOPING COUNTRIES
       New York: Praeger, 1973.

220   Little, Ian; Scitovsky, Tibor and Scott, Maurice
       INDUSTRY AND TRADE IN SOME DEVELOPING COUNTRIES: A
       COMPARATIVE STUDY
       New York: Oxford University Press, 1970.

A summary volume, analyzing the results of separately published studies of the problems of industrial development in Argentina, Brazil, Mexico, India, Pakistan, the Philippines, and Taiwan. The main theses in this book are that industry has over-encouraged in relation to agriculture, and that, although there are arguments for giving special encouragement to industry, this encouragement could be provided in forms which would not, as present policies do, discourage exports, including agricultural exports.

221   London Chamber of Commerce and Industry
        TRADE CONTACTS IN WEST AFRICAN COUNTRIES
        Nichols Publishing, 1977.

222   Lozoya, Jorge and Green, Rosario, eds.
        INTERNATIONAL   TRADE   INDUSTRIALIZATION   AND   THE   NEW
        INTERNATIONAL ECONOMIC ORDER
        New York: Pergamon Press for UNITAR and the Center for Economic and Social Studies of the Third World, 1981.

        Eight previously unpublished papers cover issues related to the establishment of the New International Economic Order (NIEO) in the fields of international trade and industrialization, emphasizing the expansion and diversification of Third World exports. Topics include: the critical role of transnational corporations, competitiveness of natural resources with synthetic substitutes, the real possibilities of establishing a world food program, the strategies of industrialized countries relevant to supplies access, appropriate technology, and the search for alternative energy sources.

223   Lundberg, Lars
        PATTERN OF BARRIERS TO TRADE IN SWEDEN: A STUDY IN THE THEORY OF PROTECTION
        Working Paper No. 494; Washington, D.C.:   World Bank, 1981.

        This report is part of an inquiry being undertaken by the World Bank in conjunction with scholars from twelve industrial countries into the penetration of the markets of industrial countries by exports of manufactures from developing countries.

224   Lydall, H. F.
        TRADE AND EMPLOYMENT: A STUDY OF THE EFFECTS OF TRADE EXPANSION ON EMPLOYMENT IN DEVELOPING AND DEVELOPED COUNTRIES
        Geneva: ILO, 1975.

225   MacBean, Alasdair I. and Balasubramanyam, V. N.
        MEETING THE THIRD WORLD CHALLENGE
        New York: St. Martin's Press for Trade Policy Research Centre, London, 1976.

Takes the position that Third World countries could do
many things internally on an individual or collective
basis to improve their living standards. Internally,
resources should be used to develop physical and human
capital as well as for investment in activities increasing
output of goods and servcies desired by the mass of their
citizens or which can be most profitably exchanged through
international trade for items needed to raise consumption
standards now or in the future. Externally, trade and
foreign investment relationships should be judged in
terms of achieving the maximum contribution to raising
present and future consumption standards of their own
citizens--not in terms of political ideology. The
developed countries have particular areas of interest
in common with the Third World--population control,
nonrenewable resources, trade along lines of comparative
advantage, etc.

226   Magee, Stephen P.
       INTERNATIONAL TRADE
       A-W, 1980.

227   Magee, Stephen P.
       INTERNATIONAL TRADE AND DISTORTIONS IN FACTOR MARKETS
       Dekker, 1976.

228   Marsden, Keith
       TRADE AND EMPLOYMENT POLICIES FOR INDUSTRIAL DEVELOPMENT
       Washington, D.C.: World Bank, 1982.

       In the last decade, the developing countries have proved
       that they can compete internationally in exporting
       manufactured goods, as well as primary products and
       services. This paper examines three sets of issues:
       (a) whether good export performance is attributable to
       special characteristics of the most successful countries
       or whether their success can be readily replicated in
       other countries; (b) whether the penetration of the markets
       of industrial countries has reached, or will soon reach,
       a limit; and (c) whether trade in manufactures among
       the developing countries can expand further. Concludes
       with a discussion of the contribution of small enterprises
       to the creation of employment and the alleviation of
       poverty.

229   Meier, Gerald M.
       EMPLOYMENT, TRADE, AND DEVELOPMENT: A   PROBLEM   IN
       INTERNATIONAL POLICY ANALYSIS
       Leiden: Sijthoff for Institut Universitaire de Hautes
       Etudes Internationales, Geneva, 1977.

       Study of the problem of absorption of surplus labor in
       LDC's, and lecture two comments on the potential of
       alleviating this unemployment problem via implementation

of policies of North-South economic cooperation. The
final selection analyzes the policy issues of employment
and development. Concludes that although the market
system can help overcome dualism within an LDC, to overcome
international dualism between rich and poor nations we
must emphasize more extensive international planning
in the crucial areas of employment, resource transfer,
and market failure.

230   Meier, Gerald M.
       INTERNATIONAL TRADE AND DEVELOPMENT
       Westport, Conn.: Greenwood Press, 1975.

231   Meyer, F. V.
       INTERNATIONAL TRADE POLICY
       New York: St. Martin's Press, 1978.

232   Milenky, Edward S.
       THE POLITICS OF REGIONAL ORGANIZATION IN LATIN AMERICA.
       THE LATIN AMERICAN FREE TRADE ASSOCIATION.
       New York and London: Praeger, 1973.

       A political scientist examines the politics of regional
       integration as seen in the case of the Latin American
       Free Trade Association (LAFTA). Discusses the development
       of the integration idea in the region, the founding
       treaties and institutions of LAFTA, the member states,
       the politics of regional trade and economic integration,
       the complementarity, coordination, planning, and
       development agreements, the problems of institutional
       reform, the politics of payments coordination, and other
       issues in regional integration and cooperation.

233   Monroe, Wilbur F.
       INTERNATIONAL TRADE POLICY IN TRANSITION
       Lexington, Mass.; Toronto and London: Heath, Lexington
       Books, 1975.

       Deals with the major problems and issues arising in the
       Tokyo Round of multilateral trade negotiations that began
       in September 1973, under the auspices of the General
       Agreement on Tariffs and Trade (GATT). It treats the
       current issues against the backdrop of the reciprocal
       trade approach that characterized and dominated trade
       policy over the last three decades, and it evaluates
       the issues both from the standpoint of less developed
       and developed countries. Furthermore, some trade policy
       problems that are likely to emerge in the future are
       discussed. Reflects the switch in attention of the
       Committee of twenty from the original target of
       comprehensive reform to the alleviation of current
       financial problems. This book is a companion to the
       author's earlier work, International Monetary
       Reconstruction.

234   Morawetz, David
WHY THE EMPEROR'S NEW CLOTHES ARE NOT MADE IN COLOMBIA:
A CASE STUDY IN LATIN AMERICAN AND EAST ASIAN MANUFACTURED
EXPORTS
New York: Oxford University Press, 1981.

Focuses on the exports of a particular commodity (clothing)
from a particular Latin American country (Colombia) in
an attempt to understnad why Latin America has been so
much less successful at exporting manufactured goods
to date than East Asia. It is the first study to go
into great detail in examining the price, and especially
the nonprice, determinants of export success.

235   Morrall, John F., III
HUMAN CAPITAL, TECHNOLOGY AND THE ROLE OF THE UNITED
STATES IN INTERNATIONAL TRADE
Gainesville, University of Florida Press, 1972.

236   Morton, Kathryn and Tulloch, Peter
TRADE AND DEVELOPING COUNTRIES
New York and Toronto: Wiley, Halsted Press, 1977.

Examines the role of international trade in the development
process and discusses the arguments for and against trade
focusing on the debate between "outward-looking" and
"inward-looking" strategies; discusses the roles of the
international organizations--GATT, UNCTAD, and others,
and those of national governments and foreign investors--in
international trade. Discusses some of the moves made
towards greater economic and trade cooperation among
developing countries. Concludes that external trade
is strategic, but not the key to economic development
and that the emphasis placed in development strategies
on trade will depend on the resource-base and the economic
characteristics of the country concerned. Contains data
for 1960-75. The authors were research officers at the
Overseas Development Institute at the time of this study.

237   Murray, Tracy
TRADE PREFERENCES FOR DEVELOPING COUNTRIES
New York and Toronto: Wiley, Halsted Press, 1977.

Discusses the origin of the concept of trade preferences
for development, its evolution, the political issues
surrounding its implementation, and the economic impact
of tariff preferences for developing countries (part
one); analyzes the operation and effects of the actual
generalized system of preferences (GSP) introduced in
1971 (part two); part three examines several issues related
to the GSP, including: the evolving trade relations
of the EEC, the impact of the GATT trade negotiations
on the GSP, and the place of the GSP in the new
international economic order. Notes that the actual

system differed quite significantly from that which was
envisaged by the developing countries, and that the trade
benefits fall far short of what was initially expected.
Concludes that in the final analysis, however, major
benefits to accelerate economic growth will be derived
from measures not dependent on international cooperation
taken within the developing countries themselves.

238   Nankani, Gobindram T.
        DEVELOPMENT PROBLEMS OF MINERAL EXPORTING COUNTRIES
        Working Paper No. 354; Washington, D.C.: World Bank,
        1979.

        A background study for World Development Report, 1979.
        Provides a perspective on the mineral economies whose
        resource, on the one hand, is readily convertible into
        a large financial flow but, on the other hand, is
        exhaustible. Discusses the problems to which this peculiar
        set of circumstances gives rise and assesses a wide array
        of policy changes to maximize these countries' benefits
        and create a diversified and growing economy.

239   Nartsupha, Chatthip
        FOREIGN TRADE, FOREIGN FINANCE AND THE ECONOMIC DEVELOPMENT
        OF THAILAND, 1956-1965
        Bangkok: Prae Pittaya Limited Partnership, 1970.

        Analyzes the impact of foreign trade and finance on growth
        and structural changes in the Thai economy; examines
        their effect on 1) internal development, and 2) patterns
        of resource allocation on foreign trade.

240   OAS
        LATIN AMERICAN TRADE AND THE INTER-AMERICAN COOPERATION
        FOR DEVELOPMENT
        OAS, 1978.

        This study is a historical presentation and analysis
        of the problems of Latin American trade with the
        industrialized nations. Chapters cover: problems in
        the evolution of Latin American trade; principal causes
        of poor trade performance; principal proposals in
        international forums on trade problems, including the
        Generalized System of Preferences (GSP), multilateral
        trade negotiations, the Integrated Program for Commodities
        (IPC), the Lome Convention, the Paris Conference, and
        producer associations; and hemisphere economic cooperation.

241   OAS
        METHODS FOR EVALUATING LATIN AMERICAN EXPORT OPERATIONS:
        A MANUAL FOR NEW EXPORTERS
        OAS, 1978.

This manual guides the business executive to the proper external source of export-related information, and describes in detail the development of a methodology by which internally-generated information is analyzed, highlighting the effect of the export operation on the structure, productivity and profitability of the firm. Chapters cover: foreign market entry strategies; methods of receiving payment; exports and the government; defining the market; financial planning; working capital analysis; production planning and control; and internal financial control.

242   OECD
ADJUSTMENT FOR TRADE: STUDIES ON INDUSTRIAL ADJUSTMENT
PROBLEMS AND POLICIES
Paris: OECD, 1975.

Includes 11 papers which review the industrial adjustment situation in particular countries or industries in light of the changing international economic order. The papers illustrate a variety of policies in industrial countries and a number of different methodological approaches. Topics covered: survey of adjustment assistance policies; costs and benefits of structural adjustments in the textile industries; adjustment policy in Germany (manufacturing sector), Belgium, the Netherlands (clothing industry), Sweden, USA, Canada, Japan and U.K. (jute industry); and developing country export potential and developed country adjustment policy (Ethiopian and Ghanian footwear production).

243   OECD
THE IMPACT OF THE NEWLY INDUSTRIALISING COUNTRIES ON
PRODUCTION AND TRADE IN MANUFACTURES
Paris: OECD, 1979.

Deals with trading patterns and policies in the advanced industrial countries (AIC's) and the newly industrialising countries (NIC's). Reports on, inter alia: OECD imports, export, and trade surplus in manufactures; the internationalization of production processes; the role of trade policies; employment; growth process and policies; and the role of NIC's in world trade. Annexes on measuring the employment effects of changes in trade flows and the methodology used in estimating the employment content of OECD trade with the NIC's.

244   OECD
COUNTERTRADE PRACTICES IN EAST-WEST ECONOMIC RELATIONS
Paris: OECD, 1979.

The East-West trade referred to as countertrade has taken the form of various types of transactions, described by interested parties or sources of information in inter-changeable terms, which entails a certain confusion. This report contains an information file on and an analysis of such countertrade practices.

245   OECD
THE DEVELOPMENT IMPACT OF BARTER IN DEVELOPING COUNTRIES
Paris: OECD, 1979.

The present study is on the general summary report of the research on the Development Impact of Barter in Developing Countries conducted by the Development Centre. Apart from a comparative analysis of the different case studies carried out in the frame of the project, it provides a theoretical discussion and general overview of the current role of barter-like trade in developing countries' foreign trade.

246   Ojala, Eric M.
IMPACT OF THE NEW PRODUCTION POSSIBILITIES ON THE STRUCTURE OF INTERNATIONAL TRADE IN AGRICULTURAL PRODUCTS
Stanford,   CA: Stanford   University,   Food   Research Institute, 1972.

247   Pagliazzi, Paolo, et al.
COMPANIES EXPORTS AND THE SOUTH
Naples: Institute for the Economic Development of Southern Italy, 1978.

Four papers, discussions, replies, and introductory and concluding remarks on problems and policies related to increasing exports of companies in the Italian South. The focus is on insurance of exports, foreign exchange, and financial aspects of law number 227 for financing development in the Third World. Meeting participants include bankers, economic advisers, entrepreneurs, and public officials.

248   Payer, Cheryl, ed.
COMMODITY TRADE OF THE THIRD WORLD
New   York   and   Toronto: Wiley,   Halsted   Press;   London: Macmillan, 1975.

Editor's introduction and afterword and seven chapters dealing with trade in selected commodities: oil, by Peter R. Odell; copper, by David N. Waite; zinc, by Ian M. Robinson; cereals, by Simon A. Harris; sugar, by G. B. Hagelberg; bananas, by Frederick F. Clairmonte; and coffee, by the editor. The book is intended for traders, policy makers, researchers, and the general reader with no advanced economics training, seeking an introduction and a basic understanding of the processes of commodity trade.

249   Pearson, Scott R. and Cownie, John with others
       COMMODITY EXPORTS AND AFRICAN ECONOMIC DEVELOPMENT
       Lexington, Mass., Toronto and London: D. C. Heath, 1974.

       Contains reports resulting from a study of the contribution
       and effects of commodity exports in the economic
       development of African countries.   The authors listed
       develop an analytical framework designed to facilitate
       comparative analysis in the first chapter which is used
       by other authors in their reports on timber, cocoa, and
       coffee in the Ivory Coast; timber and cocoa in Ghana;
       coffee in Ethiopia; cotton in Uganda; petroleum in Nigeria;
       copper in Zaire; copper in Zambia; and the mining of
       minerals in Sierra Leone.   The final chapter contains
       comparative results and analysis by Pearson and Cownie.
       The reports on exports were written by an international
       group of teachers, graduate students, and civil servants
       who conducted original research in Africa.   Some
       statistical data on exports is provided.

250   Rahman, A. H. M. Mahfuzur
       EXPORTS OF MANUFACTURES FROM DEVELOPING COUNTRIES
       The Netherlands: Academic Book Services Holland for
       Rotterdam University Press, 1973.

       One in a series of development studies examining the
       possibility of exporting and, hence, producing more
       manufactures.   In six chapters, investigation includes
       discussion of factor proportions and price competitiveness
       as a basis for exports, competitiveness among developing
       countries, the relationships of the Leontief Paradox
       and the factor proportions theory to the examination,
       export performances and composition of, trend in, and
       opportunities for exports of manufactures.   Data presented
       are primarily from the decade 1960-70.

251   Raichur, Satish and Liske, Craig, eds.
       THE POLITICS OF AID, TRADE AND INVESTMENT
       New York: Sage, 1976.

       Editor's introduction plus eight chapters written by
       ten economic and foreign policy professionals.   The text
       examines the various factors affecting bilateral economic
       and military aid, multilateral aid, private capital flows,
       trade policy, and military intervention.   The topics
       covered are: Soviet foreign economic behavior;   U.S.
       military intervention abroad;   U.S. foreign policy in
       Latin America; multilateral aid and political allegiance
       in Latin America;   U.S. direct manufacturing investment
       in Third World countries; economic and political aspects
       of U.S. multilateral aid;   U.S. commercial policy and
       export controls; and export promotion under authoritarian
       rule in Brazil.   Empirical treatment of data varies from
       descriptive documentation to the statistical estimation
       of a social field-theory model.

252   Ramaswami, V. K. (edited by Bhagwati, J. N., T. S. Harry
       Johnson and T. N. Srinivasan)
       TRADE AND DEVELOPMENT: ESSAYS IN ECONOMICS
       London: George Allen and Unwin and Cambridge, Mass.:
       MIT Press, 1971.

253   Renshaw, Geoffrey, ed.
       EMPLOYMENT, TRADE, AND NORTH-SOUTH CO-OPERATION
       Geneva: International Labor Office, 1981.

254   Reynolds, Clark W.
       CHANGING TRADE PATTERNS AND TRADE POLICY IN MEXICO: SOME
       LESSONS FOR DEVELOPING COUNTRIES
       Stanford,   CA: Food   Research   Institute,   Stanford
       University, 1970.

       A concise description and evaluation, with a historical
       flashback (1910 to 1960), of Mexico's changing trade
       structure and the commercial policies, especially those
       pursued during the past 30 years of rapid growth. After
       centuries of exporting natural resources and cultivating
       subsistence crops, Mexico has developed a successful
       import substitution program and improved her foreign
       trade position. This study provides lessons which other
       developing countries can follow in speeding the maturation
       of their domestic industry and spurring the availability
       of profitable developed natural resources.

255   Richardson, J. David
       UNDERSTANDING INTERNATIONAL ECONOMICS: THEORY AND PRACTICE
       Boston and Toronto: Little, Brown, 1980.

       Text in international economics for one-term courses
       aimed at students not having a background in intermediate
       economic theory. The book's contents, presented verbally,
       graphically, and by numerical example (with almost no
       algebraic manipulations), is in two parts: international
       finance and international trade. Chapters include a
       list of key terms and a concept review, and one or more
       explanatory supplements on particular issues related
       to the chapter's coverage.

256   Roemer, Michael
       FISHING FOR GROWTH. EXPORT-LED DEVELOPMENT IN PERU,
       1950-1967
       Cambrdige, Mass.: Harvard University Press, 1970.

       An in-depth study of export-led growth in Peru through
       the fishmeal industry which would serve as an encouraging
       model for less developed countries with export oriented
       economies. By utilizing primary product-export industries,
       these countries can successfully stimulate rapid and
       sustained economic growth. Peru's experience with the
       fishmeal industry (which spurred diversification and

industrialization, with a marked development of a substantial capital goods sector) shows that during 1950-67 her gross national product grew 5.5 percent per year. This growth record is outstanding among the less developed countries. Contains 37 tables on various statistical data.

257   Roychowdhury, Krishna Chandra
       ECONOMIC GROWTH AND INTERNATIONAL TRADE
       Delhi: S. G. Wasani for the Macmillan Company of India, 1978.

       Constructs a simple two-commodity, two-factor model of the trading world, which assumes full employment and a fixed exchange rate and, using comparative statistics, assesses the impact of economic growth on the welfare of a trading nation. Analyzes the magnification effect of factor endowment on commodity outputs at unchanged commodity prices and discusses the impact of biased technical progress and biased consumption patterns resulting from expansion. Considers how the reciprocal demand curve of a growth economy is affected by the degree of bias and level of economic growth and how trade equilibrium is obtained under conditions of complete and incomplete specialization. Also examines the relation between capital movements, the volume of trade, and the terms of trade. Finds that under certain circumstances the growth of income in a growing country may be more than offset by the loss in income due to deterioration in the terms of trade; this result can be obtained using simple assumptions with regard to demand and elasticity for imports and exports.

258   Sapir, Andre and Lutz, Ernst
       TRADE   IN   SERVICES: ECONOMIC   DETERMINANTS   AND
       DEVELOPMENT-RELATED ISSUES
       Working Paper No. 480; Washington, D.C.:   World Bank, 1981.

       A background study for World Development Report 1981. Finds that trade theories can help explain the patterns of trade in services in spite of varying and often substantial degrees of protectionism. Represents the second stage of a research project on trade in services.

259   Sarris, Alexander H. and Adelman, Irma
       INCORPORATING   UNCERTAINTY   INTO   PLANNING   OF
       INDUSTRIALIZATION STRATEGIES FOR DEVELOPING COUNTRIES
       Working Paper No. 503; Washington, D.C.:   World Bank, 1982.

       This survey of existing literature on planning under uncertainty focuses on issues of international trade and investment allocation. Various ways of incorporating uncertainty into target-planning models are discussed and proposals for possible empirical applications are outlined.

260 Savasani, Jose H.
EXPORT PROMOTION: THE CASE OF BRAZIL
New York: Praeger, 1978.

261 Schultz, George J.
FOREIGN TRADE MARKETPLACE
Gale, 1977.

262 Scobie, Grant M.
GOVERNMENT POLICY AND FOOD IMPORTS: THE CASE OF WHEAT IN EGYPT
Washington, D.C.: International Food Policy Research Institute, Research Report 29, 1981.

Before the war, Europe, the USSR, and Japan imported most of the wheat entering world trade; developing countries imported only a quarter. Now LDC's account for two-thirds of world imports and as a group have become net importers. This study provides a rigorous neo-classical framework for the aggregate econometric analysis of the wheat balance between 1949 and 1979 in Egypt, where this grain is a basic component of the real wage and the object of government control; imports have such high priority that industrial expansion becomes inversely dependent upon them while domestic supply crowds out export crops. After a decade of large subsidies, policies to encourage import substitution and curtail domestic consumption brought domestic and world prices close together in the 1960's, but in the seventies, oil exports, workers' remittances and foreign aid, allowed for the imports necessary to substantially reduce the real price to consumers.

263 Smith, Kenneth H.
INTERNATIONAL TRADE
Lerner Publications, 1970.

264 Smith, Sheila and Toye, John
TRADE AND POOR ECONOMICS
F. Cass & Company, 1979.

265 Sorenson, Vernon L.
INTERNATIONAL TRADE POLICY: AGRICULTURE AND DEVELOPMENT
East Lansing: Division of Research, Graduate School of Business Administration, Michigan State University, 1975.

Textbook treating trade and policy issues in a global framework rather than within the limited scope of U.S. self-interest. Studies the relationship of trade to efficient resource use, trade and economic development, and domestic policy implications for trading countries. Discusses trade problems, issues, and existing policies separately for advanced and less developed countries, and reviews suggested or attempted solutions. Topics such as commodity agreements, the issue of reducing trade barriers to LDC's, and trade sector planning are also covered. Many tables and figures with data, mainly on agricultural productions and trade.

266   Steedman, Ian
       TRADE AMONGST GROWING ECONOMIES
       London; New York and Melbourne: Cambridge University
       Press, 1979.

Presents a framework for a theory of trade in which produced means of production, profits, and accumulation feature prominently. Argues that the Hecksher-Ohlin-Samuelson theory of trade does not provide a firm foundation for the analysis of contemporary international trade. Discusses trade in a small economy and then how the analysis of a small economy can be expanded to allow for a choice of production methods and multiple commodities and non-traded goods. Analyzes the two-country, three commodity case and discusses the extension of the analysis to many countries. Finds that the principal proximate determinants of an international equilibrium are the alternative available methods of production, the capitalists' savings ratios and the exogenous data referring to real wages and/or growth rates.

267   Stein, Leslie
       THE GROWTH OF EAST AFRICAN EXPORTS AND THEIR EFFECT ON
       ECONOMIC DEVELOPMENT
       London: Croom Helm, 1979.

A development case study of Kenya, Uganda, and Tanzania for the period 1959-71, stressing the contribution of exports to development. Begins by summarizing the general economic conditions, policies, and trends in each country studied; examines comparatively the general export trends of the less developed countries and of East Africa; analyzes the growth of the region's major exports crops and the trade flows of the East African Common Market; evaluates East Africa's trade instability and its impact on each country's economy; and concludes with a theoretical and empirical discussion of the relationship of trade to development. Although exports in these countries grew at a rate less than that of the LDC's as a whole, concludes that the evidence supports the view that a fairly strong export-growth relationship existed.

268   Steward, Dick
        TRADE AND HEMISPHERE: THE GOOD NEIGHBOR POLICY AND
        RECIPROCAL TRADE
        University of Missouri Press, 1975.

269   Streeten, Paul, ed.
        TRADE STRATEGIES FOR DEVELOPMENT; PAPERS OF THE NINTH
        CAMBRIDGE CONFERENCE ON DEVELOPMENT PROBLEMS, SEPTEMBER
        1972
        New York and Toronto: Wiley, 1973.

        Collection of the nine papers presented at a 1972
        conference concerned with trade aspects of development,
        the conference's opening addresses (by H. G. Johnson
        and I. G. Patel), and an editor's essay which discusses
        the major themes that emerged at the conference.   Topics
        considered include: outward-looking vs. inward-looking
        strategies, the impact of the developed countries, regional
        integration of the developing countries, the impact of
        like action by developed countries, trade and technology,
        domestic farm policies and trade in agricultural goods,
        trade negotiations for manufactured goods, multinational
        enterprises,   and   some   general   formation   concerning
        international trade (given in an Overseas Development
        Administration staff paper which served as a background
        document to the conference).

270   Suh, Suk Tai
        IMPORT SUBSTITUTION AND ECONOMIC DEVELOPMENT IN KOREA
        Seoul: Korea Development Institute, 1975.

        Analyzes import substitution in the development of the
        Korean economy from the 1870's to the 1970's and focuses
        on recent performance during the post-war period.   Examines
        import substitution as an element in the growth process
        and makes international comparisons.   The Korean experience
        has led this author, who is currently with the Korean
        Development Institute,   to   conclude   that   the   most
        significant and efficient structural change can be
        accomplished by export expansion and trade liberalizing
        policies, and that import substitution was most rapidly
        achieved during the period of export expansion rather
        than during the period of import substitution in the
        early periods. Statistical data for the Korean economy
        from the 1950's to 1973.

271   Ulbrich, Holley
        INTERNATIONAL TRADE AND FINANCE: THEORY OF POLICY
        P-H, 1983.

272   United Nations
        ECONOMIC RELATIONS OF CENTRAL AMERICA AND MEXICO WITH
        THE CARIBBEAN
        New York: UN, 1982.

Presents the principal characteristics of the Caribbean market and reviews economic flows between this subregion and Mexico, the five countries of the Central American Common Market (CACM) and Panama. Each study of the seven countries includes an analysis of trade, a brief description of the contractual basis of cooperation--when it exists--and an evaluation of mercantile and economic relations. Annexes cover the foreign trade of Mexico, CACM and Panama, broken down by products, origin and destination; and terms of access to the principal markets of the Caribbean.

273   United Nations
THE RESURGENCE OF PROTECTIONISM IN THE INDUSTRIAL COUNTRIES
New York: UN, 1978.

Report on a technical analysis undertaken by the secretariat of CEPAL of the protectionist policies of industrialized countries and their effects on Latin American exports, intended as a guide for the countries of the region to adopt measures to deal with the problem of protectionism.

274   United Nations
REVIEW OF INTERNATIONAL TRADE AND DEVELOPMENT 1977: REPORT
BY THE SECRETARIAT OF UNCTAD
New York: UN, 1978.

In two parts: (a) growth and trade performance of developing countries during the 1970's in relation to UN development objectives, including the flow of resources to developing countries and the growth of debt; and (b) implementation of international development policies in the various areas of competence of UNCTAD, including trade and technology, money and finance, shipping and insurance, trade and economic cooperation between developing countries and Eastern Europe, and economic cooperation among developing countries. Includes 27 tables.

275   United Nations
INTRAREGIONAL TRADE PROJECTIONS, EFFECTIVE PROTECTION
AND INCOME DISTRIBUTION; VOLUME 1
New York: UN, 1972.

Part One contains the report of the Eighth Group of Experts on Programming Techniques--convened in Bangkok, 10-31 January 1972--evaluates the methodology employed in three studies submitted by the ECAFE secretariat's Regional Centre for Economic Projections and programming, discusses the results, sets forth some broad policy implications, and makes recommendations for future studies by the Centre. Part Two contains the Centre study on projections of intraregional trade flows of selected commodities (35 groups(among 25 developing ECAFE countries, which together in 1967 accounted for 64 percent of export trade and 67 percent of import trade. The Centre studies on effective protection and income distribution will appear in volumes 2 and 3.

276   United Nations
REVIEW OF INTERNATIONAL TRADE AND DEVELOPMENT 1975: REPORT BY THE SECRETARIAT OF UNCTAD.
New York: UN, 1976.

In two parts: (a) the recent economic experience of developing countries in relation to the goals and objectives of the International Development Strategy, covering the international economic setting, a summary of the key results so far in the Second UN Development Decade (1971-1980), and the impact of environmental issues on trade and development problems; and (b) review of the implementation of policy measures envisaged in the International Development Strategy, covering commodities, manufactures, trade and economic cooperation between socialist countries of Eastern Europe and developing countries, financial resources for development, invisibles (including shipping), least developed and land-locked developing countries, transfer of technology, the Charter of Economic Rights and Duties of States, and trade expansion, economic cooperation and regional integration among developing countries.

277   United Nations
NEW DIRECTIONS IN INTERNATIONAL TRADE AND DEVELOPMENT POLICIES: REPORT BY THE SECRETARY-GENERAL OF UNCTAD FOR THE MID-TERM REVIEW AND APPRAISAL OF THE IMPLEMENTATION OF THE INTERNATIONAL DEVELOPMENT STRATEGY.
New York: UN, 1976.

Reviews progress so far towards achieving the goals of the International Development Strategy of the Second UN Development Decade (1971-1980) which fall within the competence of UNCTAD, the field of trade and development. Also suggests appropriate changes and adaptations which might be incorporated in the Strategy as a result of changes in the world economic situation and of the objectives and policy measures of the General Assembly's Declaration and Programme of Action on the Establishment of a New International Economic Order.

278   United Nations
UNITED NATIONS CONFERENCE ON TRADE AND DEVELOPMENT: INTERNATIONSL TRADE IN COTTON TEXTILES AND THE DEVELOPING COUNTRIES: PROBLEMS AND PROSPECTS. REPORT BY THE UNCTAO SECRETARIAT.
New York: United Nations, 1974.

A review of the past decade and the current situation in the world trade of cotton, man-made, and other textiles. Contains seven chapters (policy conclusions, international trade in cotton and other textiles, demand for cotton textiles and competition from synthetics, production trends, tariff protection, non-tariff protection, an evaluation of the long-term arrangement on cotton textiles) with 33 tables and two annexes with 10 selected trade matrices and statistical notes. Data mainly from 1967-1970.

279   United Nations
       INSTITUTIONAL ARRANGEMENTS IN DEVELOPING COUNTRIES FOR INDUSTRIAL AND EXPORT FINANCE WITH A VIEW TO EXPANDING AND DIVERSIFYING THEIR EXPORTS OF MANUFACTURES AND SEMI-MANUFACTURES.
       UN, 1980.

       This report describes and discusses a number of special institutional arrangements and methods of official intermediation in the banking sector and the financial markets aimed at facilitating the provision of increased finance on adequate terms for exporting manufacturing industries in developing countries.

280   UNCTAD
A B D INDUSTRIAL COLLABORATION ARRANGEMENTS
       New York: United Nations Publications, 1978.

       Analyzes the elements of intergovernmental framework agreements on industrial and trade collaboration between developed market-economy countries and developing countries, between socialist countries of Eastern Europe and developing countries, and among developing countries.

281   United Nations
       A GLOBAL SYSTEM OF TRADE PREFERENCES AMONG DEVELOPING COUNTRIES (GSTP): STUDY BY THE SECRETARIAT
       UN, 1981.

       Examines the relationship between the efforts of developing countries to develop and strengthen their subregional and regional integration arrangements and the simultaneous efforts to develop new preferential instruments for trade (GSTP). Annex: List of Members of Subregional and Regional Integration and Economic Co-operation Groupings of Developing Countries, 1981.

282   United Nations
       TRADE AND DEVELOPMENT
       Unipub, 1982.

283   United Nations
       TRADE AND DEVELOPMENT POLICIES IN THE 1970S
       Unipub, 1973.

284   United Nations
        TRADE AND DEVELOPMENT REPORT 1981
        Unipub, 1981.

285   United Nations
        TRADE LIBERALIZATION AND THE NATIONAL INTEREST VOLS I
        AND II
        Unipub, 1980.

286   United Nations
        TRADE LIBERALIZATION, PROTECTIONISM AND INTERDEPENDENCE
        Unipub, 1980.

287   United Nations
        EXPORT PROMOTION OF SELECTED SMALL INDUSTRY PRODUCTS:
        ASIAN EXPERIENCE
        Unipub, 1981.

288   UNCTAD
        TRADE AND DEVELOPMENT: AN UNCTAD REVIEW NO. 1, SPRING
        1979
        Unipub, 1979.

289   Upadhyaya, K.K.
        IMPORT FINANCING IN INDIA: WITH SPECIAL REFERENCE TO
        THE FOURTH AND FIFTH FIVE-YEAR PLANS
        Allahabad, India: Chugh, 1980.

        Examines import financing in India for the period 1969-78.
        Surveys the theoretical literature on the relationship.
        between imports and growth, evaluates the various methods
        of import financing, and describing India's import
        requirements and strategy in the Fourth and Fifth Plans.
        Concludes with an evaluation of the development strategy
        of import substitution, which "from the point of sheer
        size...has been very impressive in India," but when
        assissed in terms of its impact on saving and capital
        formation, consumer goods, basic goods, and capital goods,
        "may be shown to be leading to negative value addition
        or perpetuation of backward technology or conspicuous
        consumption."

290   Vajda, Imre and Simai, Mihaly, eds.
        FOREIGN TRADE IN A PLANNED ECONOMY
        New York: Cambridge University Press, 1971.

291   Verbit, Gilber P.
        TRADE AGREEMENTS FOR DEVELOPING COUNTRIES
        London, Colubia University Press.

        Explains what the rules of the new trade agreements are,
        the economic experience which gave rise to them, and
        how they promote the interests of the developing countries.

292   Walsh, A.E. and Paxton, John
       TRADE AND INDUSTRIAL RESOURCES OF THE COMMON MARKET AND
       EFTA COUNTRIES
       Rothman, 1970.

293   Warnecke, Steven J., ed.
A C   INTERNATIONAL TRADE AND INDUSTRIAL POlICIES: GOVERNMENT
       INTERVENTION AND AN OPEN WORLD ECONOMY
       New York: Homes & Meier, 1978.

       Ten previously unpublished papers by economists, political
       scientists, and government officials on how national
       subsidy policies have affected the General Agreement
       on Tariffs and Trade (GATT) and what new procedures may
       be needed to deal with rising conflicts. Written from
       the perspective of the trade negotiator, the articles
       are in two parts: Part one discusses subsidies beyond
       those covered in GATT, examining them in the context
       of national industrial policies; part two considers the
       effects of national policy on the operation of GATT,
       the domestic problems caused by international commitments,
       and difficulties with subsidy negotiation, focusing on
       the EEC, the United States, Japan, and Canada. Also
       discusses problem of measuring the international effect
       of subsidies and the need to develop improved international
       laws.

294   Whitman, Marina V.N.
       INTERNATIONAL TRADE AND INVESTMENT: TWO PERSPECTIVES.
       ESSAYS IN INTERNATIONAL FINANCE, NO. 143.
       Princeton N.J.:   Princeton University, Department of
       Economics, international Finance Section, 1981.

       The Frank D. Graham Memorial Lecture given at Princeton
       University on 5 March 1981. Comments on the relationship
       between the theoretical perspective on the motivations
       and processes of international trade and investment,
       and the views of a large multinational corporation on
       these same issues from the perspective of its own
       decision-making and operations. Concentrates on the
       intricacies of intra-industry and intra-firm trade. Sets
       forth the linkage of exports, imports, domestic production,
       and world-wide investments in the global automotive
       industry. Contends that the internationalization of
       this industry does not lead to an ideal world where
       individual profit-maximizing firms make decisions and
       interact with one another without consideration of national
       boundaries. Government intervention plays an increasing
       role in influencing the pattern of international
       competition, due to the concern with jobs and exports
       and the belief that comparative advantage is dynamic
       and largely endogenous in MDC's also.

295   Wogart, Jan Peter

A C D   INDUSTRIALIZATION   IN   COLOMBIA: POLICIES,   PATTERNS,
PERSPECTIVES
Print Tubingen: J.C.B. Mohr (Paul Siebeck), 1978.

Case study of the role of foreign trade and exchange
rate policies on industrial exports of developing countries
and their impact on industrial development in advanced
countries. Focuses on (1) the relationship of Colombia's
dependence on coffee to its industrialization process;
(2) the effect of import substitution on industrial growth,
employment, and balance of payments for the period 1925-74;
(3) the origin and impact of export diversification.
Measures and quantifies some effects of Colombia's export
incentive system of the sixties and discusses patterns
and linkages of the industrialization process during
the postwar period, the major sources of industrial growth,
and the use of capital and labor in a dualistic industrial
sector. Considers the outlook for the volume and structure
of Colombian exports, predicting a growth rate of
manufactured exports of about 8 to 10 percent up to 1980,
12 percent in 1981-82, and 15 percent for the years
1983-85, amounting to $1,077 million (1976 prices) in
1985. Further suggests that Colombia's export structure
will shift from traditional to intermediate and capital
goods, with an average growth of all manufactured exports
of 14.4 percent between 1977 and 1985.

296   Wolf, Martin H. and others
INDIA'S EXPORTS
Oxford University Press, 1980.

Examines India's overall export performance, analyzes
the major constraints and policies, and explores the
key strategic options. The major conclusions are that,
while improving, India's export performance has lagged
behind need, potential, and the achievements of its main
competitors, because of failures of the domestic incentive
system and especially the anti-export bias that resulted
from a strongly inward-looking trade and industrialization
strategy, to which export incentives were merely a marginal
addition. Given the continued importance of rapid export
growth and the increasingly unfavorable world environment,
it has become more important to improve the trade policy
regime with a view to taking advantage of all available
opportunities. The book is based on an economic report
prepared between late 1975 and early 1977, and provides
more up-to-date information than that available in
competing books, as it incorporates the results of a
number of unpublished industrial studies by the World
Bank. Emphasized the central role of incentive policies
and analyzes the prospects and performance of major export
categories in detail.

297   World Bank
TRADE AND EMPLOYMENT POLICIES FOR INDUSTRIAL DEVELOPMENT

World Bank, Washington, D.C., 1982.

298   Yeager, Leland B.
FOREIGN   TRADE   AND   U.S.   POLICY: THE   CASE   FOR   FREE
INTERNATIONAL TRADE
Praeger 1976.

299   Yeats, Alexander J.
TRADE AND DEVELOPMENT POLICIES: LEADING ISSUES FOR THE
1980S.
New York: St. Martin's Press, 1981.

Second of a two-part survey of developing country trade
problems, focusing on issues in the 1980s.   (See JEL
No. 80-0405 for annotation of Trade Barriers Facing
Developing Countries (1979) and Volume 18 (December 1980)
for   review.)   Re-evaluates   trade   and   development
strategies, which have centered around outward-oriented
growth and removal of trade restraints for several decades.
Discusses growing protectionism in LDCs and the future
composition of LDC exports.   Argues that trade and other
forms of cooperation among developing countries or between
less developed countries and socialist nations will have
a much higher priority in the 1980s and that existing
international   institutions   will   require   considerable
modification to respond to conditions in the next decade.

300   Yeats, Alexander J.
SHIPPING AND DEVELOPMENT POLICY: AN INTEGRATED ASSESSMENT
New York: Prager, UK distributor Holt-Saunders, 1981.

The author points out that trade studies in developing
countries underestimate both the importance of sea freight
costs and the extent of possible policy influence over
them.   The book provides a wealth of data to substantiate
the existence of administered prices and prohibitively
high costs for South-South trade, and sound policy advice
on the formation of national shippng fleets.   The contents
include: transport   costs   and   development;   historical
perspectives   on   ocean   freight   rates   and   economic
development; institutional factors in shipping; transport
costs and exports; the influence of transportation costs
on   resource-based   industrialisation;   and   policy
recommendations.   Although   somewhat   undigested   in   its
presentation, this is a valuable study on a neglected
topic for development economists.

301   Yeats, Alexander J.
TRADE BARRIERS FACING DEVELOPING COUNTRIES
New York: St. Martin's Press, 1979.

In his comprehensive and timely analysis of the factors
that limit penetration of the world's industrial markets
by less developed countries, Yeats draws an important
distinction   between   supply   constraints   and   external

barriers, such as tariffs, quotas, export restraints, and transnational corporate policy.

II. SELECTED PERIODICAL ARTICLES

302   Abercrombie, K. C.
       Trade should make more than money; it should also make
       jobs. CERES 3 (July-August 1970): 40-44.

303   Adams, John
       India's foreign trade and payments since 1965; managing
       the nation as a peasant household. PACIFIC AFFAIRS
       53:632-42, Winter 1980-81.

304   Adelman, Irma and Sherman Robinson
       Income distribution, import substitution, and growth
       strategies in a developing country. PRINCETON UNIVERSITY.
       WOODROW WILSON SCHOOL OF PUBLIC AND INTERNATIONAL AFFAIRS.
       RESEARCH PROGRAM IN ECONOMIC DEVELOPMENT. DISCUSSION
       PAPER No. 68:1-53, Nov. 1976.

305   Ahmed, Masood
       Import substitution as a strategy of industrialization
       in Pakistan--a review. PAKISTAN ECONOMIC AND SOCIAL
       REVIEW (LAHORE) 18:56-64, Spring/Summer 1980.

306   Ahmad, Ziauddin
       Strategies of export-led growth with special reference
       to Pakistan. ECONOMIC JOURNAL 13, No. 1/2:40-60, 1980.

307   Amsden, A. H.
       Industry characteristics of intra-third world trade in
       manufactures. ECONOMIC DEVELOPMENT AND CULTURAL CHANGE
       29:1-19, October 1980.

308   Amsden, A. H.
       Trade in manufactures between developing countries.
       ECONOMIC JOURNAL 86:778-90, December 1976.

309   Atkinson, Rodney
       Overseas aid by foreign trade. JOURNAL OF ECONOMIC AFFAIRS
       2:99-102, Jan. 1982.

310   Balassa, Bela
       Trade in manufactured goods: patterns of change [trade
       between the industrialized and the developing countries;
       conference paper]. WORLD DEVELOPMENT 9:263-75, March
       1981.

311   Balassa, Bela
       Export composition and export performance in the industrial
       countries, 1953-71. REVIEW OF ECONOMICS AND STATISTICS
       61:604-07, Nov. 1979.

312   Balassa, Bela
       Exports and economic growth [their relationship in eleven
       developing countries]. JOURNAL OF DEVELOPMENT ECONOMICS
       5:181-89,, June 1978.

313   Baldwin, R. E.
       International trade and economic growth: a diagrammatic
       analysis.   AMERICAN   ECONOMIC   REVIEW   65:187-93,   March
       1975.

314   Bell, R. T.
       Productivity and foreign trade in South African development
       strategy.   SOUTH AFRICAN JOURNAL OF ECONOMICS 43:476-515,
       Dec. 1975.

       Deals with just two elements in an overall strategy of
       economic   development,   and   with   the   inter-relationship
       between them.   These elements are the rate of growth of
       factor productivity, and foreign trade policy.

315   Beyfuss, Jorg
       The trade with developing countries; its potentialities
       and limitations. INTERECONOMICS, REVIEW OF INTERNATIONAL
       TRADE AND DEVELOPMENT Nos. 11/12:287-90, Nov./Dec. 1978.

316   Bhagwati, Jagdish N. and Srinivasan, T. N.
       Trade policy and development.   INTERNATIONAL   BANK   FOR
       RECONSTRUCTION AND DEVELOPMENT.   WORLD BANK REPRINT SERIES
       No. 90:1-38, 1978.

317   Bienefeld, M. A.
       Special gains from trade with socialist countries; the
       case of Tanzania.   WORLD DEVELOPMENT 3:247-71, May 1975.

       This paper suggests that Tanzania has not derived any
       special benefits from its trade with the socialist
       countries, other than gaining access to additional export
       markets.

318   Bingham, T. R.
       Trade patterns and economic evolution.   INTERECONOMICS
       (July 1974), pp. 221-23.

319   Bird, Graham
       The terms of trade of developing countries: theory,
       evidence and policy.   ECONOMIA INTERNAZIONALE 32:399-412,
       November 1979.

320   Blair, Andrew R.
       Economic expansion, resource allocation and international
       trade theory: some empirical observations.   ECONOMIA
       INTERNAZIONALE 33:202-23, May/Aug. 1980.

       Attempts to provide some preliminary empirical responses
       to certain questions which have been raised in the

literature concerning the effects of economic expansion on the allocation of resources and on international trade, especially in developing economies.

321   Blomquist, A. G.
Tariff revenue and optimal capital accumulation in less developed countries. ECONOMIC JOURNAL 84 (March 1974): 70-90.

322   Branson, William H. and Louka T. Katseli-Papaefstratiou
Exchange rate policy for developing countries. YALE UNIVERSITY. ECONOMIC GROWTH CENTER. CENTER DISCUSSION PAPER No. 1-57, Nov. 1978.

323   Brodsky, D. A. and Sampson, G. P.
Retained value and the export performance of developing countries. JOURNAL OF DEVELOPMENT STUDIES 17:32-47, October 1980.

324   Bruton, Henry J.
Economic development with unlimited supplies of foreign exchange. WILLIAMS COLLEGE, CENTER FOR DEVELOPMENT ECONOMICS. RESEARCH MEMORANDUM SERIES RM-83:1-37, July 1981.

Focuses on three types of developing countries: countries with unlimited supplies of foreign exchange and heavy reliance on foreign workers; countries with a significant proportion of their labor force employed outside the country and an equally significant proportion of their foreign exchange receipts due to the remittance of these workers; and countries whose foreign exchange position improved greatly, virtually overnight, and which have an ample supply of labor at home.

325   Cable, V.
Britain, the new protectionism and trade with the newly industrialising countries. INTERNATIONAL AFFAIRS 55:1-17, January 1979.

326   Carlisle, E. R.
New trends in world exports. WORLD TODAY 32:428-34, November 1976.

327   Cherney, H. B.
Interactions between industrialization and exports. AMERICAN ECONOMIC REVIEW, PAPERS AND PROCEEDINGS 70:281-87, May 1980.

328   Chichilnisky, Graciela
Terms of trade and domestic distribution: export-led growth with abundant labor. HARVARD INSTITUTE FOR INTERNATIONAL DEVELOPMENT, DEVELOPMENT DISCUSSION PAPER No. 41:1-23, July 1978.

329   Christou, G. and Wilford, W. T.
       Trade intensification in the Central American common
       market. JOURNAL OF INTERAMERICAN STUDIES AND WORLD AFFAIRS
       15 (May 1973): 249-64.

330   D'Arge, Ralph C. and Kneese, Allen V.
       Environmental quality and international trade.
       INTERNATIONAL ORGANIZATIONS 26 (Spring 1972): 419-65.

331   De La Torre, Jose
       Foreign investment and export dependency. ECONOMIC
       DEVELOPMENT AND CULTURAL CHANGE 23 (October 1974): 133-50.

332   de Vries, Barend A.
       Export growth in the new world environment; the case
       of Latin America. WELTWIRTSCHAFTLICHES ARCHIV 113, No.
       2:353-79, 1977.

       Seeks to assess the role continued export growth must
       play in Latin America's development and how export policies
       can best be adapted to the changes in external as well
       as domestic conditions which have occurred since 1973.

333   Dobroczynski, Michal
       Africa's trade with developing countries. AFRICANA
       BULLETIN (1974), pp. 31-48.

334   Dobroczynski, Michal
       African trade with Eastern Europe. AFRICANA BULLETIN
       (1972), pp. 79-100.

335   Ehrlich, Thomas and Catherine Gwin
       A Third World strategy. FOREIGN POLICY No. 44:145-66,
       Fall 1981.

       The authors suggest that a central objective of U.S.
       policy toward the Third World should be to encourage
       Third World economic growth, openness to international
       trade and investment, and an orientation toward cooperation
       with the United States on global problems of common
       concern.

336   Fajana, Olufemi
       Trends and prospects of Nigerian-Japanese trade. JOURNAL
       OF MODERN AFRICAN STUDIES 14:127-36, March 1976.

337   Feder, Gershon
       Growth and external borrowing in trade gap economies
       of less developed countries. AUSSENWIRTSCHAFT (ST.
       GALLEN) 36:381-402, Dec. 1981.

338   Fels, Gerhard
       The exports of the developing world. ROUND TABLE 63
       (July 1973): 3-5-17.

339   Fiallo, Fabio R.
The negotiation strategy of developing countries in the
field of trade liberalization. JOURNAL OF WORLD TRADE
LAW 11:203-12, May/June 1977.

340   Findlay, Ronald
The terms of trade and equilibrium growth in the world
economy. AMERICAN ECONOMIC REVIEW (NASHVILLE) 70:291-99,
June 1980.

The objective of this paper is to present a highly
stylized dynamic model in which the terms of trade emerge
as the mechanism linking the growth rates of output in
the North and South.

341   Findlay, R.
Economic development and the theory of international
trade. AMERICAN ECONOMIC REVIEW, PAPERS AND PROCEEDINGS
69:186-90, May 1979.

342   Frank, Isaiah
Reciprocity and trade policy of developing countries.
FINANCE AND DEVELOPMENT 15:20-23, March 1978.

The author suggests that nonreciprocity may not be in
the best interests of the developing countries.
Reciprocity may in many cases offer them greater
opportunities to increase their exports.

343   Franko, L. G.
Adjusting to export thrusts of newly industrialising
countries: an advanced country perspective. ECONOMIC
JOURNAL 91:486-506, June 1981.

344   Friesen, Ronald L.
The determinants and implications of the demand for
imports; an econometric study of Kenya. EASTERN AFRICA
ECONOMIC REVIEW 7:49-63, June 1975.

This study is an attempt to isolate some of the empirically
relevant import demand variables for Kenya in order to
better understand the forces operative in the determination
of import volume for that country.

345   Frobel, F. and others
Export-oriented industrialization of underdeveloped
countries. MONTHLY REVIEW 30:22-27, November 1978.

346   Gabszewicz, J. Jaskold and Avner Shaked
International trade in differentiated products.
INTERNATIONAL ECONOMIC REVIEW 22:427-34, Oct. 1981.

347   Gillespie, Robert Smith
Trade information networks. INTERNATIONAL TRADE FORUM
15:11-13, 34-37, April/June 1979.

348   Glezakos, Constantine
       Export instability and economic growth: a statistical
       verification. ECONOMIC DEVELOPMENT AND CULTURAL CHANGE
       21 (July 1973): 670-78.

349   Gulati, U. C.
       Effect of capital imports on savings and growth in less
       developed countries. ECONOMIC INQUIRY 16:563-69, October
       1978.

350   Hanson, J. R.
       Tropical trade and development in the nineteenth century:
       the Brazilian experience. JOURNAL OF POLITICAL ECONOMY
       81:678-96, May 1973.

351   Hargreaves, D. Keith
       Trade among developing countries.   INTERNATIONAL
       CONCILIATION (September 1970), pp. 161-63.

352   Harris, Donald J.
       Economic growth with limited import capacity. ECONOMIC
       DEVELOPMENT AND CULTURAL CHANGE 20 (April 1972): 524-28.

353   Harris, Richard
       Trade and depletable resources: the small open economy.
       CANADIAN JOURNAL OF ECONOMICS (TORONTO) 14:649-64, Nov.
       1981.

354   Havrylyshyn, Oli and Martin Wolf
       Promoting trade among developing countries: an assessment
       [1963-77]. FINANCE AND DEVELOPMENT 19:17-21, March 1982.

355   Hay, Jorge
       Trading relations between Europe and Latin America. EURO
       COOPERATION, ECONOMIC STUDIES ON EUROPE No. 17:15-34.

       Content: 1) Latin America; the future is no longer remote;
       2) Obstacles to trade with the EEC; 3) The future of
       trading relations between the EEC and Latin America.

356   Helleiner, G. K.
       Structural aspects of Third World trade: some trends
       and some prospects. JOURNAL OF DEVELOPMENT ECONOMICS
       15:70-88, April 1979.

       Focuses on those structural aspects of Third World trade
       which are related to the policies of the industrialised
       countries' governments, and to the activities of
       transnational corporations based in these countries.

357   Helleiner, Gerald K.
       Intra-firm trade and the developing countries. New York:
       St. Martin's Press, 1981.

358   Hicks, N. L. and others
Models of trade and growth for the developing world.
EUROPEAN ECONOMIC REVIEW 87:239-55, April 1976.

359   Hidden face of third world trade. ECONOMIST 277:67,
December 20-26, 1980.

360   Hong, Wontack
Trade, growth and income distribution; the experience
of the Republic of Korea. OVERSEAS DEVELOPMENT COUNCIL,
WASHINGTON, D.C. WORKING PAPER No. 3:1-71, May 1981.

361   Hsueh, Tien-Tung and Koon-Lam Shea
Trade stability, balance, and trading partner of the
People's Republic of China. DEVELOPING ECONOMIES
19:242-54, Sept. 1981.

The purpose of this paper is to analyze the trade balance
and the trading partners of China and to compare them
with those of other countries.

362   Hughes, G. A.
Investment and trade for a developing economy with
economies of scale in industry. REVIEW OF ECONOMIC STUDIES
43:237-48, June 1976.

363   Hughes, Helen and Jean Waelbroeck
Can developing country export keep growing in the 1980's?
WORLD ECONOMY 4:127-47, June 1981.

364   Ibrahim, Tigani E.
Prospects for export growth in an African economy: the
Kenya case. WORLD BANK REPRINT SERIES No. 188:121-38,
1980.

365   International Bank for Reconstruction and Development
Trade among developing countries: theory, policy issues,
and principal trends; a background study for World
Development Report 1981. World Bank Staff Working Paper
No. 479.

366   Joen, Tae-Woong
Foreign trade and economic growth in Korea. BANK OF
KOREA, QUARTERLY ECONOMIC REVIEW p. 22-33, March 1977.

367   Johnson, Harry G.
An overview of the world crisis and international trade.
PAKISTAN ECONOMIC AND SOCIAL REVIEW 15:1-16, Spring/Summer
1977.

368   Joshi, Vijay
India's export incentive system. INDUSTRY AND DEVELOPMENT
No. 2:59-75, 1978.

369   Kanamori, Hisao
       Structure of foreign trade. DEVELOPING ECONOMIES 10
       (December 1972): 359-84.

370   Kaplinsky, Raphael
       Export-oriented growth; a large international firm in
       a small developing country. WORLD DEVELOPMENT 7:825-34,
       Aug./Sept. 1979.

       In this case study the author describes the terms
       negotiated between a large international firm and a
       small host country (Kenya) in the siting of a
       pineapple-processing plant, and examines the benefits
       arising to the respective parties. Some conclusions
       are then drawn at a more general level.

371   Karunaratne, Neil Dias
       Export oriented industrialization strategies [an
       evaluation; developing countries]. INTERECONOMICS
       15:217-23, Sept./Oct. 1980.

372   Kebschull, Dietrich
       Growth in developing countries by increasing exports?
       Critical remarks on a concept. ECONOMICS (TUBINGEN)
       14:65-82, 1976.

373   Keesing, Donald B.
       Exports and policy in Latin American countries: prospects
       for the world economy and for Latin American exports,
       1980-90. QUARTERLY REVIEW OF ECONOMICS AND BUSINESS
       21:18-47, Summer 1981.

374   Khan, Azizur Rahman
       Bangladesh's trade and economic relations with the
       socialist countries. WORLD DEVELOPMENT 3:329-34, May
       1975.

375   Khatkhate, Deena R.
       Economic development and the cost of foreign trade and
       exchange controls. JOURNAL OF ECONOMIC ISSUES 4 (Dec.
       1970): 56-67.

376   Kingston, Jerry L.
       Export concentration and export performance in developing
       countries, 1954-67. JOURNAL OF DEVELOPMENT STUDIES
       12:311-19, July 1976.

377   Kirkpatrick, C. and Yamin, M.
       Determinants of export subsidiary formation by U.S.
       transnationals in developing countries: an inter-industry
       analysis. WORLD DEVELOPMENT 9:373-81, April 1981.

378   Koch, C. W.
       Manufactured exports from third world countries.
       GEOGRAPHICAL REVIEW 68:230-32, April 1978.

379   Kojima, Kiyoshi
       Australia's trade with Asia: some policy issues.   PAKISTAN
       ECONOMIC AND SOCIAL REVIEW   (LAHORE)   21:1-14,   June 1980.

380   Koopmann, Georg
       Trends   in   world   trade.   INTERECONOMICS,   REVIEW   OF
       INTERNATIONAL   TRADE   AND   DEVELOPMENT   No.   5:207-13,
       Sept./Oct. 1981.

381   Kouri, Pentti J. K.
       Trade   in   primary   commodities   and   the   new   international
       economic order.   UNITAS 49:71-93, no. 2, 1977.

382   Krishnamurti, R.
       Multilateral   trade   negotiations   and   the   developing
       countries.   THIRD WORLD QUARTERLY 2:251-69, April 1980.

       The main purpose of this paper is to give a brief and
       general picture of thé concerns of developing countries
       in the MTN's, their initial objectives, and expectations;
       the efforts made by them to achieve those objectives,
       the modalities and processes involved in the negotiations,
       and the results obtained.

383   Krishnamurti, R.
       Tariff   preferences   in   favour   of   developing   countries.
       JOURNAL OF WORLD TRADE LAW 4 (May-June 1970): 447-59.

384   Krueger, Anne O.
       Trade policy as an input to development.   NATIONAL BUREAU
       OF ECONOMIC RESEARCH, WORKING PAPER SERIES No. 466:1-9,
       April 1980.

       Examines the relationship between a developing country's
       policies with respect to its trade and payments regime
       and its rate of economic growth.

385   Krueger, Anne O.
       Alternative   trade   strategies   and   employment   in   LDC's.
       AMERICAN ECONOMIC REVIEW, PAPERS AND PROCEEDINGS 68:270-74,
       280-83, May 1978.

386   Krugman, Paul
       Trade,   accumulation,   and   uneven   development.   YALE
       UNIVERSITY.   ECONOMIC GROWTH CENTER.   CENTER DISCUSSION
       PAPER No.   311:1-18, May 1979.

387   Langhammer, Rolf J.
       Multilateral   trade   liberalization   among   developing
       countries.   JOURNAL OF WORLD TRADE LAW 14:508-15, Nov./Dec.
       1980.

388   Lee, J. K.
       Exports and the propensity to save in LDC's.   ECONOMIC
       JOURNAL 81 (June 1971): 341-51.

389   Levy, Santiago
       Foreign trade and its impact on employment; the Mexican
       case. JOURNAL OF DEVELOPMENT ECONOMICS 10:47-65, Feb.
       1982.

390   Lim, David
       Export instability and economic growth; a return to
       fundamentals. OXFORD BULLETIN OF ECONOMICS AND STATISTICS
       38:311-22, Nov. 1976.

391   Long, Millard F.
       External debt and the trade imperative in Latin America.
       QUARTERLY REVIEW OF ECONOMICS AND BUSINESS 21:280-301,
       Summer 1981.

392   Majumdar, Badiul Alam
       Innovations and international trade; an industry study
       of dynamic and competitive advantage. KYKLOS (BASLE)
       32, No. 3:559-70, 1979.

       Studies the relationship between technology and trade
       at a given point in time, with special reference to the
       electronic calculator industry.

393   Malima, K. A.
       International trade and economic transformation of
       Tanzania. AFRICAN REVIEW 1 (September 1971): 76-90.

394   Malmgren, H. B.
       Significance of trade policies in the world economic
       outlook. ATLANTIC COMMUNICATION QUARTERLY 15:422-34,
       Winter 1977-78.

395   McCulloch, Rachel
       Gains to Latin America from trade liberalization in
       developed and developing nations. QUARTERLY REVIEW OF
       ECONOMICS AND BUSINESS 21:231-59, Summer 1981.

396   McCulloch, Rachel
       United States-Latin American trade; the issue of
       preferential market access. HARVARD INSTITUTE OF ECONOMIC
       RESEARCH, DISCUSSION PAPER SERIES No. 517:1-22, Nov.
       1976.

397   McCulloch, R. and Pinera, J.
       Trade as aid: the poltiical economy of tariff preferences
       for developing countries. AMERICAN ECONOMIC REVIEW
       67:959-67, Dec. 1977.

398   Michalopoulos, C.
       Expanding trade among developing countries: the role
       of limited preferential arrangements. JOURNAL OF COMMON
       MARKET STUDIES 13:308-18, March 1975.

399   Michalski, Wolfgang
        Exports and economic growth. INTERECONOMICS (July 1970),
        pp. 209-11.

400   Mohammad, Sharif
        Trade, growth and income redistribution: a case study
        of India. YALE UNIVERSITY. ECONOMIC GROWTH CENTER.
        CENTER DISCUSSION PAPER No. 331:1-31, Nov. 1979.

401   Murrell, Peter
        Comparative growth and comparative advantage: tests
        of the effects of interest group behavior on foreign
        trade patterns. PUBLIC CHOICE 38, No. 1:35-53, 1982.

402   Myint, H.
        Adam Smith's theory of international trade in the
        perspective of economic development. ECONOMICA 44:231-48,
        August 1977.

403   Naini, Ahmad
        Trade and development expectations of LDC's.
        INTERECONOMICS (March 1972), pp. 79-81.

404   Nandi, Sukumar
        A note on equilibrium theory of international trade and
        underdevelopment. ECONOMIC AFFAIRS 26:117-23, April/June
        1981.

405   Navarrete, Jorge, Eduardo
        The foreign trade of Mexico; imbalance and dependence.
        COMERCIO EXTERIOR DE MEXICO, ENGLISH EDITION 22:25-33,
        Jan. 1976.

406   Nayyar, Deepak
        India's export performance in the 1970's. ECONOMIC AND
        POLITICAL WEEKLY 11:731-43, May 15, 1976.

        Analyzes export trends since 1970 and discusses the broader
        implications of the recent developments for India's export
        sector.

407   Ndongko, Wilfred A.
        Trade and development aspects of the central African
        customs and economic union. CULTURES ET DEVELOPPEMENT
        7 (1975): 337-56.

408   Nguyen, The-Hiep
        Trends in terms of trade of LDC's. JOURNAL OF ECONOMIC
        STUDIES 8, No. 2:46-56, 1981.

409   Nogues, Julio J.
        Alternative trade strategies and employment in the
        Argentine manufacturing sector. BANCO CENTRALE DE LA
        REPUBLICA ARGENTINA. CENTRO DE ESTUDIOS MONETARIOS Y
        BANCARIOS. DISCUSSION PAPER (BUENOS AIRES) No. 8:1-43,
        Sept. 1981.

410   Nowzad, Bahram
Differential trade treatment for LDC's. FINANCE AND
DEVELOPMENT 15:16-21, March 1978.

411   Nsouli, S. M.
Theoretical aspects of trade, risk and growth. JOURNAL
OF INTERNATIONAL ECONOMICS 5:239-53, August 1975.

412   Olaloku, F. Akin
The changing pattern of foreign trade. INTERECONOMICS,
MONTHLY REVIEW OF INTERNATIONAL TRADE AND DEVELOPMENT
No. 2:57-59, Feb. 1975.

413   Parkinson, F.
Latin America: Present options in the world trading
system. BOLSA REVIEW 8:2-14, Jan. 1974.

414   Perez, Lorenzo L.
Export subsidies in developing countries and the GATT
(General agreement on tariffs and trade). JOURNAL OF
WORLD TRADE LAW 10:529-45, Nov./Dec. 1976.

415   Ram, Mangat
Exports, external capital inflow and economic growth
in developing countries with special reference to South
Asian countries.   INDIAN ECONOMIC REVIEW 27:20-27,
April/June 1980.

Argues that the pragmatic approach, for the present day
developing countries, in order to achieve a substantial
increase in the overall rate of economic growth to adopt,
is that "trade is aid" in place of traditional approaches,
"trade, not aid" or "trade or aid."

416   Ranis, Gustav
Challenges   and   opportunities   posed   by   Asia's
super-exporters: implications for manufactured exports
from Latin America. YALE UNIVERSITY. ECONOMIC GROWTH
CENTER. CENTER DISCUSSION PAPER No. 358:1-31, Aug. 1980.

417   Reza, Sadrel
Trade, output and employment: a case study of Bangladesh.
THE BANGLADESH DEVELOPMENT STUDIES (DACCA) 6:1-26, Winter
1978.

Focuses attention on the output and employment potential
of alternative trade strategies for the industrial economy
of Bangladesh.

418   Richter, Peter
Are the developing countries in reality "exporters of
capital"?   INTERECONOMICS 14:172-79, July/Aug. 1979.

419   Rondos, Alex
CEAO trade patterns. WEST AFRICA No. 3295:1749-51, Sept.
15, 1980.

420   Ropke, Jochen
        Free   trade,   protection   and   economic   development.
        INTERECONOMICS,   REVIEW   OF   INTERNATIONAL   TRADE   AND
        DEVELOPMENT No. 1:26-30, Jan./Feb. 1981.

421   Samuelson, Robert J.
        Trade with developing countries creates profits and a
        backlash: trading between industrialized and developing
        nations should help both sides, but in practice, things
        are not working out so neatly. NATIONAL JOURNAL 9:823-27,
        May 28, 1977.

422   Sautter, Hermann
        Underdevelopment and dependence as a result of foreign
        trade interdependence; an economic evaluation of dependency
        theory. ECONOMICS (TUBINGEN) 18:115-48, 1980.

        This article attempts to clarify the dependency concept
        of the Latin America "dependencia school". It then goes
        on the discuss the interpretive models of this school
        for the present phase of development in Latin America.

423   Schydlowsky, Daniel M. and Martha Rodriguez
        The vulnerability of small semi-industrialized economies
        to export shocks; a simulation analysis based on Peruvian
        data.   BOSTON UNIVERSITY, CENTER FOR LATIN AMERICAN
        DEVELOPMENT STUDIES. DISCUSSION PAPER SERIES No. 41:1-35,
        June 1980.

        Content: 1) The small-industrialized economy and its
        balance of payments adjustment mechanism; 2) Multisectoral
        models of adjustment to export shortfalls; 3) Simulation
        results for Peru; 4) Policy conclusions.

424   Simai, M.
        The public sector and the international economic positions
        of developing countires.   ACTA OECONOMICA (BUDAPEST)
        22:127-41, no 1/2, 1979.

425   Singer, Hans W. and Javed Ansari
        Trade access and employment in developing countries:
        a survey. CANADIAN JOURNAL OF DEVELOPMENT STUDIES
        1:288-301, no. 2, 1980.

426   Smith, Sheila and John Troye
        Introduction: three stories about trade and poor economies.
        JOURNAL OF DEVELOPMENT STUDIES 15:1-18, April 1979.

        The authors examine three broad policy attitudes and
        the fundamental assumptions of the appropriate type of
        theory.   Then they reexamine some of these assumptions
        in order to find out why the types of theory are mutually
        incompatible; and then which assumptions are to be
        preferred as the more reasonable ones.

427   Sobhan, Rehman
       Enhancing trade between OPEC and the developing countries
       of Asia. THIRD WORLD QUARTERLY 4:719-35, Oct. 1982.

428   Srinivasan, T. N.
       Trade, development and factor movements. YALE UNIVERSITY.
       ECONOMIC GROWTH CENTER. CENTER DISCUSSION PAPER No.
       393:1-29, Jan. 1982.

429   Stein, Leslie
       The growth and implications of LDC manufactured exports
       to advanced countries. KYKLOS (BASEL) 34:36-59, 1981.

430   Stremlau, J., ed.
       International relations of developing ocuntries. JOURNAL
       OF INTERNATIONAL AFFAIRS 34:1-178, Spring 1980.

431   Tanzi, Vito
       Export taxation in developing countries; taxation of
       coffee in Haiti. SOCIAL AND ECONOMIC STUDIES 25:66-76,
       March 1976.

       Describes the organization of the coffee sector in Haiti
       since that organization is very important in the analysis
       of the incidence of the tax. Then the taxation of coffee
       is discussed and some conclusions are derived from the
       Haitian experience.

432   Taylor, Lance
       North-South trade and Southern growth; bleak prospects
       from the structuralist point of view. JOURNAL OF
       INTERNATIONAL ECONOMICS 11:589-602, Nov. 1981.

433   Thirlwall, A. P.
       When is trade more valuable than aid? JOURNAL OF
       DEVELOPMENT STUDIES 13:35-41, October 1976.

434   Tinbergen, J.
       International trade, protectionism and the Third World.
       MAANDSCHRIFT ECONOMIE (TILBURG) 44, No. 2:74-80, 1980.

435   Togan, S.
       Gains from international trade in the context of a growing
       economy. JOURNAL OF INTERNATIONAL ECONOMICS 5:229-38,
       August 1975.

436   Trade and industrialization in developing countries
       (special issue). DEVELOPING ECONOMIES 16:341-446, Dec.
       1978.

437   Tyler, W. G.
       Growth and export expansion in developing countries:
       some empirical evidence. JOURNAL OF DEVELOPING ECONOMIES
       9:121-30, August 1981.

438   United Nations Conference on Trade and Development
       The developing countries in the world economy.   OPEC
       REVIEW 4:65-84, Autumn 1980.

439   United Nations Department of International Economic and
       Social Affairs
       Supplement to World Economic Survey, 1978:   The expansion
       of exports from developing countries and policies of
       structural adjustment in developed countries.

440   Vanek, J.
       Tariffs, economic welfare and development potential.
       ECONOMIC JOURNAL 81 (December 1971): 904.

441   Verma, P. C.
       Geographical concentration of foreign trade of India,
       Bangladesh and Pakistan. MARGIN; QUARTERLY JOURNAL OF
       THE NATIONAL COUNCIL OF APPLIED ECONOMIC RESEARCH 13:62-74,
       Oct. 1980.

442   Verma, P. C.
       Commodity concentration of foreign trade of India,
       Bangladesh and Pakistan. MARGIN; QUARTERLY JOURNAL OF
       THE NATIONAL COUNCIL OF APPLIED ECONOMIC RESEARCH 13:35-46,
       April 1981.

443   Vickery, Edward
       Exports and North American economic growth:
       "structuralist" and "staple" models in historical
       perspective. CANADIAN JOURNAL OF ECONOMICS (February
       1974).

444   Walleri, R. D.
       Trade dependence and underdevelopment: a causal-chain
       analysis. COMPARATIVE POLITICAL STUDIES 11:94-127, April
       1978.

445   Walter, Ingo and Chung, Jae W.
       Non-tariff distortions and trade preferences for developing
       countries. KYKLOS 24 (1971).

446   Wionczek, Miguel S.
       Pacific trade and development cooperation with Latin
       America. ASIA PACIFIC COMMUNITY No. 9:21-41, Summer
       1980.

447   Willmore, L. N.
       Free trade in manufactures among developing countries:
       the Central American experience. ECONOMIC DEVELOPMENT
       AND CULTURAL CHANGE 20 (July 1972): 659-70.

448   Wolfe, Lindsay A.
       World trade in perspective...data show rising share for
       oil exporters, decrease for other developing countries.
       IMF SURVEY (WASHINGTON) 10:49, 58-61, 23, Feb. 1981.

Presents a statistical summary of the annual trade flows over the period 1948 through 1979 among the major areas of the world, using data stored in the master file of the IMF Bureau of Statistics.

449   World trade outlook for the Far East and South Asia. OVERSEAS BUSINESS REPORT OBR-78-37:1-11, Sept. 1978.

450   World trade outlook for Near East and North Africa. OVERSEAS BUSSINESS REPORTS OBR 78-40:1-11, Sept. 1978.

451   World trade outlook for Latin America. OVERSEAS BUSINESS REPORTS OBR 79-07:1-7, March 1979.

452   World trade outlook for Africa. OVERSEAS BUSINESS REPORTS OBR 79-06:1-7, March 1979.

453   World trade outlook for Eastern Europe, Union of Soviet Socialist Republics and People's Republic of China. OVERSEAS BUSiNESS REPORTS OBR 76-06:1-6, March 1976.

454   World trade outlook for 64 countries. OVERSEAS BUSINESS REPORTS OBR 81-24:1-45, Sept. 1981.

455   Yassin, Ibrahim H.
When is trade more valuable than aid?: revisited. WORLD DEVELOPMENT 10:161-66, Feb. 1982.

III. SPECIALIZED PUBLICATIONS
(REPORTS, DOCUMENTS AND DIRECTORIES)

456   Administration for Development: A Comparative Perspective on the Middle East and Latin America, edited by Jack W. Hopkins, contains six papers presented at a meeting on the above theme, held at Indiana University in May 1976. Copies are available from the School of Public and Environmental Affairs, Indiana University, Bloomington, Indiana 47401, USA.

457   Agricultural Development and the Rural Poor, edited by Guy Hunter, is based on an international seminar in May 1978 sponsored by the Overseas Development Institute. The meeting considered the need for a radical review of both the policies and implementation of agricultural development in the Third World. Copies are available from ODI Sales, Montagu House, Huntingdon, Cambridgeshire, United Kingdom.

458   Black Africa--A Comparative Handbook, by Donald Morrison, offers country profiles for the 32 independent black African nations. In addition, the reference provides comparative profiles in the fields of demogrphy, ecology,

social and economic development, political development,
security systems and stability, international linkages,
and urban and ethnic patterns. The document is available
from the Free Press, 866 Third Avenue, New York, New York
10022, USA. Maps and bibliographies are included for
each country profile.

459   Criteria for Evaluation of Development Projects Involving
Women was prepared by the Subcommittee on Women in
Development of the Committee on Development Assistance,
American Council of Voluntary Agencies for Foreign Service.
The criteria are set forth and then tested against six
sample development projects. The booklet is available
from the Technical Assistance Information Clearing House,
ACVAFS, 200 Park Avenue South, New York, New York 10003.

460   The Development of Development Thinking is the theme of
the OECD Development Centre's Liaison Bulletin--1977/1.
The report contains papers and discussion summaries of
the First Inter-Regional Meeting on Development Research,
Communication and Education, organized by the OECD
Development Centre and Institute of Development Studies
in 1976. "New Development Strategies," "Collective
Self-Reliance," and "Inter-Regional Co-operation" are
the major subject areas. Copies are available from OECD
Publications, 2, rue Andre-Pascal, 75775 Paris Cedex 16,
France, or from any OECD sales agent.

461   Development Planning in Ecuador, by R. J. Bromley, presents
a picture of Ecuador in the first half of 1976 against
a background of historical trends and with short-term
projections into the future. Copies are available from
Grant & Cutler Ltd., 11 Buckingham Street, London WC2N
6DQ, England.

462   Development Studies--United Kingdom Research Register
1976, edited by G. E. Gorman, is a guide to current
development studies research in Great Britain. The 450
projects listed represent a wide range of institutions
and agencies involved in development research. Copies
are available from IDS Communications, Institute of
Development Studies, University of Sussex, Brighton, Sussex
BN1 9RE, United Kingdom.

463   Directory of Activities of International Voluntary Agencies
in Rural Development in Africa (Third Edition) contains
description of thirty-seven agencies and their rural
development projects in Africa. Copies may be obtained
from the Voluntary Agencies Bureau, Social Development
Division, U.N. Economic Commission for Africa, P.O. Box
3001, Addis Ababa, Ethiopia.

464   Directory of Economic and Social Development Research
and Training Units in OECD Member Countries/1976--No.

3-4 describes some 300 economic and social development research and training institutions in OECD Member Countries. All information is valid as of January 1977. Copies of the Directory are available from any OECD Sales Office or from OECD Publications, 2, rue Andre-Pascal, 75775 Paris Cedex 16, France.

465   Directory of Financial Aids for International Activities contains information on 231 sources of grants to individuals for study abroad. The guide includes geographic, subject, type, and level of eligibility indexes. Copies are available from the Office of International Programs, University of Minnesota, 201 Nolte West, Minneapolis, Minnesota 55455.

466   A Directory of Institutional Resources: U.S. Centers of Competence for International Development describes the resources and services of U.S. universities that are involved in overseas development programs. The directory is available from TA/PPU/EUI, Room 2669, Agency for International Development, U.S. Department of State, Washington, D.C. 20523.

467   A Directory of Non-Commercial Organisations in Britain Actively Concerned with Overseas Development and Training is the third edition prepared by the British Overseas Development Institute. Some 200 agencies are described in the new edition. Copies are available from ODI Sales, Montagu House, High Street, Huntingdon, Cambs. PE18 6EP, England.

468   Directory of Social Research and Training Units--Africa was prepared by the OECD Development Centre. The document, with introductions in French and English, contains a descriptive listing of institutions in some thirty-seven African countries. Also included are a subject index, index of directors and list of institution periodicals. Copies of the document are available from OECD Publications, 2, rue Andre-Pascal, 75775 Paris Cedex 16, France.

469   A Directory of Social Science Research and Training UNITS--Latin America updates a previous listing prepared by the OECD Development Centre. The directory contains descriptive summaries of institutions classified by country and also provides an alphabetical list of institutions, index of directors, subject index, and periodical guide. It is available from OECD Publications, 2, rue Andre Pascal, 75775 Paris Cedex 16, France.

470   The Directory of United Nations Information Systems and Services lists all the information activities of the United Nations system. It contains details on more than 100 information sources, and covers subjects ranging from human rights to industry. Also listed are some

2500 addresses of local offices of organizations and information centers in 155 countries. Copies are available to organizations, universities and libraries from the Director, IOB Secretariat, Palais des Nations, CH-1211 Geneva 10, Switzerland.

471   Dissertation Abstracts Relating to International Agricultural and Rural Development, Volumes I, II, II and IV, compiled by N. S. Peabody, III contain abstracts of participants in Cornell University's Program in International Agriculture. Single copies are available from the New York State College of Agriculture and Life Sciences, Cornell University, Ithaca, New York 14850.

472   Education and Training for Public Sector Management in Developing Countries, edited by Laurence D. Stifel, James S. Coleman, and Joseph E. Black, contains nine papers on various aspects of training for development administration. Copies may be obtained from The Rockefeller Foundation, 1133 Avenue of the Americas, New York, New York 10036.

473   Employment in Developing Countries, by Edgar O. Edwards, is based on a Ford Foundation study. The report discusses the nature of the employment problem, environmental factors which limit the choice of employment programs, and various strategies for handling the problem, including program options for donor agencies. The document is available from the Ford Foundation, Office of Reports, 320 East 43rd Street, New York, New York 10017.

474   The European Community and the Third World describes in depth all the European Community programs on behalf of the developing countries. The booklet is available from the Commission of the European Communities, Rue de la Loi 200, 1049 Brussels, Belgium, or any Community press/information offices around the world.

475   Family Farms in Rural Development: A Comparative Study of Japan and Developing Countries in Asia, by Masakatsu Akino, Kazushi Ohkawa, and Saburo Yamada, is available from the International Development Center of Japan, Daini Shuwa Toranomon Bldg., 20 Sakuragawa-cho, Nishikubo, Shiba, Minato-ku, Tokyo 105, Japan.

476   Financial Resources for Industrial Projects in Developing Countries gives information on some 200 industrial development financing institutions in 100 countries, and on international banking and aid-giving institutions. The directory was compiled by the Investment Cooperative Programme Office of UNIDO. The document is available from this office, UNIDO, P.O. Box 707, A-1011, Vienna, Austria.

477   Glossary of Institutions Concerned with Latin America, 2nd Edition, is a reference guide to some 244 international, regional, governmental and private institutions concerned with Latin America and the Caribbean. The Glossary is available from the Information Centre, Canadian Association for Latin America, 42 Charles Street East, Toronto, Canada M4Y 1T4.

478   Government Finance Statistics Yearbook--1977, prepared by the International Monetary Fund, provides current data on the finances of IMF member governments. Material for each country is organized in three parts: the statistical tables, institutional tables, and where information is available, a derivation table followed by a statement on the coverage of the central government statistics. Copies of the Yearbook are available from the International Monetary Fund, Washington, D.C. 20431.

479   A Guide to the Economic Appraisal of Projects in Developing Countries is a publication of the British Ministry of Overseas Development. The Guide is designed to provide a practical basis for the economic appraisal of projects financed by the public sector and for screening private sector projects subject to public sector approval. Copies are available from Her Majesty's Stationery Office, 49 High Holborn, London WC1V 6HB, England.

480   Higher Education and Social Change--Volume 2, edited by Kenneth W. Thompson, Barbara R. Fogel, and Helen E. Danner, contains twenty-five case studies and seven special reports on higher institutions in the Third World and their approaches to development problems. The publication is available from Praeger Publishers, New York, Washington and London.

481   The Integration of Women in Development: Why? When? How?, by Ester Boserup and Christina Liljencrantz, explains how and why women's participation in development presents special problems, and makes proposals for resolving these problems. The booklet is designed for decision makers, leaders and training personnel concerned with the role of women in development. Copies are available from Room CN-300, United Nations Development Programme, New York, New York 10017.

482   International Directory of Women's Development Organizations contains information on 600 local and national women's organizations around the world, with emphasis on those in developing countries. The Directory was compiled by Franziska P. Hosken under auspices of the U.S. Agency for International Development. The guide is designed to provide basic contacts for communication among women's organizations, resource groups, and the international development community. Copies are available

from Women in Development, U.S. Agency for International Development, Washington, D.C. 20523.

483   Knowledge and Power: The Global Research and Development Budget, by Colin Norman, notes the disparities in research and development expenditures around the world, and stresses, the need to mobilize Third World R & D capacities. The publication is available from the Worldwatch Institute, 1776 Massachusetts Avenue, N.W., Washington, D.C. 20036.

484   A Management Approach to Project Appraisal and Evaluation with Special Reference to Non-Directly Productive Projects, by N. Imboden, is addressed to officials concerned with the management of development programs. The book is based on the premise that appraisal/evaluation frameworks must be adapted in the socio-economic situation of a given country. It is· available from OECD Publications, 2, rue Andre-Pascal, 75775 Paris Cedex 16, France, or from any OECD Sales Office.

485   National Objectives and Project Appraisal in Developing Countries, by Hartmut Schneider, analyzes whether and how national objectives are or might be taken into account in making project appraisals in developing countries. Major subject headings are: (1) Interrelations between national objectives; (2) Linking project appraisal to national objectives; and (3) Towards a new framework for project appraisal. Copies of the study are available from OECD Publications, 2, rue Andre-Pascal, 75775 Paris Cedex 16, France.

486   On the Strategy of Industrialization in Developing Countries and Experiences in Economic and Social Development in Socialist Countries (Parts I and II) contains papers presented at the 14th International Summer Seminar sponsored by the University of Economic Science "Bruno Leuschner" in Berlin in 1977. Both documents are available from the Institute for the Economy of Developing Countries, University of Economic Science "Bruno Leuschner", Hermann-Duncker-Strasse 8, 1157 Berlin, German Democratic Republic.

487   The Process of Development in the Middle East: Goals and Achievements is a summary of the 30th Annual Conference of The Middle East Institute, held in Washington, D.C., October 15-16, 1976. Copies are available from The Middle East Institute, 1761 N Street, N.W., Washington, D.C. 20036.

488   Promotion of Small-Scale Industries in Developing Countries, by Dr. Karl Wolfgang Menck is a report published by HWWA--Institut fur Wirtschaftforschung--Hamburg. It contains 57 abstracts of books and articles which are

concerned with various aspects of promotion of small-scale industries. Copies are available from HWWA--Institut fur Wirtschaftsforschung--Hamburg, Public Relations, Neuer Jungsfernstein 21, 2000 Hamburg 36, Germany.

489   Public Administration Training for the Less Developed Countries, edited by Irving Swerdlow and Marcus Ingle, reports on a conference sponsored by the Maxwell School of Citizenship and Public Affairs, held at Syracuse University, New York, April 18-19, 1974. The panels discussed such topics as "Agricultural Administration Training," "Public Administration and Public Enterprises," "Criteria for Improving Public Administration Training," "Urban and Rural Works Programs," and "Public Management and Development Assistance." Copies of the document may be obtained from the Maxwell School of Citizenship and Public Affairs, Syracuse University, Syracuse, New York 13210.

490   The 1978/79 Publications List of Third World Publications contains over 300 titles of pamphlets, books and teaching materials about the Third World. The listing is free from Third World Publications, Ltd., 151 Stratford Road, Birmingham B11 1RD, England.

491   Register of Development Research Projects in Africa notes 226 current development research projects in 21 African countries, classified by country and institution. It contains project descriptions as well as indexes of researchers, institutions and financial sponsors. The OECD Development Centre prepared the Register, and is also working on similar volumes for Latin America and Asia. For more information contact the OECD Development Centre, 94, rue Chardon Lagache, 75016 Paris, France.

492   Register of Research Projects in Progress in Development Studies in Selected European Countries was prepared by the Centre for Development Studies of the University of Antwerp at the request of The European Association of Development Research and Training Institutes. Copies are available from the Centre, St. Ignatius Faculties, University of Antwerp, 13 Prinsstraat, 2000 Antwerp, Belgium.

493   Report to Congress on Women in Development, prepared by the Office of Women in Development of the U.S. Agency for International Development, assesses the impact of U.S. development aid programs on the integration of women into the developing economies of countries receiving assistance. The report contains five parts: Summary and evaluation; Introduction; Specific projects in Africa, Asia, Latin America, and the Near East plus activities in the area of population; data section; and description of AID programs in the area of women in development.

Copies are available from Office of Women in Development,
Room 3243 NS, Agency for International Development, U.S.
Department of State, Washington, D.C. 20523.

494   Resources for Development: Organizations and Publications,
edited by David A. Tyler, notes agencies and publications
in the U.S., Africa, Asia and Latin America that would
be useful to Peace Corps field workers in coordinating
their programs with other local development efforts.
Copies are available from the Office of Multilateral
and Special Programs, Action/Peace Corps, 806 Connecticut
Avenue, N.W., Washington, D.C. 20525.

495   The Role of Rural Women in Development is based on a
conference sponsored by the Agricultural Development
Council, held in Princeton, New Jersey, December 2-4,
1974. The report summarizes the meeting and lists the
participants and major papers presented. Copies are
available from the Agricultural Development Council,
1290 Avenue of the Americas, New York, NY 10019.

496   Rural Development Planning in Zambia: Objectives,
Strategies and Achievements, by Joachim Luhring, is a
socioeconomic analysis with special reference to problems
of administration and regional planning. The monograph
is available from the African Training and Research Centre
in Administration for Development (CAFRAD), P.O. Box
310, Tangier, Morocco.

497   Social Development and the International Development
Strategy is a brief paper prepared by the staff of the
United Nations Research Institute for Social Development.
Copies may be obtained from the Institute, Palais des
Nations, 1211 Geneva 10, Switzerland.

498   Social and Economic Development Plans--Microfiche Project
is a cumulative catalogue listing the holdings of Inter
Documentation Company AG on social and economic development
plans around the world. About 1400 plans from over 180
countries are included. Copies of the catalogue and
other catalogues of IDC's microfiche projects are free
on request from Inter Documentation Company AG, Poststrasse
14, 6300 Zug-Switzerland.

499   Systems Approaches to Developing Countries contains the
proceedings of the First IFAC/IFORS (International
Federation of Automatic Control and International
Federation of Operational Research Societies) Symposium
on the topic, held in May 1973, in Algiers, Algeria.
The sixty-six papers in the book were written by
authorities representing twenty countries. The papers
present the systems engineering approach for the following
applications: Management and Development Policies;
Agriculture and Food; Power Generation; Water and Pollution

Control; Urban Planning, Transport and Communications; Gas, Oil and Cement Industries; Methodology; Education and Health; Human Resources; and International Cooperation and Development. The document is available from the Instrument Society of America, Publications Department, 400 Stanwix Street, Pittsburgh, Pennsylvania 15222.

500   Third World Deficits and the "Debt Crisis," prepared by the North-South Institute, is a comprehensive analysis of the debt problem of developing countries with suggestions for action in debt relief. Copies of the booklet are available from the North-South Institute, 185 Rideau Street, Ottawa, Canada K1N 5X8.

501   The United States and the Developing Countries is a report of the Atlantic Council Working Group on the United States and the Developing Countries. The report reviews U.S. development policy and suggests some guidelines for future action. Copies are available from Westview Press, Inc., 1898 Flatiron Court, Boulder, Colorado 80301.

502   The University Center for Cooperatives has issued a new Directory of International Training Programs, a listing of programs which it is offering at the University of Wisconsin. Copies are available from the University Center for Cooperatives, 524 Lowell Hall, 610 Langdon Street, Madison, Wisconsin 53706.

503   Women and World Development, edited by Irene Tinker and Michele Bo Bramsen, contains twelve essays prepared as background papers for the American Association for the Advancement of Science Seminar on Women in Development, held in Mexico City, June, 1975. Also included are the Proceedings of the Seminar. Copies are available from the Overseas Development Council, 1717 Massachusetts Avenue, N.W., Washington, D.C. 20036.

504   The World Directory of Social Science Institutions: Research, Advanced Training, Documentation and Professional Bodies has been updated by Unesco. For copies write to Unesco, 7 Place de Fontenoy, 75700 Paris, France.

IV. BIBLIOGRAPHIC SUBJECT INDEX

PART IV
DIRECTORY OF
INFORMATION
SOURCES

I. UNITED NATIONS INFORMATION SOURCES

AUDIO MATERIALS LIBRARY
United Nations, Department of Public Information, Radio and Visual
Services Division, United Nations Plaza, New York, NY 10017.

DAG HAMMARSKJOLD LIBRARY
United Nations, Department of Conference Services, United Nations
Plaza, New York, NY 10017.

UNITED NATIONS BIBLIOGRAPHIC INFORMATION SYSTEM
United Nations, Department of Conference Services, Dag Hammarskjold
Library, United Nations Plaza, New York, NY 10017.

UNBIS DATA BASE
United Nations, Department of Conference Services, Dag Hammarskjold
Library, United Nations Plaza, New York, NY 10017.

DEVELOPMENT INFORMATION SYSTEM
United Nations, Department of International Economic and Social
Affairs, Information Systems Unit, Room DC 594, New York, NY
10017.

DEVELOPMENT INFORMATION SYSTEM DATA BASE
United Nations, Department of International Economic and Social
Affairs, Information Systems Unit, Room DC 594, New York, NY
10017.

**REFERENCE UNIT OF THE OFFICE FOR DEVELOPMENT RESEARCH AND POLICY
ANALYSIS**
United Nations, Department of International Economic and Social
Affairs, Office for Development Research and Policy Analysis,
New York, NY 10017.

MACRO-ECONOMIC DATA BANK AND TABLE PROCESSING SYSTEM
United Nations, Department of International Economic and Social

Affairs, Office for Development Research and Policy Analysis, New York, NY 10017.

MACRO-ECONOMIC DATA BANK AND TABLE PROCESSING SYSTEM DATA BASE
United Nations, Department of International Economic and Social Affairs, Office for Development Research and Policy Analysis, New York, NY 10017.

UNITED NATIONS PHOTO LIBRARY
United Nations, Department of Public Information, Radio and Visual Services Division, United Nations Plaza, New York, NY 10017.

EXTERNAL TRADE STATISTICS
United Nations, Department of International Economic and Social Affairs, Statistical Office, New York, NY 10017.

INTEGRATED STATISTICAL INFORMATION SYSTEM
United Nations, Department of International Economic and Social Affairs, Statistical Office, New York, NY 10017.

UNITED NATIONS VISUAL MATERIAL LIBRARY
United Nations, Department of Public Information, Radio and Visual Services Division, United Nations Plaza, New York, NY 10017.

WORLD ENERGY SUPPLIES SYSTEM
United Nations, Department of International Economic and Social Affairs, Statistical Office, New York, NY 10017.

WORLD STATISTICS IN BRIEF
United Nations, Department of International Economic and Social Affairs, Statistical Office, New York, NY 10017.

LIBRARY OF THE UNITED NATIONS COMMISSION ON INTERNATIONAL TRADE LAW
United Nations Commission on International Trade Law, United Nations Legal Office, P.O. Box 500, Vienna International Centre, Wagramer Strasse 5, 1400 Vienna, Austria.

UNITED NATIONS LIBRARY AT GENEVA
United Nations Office at Geneva, 8-14, avenue de la Paix, Palais des Nations, 1211 Geneva 10, Switzerland.

INFORMATION SERVICES ON FACILITATION OF INTERNATIONAL TRADE PROCEDURES
Economic Commission for Europe, Trade and Technology Division, Palais des Nations, 1211 Geneva 10, Switzerland.

ESCAP LIBRARY
Economic and Social Commission for Asia and the Pacific, United Nations Building, Rajadamnern Avenue, Bangkok 2, Thailand.

ESCAP BIBLIOGRAPHIC INFORMATION MASTER FILE
Economic and Social Commission for Asia and the Pacific (ESCAP), Library, United Nations Building, Rajadamnern Avenue, Bangkok 2, Thailand.

ESCAP DOCUMENTATION INFORMATION SYSTEM
Economic and Social Commission for Asia and the Pacific, Library,
United Nations Building, Rajadamnern Avenue, Bangkok 2, Thailand.

ESCAP LIBRARY SERIALS INFORMATION SYSTEM
Economic and Social Commission for Asia and the Pacific, Library,
United Nations Building, Rajadamnern Avenue, Bangkok 2, Thailand.

ESCAP LIBRARY SERIALS DATA BASE
Economic and Social Commission for Asia and the Pacific, ESCAP
Library, United Nations Building, Rajadamnern Avenue, Bangkok
2, Thailand.

UNESCAP/STATISTICS INFORMATION SYSTEM
Economic and Social Commission for Asia and the Pacific, Statistics
Division, United Nations Building, Rajadamnern Avenue, Bangkok
2, Thailand.

FOREIGN TRADE STATISTICS OF ASIA AND THE PACIFIC
Economic and Social Commission for Asia and the Pacific, Statistics
Division, United Nations Building, Rajadamnern Avenue, Bangkok
2, Thailand.

QUARTERLY BULLETIN OF STATISTICS FOR ASIA AND THE PACIFIC
Economic and Social Commission for Asia and the Pacific, Statistics
Division, United Nations Building, Rajadamnern Avenue, Bangkok
2, Thailand.

STATISTICAL INDICATORS FOR ASIA AND THE PACIFIC
Economic and Social Commission for Asia and the Pacific, Statistics
Division, United Nations Building, Rajadamnern Avenue, Bangkok
2, Thailand.

STATISTICAL YEARBOOK FOR ASIA AND THE PACIFIC
Economic and Social Commission for Asia and the Pacific, Statistics
Division, United Nations Building, Rajadamnern Avenue, Bangkok
2, Thailand.

TRADE INFORMATION SERVICE
Economic and Social Commission for Asia and the Pacific, Trade
Promotion Centre (TPC), International Trade Division, United
Nations Building, Rajadamnern Avenue, Bangkok 2, Thailand.

LATIN AMERICAN FOREIGN TRADE STATISTICS AND REPORTS SYSTEM
Economic Commission for Latin America, Statistics Division, Casilla
179D, Edificio Naciones Unidas, Avenida Dag Hammarskjold, Santiago,
Chile.

CARIBBEAN DOCUMENTATION CENTRE
Economic Commission for Latin America, CEPAL Office for the
Caribbean, P.O. Box 1113, Room 300 Salvatori Building, Port of
Spain, Trinidad and Tobago.

JOINT CEPAL/ILPES LIBRARY
Economic Commission for Latin America, Latin American Institute

for Economic and Social Planning, Casilla 179-D, Edificio Naciones Unidas, Avenida Dag Hammarskjold, Santiago, Chile.

DATA BANK
Economic Commission for Africa, Statistics Division, P.O. Box 3001, Africa Hall, Addis Ababa, Ethiopia.

EXTERNAL TRADE DATA BASE
Economic Commission for Africa, Statistics Division, P.O. Box 3001, Africa Hall, Addis Ababa, Ethiopia.

ECA LIBRARY
Economic Commission for Africa, P.O. Box 3001, Africa Hall, Addis Ababa, Ethiopia.

ECWA LIBRARY
Economic Commission for Western Asia, Administration, P.O. Box 4656, United Nations Building, Bir Hassan, Beirut, Lebanon.

UNITAR LIBRARY
United Naitons Institute for Training and Research, 801 United Nations Plaza, New York, NY 10017.

SOIL FERTILITY DATA FILE
Food and Agriculture Organization of the United Nations, Agriculture Department, Land and Water Development Division, Via delle Terme di Caracalla, 00100 Rome, Italy.

EXTERNAL PUBLIC DEBT
The World Bank, Economic Analysis and Projections Department, External Debt Division, 1818 H Street, N.W., Washington, D.C. 20433.

IMF DATA FUND SYSTEM
International Monetary Fund, Bureau of Statistics, 700 19th Street, N.W., Washington, D.C. 20431.

IMF DATA FUND SYSTEM DATA BASE
International Monetary Fund, Bureau of Statistics, 700 19th Street, N.W., Washington, D.C. 20431.

JOINT BANK-FUND LIBRARY
International Monetary Fund, 700 19th Street, N.W., Washington, D.C. 20431.

II. BIBLIOGRAPHY OF BIBLIOGRAPHIES

ANNOTATED BIBLIOGRAPHY OF COUNTRY SERIALS is a listing of periodicals, annuals and other serials containing information of economic, business or trade interest. The listing is organized on a regional and country basis. Copies are available from the Documentation Service, International Trade Centre UNCTAD/GATT, 1211 Geneva 10, Switzerland.

BASIC-NEEDS APPROACH: A SURVEY OF ITS LITERATURE, edited by M. Rutjes, contains a brief analysis of the concept of basic needs, its targets, its strategy and implications, followed by a concise bibliography related to the topic. Copies may be obtained from the Centre for the Study of Education in Developing Countries, Badhuisweg 251, The Hague, The Netherlands.

DEVELOPMENT PLANS AND PLANNING - BIBLIOGRAPHIC AND COMPUTER AIDS TO RESEARCH, by August Schumacher, is arranged in three parts. The first contains more than 100 selected bibliographies on development plans and planning, the second is concerned with a new source of empirical materials for the development planner - the automated documentation centre, and the third analyzes recent work on computer aids for the research library. The publication is available from Seminar Press Ltd., 24-28 Oval Road, London NW1, England.

BIBLIOGRAPHY ON DEVELOPMENT EDUCATION lists books, manuals, resource materials, magazines, and articles in the field of development education. The listing was prepared by the Dutch Central Bureau of Catholic Education. Copies are available from the Central Bureau of Catholic Education, G. Verstijnen, Secretary Foreign Department, Bezuidenhoutseweg 275, The Hague, Netherlands.

BIBLIOGRAPHY OF GERMAN RESEARCH ON DEVELOPING COUNTRIES, prepared by the German Foundation for International Development, is divided into two sections: Part A contains an index of research institutes, author index, subject-matter index, and a geographical index. Part B contains specific information on each of the studies listed. The text is in German with explanatory notes in German, English, French and Spanish. Copies may be obtained from the Deutsche Stiftung fur Internationale Entwicklung (DSE), Endenicher Strasse 41, 53 Bonn, Federal Republic of Germany.

BIBLIOGRAPHY OF SELECTED LATIN AMERICAN PUBLICATIONS ON DEVELOPMENT is a listing of over 200 titles in Latin American development literature, including subject and author indexes. The document was prepared by the Institute of Development Studies Library. Copies are available from the Librarian, Institute of Development Studies, University of Sussex, Brighton BN1 9RE, England.

CANADIAN DEVELOPMENT ASSISTANCE: A SELECTED BIBLIOGRAPHY 1950-70, compiled by Shirley B. Seward and Helen Janssen, covers Canada's foreign aid programs and policies from 1950 to 1970. Copies are available from the Distribution Unit, International Development Research Centre, P.O. Box 8500, Ottawa, Canada KIG 3H9.

DEVINDEX CANADA is a bibliography of literature on social and economic development in Third World countries, which originated in Canada in 1975. Copies may be obtained from the International Development Research Centre, Box 8500, Ottawa, Canada KIG 3H9.

The UNESCO Division of Scientific Research and Higher Education has compiled **A DIRECTORY AND BIBLIOGRAPHY ON THE THEME "RESEARCH AND HUMAN NEEDS"**, listing organizations, journals, newsletters, reports ard papers, information services and data banks. The bibliographical section includes headings such as food and nutrition, health, housing and sanitation, environment, energy, technology. For copies contact "Research and Human Needs", Division of Scientific Research and Higher Education, UNESCO, Place de Fontenoy, 75007 Paris, France.

GUIDE TO CURRENT DEVELOPMENT LITERATURE ON ASIA AND THE PACIFIC is published every two months by the Library and Documentation Centre of the Asia Pacific Development Information Service. For more information write to the Centre, United Nations Asian and Pacific Development Institute, P.O. Box 2-136, Sri Aydudhya Road, Bangkok, Thailand.

Hald, Marjorie W.
A SELECTED BIBLIOGRAPHY ON ECONOMIC DEVELOPMENT AND FOREIGN AID, rev. ed., Santa Monica, CA: The Rand Corporation, 1958.

Hazelwood, Arthur
THE ECONOMICS OF "UNDERDEVELOPED" AREAS: AN ANNOTATED READING LIST OF BOOKS, ARTICLES, AND OFFICIAL PUBLICATIONS. London: Oxford University Press for the Institute of Colonial Studies, 1954. 623 titles.

THE ECONOMICS OF DEVELOPMENT: AN ANNOTATED LIST OF BOOKS AND ARTICLES PUBLISHED 1958-1962. London: Oxford University Press, for the Institute of Commonwealth Studies, 1964.

INTERNATIONAL BIBLIOGRAPHY, INFORMATION DOCUMENTATION (IBID) provides bibliographic details and annotations necessary to identify the full range of publications prepared by the United Nations and its related agencies, plus those of ten organizations outside the UN system. IBID is published quarterly by Unipub. Available from Unipub, Box 433, Murray Hill Station, New York, New York 10016, USA.

THE 1978/79 PUBLICATIONS LIST OF THIRD WORLD PUBLICATIONS contains over 300 titles of pamphlets, books and teaching materials about the Third World. The listing is available from Third World Publications, Ltd., 151 Stratford Road, Birmingham B11 1RD, England.

A list of 200 books on **NORTH-SOUTH WORLD RELATIONS** has been compiled by the Developing Country Courier. The listing is organized by subject and region. For copies write to the Courier, P.O. Box 239, McLean, Virginia 22101, USA.

United States Agency for International Development
A PRACTICAL BIBLIOGRAPHY FOR DEVELOPING AREAS. Washington, D.C., 1966. 2 vols. (Vol. 1 - A selective, annotated and graded list of United States publications in the social sciences. 202 pp.) (Vol. 2 - A selective, annotated and graded list of United States publications in the physical and applied sciences. 332 pp.)

PUBLIC ADMINISTRATION--A SELECT BIBLIOGRAPHY, prepared by the British Ministry of Overseas Development Library is the second supplement to the 1973 revised edition. Copies may be obtained from Eland House, Stag Place, London SW1E 5DH, England.

PUBLIC ADMINISTRATION--A SELECT BIBLIOGRAPHY, prepared by the Library of the British Ministry of Overseas Development, is a supplement to the revised edition which appeared in 1973. It includes material published in the period 1972-1975 with 1,600 references. Copies may be obtained from the Library, British Ministry of Overseas Development, Eland House, Stag Place, London SW1E 5DH, England.

The OECD Development Centre has gathered together in the catalog **PUBLICATION AND DOCUMENT, 1962-1979** all the books and documents it has published since its establishment in 1962 up to August 1979. Copies available from OECD Development Centre, 94 rue Chardon Lagache, 75016 Paris, France.

REGISTER OF RESEARCH PROJECTS IN PROGRESS IN DEVELOPMENT STUDIES IN SELECTED EUROPEAN COUNTRIES was prepared by the Centre for Development Studies of the University of Antwerp at the request of the European Association of Development Research and Training Institutes. Copies are available from the Centre, St. Ignatius

Faculties, University of Antwerp, 13 Prinsstraat, 2000 Antwerp, Belgium.

Re Qua, Eloise and Statham, Jane
THE DEVELOPING NATIONS: A GUIDE TO INFORMATION SOURCES CONCERNING THEIR ECONOMIC, POLITICAL, TECHNICAL AND SOCIAL PROBLEMS. Detroit: Gale Research Company, 1965.

The East African Academy has published two new bibliographies. **SCIENCE AND TECHNOLOGY IN EAST AFRICA** contains more than 5,000 titles about research in the agriculture, medical technological, and related fields in East Africa, with short summaries on the problems and progress of research in these areas. **TANZANIA EDUCATION SINCE UHURU: A BIBLIOGRAPHY--1961-1971** was compiled by Dr. George A. Auger of the University of Dar es Salaam. Both publications are available from the East African Academy, RIPS, P.O. Box 47288, Nairobi, Kenya.

SELECTIVE ANNOTATED BIBLIOGRAPHY ON BRAZILIAN DEVELOPMENT has been prepared by the SID Sao Paulo Chapter. This first issue contains only references that have appeared in 1975. Copies are available from the Society for International Development, Sao Paulo Chapter, Caixa Postal 20.270-Vila Clementino, 04023-Sao Paulo-S.P. Brazil.

A SELECTED ANNOTATED BIBLIOGRAPHY: INDIGENOUS TECHNICAL KNOWLEDGE IN DEVELOPMENT, compiled by Liz O'Keefe and Michael Howes, is contained in the January 1979 IDS BULLETIN. This issue of the BULLETIN is devoted to the importance of indigenous technical knowledge in rural areas. Single copies of the BULLETIN are from the Communications Office, Institute of Development Studies, University of Sussex, Brighton N1 9RE, United Kingdom.

SELECTED BIBLIOGRAPHY OF RECENT ECONOMIC DEVELOPMENT PUBLICATIONS covers a period of one year, from July 1977 to June 1978 and contains two main sections, one for general and theoretical works, the other for literature related to regions and countries. For copies write to the Graduate Program in Economic Development, Vanderbilt University, Nashville, Tennessee 37235, USA.

International Bank for Reconstruction and Development; Economic Development Institute
SELECTED READINGS AND SOURCE MATERIALS ON ECONOMIC DEVELOPMENT.
A list of books, articles, and reports included in a small library assembled by the Economic Development Institute, Washington, D.C., 1961.

SOCIAL AND ECONOMIC DEVELOPMENT PLANS - MICROFICHE PROJECT is a cumulative catalogue listing the holdings of Inter Documentation Company AG on social and economic development plans around the world. About 1400 plans from over 180 countries are included. Copies of the catalogue and other catalogues of IDC's microfiche projects are free on request from Inter Documentation Company AG, Poststrasse 14, 6300 Zug-Switzerland.

Powelson, John
A SELECT BIBLIOGRAPHY ON ECONOMIC DEVELOPMENT.   Boulder, Colorado:
Westview Press, 1979.

THIRD WORLD BIBLIOGRAPHY AND RESOURCE GUIDE features a wide range
of material on Third World issues.   It is designed for students
and general readers.   Copies may be obtained from the Development
Education Library Project, c/o OSFAM/Ontario, 175 Carlton Street,
Toronto, Canada.

The United Nations Asian and Pacific Development Institute has
prepared a SPECIAL BIBLIOGRAPHY ON ALTERNATIVE STRATEGIES FOR
DEVELOPMENT WITH FOCUS ON LOCAL LEVEL PLANNING AND DEVELOPMENT
in connection with a UNAPDI meeting, held in Bangkok, October
31 - November 4, 1978.   Copies are available from the APDI Library
and Documentation Centre.   UNAPDI, P.O. Box 2-136, Sri Ayudhya
Road, Bangkok, Thailand.

Vente, Role and Dieter Seul
MACRO-ECONOMIC   PLANNING: A   BIBLIOGRAPHY.   Nomos
Verlagsgesellshaft, Baden-Baden, 1970.

Volunteers in Technical Assistance (VITA) has published its
1979 CATALOGUE OF BOOKS, BULLETINS AND MANUALS. The listing
contains VITA documents related to appropriate technology, as
well as materials published by other development organizations
around the world.   Copies are available from VITA, 2706 Rhode
Island Avenue, Mt. Ranier, Maryland 20822, USA.

DEVELOPMENT--A BIBLIOGRAPHY, was compiled by Vaptistis-Titos
Patrikios (Rome: FAO, 1974) and updates the first edition,
published in 1970, to cover the 1970/73 period.   Contains eight
sections relating to development: theories and problems;
perspectives of the Third World countries; population and food
production; aid, trade and international cooperation; agriculture;
manpower and employment; education; and environment.   A ninth
section lists bibliographies.

III. DIRECTORY OF PERIODICALS

ACTUEL DEVELOPPEMENT, English Digest Edition, Paris.

AFRICA, London, Africa Journal, Ltd.

AFRICA INSTITUTE, Pretoria, Africa Institute.

AFRICA QUARTERLY, New Delhi, India Council for Africa.

AFRICA RESEARCH BULLETIN, Exeter, Eng. Africa Research, Ltd.

AFRICA, SOUTH OF THE SAHARA, London, Europa Publications.

AFRICA TODAY, New York, American Committee on Africa.

AFRICAN AFFAIRS, London, Journal of the Royal African Society.

AFRICAN DEVELOPMENT, London.

AFRICAN DEVELOPMENT BANK, Annual Report, Ibadan.

AFRICAN ENVIRONMENT, Dakar, United Nations Environmental Program.

AFRICAN STATISTICAL YEARBOOK, Addis Ababa, Economic Commission for Africa.

AFRICAN STUDIES REVIEW, Stanford, Boston, East Lansing, African Studies Association.

AFRICAN URBAN STUDIES, East Lansing, Mich., African Studies Center.

AGENDA, Washington, D.C., U.S. Agency for International Development.

APPROPRIATE   TECHNOLOGY,   London,   Intermediate   Technology
Publications, Ltd.

APPROTECH, Ann Arbor, Mich., International Association for the
Advancement of Appropriate Technology for Developing Countries.

ARTHA VIJNANA, Poona, Gokhale Institute of Politics and Economics.

ASIA AND THE WORLD MONOGRAPHS, Taipei, Asia and the World Forum.

ASIA YEARBOOK, Hong Kong, Far Eastern Economic Review.

ASIAN AFFAIRS, London, Royal Central Asian Society.

ASIAN DEVELOPMENT BANK, Annual Report, Manila.

ASIAN REGIONAL CONFERENCE OF THE INTERNATIONAL LABOR ORGANIZATION,
Proceedings, Geneva, ILO.

ASIAN SURVEY, Berkeley, Institute of International Studies.

BANGLADESH DEVELOPMENT STUDIES, Dhaka, Bangladesh Institute of
Development Studies.

BANGLADESH ECONOMIC REVIEW, Dhaka, Bangladesh Institute of
Development Economics.

BULLETIN OF INDONESIAN ECONOMIC STUDIES, Canberra, Dept. of
Economics, Australian National University.

CEPAL REVIEW, Santiago, Chile.

CANADIAN JOURNAL OF AFRICAN STUDIES, Montreal, Loyola College.

COMMUNITY DEVELOPMENT JOURNAL, Manchester, U.K., Oxford University
Press.

DEVELOPING ECONOMIES, Tokyo, The Institute of Asian Economic
Affairs.

DEVELOPMENT, Rome, Society for International Development.

DEVELOPMENT CENTER STUDIES, OECD, Paris.

DEVELOPMENT AND CHANGE, Beverly Hills, Calif.: Sage Publications.

DEVELOPMENT CO-OPERATION, Paris, OECD.

DEVELOPMENT DIGEST, Washington, D.C., U.S. Agency for International
Development.

DEVELOPMENT DIALOGUE, Uppsala, Sweden, Dag Hammarskjold Foundation.

EASTERN AFRICA ECONOMIC REVIEW, Nairobi, Oxford University Press.

ECONOMIC DEVELOPMENT AND CULTURAL CHANGE, Chicago, University of Chicago Press.

ETHIOPIAN JOURNAL OF DEVELOPMENT RESEARCH, Addis Ababa, Institute of Development Research.

FAR EASTERN ECONOMIC REVIEW, Hong Kong.

FINANCE AND DEVELOPMENT, Washington, D.C.

IDS BULLETIN, Institute of Development Studies, University of Sussex, U.K.

IMPACT OF SCIENCE ON SOCIETY, Paris, UNESCO.

INDIAN JOURNAL OF INDUSTRIAL RELATIONS, New Delhi, India.

INDUSTRY AND DEVELOPMENT, Vienna, UNIDO.

INTERNATIONAL DEVELOPMENT REVIEW, Rome, Society for International Development.

INTERNATIONAL LABOR REVIEW, Geneva, ILO.

INTERNATIONAL STUDIES QUARTERLY, San Francisco.

JOURNAL OF AFRICAN STUDIES, Los Angeles, UCLA African Studies Center.

JOURNAL OF DEVELOPING AREAS, Macomb, IL, Western Illinois Univ.

JOURNAL OF DEVELOPMENT ECONOMICS, Amsterdam, North Holland Publishing Co.

JOURNAL OF DEVELOPMENT STUDIES, London, U.K.

JOURNAL OF ECONOMIC DEVELOPMENT, JOURNAL OF INTERNATIONAL AFFAIRS, New York, Columbia University.

JOURNAL OF MODERN AFRICAN STUDIES, New York, Cambridge University Press.

LATIN AMERICAN RESEARCH REVIEW, Chapel Hill, North Carolina.

MODERN ASIAN STUDIES, New York, Cambridge University Press.

MONOGRAPH, DEVELOPMENT STUDIES CENTER, AUSTRALIAN NATIONAL UNIVERSITY.

MONOGRAPH, OVERSEAS DEVELOPMENT COUNCIL, Washington, D.C.

ODI REVIEW, Overseas Development Institute, London, U.K.

OXFORD ECONOMIC PAPERS, Oxford, U.K.

PAKISTAN DEVELOPMENT REVIEW, Karachi, Pakistan.

PUBLIC ADMINISTRATION AND DEVELOPMENT, Sussex, U.K., Royal Institute of Public Administration.

THIRD WORLD QUARTERLY, London, Third World Foundation for Social and Economic Studies.

WORLD BANK STAFF WORKING PAPER, IBRD, Washington, D.C.

WORLD DEVELOPMENT, Pergamon Press, N.Y.

NOTE:

For more information on relevant periodicals please consult:

1. **DIRECTORY OF UNITED NATIONS INFORMATION SYSTEMS**

2. **REGISTER OF UNITED NATIONS SERIAL PUBLICATIONS**

Public by **Inter-Organization Board for Information Systems,** IOB Secretariat, Palais des Nations, CH-1211 Geneva 10, Switzerland.

IV. RESEARCH INSTITUTIONS

INTERNATIONAL (GENERAL)

AFRICAN INSTITUTE FOR ECONOMIC DEVELOPMENT AND PLANNING
United Nations Economic Commission for Africa, Dakar, Senegal.

AFRO-ASIAN ORGANIZATION FOR ECONOMIC CO-OPERATION
Chairo Chamber of Commerce Building, Midan el-Falsky, Cairo, Egypt.

ASIAN ASSOCIATION OF DEVELOPMENT RESEARCH AND TRAINING INSTITUTES
P.O. Box 2-136, Sri Ayudhya Road, Bangkok, Thailand.

ASIAN DEVELOPMENT CENTER
11th Floor, Philippines Banking Corporation Building, Anda Circle, Port Area, Manila, Philippines.

ASIAN INSTITUTE FOR ECONOMIC DEVELOPMENT AND PLANNING
P.O. Box 2-136, Sri Ayudhya Road, Bangkok, Thailand.

ATLANTIC INSTITUTE FOR INTERNATIONAL AFFAIRS
120, rue de Longchamp, 75016 Paris, France.

CARIBBEAN STUDIES ASSOCIATION
Inter-American University of Puerto Rico, P.O. Box 1293, Hato Rey, Puerto Rico 00919.

CENTRE FOR STUDIES AND RESEARCH IN INTERNATIONAL LAW AND INTERNATIONAL RELATIONS
The Hague Academy of International Law, The Hague, Netherlands.

CENTRE FOR THE CO-ORDINATION OF SOCIAL SCIENCE RESEARCH AND DOCUMENTATION IN AFRICA SOUTH OF THE SAHARA
B.P. 836, Kinshasa XI, Zaire.

CLUB OF ROME
Via Giorgione 163, 00147 Roma, Italy.

COMMITTEE ON SOCIETY, DEVELOPMENT AND PEACE
Oecumenical Centre, 150, route de Ferney, 1211 Geneve 20, Suisse.

COUNCIL FOR ASIAN MANPOWER STUDIES
P.O. Box 127, Quezon City, Philippines.

COUNCIL FOR THE DEVELOPMENT OF ECONOMIC AND SOCIAL RESEARCH IN
AFRICA
B.P. 3186, Dakar, Senegal.

EAST AFRICAN ACADEMY RESEARCH INFORMATION CENTRE
Regional Building of East African Community, Ngong Road (rooms
359-60), Nairobi, Kenya.

EASTERN REGIONAL ORGANIZATION FOR PLANNING AND HOUSING
Central Office: 4a, Ring Road, Indraprastha Estate, New Delhi,
India.

EASTERN REGIONAL ORGANIZATION FOR PUBLIC ADMINISTRATION
Rizal Hall, Padre Faura Street, Manila, Philippines.

ECONOMIC DEVELOPMENT INSTITUTE
1818 H Street, N.W., Washington, D.C. 20433, U.S.A.

EUROPEAN FOUNDATION FOR MANAGEMENT DEVELOPMENT
51, rue de la Concorde, Bruxelles, Belgique.

EUROPEAN INSTITUTE FOR TRANSNATIONAL STUDIES IN GROUP AND
ORGANIZATIONAL DEVELOPMENT
Viktorgasse 9, 1040 Vienna, Austria.

EUROPEAN INSTITUTE OF BUSINESS ADMINISTRATION
Boulevard de Constance, 77 Fontainebleau, France.

EUROPEAN RESEARCH GROUP ON MANAGEMENT
Predikherenberg 55, 3200 Kessel-Lo, Belgique.

INSTITUTE OF INTERNATIONAL LAW
82, avenue de Castel, 1200 Bruxelles, Belgique.

INTERNATIONAL AFRICAN INSTITUTE
210, High Holborn, London WC1V 7BW, United Kingdom.

INTERNATIONAL ASSOCIATION FOR METROPOLITAN RESEARCH AND DEVELOPMENT
Suite 1200, 130 Bloor Street West, Toronto 5, Canada.

INTERNATIONAL CENTRE OF RESEARCH AND INFORMATION ON PUBLIC AND
CO-OPERATIVE ECONOMY
45, quai de Rome, Liege, Belgique.

INTERNATIONAL CO-OPERATION FOR SOCIO-ECONOMIC DEVELOPMENT
59-61, rue Adolphe-Lacombie, Bruxelles 4, Belgique.

INTERNATIONAL INSTITUTE FOR LABOUR STUDIES
154, rue de Lausanne, Case Postale 6, 1211 Geneve, Suisse.

INTERNATIONAL INSTITUTE FOR STRATEGIC STUDIES
18, Adam Street, London WC2N 6AL, United Kingdom.

INTERNATIONAL INSTITUTE OF ADMINISTRATIVE SCIENCES
25, rue de la Charite, Bruxelles 4, Belgique.

INTERNATIONAL MANAGEMENT DEVELOPMENT INSTITUTE
4, Chemin de Conches, 1200 Geneve, Suisse.

INTERNATIONAL SCIENCE FOUNDATION
2, rue de Furstenberg, 75006 Paris, France.

INTERNATIONAL SOCIAL SCIENCE COUNCIL
1, rue Miollis, 75015 Paris, France.

INTERNATIONAL STATISTICAL INSTITUTE
Prinses Beatrixlaan 428, Voorburg, Netherlands.

INTERNATIONAL TRAINING AND RESEARCH CENTER FOR DEVELOPMENT
47, rue de la Glaciere, 75013 Paris, France.

LATIN AMERICAN CENTRE FOR ECONOMIC AND SOCIAL DOCUMENTATION
Casilla 179-D, Santiago, Chile.

ORGANIZATION FOR ECONOMIC CO-OPERATION AND DEVELOPMENT
Chateau de la Muette, 2, rue Andre Pascal, 75775 Paris Cedex
16, France.

REGIONAL ECONOMIC RESEARCH AND DOCUMENTATION CENTER
B.P. 7138, Lome, Togo.

RESEARCH CENTRE ON SOCIAL AND ECONOMIC DEVELOPMENT IN
ASIA--INSTITUTE OF ECONOMIC GROWTH
University Enclave, Delhi 7, India.

SOCIETY FOR INTERNATIONAL DEVELOPMENT
1346 Connecticut Avenue, N.W., Washington, D.C. 20036, USA.

SOUTHEAST ASIAN SOCIAL SCIENCE ASSOCIATION
Chulalongkorn University, c/o Faculty of Political Science,
Bangkok, Thailand.

UNITED NATIONS INSTITUTE FOR TRAINING AND RESEARCH
801 United Nations Plaza, New York, NY, USA.

UNITED NATIONS RESEARCH INSTITUTE FOR SOCIAL DEVELOPMENT
Palais des Nations, 1211 Geneve, Suisse.

AUSTRALIA

AUSTRALIAN INSTITUTE OF INTERNATIONAL AFFAIRS
P.O. Box E181, Canberra, ACT 2600.

INSTITUTE OF ADVANCED STUDIES
The Australian National University, P.O. Box 4, Canberra ACT
2600.

STRATEGIC AND DEFENSE STUDIES CENTER
Research School of Pacific Studies, Australian National University,
P.O. Box 4, Canberra ACT 2600.

AUSTRIA

AUSTRIAN FOUNDATION FOR DEVELOPMENT RESEARCH (OFSE)
Turkenstrasse 3, 1090 Vienna, Austria.

VIENNA INSTITUTE FOR DEVELOPMENT
Karntner Strasse 25, 1010 Vienna, Austria.

BANGLADESH

BANGLADESH INSTITUTE OF DEVELOPMENT STUDIES
Adamjee Court, Motijheel Commercial Area, Dacca 2.

BELGIUM

CATHOLIC UNIVERSITY OF LOUVAIN
Center for Economic Studies, Van Evenstraat 2b, 3000 Louvain,
Belgium.

FREE UNIVERSITY OF BRUSSELS
Department of Applied Economics, Avenue F-D Roosevelt 50, 1050
Brussels, Belgium.

UNIVERSITY OF ANTWERP
Centre for Development Studies, 13 Prinsstratt, 2000 Antwerp,
Belgium.

BRAZIL

BRAZILIAN INSTITUTE OF ECONOMICS
Fundacao Getulio Vargas Caixa Postal 4081-ZC-05, Rio de Janeiro,
Brazil.

PROGRAMME OF JOINT STUDIES ON LATIN AMERICAN ECONOMIC INTEGRATION
Caixa Postal 740, Rio de Janeiro, Brazil.

BULGARIA

SCIENTIFIC RESEARCH CENTRE FOR AFRICA AND ASIA
Academy of Social Science, ul. Gagarin 2, Sofia 13, Bulgaria.

INSTITUTE FOR INTERNATIONAL RELATIONS AND SOCIALIST INTEGRATION
Bulgarian Academy of Sciences, Boul. Pencho Slaveicov, 15, Sofia,
Bulgaria.

CANADA

CANADIAN ASSOCIATION OF AFRICAN STUDIES
Geography Department, Carleton University, Ottawa, K1S 5B6.

CANADIAN COUNCIL FOR INTERNATIONAL CO-OPERATION
75 Sparks Street, Ottawa 4, Ontario.

CANADIAN INSTITUTE OF INTERNATIONAL AFFAIRS
Edgar Tarr House, 31 Wellesley Street East, Toronto 284, Ontario.

CENTRE FOR DEVELOPING-ASIA STUDIES
McGill University, Montreal.

INSTITUTE OF INTERNATIONAL RELATIONS
University of British Columbia, Vancouver 8.

INTERNATIONAL DEVELOPMENT RESEARCH CENTRE
60 Queen Street, P.O. Box 8500, Ottawa K1G 3H9.

REGIONAL DEVELOPMENT RESEARCH CENTER
University of Ottawa, Ottawa 2, Ontario.

CHILE

CATHOLIC UNIVERSITY OF CHILE
Institute of Economics, Avda. Libertador Bernardo O'Higgins, No. 340, Santiago, Chile.

CATHOLIC UNIVERSITY OF CHILE
Center for Planning Studies (CEPLAN), Avda. Libertador Bernardo O'Higgins, No. 340, Santiago, Chile.

UNIVERSITY OF CHILE
Planning Centre (CEPLA), Avda. Libertador Bernardo O'Higgins, No. 1058, Santiago, Chile.

COLOMBIA

UNIVERSITY OF ANTIOQUIA
Economic Research Centre, Apartado Aereo 1226, Medellin, Colombia.

CZECHOSLOVAKIA

INSTITUTE OF INTERNATIONAL RELATIONS
Praha 1 - Mala Strana, Nerudova 3, Czechoslovakia.

DENMARK

INSTITUTE FOR DEVELOPMENT RESEARCH
V. Volgade 104, DK-1552 Kobenhavn.

CENTRE FOR DEVELOPMENT RESEARCH
9, NY Kongensgade, 4K-1472 Copenhagen K, Denmark.

FRANCE

UNIVERSITY OF PARIS, INSTITUTE OF ECONOMIC AND SOCIAL DEVELOPMENT
STUDIES
58 Boulevard Arago, 75013 Paris, France.

INSTITUTE FOR RESEARCH INTO THE ECONOMICS OF PRODUCTION
2 rue de Rouen, 92000 Nanterre, France.

INTERNATIONAL CENTRE OF ADVANCED MEDITERRANEAN AGRONOMIC STUDIES
Route de Mende, 34000 Montpellier, France.

INSTITUTE FOR ECONOMIC RESEARCH AND DEVELOPMENT PLANNING
B.P. 47, 38040 Grenoble Cedex, France.

GERMANY, FEDERAL REPUBLIC OF

INSTITUTE FOR DEVELOPMENT RESEARCH AND DEVELOPMENT POLICY
Ruhr-Universitat Bochum, 463 Bochum-Querenburg, Postifach 2148,
Federal Republic of Germany.

INTERNATIONAL INSTITUTE OF MANAGEMENT
Wissenschaftszentrum Berlin, Criegstrasse 5-7, Berlin 33, D-1000.

GERMAN ASSOCIATION FOR EAST ASIAN STUDIES
Rothenbaumchaussee 32, 2 Hamburg 13.

GHANA

INSTITUTE OF AFRICAN STUDIES
University of Ghana, P.O. Box 73, Legon, Accra.

HUNGARY

INSTITUTE FOR WORLD ECONOMICS OF THE HUNGARIAN ACADEMY OF SCIENCES
P.O. Box 36, 1531 Budapest, Hungary.

INSTITUTE FOR ECONOMIC AND MARKET RESEARCH
P.O. Box 133, Budapest 62, Hungary.

INDIA

CENTRE FOR THE STUDY OF DEVELOPING SOCIETIES
29, Rajpur Road, Delhi 6, India.

INDIA INTERNATIONAL CENTRE
40 Lodi Estate, New Delhi 110003, India.

INDIAN COUNCIL FOR AFRICA
Nyaya Marg, Chankyapuri, New Delhi 21, India.

INDIAN COUNCIL OF WORLD AFFAIRS
Sapru House, Barakhamba Road, New Delhi 110001, India.

INDIAN INSTITUTE OF ASIAN STUDIES
23/354, Azad Nagar, Jaiprakash Road, Andheri, Bombay 38, India.

INDIAN SCHOOL OF INTERNATIONAL STUDIES
35, Ferozeshah Road, New Delhi 1, India.

INSTITUTE OF ECONOMIC GROWTH
University of Enclave, Delhi 7, India.

MADRAS INSTITUTE OF DEVELOPMENT STUDIES
74, Second Main Road, Gandhinagar Adyar, Madras 20, India.

INDONESIA

NATIONAL INSTITUTE OF ECONOMIC AND SOCIAL RESEARCH
Leknas, UC, P.O. Box 310, Djakarta, Indonesia.

ISRAEL

DAVID HOROWITZ INSTITUTE FOR THE RESEARCH OF DEVELOPING COUNTRIES
Tel-Aviv University, Ramat-Aviv, Tel-Aviv.

AFRO-ASIAN INSTITUTE FOR CO-OPERATIVE AND LABOUR STUDIES
P.O. Box 16201, Tel-Aviv.

ISRAELI INSTITUTE OF INTERNATIONAL AFFAIRS
P.O. Box 17027, Tel-Aviv 61170.

JAPAN

INSTITUTE OF DEVELOPING ECONOMIES
42 Ichigaya-Hommura-cho, Sinjuku-ku, Tokyo 162, Japan.

JAPAN CENTER FOR AREA DEVELOPMENT RESEARCH
Iino Building, 2-1-1 Uchisaiwai-cho, Chiyoda-ku, Tokyo, Japan.

KENYA

INSTITUTE FOR DEVELOPMENT STUDIES
University of Nairobi, P.O. Box 30197, Nairobi.

KOREA

INDUSTRIAL MANAGEMENT RESEARCH CENTRE
Yonsei University, Sodaemoon-ku-Seoul.

INSTITUTE OF OVERSEAS AFFAIRS
Hankuk University of Foreign Studies, 270 Rimoon-dong, Seoul.

INSTITUTE OF THE MIDDLE EAST AND AFRICA
Rom. 52, Dong-A Building, No. 55, 2nd-ka, Sinmoonro, Congro-ku, Seoul.

MEXICO

CENTRE FOR ECONOMIC RESEARCH AND TEACHING
Av. Country Club No. 208, Apdo. Postal 13628, Mexico 21, D. F.

NEPAL

CENTRE FOR ECONOMIC DEVELOPMENT AND ADMINISTRATION (CEDA)
Tribhuvan University, Kirtipur, P.O. Box 797, Kathmandu, Nepal.

NETHERLANDS

CENTRE FOR LATIN AMERICAN RESEARCH AND DOCUMENTATION
Nieuwe Doelenstraat 16, Amsterdam 1000, Netherlands.

INSTITUTE OF SOCIAL STUDIES
Badhuisweg 251, P.O. Box 90733, 2509 LS The Hague, Netherlands.

FREE UNIVERSITY, DEPARTMENT OF DEVELOPMENT ECONOMICS
De Boelelaan 1105, Amsterdam 1000, Netherlands.

CENTRE FOR DEVELOPMENT PLANNING
Erasmus University, Postbus 1738, Rotterdam, Netherlands.

DEVELOPMENT RESEARCH INSTITUTE
Hogeschoollaan 225, Tiburg 4400, Netherlands.

NEW ZEALAND

NEW ZEALAND INSTITUTE OF INTERNATIONAL AFFAIRS
P.O. Box 196, Wellington, New Zealand.

NEW ZEALAND INSTITUTE OF ECONOMIC RESEARCH
26, Kelburn Parade, P.O. Box 3749, Wellington, New Zealand.

NIGERIA

INSTITUTE OF AFRICAN STUDIES, UNIVERSITY OF NIGERIA
University of Nigeria, Nsukka, Nigeria.

NIGERIAN INSTITUTE OF INTERNATIONAL AFFAIRS
Kofo Abayomi Road, Victoria Island, G.P.O. Box 1727, Lagos,
Nigeria.

NIGERIAN INSTITUTE OF SOCIAL AND ECONOMIC RESEARCH
Private Mail Bag No. 5, U.I. University of Ibadan, Ibadan, Nigeria.

NORWAY

INTERNATIONAL PEACE RESEARCH INSTITUTE
Radhusgt 4, Oslo 1, Norway.

NORWEGIAN AGENCY FOR INTERNATIONAL DEVELOPMENT (NORAD)
Planning Department, Boks 18142 Oslo Dep., Oslo 1, Norway.

THE CHR. MICHELSEN INSTITUTE (DERAP)
Fantoftvegen 38, 5036 Fantoft, Bergen, Norway.

PAKISTAN

DEPARTMENT OF INTERNATIONAL RELATIONS
University of Karachi, Karachi-32, Pakistan.

PHILIPPINES

ASIAN CENTER
University of the Philippines, Palma Hall, Diliman D-505, Quezon
City, Philippines.

ASIAN INSTITUTE OF INTERNATIONAL STUDIES
Malcolm Hall, University of the Philippines, Diliman, Quezon
City, Philippines.

INSTITUTE OF ECONOMIC DEVELOPMENT AND RESEARCH
School of Economics, University of the Philippines, Diliman,
Quezon City, Philippines.

POLAND

RESEARCH INSTITUTE FOR DEVELOPING COUNTRIES
Rakowiecka 24, Warsaw, Poland.

CENTRE OF AFRICAN STUDIES
University of Warsaw, Al. Zwirki i Wigury 93, 02-089 Warsaw,
Poland.

SINGAPORE

INSTITUTE OF ASIAN STUDIES
Nanyang University, Jurong Road, Singapore 22.

INSTITUTE OF SOUTH-EAST ASIAN STUDIES
Campus of University of Singapore, House No. 8, Cluny Road,
Singapore 10.

SRI LANKA

MARGA INSTITUTE
P.O. Box 601, 61 Isipathana Mawatha, Colombo 5, Sri Lanka.

SUDAN

INSTITUTE OF AFRICAN AND ASIAN STUDIES
Faculty of Arts, University of Khartoum, P.O. Box 321, Khartoum,
Sudan.

SWEDEN

INSTITUTE FOR INTERNATIONAL ECONOMIC STUDIES
Fack S-104 05, Stockholm 50, Sweden.

STOCKHOLM SCHOOL OF ECONOMICS, ECONOMIC RESEARCH INSTITUTE
Box 6501, 11383 Stockholm, Sweden.

UNITED KINGDOM

CENTRE FOR SOUTH-EAST ASIAN STUDIES
University of Hull, Hull HU6 7RX.

CENTRE OF AFRICAN STUDIES
University of Edinburgh, Adam Ferguson Building, George Square,
Edinburgh 8.

CENTRE OF LATIN AMERICAN STUDIES (CAMBRIDGE)
University of Cambridge, History Faculty Building, West Road,
Cambridge CB3 9ES, England.

CENTRE OF LATIN AMERICAN STUDIES (OXFORD)
Oxford University, St. Antony's College, Oxford OX2 6JF, England.

CENTRE OF WEST AFRICAN STUDIES
University of Birmingham, P.O. Box 363, Birmingham B15 2TT.

INSTITUTE FOR THE STUDY OF INTERNATIONAL ORGANISATION
University of Sussex, Stanmer House, Stanmer Park, Brighton
BN1 9QA, England.

INSTITUTE OF DEVELOPMENT STUDIES
University of Sussex, Falmer, Brighton BN1 9QN, England.

INSTITUTE OF LATIN AMERICAN STUDIES
University of London, 31 Tavistock Square, London WC1, England.

INSTITUTE OF LATIN AMERICAN STUDIES (GLASGOW)
University of Glasgow, Glasgow.

ROYAL INSTITUTE OF INTERNATIONAL AFFAIRS
Chatham House, St. James' Square, London SW1Y 4LE, England.

UNITED STATES

AFRICAN STUDIES CENTER (BOSTON)
Boston University, 10 Lenos Street, Brookline MA 02146.

BROOKINGS INSTITUTION
1775 Massachusetts Avenue, N.W., Washington, D.C. 20036.

CENTER FOR ASIAN STUDIES
Arizona State University, Tempe, AZ 85281.

CENTER FOR COMPARATIVE STUDIES IN TECHNOLOGICAL DEVELOPMENT AND
SOCIAL CHANGE
University of Minnesota, Minneapolis, Minnesota 55455.

CENTER FOR DEVELOPMENT ECONOMICS
Williams College, Williamston, MA 01267.

CENTER FOR INTERNATIONAL AFFAIRS
Harvard University, 6 Divinity Avenue, Cambridge, MA 02138.

CENTER FOR INTERNATIONAL STUDIES
Massachusetts Institute of Technology, Cambridge, MA 02139.

CENTER FOR LATIN AMERICAN STUDIES, ARIZONA STATE UNIVERSITY
Arizona State University, Tempe, AZ 85281.

CENTER FOR LATIN AMERICAN STUDIES, UNIVERSITY OF FLORIDA
University of Florida, Room 319 LAGH, Gainesville, FL 39611.

CENTER FOR RESEARCH IN ECONOMIC DEVELOPMENT
506 East Liberty Street, Ann Arbor, MI 48108.

CENTER FOR STRATEGIC AND INTERNATIONAL STUDIES
Georgetown University, 1800 K Street, N.W., Washington, D.C. 20006.

CENTER OF INTERNATIONAL STUDIES, PRINCETON UNIVERSITY
Princeton University, 118 Corwin Hall, Princeton, NJ 08540.

HARVARD INSTITUTE FOR INTERNATIONAL DEVELOPMENT
Harvard University, 1737 Cambridge Street, Cambridge MA 02138.

INSTITUTE FOR WORLD ORDER
1140 Avenue of the Americas, New York, New York 10036.

INSTITUTE OF LATIN AMERICAN STUDIES
University of Texas at Austin, Sid. W. Richardson Hall, Austin, TX 78705.

STANFORD INTERNATIONAL DEVELOPMENT EDUCATION CENTER
P.O. Box 2329, Stanford, CA 94305.

UNIVERSITY CENTER FOR INTERNATIONAL STUDIES
University of Pittsburgh, Social Sciences Building, Pittsburgh, PA 15213.

WORLD FUTURE SOCIETY
4916 St. Elmo Avenue, Bethesda Branch, Washington, D.C. 20014.

UNIVERSITY OF HAWAII
Centre for Development Studies, Department of Economics, Porteus Hall, 2424 Maile Way, Honolulu, Hawaii 96822.

URUGUAY

LATIN AMERICAN CENTRE FOR HUMAN ECONOMY
Cerrito 475, P.O. Box 998, Montevideo, Uruguay.

VENEZUELA

UNIVERSITY OF ZULIA
Department of Economic Research, Faculty of Economic and Social Sciences, Maracaibo, Venezuela.

YUGOSLAVIA

INSTITUTE FOR DEVELOPING COUNTRIES
41000 Zagreb, Ul. 8 Maja 82, Yugoslavia.

RESEARCH CENTRE FOR CO-OPERATION WITH DEVELOPING COUNTRIES
61 109 Ljubljana, Titova 104 P.O. Box 37, Yugoslavia.

INSTITUTE OF WORLD ECONOMICS AND INTERNATIONAL RELATIONS OF THE
ACADEMY OF SCIENCES OF THE U.S.S.R.
Yaroslavskaya Ul. 13, Moskva I-243.

Appendix

COUNTRIES BY INCOME GROUP
(based on 1976 GNP per capita in 1976 US dollars)

INDUSTRIALIZED COUNTRIES

Australia
Austria
Belgium
Canada
Denmark
Finland
France
Germany, Fed. Rep. of
Iceland
Ireland
Italy
Japan
Luxembourg
Netherlands
New Zealand
Norway
South Africa
Sweden
Switzerland
United Kingdom
United States

DEVELOPING COUNTRIES BY INCOME GROUP
(Excluding Capital Surplus Oil Exporters)

High Income (over $2500)

American Samoa
Bahamas
Bermuda
Brunei
Canal Zone
Channel Islands
Faeroe Islands
French Polynesia
Gabon
Gibraltar
Greece
Greenland
Guam
Israel
Martinique
New Caledonia
Oman
Singapore
Spain
Venezuela
Virgin Islands (U.S.)

Upper Middle Income ($1136-2500)

Argentina
Bahrain
Barbados
Brazil
Cyprus
Djibouti
Fiji

French Guiana
Guadeloupe
Hong Kong
Iran
Iraq
Isle of Man
Lebanon
Malta
Netherlands Antilles
Panama
Portugal
Puerto Rico
Reunion
Romania
Surinam
Trinidad & Tobago
Uruguay
Yugoslavia

Intermediate Middle Income ($551-1135)

Algeria
Antigua
Belize
Chile
China, Rep. of
Colombia
Costa Rica
Dominica
Dominican Republic
Ecuador
Ghana
Gilbert Islands
Guatemala
Ivory Coast
Jamaica
Jordan
Korea, Rep. of
Macao
Malaysia
Mauritius
Mexico
Namibia
Nicaragua
Paraguay
Peru
Seychelles
St. Kitts-Nevis
St. Lucia
Syrian Arab Rep.
Trust Territory of the Pacific
  Islands
Tunisia
Turkey

Lower Middle Income ($281-550)

Angola
Bolivia
Botswana
Cameroon
Cape Verde
Congo, P.R.
El Salvador
Equatorial Guinea
Grenada
Guyana
Honduras
Liberia
Mauritania
Morocco
New Hebrides
Nigeria
Papua New Guinea
Philippines
Rhodesia
Sao Tome & Principe
Senegal
St. Vincent
Sudan
Swaziland
Thailand
Tonga
Western Samoa
Zambia

Low   Income   ($280   or   less)

Afghanistan
Bangladesh
Benin
Bhutan
Burma
Burundi
Cambodia
Central African Empire
Chad
Comoros
Egypt
Ethiopia
Gambia, The
Guinea
Guinea-Bissau
Haiti
India
Indonesia
Kenya
Lesotho
Madagascar
Malawi

Maldives
Mali
Mozambique
Nepal
Niger
Pakistan
Rwanda
Sierra Leone
Solomon Islands
Somalia
Sri Lanka
Tanzania
Togo
Uganda
Upper Volta
Viet Nam
Yemen Arab Rep.
Yemen P.D.R.
Zaire

**CAPITAL SURPLUS OIL EXPORTING
DEVELOPING COUNTRIES**

Kuwait
Libya
Qatar
Saudi Arabia
United Arab Emirates

CENTRALLY PLANNED COUNTRIES

Albania
Bulgaria
China, People's Rep. of
Cuba
Czechoslovakia
German Dem. Rep.
Hungary
Korea, Dem. Rep. of
Lao People's Dem. Rep.
Mongolia
Poland
U.S.S.R.

Index

About the Editor

Pradip K. Ghosh is President of the World Academy of Development and Cooperation, Washington, D.C. and Adjunct Associate Professor and Visiting Fellow at the Center for International Development at the University of Maryland, College Park. He is the author of *Thinking Sociology* and *Land Use Planning,* and editor of the International Development Resource Books series for Greenwood Press.